MEDICAL AND DISABILITY APPEAL TRIBUNALS: THE LEGISLATION

AUSTRALIA
LBC Information Services
Sydney

CANADA AND USA
Carswell
Toronto, Ontario

NEW ZEALAND
Brooker's
Auckland

SINGAPORE AND MALAYSIA
Thomson Information (S.E. Asia)
Singapore

MEDICAL AND DISABILITY APPEAL TRIBUNALS: THE LEGISLATION

By

Mark Rowland, LL.B.

Social Security Commissioner

LONDON
SWEET & MAXWELL
1998

Published in 1998 by
Sweet & Maxwell Limited
100 Avenue Road
London NW3 3PF

Computerset by
Wyvern 21, Bristol.
Printed and bound in Great Britain by
Clays Ltd, of St Ives plc

No natural forests were destroyed to make this product;
only farmed timber was used and re-planted.

ISBN 0 421 608803

A CIP catalogue record for this book is available from the British Library

PREFACE

The purpose of this book is to present in one volume all the legislation which is relevant to hearings before medical appeal tribunals and disability appeal tribunals. I have annotated the legislation of direct relevance but I have also included a substantial amount of material that is only of indirect relevance and I have not sought to lengthen the book further by adding notes to that material. Nor have I attempted to comment on medical matters upon which I cannot claim any expertise.

It is a feature of both medical appeal tribunals and disability appeal tribunals that they have among their members both lawyers and doctors. Disability appeal tribunals also have lay members with experience of dealing with the needs of people with disabilities and who therefore contribute their own form of medical expertise. The mix of backgrounds and expertise is an important factor in the quality of decision-making by the tribunals which is, in my view, generally of a high standard. I would be disappointed if the more extreme suggestions in the previous Government's Green Paper, *Improving decision making and appeals in Social Security*, Cm. 3328, were to be introduced for appeals on issues now considered by medical appeal tribunals and disability appeal tribunals. From a lawyer's point of view, having a written medical report is seldom an adequate substitute for actually being able to discuss a case with a doctor, particularly if the doctor has had the opportunity of examining the claimant. Equally, a doctor's opinion must be directed towards answering the correct legal questions and those are best formulated in discussion in the light of the issues arising in each particular case. There is a limit to the extent to which appeals relating to any area of human life can be decided on the basis of simple codes of general application. Every person is different and attempts to process cases, at an appellate level, through the use of simplistic formulae are apt to produce injustice. That is not to say that both the substantive law and the procedural law administered by medical appeal tribunals and disability appeal tribunals could not be simplified, but it is unlikely that any system that provides adequate resources for those with disabilities at a cost that can be afforded will eliminate complicated disputes.

It should not be thought that all answers to disputes about the present law can be found in this book. The annotations to the Acts and Regulations represent my personal attempts at comprehending the legislation as it stands at October 13, 1997. Any tribunal must, of course, reach their own view on the law, aided by decisions of the Commissioners and the courts but aware that every case turns on its own facts. Nonetheless, I hope the book will be of use both to members of tribunals and to those who appear before them.

I am, as always, indebted to all those at Sweet & Maxwell who have been involved in the production of this book and to my wife, Eileen, and my daughters, Emma and Clare, who have had to put up with me taking time to write it. I am also grateful to Penny Wood for her many helpful comments and suggestions made while I was writing this edition and to those who took the trouble to comment on the last edition. Further comments are always welcome and may be addressed to me c/o Sweet & Maxwell Limited, 100 Avenue Road, London NW3 3PF.

December 1997 Mark Rowland

TABLE OF CONTENTS

PART IV: LEGISLATION RELATING TO VACCINE DAMAGE PAYMENTS

PART V: PRESIDENT'S CIRCULARS

TABLE OF CASES

TABLE OF STATUTES

References in **bold** type indicate legislation reproduced in full.

TABLE OF STATUTORY INSTRUMENTS

References in **bold** type indicate legislation reproduced in full.

TABLE OF SOCIAL SECURITY COMMISSIONER'S DECISIONS

PART I

Statutes

Social Security Contributions and Benefits Act 1992

(1992 c. 4)

ARRANGEMENT OF SECTIONS

Disablement pension

Other benefits and increases

Successive accidents

Prescribed industrial diseases etc.

PART VI

MISCELLANEOUS PROVISIONS RELATING TO PARTS I TO V

Disqualification and suspension

Interpretation

PART VII

INCOME-RELATED BENEFITS

General

Disability working allowance

General

PART X

CHRISTMAS BONUS FOR PENSIONERS

PART XIII

GENERAL

Interpretation

An Act to consolidate certain enactments relating to social security contributions and benefits with amendments to give effect to recommendations of the Law Commission and the Scottish Law Commission.

[13th February 1992]

1.—62. *Omitted.*

PART III

NON-CONTRIBUTORY BENEFITS

Descriptions of non-contributory benefits

63.—Non-contributory benefits under this Part of this Act are of the following descriptions, namely—

(a) attendance allowance;
(b) severe disablement allowance (with age related addition and increase for adult and child dependants);
(c) invalid care allowance (with increase for adult and child dependants);
(d) disability living allowance;

(e) guardian's allowance;
(f) retirement pensions of the following categories—
 (i) Category C, payable to certain persons who were over pensionable age on 5th July, 1948 and their wives and widows (with increase for adult and child dependants), and
 (ii) Category D, payable to persons over the age of 80;
(g) age addition payable, in the case of persons over the age of 80, by way of increase of a retirement pension of any category or of some other pension or allowance from the Secretary of State.

DERIVATION

Social Security Act 1975, s.34.

Attendance allowance

Entitlement

64.—(1) A person shall be entitled to an attendance allowance if he is aged 65 or over, he is not entitled to the care component of a disability living allowance and he satisfies either—
(a) the condition specified in subsection (2) below ("the day attendance condition"), or
(b) the condition specified in subsection (3) below ("the night attendance condition"),

and prescribed conditions as to residence and presence in Great Britain.

(2) A person satisfies the day attendance condition if he is so severely disabled physically or mentally that, by day, he requires from another person either—
(a) frequent attention throughout the day in connection with his bodily functions, or
(b) continual supervision throughout the day in order to avoid substantial danger to himself or others.

(3) A person satisfies the night attendance condition if he is so severely disabled physically or mentally that, at night,—
(a) he requires from another person prolonged or repeated attention in connection with his bodily functions, or
(b) in order to avoid substantial danger to himself or others he requires another person to be awake for a prolonged period or at frequent intervals for the purpose of watching over him.

DERIVATION

Social Security Act 1975, s.35(1).

GENERAL NOTE

Attendance allowance was originally introduced in 1970 and was then payable at just one rate to those who needed attention or supervision both day and night. In 1972, the lower rate was introduced for those who required attention or supervision by day or at night but not both.

The Disability Living Allowance and Disability Working Allowance Act 1991 substantially reduced the scope of attendance allowance so that now it is applicable only to those people over 65 who are not entitled under what is now s.72 of the Social Security Contributions and Benefits Act to the care component of disability living allowance. Since those who have become entitled to the care component of disability living allowance while under 65 remain entitled to it thereafter, attendance allowance is now payable only to those who become disabled after reaching that age or who, though disabled earlier, fail to claim before they are 66 (to be reduced to 65 from October 6, 1997). Attendance allowance is less generous than the care component of disability living allowance in two respects. First, it has a six-month qualifying period (s.65(1)(b)) as opposed to the three-month period for the care component (s.72(2)(a)) although neither qualifying period applies in the case of a person who is terminally ill. Secondly, there are only two rates of attendance allowance, which are the same as the highest and middle rate of the care component. There is no equivalent to the lowest rate of the care component.

Subs. (1). For the circumstances in which a person over 65 is entitled to the care component of a disability living allowance, see s.75 and also reg. 3 of and Sched. 1 to the Disability Living Allowance Regulations. The general condition is that the claimant must have satisfied the conditions for the component before reaching the age of 65 and have claimed disability living allowance before reaching the age of 66 (65 from October 6, 1997). For prescribed conditions as to residence and presence, see reg. 2 of the Social Security (Attendance Allowance) Regulation 1991.

Subss. (2) and (3). Subs. (3) contains two alternative "day" conditions and subs. (3) contains two alternative "night" conditions. Subject to the waiting period imposed by s.65(1)(b), attendance allowance is paid at the higher rate if both a "day" and a "night" condition are satisfied and at the lower rate if the conditions are satisfied only for the day or the night (s.65(3)).

The attendance conditions in subss. (2) and (3) are the same as those in paras (b) and (c) of s.72(1) and reference should be made to the notes to that subsection.

Note that both conditions may be deemed to be satisfied in the case of a person who is terminally ill and can reasonably be expected to die within six months (s.66).

Note also that reg. 5 of the Attendance Allowance Regulation provides that certain people undergoing renal dialysis are deemed to satisfy either the day or the night attention condition so as to qualify them for attendance allowance at the lower rate. There is no reason why they should not satisfy another condition for other reasons and so qualify for the higher rate.

Before March 15, 1988, the night condition was different. S.35(1)(b) of the Social Security Act 1975 provided as follows:

(b) he is so severely disabled physically or mentally that, at night, he requires from another person either—
   (i) prolonged or repeated attention during the night in connection with his bodily functions, or
   (ii) continual supervision throughout the night in order to avoid substantial danger to himself or others."

By virtue of s.1(2) of the Social Security Act 1988 (now Social Security (Consequential Provisions) Act 1992, Sched. 3, para. 19), the amendment did not affect a determination on any claim made before March 15, 1988, or any review following either an application made before that date or a decision by the Board or a delegated medical practitioner to conduct such a review made before that date. This enabled such determinations to be made applying the old law in respect of a period stretching beyond March 15, 1988. However, it does not follow that the amendment applies to any review following an application, or a decision to conduct such a review, made on or after that date but *in respect of a period before it.* S.16(1)(c) of the Interpretation Act 1978 would seem to preserve the earlier legislation in force in respect of the period before March 15, 1988, in all cases as s.1(2) of the 1988 Act does not show a "contrary intention" in sufficiently strong terms because the saving is apt to apply to future determinations in respect of periods which extend beyond the date of the amendment and need not necessarily apply to past periods. It is therefore doubtful whether it can outweigh the strong presumption against retrospectivity. There may still be one or two cases to which the old legislation still applies, as is recognised by the continuation of the saving provision by para. 19 of Sched. 3 to the Social Security (Consequential Provisions) Act 1992. The difference between the old legislation and the new is that s.35(1)(b)(ii) of the 1975 Act formerly provided for a night supervision condition identical to the day supervision condition, whereas now the condition is that there be a requirement for a person to be awake for a prolonged period or at frequent intervals for the purpose of watching over the claimant. The change was made after the Court of Appeal held, in *Moran v. Secretary of State for Social Services*, reported as an appendix to *R(A) 1/88*, that a person might, in some circumstances, be exercising supervision over another even while asleep.

Period and rate of allowance

65.—(1) Subject to the following provisions of this Act, the period for which a person is entitled to an attendance allowance shall be—

(a) a period throughout which he has satisfied or is likely to satisfy the day or the night attendance condition or both; and

(b) a period preceded immediately, or within such period as may be prescribed, by one of not less than six months throughout which he satisfied, or is likely to satisfy, one or both of those conditions.

(2) For the purposes of subsection (1) above a person who suffers from renal failure and is undergoing such form of treatment as may be prescribed shall, in such circumstances as may be prescribed, be deemed to satisfy or to be likely to satisfy the day or the night attendance condition or both.

(3) The weekly rate of the attendance allowance payable to a person for any period shall be the higher rate specified in Schedule 4, Part III, paragraph 1, if both as regards that period and as regards the period of six months mentioned in subsection (1)(b) above he has satisfied or is likely to satisfy both the day and the night attendance conditions, and shall be the lower rate in any other case.

(4) A person shall not be entitled to an attendance allowance for any period preceding the date on which he makes or is treated as making a claim for it.

(5) Notwithstanding anything in subsection (4) above, provision may be made by regulations for a person to be entitled to an attendance allowance for a period preceding the date on which he makes or is treated as making a claim for it if such an allowance has previously been paid to or in respect of him.

(6) Except in so far as regulations otherwise provide and subject to section 66(1) below—

(a) a claim for an attendance allowance may be made during the period of six months immediately preceding the period for which the person to whom the claim relates is entitled to the allowance; and

(b) an award may be made in pursuance of a claim so made, subject to the condition that, throughout that period of six months, that person satisfies—

(i) both the day and the night attendance conditions, or

(ii) if the award is at the lower rate, one of those conditions.

Derivation

Social Security Act 1975, s.35(2), (2A), (3), (4) and (4A).

General Note

Subs. (1). Para. (a) has the effect that an award of attendance allowance should be for the period for which the claimant has satisfied or is *likely* to satisfy one or both of the attendance conditions. An award may be for life or for a specified period. There is no minimum period specified but it will seldom be appropriate to make an award for less than six months which is the minimum period for an award of the care component of a disability living allowance (see s.72(2)(b)). In this case, "likely" can be read as "more likely than not" since the subsection is concerned with the continued satisfaction of the conditions of entitlement. If the prognosis is uncertain, the award should be limited in time.

It is not necessary that the conditions are likely to be satisfied in respect of every day. *R(A) 2/74* concerned a claimant who had to undergo renal dialysis for 10 hours on three nights a week, at a time before any specific provision was made for such claimants (see now reg. 5 of the Social Security (Attendance Allowance) Regulations 1991). The Commissioner held that it was wrong to take a purely arithmetical approach and that the claimant was not, as a matter of law, excluded from entitlement. Variations in a claimant's condition present greater problems because they are irregular and difficult to predict. "These are matters for the good sense and judgment of the [decision maker]."

Both attendance conditions are deemed to be satisfied for the remainder of the life of a person suffering from a progressive disease and likely to die within six months (s.66(1)(a)(i)).

Para. (b) provides for the six-month qualifying period. A person is not entitled to attendance allowance until he or she has satisfied an attendance condition for six months. The combined effect of this subsection and subs. (3) is that, if a person has been receiving the lower rate because he or she satisfies only, say, the day attendance condition and then his or her condition deteriorates so that he or she also satisfies the night condition, he or she does not become entitled to the higher rate until six months have elapsed. This six-month qualifying period is waived in the case of a person who is suffering from a progressive disease and likely to die within six months (s.66(1)(a)(ii)). Other claimants may make their claims during the qualifying period so that a decision can be made straightaway and payment can start as soon as the qualifying period has been completed (subs. (4)(a)).

Usually the six-month qualifying period immediately precedes the period of entitlement but it may fall within such other period as may be prescribed. Reg. 3 of the Social Security (Attendance Allowance) Regulations 1991 prescribes the period of two years.

Subs. (2). This enables regulations to be made so that a person who undergoes renal dialysis is deemed to satisfy either or both the day and the night attendance conditions. Reg. 5 of the Social Security (Attendance Allowance) Regulations 1991 allows a person having such treatment at least twice a week to be deemed, in some circumstances, to satisfy one, but not both, of the attendance conditions. Any question whether a person suffers renal failure is determined by a disability appeal tribunal on appeal from an adjudication officer.

Subs. (3). From April 7, 1997, the higher rate is £49.50 pw and the lower rate is £33.10 pw.

Subss. (4) and *(5).* Awards of attendance allowance cannot usually be made in respect of a period before the date of claim. Reg. 6 of the Social Security (Claims and Payments) Regulations 1987 deems a claim to be made on the date it is received in the appropriate office, makes provision to deal with defective claims that are corrected within a reasonable time and effectively treats the date of receipt of a request for a claim form on the date of claim if the claim form is returned within the specified time. Reg. 6(5) allows a claim delayed in the post through industrial action to be treated as having been made on the day on which it would have been received if it had been delivered in the ordinary course of post.

Reg. 4 of the Social Security (Attendance Allowance) Regulations 1991, treated as made under subs. (5), allowed an award to be made from the end of a previous period of entitlement if the renewal claim was made within six months but that regulation was revoked from September 1, 1997.

Subs. (6). A claim may be made in advance during the six-month waiting period. The award is, of course, conditional on the claimant continuing to satisfy the attendance conditions.

Attendance allowance for the terminally ill

66.—(1) If a terminally ill person makes a claim expressly on the ground that he is such a person, then—

(a) he shall be taken—

(i) to satisfy, or to be likely to satisfy, both the day attendance condition and the night attendance condition for the remainder of his life, beginning with the date of the claim or, if later, the first date on which he is terminally ill; and

(ii) to have satisfied those conditions for the period of six months immediately preceding that date (so however that no allowance shall be payable by virtue of this sub-paragraph for any period preceding that date); and

(b) the period for which he is entitled to attendance allowance shall be the remainder of the person's life, beginning with that date.

(2) For the purposes of subsection (1) above—

(a) a person is "terminally ill" at any time if at that time he suffers from a progressive disease and his death in consequence of that disease can reasonably be expected within six months; and

(b) where a person purports to make a claim for an attendance allowance by virtue of that subsection on behalf of another, that other shall be regarded as making the claim, notwithstanding that it is made without his knowledge or authority.

DERIVATION

Social Security Act 1975, s.35(2B), (2C).

GENERAL NOTE

There had been much criticism of the difficulties facing terminally ill people claiming attendance allowance. Many died during the qualifying period and others had died before awards were made because of the delay caused by the necessity for medical examinations to determine whether the claimant satisfied the attendance conditions. These difficulties are removed by deeming terminally ill people to satisfy both the day and the night attendance conditions and to be likely to satisfy them for the remainder of their lives and also by removing the qualifying period. Such people therefore automatically qualify for attendance allowance at the higher rate subject to the usual conditions relating to residence and presence in Great Britain and the exclusions for those residing in hospitals and certain other accommodation.

There are two conditions for entitlement under these provisions. Firstly, the claimant must be a "terminally ill" person within the definition provided by subs. (2)(a) and, secondly, the claim must be made expressly on the ground that the claimant is such a person. To be "terminally ill" it is necessary that the claimant's death "can reasonably be expected within six months". The precise meaning of this phrase is a little obscure. It is fairly clear that a person who is more likely to die within that period than not is covered by the provision. But what about the person who could die at any time and might equally well survive the period as die within it? Does "can reasonably be expected" mean the same as "is expected", or does it suggest a likelihood falling short of probability? In any event, death must be expected as a result of a progressive disease, rather than some other cause. This may be a significant qualification for a few very elderly people. A question whether a person is terminally ill is decided by a disability appeal tribunal in the event of an appeal from an adjudication officer. Although a claim must be made expressly on the ground that the claimant is terminally ill, the Secretary of State may accept any notification that a person is terminally ill as being sufficient to amount to a claim (reg. 4 of the Social Security (Claims and Payments) Regulations 1987). Presumably, in the case of a claimant with an existing award of attendance allowance at the lower rate, an application for a review on this ground counts as a claim for the purposes of s.66. The distinction may be important because, whereas it is for the Secretary of State to determine whether a document may be accepted as a claim, an application for a review does not have to be in any particular form, and it is for an adjudication officer or tribunal to decide whether a document furnishes sufficient grounds for a review. Subs. (2)(b) allows someone else to make a claim on this basis on behalf of the claimant, which enables a claim to be made in a case where the claimant's prognosis is being kept from him or her.

Exclusions by regulation

67.—(1) Regulations may provide that, in such circumstances, and for such purposes as may be prescribed, a person who is, or is treated under the regulations as, undergoing treatment for renal failure in a hospital or other similar institution otherwise than as an in-patient shall be deemed not to satisfy or to be unlikely to satisfy the day attendance condition or the night attendance condition, or both of them.

(2) Regulations may provide that an attendance allowance shall not be payable in respect of a person for any period when he is a person for whom accommodation is provided—

(a) in pursuance—
 (i) of Part III of the National Assistance Act 1948; or
 (ii) of paragraph 2 of Schedule 8 to the National Health Service Act 1977; or
 (iii) of Part IV of the Social Work (Scotland) Act 1968; or
 (iv) of section 7 of the Mental Health (Scotland) Act 1984; or

(b) in circumstances in which the cost is, or may be, borne wholly or partly out of public or local funds, in pursuance of those enactments or of any other enactment relating to persons under disability.

Derivation

Social Security Act 1975, s.35(5A), (6).

General Note

Subs. (1). See reg. 5(3) and 5(4) of the Social Security (Attendance Allowance) Regulations 1991.
Subs. (2). See regs. 6–8 of the Social Security (Attendance Allowance) Regulations 1991.

Severe disablement allowance

Entitlement and rate

68.—(1) Subject to the provisions of this section, a person shall be entitled to a severe disablement allowance for any day (''the relevant day'') if he satisfies—

(a) the conditions specified in subsection (2) below; or
(b) the conditions specified in subsection (3) below.

(2) The conditions mentioned in subsection (1)(a) above are that—

(a) on the relevant day he is incapable of work; and
(b) he has been incapable of work for a period of not less than 196 consecutive days—
  (i) beginning not later than the day on which he attained the age of 20; and
  (ii) ending immediately before the relevant day.

(3) The conditions mentioned in subsection (1)(b) above are that—

(a) on the relevant day he is both incapable of work and disabled; and
(b) he has been both incapable of work and disabled for a period of not less than 196 consecutive days ending immediately before the relevant day.

(4) A person shall not be entitled to a severe disablement allowance if—

(a) he is under the age of 16; or
(b) he is receiving full-time education; or
(c) he does not satisfy the prescribed conditions—
  (i) as to residence in Great Britain; or
  (ii) as to presence there; or
(d) he has attained [2the age of 65] and—
  (i) was not entitled to a severe disablement allowance immediately before he attained that age; and
  (ii) is not treated by regulations as having been so entitled immediately before he attained that age.

[1(4ZA) In determining whether the person satisfies any conditions prescribed under paragraph (c) of subsection (4) above—

(a) any period during which the person is absent from Great Britain by reason only of the fact that—
  (i) he is abroad in his capacity as a serving member of the forces, or
  (ii) he is living with a person mentioned in sub-paragraph (i) and is the spouse, son, daughter, father, father-in-law, mother or mother-in-law of that person,

  shall be treated as a period during which the person was resident in Great Britain; and
(b) any day on which the person is absent from Great Britain by reason only of the fact that on that day—
  (i) he is abroad in his capacity as a serving member of the forces, or
  (ii) he is living with a person mentioned in sub-paragraph (i) and is the spouse, son, daughter, father, father-in-law, mother or mother-in-law of that person, or
  (iii) he is in employment prescribed for the purposes of section 132 of the Act in connection with continental shelf operations, or
  (iv) he is abroad in his capacity as an airman or mariner within the meaning of regulation 81 and regulation 86 respectively of the Social Security (Contributions) Regulations 1979;

shall be treated as a day on which the person is present in Great Britain; and for the purposes of this provision, the expression ''serving member of the forces'' has the same meaning as in regulation 1(2) of the Social Security (Contributions) Regulations 1979.]

(5) A person shall not be entitled to a severe disablement allowance for any day which as between him and his employer falls within a period of entitlement for the purposes of statutory sick pay.

(6) A person is disabled for the purposes of this section if he suffers from loss of physical or mental faculty such that the extent of the resulting disablement assessed in accordance with Schedule 6 to this Act amounts to not less than 80 per cent.

(7) A severe disablement allowance shall be paid at the weekly rate specified in Schedule 4, Part III, paragraph 2.

(8) The amount of severe disablement allowance payable for any relevant day shall be [[3]1/7th of the weekly rate].

(9) In any case where—

(a) a severe disablement allowance is payable to a woman in respect of one or more relevant days in a week; and
(b) an amount of statutory maternity pay becomes payable to her on any day in that week,

the amount of the severe disablement allowance (including any increase for a child or adult dependant under section 90(a) below) so payable shall be reduced by the amount of the statutory maternity pay, and only the balance (if any) shall be payable.

(10) Where—

(a) a person who is engaged and normally engaged in remunerative work ceases to be so engaged; and
(b) he is entitled to a disability working allowance for the week in which there falls the last day on which he is so engaged; and
(c) he qualified for a disability working allowance for that week by virtue of a severe disablement having been payable to him; and
(d) the first day after he ceases to be engaged as mentioned in paragraph (a) above is a day on which he is incapable of work and falls no later than the end of the period of two years beginning with the last day for which he was entitled to a severe disablement allowance,

any day since that day which fell within a week for which he was entitled to a disability working allowance shall be treated for the purposes of any claim for a severe disablement allowance for a period commencing after he ceases to be engaged as mentioned in paragraph (a) above as having been a day on which he was both incapable of work and disabled.

[[3](10A) Where—

(a) a person becomes engaged in training for work, and
(b) he was entitled to a severe disablement allowance for one or more of the 56 days immediately before he becomes so engaged, and
(c) the first day after he ceases to be so engaged is for him a day on which he is incapable of work and falls not later than the end of the period of two years beginning with the last day for which he was entitled to a severe disablement allowance,

any day since that day in which he was engaged in training for work shall be treated for the purposes of any claim for a severe disablement allowance as having been a day on which he was both incapable of work and disabled.]

(11) Regulations—

(a) may direct that persons who—
   (i) have attained [[2] the age of 65]; and
   (ii) were entitled to a severe disablement allowance immediately before they attained that age,

   shall continue to be so entitled notwithstanding that they do not satisfy the conditions specified in subsection (2) or (3) above;
(b) may direct—
   (i) that persons who have previously been entitled to a severe disable-

ment allowance shall be entitled to such an allowance notwithstanding that they do not satisfy the conditions specified in subsection (2)(b) or (3)(b) above;

(ii) that subsections (2)(b) and (3)(b) above shall have effect in relation to such persons subject to such modifications as may be specified in the regulations;

[[3](ca) may prescribe circumstances in which a person is or is not to be treated as incapable of work;

(cb) may prescribe circumstances in which a person is or is not to be treated as receiving full-time education;

(cc) may prescribe evidence which is to be treated as establishing that a person suffers from loss of physical or mental faculty such that the extent of the resulting disablement amounts to not less than 80 per cent; and

(d) may make in relation to severe disablement allowance any such provision as is made in relation to incapacity benefit by section 30E above.]

(e) [[3] . . .]

(12) [[4] . . .]

(13) [[4] . . .]

DERIVATION

Social Security Act 1975, s.36.

AMENDMENTS

1. This subsection was inserted in s.36 of the Social Security Act 1975 by reg. 3(2) of the Social Security (Severe Disablement Allowance) Regulations 1984 (S.I. 1984 No. 1303) as substituted by reg. 2 of the Social Security (Severe Disablement Allowance) Amendment Regulations 1991 (S.I. 1991 No. 1747) (October 14, 1991).

2. Social Security (Severe Disablement Allowance and Invalid Care Allowance) Amendment Regulations 1994 (S.I. 1994 No. 2556), reg. 2(2)(a) (October 28, 1994).

3. Social Security (Incapacity for Work) Act 1994, s.9 and Sched. 1, paras. 11(5) and 18 (April 13, 1995).

4. Social Security (incapacity for Work) Act 1994, Sched. 1, para. 11(6) and Sched. 2, as amended by Social Security (Severe Disavblement Allowance and Invalid Care Allowance) Amendment Regulations 1994 (S.I. 1994 No. 2556), reg. 3 April 13, 1995).

GENERAL NOTE

Severe disablement allowance (SDA) is a weekly benefit paid to those who are incapable of work and have been for at least 28 weeks. It is paid to those whose contribution record is not sufficient to entitle them to benefit.

SDA is intended as an earnings-replacement benefit. Therein lies a difficulty, from the Government's point of view, because a non-contributory benefit for people incapable of work is likely to be payable to a large number of people who would not have been working even if they had been able to do so. However, it is impossible to identify who those people are because the question is hypothetical. When the Social Security Act 1975 was originally enacted, s.36 provided for a benefit known as non-contributory invalidity pension. For that benefit, an assumption was made that married and cohabiting women who were fit to do housework would not be in paid employment even if they were capable of it. Therefore, whereas the benefit was paid to a man or a single woman simply on the ground of their incapacity for work, a married or cohabiting woman had also to show that she was incapable of performing normal household duties. That plainly amounted to discrimination on grounds of sex.

SDA was therefore introduced by the Social Security Act 1984 in anticipation of the coming into effect of Council Directive 79/7 *on the progressive implementation of the principle of equal treatment for men and women in matters of social security*. Entitlement to SDA requires that all claimants be not only incapable of work but also severely disabled, unless they have been incapable of work since before they reached the age of 20 (in which case they are unlikely to have satisfied the contribution conditions for incapacity benefit even if they were working) or unless they are assisted by transitional provisions concerned with prior entitlement to non-contributory invalidity pension.

The assessment of disablement falls to adjudicating medical practitioners and, on appeal, to medical appeal tribunals (see Social Security Administration Act 1992, s.45).

Subs. (1). SDA is paid weekly but is paid in respect of individual days of the weekly rate is paid for each day (subs. (8)).

Subs. (2). The first basis of entitlement is that the claimant both is incapable of work and has been for a continuous period of 196 days beginning on or before his 20th birthday. For the meaning of "incapable of work", see reg. 7(1) of the SDA Regulations.

The period of 196 days is calculated by including Sundays so it amounts to 28 weeks.

The 196-day qualifying period does not have to be satisfied if the claimant has previously been entitled to SDA in the same period of incapacity for work—see SDA Regulations, reg. 6. Because of the way periods of incapacity for work separated by less than eight weeks are linked together, this means that a person who has been entitled to SDA may go back to work and will still be able to claim SDA immediately if he becomes incapable of work within the first eight weeks.

Subs. (3). The second basis of entitlement requires that the claimant be "disabled" as well as incapable of work both on the day for which the claim is made and throughout the 196-day qualifying period.

As to the 196-day qualifying period, see above.

A person is "disabled" if assessed as suffering from disablement amounting to at least 80 per cent (subs. (5)). The assessment is carried out by an adjudicating medical authority and, on appeal, by a MAT in the same way as in industrial injuries cases (subs. (6) which applies Sched. 6). Under reg. 10 of the SDA Regulations, a person may be treated as "disabled" on other grounds. The effect of reg. 10(2)(ab) of the Social Security (Incapacity for Work) (General) Regulations 1995, introduced by reg. 2 of the Social Security (Incapacity for Work and Severe Disablement Allowance) Regulations 1997 from April 1, 1997, is that a person who is "disabled" is treated as being "incapable of work".

Subs. (4). For the meaning of "full-time education", see reg. 8 of the SDA Regulations. In particular, it should be noted that only those under the age of 19 are disentitled under this provision.

For residence and presence conditions, see reg. 3.

For people over the age of 65, see regs. 4 and 5.

Subs. (5). It is rare for a person to be entitled to SSP at a time when he would otherwise be entitled to SDA because periods of entitlement to SSP correspond roughly with the 196-day qualifying period for SDA and entitlement to SSP does not arise within eight weeks of previous entitlement to SDA (see Social Security Contributions and Benefits Act 1992, Sched. 11, para. 2(d)).

Subs. (6). Disablement is assessed under Sched. 6 according to the same principles as in industrial injuries cases. Under s.45 of the Social Security Administration Act 1992 the disablement questions, including the assessment of disablement, are referred to and determined by an adjudicating medical authority or a MAT.

Subs. (7). In addition to the basic allowance, there are increases for dependants (s.90; and the Social Security Benefits (Dependency) Regulations 1977, reg. 12, *see Non-means-tested Benefits: The Legislation*, Bonner *et al.*) and there is also an age-related addition payable under s.69. From April 17, 1997, the rates are: claimant £37.75 pw; adult dependant £22.40 pw; child dependant £11.20 pw (reduced by £2.05 for any child for whom the higher rate of child benefit is paid).

Severe disablement allowance: age related addition

69.—(1) If a person was under the age of 60 on the day on which he qualified for severe disablement allowance, the weekly rate of his severe disablement allowance shall be increased by an age related addition at whichever of the weekly rates specified in the second column of paragraph 3 of Part III of Schedule 4 to this Act is applicable in his case, that is to say—

(a) the higher rate, if he was under the age of 40 on the day on which he qualified for severe disablement allowance;

(b) the middle rate, if he was between the ages of 40 and 50 on that day; or

(c) the lower rate, if he was between the ages of 50 and 60 on that day.

(2) Subject to subsection (4) below, for the purposes of this section the day on which a person qualified for severe disablement allowance is his first day of incapacity for work in the period of not less than 196 consecutive days mentioned in section 68(2)(b) or (3)(b) above, as the case may be, which preceded the first day in his current period of entitlement.

(3) For the purposes of this section, a person's "current period of entitlement" is a current period—

(a) which consists of one or more consecutive days on which he is or has been entitled to a severe disablement allowance; and

(b) which begins immediately after the last period of one or more consecutive days for which he was not entitled to such an allowance.

(4) Regulations—

(a) may prescribe cases were a person is to be treated for the purposes of this section as having qualified for severe disablement allowance on a prescribed day earlier than the day ascertained in accordance with subsection (2) above;

(b) may provide for days which are not days of incapacity for work in relation to a person to be treated as days of incapacity for work for the purpose of determining under this section the day on which he qualified for severe disablement allowance; and

(c) may make provision for disregarding prescribed days in computing any period of consecutive days for the purposes of subsection (3) above.

DERIVATION

Social Security Act 1975, s.36A.

GENERAL NOTE

The younger a person is when he or she first becomes disabled, the greater the amount of benefit he or she receives. This reflects the fact that he or she will have had less opportunity to make other provision before becoming disabled.

Although, the predecessor of this section came into force only on December 3, 1990, it applies also to people who first qualified for severe disablement allowance before then.

Subs. (1). From April 7, 1997 the rates are: higher £13.15 pw; middle £8.30 pw; lower £4.15 pw.

Subs. (4). See regs. 10A and 10B of the SDA Regs.

Invalid care allowance

Invalid care allowance

70.—(1) A person shall be entitled to an invalid care allowance for any day on which he is engaged in caring for a severely disabled person if—

(a) he is regularly and substantially engaged in caring for that person;

(b) he is not gainfully employed; and

(c) the severely disabled person is either such relative of his as may be prescribed or a person of any such other description as may be prescribed.

(2) In this section, "severely disabled person" means a person in respect of whom there is payable either an attendance allowance or a disability living allowance by virtue of entitlement to the care component at the highest or middle rate or such other payment out of public funds on account of his need for attendance as may be prescribed.

(3) A person shall not be entitled to an allowance under this section if he is under the age of 16 or receiving full-time education.

(4) A person shall not be entitled to an allowance under this section unless he satisfies prescribed conditions as to residence or presence in Great Britain.

(5) Subject to subsection (6) below, a person who has attained [[1]the age of 65] shall not be entitled to an allowance under this section unless he was so entitled (or is treated by regulations as having been so entitled) immediately before attaining that age.

(6) Regulations may make provision whereby a person who has attained [[1]the age of 65], and was entitled to an allowance under this section immediately

before attaining that age, continues to be so entitled notwithstanding that he is not caring for a severely disabled person or no longer satisfies the requirements of subsection (1)(a) or (b), above.

(7) No person shall be entitled for the same day to more than one allowance under this section; and where, apart from this subsection, two or more persons would be entitled for the same day to such an allowance in respect of the same severely disabled person, one of them only shall be entitled and that shall be such one of them—

(a) as they may jointly elect in the prescribed manner, or
(b) as may, in default of such an election, be determined by the Secretary of State in his discretion.

(8) Regulations may prescribe the circumstances in which a person is or is not to be treated for the purposes of this section as engaged, or regularly and substantially engaged, in caring for a severely disabled person, as gainfully employed or as receiving full-time education.

(9) An invalid care allowance shall be payable at the weekly rate specified in Schedule 4, Part III, paragraph 4.

(10)[[1]. . .]

DERIVATION

Social Security Act 1975, s.37.

AMENDMENTS

1. Social Security (Severe Disablement Allowance and Invalid Care Allowance) Amendment Regulations 1994 (S.I. 1994 No. 2556), reg. 2(3) (October 28, 1994).

GENERAL NOTE

Invalid care allowance is a weekly benefit for those who spend at least 35 hours a week caring for another person who is in receipt of attendance allowance, disability living allowance at the higher or middle rate, or constant attendance allowance under industrial injuries or war disablement schemes.

Like severe disablement allowance (s.68), ICA is an earnings replacement benefit and there is a difficulty in deciding whether a person would have been working but for the need to care for an invalid. It was decided that there should be no requirement that a person should have given up work in order to look after an invalid. However, when first enacted, s.37 of the Social Security Act 1975 excluded married or cohabiting women from entitlement. In *Drake v. Chief Adjudication Officer* (Case 150/85) [1987] Q.B. 166 that exclusion was held to be contrary to Council Directive 79/7 *on the progressive implementation of equal treatment for men and women in matters of social security* so the offending words were removed from subs. (3) retrospectively by the Social Security Act 1986.

Subs. (1). Reg. 6 of the ICA Regulations has the effect that any person, whether related to the carer or not, is prescribed for the purposes of para. (c).

Subs. (2). For prescribed payments out of public funds, see reg. 3 of the ICA Regulations.

Subs. (3). See reg. 5 of the ICA Regulations.

Subs. (4). See reg. 9 of the ICA Regulations.

Subs. (5). The amendment gives effect to the decision of the European Court of Justice in *Thomas v. Chief Adjudication Officer* (Case C 328/91) [1993] Q.B. 747.

Reg. 10 of the ICA Regulations deems people to have been entitled to ICA if they would have been but for an overlapping benefit.

Subs. (6). See reg. 11 of the ICA Regulations.

Subs. (7). See reg. 7 of the ICA Regulations.

Subs. (8). See regs. 4, 5 and 8 of the ICA Regulations.

Subs. (9). In addition to the basic allowance, there are increases for dependants (s.90: and the Social Security Benefits (Dependency) Regulations 1977, reg. 12: see *Non-means-tested Benefits: The Legislation*, Bonner *et al.*). From April 7, 1997 the rates are: claimant £37.75 pw; adult dependant £22.40 pw; child dependant £11.20 pw (reduced by £2.05 for any child for whom the higher rate of child benefit is paid.

Disability living allowance

71.—(1) Disability living allowance shall consist of a care component and a mobility component.

(2) A person's entitlement to a disability living allowance may be an entitlement to either component or to both of them.

(3) A person may be awarded either component for a fixed period or for life, but if his award of a disability living allowance consists of both components, he may not be awarded the components for different fixed periods.

(4) The weekly rate of a person's disability living allowance for a week for which he has only been awarded one component is the appropriate weekly rate for that component as determined in accordance with this Act or regulations under it.

(5) The weekly rate of a person's disability living allowance for a week for which he has been awarded both components is the aggregate of the appropriate weekly rates for the two components as so determined.

(6) A person shall not be entitled to a disability living allowance unless he satisfies prescribed conditions as to residence and presence in Great Britain.

DERIVATION

Social Security Act 1975, s.37ZA.

GENERAL NOTE

This section is introductory. Disability living allowance (DLA) was introduced from April 6, 1992 by the Disability Living Allowance and Disability Working Allowance Act 1991 to give effect to part of the third stage of the programme announced by the Government in *The Way Ahead: Benefits for Disabled People* (Cmnd. 917).

DLA replaced attendance allowance and mobility allowance (formerly payable under ss. 35 and 37A respectively of the Social Security Act 1975) for those under the age of 65. Attendance allowance remains (ss.64–67) for those becoming disabled after that age. There is provision (s.75) for DLA to continue to be paid after a person reaches that age provided the person had been awarded the allowance before reaching that age. There was a similar, but not identical, provision in relation to mobility allowance which was not otherwise payable to those over 65.

There are two components to DLA. The care component (s.72) is similar to attendance allowance. The principal differences are that there is a shorter qualifying period for those not terminally ill (three months instead of six) and there are three rates of payment rather than two, with the introduction of a new lower rate. The mobility component (s.73) is similar to mobility allowance but, again, there are differences. The three-month qualifying period applies to the mobility component as it does to the care component (there was no such period for mobility allowance) but the minimum period for an award is reduced from a year to six months and there are now two rates of payment rather than one. Again, the new rate is a lower one.

The main effect of the changes is to make some provision for those who just failed to qualify in the past. However, fears have been expressed that many of those who will be awarded the new lower rates would previously have been awarded attendance allowance or mobility allowance and that the changes may not prove to have been as advantageous as they seem at first sight.

More general criticism has been made of the limited scope of the reforms promised in *The Way Ahead*. In particular, DLA is available only to those disabled people who need attention or supervision as a result of disability or who are likely to have greater mobility costs. Those who have other costs such as an expensive diet or large laundry costs may not qualify for any assistance. Furthermore, those severely disabled people who must pay for those who care for them are likely to find that DLA does not go very far.

Subss. (2)–(5). Although a person may be awarded either just one component or both, the components are not entirely separate benefits. On an appeal, a disability appeal tribunal must usually consider both components, unless s. 33(4) to (6) of the Social Security Administration Act 1992 applies, but, in *CSDLA/180/94*, it was held:

"Where a claim under appeal relates only to one component and there is no award of the other component and no evidence of substance relating to that other component, a tribunal may safely accept, record and proceed upon a restriction of the appeal to the component claimed."

See also *R(DLA)1/95*. Where an appeal *does* involve both components, a tribunal may determine entitlement to one component and adjourn consideration of the other component (*CSDLA/102/95* where a tribunal awarded the lowest rate of the care component but adjourned the appeal relating to the mobility component to await a medical report).

It is suggested that a tribunal must consider whether the advantages in terms of the efficient use of tribunal time and the speed of the first decision outweigh the risk of there being inconsistent decisions if a differently constituted tribunal deals with the second issue in the light of further evidence. If a person is awarded both components, there is one award of DLA at a rate calculated by aggregating the appropriate rates of the components and the award must be for one common period and not different periods for the different components. It follows that, if one component has been awarded and the claimant appeals against refusal of the other, the tribunal must be informed of the period of the award (*CDLA/52/94*). DLA may be paid at any one of 11 different rates or, more strictly, 10 since two are the same:

care component	mobility component	From April 7, 1997 £
highest	higher	84.10
middle	higher	67.70
highest	lower	62.65
highest	—	49.50
lowest	higher	47.75
middle	lower	46.25
—	higher	34.60
middle	—	33.10
lowest	lower	26.30
lowest	—	13.15
—	lower	13.15

Subs. (6). See reg. 2 of the DLA Regulations

The care component

72.—(1) Subject to the provisions of this Act, a person shall be entitled to the care component of a disability living allowance for any period throughout which—

(a) he is so severely disabled physically or mentally that—

(i) he requires in connection with his bodily functions attention from another person for a significant portion of the day (whether during a single period or a number of periods); or

(ii) he cannot prepare a cooked main meal for himself if he has the ingredients; or

(b) he is so severely disabled physically or mentally that, by day, he requires from another person—

(i) frequent attention throughout the day in connection with his bodily functions; or

(ii) continual supervision throughout the day in order to avoid substantial danger to himself or others; or

(c) he is so severely disabled physically or mentally that, at night,—

(i) he requires from another person prolonged or repeated attention in connection with his bodily functions; or

(ii) in order to avoid substantial danger to himself or others he requires another person to be awake for a prolonged period or at frequent intervals for the purpose of watching over him.

(2) Subject to the following provisions of this section, a person shall not be entitled to the care component of a disability living allowance unless—

(a) throughout—

(i) the period of three months immediately preceding the date on which the award of that component would begin; or

(ii) such other period of three months as may be prescribed,

he has satisfied or is likely to satisfy one or other of the conditions mentioned in subsection (1)(a) to (c) above; and

(b) he is likely to continue to satisfy one or other of those conditions throughout—

(i) the period of six months beginning with that date; or

(ii) (if his death is expected within the period of six months beginning with that date) the period so beginning and ending with his death.

(3) Three weekly rates of the care component shall be prescribed.

(4) The weekly rate of the care component payable to a person for each week in the period for which he is awarded that component shall be—

(a) the highest rate, if he falls within subsection (2) above by virtue of having satisfied or being likely to satisfy both the conditions mentioned in subsection (1)(b) and (c) above throughout both the period mentioned in paragraph (a) of subsection (2) above and that mentioned in paragraph (b) of that subsection;

(b) the middle rate, if he falls within that subsection by virtue of having satisfied or being likely to satisfy one or other of those conditions throughout both those periods; and

(c) the lowest rate in any other case.

(5) For the purposes of this section, a person who is terminally ill, as defined in section 66(2) above, and makes a claim expressly on the ground that he is such a person, shall be taken—

(a) to have satisfied the conditions mentioned in subsection (1)(b) and (c) above for the period of three months immediately preceding the date of the claim, or, if later, the first date on which he is terminally ill (so however that the care component shall not be payable by virtue of this paragraph for any period preceding that date); and

(b) to satisfy or to be likely to satisfy those conditions for the remainder of his life beginning with that date.

(6) For the purposes of this section in its application to a person for any period which he is under the age of 16—

(a) sub-paragraph (ii) of subsection (1)(a) above shall be omitted; and

(b) neither the condition mentioned in sub-paragraph (i) of that paragraph nor any of the conditions mentioned in subsection (1)(b) and (c) above shall be taken to be satisfied unless—

(i) he has requirements of a description mentioned in subsection (1)(a), (b) or (c) above substantially in excess of the normal requirements of persons of his age; or

(ii) he has substantial requirements of any such description which younger persons in normal physical and mental health may also have but which persons of his age and in normal physical and mental health would not have.

(7) Subject to subsections (5) and (6) above, circumstances may be prescribed in which a person is to be taken to satisfy or not to satisfy such of the conditions mentioned in subsection (1)(a) to (c) above as may be prescribed.

(8) Regulations may provide that a person shall not be paid any amount in respect of a disability living allowance which is attributable to entitlement to the care component for a period when he is a person for whom accommodation is provided—

(a) in pursuance—

(i) of Part III of the National Assistance Act 1948 or paragraph 2 of Schedule 8 to the National Health Service Act 1977; or

(ii) of Part IV of the Social Work (Scotland) Act 1968 or section 7 of the Mental Health (Scotland) Act 1984; or

(b) in circumstances in which the cost is, or may be, borne wholly or partly out of public or local funds, in pursuance of those enactments or of any other enactment relating to persons under disability or to young persons or to education or training.

Derivation

Social Security Act 1975, s.37ZB

General Note

This section makes basic provision for the care component of DLA.

Subs. (1). This subsection sets out the conditions of entitlement. Para. (b) reproduces the "day" conditions of attendance allowance and para. (c) reproduces the "night" conditions for attendance allowance. Para. (a) contains the conditions for the lowest rate of the care component of DLA first introduced on April 6, 1992 and, being concerned with attendance needs during the day, is intended as a less stringent alternative to para. (b)(i). The lowest rate is paid to a person who satisfies only the condition of para. (a), the middle rate is paid to those who satisfy the conditions of either one of paras. (b) or (c) and the highest rate is payable to a person who satisfies the conditions of both paras. (b) and (c) (see subs. (4)). It is to be noted that a person who satisfies para. (c) does not receive any more benefit if he or she also satisfies para. (a) so that a person who requires prolonged attention at night and also attention for a significant portion of the day (but not throughout the day) receives only the middle rate. It is therefore necessary for an adjudication officer or tribunal to consider para. (a) only if neither paras. (b) or (c) is satisfied and in most cases it will be sensible to consider paras. (b) and (c) first.

Para. (a) provides two different and alternative attention conditions. Paras. (b) and (c) each provide one attention condition and an alternative condition directed to the claimant's need to be supervised or watched over. The day attention condition (para. (b)(i)) is more stringent than the night attention condition (para. (c)(i)) because during the day the need for attention must be "frequent . . . throughout the day" whereas at night the attention required need only be "prolonged or repeated". Thus one substantial, or two or three shorter, periods of attention suffice to satisfy the night condition but more frequent periods are needed during the day. That reflects the greater disruption caused by the need for attention at night. The differences between paras. (b)(ii) and (c)(ii) are more complicated. The requirement for "supervision" during the day is less stringent than the requirement for "watching over" at night. However, the supervision during the day must be "continual . . . throughout the day" whereas the watching over at night need only be "for a prolonged period or at frequent intervals" which need not necessarily be spread throughout the night.

Note that reg. 7 of the DLA Regulations deems certain people undergoing renal dialysis to satisfy either the day or the night attention condition and so qualify for the middle rate of the care component.

Note also that, under subs. (5), terminally ill claimants may be deemed to satisfy both the day and night conditions and so qualify for the highest rate of the care component for the rest of their lives.

any period throughout which: These words require some consistency in the claimant's need for attendance over the whole period of an award but they do not require that the conditions should be satisfied on every day. The Attendance Allowance Board's *Handbook for Delegated Medical Practitioners* suggested that a man satisfies the night attention condition if he "invariably requires prolonged or repeated attention on more nights of the week than he does not". Although DLA is a weekly benefit, there does not seem to be any particular reason for requiring that it should *invariably* be the case that a person should satisfy the statutory criteria in the majority of the days of a week. In *R(A) 2/74*, the Commissioner said:

> "I think that the delegate should take a broad view of the matter, asking himself some such question as whether in the whole circumstances the words of the statute do or do not as a matter of the ordinary usage of the English language cover or apply to the facts. These are matters for the good sense and judgment of the delegate."

Thus, it may be appropriate in some cases to make an award covering a substantial period notwithstanding that there may be expected to be periods of remission in the claimant's condition lasting longer than a week. Both the length of the periods of remission and their frequency are likely to be relevant considerations as, perhaps, is the severity of the disablement during other periods. If the disability is one from which a substantial period of remission is quite likely, an award for a short period may be appropriate. If at the end of that period the claimant no longer satisfies the conditions for an award, or an award at the same rate, but the period of remission lasts less than two years, reg. 6 of the DLA Regulations enables the claimant to qualify again without having to wait the usual three months (or six months if the claimant is over 65).

so severely disabled physically or mentally: The purpose of the phrase appears to be to limit payment to those cases where the requirement for attendance arises from a condition of body or mind rather than from any convention, religious belief, cultural habit or other possible cause. *CA/137/84* concerned a child who was severely physically disabled in that, among other disabilities, his right arm was shorter than his left one and he had severe weakness of grip in his right hand. The issue was whether he reasonably required attention in connection with the bodily function of eating because he could not use his right hand for that purpose. He was a Muslim and there was evidence that, according to Muslim law, food is eaten using the right hand only, the left hand being considered unclean because it is used when washing the private parts after defecation. The Chief Commissioner held that the requirement for attention must be in consequence of the severe disablement and not from the combined effect both of the severe disablement and the religious or cultural beliefs of the claimant.

However this phrase has recently been given greater significance as it has been suggested that it gives rise to a preliminary question as to whether the claimant is suffering from a severe physical or mental disability. In *R(A) 2/92*, the Chief Commissioner, giving leave to appeal in an attendance allowance case, asked:

> "Is it right . . . to reframe the statutory words 'so severely disabled physically or mentally that . . . he requires . . .' into a question treated as determinitive whether a person is suffering from a severe mental or physical disability and to sever the language of the subsection?"

He may have had in mind the warning against analysing these provisions word by word given by Lord Bridge in *Re Woodling* [1984] 1 W.L.R. 348 at 352 (reported also as App. 2 to *R(A) 2/80*) where, in a case concerning attendance allowance, he said:

> "Again, it seems a reasonable inference that the policy of the enactment was to provide a financial incentive to encourage families or friends to undertake the difficult and sometimes distasteful task of caring within the home for those who are so severely disabled that they must otherwise become a charge on some public institution.
>
> The language of the section should, I think, be considered as a whole, and such consideration will, I submit, be more likely to reveal the intention than an attempt to analyse each word or phrase separately."

Nevertheless, in *R(A) 2/92* the Chief Commissioner's question was answered in the affirmative and it was held (para. 10) that "where a person indulges in aggressive or seriously irresponsible conduct the Board has to consider whether that arises from some recognised disordered mental condition or whether it merely arises from a defective character". In *CA/123/91*, the Commissioner appears to have accepted a submission that a claimant must be suffering from a "diagnosable disease" and said that the "phrase 'severely disabled physically or mentally' relates to a condition of body or mind that can be defined medically and it is not meant to encompass unsociable behaviour which is not related to serious mental illness". In *Re H (A Minor)* (unreported, February 17, 1994, C. A., on appeal from *CA/648/91*), it was argued that a delegated medical practitioner had erred in law in concluding that, because a child's symptoms were "behavioural in origin", the psychological condition from which she was suffering could not amount to a mental disability. The claimant's appeal was dismissed without the court having called on counsel for the Secretary of State. The court purported to determine the appeal solely upon the construction of the delegated medical practitioner's decision, without determining the point of principle. However, they held that the delegated medical practitioner had been entitled to find that the psychological condition from which the claimant was suffering did not amount to a mental disability, taking into account the medical opinion which, they thought, implicitly suggested that the condition was not serious. In other words, not all psychological conditions amount to mental disability and the distinction is a medical question rather than a question of law. It is difficult to read the decision as a whole as being anything other than a confirmation of the approach taken in *R(A) 2/92*. The difficulty with this approach is that mental illness may be defined by reference to a person's behaviour (see Mental Health Act 1983, s.1). In *W v. L* [1974] Q.B. 711 at 719, Lawton L.J. said:

> "I ask myself, what would the ordinary sensible person have said about the patient's condition in this case if he had been informed of his behaviour to the dogs, the cat and his wife? In my judgment such a person would have said: 'Well, the fellow is obviously mentally ill.' . . . and there is the added medical fact that when the EEG was taken there were indications of a clinical character showing some abnormality of the brain. It is that application of the sensible person's assessment of the condition, plus the medical indication, which in my judgment brought the case within the classification of mental illness. . . ."

It may be relevant that there is no such word as "specific", whereas s.17(1)(a)(ii) provides that a day of incapacity arises only if a person is, or is deemed to be, "incapable of work by reason of some specific disease or bodily or mental disablement". On the other hand, it is difficult to understand the concept of "specific . . . mental disablement" (see John Mesher's comments at [1982] J.S.W.L. 48) and, in *CS 7/82*, the term "personality disorder" was held to convey a mental disability within s.17(1)(a)(ii). This point does not appear to have been taken in *R(A) 4/90* where the diagnoses included "anxiety state" and "personality disorder".

The question whether disablement is "severe" is plainly to be determined by reference to the need for attendance because the phrase reads: "*so severely* disabled physically or mentally *that* . . . he requires. . . ." In *Re H (A Minor)*, the Court of Appeal was prepared to assume that a submission along these lines was correct without hearing argument on the point.

requires: "Requires" means "reasonably requires" (see *Mallinson v. Secretary of State for Social Security* [1994] 1 W.L.R. 630, H.L. also reported as an appendix to *R(A)3/94*) and not "medically requires", (see *R(A) 3/86* following *R. v. Social Security Commissioner, ex p. Connolly* [1986] 1 W.L.R. 424). In *CA/96/84* the fact that it was considered that an eight-year old girl who suffered from nocturnal eneuresis would come to no harm if left in her wet bedding and nightclothes did not necessarily mean that she did not require the attention necessary to change them. The Commissioner pointed out that otherwise it might be said of a person who could not dress himself and was housebound that he did not require assistance with dressing as he could easily remain without medical harm in his dressing gown all day.

In *R(A) 1/73*, the Chief Commissioner observed that "The question of course is whether supervision was required, not whether it was in fact provided. But the Board would probably agree that evidence that supervision (or attention) was in fact provided is strong evidence that it was required; mothers would be unlikely to exhaust themselves by providing it unnecessarily *for years*." On the other hand, if a claimant lives with his wife and she cares for him, a tribunal are entitled to assume that he does not require more attention than she gives him, unless a submission is specifically made to the contrary (*CDLA/5221/95*).

It is often suggested that, because claimants are aware of dangers, they can take steps to avoid placing themselves in positions of danger and so can avoid any requirement for attention and supervision. However, claimants can be said reasonably to require supervision if otherwise they would have to make unreasonable changes in their lifestyles. In *R(A) 3/89*, the Commissioner adopted observations made in *CSA/4/87*:

> "If she is at risk of falling and indeed there is evidence that she has fallen it is simply not enough to say, as the DMP does, that she should take precautions and undertake only those activities which are within the limits imposed by her disabilities. Is he suggesting that when she has fallen she has been engaged in activities she should not sensibly have undertaken? Is she not to move from her chair without assistance? Is she expected to remain chairbound until assistance is available? If whenever she moves from her chair she needs supervision why does that not satisfy the condition?"

In *R(A) 5/90*, a Tribunal of Commissioners has said that any determination in a case where it is suggested that a claimant can take steps to avoid the necessity for supervision should identify the precautions to be taken or the activities to be refrained from; otherwise the reasons given are certain to be insufficient. This requires that a tribunal should explain how the suggestion is practical and compatible with reasonable normal domestic arrangements. In *R(A) 4/90*, the claimant's need for attention arose, at least in part, from her inordinate self-dosages of laxatives. The delegated medical practitioner took the view that "reduced dosage of aperients would have facilitated less frequent bowel action". The Tribunal of Commissioners held that he had erred because it was not clear to what extent he had considered whether her psychiatric position was such that she no longer had "any effective control over that aspect of her life". In *Secretary of State v. Fairey* (decided by the House of Lords with *Cockburn v. Chief Adjudication Officer* [1997] 1 W.L.R. 799) the claimant was profoundly deaf and one issue was whether she "required" interpretation by sign language for the purpose of carrying out social activities. Lord Slynn of Hadley said, at 815:

> "In my opinion the yardstick of a 'normal life' is important; it is a better approach than adopting the test as to whether something is 'essential' or 'desirable.' Social life in the sense of mixing with others, taking part in activities with others, undertaking recreation and cultural activities can be part of normal life. It is not in any way unreasonable that the severaly disabled person should wish to be involved in them despite his disability. What is reasonable will depend on the age, sex, interests of the applicant and other circumstances. To take part in such activities sight and hearing are nomrally necessary and if they are impaired attention is required in connection with the bodily functions of seeing and hearing to enable the person to overcome his disability. As Swinton Thomas L.J. in the Court of Appeal said: 'Attention given to a profoundly deaf person to enable that person to carry on, so far as possible in the circumstances, an ordinary life is capable of being attention that is reasonable required.'
>
> How much attention is reasonably required and how frequently it is required are questions of fact for the adjudication officer."

In *CDLA/267/94*, it was suggested that the decision of the Court of Appeal in *Fairey*, which was to the same effect as the decision of the House of Lords, did not have the effect that a claimant who is blind must be placed in the same position as a person without disability.

> "In the present case, for instance, it is said that the claimant requires attention to help him find things that he has lost. That may well be so, but the tribunal to whom this case is now referred must consider whether that implies a requirement for frequent attention or whether, when the claimant has lost something, he could reasonably be expected to wait until infrequent attention was to hand."

Furthermore, many of the tasks required to be performed for a person with disability do not amount to the provision of "attention . . . in connection with his bodily functions" (see below).

A tribunal are entitled to suggest sensible steps that a claimant might take to avoid a requirement for someone to provide attention or supervision, but the claimant should be given the opportunity of commenting on the suggestion (*CSA/50/87*) because the steps may be impractical or unreasonable.

attention . . . in connection with his bodily functions: These words appear in paras. (a)(i), (b)(i) and (c)(i) but not always in the same order. Bodily functions "include breathing, hearing, seeing, eating, drinking, walking, sitting, sleeping, getting out of bed, dressing, undressing, eliminating waste products—and the like—all of which an ordinary person—who is not suffering from any disability—does for himself. But they do not include cooking, shopping or any other things which a wife or daughter does as part of her domestic duties: or generally which one member of the household normally does for the rest of the family" (*per* Lord Denning M.R. in *R. v. National Insurance Commissioner, ex p. the Secretary of State for Social Services* [1981] 1 W.L.R. 1017 and also reported as an appendix to *R(A) 2/80*). As Lord Denning noted, it is the words "in connection with" which give rise to the difficulty. Although cooking obviously has some connection with eating, the connection is regarded as too remote. Lord Denning held that "shopping, cooking meals, making tea or coffee, laying the table or the tray, carrying it into the room, making the bed or filling the hot water bottle" did not qualify as being attention in connection with bodily functions whereas "cutting up food, lifting the cup to the mouth, helping to dress and undress or at the toilet" all did qualify. The House of Lords in *Re Woodling* [1984] 1 W.L.R. 348 (also reported as app. 2 to *R(A) 2/80*) agreed that domestic tasks (including cooking) did not qualify and considered that attention in connection with bodily functions connoted "a high degree of physical intimacy between the person giving and the person receiving the attention". The new condition in para. (a)(ii) assists those who require assistance with cooking.

Assistance provided to enable a claimant to cook for himself could possibly be attention in connection with his bodily function of, say, lifting but there would be a question whether that attention was reasonably required or whether it could reasonably be obviated by having someone else do the cooking (*CDLA/267/94*). In *Cockburn*, the House of Lords held that dealing with the additional laundry generated by a claimant's incontience was not capable of being attention in connection with her bodily functions but that changing her night clothes and bedding and taking the soiled bedding to be rinsed and hung out to dry would be. "I see here a sufficient continuity between the applicant's incontinence and the presence of the other person to deal with the consequences on the spot to satisfy the section" (at 804). It follows from *Cockburn* that R(A) 1/91 can no longer be regarded as good law. In *CSDLA/160/95*, the Commissioner decided that the selection, preparation and cooking of special foods and supplements for a person suffering from pheylketonuria did not amount to attention in connection with the cliamant's bodily function. This decision appears to be in conflict with *R/A 1/87* where a Commissioner had reached the opposite conclusion in respect of a child but had not been referred to *Re Woodling*. *Mallinson, Cockburn* and *Fairey* all followed *Re Woodling* in stressing the need for physical initmacy between the person giving and the person receiving the attention but it is clear from *Mallinson* and *Fairey* that that need not involve physical contact. Oral guidance of a blind man would amount to attention in connection with a bodily function (*Mallinson*) and interpreting for a deaf person by sign language would also amount to attention in connection with a bodily function (*Fairey*). In *Fairey*, the Commissioner (*CA/780/91*) drew a distinction (also drawn in *CDLA/240/94*) between communication through an interpreter and communication directly with another person "reasonably skilled in the use of sign language". The interpreter would be providing attention but the other party to the "conversation" would not usually be doing so, although there might be exceptions when a claimant's disability meant that a considerable amount of effort would be required in comprehending what he or she wanted to communicate. The Court of Appeal dismissed the claimant's cross-appeal on this issue (*Secretary of State v. Fairey* June 15, 1995) and the claimant abandoned the point before the House of Lords. The Commissioner also pointed out that a profoundly deaf person may require more attention as a child, while learning to sign, than he or she does in later life. Cajoling a person suffering from mental illness so that he or she avoids self-neglect may amount to attention (*CDLA/14696/96*).

In *Fairey*, Lord Slynn of Hadley said, at 814:

> "It may well be that, on a strict analysis and in logic, attention cannot be in connection with a bodily function which does not function and never has functioned since birth, but it seems to me impossible to attribute to Parliament the intention to exclude from the section attention given to a person whose bodily functions (sight or hearing) are wholly impaired and to limit it to someone whose bodily functions are partially impaired. If an over-fine analysis leads to such an absurd result it is necessary, as Lord Bridge stressed in *Re Woodling*, to look at the language of the section as a whole to find the intention."

It may be important correctly to identify the bodily function relevant to any particular case. In *Mallinson* the House of Lords were considering an appeal by a blind claimant who said that he required attention in the form of guidance when out walking, so that he would not injure himself. The majority took the view that the case should be considered as one where the claimant needed attention in connection with the bodily function of seeing. Lord Lloyd, with whom Lord Mustill agreed, considered that that could not be right because the claimant was unable to see, however much attention he received. They took the view that the only relevant bodily function was walking and that, as the claimant could walk – in the sense of making progress on foot – without attention, the appeal should be dismissed. He suggested that if "you were to ask a blind man's guide what his purpose was he would reply 'I am helping him walk because he cannot see;' he would not say 'I am helping him see to walk." On the other hand, Lord Woolf, with whom Lord Templeman and Lord Browne-Wilkinson agreed, said:

> "The fact that your disability is so severe that you are incapable of exercising a bodily function does not mean that the attention you receive is not in connection with that bodily function. The attention is in connection with the bodily function if it provides a substitute method of providing what the bodily function would provide if it were not totally or partially impaired."

At first sight it is not easy to reconcile Lord Woolf's approach with the language of the statute which does seem to refer to the functions still performed by the claimant or, as Lord Lloyd observed, with the approach taken in *Re Woodling*. However, the result appears more obviously consistent with the presumed purpose of the legislation and the approaches can be reconciled if bodily functions are appropriately defined in terms of what they enable a person to do. Seeing enables a person to avoid obstacles. Lord Lloyd's blind man's guide might well say "I am helping him to avoid obstacles".

The distinction between "attention" (paras. (a)(i), (b)(i) and (c)(i)) and "supervision" (paras. (b)(ii) and (c) (ii)) was explained in a helpful passage in *CA 6/72* approved in *R(A) 3/74*:

> "In my judgment, the word 'attention' denotes a concept of some personal service of an active nature; for example, helping the disabled person to bath or eat his food, cooking for him, or dressing a wound. On the other hand the word 'supervision' denotes a more passive concept, such as being in the same room with the disabled person so as to be prepared to intervene if necessary; but not actually intervening save in emergencies."

Cooking, if attention, is not in connection with bodily functions, but in other respects that passage holds good and that distinction between the concepts of attention and supervision was accepted by the Court of Appeal in *Moran v. Secretary of State for Social Services* (reported as an appendix to *R(A) 1/88*) and approved in *Mallinson* where it was said that the two concepts were not mutally exclusive. A person providing supervision to an epileptic also provides attention when giving assistance during or after an attack. A person supervising a blind person gives attention when providing guidance.

To satisfy the condition of para. (a)(i), the attention must be required *for a significant portion of the day* and it is expressly provided that that may be during a single period or a number of periods. Read literally, however, that suggests that the actual giving of attention must add up to a significant portion of the day but it is arguable that the sub-paragraph is also intended to cover several short, momentary, instances of attention which may not themselves last for a significant portion of the day but can be said to occur within one. If that be right, a person who does not require any help when at home but does need escorting outside when it is usual for the escort to have to intervene to provide support or guidance several times, each for a few seconds, may satisfy the condition if such trips out themselves last for a significant portion of the day. No guidance is given in the legislation as to the meaning of "significant portion" save that it is arguable that para. (a)(i) should be satisfied if the attention is spread over a period as long as that needed to prepare a cooked main meal and satisfy para. (a)(ii). This would be consistent with the Government's suggestion that a significant portion of the day would be interpreted as "an hour or thereabouts" so that people who need help getting in and out of bed or a bath or with administering a course of injections or medicines might qualify (see *Hansard*, HL Vol. 526 col. 884). In *CDLA/58/93* the Commissioner declined to take account of what was said in Parliament, holding that the conditions for doing so (see *Pepper v. Hart* [1993] A.C. 593, HL) were not met. The meaning of "a significant portion of the day" therefore fell to be considered in the light of ordinary usage, but he "would not dissent" from a suggestion made on behalf of the adjudication officer that the length of time in question could be "a minimum of an hour". He rejected a submission made on behalf of the claimant that "significant" could refer to the importance to the claimant of the attention and he held that it referred only to the length of time for which attention was given. In *CSDLA/29/94* the Commissioner said that "attention for a lesser period [than one hour] could be 'significant', depending on the circumstances. Thus if it consists of many short periods of attention the total significance in time terms may be greater. The attention must be 'for a significant portion of the day' and the preposition 'for' seems to me to open up to consideration the position of the attender. If for that individual to provide the attention necessary on a considerable number of small occasions produces other disruption to his or her own affairs then that *may* elevate those periods from relative insignificance to an overall and collective significance." The Commissioner also held that the word "portion" suggested that one must look at the proportion of the day the total amount of attention took up. It was unnecessary for a tribunal to decide exactly how much time was taken by each bit of attention. What the tribunal had to do was to consider the total amount of attention and "make a broad determination, recorded . . . as a finding, of the percentage or fraction of the normal day for this household that total involved."

To satisfy the condition of para. (b)(i), the attention must be *frequent . . . throughout the day*. Frequent connotes "several times—not once or twice" (*per* Lord Denning M.R. in *R. v. National Insurance Commissioner, ex p. the Secretary of State for Social Services* [1981] 1 W.L.R. 1017 and also reported as an appendix to *R(A) 2/80*). In *CA/147/84*, the Commissioner held that the phrase consisted of ordinary words, not used in any unusual sense, and he refused to hold a delegated medical practitioner to have been wrong in law when he had decided that a girl who required catheterisation for 10 to 15 minutes, four times a day at 8 a.m., 12.30 p.m., 5 p.m. and 8.30 p.m. did not require frequent attention throughout the day. In *CA/281/89*, the Commissioner held that attention should be required "at intervals spread over the day". It is not necessary that the frequent attention be needed throughout the day in connection with the same bodily function so that the various types of attention required during the day in connection with different bodily functions must be added together (see *Mallinson*). The fact that there are lengthy periods when no attention is required does not mean that attention is not required frequently throughout the day and in *CA/140/85*, the Chief Commissioner stressed the need to have regard to the claimant's normal routine and the fact that a claimant's need for attention was "in the main" at the beginning and end of the day did not justify adopting a *de minimis* conclusion in relation to his needs in the remainder of the day. The evidence suggested that the claimant, who was blind, needed help with dressing and some, although perhaps not very much, help at meal-times. The Chief Commissioner said that it was erroneous "to specify, given the pattern of this gentleman's daily activity, that once dressed in the morning there was no significant need for dressing subsequently; he went out every day and could hardly be expected to get up in the morning in his mackintosh. What happened if he got up in slippers, who was to choose the shoes of a pair so that he avoided wearing either two left shoes or one brown and one black one? As for eating or drinking he had the ordinary three meals a day with tea in the morning and apparently on occasions some late evening drink before going to bed." In some cases like that it might be that a person could manage throughout the day without any attention if everything were arranged properly at the beginning of the day but as long as some attention is still required at other times during the day a claimant may qualify even if the amount of attention is spread unevenly.

To satisfy para (c)(i), the attention must be *at night . . . prolonged or repeated*. "'Prolonged' means some little time. 'Repeated' means more than once at any rate" (*per* Lord Denning M.R. in *R. v. National Insurance Commissioner, ex p. the Secretary of State for Social Services* [1981] 1 W.L.R. 1017 and also reported as an appendix to *R(A) 2/80*). The Attendance Allowance Board used to take "prolonged" to mean at least 20 minutes and in *CA/271/88* a Commissioner refused to hold a delegated medical practitioner to have erred in law when he decided that attention for 15 minutes was not prolonged. Note that one "prolonged" period of attention suffices and that if there are "repeated" periods, they need not be throughout the night but might all be concentrated in one part of it and, of course, they need not all be in connection with the same bodily function. In a Northern Ireland case, *R 1/72 (A.A.)*, the Commissioner held the Attendance Allowance Board to have erred in applying the criterion of "constant and regular attendance" instead of "prolonged or repeated attention" and also in suggesting that the condition had to be satisfied every night. Time spent soothing a child back to sleep after a fit counts (*R(A) 3/78*).

cannot prepare a cooked main meal for himself if he has the ingredients: This new condition enables people to qualify for the lower rate despite *Woodling*. The reference to ingredients is intended to exclude any suggestion that a person who needs assistance with shopping might qualify on this ground (although he or she might qualify under para. (a)(i) if he or she reasonably requires attention to enable him or her to do the shopping, rather than having someone else do it). The "cooking test" was considered at length in *R(DLA)2/95*, where the Commissioner said:

"... In my view the 'cooking test' is a hypothetical test to be determined objectively. Factors such as the type of facilities or equipment available and a claimant's cooking skills are irrelevant.

8. The nature of the 'cooked main meal' which the claimant 'cannot prepare' is crucial. In my view it is a labour intensive reasonable main daily meal freshly cooked on a traditional cooker. What is reasonable is a question of fact to be determined by reference to what is reasonable for a member of the community to which the claimant belongs, *e.g.* a vegetarian meal as opposed to one which is not. The use of the phrase 'for himself' shows that the meal is intended to be just for one person, not for the whole family. The 'main meal' at issue is therefore a labour intensive, main reasonable daily meal for one person, not a celebration meal or a snack. The main meal must be cooked on a daily basis and it is irrelevant that a claimant may prepare, cook and freeze a number of main meals on the days that help is provided and then defrost and heat them in a microwave on subsequent days. The test depends on what a claimant cannot do without help on each day. Because the main meal has to be cooked, the test includes all activities auxiliary to the cooking such as reaching for a saucepan, putting water in it and lifting it on and off the cooker. All cooking utensils must of course be placed in a reasonable position.

9. The word 'prepare' emphasises a claimant's ability to make all the ingredients ready for cooking. This includes the peeling and chopping of fresh vegetable as opposed to frozen vegetables, which require no real preparation. However in my view a chop, a piece of fish or meat ready minced does not fall in the category of 'convenience foods' and are permissible as basic ingredients. I should add for completeness that because the test is objective it is irrelevant that a claimant may never wish to cook such a meal or that it is considered financially impossible."

In *CDLA/2267/95*, the same Commissioner said:

"It cannot be overstressed that the 'main meal' at issue is a main reasonable daily meal for *one* person. It follows that the use of heavy pans or dishes is not necessary for the preparation of such a meal. Nor is it necessary to use the oven. If the claimant is unable to stand for any length of time, such a meal can be prepared and cooked while sitting on a high stool or chair if necessary. It is all a question of what is reasonable in the circumstances of the case."

As long as there is a reasonable variety of meals that can be prepared by the claimant, the range need not be unlimited (*CDLA/17329/96*). The possibility of the claimant obtaining devices and appliances that he or she does not have and which he or she could not reasonably be expected to obtain must be ignored (*R(DLA)2/95*), but there is no reason why the fact that a claimant has had a kitchen adapted or has special appliances actually available should not be taken into account when considering his or her capacity to prepare a cooked main meal (*CDLA/17329/96*). In *CDLA/902/94*, it was held that a person could satisfy the test in s. 72(1)(a)(ii) if it was not *reasonable* to expect him or her to prepare a cooked main meal, but that reasonableness had to be judged only in relation to the claimant carrying out the hypothetical function identified in *R(DLA)2/95*. The Commissioner, determining the factual issues arising in the case in which the claimant suffered from haemophilia, said:

"Clearly it takes the claimant rather longer to prepare a meal than it would for most people and clearly also he suffers some anxiety when he does so, but the fact remains that he can and does prepare traditional cooked main meals. To say that he acts unreasonably in doing so would be to imply that a person in his position acts reasonably only if he or she gives up traditional meals or cooking methods or has someone else cook such meals. It is not unreasonable for a person with a disability to try and pursue as normal a life as possible unless the risks involved in carrying out a particular task make it so. I do not think that the additional risk and associated anxiety involved in cooking, over and above the risk attending all the claimant's activities, justifies a finding that it is unreasonable to expect him to prepare a cooked main meal."

A person who is unable to cook because the heat from the cooker brings on an asthma attack is just as unable to cook a meal as one who has lost both hands (*CDLA/20/94*). The cooking test under s.72(1)(a)(ii) is not applicable to a child under 16 (see subs. (6)(a)).

day and *night*: It is right to regard night as "that period of inactivity or that principal period of inactivity through which each household goes in the dark hours and to measure the beginning of the night from the time at which the household, as it were, closed down for the night" (*R. v. National Insurance Commissioner, ex p. Secretary of State for Social Services* [1974] 1 W.L.R. 1290 and also reported as an appendix to *R(A) 4/74*). It was also held that dressing in the morning and undressing before going to bed were activities carried on during the day. In the case of a child, "night" is the same as for the adults in the household so that attention given after the child has gone to bed but before its parents have retired is attributable to the "day" (*R(A) 3/78*).

continual supervision . . . in order to avoid substantial danger to himself or others: The distinction between "attention" and "supervision" has been noted above. "The object of supervision is to avoid substantial danger which may or may not in fact arise; so supervision may be precautionary and anticipatory, yet never result in intervention, or it may be ancillary to and part of active assistance given on specific occasions to the claimant" (*R(A) 2/75*). An example of supervision which is precautionary and anticipatory is that provided by a person who is on hand to give assistance when the claimant has a fit. An example of supervision which is ancillary to and part of active assistance given on specific occasions is that provided by a person who is escorting a blind claimant and giving guidance. The former type of supervision may well be provided by someone who is getting on with something else in between any such calls for assistance that there might be. He or she may be in another room. Indeed, someone may be supervising a claimant even while asleep if the circumstances are such that the claimant can wake him or her up when necessary or his or her "antennae" are so attuned that, without any conscious call from the claimant, he or she awakes at the onset of a fit (*Moran*). If the danger is always there, the supervision needed is likely to be continual even though intervention may never be required.

However, in *Moran*, Nicholls L.J. draws a distinction between a need for supervision and a need for someone to be "on call".

> "A person who is in the same room or another room in the same house or in a nearby property and keeps himself available to be called by such a sufferer, in person or by bell or by telephone, may not be exercising 'supervision' over the sufferer. It will all depend upon the particular facts of the case."

In *CDLA/42/94*, the Commissioner said:

> "Supervision may be passive by nature, but it is not constituted by mere presence. In the context of the care component of DLA and of attendance allowance it implies sufficient monitoring to be able to detect signs of a need for assistance."

The ability and willingness of the claimant to summon help which will arrive in time to avoid substantial danger will be important in determining whether he or she requires supervision rather than merely the presence of someone in the vicinity. The frequency of the interventions may also be relevant to the distinction between supervision and mere presence; someone who may expect to be called upon several times a day may, perhaps, be more likely to be exercising supervision than someone who may expect to be called upon once a month. However, where a claimant needs a degree of monitoring, it is clear from *Moran* that "the relative frequency or infrequency of attacks is immaterial so long as the risk of 'substantial' danger is not so remote a possibility that it ought reasonably to be disregarded". In both *R(A) 1/81* and *R(A) 5/81* the point was made that it only required a child to run into traffic once for it to be killed and it was said that two questions should be asked: Is there a relevant (*i.e.* not remote) risk of such an incident occurring? If so, is it likely to give rise to substantial danger to the disabled person concerned or others? This appears, at first sight, to separate the remoteness of the risk from the degree of danger involved, but that does not appear to be the right approach. In *R(A) 2/89*, the Commissioner pointed out that the claimant, a tetraplegic, would be unable to fend for himself if left alone in a house which then caught fire. "This may be a remote contingency but it is not fanciful. And anyone who left the claimant alone in a house where such an emergency arose would be criticised. The result could be catastrophic." This is consistent with the test suggested by the Chief Commissioner in *R(A) 1/73* (above) and with the construction of "requires" as meaning "reasonably requires", but the Commissioner in *R(A) 2/89* appears to use "remote" in a different sense from that used in *R(A) 1/81*, *R(A) 5/81*, *R(A) 3/89* and, in particular, *R(A) 6/89* where the Commissioner made it clear that the question whether substantial danger is so remote that it may reasonably be disregarded itself requires consideration of the degree of danger as well as the chance of the event occurring. However, the decisions are consistent even if the language used is not. An unlikely, but nonetheless possibly life-threatening event needs guarding against whereas a risk of much less serious harm may have to be more likely before it must be taken into account.

To satisfy the condition in para. (b)(ii), the supervision needed must be "continual", but that word is wider than "continuous" (*R(A) 1/73*) so that the condition may be satisfied even though the claimant may safely be left alone for short periods.

In *R(A) 1/73*, the Chief Commissioner also pointed to "a danger of not starting the enquiry at an early enough point. If one starts with the fact that the disabled person is living with relatives who are looking after him, and then asks oneself to what extent he requires supervision, that is beginning at the wrong point. It might indeed be helpful to ask also whether without substantial danger the disabled person could be by himself in a house at any rate for periods long enough to make any supervision that there was not continual." In *CA/60/91*, a Tribunal of Commissioners has pointed out that the Court of Appeal in *Connolly* approved a submission along the same lines.

In *R(A) 1/73*, the Chief Commissioner also said that the phrase "substantial danger" should not be narrowly construed but he quoted from the speech of Viscount Simon L.C. in *Palser v. Grinling* [1948] A.C. 291 at 317 to the effect that "substantial" does not mean just enough to avoid the "*de minimis*" principle but is equivalent to considerable, solid or big and that its applicability is a matter of judgment. The danger certainly need not be life-threatening. In *R(A) 11/83*, a Tribunal of Commissioners were not convinced that biting the tongue during a fit was a minor injury. In *CSA/68/89*, it was suggested that there may well be substantial danger in a suicide attempt which was merely impulsive and not intended to be successful as well as one which was intended to succeed. In *R(A) 3/92* it was held that supervision is required to "avoid" substantial danger if it is required to effect a real reduction in the risk of harm to the claimant. It is not a condition that the supervision should eliminate all substantial danger. Avoiding substantial danger to himself or others includes avoiding the risk of injury to the claimant *by* others (*R(A) 5/81*).

In cases concerning the risk of falling, a Commissioner (in *R(A) 3/89*) has suggested the following questions should be determined:

> "(i) Are the situations in which the claimant may fall predictable or unpredictable? That is to say, does the claimant have a liability to fall anywhere at any time? Or does he fall only in certain circumstances or situations? This is, of course, a matter of medical opinion: but the opinion must be based on evidence.
>
> (ii) If the falling is predictable, can the claimant reasonably be expected to avoid the risk of falling or to place himself at such risk only when adequately supervised? That again is a matter of medical opinion. If the claimant cannot reasonably be expected either to avoid the risk or to place himself at risk only when adequately supervised, the DMP should treat the case as one in which the falling was unpredictable.
>
> (iii) If the falling is unpredictable, will the falling give rise to substantial danger to himself? This is again, of course, a matter of medical opinion. Nevertheless it must be borne in mind that a person, particularly a disabled person, may when falling hit his head on the corner of a cupboard or on a fire kerb or radiator; and whether or not he is injured in the course of falling, he may by reason of his disability be unable to rise or be unable to summon help. Or he may be of such an age that a fall will be likely to have serious consequences. Clearly such matters ought in an appropriate case to be taken into account.
>
> (iv) Is the substantial danger too remote? In the present case, the DMP stated that in his medical opinion the risk of substantial danger arising from a fall 'is so remote a possibility that it ought to be reasonably disregarded.' But he has failed to give any indication why he reached that conclusion or to indicate on what evidence he relied to support that conclusion. Although, as I have said, those questions are matters of medical opinion, it is incumbent upon a DMP to consider all the evidence, including the evidence of the claimant, to make the relevant findings of fact and to give adequate reasons for the conclusions which he reaches upon those findings of fact so that the claimant 'looking at the decision should be able to discern on the face of it the reasons why' the evidence failed to satisfy the DMP: *R(A) 1/72* at paragraph 8. In my judgment the DMP has failed to do so in the present case."

In *R(A) 5/90*, the Tribunal of Commissioners held that those particular questions should not be treated as statutory requirements and that a delegated medical practitioner was not bound, as a matter of law, to answer them but that there "will no doubt be many cases in which it would be helpful in relation to sufficiency of reasons if he did".

A single instance of falling does not necessarily show a propensity to fall such as might give rise to a requirement for supervision to avoid danger (*CA/233/95*). In *CDLA/899/94*, the Commissioner held that, despite a propensity on the claimant's part to fall from time to time, it was not arguable on the undisputed facts of the case that there was a requirement for continual supervision to avoid danger.

> "10. . . . This is not a case of a person who is so unsteady that he requires to be supported whenever he stands, which may have been the case in *R(A) 3/89*. It is always possible that a person who falls may suffer some injury. However, that is far more likely in the case of a person who falls due to a fit or loss of consciousness and therefore cannot take any steps to mitigate the effects of the fall. In the present case, the risk of falling at home is slight and the risk of serious injury when falling at home is even slighter. This is not the case of an elderly person who is particularly frail. It really cannot be said that the claimant reasonably requires someone to be so close to him the whole time as to be able to catch him should he fall.
>
> "11. It is of course theoretically possible that a person falls and the effects of the fall are made worse by the lack of immediate response. Supervision may be required in some case in order to avoid the risk of danger arising after a fall. However, one must have regard to the

relative frequency of falls and the likelihood of serious injury, *of a type that might be avoided if there were supervison*, arising from them."

In *R(A) 4/92*, the claimant had blackouts during which he was liable to fall. The blackouts were unpredictable and the Attendance Allowance Board considered that he did not need supervision because the lack of any warning would prevent intervention quickly enough to avoid the fall. The Commissioner did not accept that approach. "If the claimant were to have an attack on going up a staircase, the presence of another person immediately below him on the staircase might well be capable of preventing substantial damage to the claimant. It is not in my view within the purpose of the Act that, where a person suffers from epileptic attacks without any previous warning, they are thereby not entitled to receive attendance allowance. If the presence of another person is sufficient to reduce the amount of danger involved in the happening of a sudden attack, that may well be sufficient to comply with the conditions of entitlement."

Some medical evidence is likely to be required before it is accepted that somone is suffering from such severe mental disablement that he or she requires continual supervision within this section. Merely being concerned about someone is obviously not enough (*CA/147/84*). It was held in *CSA/68/89* that an impulsive suicide attempt, not intended to succeed, could give rise to substantial danger and that encouragement, support, comfort and reassurance given to the potential suicide could amount to supervision. In the light of *Mallinson*, it is probably more accurate to say that that sort of assistance may amount to attention but that an unpredictable need for it may show a need for continual supervision to avoid substantial danger to the claimant. In *R(A) 2/91* a consultant psychiatrist had said the claimant was "at times significantly depressed and potentially at risk to herself". The Commissioner held that the fact that she had not been detained in hospital was not sufficient to show that there would be no serious risk of substantial danger to herself in the absence of supervision. In *R(A) 3/92* the Commissioner held that a view that nothing would stop a really determined suicide attempt was not a ground for concluding that there was no requirement for continual supervision to avoid substantial danger to the claimant. The question should be whether continual supervision is required "in order to effect a real reduction in the risk of harm to the claimant".

to be awake . . . for the purpose of watching over him: Following the Court of Appeal's decision in *Moran* to the effect that a person might exercise supervision while asleep, the former night supervision condition (see the note to s.64, above) was replaced by this "watching over" condition which requires that the supervisor be awake for a prolonged period or at frequent intervals. For the meaning of "prolonged" and "frequent" see under "attention . . . in connection with bodily functions" above. Note that the frequent intervals need not be "throughout" the night but could be concentrated in one part of the night. As long as a person is awake for the requisite period or periods and the wakefulness is for the purpose of watching over the claimant, it does not appear necessary that the person be actually looking at the claimant for the whole of that time.

Subs. (2). Para. (a) imposes the three-month qualifying period but this is deemed to be satisfied in the case of a person who is terminally ill (see subs. (5)). If a person's condition deteriorates so that he or she satisfies a further condition and would qualify for a higher rate of the care component, the effect of subs. (4) is that the claimant must still wait three months before qualifying for the higher rate unless terminally ill. Under s.76(1), an award cannot usually be made before the date of claim but this does not prevent the three-month qualifying period imposed by s.72(2)(a) from being satisfied as at the date of claim if the conditions were met during the three months before the date of claim. The date of claim is determined in accordance with regs. 6(1) and 6(5) of the Social Security (Claims and Payments) Regulations 1987 as being the date a claim is received in the local office, although it may be treated as having been received earlier if delayed due to postal disruption as the result of industrial action. See also reg. 6(8) under which a claim is treated as made when a claim form was requested. Reg. 5 of the DLA Regulations allowed (until September 1, 1997 when it was revoked) a repeat claim to be made within six months of a previous period of entitlement to DLA. Reg. 6 of the DLA Regulations prescribes, for the purpose of para.(a)(ii) a period of three months ending on the day on which the claimant was last entitled to the component or to attendance allowance if that was not more than two years before the current period of entitlement would otherwise begin. This has the practical effect in most cases that the three month qualifying period is deemed to be satisfied if the current claim is within two years of a previous period of entitlement at the relevant rate.

Under paras. 3(2) and 7(2) of Sched. 1 to the DLA Regulations, a period of six months is substituted for the period of three months in subs. (2) in the case of a person over the age of 65 who makes a renewal claim for DLA or whose entitlement is to be revised on review.

Para. (b) requires that a person should be expected to satisfy the conditions for the component for six months, unless he or she is expected to die sooner. Six months is therefore the minimum period for an award. This period of six months begins as the three-month (or six-month for those over 65) qualifying period ends and both conditions are intended to ensure that only the chronically disabled are entitled to DLA. There is no minimum period for attendance allowance and the minimum award for mobility allowance was for 12 months. For mobility allowance there was no equivalent to para. (b)(ii) dealing with the case of a person not expected to live for a year but in *CM/83/84* it was held that the fact that a person had died before the end of the period of 12 months should be ignored. Death was a supervening event. Are there circumstances in which an operation, which will probably be performed so as to reduce the claimant's disablement within six months, might be regarded as a supervening event so that an award should be made in the expectation that it might be reviewed if the operation does take place successfully?

Subss. (3) and (4). Reg. 4(1) of the DLA Regulations provides for the following rates from April 7, 1997: highest £49.50 pw; middle £33.10 pw; lowest £13.15 pw.

Despite the strange use of the words "in any other case" in subs. (4)(c) it is plain that it is intended that the lowest rate is applicable only if a claimant satisfies the condition mentioned in subs. (1)(a) without also satisfying the condition in either subs. (1)(b) or (1)(c) If he or she were to satisfy the conditions in, say, both subs. (1)(a) and (1)(c), the middle rate would be applicable.

Subs. (5). Under s.66(2), a person is "terminally ill" if "he suffers from a progressive disease and his death in consequence of that disease can reasonably be expected within six months". See the notes to that section. Note also that someone may make a claim on this ground on behalf of the claimant without the claimant's knowledge or authority s.76(3)).

The effect of this subsection is that a terminally ill person is deemed to satisfy the three month (or six month in the case of a person over 65) qualifying period and is entitled to an award of the highest rate of the care component for the remainder of his or her life, subject only to satisfying presence and residence conditions and the rules about people in hospital and other accommodation. Even those are relaxed. Reg. 2(4) of the DLA Regulations relaxes the presence conditions for terminally ill claimants so that it is not necessary for them to have been in Great Britain before the day in respect of which the claim is made. Reg. 9(3) also enables such claimants to receive the care component even though they are in accommodation where the cost could be, but is not, borne wholly or partly out of public or local funds.

Subs. (6). There is no lower age limit for the care component but, since all young children need a certain amount of attention and supervision, a disabled child qualifies for the care component only if he or she requires more attention or supervision than children of the same age who are not disabled. Note that the child is now the claimant although an adult will be appointed to act on his or her behalf. When attendance allowance was payable in respect of children, the adult was actually the claimant but now the old mobility allowance practice has been adopted for both components of DLA.

Para. (a) provides that claim for the lowest rate cannot be based on a child's inability to prepare a main meal, even if the child is 15.

Para. (b) provides that a child may be taken to satisfy the usual conditions for entitlement to the care component only if either he or she has usbstantial requirements that children of his or her age do not usually have at all (sub-para. (ii)) or else his or her requirements are substantially in excess of the normal requirements of children of his or her age (sub-para. (i)). The fact that younger children than the claimant require as much attention or supervision is irrelevant. Obviously, the younger a child is, the more difficult it is for him or her to satisfty the additional conditions. However, in *CDLA/92/92* the Deputy Commissioner, considering earlier legislation which was in similar, but not idential, terms, said:

> "5. In the case of a child, it is to be noted that the attention or supervision required must be 'substantially in excess of that normally required by a child of the same age and sex.' Attention or supervision may be required 'substantially in excess of that normally required' either by virtue of the time over which it is required or by virtue of the quality or degree of attention or supervision which is required.
>
> 6. The idea of a greater quality or degree of attention can be illustrated by considering meal times. A young child may require attention in connection with eating because he or she requires the food to be cut up. A disabled child of the same age may require attention in excess of that normally required by a child of the same age because he or she not only requires the food to be cut up but also requires it to be spooned into the mouth. The fact that the child will be supervised anyway is irrelevant: there is still an additional requirement for attention. Whether such additional attention, taken with any other additional attention requirements, is 'substantial' and 'frequent . . . throughout the day' are matters of judgement to be determined in each case where the condition in section 35(1)(a)(i) [of the Social Security Act 1975—now s.72(1)(b)(i) of the 1992 Act] is being considered. Those may be significant limiting factors.
>
> 7. When considering the condition in section 35(1)(a)(ii) [of the 1975 Act—now s.72(1)(b)(ii) of the 1992 Act], the additional condition that the supervision required must be substantially

STRICT, BINDING

in excess of that normally required by a child of the same age is indeed 'stringent' as it was described in *CA/21/88*. Because young children normally require continual supervision throughout the day in order to avoid substantial danger to themselves, the focus will be on the quality or degree of supervision. Thus a very young immobile baby or an older child might normally be regarded as being adequately supervised by a person who was getting on with his or her own chores in a different part of the home. On the other hand, a disabled child of the same age may need much closer supervision amounting, perhaps, to being watched over. That would be supervision in excess of that normally required. Again, it is necessary to consider whether such additional supervision is 'substantial' and 'continual . . . throughout the day' and those may be significant limiting factors.

8. Similar considerations apply to the night conditions in section 35(1)(b) [of the 1975 Act—now s.72(1)(c) of the 1992 Act], although it may in practice be more difficult for claimants to qualify on the basis of the additional quality or degree of attention or watching over rather than on the basis of the additional frequency or length of time for which attention or watching over is required.

9. The other general question raised by this appeal is how one judges what attention of supervision is normally required by a child of the same age and sex. Children vary considerably in their requirements for attention and supervision, particularly when they are young. At any age, there is a range of requirements for attention or supervision. It is significant that the legislation does not speak of attention or supervision substantially in excess of that which would be required by the particular child being considered were he not physically or mentally disabled. So that, if it were possible to ascribe tantrums to frustration arising out of a disability, that would not be enough for the child to qualify unless the attention or supervision was substantially in excess of that normally required by a child of the same age and sex. It seems to me that the legislation contemplates a yardstick of an average child, neither particularly bright or well behaved nor particularly dull or badly behaved, and then the attention or supervision required by the child whose case is being considered must be judged to decide whether it is 'substantially' more than would normally be required by the average child. That, I think, comes to much the same thing as saying that the attention or supervision required must be substantially more than that normally required by *most* children, which is the way the delegated medical practitioner put it in paragraph 4 of his decision in this case. Attention or supervision is not to be regarded as 'substantially' in excess of that normally required unless it is outside the whole range of attention or supervision that would normally be required by the average child. However, it need not necessarily be substantially in excess of that which would be required by a particularly dull or badly behaved, but not physically or mentally disabled, child. I appreciate that all this is pitched at a fairly theoretical level and that there may be significant evidential problems and problems of judgement in individual cases, but it seems desirable to provide some sort of theoretical framework within which the present case can be considered.''

A child who is terminally ill is taken to satisfy paragraphs (b) and (c) of subs. (1) by virtue of subs. (5). Subs. (6)(b) has no application in such a case (*CDLA/1304/95*).

Subs. (7). Reg. 7 of the DLA Regulations deems people undergoing renal dialysis to satisfy the condition of either subs. (1)(b) or (1)(c).

Subs. (8). See regs. 8–10 of the DLA Regulations.

The mobility component

73.—(1) Subject to the provisions of this Act, a person shall be entitled to the mobility component of a disability living allowance for any period in which he is over the age of five and throughout which—

(a) he is suffering from physical disablement such that he is either unable to walk or virtually unable to do so; or
(b) he falls within section (2) below; or
(c) he falls within subsection (3) below; or
(d) he is able to walk but is so severely disabled physically or mentally that, disregarding any ability he may have to use routes which are familiar to him on his own, he cannot take advantage of the faculty out of doors without guidance or supervision from another person most of the time.

(2) A person falls within this subsection if—
(a) he is both blind and deaf; and
(b) he satisfies such other conditions as may be prescribed.

(3) A person falls within this subsection if—

(a) he is severely mentally impaired; and

(b) he displays severe behavioural problems; and

(c) he satisfies both the conditions mentioned in section 72(1)(b) and (c) above.

(4) For the purposes of this section in its application to a person for any period in which he is under the age of 16, the condition mentioned in subsection (1)(d) above shall not be taken to be satisfied unless—

(a) he requires substantially more guidance or supervision from another person than persons of this age in normal physical and mental health would require; or

(b) persons of his age in normal physical and mental health would not require such guidance or supervision.

(5) Subject to subsection (4) above, circumstances may be prescribed in which a person is to be taken satisfy or not to satisfy a condition mentioned in subsection (1)(a) or (d) or subsection (2)(a) above.

(6) Regulations shall specify the cases which fall within subsection (3)(a) and (b) above.

(7) A person who is to be taken for the purposes of section 72 above to satisfy or not to satisfy a condition mentioned in subsection (1)(b) or (c) of that section is to be taken to satisfy or not to satisfy it for the purposes of subsection (3)(c) above.

(8) A person shall not be entitled to the mobility component for a period unless during most of that period his condition will be such as permits him from time to time to benefit from enhanced facilities for locomotion.

(9) A person shall not be entitled to the mobility component of a disability living allowance unless—

(a) throughout—

(i) the period of three months immediately preceding the date on which the award of that component would begin; or

(ii) such other period of three months as may be prescribed,

he has satisfied or is likely to satisfy one or other of the conditions mentioned in subsection (1) above; and

(b) he is likely to continue to satisfy one or other of those conditions throughout—

(i) the period of six months beginning with that date; or

(ii) (if his death is expected within the period of six months beginning with that date) the period so beginning and ending with his death.

(10) Two weekly rates of the mobility component shall be prescribed.

(11) The weekly rate of the mobility component payable to a person for each week in the period for which he is awarded that component shall be—

(a) the higher rate, if he falls within subsection (9) above by virtue of having satisfied or being likely to satisfy one or other of the conditions mentioned in subsection (1)(a), (b) and (c) above throughout both the period mentioned in paragraph (a) of subsection (9) above and that mentioned in paragraph (b) of that subsection; and

(b) the lower rate in any other case.

(12) For the purposes of this section in its application to a person who is terminally ill, as defined in section 66(2) above, and who makes a claim expressly on the ground that he is such a person—

(a) subsection (9)(a) above shall be omitted; and

(b) subsection (11)(a) above shall have effect as if for the words from "both" to "subsection", in the fourth place where it occurs, there were substituted the words "the period mentioned in subsection (9)(b) above".

(13) Regulations may prescribe cases in which a person who has the use—

(a) of an invalid carriage or other vehicle provided by the Secretary of State under section 5(2)(a) of the National Health Service Act 1977 and Schedule 2 to that Act or under section 46 of the National Health Service (Scotland) Act 1978 or provided under Article 30(1) of the Health and Personal Social Services (Northern Ireland) Order 1972; or

(b) of any prescribed description of appliance supplied under the enactments relating to the National Health Service being such an appliance as is primarily designed to afford a means of personal and independent locomotion out of doors,

is not to be paid any amount attributable to entitlement to the mobility component or is to be paid disability living allowance at a reduced rate in so far as it is attributable to that component.

(14) A payment to or in respect of any person which is attributable to his entitlement to the mobility component, and the right to receive such a payment, shall (except in prescribed circumstances and for prescribed purposes) be disregarded in applying any enactment or instrument under which regard is to be had to a person's means.

DERIVATION

Social Security Act 1975, s.37ZC.

GENERAL NOTE

This section makes basic provision for the mobility component of DLA.

Subs. (1). This lays down the basic conditions which are that the claimant be over the age of five years and satisfy one of four other conditions. Paras. (a) and (b) reproduce grounds of entitlement to mobility allowance and paras. (c) and (d) introduce conditions that were new from April 6, 1992. Both new grounds of entitlement allow claimants suffering from mental disablement to qualify whereas, for mobility allowance, only physical disablement could be taken into account. Under subs. (11), the higher rate of the mobility component is payable to those who satisfy the conditions of paras. (a), (b) or (c) and the lower rate to those who satisfy only para. (d).

The lower age limit of five years is the age at which children must attend school and below which children ought usually to be supervised when walking outdoors. S.75 imposes an upper age limit of 65 unless a claimant satisfies the conditions before reaching that age and makes a claim before reaching the age of 66 (65 from October 6, 1997). Thus the mobility component is confined to the period which would generally be a person's school and working life. Sched. 2 to the DLA Regulations permits a person over the upper age limit to qualify if he or she is a former beneficiary under an invalid vehicle scheme.

A person satisfies the condition of para (a) only in the circumstances set out in reg. 12(1) of the DLA Regulations 1991, made under subs. (5). Reg. 12(4), made under the same provision, provides that the ability to wear or use an prosthesis or artificial aid must be taken into account but there is separate provision for people who have lost both legs. Reference should be made to the notes to that regulation.

Para. (d) assists those claimants who can walk and do not fall within subss. (2) and (3) and yet need assistance from someone else to enable them to walk. In *Lees v. Secretary of State for Social Services* [1985] 1 A.C. 930 (also reported as App. 2 to *R(M) 1/84*), the House of Lords had considered the case of a blind woman who suffered from marked impairment of capacity for spatial orientation and who had claimed mobility allowance. Outdoor walking was only feasible for her if she had an intelligent adult to pilot her because otherwise she could not tell in which direction she should go. An argument that she was virtually unable to walk because she could not make use of her physical capacity for walking was rejected. Some claimants in a similar position were assisted by the introduction of the provision that enabled blind and deaf claimants to qualify (reg. 3(1)(b) of the Mobility Allowance Regulations—see now subs. (2)) but that would not have helped Miss Lees who was not, so far as reports show, deaf. Para. (d) would enable her to qualify. The paragraph applies in cases of mental disability as well as physical disability and applies in cases where mere supervision is required in order for the claimant to take advantage of the ability to walk. Thus a mentally handicapped adult who requires supervision before he or she can safely be allowed to walk near traffic would appear to qualify. This approach is reinforced by subs. (4) which makes it an additional condition in the case of a child under 16 that he or she should require substantially more guidance or supervision than a child of the same age in normal health. That makes it clear that the sort of supervision normally required by children may well be sufficient to enable an adult to qualify. Note that ability to use familiar routes is to be ignored so that the fact that a claimant can get to and from a local shop may not be a bar to entitlement. In *CDLA/52/94* the Commissioner said that "the only people who can satisfy the condition of s.73(1)(d) are those who, along unfamiliar routes, cannot reasonably be expected to walk without guidance or supervision even to the fairly limited extent relevant when considering virtual inability to walk under s.73(1)(a). On the other hand, a person who could not reasonably be expected to walk to that extent without guidance or supervision satisfies the condition of s.73(1)(d) even if, when guided or supervised, he or she can reasonably be expected to walk as far as most other people." The meaning of "guidance" and "supervision" in this context was considered in *CDLA/42/94* in which the Commissioner summarised his conclusions as follows:

"(i) The meaning of guidance or supervision must be considered within the context of action which is aimed at enabling the claimant to take advantage of the faculty of walking despite the limits imposed by her physical or mental condition. It is not a condition that guidance or supervision should be necessary to avoid a risk of danger to the claimant or others.

(j) Guidance means the action of directing or leading. It may, for example, be constituted by physically directing or leading the claimant or by oral direction, persuasion or suggestion.

(k) Supervision, in the context of section 73(1)(d), means accompanying the claimant and at the least monitoring the claimant or the circumstances for signs of a need to intervene so as to prevent the claimant's ability to take advantage of the faculty of walking being compromised. Other, more active, measures may also amount to supervision. The monitoring does not cease to fall within the meaning of supervision by reason only that intervention by the person accompanying the claimant has not in the past actually been necessary.

(l) The fact that the claimant derives reassurance from the presence of the other person does not prevent action which would otherwise fall within point (j) or (k) from being guidance or supervision."

In *CDLA/52/94* the claimant suffered from epilepsy and the Commissioner said:

"7. Where a person has only occasional fits, the expression 'most of the time' focuses attention on the needs of the claimant between fits, rather than during or immediately after them. Therefore, so far as epilepsy is concerned, guidance may be of little relevance. The question then arises whether a person who is accompanying the claimant is thereby exercising 'supervision'. . . .

8. It is likely that a claimant who, due to epilepsy, satisfies the condition of section 72(1)(b)(ii) and is entitled to the care component of disability living allowance on the ground that he or she 'requires from another person . . . continual supervision throughout the day in order to avoid substantial danger to himself or others' will also satisfy the condition of section 73(i)(d). What is less clear is whether a person who fails to satisfy the condition of section 72(1)(b)(ii), because he or she merely needs a person to be nearby, will also fail to satisfy the condition of section 73(1)(d), because all that can be shown is a need to be accompanied when walking. Is a person accompanying such a claimant out walking in any different position from that of a person 'who keeps himself available to be called' while the claimant is at home?

9. It is, I think, important to bear in mind that Nicholls L.J. [in *Moran*—see note to s.72(1) *supra*] did not exclude the possibility that a person 'who keeps himself available to be called' *might* be exercising supervision. 'It will all depend on the facts of the case.' In my view, the most significant factor is that a person who is keeping himself available while the claimant is at home (or at work) is likely to be able to get on with his or her own activities, whereas having to accompany a claimant is likely to preclude that and, unless he or she wishes to go on the same journey anyway, there is inevitably an element of service involved. It is that element of service that is significant. In my view, the use of the word 'monitoring' by the Commissioner in *CDLA/042/94* reflects the facts of the case before the Commissioner and the need for there to be some element of service rather than mere presence. In a case where a claimant can give warning to a person who is accompanying him or her, I do not think that it can reasonably be said that the accompanying person is 'monitoring' the claimant. However, even though there may be an absence of monitoring, I take the view that a need to be accompanied when walking may amount to a need for supervision. In practice, where epilepsy is concerned, the focus is likely to be on the reasonableness of the claim that there is a *need* to be accompanied when walking a modest distance. Relevant issues will be the likelihood of a fit occurring when the claimant is out walking and the risk of substantial danger if one does occur then. There may well be a greater risk of danger when the claimant has a fit out in the street than when he or she is at home."

However, in *CDLA/757/95*, a Commissioner held that a person, who was in receipt of the care component under s.72(1)(b)(ii) on the ground that continual supervision was required due to a propensity to fall, did not *ipso facto* satisfy the condition of s.73(1)(d). He said:

"... in the present case there was nothing to prevent the claimant from walking out of doors. She might not want to, by reason of her alleged propensity to fall four or five times a day, and such a fall might occur while she was walking outside, but the choice was entirely hers. Supervision was not a pre-requisite for her exercising her power of walking; it was an additional advantage rendering her walking less open to risk. But s.73(1)(d) is not concerned with supervision to avoid danger to the claimant; that type of supervision is provided for under s.72(1)(b)(ii)."

The approaches adopted in *CDLA/52/94* and *CDLA/757/95* appear to be irreconcilable. The question that will have to be answered is whether s.73(1)(d) should be construed so that a person is regarded as one who "cannot" take advantage of any ability to walk without guidance or supervision if he or she cannot *reasonably* be expected to take advantage of it without guidance or supervision.

In *CDLA/240/94*, the Commissioner held that a profoundly deaf person who required an interpreter to communicate effectively did not satisfy the condition of s.73(1)(d) because, even if the claimant reasonably required someone to accompany him to act as an interpreter in the event of his getting lost, there was no element of supervision. It was conceded on behalf of the claimant that he could not show a need for guidance most of the time. However, in *CDLA/206/94*, the Commissioner did not rule out the possibility that the claimant with problems of hearing, language and learning might qualify. He directed the tribunal "to concentrate only upon the extent to which the claimant may require guidance or supervision through becoming lost, confused or disorientated and whether that would be required 'most of the time' that he went *walking* on an unfamiliar route." It is suggested that it will be difficult for a profoundly deaf claimant without learning difficulties to show that he cannot walk without guidance most of the time.

Nevertheless, an adjudication officer's appeal against a decision of a disability appeal tribunal who had, by a majority, awarded the lower rate of the mobility component to a profoundly deaf person was dismissed in *CDLA/1430/96*. The Commissioner could find no error of law and, in particular, held that the tribunal were entitled to find that the claimant required guidance *most of the time* while using unfamiliar routes. In *CDLA/494/94*, the Commissioner accepted that a claimant who suffered from considerable incontinence, both urinary and faecal, and who never went out on her own might satisfy the test in section 73(1)(d): "It is, of course, walking out of doors, particularly in an unfamiliar area, that may give rise to a crisis and panic over a sudden attack of incontinence. To have supervision from a companion would enable the claimant to walk out of doors in an unfamiliar area in circumstances where she might feel terrified to undertake such a walk on her own."

Commissioners have differed as to whether guidance or supervision will only be relevant if it will enable the cliamant to overcome his or her inability to make use of the faculty of walking. In *CDLA/42/94* the Commissioner said that "it would be absurd if a claimant whose disablement was so severe that she was not able to take advantage of the faculty of walking on unfamiliar routes out of doors even with guidance or supervision was excluded from section 73(1)(d). Because of the negative formulation of the provision, a claimant does not necessarily have to show an ability to take advantage of that faculty with guidance or supervision." However, in *CDLA/2364/95*, the Commissioner rejected that approach and decided that a person who suffered from claustrophobia and agoraphobia and who could not be persuaded to walk outdoors would not be entitled to the lower rate of the mobility component.

Subs. (2). Reg. 12(2) of the DLA Regulations 1991, made under subs. (5), defines blindness and deafness for the purposes of para. (a). It is not necessary for the claimant to have total loss of vision and hearing. See the note to that regulation. Reg. 12(3), made under para. (b) makes it a further condition of entitlement that the combined effects of the claimant's blindness and deafness should make him unable, without the assistance of another, to walk to any intended or required destination while out of doors.

Subs. (3). This provision is intended to reduce the immense difficulties caused in mobility allowance cases by the fact that only virtual inability to walk due to *physical* disablement could be taken into account. Some of those who would qualify under this subsection would also qualify under subs. (1) (a) but adjudication in such cases is made much simpler by this new provision. The conditions imposed by this subsection are quite stringent but those who fail to qualify may be able to qualify under subs. (1) (a) for the higher rate (if they can show physical disablement) or under subs. (1) (d) for the lower rate.

Regs. 12(5) and 12(6) of the DLA Regulations 1991, made under subs. (6), specify who falls within paras (a) and (b) as suffering from mental impairment and displaying severe behavioural problems. A person falls within para (a) if "he suffers from a state of arrested development or incomplete physical development of the brain, which results in severe impairment of intelligence and social functioning''. A person falls within para. (b) if the disruptive behaviour ''(a) is extreme, (b) regularly requires another person to intervene and physically restrain him in order to prevent him causing physical injury to himself or another, or damage to property, and (c) is so unpredicable that he requires another person to be present and watching over him whenever he is awake.''

Under para. (c), it is also necessary for the claimant to satisfy the conditions for the higher rate of the care component. It is not clear why entitlement to an allowance in respect of mobility outdoors should require satisfaction of the night attendance condition for the care component, and this may be a major obstacle for some claimants. Subs. (7) has the effect that those who are deemed to satisfy one or both the attendance conditions for the care component because they undergo renal dialysis or are terminally ill may rely on the same provisions for the purpose of satisfying para. (c)

Subss. (4) and (5). See regs. 12 to 12C of the DLA Regulations 1991.

Subs. (8). This is in the same terms as s.37A(2)(b) of the Social Security Act 1975 relating to mobility allowance which was considered by a Commissioner in *R(M) 2/83*. He approved a passage in the second edition Ogus and Barendt, *The Law of Social Security*, in which they said:

> ''This obviously excludes human vegetables and those whom it is unsafe to move, but it is arguable that of the remainder there will be few who will not receive some benefit from the occasional sortie, and it is not easy to draw a line between the deserving and the undeserving except on some arbitrary basis.''

The Commissioner pointed out that the word ''benefit'' was a wide one and that the provision contained the words ''from time to time'' but he added a further category of excluded persons, ''that is persons so severely mentally deranged that a high degree of supervision and restraint would be required to prevent them either injuring themselves or other''.

Subs. (9). Para. (a) imposes the three-month qualifying period but this is deemed to be satisfied in the case of a person who is terminally ill (see subs. (12)). If a person is entitled to the lower rate of the mobility component by virtue of satisfying the condition in subs. (1) (d) and his or her condition deteriorates so that he or she would satisfy one or other of the conditions in subs. (1) (a), (b) or (c) the effect of subs. (11) (a) is that the claimant must still wait three months before qualifying for the higher rate unless terminally ill. Under s.76(1), an award cannot usually be made before the date of claim which is determined in accordance with reg. 6(1) and (5) of the Social Security (Claims and Payments) Regulations 1987 as being the date a claim is received in the local office, although it may be treated as having been received earlier if delayed due to postal disruption as the result of industrial action and a request for a claim form may effectively be treated as a claim if the claim form is returned within the specified time. Reg. 5 of the DLA Regulations allowed (until September 1, 1997 when it was revoked) a repeat claim to be made within six months of a previous period of entitlement to DLA. Reg. 11 of the DLA Regulations prescribes, for the purpose of para. (a) (ii) a period of three months ending on the day on which the claimant was last entitled to the component or to attendance allowance if that was not more than two years before the current period of entitlement would otherwise begin. This has the practical effect in most cases that the three-month qualifying period is deemed to be satisfied if the current claim is within two years of a previous period of entitlement at the relevant rate.

Under para. 4(2) of Sched. 1 to the DLA Regulations, a period of six months is substituted for the period of three months in para. (a) in the case of a person over the age of 65 who makes a claim for the mobility component and is entitled to do so because he or she was formerly entitled to a car or other assistance under an invalid vehicle scheme.

Para. (b) requires that a person should be expected to satisfy the conditions for the component for six months, unless he or she is expected to die sooner. Six months is therefore the minimum period for an award. This period of six months begins as the three-month (or six-month for those over 65) qualifying period ends and both conditions are intended to ensure that only the chronically disabled are entitled to DLA. The minimum award for mobility allowance was for 12 months, but there was no equivalent to para. (b) (ii) dealing with the case of a person not expected to live for a year. In *CM/83/84* it was held that the fact that a person had died before the end of the period of 12 months should be ignored. Death was a supervening event. This raises the question whether there are circumstances in which an operation, which will probably be performed so as to reduce the claimant's disablement within six months, might be regarded as a supervening event so that an award should be made in the expectation that it might be reviewed if the operation does take place successfully.

Subss. (10) and (11). From April 7, 1997, reg. 4(2) of the DLA regulations provides for a higher rate of £34.60 pw and a lower rate of £13.15 pw. The higher rate is payable if one or other of the conditions in subs. (1)(a), (b) or (c) is satisfied and the lower rate is payable if the condition in subs. (1) (d) is satisfied. To be entitled at the higher rate, it is not necessary that the *same* condition should have been satisfied throughout the qualifying period and the period of the award.

Subs. (12). Under s.66(2), a person is "terminally ill" if "he suffers from a progressive disease and his death in consequence of that disease can reasonably be expected within six months". See the notes to that section.

The effect of this subsection is that a terminally ill person is deemed to satisfy the three-month qualifying period (or the six-month period in the case of a person over 65 formerly entitled to an invalid vehicle). Note also that reg. 2(4) of the DLA Regulations relaxes the presence conditions for terminally ill claimants so that it is not necessary for them to have been in Great Britain before the day in respect of which the claim is made. However, while terminally ill claimants are deemed to satisfy the conditions for the highest rate of the care component, they are not deemed to satisfy any of the conditions for the mobility component except subs. (3)(c) (see Subs. (7)).

Subs. (13). Sched. 2 to the DLA Regulations makes provision allowing former invalid vehicle scheme beneficiaries to be deemed to satisfy the conditions for the higher rate of the mobility component and Sched. 1, para. 4 permits them to claim the mobility component event if they are aged over 65.

Subs. (14). There is specific provision in the legislation governing disability working allowance which ensures that disability living allowance is not to be treated as income (Sched. 3, para. 4 to the Disability Working Allowance (General) Regulations 1991). But *quaere* whether para. 8 (a) of Sched. 4 to those Regulations (which allows arrears of disability living allowance to be disregarded as capital only for 52 weeks and so implies it should be taken into account after that) is overridden by this subsection so that the arrears may continue to be disregarded for longer. The power to make regulations under this subsection is not referred to in the preamble to those Regulations. This provision also applies to any local authority scheme applying a means test where there is a statutory power to make charges for services, *e.g.* charges for home helps under para. 3 of Sched. 8 to the National Health Service Act 1977.

Mobility component for certain persons eligible for invalid carriages

74.—(1) Regulations may provide for the issue, variation and cancellation of certificates in respect of prescribed categories of persons to whom this section applies; and a person in respect of whom such a certificate is issued shall, during any period while the certificate is in force, be deemed for the purposes of section 73 above to satisfy the condition mentioned in subsection (1)(a) of that section and to fall within paragraphs (a) and (b) of subsection (9) by virtue of having satisfied or being likely to satisfy that condition throughout both the periods mentioned in those paragraphs.

(2) This section applies to any person whom the Secretary of State considers—

(a) was on 1st January 1976 in possession of an invalid carriage or other vehicle provided in pursuance of section 33 of the Health Services and Public Health Act 1968 (which related to vehicles for persons suffering from physical defect or disability) or receiving payments in pursuance of subsection (3) of that section; or

(b) had at that date, or at a later date specified by the Secretary of State, made an application which the Secretary of State approved for such a carriage or vehicle or for such payments; or

(c) was, both at some time during a prescribed period before that date and at some time during a prescribed period after that date, in possession of such a carriage or vehicle or receiving such payments; or

(d) would have been, by virtue of any of the preceding paragraphs, a person to whom this section applies but for some error or delay for which in the opinion of the Secretary of State the person was not responsible and which was brought to the attention of the Secretary of State within the period of one year beginning with 30th March 1977 (the date of the passing of the Social Security (Miscellaneous Provisions) Act 1977, section 13 of which made provisions corresponding to the provision made by this section).

Derivation

Social Security (Miscellaneous Provisions) Act 1977, s.13.

General Note

For regulations, see reg. 13 of, and Sched. 2 to, the Social Security (Disability Living Allowance) Regulations 1991, which are treated by s.2(2) of the Social Security (Consequential Provisions) Act 1992 as having been made under this section.

Mobility allowance (which was introduced by s.22 of the Social Security Pensions Act 1975 and has now been replaced by the higher rate of the mobility component of disability living allowance) was intended to replace the provision of invalid vehicles and the alternative system of paying for vehicles. Those who were already entitled to vehicles or payments under the Health Services and Public Health Act 1968 on January 1, 1976, have retained the right to them but may at any time exchange them for the higher rate of the mobility component of disability living allowance, even if they are over the usual maximum age of 65.

Persons 65 or over

75.—(1) Except to the extent to which regulations provide otherwise, no person shall be entitled to either component of a disability living allowance for any period after he attains the age of 65 otherwise than by virtue of an award made before he attains that age.

(2) Regulations may provide in relation to persons who are entitled to a component of a disability living allowance by virtue of subsection (1) above that any provisions of this Act which relates to disability living allowance, other than section 74 above, so far as it so relates, and any provision of the Administration Act which is relevant to disability living allowance—

(a) shall have effect subject to modifications, additions or amendments; or
(b) shall not have effect.

Derivation

Social Security Act 1975, s.37ZD

General Note

The general rule established by this subsection is that a person is not entitled to DLA for any period after reaching the age of 65 unless entitled by virtue of an award made before he or she reaches that age. Reg. 3 of, and Sched. 1 to, the DLA Regulations are made under this section.

Reg. 3 originally provided for two exceptions to the general rule. First, a person who would have qualified at the age of 65 could be awarded DLA provided a claim was made before he or she reached the age of 66. That provision was revoked from October 6, 1997. Secondly, if a claimant reaches the age of 65 during the three-month qualifying period for either component, having claimed before reaching that age, then the claimant is not prejudiced by the fact that the award is not made, or effective, until after his or her 65th birthday. There is a further exception under para. 4 of Sched. 1 to the DLA Regulations allowing a former invalid vehicle scheme beneficiary to qualify for the mobility component. Sched. 1 to the DLA Regulations also enables further awards to be made to those people who have established entitlement to DLA beyond the age of 65, although there are some restrictions. A person who ceases to be entitled to the care component at the middle or higher rate cannot qualify for the lower rate. The qualifying period for the middle and highest rates of care component are extended to six months. A person who ceases to be entitled to the mobility component at the higher rate cannot qualify for the lower rate. A person who has been entitled to the mobility component at the lower rate cannot qualify for the higher rate.

People over 65 who are not entitled to DLA may instead qualify for attendance allowance under s.64.

Disability living allowance—supplementary

76.—(1) Subject to subsection (2) below, a person shall not be entitled to a disability living allowance for any period preceding the date on which a claim for it is made or treated as made by him or on his behalf.

(2) Notwithstanding anything in subsection (1) above, provision may be made by regulations for a person to be entitled to a component of a disability living allowance for a period preceding the date on which a claim for such an allowance is made or treated as made by him or on his behalf if he has previously been entitled to that component.

(3) For the purposes of sections 72(5) and 73(12) above where—

(a) a person purports to make a claim for a disability living allowance on behalf of another; and

(b) the claim is made expressly on the ground that the person on whose behalf it purports to be made is terminally ill,

that person shall be regarded as making the claim notwithstanding that it is made without his knowledge or authority.

Derivation

Social Security Act 1975, s.37ZE.

General Note

This section makes provision for claims to DLA.

Subss. (1) and (2). This states the general rule that claims for DLA cannot be backdated to cover a period before the date on which a claim is made or *is treated as made*. The general rule has been criticised as unduly severe. Claims for most other social security benefits can be backdated, including benefits in respect of incapacity for work which suggests that the gathering of medical evidence in respect of past periods is not an insuperable problem. It should, however, be noted that the three-month qualifying period (six month for people over 65) is normally before the date of claim, so to that extent, claims can be regarded as being backdated over that period. There is also some further flexibility. Reg. 6(1)(a) of the Claims and Payments Regulations 1987 provides that a claim shall be treated as made on the date it is received in an appropriate office of the Department of Social Security. Reg. 4(1) requires a claim to be made in writing either on a claim form or in such other manner as the Secretary of State may accept as sufficient. If the Secretary of State does not accept a document as a claim, he may ask the claimant to complete a proper claim form or simply to give further information. If that is done within a reasonable period, the claim is then treated as having been made when the original document was received (regs. 4(7) and 6(1)(b)). More specific provision is made in respect of DLA and attendance allowance in reg. 6(8) under which a claim is treated as having been made when a request for a claim form is received by the Department, provided that the claimant duly completes and returns the claim form within six weeks or such longer period as the Secretary of State considers reasonable. Leaflets widely available to claimants include requests for claim forms rather than claim forms themselves which are bulky documents. If a claim is delayed in the post due to industrial action, it is treated as having been made on the date it would have arrived in the ordinary course of post (reg. 6(7)). Until October 6, 1997, reg. 5 of the DLA Regulations, made under subs. (2), allowed a claim to be backdated to the end of a previous period of entitlement to the same component of DLA, provided that the renewal claim was made within six months of the end of that period of entitlement and the claimant satisfied the conditions of entitlement throughout the intervening period. For these purposes, a previous period of entitlement to attendance allowance was treated as a period of entitlement to the care component and a previous period of entitlement to mobility allowance was treated as a period of entitlement to the mobility component.

Subs. (3). This is necessary to enable a person to make a claim for DLA on behalf of someone who is terminally ill in a case when the claimant is not to be told of the prognosis in his case.

77.—93. *Omitted.*

Part V

Benefit For Industrial Injuries

General provisions

Right to industrial injuries benefit

94.—(1) Industrial injuries benefit shall be payable where an employed earner suffers personal injury caused after 4th July 1948 by accident arising out of and in the course of his employment, being employed earner's employment.

(2) Industrial injuries benefit consists of the following benefits—

(a) disablement benefit payable in accordance with sections 103 to 105 below, paragraphs 2 and 3 of Schedule 7 below and Parts II and III of that Schedule;

(b) reduced earnings allowance payable in accordance with Part IV;

(c) retirement allowance payable in accordance with Part V; and

(d) industrial death benefit, payable in accordance with Part VI.

(3) For the purposes of industrial injuries benefit an accident arising in the course of an employed earner's employment shall be taken, in the absence of evidence to the contrary, also to have arisen out of that employment.

(4) Regulations may make provision as to the day which, in the case of night workers and other special cases, is to be treated for the purposes of industrial injuries benefit as the day of the accident.

(5) Subject to sections 117, 119 and 120 below, industrial injuries benefit shall not be payable in respect of an accident happening while the earner is outside Great Britain.

(6) In the following provisions of this Part of this Act "work" in the contexts "incapable of work" and "incapacity for work" means work which the person in question can be reasonably expected to do.

DERIVATION

Social Security Act 1975, s.50.

DEFINITIONS

For "employed earner", see ss.2 and 95(4).
For "employed earner's employment", see ss.95 and 97.
For "benefit", "employment" and "industrial injuries benefit", see s.122(1).
For "work", see subs. (6).

GENERAL NOTE

Subs. (1). This provides that the benefits listed in subs. (2) shall be payable to certain people who have suffered personal injury caused by an industrial *accident.* Similar provision is made by s.108(1) in respect of industrial *diseases* and injuries not caused by accident. The extremely complicated questions thrown up by this provision do not fall within the jurisdiction of medical appeal tribunals so only a basic summary is given here.

Whether a person is an "employed earner" is a matter to be determined by the Secretary of State under s.18 of the Social Security Administration Act 1992. S.2(1)(a) defines an "employed earner" as "a person who is gainfully employed in Great Britain either under a contract of service, or in an office (including elective office) with emoluments chargeable to income tax under Schedule E" and distinguishes between such a person and a "self-employed earner". The latter is not within the scope of the industrial injuries scheme. For guidance as to the distinction, see *Ready Mixed Concrete South East Ltd v. Ministry of Pensions and National Insurance* [1968] 2 Q.B. 497 and *Global Plant v. Secretary of State for Health and Social Security* [1971] 3 All E.R. 385. The Social Security (Categorisation of Earners) Regulations 1978 (S.I. 1978 No. 1689) deem certain people to be or not to be employed earners. S.95 provides that regulations may be made prescribing what is or is not to be "employed earner's employment" (see the Social Security (Employed Earners' Employments for Industrial Injuries Purposes) Regulations 1975 (S.I. 1975 No. 467)).

Whether a person has suffered personal injury caused by accident is determined by an adjudication officer or a social security appeal tribunal. However, a declaration by such a body that there has been an industrial accident does not import a decision as to the origin of any injury or disability suffered by the claimant (see s.60(3) of the Social Security Administration Act 1992). The question whether an accident has resulted in a loss of faculty is to be determined by an adjudicating medical authority or a medical appeal tribunal (see s.45(1) of the Social Security Administration Act 1992). An increase in pain is not, of itself, an injury because there must be physiological change for the worse and any aggravation of a pre-existing condition must be of some substance (*R(I) 1/76*). Damage to spectacles (*R(I) 1/82*) or an artificial limb (*R(I) 7/56*) have been held not to be personal injuries but damage to an artificial hip (*R(I) 8/81*) was accepted on the ground that the artificial joint was so intimately linked with the living body as to have become part of it. Assessment of disablement in such a case may not be easy. An assault is an accident for these purposes (*Trim Joint District School Board v. Kelly* [1914] A.C. 667). So also is a strain or heart attack caused by heavy work (*Fenton v. Thorley* [1903] A.C. 443, *Jones v. Secretary of State for Social Services* [1972] A.C. 944 and also reported as an appendix to *R(I) 3/69*). On the other hand, the word "accident" connotes one or more particular events rather than a continuous process. Some fine distinctions have been drawn over the years between series of events (*R(I) 77/51, R(I) 43/55, CI/ 71/87*) and continuous processes (*Roberts v. Dorothea Slate Quarries Ltd* [1948] 2 All E.R. 201, *R(I) 42/51, R(I) 19/56, R. v. Industrial Injuries Commissioner, ex p. Starr* reported as an appendix to *R(I) 11/74*). Even if a disease is caused by an accident rather than a process, if it is prescribed in relation to the claimant he or she must claim under s.108 and not under s.94 (see s.108(5)).

An accident occurs in the course of a man's employment "if it occurs while he is doing what a man so employed may reasonably do within a time during which he is employed, and at a place where he may reasonably be during that time to do that thing" (*Moore v. Manchester Liners Ltd* [1910] A.C. 498). This gives rise to nice questions of judgment and the Court of Appeal in *Nancollas v. Insurance Officer* [1985] 2 All E.R. 833 (also reported as an appendix to *R(I) 7/85*) has drawn attention to the fact that what might have been regarded as unreasonable 30 years ago might now be regarded as reasonable because the relationship between employer and employee has changed over the years. Therefore, old cases on this issue should be treated with caution. However, in *Smith v. Stages* [1989] A.C. 928 the House of Lords rejected a suggestion in *Nancollas* that there are no rules at all to be derived from those cases. Misconduct takes a person outside his or her course of employment. In *R. v. Industrial Injuries Commissioner, ex p. A E U (No. 2)* [1966] 2 Q.B. 31 also reported as an appendix to *R(I) 4/66*, a man was not in the course of employment when he had overstayed a smoking break. However, by s.98, a person is deemed still to be in the course of employment even when acting in breach of regulations if the act is done for the purposes of or in connection with the employer's trade or business. People with fixed places of employment are likely to be regarded as in the course of employment once they arrive on the premises, even well before the time at which work should start (*R(I) 3/62*) unless their early arrival was purely for their own purposes (*R(I) 11/54, R(I) 1/59*). Travelling to and from a normal place of employment is not part of the course of employment unless deemed to be so by s.99 because the transport is provided by, or in pursuance of arrangements made by, the employer. Injuries while travelling to other places may well be covered (see *Nancollas, Smith v. Stages* and *R(I) 1/88*).

The accident must arise out of the employment so that a person who has a heart attack at work but not caused by the work is not covered by the industrial injuries scheme. The same applies to a person who just "goes over" on his ankle (*R(I) 6/82*) but a person who is injured by coming into contact with his or her employer's plant, premises or machinery is covered (*Brooker v. Thomas Borthwick and Sons Ltd* [1933] A.C. 669). Ss.100 and 101 deem certain accidents to arise out of employment if caused by another person's misconduct, the behaviour or presence of an animal (including a bird, fish or insect), being struck by lightning or assisting in an emergency.

Subs. (2) Industrial death benefit is no longer payable except in respect of deaths occurring before April 11, 1988.

Subs. (5). The effect of this is reduced considerably by reg. 10C(5) of the Social Security Benefit (Persons Abroad) Regulations 1975. For the relevance of this subsection to industrial accident declarations, see s.44(6)(c) of the Social Security Administration Act 1992.

Relevant employments

95.—(1) In section 94 above, this section and sections 98 to 109 below "employed earner's employment" shall be taken to include any employment by virtue of which a person is, or is treated by regulations as being for the purposes of industrial injuries benefit, an employed earner.

(2) Regulations may provide that any prescribed employment shall not be treated for the purposes of industrial injuries benefit as employed earner's employment notwithstanding that it would be so treated apart from the regulations.

(3) For the purposes of the provisions of this Act mentioned in subsection (1) above an employment shall be an employed earner's employment in relation to an accident if (and only if) it is, or is treated by regulations as being, such an employment when the accident occurs.

(4) Any reference in the industrial injuries and diseases provisions to an "employed earner" or "employed earner's employment" is to be construed,

in relation to any time before 6th April 1975, as a reference respectively to an "insured person" or "insurable employment" within the meaning of the provisions relating to industrial injuries and diseases which were in force at that time.

(5) In subsection (4) above "the industrial injuries and diseases provisions" means—

(a) this section and sections 96 to 110 below;
(b) any other provisions of this Act so far as they relate to those sections; and
(c) any provisions of the Administration Act so far as they so relate.

DERIVATION

Social Security Act 1975, s.51; Social Security (Miscellaneous Provisions) Act 1977, s.17(3).

DEFINITIONS

For "employed earner", see s.2.
For "employment", "industrial injuries benefit" and "prescribe", see s.122(1).
For "the industrial injuries and diseases provisions", see subs. (5).

Persons treated as employers for certain purposes

96. In relation to—

(a) a person who is an employed earner for the purposes of this Part of this Act otherwise than by virtue of a contract of service or apprenticeship; or
(b) any other employed earner—
  (i) who is employed for the purpose of any game or recreation and is engaged or paid through a club; or
  (ii) in whose case it appears to the Secretary of State there is special difficulty in the application of all or any of the provisions of this Part of this Act relating to employers,

regulations may provide for a prescribed person to be treated in respect of industrial injuries benefit and its administration as the earner's employer.

DERIVATION

Social Security Act 1975, s.157.

DEFINITIONS

For "employed earner", see ss.2 and 95(4).
For "contract of service", "employed", "industrial injuries benefit" and "prescribe", see s.122(1).

Accidents in course of illegal employments

97.—(1) Subsection (2) below has effect in any case where—

(a) a claim is made for industrial injuries benefit in respect of an accident, or of a prescribed disease or injury; or
(b) an application is made under section 44 of the Administration Act for a declaration that an accident was an industrial accident, or for a corresponding declaration as to a prescribed disease or injury.

(2) The Secretary of State may direct that the relevant employment shall, in relation to that accident, disease or injury, be treated as having been employed earner's employment notwithstanding that by reason of a contravention of, or non-compliance with, some provision contained in or having effect under an enactment passed for the protection of employed persons or any class of employed persons, either—

(a) the contract purporting to govern the employment was void; or

(b) the employed person was not lawfully employed in the relevant employment at the time when, or in the place where, the accident happened or the disease or injury was contracted or received.

(3) In subsection (2) above "relevant employment" means—

(a) in relation to an accident, the employment out of and in the course of which the accident arises; and

(b) in relation to a prescribed disease or injury, the employment to the nature of which the disease or injury is due.

DERIVATION

Social Security Act 1975, s. 156.

DEFINITIONS

For "employed earner", see ss.2 and 95(4).
For "employed earner's employment", see s.95.
For "claim", "employed", "employment", "industrial injuries benefit" and "prescribe", see s.122(1).
For "relevant employment", see subs. (3).

Earner acting in breach of regulations, etc

98. An accident shall be taken to arise out of and in the course of an employed earner's employment, notwithstanding that he is at the time of the accident acting in contravention of any statutory or other regulations applicable to his employment, or of any orders given by or on behalf of his employer, or that he is acting without instructions from his employer, if—

(a) the accident would have been taken so to have arisen had the act not been done in contravention of any such regulations or orders, or without such instructions, as the case may be; and

(b) the act is done for the purposes of and in connection with the employer's trade or business.

DERIVATION

Social Security Act 1975, s.52.

DEFINITIONS

For "employed earner's employment", see ss.95 and 97.
For "employer", see s.96.
For "employed earner", see ss.2 and 95(4).
For "employment" and "trade or business", see s.122(1).

Earner travelling in employer's transport

99.—(1) An accident happening while an employed earner is, with the express or implied permission of his employer, travelling as a passenger by any vehicle to or from his place of work shall, notwithstanding that he is under no obligation to his employer to travel by that vehicle, be taken to arise out of and in the course of his employment if—

(a) the accident would have been taken so to have arisen had he been under such an obligation; and

(b) at the time of the accident, the vehicle—

(i) is being operated by or on behalf of his employer or some other person by whom it is provided in pursuance of arrangements made with his employer; and

(ii) is not being operated in the ordinary course of a public transport service.

(2) In this section references to a vehicle include a ship, vessel, hovercraft or aircraft.

DERIVATION

Social Security Act 1975, s.53.

DEFINITIONS

For "employer", see s.96.
For "employed earner", see ss.2 and 95(4).
For "employment", see s.122(1).
For "vehicle", see subs. (2).

Accidents happening while meeting emergency

100. An accident happening to an employed earner in or about any premises at which he is for the time being employed for the purposes of his employer's trade or business shall be taken to arise out of and in the course of his employment if it happens while he is taking steps, on an actual or supposed emergency at those premises, to rescue, succour or protect persons who are, or are thought to be or possibly to be, injured or imperilled, or to avert or minimise serious damage to property.

DERIVATION

Social Security Act 1975, s.54.

DEFINITIONS

For "employer", see s.96.
For "employed earner", see ss.2 and 95(4).
For "employed", "employment" and "trade or business", see s.122(1).

Accident caused by another's misconduct etc

101. An accident happening after 19th December 1961 shall be treated for the purposes of industrial injuries benefit, where it would not apart from this section be so treated, as arising out of an employed earner's employment if—

(a) the accident arises in the course of the employment; and
(b) the accident either is caused—
   (i) by another person's misconduct, skylarking or negligence, or
   (ii) by steps taken in consequence of any such misconduct, skylarking or negligence, or
   (iii) by the behaviour or presence of an animal (including a bird, fish or insect),

   or is caused by or consists in the employed earner being struck by any object or by lightning; and
(c) the employed earner did not directly or indirectly induce or contribute to the happening of the accident by his conduct outside the employment or by any act not incidental to the employment.

DERIVATION

Social Security Act 1975, s.55.

(1992 c. 4 s.101)

DEFINITIONS

For "employed earner's employment", see ss.95 and (7).
For "employed earner", see ss.2 and 95(4).
For "employment" and "industrial injuries benefit", see s.122(1).

Sickness benefit

Sickness benefit in respect of industrial injury

102. *Repealed from April 13, 1995 by Social Security (Incapacity for Work) Act 1994, Sched.1, para. 29.*

Disablement pension

Disablement pension

103.—(1) Subject to the provisions of this section, an employed earner shall be entitled to disablement pension if he suffers as the result of the relevant accident from loss of physical or mental faculty such that the assessed extent of the resulting disablement amounts to not less than 14 per cent. or, on a claim made before 1st October 1986, 20 per cent.

(2) In the determination of the extent of an employed earner's disablement for the purposes of this section there may be added to the percentage of the disablement resulting from the relevant accident the assessed percentage of any present disability of his—

(a) which resulted from any other accident after 4th July 1948 arising out of and in the course of his employment, being employed earner's employment, and
(b) in respect of which a disablement gratuity was not paid to him after a final assessment of his disablement,

(as well as any percentage which may be so added in accordance with regulations under subsection (2) of section 109 below made by virtue of subsection (4)(b) of that section).

(3) Subject to subsection (4) below, where the assessment of disablement is a percentage between 20 and 100 which is not a multiple of 10, it shall be treated—

(a) if it is a multiple of 5, as being the next higher percentage which is a multiple of 10, and
(b) if it is not a multiple of 5, as being the nearest percentage which is a multiple of 10,

and where the assessment of disablement on a claim made on or after 1st October 1986 is less than 20 per cent., but not less than 14 per cent., it shall be treated as 20 per cent.

(4) Where subsection (2) above applies, subsection (3) above shall have effect in relation to the aggregate percentage and not in relation to any percentage forming part of the aggregate.

(5) In this Part of this Act "assessed", in relation to the extent of any disablement, means assessed in accordance with Schedule 6 to this Act; and for the purposes of that Schedule there shall be taken to be no relevant loss of faculty when the extent of the resulting disablement, if so assessed, would not amount to 1 per cent.

(6) A person shall not be entitled to disablement pension until after the expiry of the period of 90 days (disregarding Sundays) beginning with the day of the relevant accident.

(7) Subject to subsection (8) below, where disablement pension is payable for a period, it shall be paid at the appropriate weekly rate specified in Schedule 4, Part V, paragraph 1.

(8) Where the period referred to in subsection (7) above is limited by reference to a definite date, the pension shall cease on the death of the beneficiary before that date.

DERIVATION

Social Security Act 1975, s.57.

DEFINITIONS

For "employed earner", see ss.2 and 95(4).
For "employed earner's employment", see s.95.
For "claim", "employment", "entitled", "loss of physical faculty", "relevant accident" and "relevant loss of faculty", see s.122(1).
For "assessed", see subs. (5).

GENERAL NOTE

Subs. (1). Disablement benefit is payable in respect of disablement even if the claimant's capacity for work is unimpaired. The practice of the Benefits Agency has been to require a separate claim for disablement benefit in respect of each industrial accident. However, in *CI/6872/95*, following the approach he had taken in *CI/420/94*, the Commissioner held that, where disablement benefit had been claimed in respect of one accident but had not been finally determined, a further claim in respect of another accident was not required. If disablement benefit is already in payment in respect of one accident, a further "claim" in respect of another accident is really an application for review. Equally, if there is in existence an assessment of disablement but disablement benefit is not payable because the assessment is below 14 per cent, an application for review of the assessment must be treated as a claim for disablement benefit if benefit is to be paid.

employed earner: See the note to s.94.

accident: See the note to s.94. S.108 has the effect that disablement benefit is also payable in respect of prescribed diseases and prescribed personal injuries not caused by accident.

loss of physical or mental faculty: This means "an impairment of the proper functioning of part of the body or mind" (*Jones v. Secretary of State for Social Services* [1972] A.C. 944 at 1009 also reported as an appendix to *R(I) 3/69*). Thus a loss of a kidney by a claimant, which necessarily results in a loss of useful function, must, as a matter of law, mean he or she has suffered a loss of faculty even if the claimant can live normally in every way (*R(I) 14/66*). It was pointed out in *R(I) 14/66* that it does not follow that there is any resulting disablement. Nevertheless, adjudicating medical authorities have been advised to assess a "loss of reserve function" which in the case of a kidney is usually put at between 5 and 10 per cent. It is doubtful whether that is correct since that seems to be an assessment of loss of faculty rather than an assessment of disablement. The Deputy Commissioner in *R(I) 14/66* expressed concern that a claimant's assessment of disablement could not be increased if he or she lost the other kidney due to a non-industrial disease or accident. Although *R(I) 11/66*, to which he referred, was overturned in the Court of Appeal (*R. v. Medical Appeal Tribunal, ex p. Cable*, appendix to *R(I) 11/66*), reg. 11(4) of the Social Security (General Benefit) Regulations 1982 appears to limit the effect of *Cable* to cases where the assessment of disablement before the loss of the second kidney has been assessed at not less than 11 per cent.

The definition of "loss of physical faculty" in s.122(1) makes special provision so that it includes disfigurement whether or not accompanied by any actual loss of faculty.

resulting disablement amounts to not less than 14 per cent: It is disablement which must be assessed and not loss of faculty. In *R(I) 3/76*, it was held that:

> " 'disability' means inability to do something which persons of the same age and sex and normal physical and mental powers can do; 'disablement' means a collection of disabilities, that is to say the sum total of all the relevant disabilities found present in a given case."

"14 per cent" was substituted for "one per cent" in s.57(1) of the Social Security Act 1975 from October 1, 1986 (Social Security Act 1986, Sched. 3, para. 3). Before that date, disablement benefit was paid in the form of a gratuity if the assessment was less than 20 per cent and in the form of a pension if the assessment was 20 per cent or more. That remains the case where a claim was made before that date (Social Security (Industrial Injuries and Diseases) Miscellaneous Provisions

Regulations 1986, reg. 14). Any pension is payable under this section and any gratuity is payable under Sched. 7, para. 9. This remains important where, on a claim made before October 1, 1986, there have been a series of provisional assessments. If a claim is made after October 1, 1986 in respect of a period before that date, the new legislation applies (*R(I) 1/90, CI/509/94*).

Disablement benefit is also payable where the assessment is less than 14 per cent, but at least one percent, if it is due to pneumoconiosis, byssinosis or diffuse mesothelioma (Social Security (Industrial Injuries) (Prescribed Diseases) Regulations 1985, reg. 20(1)).

Subs. (5). There is deemed to be no loss of faculty if the resulting disablement is assessed at less than 1 per cent. In *R(I) 6/61*, the Commissioner held that it was desirable that a medical appeal tribunal should indicate whether they have concluded that there is *no* loss of faculty or whether they have concluded that there *is* a loss of faculty, but that the resulting disablement does not amount to 1 per cent. Note that, under s.110(3), a person suffering from pneumoconiosis *shall* be treated as suffering from a loss of faculty such that the assessed extent of disablement amounts to not less than 1 per cent.

For notes on the assessment of disablement, see the annotations to Sched. 6 to the Act and to reg. 11 of the Social Security (General Benefit) Regulations 1982.

Subs. (6). This does not apply where a person is awarded disablement benefit in respect of occupational deafness (reg. 28 of the Social Security (Industrial Injuries) (Prescribed Diseases) Regulations 1985) where a claim is made in respect of diffuse mesothelioma, see *ibid.* reg. 20(4).

Subs. (7). Under Sched. 4, the amount of the pension depends on whether the claimant is over 18 and the extent of disablement. A person over 18 whose disablement is assessed at 100 per cent receives £101.10 per week. The amount paid to people with lower assessments is proportionately less.

Increase where constant attendance needed

104.—(1) Where a disablement pension is payable in respect of an assessment of 100 per cent., then, if as the result of the relevant loss of faculty the beneficiary requires constant attendance, the weekly rate of the pension shall be increased by an amount, not exceeding the appropriate amount specified in Schedule 4, Part V, paragraph 2 determined in accordance with regulations by reference to the extent and nature of the attendance required by the beneficiary.

(2) An increase of pension under this section shall be payable for such period as may be determined at the time it is granted, but may be renewed from time to time.

(3) The Secretary of State may by regulations direct that any provision of sections 64 to 67 above shall have effect, with or without modifications, in relation to increases of pension under this section.

(4) In subsection (3) above, "modifications" includes additions and omissions.

DERIVATION

Social Security Act 1975, s.61.

DEFINITIONS

For "beneficiary" and "relevant loss of faculty", see s.122(1).
For "modifications", see subs. (4).

GENERAL NOTE

See regs. 19–21 of the Social Security (General Benefit) Regulations 1982 for further provisions relating to constant attendance allowance. Note that, under para. 5 of Sched. 1 to the Social Security (Overlapping Benefits) Regulations 1979, constant attendance allowance overlaps with attendance allowance under s.35 and the care component of disability living allowance.

Under reg. 17(1)(a)(i) of the Social Security (Adjudication) Regulations 1995, any question whether constant attendance allowance is to be granted is to be determined by the Secretary of State.

Increase for exceptionally severe disablement

105.—(1) Where a disablement pension is payable to a person—

(a) who is or, but for having received medical or other treatment as an in-

patient in a hospital or similar institution, would be entitled to an increase of the weekly rate of the pension under section 104 above, and the weekly rate of the increase exceeds the amount specified in Schedule 4, Part V, paragraph 2(a); and
(b) his need for constant attendance of an extent and nature qualifying him for such an increase at a weekly rate in excess of that amount is likely to be permanent.

the weekly rate of the pension shall, in addition to any increase under section 104 above, be further increased by the amount specified in Schedule 4, Part V, paragraph 3.

(2) An increase under this section shall be payable for such period as may be determined at the time it is granted, but may be renewed from time to time.

Derivation

Social Security Act 1975, s.63.

Definitions

For ''medical treatment'', see s.122(1).

General Note

Under reg. 17(1)(a)(ii) of the Social Security (Adjudication) Regulations 1995, any question whether exceptionally severe disablement allowance is to be granted is to be determined by the Secretary of State.

Other benefits and increases

Benefits and increases subject to qualifications as to time

106. Schedule 7 to this Act shall have effect in relation—
(a) to unemployability supplement;
(b) to disablement gratuity;
(c) to increases of disablement pension during hospital treatment;
(d) to reduced earnings allowance;
(e) to retirement allowance; and
(f) to industrial death benefit,

for all of which the qualifications include special qualifications as to time.

Successive accidents

Adjustments for successive accidents

107.—(1) Where a person suffers two or more successive accidents arising out of and in the course of his employed earner's employment—
(a) he shall not for the same period be entitled (apart from any increase of benefit mentioned in subsection (2) below) to receive industrial injuries benefit by way of two or more disablement pensions at an aggregate weekly rate exceeding the appropriate amount specified in Schedule 4, Part V, paragraph 4; and
(b) regulations may provide for adjusting—
(i) disablement benefit, or the conditions for the receipt of that benefit, in any case where he has received or may be entitled to a disablement gratuity;
(ii) any increase of benefit mentioned in subsection (2) below, or the conditions for its receipt.

(2) The increases of benefit referred to in subsection (1) above are those under the following provisions of this Act—
section 104,
section 105,
paragraph 2, 4 or 6 of Schedule 7.

DERIVATION

Social Security Act 1975, s.91.

DEFINITIONS

For "employed earner", see ss.2 and 95(4).
For "employed earner's employment", see ss.95 and 97.
For "entitled", "employment" and "industrial injuries benefit", see s.122(1).

GENERAL NOTE

In the light of *CI/420/94*, this section now appears to be of relevance only where the last claim was made before October 1, 1986.

Regs. 38 and 39 of the Social Security (General Benefit) Regulations 1982 are treated as made under this section (Social Security (Consequential Provisions) Act 1992, s.2(2)).

Prescribed industrial diseases etc.

Benefit in respect of prescribed industrial diseases, etc

108.—(1) Industrial injuries benefits shall, in respect of a person who has been in employed earner's employment, be payable in accordance with this section and sections 109 and 110 below in respect of—
(a) any prescribed disease, or
(b) any prescribed personal injury (other than an injury caused by accident arising out of and in the course of his employment),
which is a disease or injury due to the nature of that employment and which developed after 4th July 1948.

(2) A disease or injury may be prescribed in relation to any employed earners if the Secretary of State is satisfied that—
(a) it ought to be treated, having regard to its causes and incidence and any other relevant considerations, as a risk of their occupations and not as a risk common to all persons; and
(b) it is such that, in the absence of special circumstances, the attribution of particular cases to the nature of the employment can be established or presumed with reasonable certainty.

(3) Regulations prescribing any disease or injury for those purposes may provide that a person who developed the disease or injury on or at any time after a date specified in the regulations (being a date before the regulations come into force but not before 5th July 1948) shall be treated, subject to any prescribed modifications of this section or section 109 or 110 below, as if the regulations had been in force when he developed the disease or injury.

(4) Provision may be made by regulations for determining—
(a) the time at which a person is to be treated as having developed any prescribed disease or injury; and
(b) the circumstances in which such a disease or injury is, where the person in question has previously suffered from it, to be treated as having recrudesced or as having been contracted or received afresh.

(5) Notwithstanding any other provision of this Act, the power conferred by subsection (4)(a) above includes power to provide that the time at which a

person shall be treated as having developed a prescribed disease or injury shall be the date on which he first makes a claim which results in the payment of benefit by virtue of this section or section 110 below in respect of that disease or injury.

(6) Nothing in this section or in section 109 or 110 below affects the right of any person to benefit in respect of a disease which is a personal injury by accident within the meaning of this Part of this Act, except that a person shall not be entitled to benefit in respect of a disease as being an injury by accident arising out of and in the course of any employment if at the time of the accident the disease is in relation to him a prescribed disease by virtue of the occupation in which he is engaged in that employment.

DERIVATION

Social Security Act 1975, s.76.

DEFINITIONS

For "employed earner", see ss.2 and 95(4).
For "employed earner's employment", see ss.95 and 97.
For "entitled", "employment", "industrial injuries benefit" and "prescribe", see s.122(1).

GENERAL NOTE

This section makes general provision for payment of industrial injuries benefits to employed earners who are suffering from a disease or personal injury which was *not* caused by accident and so could not give rise to entitlement under s.94. S.109 makes more detailed provision. For the prescribed diseases, see column 1 of Sched. 1 to the Social Security (Industrial Injuries) (Prescribed Diseases) Regulations 1985. Each disease is prescribed in relation to a fairly narrowly defined occupation. Under regs. 43–54 of the Social Security (Adjudication) Regulations 1995, a question whether a person is suffering from a prescribed disease falls to be determined by an adjudication officer in the first instance with appeals to an adjudicating medical authority and then to a medical appeal tribunal. However, an appeal on a question whether a person was engaged in a prescribed occupation falls to be determined by a social security appeal tribunal.

Subs. (3). See reg.43 of, and Sched. 4 to, the Social Security (Industrial Injuries) (Prescribed Diseases) Regulations 1985.

Subss. (4) and (5). See regs. 6 and 7 of the Social Security (Industrial Injuries) (Prescribed Diseases) Regulations 1985.

Subs (6). This makes it clear that a person who develops, as the result of an accident, a disease which *is not* prescribed in relation to him or her remains entitled to benefit under s.94. On the other hand, if the disease *is* prescribed in relation to the claimant, he or she must rely on the provisions relating to prescribed diseases and cannot claim benefit under s.94.

General provisions relating to benefit under section 108

109.—(1) Subject to the power to make different provision by regulations, and to the following provisions of this section and section 110 below—

(a) the benefit payable under section 108 above in respect of a prescribed disease or injury, and

(b) the conditions for receipt of benefit,

shall be the same as in the case of personal injury by accident arising out of and in the course of employment.

(2) In relation to prescribed diseases and injuries, regulations may provide—

(a) for modifying any provisions contained in this Act or the Administration Act which relate to disablement benefit or reduced earnings allowance or their administration; and

(b) for adapting references in this Act and that Act to accidents,

and for the purposes of this subsection the provisions of the Administration Act which relate to the administration of disablement benefit or reduced earnings allowance shall be taken to include section 1 and any provision which relates to the administration of both the benefit in question and other benefits.

(3) Without prejudice to the generality of subsection (2) above, regulations under that subsection may in particular include provision—

(a) for presuming any prescribed disease or injury—

(i) to be due, unless the contrary is proved, to the nature of a person's employment where he was employed in any prescribed occupation at the time when, or within a prescribed period or for a prescribed length of time (whether continuous or not) before, he developed the disease or injury,

(ii) not to be due to the nature of person's employment unless he was employed in some prescribed occupation at the time when, or within a prescribed period or for a prescribed length of time (whether continuous or not) before, he developed the disease or injury;

(b) for such matters as appear to the Secretary of State to be incidental to or consequential on provisions included in the regulations by virtue of subsection (2) and paragraph (a) above.

(4) Regulations under subsection (2) above may also provide—

(a) that, in the determination of the extent of an employed earner's disablement resulting from a prescribed disease or injury, the appropriate percentage may be added to the percentage of that disablement; and

(b) that, in the determination of the extent of an employed earner's disablement for the purposes of section 103 above, the appropriate percentage may be added to the percentage of disablement resulting from the relevant accident.

(5) In subsection (4)(a) above "the appropriate percentage" means the assessed percentage of any present disablement of the earner which resulted—

(a) from any accident after 4th July 1948 arising out of and in the course of his employment, being employed earner's employment, or

(b) from any other prescribed disease or injury due to the nature of that employment and developed after 4th July 1948,

and in respect of which a disablement gratuity was not paid to him after a final assessment of his disablement.

(6) In subsection (4)(b) above "the appropriate percentage" means the assessed percentage of any present disablement of the earner—

(a) which resulted from any prescribed disease or injury due to the nature of his employment and developed after 4th July 1948, and

(b) in respect of which a disablement gratuity was not paid to him after a final assessment of his disablement.

(7) Where regulations under subsection (2) above—

(a) make provision such as is mentioned in subsection (4) above, and

(b) also make provision corresponding to that in section 103(3) above, they may also make provision to the effect that those corresponding provisions shall have effect in relation to the aggregate percentage and not in relation to any percentage forming part of the aggregate.

DERIVATION

Social Security Act 1975, s.77.

DEFINITIONS

For "employed earner", see ss.2 and 95(4).
For "employed earner's employment", see ss.95 and 97.
For "assessed", see s.103(5).
For "employment", "employed", "prescribe" and "relevant accident", see s.122(1).

General Note

In general the same benefits are payable in respect of prescribed diseases as are payable in respect of injuries caused by accident. For regulations, see the Social Security (Industrial Injuries) (Prescribed Diseases) Regulations 1985. The practice of the Benefits Agency has been to require a separate claim for disablement benefit in respect of each disease. However, in *CI/420/94*, it was held that, where disablement benefit was in payment in respect of one disease, a "claim" in respect of another disease was really an application for review. The concluding words of subs. (2) were added to s.77(2) of the Social Security Act 1975 in order to reverse the effect of *McKiernon v. Secretary of State for Social Security* (*The Times*, November 1, 1989) in which reg. 25 of the 1985 Regulations had been held to be *ultra vires*. In *Chatterton v. Chief Adjudication Officer, McKiernon v. Chief Adjudication Officer* (unreported, July 8, 1993), the Court of Appeal held that the amendment did have the intended effect.

Respiratory diseases

110.—(1) As respects pneumoconiosis, regulations may further provide that, where a person is found to be suffering from pneumoconiosis accompanied by tuberculosis, the effects of the tuberculosis shall be treated for the purposes of this section and sections 108 and 109 above as if they were effects of the pneumoconiosis.

(2) Subsection (1) above shall have effect as if after "tuberculosis" (in both places) there were inserted "emphysema or chronic bronchitis", but only in relation to a person the extent of whose disablement resulting from pneumoconiosis, or from pneumoconiosis accompanied by tuberculosis, would (if his physical condition were otherwise normal) be assessed at not less than 50 per cent.

(3) A person found to be suffering from pneumoconiosis shall be treated for the purposes of this Act as suffering from a loss of faculty such that the assessed extent of the resulting disablement amounts to not less than 1 per cent.

(4) In respect of byssinosis, a person shall not (unless regulations otherwise provide) be entitled to disablement benefit unless he is found to be suffering, as the result of byssinosis, from loss of faculty which is likely to be permanent.

Derivation

Social Security Act 1975, s.78.

Definitions

For "assessed", see s.103(5).
For "pneumoconiosis", see s.122(1).

General Note

Subss. (1) and (2). See regs. 21 and 22 of the Social Security (Industrial Injuries) (Prescribed Diseases) Regulations 1985.

Subs. (3). This requires that a person suffering from pneumoconiosis *shall* be treated as being disabled to the extent of at least 1 per cent, even if the disablement is in fact negligible. Under reg. 20(1) of the Social Security (Industrial Injuries) (Prescribed Diseases) Regulations 1985 a person suffering from pneumoconiosis is entitled to disablement benefit if the resulting disablement is at least 1 per cent.

Subs. (4). This subsection is disapplied by reg. 20(2) of the Social Security (Industrial Injuries) (Prescribed Diseases) Regulations 1985.

111. *Omitted.*

Part VI

Miscellaneous Provisions relating to Parts I to V

112. *Omitted.*

Disqualification and suspension

General provisions as to disqualification and suspension

113.—(1) Except where regulations otherwise provide, a person shall be disqualified for receiving any benefit under Parts II to V of this Act, and an increase of such benefit shall not be payable in respect of any person as the beneficiary's wife or husband, for any period during which the person—

(a) is absent from Great Britain; or

(b) is undergoing imprisonment or detention in legal custody.

(2) Regulations may provide for suspending payment of such benefit to a person during any period in which he is undergoing medical or other treatment as an in-patient in a hospital or similar institution.

(3) Regulations may provide for a person who would be entitled to any such benefit but for the operation of any provisions of this Act or the Administration Act to be treated as if entitled to it for the purposes of any rights or obligations (whether his own or another's) which depend on his entitlement, other than the right to payment of the benefit.

Derivation

Social Security Act 1975, ss.82(5) and (6), 83.

Definitions

For "beneficiary", "benefit", "entitled" and "medical treatment", see s.122(1).

General Note

Under the Social Security (Consequential Provisions) Act 1992, s.2(2), a considerable number of statutory instruments made under the Social Security Act 1975 are treated as having effect under this section. See in particular the Social Security Benefit (Persons Abroad) Regulations 1975, the Social Security (General Benefit) Regulations 1982 (for disqualification or suspension while in prison or other legal custody) and the Social Security (Hospital In-patients) Regulations 1975 (S.I. 1975 No. 555—not reproduced in this book).

114.—121. *Omitted.*

Interpretation

Interpretation of Parts I to VI and supplementary provisions

122.—(1) In Parts I to V above and this Part of this Act, unless the context otherwise requires—

"beneficiary", in relation to any benefit, means the person entitled to that benefit;

"benefit" means—

(a) benefit under Parts II to V of this Act other than Old Cases payments;

(b) as respects any period before 1st July 1992 but not before 6th April 1975, benefit under Part II of the 1975 Act; or

(c) as respects any period before 6th April 1975, benefit under—
(i) the National Insurance Act 1946 or 1965; or
(ii) the National Insurance (Industrial Injuries) Act 1946 or 1965;

"child" means a person under the age of 19 who would be treated as a child for the purposes of Part IX of this Act or such other person under that age as may be prescribed;

"claim" is to be construed in accordance with "claimant";

"claimant", in relation to benefit other than industrial injuries benefit, means a person who has claimed benefit;

"claimant", in relation to industrial injuries benefit, means a person who has claimed industrial injuries benefit;

"contract of service" means any contract of service or apprenticeship whether written or oral and whether express or implied;

[[3]"contribution-based jobseeker's allowance" has the same meaning as in the Jobseeker's Act 1995;]

"current", in relation to the lower and upper earnings limits under section 5(1) above, means for the time being in force;

[[1]"day of interruption of employment" has the meaning given by section 25A(1)(c) above];

"deferred" and "period of deferment" have the meanings assigned to them by section 55 above;

"earner" and "earnings" are to be construed in accordance with sections 3, 4 and 112 above;

"employed earner" has the meaning assigned to it by section 2 above;

"employment" includes any trade, business, profession, office or vocation and "employed" has a corresponding meaning;

"entitled", in relation to any benefit, is to be construed in accordance with—
(a) the provisions specifically relating to that benefit;
(b) in the case of a benefit specified in section 20(1) above, section 21 above; and
(c) sections 1 to 3 and 68 of the Administration Act;

"industrial injuries benefit" means benefit under Part V of this Act, other than under Schedule 8;

"initial primary percentage" is to be construed in accordance with section 8(1) and (2) above and as referring to the percentage rate from time to time specified in section 8(2)(a) above as the initial primary percentage;

"the Inland Revenue" means the Commissioners of Inland Revenue;

"late husband", in relation to a woman who has been more than once married, means her last husband;

"long-term benefit" has the meaning assigned to it by section 20(2) above;

"loss of physical faculty" includes disfigurement whether or not accompanied by any loss of physical faculty;

"lower earnings limit" and "upper earnings limit" are to be construed in accordance with section 5(1) above and references to the lower or upper earnings limit of a tax year are to whatever is (or was) for that year the limit in force under that subsection;

"main primary percentage" is to be construed in accordance with section 8(1) and (2) above and as referring to the percentage rate from time to time specified in section 8(2)(b) above as the main primary percentage;

"medical examination" includes bacteriological and radiographical tests and similar investigations and "medically examined" has a corresponding meaning;

"medical treatment" means medical, surgical or rehabilitative treatment (including any course or diet or other regimen), and references to a person receiving or submitting himself to medical treatment are to be construed accordingly;

"the Northern Ireland Department" means the Department of Health and Social Services for Northern Ireland;

"Old Cases payments" means payments under Part I or II of Schedule 8 to this Act;

"payments by way of occupational or personal pension" means, in relation to a person, periodical payments which, in connection with the coming to an end of an employment of his, fall to be made to him—

(a) out of money provided wholly or partly by the employer or under arrangements made by the employer; or

(b) out of money provided under an enactment or instrument having the force of law in any part of the United Kingdom or elsewhere; or

(c) under a personal pension scheme as defined in section 84(1) of the 1986 Act; or

(d) under a contract or trust scheme approved under Chapter III of Part XIV of the Income and Corporation Taxes Act 1988; or

(e) under a personal pension scheme approved under Chapter IV of that Part of that Act,

and such other payments as are prescribed;

[[2]"pensionable age" has the meaning given by the rules in paragraph 1 of Schedule 4 to the Pensions Act 1995;]

"pneumoconiosis" means fibrosis of the lungs due to silica dust, asbestos dust, or other dust, and includes the condition of the lungs known as dust-reticulation;

"prescribe" means prescribe by regulations;

"primary percentage" is to be construed in accordance with section 8(1) and (2) above;

"qualifying earnings factor" means an earnings factor equal to the lower earnings limit for the tax year in question multiplied by 52;

"relative" includes a person who is a relative by marriage;

"relevant accident" means the accident in respect of which industrial injuries benefit is claimed or payable;

"relevant injury" means the injury in respect of which industrial injuries benefit is claimed or payable;

"relevant loss of faculty" means—

(a) in relation to severe disablement allowance, the loss of faculty which results in the disablement; or

(b) in relation to industrial injuries benefit, the loss of faculty resulting from the relevant injury;

"self-employed" has the meaning assigned to it by section 2 above;

"short-term benefit" has the meaning assigned to it by section 20(2) above;

"tax week" means one of the successive periods in a tax year beginning with the first day of that year and every seventh day thereafter, the last day of a tax year (or, in the case of a tax year ending in a leap year, the last two days) to be treated accordingly as a separate tax week;

"tax year" means the 12 months beginning with 6th April in any year, the expression "1978–79" meaning the tax year beginning with 6th April 1978, and any correspondingly framed reference to a pair of successive years being construed as a reference to the tax year beginning with 6th April in the earlier of them;

"trade or business" includes, in relation to a public or local authority, the exercise and performance of the powers and duties of that authority;

"trade union" means an association of employed earners;

"week", except in relation to disability working allowance, means a period of seven days beginning with Sunday;

[2 "working life" has the meaning given by paragraph 5(8) of Schedule 3 to this Act.]

(2) Regulations may make provision modifying the meaning of "employment" for the purposes of any provision of Parts I to V and this Part of this Act.

(3)—(6) *Omitted.*

DERIVATION

Social Security Act 1975, s.168(1) and Sched. 20.

AMENDMENTS

1. Social Security (Incapacity for Work) Act 1994, Sched. 1, para. 30 (April 13, 1995).
2. Pensions Act 1995, s. 134(4) and Sched. 4, para. 13(a) (July 19, 1995).
3. Jobseekers Act 1995, Sched. 2, para. 29 (October 7, 1996).

PART VII

INCOME-RELATED BENEFITS

General

Income-related benefits

123.—(1) Prescribed schemes shall provide for the following benefits (in this Act referred to as "income-related benefits")—

(a) income support;
(b) family credit;
(c) disability working allowance;
(d) housing benefit; and
[1(e) council tax benefit.]

(2) The Secretary of State shall make copies of schemes prescribed under subsection (1)(a), (b) or (c) above available for public inspection at local offices of the Department of Social Security at all reasonable hours without payment.

(3)—(6) *Omitted.*

DERIVATION

Social Security Act 1986, s. 20(1) and (2).

AMENDMENT

1. Local Government Finance Act 1992, Sched. 9, para. 1(1) (April 1, 1993).

124.—128. *Omitted.*

Disability working allowance

Disability working allowance

129.—(1) A person in Great Britain who has attained the age of 16 and [2 qualifies under subsection (2) or (2A) below] is entitled to a disability working allowance if, when the claim for it is made or is treated as made—

(a) he is engaged and normally engaged in remunerative work;

(b) he has a physical or mental disability which puts him at a disadvantage in getting a job;

(c) his income—

(i) does not exceed the amount which is the applicable amount at such date as may be prescribed; or

(ii) exceeds it, but only by such an amount that there is an amount remaining if the deduction for which subsection (5)(b) below provides is made; and

(d) except in such circumstances as may be prescribed, neither he nor, if he has a family, any member of it, is entitled to family credit.

(2) Subject to subsection (4) below, a person qualifies under this sub-section if—

(a) for one or more of the 56 days immediately preceding the date when the claim for a disability working allowance is made or is treated as made there was payable to him one or more of the following—

[[2]](i) the higher rate of short-term incapacity benefit or long-term incapacity benefit;]

(ii) a severe disablement allowance;

(iii) income support [[3]an income-based jobseeker's allowance], housing benefit or [[1] council tax benefit],

or a corresponding benefit under any enactment having effect in Northern Ireland;

(b) when the claim for a disability working allowance is made or is treated as made, there is payable to him one or more of the following—

(i) an attendance allowance;

(ii) a disability living allowance;

(iii) an increase of disablement pension under section 104 above;

(iv) an analogous pension increase under a war pension scheme or an industrial injuries scheme.

or a corresponding benefit under any enactment having effect in Northern Ireland; or

(c) when the claim for a disability working allowance is made or is treated as made, he has an invalid carriage or other vehicle provided by the Secretary of State under section 5(2)(a) of the National Health Service Act 1977 and Schedule 2 to that Act or under section 46 of the National Health Service (Scotland) Act 1978 or provided under Article 30(1) of the Health and Personal Social Services (Northern Ireland) Order 1972.

[[2]](2A) A person qualifies under this subsection if—

(a) on one or more of the 56 days immediately preceding the date when the claim for a disability working allowance is made or is treated as made he was engaged in training for work and

(b) a relevant benefit was payable to him for one or more of the 56 days immediately preceding—

(i) the first day of training for work falling within the 56 days mentioned in paragraph (a) above or

(ii) an earlier day of training for work which formed part of the same period of training for work as that day.

(2B) For the purposes of subsection (2A) above—

(a) the following are relevant benefits—

(i) the higher rate of short-term incapacity benefit

(ii) long-term incapacity benefit

(iii) a severe disablement allowance,

or a corresponding benefit under any enactment having effect in Northern Ireland;

(b) "training for work" means training for work in pursuance of arrangements made under section 2(1) of the Employment and Training Act

1973 or section 2(3) of the Enterprise and New Towns (Scotland) Act 1990 or training of such other description as may be prescribed; and

(c) a period of training for work means a series of consecutive days of training for work, there being disregarded for this purpose such days as may be prescribed.]

(3) For the purposes of subsection (1) above a person has a disability which puts him at a disadvantage in getting a job only if he satisfies prescribed conditions or prescribed circumstances exist in relation to him.

(4) If the only benefit mentioned in paragraph (a) of subsection (2) above which is payable to a person as there mentioned is—

(a) a benefit mentioned in sub-paragraph (iii) of that paragraph; or

(b) a corresponding benefit under any enactment having effect in Northern Ireland,

he only qualifies under that subsection in prescribed circumstances.

(5) Where a person is entitled to a disability working allowance, then—

(a) if his income does not exceed the amount which is the applicable amount at the date prescribed under subsection (1)(c)(i) above, the amount of the disability working allowance shall be the amount which is the appropriate maximum disability working allowance in his case; and

(b) if his income exceeds that amount, the amount of the disability working allowance shall be what remains after the deduction from the appropriate maximum disability working allowance of a prescribed percentage of the excess of his income over that amount.

(6) A disability working allowance shall be payable for a period of 26 weeks or such other period as may be prescribed and, subject to regulations, an award of a disability working allowance and the rate at which it is payable shall not be affected by any change of circumstances during that period or by any order under section 150 of the Administration Act.

(7) Regulations may provide that an award of a disability working allowance to a person shall terminate if—

(a) a disability working allowance becomes payable in respect of some of other person who was a member of his family at the date of his claim for a disability working allowance; or

(b) income support [[3], an income-based jobseeker's allownace] or family credit becomes payable in respect of a person who was a member of the family at that date.

(8) Regulations shall prescribe the manner in which the appropriate maximum disability working allowance is to be determined in any case.

(9) The provisions of this Act relating to disability working allowance apply in relation to persons employed by or under the Crown as they apply in relation to persons employed otherwise than by or under the Crown.

DERIVATION

Subs. (1): Social Security Act 1986, s.20(6A) and (6D).
Subs. (2): Social Security Act 1986, s.20(6B).
Subs. (3): Social Security Act 1986, s.20(6C).
Subs. (4): Social Security Act 1986, s.20(6E).
Subs. (5): Social Security Act 1986, s.21(3A) and (3B).
Subs. (6): Social Security Act 1986, s.20(6F).
Subs. (7): Social Security Act 1986, s.27B(4).
Subs. (8): Social Security Act 1986, s.21(6)(aa).
Subs. (9): Social Security Act 1986, s.79(3).

AMENDMENTS

1. Local Government Finance Act 1992, Sched. 9, para. 2 (April 1, 1993).

2. Social Security (Incapacity for Work) Act 1994, s.10 and Sched. 1, para. 32 (November 18, 1994 for regulation-making purposes and April 13, 1995 for other purposes).
3. Jobseekers Act 1995, Sched. 2, para. 34 (October 7, 1996).

GENERAL NOTE

Subs.(1). This sets out the principal conditions for entitlement to disability working allowance.

(i) The claimant must be in Great Britain. However, reg. 5 of the Disability Working Allowance (General) Regulations 1991 provides that a claimant shall be treated as being in Great Britain if the claimant is ordinarily resident in Great Britain, his or her partner is ordinarily resident in the United Kingdom and any earnings of either derive at least in part from remunerative work in the United Kingdom and not wholly from work outside the United Kingdom.

(ii) The claimant must be at least 16.

(iii) The claimant must have been, or be, entitled to one of the incapacity or disability benefits listed in subs. (2).

(iv) The claimant must be engaged in remunerative work which is defined in reg. 6 of the Disability Working Allowance (General) Regulations 1991 as work for at least 16 hours per week done for or in expectation of payment. Under reg. 6(6) the work must be work which the claimant normally does and it must be likely to last for at least five weeks from the week in which the claim is made. Note that, unlike family credit, it is the claimant's work that is relevant and not the work of any partner.

(v) The claimant must have a physical or mental disability which puts him at a disadvantage in getting a job. See reg. 3 of, and Sched. 1 to, the Disability Working Allowance (General) Regulations 1991.

(vi) The claimant's income must not be so high that the application of the means-test prescribed by subs. (5) results in no entitlement. Under reg. 52(2) of the Disability Working Allowance (General) Regulations 1991, the prescribed date is the date on which the period of the award begins.

(vii) The claimant must not be entitled to family credit save in the circumstances outlined in reg. 57 of the Disability Working Allowance (General) Regulations 1991 which allows a claim for disability working allowance to be made during the last 28 days of a period of entitlement to family credit so as to begin at the end of that period.

Subs. (2). This sets out the qualifying benefits. There are three groups. The claimant need have been, or be, entitled to only one benefit from only one of the three groups.

The benefits listed in para. (a) are all benefits for which it is a condition of entitlement that the claimant be incapable of work. Since the claimant must be working in order to qualify for disability working allowance, the claimant is unlikely to be entitled to these benefits while actually working so the condition is satisfied if the claimant was entitled to one or more of the benefits within the eight weeks preceding the date of claim. Note that, by virtue of subs. (4) and reg. 7 of the Disability Working Allowance (General) Regulations 1991, income support, housing benefit and community charge benefit are qualifying benefits only if the claimant's applicable amount included a higher pensioner premium or disability premium in respect of him or her.

The benefits listed in para. (b) are all disability benefits receipt of which is not necessarily inconsistent with capacity for work. Accordingly, the claimant must be entitled to one or more of them at the date of claim.

Para. (c) enables a person to qualify if he or she has, at the date of claim, an invalid carriage or other vehicle provided under a statutory scheme.

Subs. (3). See reg. 3 of, and Sched. 1 to, the Disability Working Allowance (General) Regulations 1991.

Subs. (4). See reg. 7 of the Disability Working Allowance (General) Regulations 1991.

Subs. (6). No period other than 26 weeks has been prescribed. Once an award has been made, it continues for the 26-week period irrespective of any changes in the claimant's circumstances, whether favourable or unfavourable except in the circumstances provided for in regs. 54–56 of the Disability Working Allowance (General) Regulations 1991 (death of claimant and overlapping awards).

Subs. (7). See reg. 55 of the Disability Working Allowance (General) Regulations 1991.

Subs. (8). See reg. 51 of, and Sched. 5 to, the Disability Working Allowance (General) Regulations 1991.

130.—133. *Omitted.*

Exclusions from benefit

134.—(1) No person shall be entitled to an income-related benefit if his capital or a prescribed part of it exceeds the prescribed amount.

(2) Except in prescribed circumstances the entitlement of one member of a family to any one income-related benefit excludes entitlement to that benefit for any other member for the same period.

(3)[1. . .]

(4) Where the amount of any income-related benefit would be less than a prescribed amount, it shall not be payable except in prescribed circumstances.

DERIVATION

Subs. (1): Social Security Act 1986, s.22(6).
Subs. (2): Social Security Act 1986, s.20(9).
Subs. (4): Social Security Act 1986, s.21(7).

AMENDMENT

1. Local Government Finance Act 1992, Sched. 9, para. 7 and Sched. 14 (April 1, 1993).

DEFINITIONS

For "family", see s.137(1).

GENERAL NOTE

Subs. (1). The capital limit for disability working allowance is £16,000 (Disability Working Allowance (General) Regulations 1991, reg. 31).

Subs. (2). No regulations have been made under this subsection in order to provide an exception to the general rule.

Subs. (4). The minimum amount of disability working allowance that is payable is 50 pence per week (Social Security (Claims and Payments) Regulations 1987, reg. 27(2)).

The applicable amount

135.—(1) The applicable amount, in relation to any income-related benefit, shall be such amount or the aggregate of such amounts as may be prescribed in relation to that benefit.

(2) The power to prescribe applicable amounts conferred by subsection (1) above includes power to prescribe nil as an applicable amount.

(3) to (6) *Omitted.*

DERIVATION

Social Security Act 1986, s.22(1) and (2).

GENERAL NOTE

See reg. 52(1) of the Disability Working Allowance (General) Regulations 1991.

Income and capital

136.—(1) Where a person claiming an income-related benefit is a member of a family, the income and capital of any member of that family shall, except in prescribed circumstances, be treated as the income and capital of that person.

(2) Regulations may provide that capital not exceeding the amount prescribed under section 134(1) above but exceeding a prescribed lower amount shall be treated, to a prescribed extent, as if it were income of a prescribed amount.

(3) Income and capital shall be calculated or estimated in such manner as may be prescribed.

(4) A person's income in respect of a week shall be calculated in accordance with prescribed rules; and the rules may provide for the calculation to be made by reference to an average over a period (which need not include the week concerned).

(5) Circumstances may be prescribed in which—

(a) a person is treated as possessing capital or income which he does not possess;

(b) capital of income which a person does possess is to be disregarded;

(c) income is to be treated as capital;

(d) capital is to be treated as income.

DERIVATION

Social Security Act 1986, s.22(5) and (7) (9).

GENERAL NOTE

Subs. (1). Capital of a child or young person is not treated as capital of the claimant (Disability Working Allowance (General) Regulations 1991, reg. 33). There are also some circumstances in which the income of a child or young person is not treated as income of the claimant (*ibid.* reg. 30).

Sub. (2). ibid. reg. 40.

Subs. (3)–(5). See generally *ibid.* regs. 12–50.

Interpretation of Part VII and supplementary provisions

137.—(1) In this Part of this Act, unless the context otherwise requires—

[. . .]

"child" means a person under the age of 16;

[. . .]

"family" means—

(a) a married or unmarried couple;

(b) a married or unmarried couple and a member of the same household for whom one of them is or both are responsible and who is a child or a person of a prescribed description;

(c) except in prescribed circumstances, a person who is not a member of a married or unmarried couple and a member of the same household for whom that person is responsible and who is a child or a person of a prescribed description;

[[1]"income-based jobseeker's allowance" has the same meaning as in the Jobseekers Act 1995;]

"industrial injuries scheme" means a scheme made under Schedule 8 to this Act or section 159 of the 1975 Act or under the Old Cases Act;

[. . .]

"married couple" means a man and woman who are married to each other and are members of the same household;

[. . .]

"prescribed" means specified in or determined in accordance with regulations;

"unmarried couple" means a man and woman who are not married to each other but are living together as husband and wife otherwise than in prescribed circumstances;

"war pension scheme" means a scheme under which war pensions (as defined in section 25 of the Social Security Act 1989) are provided;

[. . .]

(2) Regulations may make provision for the purposes of this Part of this Act—

(a) as to circumstances in which a person is to be treated as being or not being in Great Britain;

(b) continuing a person's entitlement to benefit during periods of temporary absence from Great Britain;

(c) as to what is or is not to be treated as remunerative work or as employment;

[[1](d) as to circumstances in which a person is or is not to be treated as engaged or normally engaged in remunerative work;]

(e) as to what is or is not to be treated as relevant education;

(f) as to circumstances in which a person is or is not to be treated as receiving relevant education;

(g) specifying the descriptions of pension increases under war pension schemes or industrial injuries schemes that are analogous to the benefits mentioned in section 129(b)(i) to (iii) above;

(h) as to circumstances in which a person is or is not to be treated as occupying a dwelling as his home;

(i) for treating any person who is liable to make payments in respect of a dwelling as if he were not so liable;

(j) for treating any person who is not liable to make payments in respect of a dwelling as if he were so liable;

(k) for treating as included in a dwelling any land used for the purposes of the dwelling;

(l) as to circumstances in which persons are to be treated as being or not being members of the same household;

(m) as to circumstances in which one person is to be treated as responsible or not responsible for another.

Derivation

Social Security Act 1986, s.20(11) and (12).

Amendment

1. Jobseekers Act 1995, Sched. 2, para. 35 (October 7, 1996).

General Note

Subs. (1). These definitions are of considerable importance for all income-related benefits, including disability working allowance.

family: This definition is important because, under s.136(1), the income and capital of members of a family are usually aggregated. A family consists either of a couple, or a couple and child(ren) or a single person and child(ren). A child is defined as a person under 16, but an older dependent child is included as "a person of a prescribed description" if under 19 and receiving full-time education within s.2(1)(b) of the Child Benefit Act 1975 (see reg.8 of the Disability Working Allowance (General) Regulations 1991 by virtue of which such a person is known as a "young person"). Reg. 9 of those Regulations provides for circumstances in which a person is treated as responsible for or not responsible for a child or young person. Reg. 10 has the effect that a child or young person is usually deemed to be a member of the same household as the person who is responsible for him or her.

married couple: A man and a woman who are married to each other are treated as a "married couple" only if they are members of the same household. Two people who lead separate lives, albeit they live under the same roof, will be in separate households; "house" relates to something physical but "household" has an abstract meaning (*Santos v. Santos* [1972] Fam. 247). So, in the not uncommon situation where spouses remain in the matrimonial home following the breakdown of a marriage, they may cease to be a "married couple" for the purposes of disability working allowance. On the other hand, a married couple who are temporarily living in different places because, for instance, one spouse is working away from home, will generally still be regarded as living in the same household until one decides that the marriage is at an end (*Santos v. Santos).* Reg. 11 of the Disability Working Allowance (General) Regulations 1991 makes specific provision for cases where one member of a couple is living in accommodation provided under the National Assistance Act 1948 (*e.g.* a local authority old people's home) or is in hospital or in custody.

unmarried couple: Deciding whether two people are living together as husband and wife can raise all sorts of delicate questicns and tribunals should remember that, under reg. 4(4) of the Social Security (Adjudication) Regulations 1986, a hearing need not be in public if the chairman "is satisfied that intimate personal or financial circumstances may have to be disclosed".

In considering whether two people are an unmarried couple, adjudication officers refer to six "criteria", which Woolf J. in *Crake v. Supplementary Benefits Commission, Butterworth v. Supplementary Benefits Commission* (1981) 2 F.L.R. 264 said were better described as "admirable signposts to help a tribunal, or indeed the Commission, to come to a decision whether in fact the parties should be regarded as being within the words 'living together as husband and wife'". In *R(SB) 35/85*, it was pointed out that the criteria have not always remained the same. In any event, it is the statute that must be construed; not the Adjudication Officer's Guide. In *CIS/87/93* (reported *sub nom. Re J (Income Support: Cohabitation)* [1995] 1 F.L.R. 660) the criteria were criticised as being inadequate and not entirely accurate in their reflection of the law. The Commissioner emphasised the importance of the parties' general relationship. The six criteria are common household, stability, financial support, sexual relationship, children and public acknowledgement.

common household: Two people can be living together only if they are members of the same household (*Butterworth*). "A person who has, and lives in, his own separate home cannot reasonably be regarded as being a member of someone else's household" (*R(SB) 4/83*). See also the references above to *Santos* and to reg. 11 of the Disability Working Allowance (General) Regulations 1991. The mere fact that two people are members of the same household is not conclusive. In *Robson v. Secretary of State for Social Services* (1982) 3 F.L.R. 232, Webster J. said: "It does seem that the legislation provides for three different situations: two persons living together being husband and wife is the first; two persons living together as husband and wife is the second; and two persons living together not as husband and wife is the third." It is therefore necessary to consider the nature of the relationship. In *R(G) 3/71*, it was said to be necessary to consider the sexual relationship, the financial relationship and the general relationship.

stability: This rather begs the question of the nature of the relationship. It is difficult to see how stability can, of itself, indicate that a relationship is "as husband and wife", since there are many other types of relationship that might be stable (*e.g.* lodger and landlady). On the other hand, if a relationship could be regarded as being as "husband and wife" on the basis of other considerations, the stability of the relationship is another relevant factor.

financial support: The fact that one party was not supporting another while that other party was entitled to benefit is not a matter of great weight. It may be more relevant to ask whether the relationship is such that one party would support the other in the absence of any other source of income. Even then, regard has to be had to the reasons for such support. People may be friends without living together as husband and wife.

sexual relationship: This is an important, as well as a normal, part of marriage. If two people have never had a sexual relationship, it is unlikely that their relationship is "as husband and wife" (see *R(SB) 35/85*). In *CSB/150/85*, it was held that a claimant and his fiancee, who lived together but refrained on religious principle from any sexual relationship, were not living together as husband and wife. One difficulty facing tribunals is that adjudication officers are instructed not to raise questions relating to a couple's sexual relationship. In *CIS/87/93* (reported *sub nom. Re J (Income Support: Cohabitation)* [1995] 1 F.L.R. 660), it was held that, in an inquisitorial jurisdiction, it is not desirable for tribunals to take the same approach because the issue is important, although any questioning must, of course, be conducted with sensitivity and should not probe further than is necessary.

children: If a couple are living in the same household to care for their children, they are likely to be living together as husband and wife.

public acknowledgment: Use of the same surname is likely to lead to an inference that a couple are living together as husband and wife (*R(G) 1/74, R(G) 1/79*). However, describing the other person as "her common-law husband" was not fatal in *Robson*. The right approach is to ask what inferences about the private relationship can properly be drawn from the public behaviour.

Butterworth, Robson and *R(SB) 35/85* were all cases in which it was made plain that the fact that two people live together so that one can provide support for the other who is disabled does not lead to the conclusion that they are living together as husband and wife.

138.—147. *Omitted.*

PART X

CHRISTMAS BONUS FOR PENSIONERS

Entitlement of pensioners to Christmas bonus

148.—(1) Any person who in any year—

(a) is present or ordinarily resident in the United Kingdom or any other member State at any time during the relevant week; and

(b) is entitled to a payment of a qualifying benefit in respect of a period which includes a day in that week or is to be treated as entitled to a payment of a qualifying benefit in respect of such a period,

shall, subject to the following provisions of this Part of this Act and to section 1 of the Administration Act, be entitled to payment under this subsection in respect of that year.

(2) Subject to the following provisions of this Part of this Act, any person who is a member of a couple and is entitled to a payment under subsection (1) above in respect of a year shall also be entitled to payment under this subsection in respect of that year if—

(a) both members have attained pensionable age not later than the end of the relevant week; and

(b) the other member satisfies the condition mentioned in subsection (1)(a) above; and

(c) either—

(i) he is entitled or treated as entitled, in respect of the other member, to an increase in the payment of the qualifying benefit; or

(ii) the only qualifying benefit to which he is entitled is income support.

(3) A payment under subsection (1) or (2) above—

(a) is to be made by the Secretary of State; and

(b) is to be of £10 or such larger sum as the Secretary of State may by order specify.

(4) Where the only qualifying benefit to which a person is entitled is income support, he shall not be entitled to a payment under subsection (1) above unless he has attained pensionable age not later than the end of the relevant week.

(5) Only one sum shall be payable in respect of any person.

DERIVATION

Social Security Act 1986, s.66 and Sched. 6, para. 2.

Provisions supplementary to section 148

149.—(1) For the purposes of section 148 above the Channel Islands, the Isle of Man and Gibraltar shall be treated as though they were part of the United Kingdom.

(2) A person shall be treated for the purposes of section 148(1)(b) above as entitled to a payment of a qualifying benefit if he would be so entitled—

(a) in the case of a qualifying benefit other than income support, but for the fact that he or, if he is a member of a couple, the other member is entitled to receive some other payment out of public funds;

(b) in the case of income support, but for the fact that his income or, if he is a member of a couple, the income of the other member was exceptionally of an amount which resulted in his having ceased to be entitled to income support.

(3) A person shall be treated for the purposes of section 148(2)(c)(i) above as entitled in respect of the other member of the couple to an increase in a payment of a qualifying benefit if he would be so entitled—

(a) but for the fact that he or the other member is entitled to receive some other payment out of public funds;

(b) but for the operation of any provision of section 83(2) or (3) above or paragraph 6(4) of Schedule 7 to this Act or any regulations made under paragraph 6(3) of that Schedule whereby entitlement to benefit is affected by the amount of a person's earnings in a given period.

(4) For the purposes of section 148 above a person shall be taken not to be entitled to a payment of a war disablement pension unless not later than the end of the relevant week he has attained the age of [[1]65].

(5) A sum payable under section 148 above shall not be treated as benefit for the purposes of any enactment or instrument under which entitlement to the relevant qualifying benefit arises or is to be treated as arising.

(6) A payment and the right to receive a payment—

(a) under section 148 above or any enactment corresponding to it in Northern Ireland; or

(b) under regulations relating to widows which are made by the Secretary of State under any enactment relating to police and which contain a statement that the regulations provide for payments corresponding to payments under that section,

shall be disregarded for all purposes of income tax and for the purposes of any enactment or instrument under which regard is had to a person's means.

DERIVATION

Social Security Act 1986, s.66 and Sched. 6, para. 3.

AMENDMENT

1. Pensions Act 1995, Sched. 4, para. 8 (19 July 1995).

Interpretation of Part X

150.—(1) In this Part of this Act "qualifying benefit" means—

(a) a retirement pension;

[[1](b) long-term incapacity benefit;]

(c) a widowed mother's allowance or window's pension;

(d) a severe disablement allowance;

(e) an invalid care allowance;

(f) industrial death benefit;

(g) an attendance allowance;

(h) an unemployability supplement or allowance;

(i) a war disablement pension;

(j) a war widow's pension;

(k) income support.

[[2](1) a mobility supplement].

(2) In this Part of this Act—

"attendance allowance" means—

(a) an attendance allowance;

(b) a disability living allowance;

(c) an increase of disablement pension under section 104 or 105 above;

(d) a payment under regulations made in exercise of the powers in section 159(3)(b) of the 1975 Act or paragraph 7(2) of Schedule 8 to this Act;

(e) an increase of allowance under Article 8 of the Pneumoconiosis, Byssinosis and Miscellaneous Diseases Benefit Scheme 1983 (constant attendance allowance for certain persons to whom that Scheme applies) or under the corresponding provision of any Scheme which may replace that Scheme.

(f) an allowance in respect of constant attendance on account of disablement for which a person is in receipt of war disablement pension, including an allowance in respect of exceptionally severe disablement;

[2"mobility supplement" means a supplement awarded in respect of disablement which affects a person's ability to walk and for which the person is in receipt of war disablement pension;]

[2"pensionable age" has the meaning given by the rules in paragraph 1 of Schedule 4 to the Pensions Act 1995];

"retirement pension" includes graduated retirement benefit, [2. . .];

"unemployability supplement or allowance" means—

(a) an unemployability supplement payable under Part I of Schedule 7 to this Act; or

(b) any corresponding allowance payable—

(i) by virtue of paragraph 6(4)(a) of Schedule 8 to this Act;

(ii) by way of supplement to retired pay or pension exempt from income tax under section 315(1) of the Income and Corporation Taxes Act 1988;

(iii) under the Personal Injuries (Emergency Provisions) Act 1939; [2. . .]

(iv) by way of supplement to retired pay or pension under the Polish Resettlement Act 1947; [2or

(v) under the Pensions (Navy, Army, Air Force and Mercantile Marine) Act 1939];

"war disablement pension" means—

(a) any retired pay, pension or allowance granted in respect of disablement under powers conferred by or under the Air Force (Constitution) Act 1917, the Personal Injuries (Emergency Provisions) Act 1939, the Pensions (Navy, Army, Air Force and Mercantile Marine) Act 1939, the Polish Resettlement Act 1947, or Part VII or section 151 of the Reserve Forces Act 1980;

(b) without prejudice to paragraph (a) of this definition, any retired pay or pension to which subsection (1) of section 315 of the Income and Corporation Taxes Act 1988 applies;

"war widow's pension" means any widow's pension or allowance granted in respect of a death due to service or war injury and payable by virtue of any enactment mentioned in paragraph (a) of the preceding definition or a pension or allowance for a widow granted under any scheme mentioned in subsection (2) (e) of the said section 315;

and each of the following expressions, namely "attendance allowance", "unemployability supplement or allowance", "war disablement pension" and "war widow's pension", includes any payment which the Secretary of State accepts as being analogous to it.

(3) References in this Part of this Act to a "couple" are references to a married or unmarried couple; and for this purpose "married couple" and "unmarried couple" are to be construed in accordance with Part VII of this Act and any regulations made under it.

(4) In this Part of this Act "the relevant week", in relation to any year, means the week beginning with the first Monday in December or such other week as may be specified in an order made by the Secretary of State.

DERIVATION

Social Security Act 1986, ss.66, 84(1) and Sched. 6, para. 1.

AMENDMENTS

1. Social Security (Incapacity for Work) Act 1994, Sched. 1, para. 33 (April 13, 1995).
2. Pensions Act 1995, s. 132 and Sched. 4, para. 13 (July 19, 1995).

GENERAL NOTE

Disability living allowance is a qualifying benefit because it is included within the definition of "attendance allowance" in subs. (2).

151.—171G. *Omitted.*

PART XIII

GENERAL

Interpretation

Application of Act in relation to territorial waters

172. In this Act—
(a) any reference to Great Britain includes a reference to the territorial waters of the United Kingdom adjacent to Great Britain;
(b) any reference to the United Kingdom includes a reference to the territorial waters of the United Kingdom.

DERIVATION

Social Security and Housing Benefits Act 1982, ss.26(7) and 44; Social Security Act 1986, s.84(4).

Age

173. For the purposes of this Act a person—
(a) is over or under a particular age if he has or, as the case may be, has not attained that age; and
(b) is between two particular ages if he has attained the first but not the second;
and in Scotland (as in England and Wales) the time at which a person attains a particular age expressed in years is the commencement of the relevant anniversary of the date of his birth.

DERIVATION

Social Security Act 1975, s.168(1) and Sched. 20.

References to Acts

174. In this Act—
"the 1975 Act" means the Social Security Act 1975;
"the 1986 Act" means the Social Security Act 1986;

"the Administration Act" means the Social Security Administration Act 1992;
"the Consequential Provisions Act" means the Social Security (Consequential Provisions) Act 1992;
"the Northern Ireland Contributions and Benefits Act" means the Social Security Contributions and Benefits (Northern Ireland) Act 1992;
"the Old Cases Act" means the Industrial Injuries and Diseases (Old Cases) Act 1975; and
"the Pensions Act" means the [[1]Pension Schemes Act 1993].

AMENDMENT

1. Pension Schemes Act 1993, Sched. 8, para. 41 (February 7, 1994).

Subordinate legislation

Regulations, orders and schemes

175.—(1) Subject to section 145(5) above, regulations and orders under this Act shall be made by the Secretary of State.

(2) Powers under this Act to make regulations, orders or schemes shall be exercisable by statutory instrument.

(3) Except in the case of an order under section 145(3) above and in so far as this Act otherwise provides, any power under this Act to make regulations or an order may be exercised—

(a) either in relation to all cases to which the power extends, or in relation to those cases subject to specified exceptions, or in relation to any specified cases or classes of case;
(b) so as to make, as respects the cases in relation to which it is exercised—
  (i) the full provision to which the power extends or any less provision (whether by way of exception or otherwise),
  (ii) the same provision for all cases in relation to which the power is exercised, or different provision for different cases or different classes of case or different provision as respects the same case or class of case for different purposes of this Act,
  (iii) any such provision either unconditionally or subject to any specified condition;

and where such a power is expressed to be exercisable for alternative purposes it may be exercised in relation to the same case for any or all of those purposes; and powers to make regulations or an order for the purposes of any one provision of this Act are without prejudice to powers to make regulations or an order for the purposes of any other provision.

(4) Without prejudice to any specific provision in this Act, any power conferred by this Act to make regulations or an order (other than the power conferred in section 145(3) above) includes power to make thereby such incidental, supplementary, consequential or transitional provision as appears to the Secretary of State to be expedient for the purposes of the regulations or order.

(5) Without prejudice to any specific provisions in this Act, a power conferred by any provision of this Act except—

(a) sections [[1]5B(2)(a)] 30, 47(6), and 145(3) above and paragraph 3(9) of Schedule 7 to this Act;

(b) section 122(1) above in relation to the definition of "payments by way of occupational or personal pension"; and

(c) Part XI,

to make regulations or an order includes power to provide for a person to exercise a discretion in dealing with any matter.

(6) *Omitted*

(7) Any power of the Secretary of State under any provision of this Act, except the provisions mentioned in subsection (5)(a) and (b) above and Part IX, to make any regulations or order, where the power is not expressed to be exercisable with the consent of the Treasury, shall if the Treasury so direct be exercisable only in conjunction with them.

(8) Any power under any of sections 116 to 120 above to modify provisions of this Act or the Administration Act extends also to modifying so much of any other provision of this Act or that Act as re-enacts provisions of the 1975 Act which replaced provisions of the National Insurance (Industrial Injuries) Acts 1965 to 1974.

(9) A power to make regulations under any of sections 116 to 120 above shall be exercisable in relation to any enactment passed after this Act which is directed to be construed as one with this Act; but this subsection applies only so far as a contrary intention is not expressed in the enactment so passed, and is without prejudice to the generality of any such direction.

(10) Any reference in this section or section 176 below to an order or regulations under this Act includes a reference to an order or regulations made under any provision of an enactment passed after this Act and directed to be construed as one with this Act; but this subsection applies only so far as a contrary intention is not expressed in the enactment so passed, and without prejudice to the generality of any such direction.

Derivation

Social Security Act 1975, ss.162, 166 and 168(1) and Sched. 20; Social Security Act 1986, ss.83 and 84(1).

Amendment

1. Social Security (Incapacity for Work) Act 1994, Sched. 1, para. 36 (April 13, 1995).

Parliamentary Control

176.—(1) Subject to the provisions of this section, a statutory instrument containing (whether alone or with other provisions)—

(a) regulations made by virtue of—
[. . .]
section 104(3);
[. . .]

(b) *Omitted.*

(c) *Omitted.*

shall not be made unless a draft of the instrument has been laid before Parliament and been approved by a resolution of each House.

(2) Subsection (1) above does not apply to a statutory instrument by reason only that it contains—

(a) *Omitted.*

(b) regulations under powers conferred by any provision mentioned in paragraph (a) of that subsection [[1]. . .] which are to be made for the purpose of consolidating regulations to be revoked in the instrument;

(c) regulations which, in so far as they are made under powers conferred by any provision mentioned in paragraph (a) of that subsection (other than section 145 [1...]), only replace provisions of previous regulations with new provisions to the same effect.

(3) A statutory instrument—

(a) which contains (whether alone or with other provisions) any order, regulations or scheme made under this Act by the Secretary of State, other than an order under section 145(3) above; and

(b) which is not subject to any requirement that a draft of the instrument shall be laid before and approved by a resolution of each House of Parliament,

shall be subject to annulment in pursuance of a resolution of either House of Parliament.

Derivation

Social Security Act 1975, s.167.

Amendment

1. Statutory Sick Pay Percentage Threshold Order 1995 (S.I. 1995 No. 521), art 6(1)(a) (April 6, 1995).

Short title, commencement and extent

Short title, commencement and extent

177.—(1) This Act may be cited as the Social Security Contributions and Benefits Act 1992.

(2) This Act is to be read, where appropriate, with the Administration Act and the Consequential Provisions Act.

(3) The enactments consolidated by this Act are repealed, in consequence of the consolidation, by the Consequential Provisions Act.

(4) Except as provided in Schedule 4 to the Consequential Provisions Act, this Act shall come into force on 1st July 1992.

(5) The following provisions extend to Northern Ireland—

section 16 and Schedule 2;

section 116(2); and

this section.

(6) Except as provided by this section, this Act does not extend to Northern Ireland.

SCHEDULES

Schedules 1.—3. *Omitted.*

[1Schedule 4

Rates of benefits, etc

Parts I and **II** *Omitted.*

Part III

Non-contributory periodical benefits

Description of benefit	*Weekly rate*
1. Attendance allowance.	(a) higher rate .... £49.50 (b) lower rate .... £33.10 (the appropriate rate being determined in accordance with section 65(3)).
2. Severe disablement allowance.	£37.75
3. Age related addition.	(a) higher rate .... £13.15 (b) middle rate .... £8.30 (c) lower rate .... £4.15 (the appropriate rate being determined in accordance with section 69(1)).
4. Invalid care allowance.	£37.75
5. to 8. *omitted.*	

Part IV *Omitted.*

Part V

Rates of industrial injuries benefit

Description of benefit, etc.	*Rate*
1. Disablement pension (weekly rates).	For the several degrees of disablement set out in column (1) of the following Table, the respective amounts in that Table, using— (a) column (2) for any period during which the beneficiary is over the age of 18 or is entitled to an increase of benefit in respect of a child or adult dependant; (b) Column (3) for any period during which the beneficiary is not over the age of 18 and not so entitled;

Table

Degree of disablement	*Amount*	
(1)	(2)	(3)
Per cent.	£	£
100	101.10	61.90
90	90.99	55.71
80	80.88	49.52
70	70.77	43.33
60	60.66	37.14
50	50.55	30.95
40	40.44	24.76
30	30.33	18.57
20	20.22	12.38

2. Maximum increase of weekly rate of disablement pension where constant attendance needed.	(a) except in cases of exceptionally severe disablement .... £40.50 (b) in any case £81.00
3. Increase of weekly rate of disablement pension (exceptionally severe disablement).	£40.50
4. Maximum of aggregate of weekly benefit payable for successive accidents.	(a) for any period during which the beneficiary is over the age of 18 or is entitled to an increase in benefit in respect of a child or adult dependant .... £101.10 (b) for any period during which the beneficiary is not over the age of 18 and not so entitled £61.90
5. Unemployability supplement under paragraph 2 of Schedule 7.	£62.45
6. Increase under paragraph 3 of Schedule 7 of weekly rate of unemployability supplement.	(a) if on the qualifying date the beneficiary was under the age of 35 or if that date fell before 5th July 1948 .... £13.15 (b) if head (a) above does not apply and on the qualifying date the beneficiary was under the age of 40 and he had not attained pensionable age before 6th April 1979 .... £13.15 (c) if heads (a) and (b) above do not apply and on the qualifying date the beneficiary was under the age of 45 .... £8.30 (d) if heads (a), (b) and (c) above do not apply and on the qualifying date the beneficiary was under the age of 50 and had not attained pensionable age before 6th April 1979 .... £8.30 (e) in any other case £4.15
7. Increase under paragraph 4 of Schedule 7 of weekly rate of disablement pension.	£11.20
8. Increase under paragraph 6 of Schedule 7 of weekly rate of disablement pension.	£37.35
9. Maximum disablement gratuity under paragraph 9 of Schedule 7.	£6,720.00

10.—12. *omitted.*]

Derivation

Social Security Act 1975, Sched. 4.

Amendment

1. The whole Schedule was substituted by the Social Security Benefits Up-rating Order 1997 (S.I. 1997 No. 543, art. 3(1) (April 17, 1997).

Schedule 5. *Omitted.*

SCHEDULE 6

ASSESSMENT OF EXTENT OF DISABLEMENT

General provisions as to method of assessment

1. For the purposes of section 68 or 103 above and Part II of Schedule 7 to this Act, the extent of disablement shall be assessed, by reference to the disabilities incurred by the claimant as a result of the relevant loss of faculty in accordance with the following general principles—

(a) except as provided in paragraphs (b) to (d) below, the disabilities to be taken into account shall be all disabilities so incurred (whether or not involving loss of earning power or additional expense) to which the claimant may be expected, having regard to his physical and mental condition at the date of the assessment, to be subject during the period taken into account by the assessment as compared with a person of the same age and sex whose physical and mental condition is normal;

(b) except in the case of an assessment for the purposes of section 68 above, regulations may make provision as to the extent (if any) to which any disabilities are to be taken into account where they are disabilities which, though resulting from the relevant loss of faculty, also result, or without the relevant accident might have been expected to result, from a cause other than the relevant accident;

(c) the assessment shall be made without reference to the particular circumstances of the claimant other than age, sex, and physical and mental condition;

(d) the disabilities resulting from such loss of faculty as may be prescribed shall be taken as amounting to 100 per cent. disablement and other disabilities shall be assessed accordingly.

2. Provisions may be made by regulations for further defining the principles on which the extent of disablement is to be assessed and such regulations may in particular direct that a prescribed loss of faculty shall be treated as resulting in a prescribed degree of disablement; and, in connection with any such direction, nothing in paragraph 1(c) above prevents the making of different provision, in the case of loss of faculty in or affecting hand or arm, for right-handed and for left-handed persons.

3. Regulations under paragraph 1(d) or 2 above may include provision—

(a) for adjusting or reviewing an assessment made before the date of the coming into force of those regulations;

(b) for any resulting alteration of that assessment to have effect as from that date;

so however that no assessment shall be reduced by virtue of this paragraph.

Severe disablement allowance

4.—(1) In the case of an assessment of any person's disablement for the purposes of section 68 above, the period to be taken into account for any such assessment shall be the period during which that person has suffered and may be expected to continue to suffer from the relevant loss of faculty beginning not later than—

(a) the first claim day, if his entitlement to benefit falls to be determined in accordance with section 68(3)(b) above as modified by regulations under section 68(11)(b);

(b) where his disablement has previously been assessed for the purposes of section 68 above at a percentage which is not less than 80 per cent.—

  (i) if the period taken into account for that assessment was or included the period of 196 days ending immediately before the first claim day, the first claim day, or

  (ii) If the period so taken into account included any day falling within that period of 196 days, the day immediately following that day or, if there is more than one such day, the last such day;

(c) in any other case, 196 days before the first claim day;

and, in any case, ending not later than the day on which that person attains the age of 65 [[1] . . .].

(2) In this paragraph "the first claim day" means the first day in respect of which the person concerned has made the claim in question for a severe disablement allowance.

5.—(1) An assessment of any person's disablement for the purposes of section 68 above shall state the degree of disablement in the form of a percentage and shall specify the period taken into account by the assessment.

(2) For the purposes of any such assessment—

(a) a percentage which is not a whole number shall be rounded to the nearest whole number or, if it falls equally near two whole numbers, shall be rounded up to the higher; and

(b) a percentage between 5 and 100 which is not a multiple of 10 shall be treated, if it is a multiple of 5, as being the next higher percentage which is a multiple of 10 and, in any other case, as being the nearest percentage which is a multiple of 10.

(3) If on the assessment the person's disablement is found to be less than 5 per cent., that degree of disablement shall for the purposes of section 68 above be disregarded and, accordingly, the assessment shall state that he is not disabled.

Disablement benefit

6.—(1) Subject to sub-paragraphs (2) and (3) below, the period to be taken into account by an assessment for the purposes of section 103 above and Part II of Schedule 7 to this Act of the extent of a claimant's disablement shall be the period (beginning not earlier than the end of the period of 90 days referred to in section 103(6) above and in paragraph 9(3) of that Schedule and limited by reference either to the claimant's life or to a definite date) during which the claimant has suffered and may be expected to continue to suffer from the relevant loss of faculty.

(2) If on any assessment the condition of the claimant is not such, having regard to the possibility of changes in that condition (whether predictable or not), as to allow of a final assessment being made up to the end of the period provided by sub-paragraph (1) above, then, subject to sub-paragraph (3) below—

(a) a provisional assessment shall be made, taking into account such shorter period only as seems reasonable having regard to his condition and that possibility; and

(b) on the next assessment the period to be taken into account shall begin with the end of the period taken into account by the provisional assessment.

(3) Where the assessed extent of a claimant's disablement amounts to less than 14 per cent., then, subject to sub-paragraphs (4) and (5) below, that assessment shall be a final assessment and the period to be taken into account by it shall not end before the earliest date on which it seems likely that the extent of the disablement will be less than 1 per cent.

(4) Sub-paragraph (3) above does not apply in any case where it seems likely that—

(a) the assessed extent of the disablement will be aggregated with the assessed extent of any present disablement, and

(b) that aggregate will amount to 14 per cent. or more.

(5) Where the extent of the claimant's disablement is assessed at different percentages for different parts of the period taken into account by the assessment, then—

(a) sub-paragraph (3) above does not apply in relation to the assessment unless the percentage assessed for the latest part of that period is less than 14 per cent., and

(b) in any such case that sub-paragraph shall apply only in relation to that part of that period (and subject to sub-paragraph (4) above).

7. An assessment for the purposes of section 103 above and Part II of Schedule 7 to this Act shall—

(a) state the degree of disablement in the form of a percentage;

(b) specify the period taken into account by the assessment; and

(c) where that period is limited by reference to a definite date, specify whether the assessment is provisional or final;

but the percentage and the period shall not be specified more particularly than is necessary for the purpose of determining in accordance with section 103 above and Parts II and IV of Schedule 7 to this Act the claimant's rights as to disablement pension or gratuity and reduced earnings allowance (whether or not a claim has been made).

Special provision as to entitlement to constant attendance allowance, etc.

8—(1) For the purpose of determining whether a person is entitled—

(a) to an increase of a disablement pension under section 104 above; or

(b) to a corresponding increase of any other benefit by virtue of paragraph 6(4) (b) or 7(2) (b) of Schedule 8 to this Act,

regulations may provide for the extent of the person's disablement resulting from the relevant injury or disease to be determined in such manner as may be provided for by the regulations by reference to all disabilities to which that person is subject which result either from the relevant injury or disease or from any other injury or disease in respect of which there fall to be made to the person payments of any of the descriptions listed in sub-paragraph (2) below.

(2) Those payments are—

(a) payments by way of disablement pension;

(b) payments by way of benefit under paragraph 4 or 7(1) of Schedule 8 to this Act; or

(c) payments in such circumstances as may be prescribed by way of such other benefit as may be prescribed (being benefit in connection with any hostilities or with service as a member of Her Majesty's forces or of such other organisation as may be specified in the regulations).

DERIVATION

Social Security Act 1975, Sched. 8.

AMENDMENT

1. Social Security (Severe Disablement Allowance and Invalid Care Allowance) Amendment Regulations 1994, reg.2(4) (October 28, 1994).

GENERAL NOTE

Reg. 11 of the Social Security (General Benefit) Regulations 1982 is treated (by s.2(2) of the Social Security Consequential Provisions) Act 1992) as having been made under this Schedule to further define the principles on which the extent of disablement is to be assessed.

In the case of some prescribed diseases, special provision is made by the Social Security (Prescribed Diseases) Regulations 1985 and this Sched. and reg. 11 of the Social Security (General Benefit) Regulations 1982 must be read as subject to that.

Para. 1. Sub-paras (a) and (c) make it plain that disablement is to be assessed by comparing the claimant with a person of the same age and sex whose physical and mental condition is normal *without* taking into account loss of earning power, additional expense or other circumstances peculiar to the claimant (*e.g.* the distance from home to public transport or other facilities) other than, of course, age, sex and physical and mental condition. The one exception is allowed by sub-para. (b) which permits the taking into account of disabilities which are due not only to the relevant accident or disease but also to another cause (see reg. 11(2)–(4) of the Social Security (General Benefit) Regulations 1982).

Sub-para. (d) enables regulations to prescribe disabilities amounting to 100 per cent. Other disabilities must be assessed accordingly (see reg. 11(7) of, and Sched. 2 to, the Social Security (General Benefit) Regulations 1982). In *R(I) 30/61*, it was made clear that "a man entitled to an assessment of 100 per cent is not necessarily totally disabled, and that any scale of values which a member of an assessing body has in the back of his mind should take account of that fact".

Para. 2. Reg 11 of the Social Security (General Benefit) Regulations 1982 is made under this paragraph. There is no specific provision for compensating for the loss of the "dominant hand" but, even in a case where the injury is one specified in Sched. 2 to the Regulations, reg. 11(6) permits "such increase or reduction in [the prescribed] degree of disablement as may be reasonable in the circumstances in the case".

Para. 6. The period of the assessment should cover the whole period during which it is expected that the claimant will continue to suffer from the relevant loss of faculty resulting in disablement of at least 1 per cent. If the prognosis is uncertain and the assessment is at least 14 per cent a provisional assessment should be made so that, under s.45(3) of the Social Security Administration Act 1992, the extent of the claimant's disability is automatically reassessed at the end of the period of the provisional assessment. A final assessment which is for a definite period rather than "life" implies *either* that the claimant will be suffering from no loss of faculty *or* the resulting disablement will be less than 1 per cent) from the end of the period of assessment *or* that any disablement from which the claimant may be expected to be suffering at the end of the period of assessment would have been present even if the relevant accident had not occurred. If the claimant is still disabled at the end of the period, he or she may apply for a review under s.47(4) of the Social Security Administration Act 1992. There is no reason why the claimant's disablement should not be assessed at different percentages for different parts of the period; nor why those parts should be lengthy. In *R(I) 30/61*, the medical appeal tribunal assessed disablement from January 11, to March 25, 1960, at 30 per cent, March 26 to June 24, 1960, at 100 per cent, June 25, to July 24, 1960, at 40 per cent, from June 25, 1960, to January 24, 1961, at 30 per cent. That was a provisional assessment and reflected the fact that the claimant had been in hospital from March to June and was then recuperating. Although an appeal was allowed on the ground of inadequate reasons, the tribunal's general approach was not criticised and the Commissioner said, "the disabilities resulting from the relevant loss of faculty must be related to the period covered by the assessment, and . . . the assessing body must not be misled by the fact that a very serious disability is expected not to last long. The answer to that situation is a high assessment for a short period." Since disablement benefit is calculated on a weekly basis, it might be slightly more convenient for adjudication officers if short periods were calculated in weeks rather than months if the evidence permits it.

Sub-paras. (3)–(5) normally prevent a provisional assessment if the assessment, at least for the last part of the period, is less than 14 per cent. If the extent of the claimant's disablement resulting from the relevant loss of faculty is likely to become less over time, the adjudicating medical authority is then bound to determine a date from which the claimant's extent of disablement may be expected to be less than 1 per cent. If the extent of disablement is expected to become greater but the adjudicating medical authority cannot tell when and so is unable to include an assessment of at least 14 per cent within the period of assessment, a life assessment should be made and the burden rests upon the claimant to make an application for review under s.47(4) of the Social Security Administration Act 1992 when the extent of disablement does become at least 14 per cent. An exception is made by sub-para. (4) if the assessment of the extent of disablement may be aggregated with another assessment and the aggregate may amount to 14 per cent or more. In such a case, a provisional assessment may be made if the prognosis is uncertain.

Reg. 20(3) of the Social Security (Industrial Injuries) (Prescribed Diseases) Regulations 1985 provides that the minimum period of assessment in a case of byssinosis shall be one year. Reg. 29 provides that the initial assessment in a case of occupational deafness shall always be provisional and for a period of five years and that all subsequent assessments shall be for a period of at least five years.

Para. 6. Where a claim is made in respect of diffuse mesothelioma, see reg. 20(4) of the Social Security (Industrial Injuries) (Prescribed Diseases) Regulations 1985.

Para. 7. An assessment shall not specify the percentage or period more particularly than is necessary for the purpose of determining entitlement to industrial injuries benefits. This means that, where the assessment is under 14 per cent but not under 1 per cent, it is not necessary for the adjudicating medical authority to go into greater detail unless either the assessment may be aggregated with another and the aggregate might be more than 14 per cent or else the claimant is suffering from pneumoconiosis, byssinosis or diffuse mesothelioma in which case it matters whether the assessment is greater than 10 per cent or not for the purpose of determining the amount of disablement benefit payable (reg. 20 of the Social Security (Prescribed Diseases) Regulations 1985). The rounding of assessments of disablement under s.103(3) would appear to be a matter for an adjudication officer because it is to be carried out after any aggregation (s. 103(4)) and aggregation is certainly a matter for an adjudication officer rather than an adjudicating medical authority (s.45(1) of the Social Security Administration Act 1992).

Para. 8. See reg. 20 of the Social Security (General Benefit) Regulations 1982.

Schedule 7

Industrial Injuries Benefits

Part I

Unemployability Supplement

Availability

1. This Part of this Schedule applies only in relation to persons who were beneficiaries in receipt of unemployability supplement under section 58 of the 1975 Act immediately before 6th April 1987.

Rate and duration

2.—(1) The weekly rate of a disablement pension shall, if as the result of the relevant loss of faculty the beneficiary is incapable of work and likely to remain so permanently, be increased by the amount specified in Schedule 4, Part V, paragraph 5.

(2) An increase of pension under this paragraph is referred to in this Act as an "unemployability supplement".

(3) For the purposes of this paragraph a person may be treated as being incapable of work and likely to remain so permanently, notwithstanding that the loss of faculty is not such as to prevent him being capable of work, if it is likely to prevent his earnings in a year exceeding a prescribed amount not less than £104.

(4) An employability supplement shall be payable for such period as may be determined at the time it is granted, but may be renewed from time to time.

Increase of unemployability supplement

3.—(1) Subject to the following provisions of this paragraph, if on the qualifying date the beneficiary was—

(a) a man under the age of 60, or

(b) a woman under the age of 55,

the weekly rate of unemployability supplement shall be increased by the appropriate amount specified in Schedule 4, Part V, paragraph 6.

(2) Where for any period the beneficiary is entitled to a Category A or Category B retirement pension [[4]. . .] and the weekly rate of the pension includes an additional pension such as is mentioned in section 44(3)(b) above, for that period the relevant amount shall be deducted from the amount that would otherwise be the increase under this paragraph and the beneficiary shall be entitled to an increase only if there is a balance after that deduction and, if there is such a balance, only to an amount equal to it.

(3) In this paragraph "the relevant amount" means an amount equal to the additional pension reduced by the amount of any reduction in the weekly rate of the retirement [[4]. . .] made by virtue of [[2]section 46] of the Pensions Act.

(4) In this paragraph references to an additional pension are references to that pension after any increase under section 52(3) above but without any increase under paragraphs 1 and 2 of Schedule 5 to this Act.

(5) In this paragraph "the qualifying date" means, subject to sub-paragraphs (6) and (7) below, the beginning of the first week for which the beneficiary qualified for unemployability supplement.

(6) If the incapacity for work in respect of which unemployability supplement is payable forms part of a period of interruption of employment which has continued from a date earlier than the date fixed under sub-paragraph (5) above, the qualifying date means the first day in that period which is a day of incapacity for work, or such earlier day as may be prescribed.

(7) Subjects to sub-paragraph (6) above, if there have been two or more periods for which the beneficiary was entitled to unemployability supplement, the qualifying date shall be, in relation to unemployability supplement for a day in any one of those periods, the beginning of the first week of that period.

(8) for the purposes of sub-paragraph (7) above—

(a) a break of more than 8 weeks in entitlement to unemployability supplement means that the periods before and after the break are to different periods; and

(b) a break of 8 weeks or less is to be disregarded.

(9) The Secretary of State may by regulations provide that sub-paragraph (8) above shall have effect as if for the references to 8 weeks there were substituted references to a larger number of weeks specified in the regulations.

(10) In this paragraph "period of interruption of employment" has the same meaning as [[6]a jobseeking period and any period linked to such a period has for the purposes of the Jobseekers Act 1995].

(11) The provisions of this paragraph are subject to [[2]section 46(6) and (7) (entitlement to guaranteed minimum pensions and increases of unemployability supplement).]

Increase for beneficiary's dependent children

4.—(1) Subject to the provisions of this paragraph and paragraph 5 below, the weekly rate of a disablement pension where the beneficiary is entitled to an unemployability supplement shall be increased for any period during which the beneficiary is entitled to child benefit in respect of a child or children.

(2) The amount of the increase shall be as specified in Schedule 4, Part V, paragraph 7.

(3 In any case where—

(a) a beneficiary is one of two persons who are—

(i) spouses residing together, or

(ii) an unmarried couple, and

(b) the other person had earnings in any week,

the beneficiary's right to payment of increases for the following week under this paragraph shall be determined in accordance with sub-paragraph (4) below.

(4) No such increase shall be payable—

(a) in respect of the first child where the earnings were [[7]£135] or more; and

(b) in respect of a further child for each complete [[5]£17] by which the earnings exceeded [[7]£135].

(5) The Secretary of State may by order substitute larger amounts for the amounts for the time being specified in sub-paragraph (4) above.

(6) In this paragraph "week" means such period of 7 days as may be prescribed by regulations made for the purposes of this paragraph.

Additional provisions as to increase under paragraph 4

5.—(1) An increase under paragraph 4 above of any amount in respect of a particular child shall for any period be payable only if during that period one or other of the following conditions is satisfied with respect to the child—

(a) the beneficiary would be treated for the purposes of Part IX of this Act has having the child living with him; or

(b) the requisite contributions are being made to the cost of providing for the child.

(2) The condition specified in paragraph (b) of sub-paragraph (1) above is to be treated as satisfied if, and only if—

(a) such contributions are being made at a weekly rate not less than the amount referred to in that sub-paragraph—

(i) by the beneficiary, or

(ii) where the beneficiary is one of two spouses residing together, by them together; and

(b) except in prescribed cases, the contributions are over and above those required for the purposes of satisfying section 143(1)(b) above.

Increase for adult dependants

6.—(1) The weekly rate of a disablement pension where the beneficiary is entitled to an unemployability supplement shall be increased under this paragraph for any period during which—

(a) the beneficiary is—

(i) residing with his spouse, or

(ii) contributing to the maintenance of his spouse at the requisite rate; or

(b) a person—

(i) who is neither the spouse of the beneficiary nor a child, and

(ii) in relation to whom such further conditions as may be prescribed are fulfilled,

has the care of a child or children in respect of whom the beneficiary is entitled to child benefit.

(2) The amount of the increase under this paragraph shall be that specified in Schedule 4, Part V, paragraph 8 and the requisite rate for the purposes of sub-paragraph (1)(a) above is a weekly rate not less than that amount.

(3) Regulations may provide that, for any period during which—

(a) the beneficiary is contributing to the maintenance of his or her spouse at the requisite rate, and

(b) the weekly earnings of the spouse exceed such amount as may be prescribed

there shall be no increase of benefit under this paragraph.

(4) Regulations may provide that, for any period during which the beneficiary is residing with his or her spouse and the spouse has earnings—

(a) the increase of benefit under this paragraph shall be subject to a reduction in respect of the spouse's earnings; or

(b) there shall be no increase of benefit under this paragraph.

(5) Regulations may, in a case within sub-paragraph (1)(b) above in which the person there referred to is residing with the beneficiary and fulfils such further conditions as may be prescribed, authorise an increase of benefit under this paragraph, but subject, taking account of the earnings of the person residing with the beneficiary, other than such of that person's earnings from employment by the beneficiary as may be prescribed, to provisions comparable to those that may be made by virtue of sub-paragraph (4) above.

(6) Regulations under this paragraph may, in connection with any reduction or extinguishment of an increase in benefit in respect of earnings, prescribe the method of calculating or estimating the earnings.

(7) A beneficiary shall not be entitled to an increase of benefit under this paragraph in respect of more than one person for the same period.

Earnings to include occupational and personal pensions for purposes of disablement pension

7.—(1) Except as may be prescribed, any reference to earnings in paragraph 4 or 6 above includes a reference to payments by way of occupational or personal pension.

(2) For the purposes of those paragraphs, the Secretary of State may by regulations provide, in relation to cases where payments by way of occupational or personal pension are made otherwise than weekly, that any necessary apportionment of the payments shall be made in such manner and on such basis as may be presribed.

Dependency increases: continuation of awards in cases of fluctuating earnings

8.—(1) Where a beneficiary—

(a) has been awarded an increase of benefit under paragraph 4 or 6 above, but

(b) ceases to be entitled to the increase by reason only that the weekly earnings of some other person (''the relevant earner'') exceed the amount of the increase or, as the case may be, some specified amount,

then, if and so long as the beneficiary would have continued to be entitled to the increase, disregarding any such excess of earnings, the award shall continue in force but the increase shall not be payable for any week if the earnings relevant to that week exceed the amount of the increase or, as the case may be, the specified amount.

(2) In this paragraph the earnings which are relevant to any week are those earnings of the relevant earner which, apart from this paragraph, would be taken into account in determining whether the beneficiary is entitled to the increase in question for that week.

Part II

Disablement Gratuity

9.—(1) An employed earner shall be entitled to a disablement gratuity, if—

(a) he made a claim for disablement benefit before 1st October, 1986;

(b) he suffered as the result of the relevant accident from loss of physical or mental faculty such that the extent of the resulting disablement assessed in accordance with Schedule 6 to this Act amounts to not less than 1 per cent.; and

(c) the extent of the disablement is assessed for the period taken into account as amounting to less than 20 per cent.

(2) A disablement gratuity shall be—

(a) of an amount fixed, in accordance with the length of the period and the degree of the disablement, by a prescribed scale, but not in any case exceeding the amount specified in Schedule 4, Part V, paragraph 9; and

(b) payable, if and in such cases as regulations so provide, by instalments.

(3) A person shall not be entitled to disablement gratuity until after the expiry of the period of 90 days (disregarding Sundays) beginning with the day of the relevant accident.

Part III

Increase of Disablement Pension During Hospital Treatment

10.—(1) This Part of this Schedule has effect in relation to a period during which a person is receiving medical treatment as an in-patient in a hospital or similar institution and which—

(a) commenced before 6th April 1987; or

(b) commenced after that date but within a period of 28 days from the end of the period during which he last received an increase of benefit under section 62 of the 1975 Act or this paragraph in respect of such treatment for the relevant injury or loss of faculty.

(2) Where a person is awarded disablement benefit, but the extent of his disablement is assessed for the period taken into account by the assessment at less than 100 per cent., it shall be treated as assessed at 100 per cent. for any part of that period, whether before or after the making of the assessment or the award of benefit, during which he receives, as an in-patient in a hospital or similar institution, medical treatment for the relevant injury or loss of faculty.

(3) Where the extent of the disablement is assessed for that period at less than 20 per cent., sub-paragraph (2) above shall not affect the assessment; but in the case of a disablement pension payable by virtue of this paragraph to a person awarded a disablement gratuity wholly or partly in respect of the same period, the weekly rate of the pension (after allowing for any increase under Part V of this Act) shall be reduced by the amount prescribed as being the weekly value of his gratuity.

Part IV

Reduced Earnings Allowance

11.—(1) Subject to the provisions of this paragraph, an employed earner shall be entitled to reduced earnings allowance if—

(a) he is entitled to a disablement pension or would be so entitled if that pension were payable where disablement is assessed at not less than 1 per cent.; and

(b) as a result of the relevant loss of faculty, he is either—

(i) incapable, and likely to remain permanently incapable, of following his regular occupation; and

(ii) incapable of following employment of an equivalent standard which is suitable in his case,

or is, and has at all times since the end of the period of 90 days referred to in section 103(6) above been, incapable of following that occupation or any such employment;

but a person shall not be entitled to reduced earnings allowance to the extent that the relevant loss of faculty results from an accident happening on or after 1st October 1990 (the day on which section 3 of the Social Security Act 1990 came into force) [[3]and a person shall not be entitled to reduced earnings allowance—

(i) in relation to a disease prescribed on or after 10th October 1994 under section 108(2) above; or

(ii) in relation to a disease prescribed before 10th October 1994 whose prescription is extended on or after that date under section 108(2) above but only in so far as the prescription has been so extended].

(2) A person—

(a) who immediately before that date is entitled to reduced earnings allowance in consequence of the relevant accident; but

(b) who subsequently ceases to be entitled to that allowance for one or more days,

shall not again be entitled to reduced earnings allowance in consequence of that accident; but this sub-paragraph does not prevent the making at any time of a claim for, or an award of, reduced earnings allowance in consequence of that accident for a period which commences not later than the day after that on which the claimant was last entitled to that allowance in consequence of that accident.

(3) For the purposes of sub-paragraph (2) above—

(a) a person who, apart from section 130(6) above, would have been entitled to reduced earnings allowance immediately before 1st October 1990 shall be treated as entitled to that allowance on any day (including a Sunday) on which he would have been entitled to it apart from that provision;

(b) regulations may prescribe other circumstances in which a person is to be treated as entitled, or as having been entitled, to reduced earnings allowance on any prescribed day.

(4) The Secretary of State may by regulations provide that in prescribed circumstances employed earner's employment in which a claimant was engaged when the relevant accident took place but which was not his regular occupation is to be treated as if it had been his regular occupation.

(5) In sub-paragraph (1) above—

(a) references to a person's regular occupation are to be taken as not including any subsidiary occupation, except to the extent that they fall to be treated as including such an occupation by virtue of regulations under sub-paragraph (4) above; and

(b) employment of an equivalent standard is to be taken as not including employment other than employed earner's employment;

and in assessing the standard of remuneration in any employment, including a person's regular occupation, regard is to be had to his reasonable prospect of advancement.

(6) For the purposes of this Part of this Schedule a person's regular occupation is to be treated as extending to and including employment in the capacities to which the

persons in that occupation (or a class or description of them to which he belonged at the time of the relevant accident) are in the normal course advanced, and to which, if he had continued to follow that occupation without having suffered the relevant loss of faculty, he would have had at least the normal prospects of advancement; and so long as he is, as a result of the relevant loss of faculty, deprived in whole or in part of those prospects, he is to be treated as incapable of following that occupation.

(7) Regulations may for the purposes of this Part of this Schedule provide that a person is not to be treated as capable of following an occupation or employment merely because of his working thereat during a period of trial or for purposes of rehabilitation or training or in other prescribed circumstances.

(8) Reduced earnings allowance shall be awarded—

(a) for such period as may be determined at the time of the award; and

(b) if at the end of that period the beneficiary submits a fresh claim for the allowance, for such further period, commencing as mentioned in sub-paragraph (2) above, as may be determined.

(9) The award may not be for a period longer than the period to be taken into account under paragraph 4 or 6 of Schedule 6 to this Act.

(10) Reduced earnings allowance shall be payable at a rate determined by reference to the beneficiary's probable standard of remuneration during the period for which it is granted in any employed earner's employments which are suitable in his case and which he is likely to be capable of following as compared with that in the relevant occupation, but in no case at a rate higher than 40 per cent. of that maximum rate of a disablement pension or at a rate such that the aggregate of disablement pension (not including increases in disablement pension under any provision of this Act) and reduced earnings allowance awarded to the beneficiary exceeds 140 per cent, of the maximum rate of a disablement pension.

(11) Sub-paragraph (10) above shall have effect in the case of a person who retired from regular employment before 6th April 1987 with the substitution for "140 per cent." of "100 per cent.".

(12) In sub-paragraph (10) above "the relevant occupation" means—

(a) in relation to a person who is entitled to reduced earnings allowance by virtue of regulations under sub-paragraph (4) above, the occupation in which he was engaged when the relevant accident took place; and

(b) in relation to any other person who is entitled to reduced earnings allowance, his regular occupation within the meaning of sub-paragraph (1) above.

[[1](12A) The reference in sub-paragraph (11) above to a person who has retired from regular employment includes a reference—

(a) to a person who under subsection (3) of section 27 of the 1975 Act was treated for the purposes of that Act as having retired from regular employment; and

(b) to a person who under subsection (5) of that section was deemed for those purposes to have retired from it.]

(13) On any award except the first the probable standard of his remuneration shall be determined in such manner as may be prescribed; and, without prejudice to the generality of this sub-paragraph, regulations may provide in prescribed circumstances for the probable standard of remuneration to be determined by reference—

(a) to the standard determined at the time of the last previous award of reduced earnings allowance; and

(b) to scales or indices of earnings in a particular industry or description of industries or any other data relating to such earnings.

(14) In this paragraph "maximum rate of a disablement pension" means the rate specified in the first entry in column (2) of Schedule 4, Part V, paragraph 1 and does not include increases in disablement pension under any provision of this Act.

Supplementary

12.—(1) A person who on 10th April 1988 or 9th April 1989 satisfies the conditions—

(a) that he has attained pensionable age;
(b) that he has retired from regular employment; and
(c) that he is entitled to reduced earnings allowance, shall be entitled to that allowance for life.

(2) In the case of any beneficiary who is entitled to reduced earnings allowance by virtue of sub-paragraph (1) above, the allowance shall be payable, subject to any enactment contained in Part V or VI of this Act or in the Administration Act and to any regulations made under any such enactment, at the weekly rate at which it was payable to the beneficiary on the relevant date or would have been payable to him on that date but for any such enactment or regulations.

(3) For the purpose of determining under sub-paragraph (2) above the weekly rate of reduced earnings allowance payable in the case of a qualifying beneficiary, it shall be assumed that the weekly rate at which the allowance was payable to him on the relevant date was—

(a) £25.84, where that date is 10th April 1988, or
(b) £26.96, where that date is 9th April 1989.

(4) In sub-paragraph (3) above "qualifying beneficiary" means a person entitled to reduced earnings allowance by virtue of sub-paragraph (1) above who—

(a) did not attain pensionable age before 6th April 1987, or
(b) did not retire from regular employment before that date,

and who, on the relevant date, was entitled to the allowance at a rate which was restricted under paragraph 11(10) above by reference to 40 per cent. of the maximum rate of disablement pension.

(5) For a beneficiary who is entitled to reduced earnings allowance by virtue of satisfying the conditions in sub-paragraph (1) above on 10th April 1988 the relevant date is that date.

(6) For a beneficiary who is entitled to it by virtue only of satisfying those conditions on 9th April 1989 the relevant date is that date.

[[1](7) The reference in sub-paragraph (1) above to a person who has retired from regular employment includes a reference—

(a) to a person who under subsection (3) of section 27 of the 1975 Act was treated for the purposes of that Act as having retired from regular employment; and
(b) to a person who under subsection (5) of that section was deemed for those purposes to have retired from it.]

Part V

Retirement Allowance

13.—(1) Subject to the provisions of this Part of this Schedule, a person who—

(a) has attained pensionable age; and
(b) gives up regular employment on or after 10th April 1989; and
(c) was entitled to reduced earnings allowance (by virtue either of one award or of a number of awards) on the day immediately before he gave up such employment,

shall cease to be entitled to reduced earnings allowance as from the day on which he gives up regular employment.

(2) If the day before a person ceases under sub-paragraph (1) above to be entitled to reduced earnings allowance he is entitled to the allowance (by virtue either of one award or of a number of awards) at a weekly rate or aggregate weekly rate of not less than £2.00, he shall be entitled to a benefit, to be known as "retirement allowance".

(3) Retirement allowance shall be payable to him (subject to any enactment contained in Part V or VI of this Act or in the Administration Act and to any regulations made under any such enactment) for life.

(4) Subject to sub-paragraph (6) below, the weekly rate of a beneficiary's retirement allowance shall be—

(a) 25 per cent. of the weekly rate at which he was last entitled to reduced earnings allowance; or

(b) 10 per cent. of the maximum rate of a disablement pension, whichever is the less.

(5) For the purpose of determining under sub-paragraph (4) above the weekly rate of retirement allowance in the case of a beneficiary who—

(a) retires or is deemed to have retired on 10th April 1989, and

(b) on 9th April 1989 was entitled to reduced earnings allowance at a rate which was restricted under paragraph 11(10) above by reference to 40 per cent. of the maximum rate of disablement pension,

it shall be assumed that the weekly rate of reduced earnings allowance to which he was entitled on 9th April 1989 was £26.96.

(6) If the weekly rate of the beneficiary's retirement allowance—

(a) would not be a whole number of pence; and

(b) would exceed the whole number of pence next below it by ½p or more,

the beneficiary shall be entitled to retirement allowance at a rate equal to the next higher whole number of pence.

(7) The sums falling to be calculated under sub-paragraph (4) above are subject to alteration by orders made by the Secretary of State under section 150 of the Administration Act.

(8) Regulations may—

(a) make provision with respect to the meaning of "regular employment" for the purposes of this paragraph; and

(b) prescribe circumstances in which, and periods for which, a person is or is not to be regarded for those purposes as having given up such employment.

(9) Regulations under sub-paragraph (8) above may, in particular—

(a) provide for a person to be regarded—

(i) as having given up regular employment, notwithstanding that he is or intends to be an earner; or

(ii) as not having given up regular employment, notwithstanding that he has or may have one or more days of interruption of employment; and

(b) prescribe circumstances in which a person is or is not to be regarded as having given up regular employment by reference to—

(i) the level or frequency of his earnings during a prescribed period; or

(ii) the number of hours for which he works during a prescribed period calculated in a prescribed manner.

[[6](10) "Day of interruption of employment" means a day which forms part of—

(a) a jobseeking period (as defined by the Jobseekers Act 1995), or

(b) a linked period (as defined by that Act).]

(11) In this paragraph "maximum rate of a disablement pension" means the rate specified in the first entry in column (2) of Schedule 4, Part V, paragraph 1 and does not include increases in disablement pension under any provision of this Act.

Part VI

Industrial Death Benefit

Introductory

14.—21. *Omitted.*

Derivation

Social Security Act 1975, ss.57–59B, 62, 64–64A and 84A; Social Security (No. 2) Act 1980, s.3(4); Social Security Act 1986, s.39 and Sched. 3; Social Security Act 1988, s.2.

AMENDMENTS

1. Social Security (Consequential Provisions) Act 1992, Sched. 4, paras. 10 and 11 (transitorily).
2. Pensions Schemes Act 1993, Sched. 8, para. 43 (February 7, 1994).
3. Social Security (Industrial Injuries) (Prescribed Diseases) Regulations 1985, reg. 14A (October 10, 1994).
4. Social Security (Incapacity for Work) Act 1994, Sched. 1, para. 41 (April 13, 1995).
5. Social Security (Industrial Injuries) (Dependency) (Permitted Earnings Limits) Order 1996 (S.I. 1996 No. 671), art. 2 (April 8, 1996).
6. Jobseekers Act 1995, Sched. 2, para. 36 (October 7, 1996).
7. Social Security (Industrial Injuries) (Dependency) (Permitted Earnings Limits) Order 1997 (S.I. 1997 No. 577), art. 2 (April 7, 1997).

GENERAL NOTE

This Schedule preserves for certain claimants entitlement to industrial injuries benefits that have been abolished. Part I preserves unemployability supplement, which was an increase of disablement pension for those incapable of work due to an industrial accident or prescribed disease, but only for those who were entitled to it immediately before April 6, 1987. Part II preserves disablement gratuities, which were lump sums paid instead of disablement pension for those whose disablement was assessed at between 1 per cent. and 19 per cent. It applies where the claim was made before October 1, 1986 and still has relevance where there has been a series of provisional assessments since then. Part III preserves hospital treatment allowance for those who have been more or less continuously entitled to it since April 6, 1987. Parts IV and V preserve reduced earnings allowance and retirement allowance for those who earning capacity has been reduced by an industrial accident occurring before, or an industrial disease the onset of which was before, October 1, 1990. If there is any break in entitlement to reduced earnings allownace after that date, the claimant cannot become entitled again. However, if there has been no previous entitlement since that date, a new period of entitlement may still commence. Those who were entitled to reduced earnings allowance before April 10 1989 and had retired before that date, remain entitled to the allowance for life at a frozen rate. Otherwise, people who have reached pensionable age ar no longer entitled to reduced earnings allownace and become entitled to retirment allowance instead, unless they remain in regular employment for at least 10 hours a week (see the Social Security (Industrial Injuries) (Regular Employment) Regulations 1990 (S.I. 1990 No. 256) as amended and *CI/94/94 and CI/600/94* in which the torturous history of this legislation is examined). Part VI, which is omitted, provides for industrial death benefit in relation to deaths before April 11, 1988. For a fuller commentary on Parts I to V, see *Non-means-tested Benefits: The Legislation* (Bonner, Hooker and White (eds.)).

Schedules 8.–13. *Omitted.*

Social Security Administration Act 1992

(1992 c. 5)

ARRANGEMENT OF SECTIONS

PART I

CLAIMS FOR AND PAYMENTS AND GENERAL ADMINISTRATION OF BENEFIT

Necessity of claim

1. Entitlement to benefit dependent on claim.
2. Retrospective effect of provisions making entitlement to benefit dependent on claim.

3.–4. *Omitted.*

Claims and payments regulations

5. Regulations about claims for and payments of benefit.

6.–7. *Omitted.*

Industrial injuries benefit

8. Notification of accidents, etc.
9. Medical examination and treatment of claimants.
10. Obligations of claimants.

Disability working allowance

11. Initial claims and repeat claims.
12.–16. *Omitted.*

Social Security Administration Act 1992

PART II

ADJUDICATION

Adjudication by the Secretary of State

17. Questions for the Secretary of State.
18. Appeal on question of law.
19. Review of decisions.

Adjudication by adjudication officers

20. Claims and questions to be submitted to adjudication officer.
21. Decision of adjudication officer.

Appeals from adjudication officers—general

22. Appeal to social security appeal tribunal.
23. Appeal from social security appeal tribunal to Commissioner.
24. Appeal from Commissioners on point of law.

Reviews—general

25. Review of decisions.
26. Procedure for reviews.
27. Reviews under s.25—supplementary.
28. Appeals following reviews or refusals to review.
29. Review after claimant appeals.

Attendance allowance, disability living allowance and disability working allowance

30. Reviews of decisions of adjudication officers.
31. Further reviews.
32. Reviews of decisions as to attendance allowance, disability living allowance or disability working allowance—supplementary.
33. Appeals following reviews.
34. Appeal from social security appeal tribunals or disability appeal tribunals to Commissioners and appeals from Commissioners.
35. Reviews of decisions on appeal.

Questions first arising on appeal

36. Questions first arising on appeal.

Reference of special questions

37. Reference of special questions.

Adjudication officers and the Chief Adjudication Officer

38. Adjudication officers.
39. The Chief Adjudication Officer.

Social security appeal tribunals

40. Panels for appointment to social security appeal tribunals.
41. Constitution of social security appeal tribunals.

Disability appeal tribunals

42. Panels for appointment to disability appeal tribunals.
43. Constitution of disability appeal tribunals.

Adjudication in relation to industrial injuries and disablement benefit

44. Declaration that accident is an industrial accident.
45. Disablement questions.
46. Medical appeals and references.
47. Review of medical decisions.
48. Appeal etc. on question of law to Commissioner.

Adjudicating medical practitioners and medical appeal tribunals

49. Adjudicating medical practitioners.
50. Constitution of medical appeal tribunals.

The President and full-time chairmen of tribunals

51. The President of social security appeal tribunals, medical appeal tribunals and disability appeal tribunals and regional chairmen and other full-time chairmen.

Social Security Commissioners

52. Appointment of Commissioners.

References by authorities

53. Power of adjudicating authorities to refer matters to experts.
54. Claims relating to attendance allowance, disability living allowance and disability working allowance.
55. Medical examination etc. in relation to appeals to disability appeal tribunals.

Determination of questions of special difficulty

56. Assessors.
57. Tribunal of three Commissioners.

Medical examinations

57A. Medical examinations of persons awarded attendance allowance or disability living allowance.

Regulations

58. Regulations as to determination of questions and matters arising out of, or pending, reviews and appeals.
59. Procedure.
60. Finality of decisions.
61. Regulations and supplementary matters relating to determinations.
61A. *Omitted.*

Industrial diseases

62. Adjudication as to industrial diseases.
63.–66. *Omitted.*

An Act to consolidate certain enactments relating to the administration of social security and related matters with amendments to give effect to recommendations of the Law Commission and the Scottish Law Commission.

[13th February 1992]

PART I

CLAIMS FOR AND PAYMENTS AND GENERAL ADMINISTRATION OF BENEFIT

Necessity of claim

Entitlement to benefit dependent on claim

1.—(1) Except in such cases as may be precribed, and subject to the following provisions of this section and to section 3 below, no person shall be entitled to any benefit unless, in addition to any other conditions relating to that benefit being satisfied—

(a) he makes a claim for it in the manner, and within the time, prescribed in relation to that benefit by regulations under this Part of this Act; or
(b) he is treated by virtue of such regulations as making a claim for it.

(2) Where under subsection (1) above a person is required to make a claim or to be treated as making a claim for a benefit in order to be entitled to it—

(a) if the benefit is a widow's payment, she shall not be entitled to it in respect of a death occurring more than 12 months before the date on which the claim is made or treated as made; and
(b) if the benefit is any other benefit except disablement benefit or reduced earnings allowance, the person shall not be entitled to it in respect of any period more than 12 months before that date,

except as provided by section 3 below.

(3) Where a person purports to make a claim on behalf of another—

(a) for an attendance allowance by virtue of section 66(1) of the Contributions and Benefits Act; or
(b) for a disability living allowance by virtue of section 72(5) or 73(12) of that Act,

that other shall be regarded for the purposes of this section as making the claim, notwithstanding that it is made without his knowledge or authority.

(4) In this section and section 2 below "benefit" means—

(a) benefit as defined in section 122 of the Contributions and Benefits Act;

[([1]aa) a jobseeker's allowance;]

and;

(b) any income-related benefit.

(5) This section (which corresponds to section 165A of the 1975 Act, as it had effect immediately before this Act came into force) applies to claims made on or after 1st October 1990 or treated by virtue of regulations under that section or this section as having been made on or after that date.

(6) Schedule 1 to this Act shall have effect in relation to other claims.

Derivation

Social Security Act 1975, s.165A; Social Security Act 1986, Sched. 10, para. 48(b)

Amendment

1. Jobseekers Act 1995, Sched. 2, para. 38 (April 22, 1996).

General Note

Subs. (1) makes it a condition of entitlement to benefit that there should have been a claim for benefit save in certain limited circumstances set out in reg. 3 of the Social Security (Claims and Payments) Regulations 1987 and affecting only certain retirement pensions and also invalidity pension where there has been a claim for sickness benefit. S.3 is concerned with claims for widowhood benefits where it has been difficult for the widow to establish that her husband has died.

The section was originally introduced to reverse the effect of the decision of the House of Lords in *Insurance Officer v. McCaffery* [1984] 1 W.L.R. 1353 which held that a failure to claim merely affected payability rather than entitlement. S.2 gives this section retrospective effect.

For regulations governing the making of claims, see regs. 4–19 of the Social Security (Claims and Payments) Regulations 1987. Reg. 19 provides for claims to some benefits to be backdated, but subs. (2) imposes an absolute limit of 12 months on the amount of arrears that may be paid except in the case of industrial injuries benefits.

Retrospective effect of provisions making entitlement to benefit dependent on claim

2.—(1) This section applies where a claim for benefit is made or treated as made at any time on or after 2nd September 1985 (the date on which section 165A of the 1975 Act (general provision as to necessity of claim for entitlement to benefit), as originally enacted, came into force) in respect of a period the whole or any part of which falls on or after that date.

(2) Where this section applies, any question arising as to—

(a) whether the claimant is or was at any time (whether before, on or after 2nd September 1985) entitled to the benefit in question, or to any other benefit on which his entitlement to that benefit depends; or

(b) in a case where the claimant's entitlement to the benefit depends on the entitlement of another person to a benefit, whether that other person is or was so entitled,

shall be determined as if the relevant claim enactment and any regulations made under or referred to in that enactment had also been in force, with any necessary modifications, at all times relevant for the purpose of determining the entitlement of the claimant, and, where applicable, of the other person, to the benefit or benefits in question (including the entitlement of any person to any benefit on which that entitlement depends, and so on).

(3) In this section "the relevant claim enactment" means section 1 above as it has effect in relation to the claim referred to in subsection (1) above.

(4) In any case where—
(a) claim for benefit was made or treated as made (whether before, on or after 2nd September 1985, and whether by the same claimant as the claim referred to in subsection (1) above or not), and benefit was awarded on that claim, in respect of a period falling wholly or partly before that date; but
(b) that award would not have been made had the current requirements applied in relation to claims for benefit, whenever made, in respect of periods before that date; and
(c) entitlement to the benefit claimed as mentioned in subsection (1) above depends on whether the claimant or some other person was previously entitled or treated as entitled to that or some other benefit,

then, in determining whether the conditions of entitlement to the benefit so claimed are satisfied, the person to whom benefit was awarded as mentioned in paragraphs (a) and (b) above shall be taken to have been entitled to the benefit so awarded, notwithstanding anything in subsection (2) above.

(5) In subsection (4) above "the current requirements" means—
(a) the relevant claim enactment, and any regulations made or treated as made under that enactment, or referred to in it, as in force at the time of the claim referred to in subsection (1) above, with any necessary modifications; and
(b) subsection (1) (with the omission of the words following "at any time") and subsections (2) and (3) above.

DERIVATION

Social Security Act 1975, s.165B; Social Security Act 1986, Sched. 10, para. 48(b).

3. and **4.** *Omitted.*

Claims and payments regulations

Regulations about claims for and payments of benefit

5.—(1) Regulations may provide—
(a) for requiring a claim for a benefit to which this section applies to be made by such person, in such manner and within such time as may be prescribed;
(b) for treating such a claim made in such circumstances as may be prescribed as having been made at such date earlier or later than that at which it is made as may be prescribed;
(c) for permitting such a claim to be made, or treated as if made, for a period wholly or partly after the date on which it is made;
(d) for permitting an award on such a claim to be made for such a period subject to the condition that the claimant satisfies the requirements for entitlement when benefit becomes payable under the award;
(e) for a review of any such award if those requirements are found not to have been satisfied;
(f) for the disallowance on any ground of a person's claim for a benefit to which this section applies to be treated as a disallowance of any further claim by that person for that benefit until the grounds of the original disallowance have ceased to exist;
(g) for enabling one person to act for another in relation to a claim for a benefit to which this section applies and for enabling such a claim to be made and proceeded with in the name of a person who has died;
(h) for requiring any information or evidence needed for the determination

of such a claim or of any question arising in connection with such a claim to be furnished by such person as may be prescribed in accordance with the regulations;

(i) for the person to whom, time when and manner in which a benefit to which this section applies is to be paid and for the information and evidence to be furnished in connection with the payment of such a benefit;

(j) for notice to be given of any change of circumstances affecting the continuance of entitlement to such a benefit or payment of such a benefit;

(k) for the day on which entitlement to such a benefit is to begin or end;

(l) for calculating the amounts of such a benefit according to a prescribed scale or otherwise adjusting them so as to avoid fractional amounts or facilitate computation;

(m) for extinguishing the right to payment of such a benefit if payment is not obtained within such period, not being less than 12 months, as may be prescribed from the date on which the right is treated under the regulations as having arisen;

(n) for suspending payment, in whole or in part, where it appears to the Secretary of State that a question arises whether—

(i) the conditions for entitlement are or were fulfilled;

(ii) an award ought to be revised;

(iii) an appeal ought to be brought against an award;

(o) for withholding payments of a benefit to which this section applies in prescribed circumstances and for subsequently making withheld payments in prescribed circumstances;

(p) for the circumstances and manner in which payments of such a benefit may be made to another person on behalf of the beneficiary for any purpose, which may be to discharge, in whole or in part, an obligation of the beneficiary or any other person;

(q) for the payment or distribution of such a benefit to or among persons claiming to be entitled on the death of any person and for dispensing with strict proof of their title;

(r) for the making of a payment on account of such a benefit—

(i) where no claim has been made and it is impracticable for one to be made immediately;

(ii) where a claim has been made and it is impracticable for the claim or an appeal, reference, review or application relating to it to be immediately determined;

(iii) where an award has been made but it is impracticable to pay the whole immediately.

(2) This section applies to the following benefits—

(a) benefits as defined in section 122 of the Contributions and Benefits Act;

[[1](aa) a jobseeker's allowance;]

(b) income support;

(c) family credit;

(d) disability working allowance;

(e) housing benefit;

(f) any social fund payments such as are mentioned in section 138(1)(a) or (2) of the Contributions and Benefits Act;

(g) child benefit; and

(h) Christmas bonus.

(3) The reference in subsection (1)(h) above to information or evidence needed for the determination of a claim includes a reference to information or evidence required by a rent officer under section 121 of the Housing Act 1988.

(4) Subsection (1)(n) above shall have effect in relation to housing benefit as if the reference to the Secretary of State were a reference to the authority paying the benefit.

(5) Subsection (1)(g), (i), (l), (p) and (q) above shall have effect as if statutory sick pay and statutory maternity pay were benefits to which this section applies.

[[2](6) As it has effect in relation to housing benefit subsection (1)(p) above authorises provision requiring the making of payments of benefits to another person, on behalf of the beneficiary, in such circumstances as may be prescribed.]

DERIVATION

Social Security Act 1986, s.51.

AMENDMENTS

1. Jobseekers Act 1995, Sched. 2, para. 39 (April 22, 1996).
2. Housing Act 1996, s.120 (unlimited retrospection).

6. and **7.** *Omitted.*

Industrial injuries benefit

Notification of accidents, etc.

8. Regulations may provide—

(a) for requiring the prescribed notice of an accident in respect of which industrial injuries benefit may be payable to be given within the prescribed time by the employed earner to the earner's employer or other prescribed person;

(b) for requiring employers—

(i) to make reports, to such person and in such form and within such time as may be prescribed, of accidents in respect of which industrial injuries benefit may be payable;

(ii) to furnish to the prescribed person any information required for the determination of claims, or of questions arising in connection with claims or awards;

(iii) to take such other steps as may be prescribed to facilitate the giving notice of accidents, the making of claims and the determination of claims and of questions so arising.

DERIVATION

Social Security Act 1975, s.88.

GENERAL NOTE

See regs. 24 and 25 of the Social Security (Claims and Payments) Regulations 1979, treated as made under this section by s.2(2) of the Social Security (Consequential Provisions) Act 1992.

Medical examination and treatment of claimants

9.—(1) Regulations may provide for requiring claimants for disablement benefit—

(a) to submit themselves from time to time to medical examination for the purpose of determining the effect of the relevant accident, or the treatment appropriate to the relevant injury or loss of faculty;

(b) to submit themselves from time to time to appropriate medical treatment for the injury or loss of faculty.

(2) Regulations under subsection (1) above requiring persons to submit themselves to medical examination or treatment may—

(a) require those persons to attend at such places and at such times as may be required; and

(b) with the consent of the Treasury provide for the payment by the Secretary of State to those persons of travelling and other allowances (including compensation for loss of remunerative time).

Derivation

Social Security Act 1975, s.89.

General Note

See reg. 26 of the Social Security (Claims and Payments) Regulations 1979, treated as made under this section by s.2(2) of the Social Security (Consequential Provisions) Act 1992. This provision differs from ss.53 and 54 in that it enables regulations to be made to *require* a claimant to attend an examination. It applies only to those claiming disablement benefit, but see s.57A, introduced by s.18 of the Social Security Administration (Fraud) Act 1997, which makes similar provision in respect of those who have been awarded attendance allowance or disability living allowance.

Obligations of claimants

10.—(1) Subject to subsection (3) below, regulations may provide for disqualifying a claimant for the receipt of industrial injuries benefit—

(a) for failure without good cause to comply with any requirement of regulations to which this subsection applies (including in the case of a claim for industrial death benefit, a failure on the part of some other person to give the prescribed notice of the relevant accident);

(b) for wilful obstruction of, or other misconduct in connection with, any examination or treatment to which he is required under regulations to which this subsection applies to submit himself, or in proceedings under this Act for the determination of his right to benefit or to its receipt,

or for suspending proceedings on the claim or payment of benefit as the case may be, in the case of any such failure, obstruction or misconduct.

(2) The regulations to which subsection (1) above applies are—

(a) any regulations made by virtue of section 5(1)(h), (i) or (l) above, so far as relating to industrial injuries benefit; and

(b) regulations made by virtue of section 8 or 9 above.

(3) Regulations under subsection (1) above providing for disqualification for the receipt of benefit for any of the following matters, that is to say—

(a) for failure to comply with the requirements of regulations under section 9(1) or (2) above;

(b) for obstruction of, or misconduct in connection with, medical examination or treatment,

shall not be made so as to disentitle a claimant to benefit for a period exceeding six weeks on any disqualification.

Derivation

Social Security Act 1975, s.90(2)–(4).

General Note

See reg. 40 of the Social Security (General Benefit) Regulations 1982, treated as made under this section by s.2(2) of the Social Security (Consequential Provisions) Act 1992.

Disability working allowance

Initial claims and repeat claims

11.—(1) In this section—

"initial claim" means a claim for a disability working allowance made by a person—

(a) to whom it has not previously been payable; or

(b) to whom it has not been payable during the period of two years immediately preceding the date on which the claim is made or is treated as made; and

"repeat claim" means any other claim for a disability working allowance.

(2) On an initial claim a declaration by the claimant that he has a physical or mental disability which puts him at a disadvantage in getting a job is conclusive, except in such circumstances as may be prescribed, that for the purposes of section 129(1)(b) of the Contributions and Benefits Act he has such a disability (in accordance with regulations under section 129(3) of that Act).

(3) If—

(a) a repeat claim is made or treated as made not later than the end of the period of eight weeks commencing with the last day of the claimant's previous award; and

(b) on the claim which resulted in that award he qualified under section 129(2) of the Contributions and Benefits Act by virtue—

(i) of paragraph (a) of that subsection; or

(ii) of there being payable to him a benefit under an enactment having effect in Northern Ireland and corresponding to a benefit mentioned in that paragraph,

he shall be treated on the repeat claim as if he still so qualified.

Derivation

Social Security Act 1986, s.27B(1)–(3).

General Note

Subs. (1). An "initial claim" is one made by a person who either has never before been entitled to disability working allowance or else has not been entitled during the two years before the date of claim. Any other claim is treated as a "repeat claim".

Subs. (2). The emphasis on claims for disability working allowance is on self-assessment. On an "initial claim", a claimant's declaration on the detailed claim form that he or she has a physical or mental disability which puts him at a disadvantage is usually conclusive. The only exceptions are where the claim itself contains contrary indications or the adjudication officer has before him or her other evidence which contradicts that declaration (reg. 4 of the Disability Working Allowance (General) Regulations 1991).

Subs. (3). Where a person has qualified for disability working allowance because he or she was entitled to an incapacity benefit within eight weeks before the date of claim, he or she continues to qualify for disability working allowance on any repeat claim made within eight weeks of the expiry of the previous award. This may continue indefinitely as long as there is never a gap in entitlement exceeding eight weeks.

12.—16. *Omitted.*

Part II

Adjudication

Adjudication by the Secretary of State

Questions for the Secretary of State

17.—(1) Subject to this Part of this Act, any of the following questions shall be determined by the Secretary of State—

(a) a question whether a person is an earner and, if he is, as to the category of earners in which he is to be included;
(b) subject to subsection (2) below, a question whether the contribution conditions for any benefit are satisfied, or otherwise relating to a person's contributions or his earnings factor;
(c) a question whether a Class 1A contribution is payable or otherwise relating to a Class 1A contribution;
(d) a question whether a person is or was employed in employed earner's employment for the purposes of Part V of the Contributions and Benefits Act;
(e) a question as to whether a person was, within the meaning of regulations, precluded from regular employment by responsibilities at home;
(f) any question as to which surpluses are to be taken into account under section 45(1) of the Contributions and Benefits Act;
(g) any question arising under any provision of Part XI of the Contributions and Benefits Act or this Act, or under any provision of regulations [[1]or and order] under that Part, as to—
   (i) whether a person is, or was, an employee or employer of another;
   (ii) whether an employer is entitled to make any deduction from his contribution payments in accordance with [[1]an order under section 159A] of the Contributions and Benefits Act;
   (iii) whether a payment falls to be made to an employer in accordance with the regulations [[1]or order];
   (iv) the amount that falls to be so deducted or paid;
   (v) the amount of an employer's contributions payments for any period for the purposes of regulations under section 158(3) of the Contributions and Benefits Act; or
   (vi) whether two or more employers or two or more contracts of service are, by virtue of regulations made under section 163(5) of that Act, to be treated as one; [[2]. . .]
(h) any question arising under any provision of Part XII of that Act or this Act, or under any provision of regulations under that Part, as to—
   (i) whether a person is, or was, an employee or employer of another;
   (ii) whether an employer is entitled to make any deduction from his contributions payments in accordance with regulations under section 167 of the Contributions and Benefits Act;
   (iii) whether a payment falls to be made to an employer in accordance with the regulations;
   (iv) the amount that falls to be so deducted or paid; or
   (v) whether two or more employers or two or more contracts of service are, by virtue of regulations made under section 171(2) of that Act, to be treated as one,

   and any question arising under regulations made by virtue of paragraph (c), (d) or (f) of section 164(9) of that Act [[2]and
(i) any question arising under section 27 of the Jobseekers Act 1995, or under any provisions of regulations under that section, as to—
   (i) whether a person is, or was, an employee or employer of another;
   (ii) whether an employer is entitled to make any deduction from his contributions payments in accordance with regulations under section 27 of that Act;
   (iii) whether a payment falls to be made to an employer in accordance with those regulations;
   (iv) the amount that falls to be so deducted or paid; or
   (v) whether two or more employers are, by virtue of regulations under section 27 of that Act, to be treated as one.]

(2) Subsection (1)(b) above includes any questions arising—

(a) under section 17(1) of the Contributions and Benefits Act as to whether by regulations under that subsection a person is excepted from liability for Class 4 contributions, or his liability is deferred; or

(b) under regulations made by virtue of section 17(3) or (4) or 18 of that Act;

but not any other question relating to Class 4 contributions, nor any question within section 20(1)(c) below.

(3) Regulations may make provision restricting the persons who may apply to the Secretary of State for the determination of any such question as is mentioned in subsection (1) above.

(4) The Secretary of State may, if he thinks fit, before determining any such question as is mentioned in subsection (1) above, appoint a person to hold an inquiry into the question, or any matters arising in connection with it, and to report on the question, or on those matters, to the Secretary of State.

DERIVATION

Social Security Act 1975, s.93; Social Security Act 1986, s.52(2) and Sched. 5, Pt. 2.

DEFINITION

For "employed earner's employment", see s.95 of the Social Security Contributions and Benefits Act 1992.

AMENDMENTS

1. Statutory Sick Pay Percentage Threshold Order (S.I. 1995 No. 512), art. 6(2)(a) (April 6, 1995).
2. Jobseekers Act 1995, Sched. 2, para. 41 (April 6, 1996).

GENERAL NOTE

Regs. 12–17 of the Social Security (Adjudication) Regulations 1995 (omitted from this book) make provision for decisions of the Secretary of State and for the procedure for inquiries.

Appeal on question of law

18.—(1) A question of law arising in connection with the determination by the Secretary of State of any such question as is mentioned in section 17(1) above may, if the Secretary of State thinks fit, be referred for decision to the High Court or, in Scotland, to the Court of Session.

(2) If the Secretary of State determines in accordance with subsection (1) above to refer any question of law to the court, he shall give notice in writing of his intention to do so—

(a) in a case where the question arises on an application made to the Secretary of State, to the applicant; and

(b) in any cases to such persons as appear to him to be concerned with the question.

(3) Any person aggrieved by the decision of the Secretary of State on any question of law within subsection (1) above which is not referred in accordance with that subsection may appeal from that decision to the court.

(4) The Secretary of State shall be entitled to appear and be heard on any such reference or appeal.

(5) Rules of court shall include provision for regulating references and appeals under this section and for limiting the time within which such appeals may be brought.

(6) Notwithstanding anything in any Act, the decision of the court on a reference or appeal under this section shall be final.

(7) On any such reference or appeal the court may order the Secretary of State to pay the costs (in Scotland, the expenses) of any other person, whether or not the decision is in that other person's favour and whether or not the Secretary of State appears on the reference or appeal.

DERIVATION

Social Security Act 1975, s.94.

GENERAL NOTE

For Rules of Court, see R.S.C., Ord. 111 and, in Scotland, R.C. 288. Note that there is no further appeal to the Court of Appeal or House of Lords.

Review of decisions

19.—(1) Subject to subsection (2) below, the Secretary of State may review any decision given by him on any such question as is mentioned in section 17(1) above if—

(a) new facts have been brought to his notice; or
(b) he is satisfied that the decision—
  (i) was given in ignorance of some material fact;
  (ii) was based on a mistake as to some material fact; or
  (iii) was erroneous in point of law.

(2) A decision shall not be reviewed while an appeal under section 18 above is pending against the decision of the Secretary of State on a question of law arising in connection with it, or before the time for so appealing has expired.

(3) On a review any question of law may be referred under subsection (1) of section 18 above or, where it is not so referred, may be the subject of an appeal under subsection (3) of that section, and the other provisions of that section shall apply accordingly.

DERIVATION

Social Security Act 1975, s.96.

GENERAL NOTE

The circumstances in which decisions may be reviewed under subs. (1)(b) are the same as those under s.30(2)(a) and (d) and reference should be made to the notes to s.30. The scope of subs. (1)(a) is wider than "change of circumstances".

Adjudication by adjudication officers

Claims and questions to be submitted to adjudication officer

20.—(1) Subject to section 54 below, there shall be submitted forthwith to an adjudication officer for determination in accordance with this Part of this Act—

(a) any claim for a benefit to which this section applies;
(b) subject to subsection (2) below, any question arising in connection with a claim for, or award of, such a benefit; [2. . . .]
[1(c) any question whether, if he otherwise had a right to it, a person would be disqualified under or by virtue of any provision of the Contributions and Benefits Act for receiving a benefit to which this section applies] [2and
(d) any question whether a jobseeker's allowance is not payable to a person by virtue of section 19 of the Jobseekers Act 1995.

(2) Subsection (1) above does not apply to any question which—

[[2](a) may be determined by an adjudication officer under section 9(6) or 10(5) of the Jobseekers Act 1995; or

(b)] falls to be determined otherwise than by an adjudication officer.

(3) Any question as to, or in connection with, entitlement to statutory sick pay or statutory maternity pay may be submitted to an adjudication officer—

(a) by the Secretary of State; or

(b) subject to and in accordance with regulations, by the employee concerned,

for determination in accordance with this Part of this Act.

(4) If—

(a) a person submits a question relating to the age, marriage or death of any person; and

(b) it appears to the adjudication officer that the question may arise if the person who has submitted it to him submits a claim to a benefit to which this section applies,

the adjudication officer may determine the question.

(5) Different aspects of the same claim or question may be submitted to different adjudication officers; and for that purpose this section and the other provisions of this Part of this Act with respect to the determination of claims and questions shall apply with any necessary modifications.

(6) This section applies to the following benefits—

(a) benefits as defined in section 122 of the Contributions and Benefits Act;

[[2](aa) a jobseeker's allowance;]

(b) income support;

(c) family credit;

(d) disability working allowance;

(e) any social fund payment such as is mentioned in section 138(1)(a) or (2) of the Contributions and Benefits Act;

(f) child benefit;

(g) statutory sick pay; and

(h) statutory maternity pay.

DERIVATION

Social Security Act 1975, s.98; Social Security Act 1986, s.52(3) and (3A).

AMENDMENTS

1. Social Security (Incapacity for Work) Act 1994, Sched. 1, para. 46 (April 13, 1995).
2. Jobseekers Act 1996, Sched. 2, para. 42 (June 11, 1996).

GENERAL NOTE

Subs. (1). A distinction is drawn between a "claim" and a "question". A claim may give rise to a considerable number of potential questions but there is not necessarily an individual determination of those potential questions where there does not appear to be a real issue. Under subs. (3) different aspects of a claim, or even different aspects of one question, may be referred to different adjudication officers.

The duty to submit a claim or question to an adjudication officer arises only when the Department has sufficient basic information for the determination of the issue. Once that information is available, submission of the claim or question should not be delayed pending verification of the information. However, after the claim or question has been referred, the adjudication officer is entitled to delay a determination while he or she seeks verification (*R. v. Secretary of State for Social Services, ex p. CPAG* [1990] 2 Q.B. 540).

Subs. (2). The questions which fall to be decided otherwise than by an adjudication officer are those which fall to be decided by the Secretary of State (s.17 and regulations under s.58(1)(a)) and the disablement questions which normally fall to be determined by an adjudicating medical authority (s.45(2)).

Decision of adjudication officer

21.—(1) An adjudication officer to whom a claim or question is submitted under section 20 above (other than a claim which under section 30(12) or (13) or 35(7) below falls to be treated as an application for a review) shall take it into consideration and, so far as practicable, dispose of it, in accordance with this section, and with procedure regulations under section 59 below, within 14 days of its submission to him.

(2) Subject to subsection (3) and section 37 below, the adjudication officer may decide a claim or question himself or refer it to a social security appeal tribunal.

(3) The adjudication officer must decide a claim for or question relating to an attendance allowance, a disability living allowance or a disability working allowance himself.

(4) Where an adjudication officer refers a question as to, or in connection with, entitlement to statutory sick pay or statutory maternity pay to a social security appeal tribunal, the employee and employer concerned shall each be given notice in writing of the reference.

(5) In any other case notice in writing of the reference shall be given to the claimant.

(6) Where—

(a) a case has been referred to a social security appeal tribunal ("the tribunal"); and

(b) the claimant makes a further claim which raises the same or similar questions; and

(c) that further claim is referred to the tribunal by the adjudication officer,

then the tribunal may proceed to determine the further claim whether or not notice has been given under subsection (4) or (5) above.

Derivation

Social Security Act 1975, s.99; Social Security Act 1986, s.52(3) and (3A).

General Note

Subs. (1). There is no breach of duty if an adjudication officer delays a determination either because he or she is seeking verification of information or if there is simply too much work. A decision cannot be delayed indefinitely if information is not verified. An adjudication officer must make a determination on the basis of such information as is available *(R(SB) 29/83).* If a claimant fails to provide information in circumstances when he or she could reasonably be expected to do so, an adjudication officer is entitled to draw an adverse inference.

Subss. (2) and (3). Where there is a conflict of evidence, adjudication officers frequently refer questions to social security appeal tribunals rather than determining them themselves. In those industrial disease cases where appeals are heard by medical boards there is similar power to refer a case to an adjudicating medical practitioner (reg. 46(2) of the Social Security (Adjudication) Regulations 1995). However, a case cannot be referred either to a social security appeal tribunal or to a disability appeal tribunal if it concerns attendance allowance, disability living allowance or disability working allowance. This is because it is intended that there should be hearings before tribunals in such cases only after there has been not only an original decision by an adjudication officer but also after the adjudication officer has had the opportunity to review the decision (s.33(1)).

Appeals from adjudication officers—general

Appeal to social security appeal tribunal

22.—(1) Subject to subsection (3) below, where the adjudication officer has decided a claim or question other than a claim or question relating to an attendance allowance, a disability living allowance or a disability working allowance—

(a) if it relates to statutory sick pay or statutory maternity pay, the employee and employer concerned shall each have a right to appeal to a social security appeal tribunal; and

(b) in any other case the claimant shall have a right to do so.

(2) A person with a right of appeal under this section shall be given such notice of a decision falling within subsection (1) above and of that right as may be prescribed.

(3) No appeal lies under this section where—

(a) in connection with the decision of the adjudication officer there has arisen any question which under or by virtue of this Act falls to be determined otherwise than by an adjudication officer; and

(b) the question has been determined; and

(c) the adjudication officer certifies that the decision on that question is the sole ground of his decision.

(4) Regulations may make provision as to the manner in which, and the time within which, appeals are to be brought.

(5) Where an adjudication officer has determined that any amount, other than an amount—

(a) of an attendance allowance;

(b) of a disability living allowance;

(c) of a disability working allowance;

(d) of statutory sick pay; or

(e) of statutory maternity pay,

is recoverable under or by virtue of section 71 or 74 below, any person from whom he has determined that it is recoverable shall have the same right of appeal to a social security appeal tribunal as a claimant.

(6) In any case where—

(a) an adjudication officer has decided any claim or question under Part V of the Contributions and Benefits Act; and

(b) the right to benefit under that Part of that Act of any person other than the claimant is or may be, under Part VI of Schedule 7 to that Act, affected by that decision,

that other person shall have the like right of appeal to a social security appeal tribunal as the claimant.

(7) Subsection (2) above shall apply to a person with a right of appeal under subsection (5) or (6) above as it applies to a claimant.

DERIVATION

Social Security Act 1975, s.100; Social Security Act 1986, s.52(3) and (3A).

GENERAL NOTE

The right of appeal given by this section does not apply to cases concerning attendance allowance, disability living allowance or disability working allowance. Some such cases are considered by social security appeal tribunals, but under s.33(1)(b) rather than under this section.

There is no right of appeal to a social security appeal tribunal from a decision of an adjudication officer on a diagnosis question or a recrudescence question in an industrial disease case. Appeals against those decisions are heard by adjudicating medical authorities (reg. 48 of the Social Security (Adjudication) Regulations 1995).

Appeal from social security appeal tribunal to Commissioner

23.—(1) Subject to the provisions of this section, an appeal lies to a Commissioner from any decision of a social security appeal tribunal under section 22 above on the ground that the decision of the tribunal was erroneous in point of law.

(2) In the case of statutory sick pay or statutory maternity pay an appeal lies under this section at the instance of any of the following—

(a) an adjudication officer;
(b) the employee concerned;
(c) the employer concerned;
(d) a trade union, where—
  (i) the employee is a member of the union at the time of the appeal and was so immediately before the question at issue arose; or
  (ii) the question at issue is a question as to or in connection with entitlement of a deceased person who was at the time of his death a member of the union;
(e) an association of employers of which the employer is a member at the time of the appeal and was so immediately before the question at issue arose.

(3) In any other case an appeal lies under this section at the instance of any of the following—

(a) an adjudication officer;
(b) the claimant;
(c) in any of the cases mentioned in subsection (5) below, a trade union; and
(d) a person from whom it is determined that any amount is recoverable under section 71(1) or 74 below.

(4) In a case relating to industrial injuries benefit an appeal lies under this section at the instance of a person whose right to benefit is, or may be, under Part VI of Schedule 7 to the Contributions and Benefits Act, affected by the decision appealed against, as well as at the instance of any person or body such as is mentioned in subsection (3) above.

(5) The following are the cases in which an appeal lies at the instance of a trade union—

(a) where the claimant is a member of the union at the time of the appeal and was so immediately before the question at issue arose;
(b) where that question in any way relates to a deceased person who was a member of the union at the time of his death;
(c) where the case relates to industrial injuries benefit and the claimant or, in relation to industrial death benefit, the deceased, was a member of the union at the time of the relevant accident.

(6) Subsections (2), (3) and (5) above, as they apply to a trade union, apply also to any other association which exists to promote the interests and welfare of its members.

(7) Where the Commissioner holds that the decision was erroneous in point of law, he shall set it aside and—

(a) he shall have power—
  (i) to give the decision which he considers the tribunal should have given, if he can do so without making fresh or further findings of fact; or
  (ii) if he considers it expedient, to make such findings and to give such decision as he considers appropriate in the light of them; and
(b) in any other case he shall refer the case to a tribunal with directions for its determination.

(8) Subject to any direction of the Commissioner, the tribunal on a reference under subsection (7)(b) above shall consist of persons who were not members of the tribunal which gave the erroneous decision.

(9) No appeal lies under this section without the leave—

(a) of the person who was the chairman of the tribunal when the decision was given or, in a prescribed case, the leave of some other chairman; or

(b) subject to and in accordance with regulations, of a Commissioner.

(10) Regulations may make provision as to the manner in which, and the time within which, appeals are to be brought and applications made for leave to appeal.

DERIVATION

Social Security Act 1975, s.101; Social Security Act 1986, s.52(3) and (3A).

GENERAL NOTE

Subs. (1) See note to s.34(1).

Subss. (2)–(6) Not everyone who has a right to be heard before a tribunal as being "interested in the proceedings" (see reg. 4(5) of the Social Security (Adjudication) Regulations 1995 and the definition of "party to the proceedings" in reg. 1(2)) has the right to appeal.

Subs. (7). Commissioners do not usually make findings of fact if there is a clear conflict of evidence.

Subs. (8). Any tribunal rehearing a case after an appeal to a Commissioner *must* consist of people who were not members of the tribunal whose decision has been set aside unless the Commissioner directs otherwise.

Subs. (9). Before appealing to a Commissioner, a person must first obtain a statement of the tribunal's reasons and leave to appeal from either the chairman of the tribunal or the Commissioner. Application is made to the chairman first, unless the three month time-limit has expired in which case the application must be made straight to a Commissioner. Regs. 24(4) and 32(4) of the Adjudication Regulations provide that, if it would be impracticable or would cause undue delay for a person who was chairman of the tribunal giving the decision to consider the application for leave, any other chairman may do so. If a chairman refuses leave to appeal, a further application may be made to a Commissioner. No appeal lies against a refusal by a Commissioner to grant leave although such a refusal may be challenged by way of an application for judicial review (*Bland v. Chief Supplementary Benefit Officer* [1983] 1 W.L.R. 262, also reported as *R(SB) 12/83*).

Subs. (10). See regs. 24 and 32 of the Adjudication Regulations and also the Social Security Commissioners Procedure Regulations 1987.

Appeal from Commissioners on point of law

24.—(1) Subject to subsections (2) and (3) below, an appeal on a question of law shall lie to the appropriate court from any decision of a Commissioner [[1] or given in consequence of a reference under section 112(4) of the 1975 Act (which enabled a medical appeal tribunal to refer a question of law to a Commissioner)].

(2) No appeal under this section shall lie from a decision except—

(a) with the leave of the Commissioner who gave the decision or, in a prescribed case, with the leave of a Commissioner selected in accordance with regulations; or

(b) if he refuses leave, with the leave of the appropriate court.

(3) An application for leave under this section in respect of a Commissioner's decision may only be made by—

(a) a person who, before the proceedings before the Commissioner were begun, was entitled to appeal to the Commissioner from the decision to which the Commissioner's decision relates;

(b) any other person who was a party to the proceedings in which the first decision mentioned in paragraph (a) above was given;

(c) the Secretary of State, in a case where he is not entitled to apply for leave by virtue of paragraph (a) or (b) above;

(d) any other person who is authorised by regulations to apply for leave; and regulations may make provision with respect to the manner in which and the time within which applications must be made to a Commissioner for leave under this section and with respect to the procedure for dealing with such applications.

(4) On an application to a Commissioner for leave under this section it shall be the duty of the Commissioner to specify as the appropriate court—

(a) the Court of Appeal if it appears to him that the relevant place is in England or Wales;

(b) the Court of Session if it appears to him that the relevant place is in Scotland; and

(c) the Court of Appeal in Northern Ireland if it appears to him that the relevant place is in Northern Ireland,

except that if it appears to him, having regard to the circumstances of the case and in particular to the convenience of the persons who may be parties to the proposed appeal, that he should specify a different court mentioned in paragraphs (a) to (c) above as the appropriate court, it shall be his duty to specify that court as the appropriate court.

(5) In this section—

"the appropriate court", except in subsection (4) above, means the court specified in pursuance of that subsection;

"the relevant place", in relation to an application for leave to appeal from a decision of a Commissioner, means the premises where the authority whose decision was the subject of the Commissioner's decision usually exercises its functions.

[[1](5A) In relation to a decision of a Commissioner which was given in consequence of a reference under section 112(4) of the 1975 Act subsections (3) and (5) of this section shall have effect with such modification as may be prescribed by regulations.]

(6) The powers to make regulations conferred by this section shall be exercisable by the Lord Chancellor.

DERIVATION

Social Security Act 1980, s.14.

AMENDMENT

1. Social Security (Consequential Provisions) Act 1992, Sched. 4, para. 12.

GENERAL NOTE

This section provides for an appeal to the "appropriate court" from a decision of a Commissioner. It seems fairly clear that this was intended to replace s.14 of the Social Security Act 1980 and provide for a right of appeal against any decision of a Commissioner. However, the structure of the 1992 Act makes the scope of s.24 ambiguous. It clearly provides an avenue of appeal against a decision of a Commissioner given under s.23. S.34(5) also makes it clear that it provides an avenue of appeal against a decision under s.34 It is less clear that it provides an avenue of appeal against a decision under s.48 and it is even less obvious that s.24 is concerned with appeals from Commissioners in cases arising under reg.23 of the Social Security (Introduction of Disability Living Allowance) Regulations 1991 or under the Forfeiture Act 1982 or under s.13 of the Social Security (Recovery of Benefits) Act 1997. Note that a decision of a Commissioner to refuse leave to appeal to a Commissioner is not a "decision" against which an appeal lies under this section. Instead, any challenge must be made by way of an application for judicial review (*Bland v. Chief Adjudication Officer* [1983] 1 W.L.R. 262 (also reported as *R(SB) 12/83*)).

An appeal lies on a point of law only. Leave to appeal must be obtained. If the Commissioner refuses leave, it is still necessary for him or her to identify the "appropriate court" so that an application for leave may be made to that court. For the procedure for applying to the Commissioner for leave, see reg. 31 of the Social Security Commissioners Procedure Regulations 1987. Note that the three-month time limit for making an application to the Commissioner may be extended by the Commissioner but not by the "appropriate court" (*White v. Chief Adjudication Officer* [1986] 2 All E.R. 905 (also reported as an appendix to *R(S) 8/85*)). For the procedure in the Court of Appeal, see R.S.C., Ord. 59. Under Ord. 59, r. 21, an application for leave to appeal or an appeal must be brought within six weeks of the Commissioner's refusal or grant of leave being sent to the parties, although the Court has a general power under Ord. 3, r. 5 to extend time limits. For the procedure in the Court of Session, see R.C. 290 and 293B.

In *Smith v. Cosworth Casting Processes Ltd* (Practice Note) [1997] 1 W.L.R. 1538, the Court of Appeal gave guidance as to applications for leave to appeal to the Court. The Court would only refuse leave if satisfied that the applicant had "no real prospect" of succeeding on the appeal. The Court could grant an application even if not so satisfied if, for instance, the issue was one the Court considered should, in the public interest, be examined by the Court of Appeal or if it raised an issue where the law needed clarifying. Where leave was refused, the Court would give short reasons. Where leave was granted, the Court might also identify, for the benefit of the parties and the Court hearing the appeal, a reason for giving leave, but it should not be assumed that the Court did not accept that there were other issues to be decided as well as the one identified. A person applying for a grant of leave to be set aside had a heavy onus and such applications were discouraged.

In cases where a claimant is appealing against a decision on appeal from a social security appeal tribunal or disability appeal tribunal, the respondent should be the Chief Adjudication Officer. If the appeal is being brought against a decision on appeal from a medical appeal tribunal (if this section extends to such appeal), the respondent should be the Secretary of State for Social Security. The Solicitor to the Departments of Social Security and Health will accept service on behalf of the Chief Adjudication Officer or the Secretary of State, at New Court, 48 Carey Street, London WC2A 2LS.

Reviews—general

Review of decisions

25.—(1) Subject to the following provisions of this section, any decision under this Act of an adjudication officer, a social security appeal tribunal or a Commissioner (other than a decision relating to an attendance allowance, a disability living allowance or a disability working allowance) may be reviewed at any time by an adjudication officer or, on a reference by an adjudication officer, by a social security appeal tribunal, if—

(a) the officer or tribunal is satisfied that the decision was given in ignorance of, or was based on a mistake as to, some material fact; or

(b) there has been any relevant change of circumstances since the decision was given; or

(c) it is anticipated that a relevant change of circumstances will so occur; or

(d) the decision was based on a decision of a question which under or by virtue of this Act falls to be determined otherwise than by an adjudication officer, and the decision of that question is revised; or

(e) the decision falls to be reviewed under section [[1]6(6) or 7(7) of the Jobseekers Act 1995].

(2) Any decision of an adjudication officer (other than a decision relating to an attendance allowance, a disability living allowance or a disability working allowance) may be reviewed, upon the ground that it was erroneous in point of law, by an adjudication officer or, on a reference from an adjudication officer, by a social security appeal tribunal.

(3) Regulations may provide that a decision may not be reviewed on the ground mentioned in subsection (1)(a) above unless the officer or tribunal is satisfied as mentioned in that paragraph by fresh evidence.

(4) In their application to family credit, subsection (1)(b) and (c) above shall have effect subject to section 128(3) of the Contributions and Benefits Act (change of circumstances not to affect award or rate during specified period).

(5) Where a decision is reviewed on the ground mentioned in subsection (1)(c) above, the decision given on the review—

(a) shall take effect on the day prescribed for that purpose by reference to the date on which the relevant change of circumstances is expected to occur; and

(b) shall be reviewed again if the relevant change of circumstances either does not occur or occurs otherwise than on that date.

Derivation

Social Security Act 1975, s.104(1)–(1A); Social Security Act 1986, s.52(3) and (3A).

Amendment

1. Jobseekers Act 1995, Sched. 2, para. 43 (October 7, 1996).

General Note

This section does not apply where the decision concerns attendance allowance, disability living allowance or disability working allowance. The grounds of review under s.25(1) and (2) are similar to those under s.30(2) and reference should be made to the note to that subsection. No regulations have been made under subs. (3).

Procedure for reviews

26.—(1) A question may be raised with a view to a review under section 25 above by means of an application in writing to an adjudication officer, stating the grounds of the application.

(2) On receipt of any such application, the adjudication officer shall proceed to deal with or refer any question arising on it in accordance with sections 21 to 23 above.

(3) Regulations may provide for enabling, or requiring, in prescribed circumstances, a review under section 25 above notwithstanding that no application for a review has been made under subsection (1) above.

Derivation

Social Security Act 1975, s.104(2)–(3A); Social Security Act 1986, s.52(3) and (3A).

Reviews under s.25—supplementary

27.—(1) Regulations—

(a) may prescribe what are, or are not, relevant changes of circumstances for the purposes of section 25 above; and

(b) may make provision restricting the payment of any benefit, or any increase of benefit, to which a person would, but for this subsection, be entitled by reason of a review in respect of any period before or after the review (whether that period falls wholly or partly before or after the making of the regulations).

(2) Regulations under subsection (1)(b) above shall not restrict the payment to or for a woman of so much of—

(a) any widow's benefit, any [1incapacity benefit] under section 40 of the Contributions and Benefits Act or any Category A or Category B retirement pension; or

(b) any increase of such a benefit or pension,

as falls to be paid by reason of a review which takes place by virtue of section 25(1)(a) or (1)(b) above in consequence of a claim for a widowhood benefit, within the meaning of section 3 above, which is made or treated as made by virtue of that section.

Derivation

Social Security Act 1975, s.104(5) and (6); Social Security Act 1986, s.52(3) and (3A).

AMENDMENT

1. Social Security (Incapacity for Work) Act 1994, Sched. 1, para. 48) (April 13, 1995).

Appeals following reviews or refusals to review

28. A decision given on a review under section 25 above, and a refusal to review a decision under that section, shall be subject to appeal in like manner as an original decision, and sections 21 to 23 above shall, with the necessary modifications, apply in relation to a decision given on such a review as they apply to the original decision of a question.

DERIVATION

Social Security Act 1975, s.104(4); Social Security Act 1986, s.52(3) and (3A).

Review after claimant appeals

29. Where a claimant has appealed against a decision of an adjudication officer and the decision is reviewed by an adjudication officer under section 25 above—

(a) if the adjudication officer considers that the decision which he has made on the review is the same as the decision that would have been made on the appeal had every ground of the claimant's appeal succeeded, the appeal shall lapse; but

(b) in any other case, the review shall be of no effect and the appeal shall proceed accordingly.

DERIVATION

Social Security Act 1975, s.104(3B); Social Security Act 1986, s.52(3) and (3A).

Attendance allowance, disability living allowance and disability working allowance

Reviews of decisions of adjudication officers

30.—(1) On an application under this section made within the prescribed period, a decision of an adjudication officer under section 21 above which relates to an attendance allowance, a disability living allowance or a disability working allowance may be reviewed on any ground subject, in the case of disability working allowance, to section 129(6) of the Contributions and Benefits Act.

(2) On an application under this section made after the end of the prescribed period, a decision of an adjudication officer under section 21 above which relates to an attendance allowance or a disability living allowance may be reviewed if—

(a) the adjudication officer is satisfied that the decision was given in ignorance of, or was based on a mistake as to, some material fact; or

(b) there has been any relevant change of circumstances since the decision was given; or

(c) it is anticipated that a relevant change of circumstances will so occur; or

(d) the decision was erroneous in point of law; or

(e) the decision was to make an award for a period wholly or partly after the date on which the claim was made or treated as made but subject to a condition being fulfilled and that condition has not been fulfilled,

but regulations may provide that a decision may not be reviewed on the ground mentioned in paragraph (a) above unless the officer is satisfied as mentioned in that paragraph by fresh evidence.

(3) Regulations may prescribe what are, or are not, relevant changes of circumstances for the purposes of subsection (2)(b) and (c) above.

(4) On an application under this section made after the end of the prescribed period, a decision of an adjudication officer under section 21 above that a person is or was at any time terminally ill for the purposes of section 66(1), 72(5) or 73(12) of the Contributions and Benefits Act may be reviewed if there has been a change of medical opinion with respect to his condition or his reasonable expectation of life.

(5) On an application under this section made after the end of the prescribed period, a decision of an adjudication officer under section 21 above which relates to a disability working allowance may be reviewed if—

(a) the adjudication officer is satisfied that the decision was given in ignorance of, or was based on a mistake as to, some material fact; or

(b) subject to section 129(6) of the Contributions and Benefits Act, there has been any prescribed change of circumstances since the decision was given; or

(c) the decision was erroneous in point of law; or

(d) the decision was to make an award for a period wholly or partly after the date on which the claim was made or treated as made but subject to a condition being fulfilled and that condition has not been fulfilled,

but regulations may provide that a decision may not be reviewed on the ground mentioned in paragraph (a) above unless the officer is satisfied as mentioned in that paragraph by fresh evidence.

(6) The claimant shall be given such notification as may be prescribed of a decision which may be reviewed under this section and of his right to a review under subsection (1) above.

(7) A question may be raised with a view to a review under this section by means of an application made in writing to an adjudication officer stating the grounds of the application and supplying such information and evidence as may be prescribed.

[[1](7A) The Secretary of State may undertake investigations to obtain information and evidence for the purposes of making applications under subsection (7) above.]

(8) Regulations—

(a) may provide for enabling or requiring, in prescribed circumstances, a review under this section notwithstanding that no application under subsection (7) above has been made; and

(b) if they do so provide, shall specify under which provision of this section a review carried out by virtue of any such regulations falls.

(9) Reviews under this section shall be carried out by adjudication officers.

(10) Different aspects of any question which arises on such a review may be dealt with by different adjudication officers; and for this purpose this section and the other provisions of this Part of this Act which relate to reviews under this section shall apply with any necessary modifications.

(11) If a review is under subsection (1) above, the officer who took the decision under review shall not deal with any question which arises on the review.

(12) Except in prescribed circumstances, where a claim for a disability living allowance in respect of a person already awarded such an allowance by an adjudication officer is made or treated as made during the period for which he has been awarded the allowance, it shall be treated as an application for a review under this section.

(13) Where—

(a) a claim for an attendance allowance, a disability living allowance or a disability working allowance in respect of a person has been refused; and

(b) a further claim for the same allowance is made in respect of him within the period prescribed under subsection (1) above,

the further claim shall be treated as an application for a review under that subsection.

DERIVATION

Social Security Act 1975, s.100A; Social Security Act 1986, s.52(3A).

AMENDMENT

1. Social Security Administration (Fraud) Act 1997, s.17(1) (July 1, 1997).

GENERAL NOTE

This section is concerned only with reviews of decisions of adjudication officers. Decisions of social security appeal tribunals, disability appeal tribunals and Social Security Commissioners may be reviewed under s.35.

One curious feature of this section is that the power to review decisions under subs. (1), (2), (4) or (5) arises only "[o]n an application under this section". In the absence of any regulations under subs. (8), this precludes an adjudication officer from reviewing a decision of his or her own motion. There is no indication as to who may apply for a review. Presumably, an applicant would have to show a sufficient interest. It is generally accepted that the Secretary of State for Social Security has a right to apply for a review. He does so on Form LT54. In *CDLA/14884/96* it was stated that any application for review should be included in the papers before a tribunal, should it lead to an appeal. It was also held that there was no general duty on an adjudication officer to seek representations from a claimant before reviewing and revising a decision. However, the general duty to investigate a matter before reaching a decision may make it appropriate to seek representations in some cases.

Subs. (1). This power to review is most important because appeals in attendance allowance, disability living allowance and disability working allowance cases may be made only against decisions on review under this subsection (s.33(1)).

The idea that the original determining authority should have another look at a case before it is considered at a higher level is taken from the old attendance allowance legislation (s.106 of the Social Security Act 1975). More than half of reviews under the former provision were successful. There is a similar provision in housing benefit legislation (reg. 79(2) of the Housing Benefit (General) Regulations 1987).

The review must be by a different adjudication officer (subs. (11)) and the decision may be reviewed simply because the second adjudication officer takes a different overall view of the case. The limitations usually applied to reviews under subs. (2) or s.25 do not apply.

The "prescribed period" is the period of three months beginning with the date on which the adjudication officer's decision was given to the claimant (reg. 25 of the Social Security (Adjudication) Regulations 1995). The time is extended in the event of a postal delay caused by industrial action but not otherwise. If a claimant wishes after the prescribed period to challenge a decision of an adjudication officer, he or she must either seek a review under subs. (2), (4) or (5) or, if the adjudication officer has refused benefit altogether, make a new claim. In the case of either a review under subs. (2) or a new claim, there may be a limit to the extent to which benefit may be backdated and the grounds for review under subs. (2) are relatively limited.

The power to review decisions under subs. (1) applies not only to original decisions of adjudication officers made under s.21 but also to decisions made on reviews under subss. (2), (4), or (5) (see s.31(2)). However it does not apply to a previous decision under subs. (1) so it is not possible for a claimant to keep applying for reviews by different adjudication officers in the hope of obtaining a favourable decision. After one review under subs. (1) a claimant must either appeal or seek a review under subss. (2), (4) or (5). This point is stressed in *CSDLA/128/94*. The Commissioner was obliged to set aside a decision of a tribunal who had failed to note that there was before them an appeal from a decision under s.30(1) reviewing a decision given on an application for review which had had to be made under s.30(2) because the application was outside the "prescribed period". The tribunal had erroneously looked at the simple merits of the original claim without considering whether there were grounds for review under s.30(2).

When reviewing under s.30(1) a decision made on an application for review under s.30(2) of an initial decision given on a claim, the adjudication officer carrying out the s.30(1) review must consider the merits of the decision given on the application for the s.30(2) review and therefore must consider whether there are grounds for reviewing under s.30(2) the initial decision.

Subs. (2). This provides for review on grounds similar to those contained in s.25. This subsection applies only to attendance allowance and disability living allowance—see subs. (5) for disability working allowance. Note also that only an adjudication officer's decision may be reviewed under this subsection. The power to review a decision of a tribunal or a Commissioner is to be found in s.35(1). Even if any of these grounds is made out, a review of an adjudication officer's decision within the "prescribed period" (see above) is always carried out under subs. (1) rather than subs. (2) so that an appeal lies from the review decision. However, there is no "prescribed period" if the decision now under review was itself made under subs. (1) (see s.31(1)).

A claimant who is dissatisfied with a decision on review under subs. (2) must seek a further review under subs. (1) before being able to appeal under s.33(1). A refusal to review a decision may be challenged in the same way (see s.31(2)).

The term "review" is commonly, and confusingly, used in two senses. There are two possible stages in the process. First, an adjudication officer must decide whether any of the grounds justifying a review is made out. Secondly, if one of the grounds is made out, the adjudication officer must decide whether the original decision of the adjudication officer should be altered. This second stage is the review. If it is altered, the decision is said to have been reviewed and revised. Commonly, a decision is regarded as having been reviewed only if it has been revised, but that is not necessarily so. An adjudication officer might consider that an earlier decision had been made in ignorance of a material fact but also decide that, looking at all the other circumstances of the case, the original decision should still not be revised. Despite the lack of revision, there would still have been a review. There is technically a refusal to review a decision only if an adjudication officer has held that none of the grounds for review has been made out and he or she has not proceeded to the second stage.

The burden of proof in review cases lies upon the person initiating the review, whether it be the secretary of state or the claimant. That person must prove not only that the grounds for a review are made out but also that the original decision should be revised (*R(I) 1/71*). In *CDLA/14884/96*, it was pointed out that the Secretary of State did not have any standing before a tribunal and that it fell to the adjudication officer to justify any review carried out at the behest of the Secretary of State. In *R(A) 2/90*, it was held that once grounds for a review are made out, the whole of the determination under review may be considered. That was on the ground that, in attendance allowance cases, there was not a series of determinations but only one determination by the Attendance Allowance Board. Therefore, if there were grounds for a review relating to the night attention condition, the day attention condition could also be reviewed. On the other hand, it is plain from s.20(5) that there may be a series of determinations by different adjudication officers on the same claim, so it may now be particularly important to identify the precise determination under review in order to discover the possible scope of the review.

ignorance of, or . . . mistake as to, some material fact: A fact is "material" if it *could* but not necessarily *would* have made a difference to the decision under consideration. In *Saker v. Secretary of State for Social Services* (reported as an appendix to *R(I) 2/88*) Nicholls L.J. said that a fact was material "if it is one which, had it been known to the medical board, would have called for serious consideration by the board and might well have affected its decision". Hence the possibility of deciding that a decision should be reviewed but not revised. However, in *CDLA/1715/95*, it was held that "reviewed" in s.30(2) meant "revised" rather than merely "looked at again". It is difficult to reconcile that view with what was said in *Saker* but in *CCS/511/94* the Child Support Commissioner suggested that the discussion in *Saker* was wholly academic and that there was no practical distinction between a refusal to review a decision and a decision to review but not revise a decision. In practice, it is rare to be able to identify facts found by adjudication officers save by inference from the evidence before them, because they are obliged by reg.18(1) of the Social Security (Adjudication) Regulations 1995 to record the reasons for their decision but not their findings of fact. This is not a problem in most cases since most reviews seem to be carried out as a result of new evidence disclosing totally new facts. The concluding words of subs. (2) enable the Secretary of State to make regulations requiring "fresh evidence" before a decision may be reviewed on the ground of mistake or ignorance of fact, but no such regulations have been made.

The ignorance or mistake must be as to a primary fact and not merely as to an inference or conclusion of fact. Thus a decision cannot be reviewed simply on the ground that an adjudication officer is now satisfied that the original decision as to, say, the claimant's ability to walk was wrong. "He must go further and assert and prove that the inference might not have been drawn, if the determining authority had not been ignorant of some specific fact of which it could have been aware, or had not been mistaken as to some specific fact which it took into consideration" (*R(I) 3/75*) A medical report may or may not give grounds for a review. It may provide evidence of facts about the claimant's disabilities as to which the adjudication officer making the earlier decision may have been ignorant or mistaken. On the other hand, a new medical opinion does not justify a review (*R(S) 4/86*, but see subs. (4) in respect of medical opinions concerning the terminally ill).

relevant change of circumstances: In *R(I) 56/54*, the Commissioner said "A relevant change of circumstances postulates that the decision has ceased to be correct". However, that approach has been rejected by another Commissioner, in *R(A) 2/90*. He adopted the approach of Nicholls L.J. in *Saker* (above) and held that a change of circumstances is relevant if it is such that the body giving the decision on review "would need to give those circumstances serious consideration to the extent that they might well affect [its] decision". He went on to say:

> "In my view the new circumstances must not only be in their substance in the area of what is relevant but there must also be sufficiency with regard to quantity. It is thus not enough that the new circumstances relate to night attention. They must also be such as to raise a serious question as to whether the requirement for night attention can be said to be a requirement for prolonged or repeated attention."

R(I) 56/54 had been followed in *R(A) 2/81* and *R(A) 4/81* but there is clearly force in the view expressed in *R(A) 2/90* that "relevant" should mean the same as "material" and that the Court of Appeal's approach in *Saker* should apply to both grounds of review. This may seem academic because if a decision is reviewed and not revised the outcome is the same as if it had not been reviewed at all. However, in *R(A) 2/90*, the claimant sought a review of a decision that he satisfied the day supervision condition for attendance allowance on the ground that he now satisfied the night attention condition as well. The Commissioner held that, as long as the claimant's change of circumstances raised a serious question that he might satisfy the night condition, it was open to the Attendance Allowance Board to review the decision so as to decide that the claimant satisfied neither the night nor the day conditions. Had the evidence before the Board when reviewing the decision in respect of the night condition also shown, say, ignorance of a fact material to the day condition, there could not possibly have been any objection to the Board then reviewing the decision in respect of both conditions. However, the Commissioner's decision suggests that the decision in respect of the day condition could be reviewed even if there had not been any ground for review relevant to that aspect of the case. Ought "relevant change of circumstances" mean "change of circumstances relevant to the contemplated revision"? The Commissioner had pointed out that the Board made only one determination rather than separate determinations in respect of the day and the night conditions and so he considered that once there were grounds for review of the determination, the whole determination was thrown wide open. However, under the new regime, different adjudication officers may deal with different aspects of a claim or question (s.20(5)) and they, of course, deal with all the various questions that may arise and not just disability questions. If *R(A) 2/90* is applied to adjudication officers' decisions, a change of circumstances relevant to one aspect of a decision would justify a review of a completely different aspect if, and only if, they had originally both been dealt with in the same determination. That would seem likely to produce anomalies since the scope of the possible review would depend on the procedural history of the claim rather than its merits.

A change in the legislation is a change of circumstances (*R(A) 4/81*) but an unexpected decision of a court is not (*Chief Adjudication Officer v. McKiernon*, unreported, July 8, 1993). However, s.155(3) provides that it is unnecessary for an adjudication officer to review a decision in order to give effect to a change in benefit rates. If the decision was erroneous in point of law at the time it was made, it should be reviewed under subs. (2)(d) rather than (2)(b). No regulations have been made under subs. (3) to prescribe what are, or are not, changes of circumstances.

anticipated changes of circumstances: If a decision is reviewed under subs. (2)(c) and the change of circumstances does not occur, or occurs on a date different from the one anticipated, the decision is reviewed again under s.32(6)(b).

Subs. (3). See reg. 67A of the Social Security (Adjudication) Regulations 1995.

Subs. (4). This enables a determination that a person is "terminally ill" to be reviewed simply on the grounds of a change of medical opinion which would not ordinarily amount to a change of circumstances justifying a review under subs. (2)(b). Under s.66(1) of the Social Security Contributions and Benefits Act 1992 a person is "terminally ill" if he suffers from a progressive disease and his death in consequence of that disease can reasonably be expected within six months. So a change in a medical opinion as to the nature of a claimant's illness or his or her life expectancy may give rise to a review under this subsection.

Unfortunately, the subsection does not allow for the review on ground of change of medical opinion of a decision that a person is *not* terminally ill. If the claimant was originally refused benefit altogether, that is not of importance because it is possible simply to make a new claim. It also does not matter if a review is sought during the "prescribed period" of three months after the original decision because a review under subs. (1) may be based on a change of opinion. The difficulty arises if the claimant is receiving an allowance at a rate other than the highest and seeks a review after the prescribed period. He or she must then show grounds for a review under subs. (2). Generally that is likely to be possible (ignorance or mistake as to the nature of the disease, or change of circumstances in that the claimant's death can now be expected within six months whereas before it was longer) but there may be the occasional hard case.

This subsection applies to review decisions under subs. (1) as it does to original decisions under s.21 but then there is no prescribed period (s.31(1)).

Subs. (5). This applies to disability working allowance only. It is the same as subs. (2) save that there is only a very limited power to review on the ground of change of circumstances and no power to anticipate such a change. See regs. 54–56 of the Disability Working Allowance (General) Regulations 1991 for the prescribed changes of circumstances.

Subs. (6). See reg. 18 of the Social Security (Adjudication) Regulations 1995.

Subs. (7). This is in similar terms to s.104(2) of the Social Security Act 1975 and it was held that a request for a review under s.104 might still be made orally (*CSB/336/87*). However, applications for reviews are required under s.30 but were not under s.104 so it is arguable that different considerations apply. No regulations have been made prescribing information and evidence to be supplied. Since adjudication officers can always write to ask for further details, the requirement that the application should state the grounds of the application is not to be construed too severely (*CSB/1182/89* which was concerned with the similar requirement to give grounds in a letter of appeal). Where the Secretary of State applies for a review, this subsection applies and he or she must give reasons for the application but is not obliged to provide evidence (see *CDLA/14884/96*).

Subss. (12) and (13) provide that inappropriate claims shall be treated as applications for review. Inappropriate claims not covered by those provisions may also be treated as applications for review because applications for benefit should not be defeated by legal technicalities (*R(I) 50/56*).

Subs. (7A). Where the Secretary of State is undertaking an investigation in connection with an award of attendance allowance or disability living allowance, the claimant may be *required* to attend for, or submit to, a medical examination and benefit may be withheld if he or she does not do so (see regs. 8C to 8E of the Social Security (Attendance Allowance) Regulations 1991 and regs. 5A to 5C of the Social Security (Disability Living Allowance) Regulations 1991).

Subs. (8). No regulations have yet been made under this subsection.

Subss. (9) and (10). These apply to review decisions provisions similar to those of s.20. In particular, different adjudication officers may deal with different aspects of the review.

Subs. (11). Because a review under subs. (1) may involve no more than an adjudication officer having another look at the same evidence as was available when the original decision was made, the review is to be carried out by a different adjudication officer who may reach a different judgment on it. Different considerations apply to reviews under subss. (2) and (4) so the same adjudication officer may carry out a review of his or her own original decision under those provisions.

Subs. (12). Once an award of disability living allowance has been made, any application for a higher rate should be by way of review rather than a fresh claim. Therefore, any claim for the allowance in those circumstances must be treated as an application for a review. It is not clear why subs. (12) does not also apply to attendance allowance cases where the same principle applies. However, a claim for the higher rate of attendance allowance by a person already receiving the lower rate will presumably still be treated as an application for review applying the approach suggested in *R(I) 50/56* of not defeating applications for benefit on technical grounds if that can be avoided. A *renewal* claim is usually treated as made only at the end of the current award (reg. 13C of the Social Security (Claims and Payments) Regulations 1987) but, in *CDLA/14895/96*, it was held that, if an adjudication officer or tribunal is minded to award a component at a higher rate on such a claim, it should first be considered whether the claim should be treated as made on the day it was received or the claim pack was requested, so that this subsection would apply.

Subs. (13). If attendance allowance, disability living allowance or disability working allowance is refused, any new claim within the three-month "prescribed period" is automatically treated as an application for a review. After that period, a person may either make a new claim or may apply for a review under subs. (2) or (5) or may do both. Then, the advantage of a review is that it may be possible to obtain an award of benefit from an earlier date but the disadvantage is that it is first necessary to make out one of the grounds for review under subs. (2).

The application of this provision to disability working allowance gives rise to complications because entitlement to disability working allowance depends very much on the claimant's circumstances at the date of claim. The main difficulty has been overcome by amending reg. 66(1) of the Social Security (Adjudication) Regulations 1995 so that a claimant is not prejudiced if he or she was rightly refused the allowance on the original claim but qualified by the date of the second claim. For difficulties that still arise where the claimant was wrongly refused the allowance on his or her first claim, see the note to reg. 6(11) of the Social Security (Claims and Payments) Regulations 1987.

Further reviews

31.—(1) Subsections (2), (4) and (5) of section 30 above shall apply to a decision on a review under subsection (1) of that section as they apply to a decision of an adjudication officer under section 21 above but as if the words "made after the end of the prescribed period" were omitted from each subsection.

(2) Subsections (1), (2), (4) and (5) of section 30 above shall apply—

(a) to a decision on a review under subsection (2), (4) or (5) of that section; and

(b) to a refusal to review a decision under subsection (2), (4) or (5) of that section,

as they apply to a decision of an adjudication officer under section 21 above.

(3) The claimant shall be given such notification as may be prescribed—

(a) of a decision on a review under section 30 above;

(b) if the review was under section 30(1), of his right of appeal under section 33 below; and

(c) if it was under section 30(2), (4) or (5), of his right to a further review under section 30(1).

Derivation

Social Security Act 1975, s.100B; Social Security Act 1986, s.52(3A).

General Note

Subss. (1) and (2). These are concerned with allowing review decisions to be reviewed in the same way as initial decisions by adjudication officers. A review decision under s.30(1) cannot be further reviewed under the same provision but may be reviewed under s.30(2), (4) or (5) as though it were an original decision. Since there is no possibility of a further review under s.30(1), an application for review on other grounds may take place at any time and the "prescribed period" is removed. A review decision under s.30(2), (4) or (5) may be reviewed in the same way as an initial decision, so any review within the prescribed period is made under s.30(1). A refusal to review is treated as a decision.

Subs. (3). Reg. 18 of the Social Security (Adjudication) Regulations 1995 provides that a claimant shall be notified in writing of any decision of an adjudication officer and of his or her right of appeal or to apply for a further review.

Reviews of decisions as to attendance allowance, disability living allowance or disability working allowance—supplementary

32.—(1) An award of an attendance allowance, a disability living allowance or a disability working allowance on a review under section 30 above replaces any award which was the subject of the review.

(2) Where a person who has been awarded a disability living allowance consisting of one component applies or is treated as applying for a review under section 30 above and alleges that he is also entitled to the other component, the adjudiction officer need not consider the question of his entitlement to the component which he has already been awarded or the rate of that component.

(3) Where a person who has been awarded a disability living allowance consisting of both components applies or is treated as applying for a review under section 30 above and alleges that he is entitled to one component at a rate higher than that at which it has been awarded, the adjudication officer need not consider the question of his entitlement to the other component or the rate of that component.

(4) Where a person has been awarded a component for life, on a review under section 30 above the adjudication officer shall not consider the question of his

entitlement to that component or the rate of that component or the period for which it has been awarded unless—

(a) the person awarded the component expressly applies for the consideration of that question; or

(b) [[1]there has been supplied to the adjudication officier by the Secretary of State, or is otherwise available to him, information] which gives him reasonable grounds for believing that entitlement to the component, or entitlement to it at the rate awarded or for that period, ought not to continue.

(5) No decision which relates to an attendance allowance or a disability living allowance shall be reviewed under section 30 above on the ground that the person is or was at any time terminally ill, within the meaning of section 66(2) of the Contributions and Benefits Act, unless an application for review is made expressly on that ground either—

(a) by the person himself; or

(b) by any other person purporting to act on his behalf, whether or not that other person is acting with his knowledge or authority;

and a decision may be so reviewed on such an application, notwithstanding that no claim under section 66(1) or 72(5) or 73(12) of that Act has been made.

(6) Where a decision is reviewed under section 30 above on the ground that it is anticipated that a change of circumstances will occur, the decision given on review—

(a) shall take effect on the day prescribed for that purpose by reference to the date on which the change of circumstances is expected to occur; and

(b) shall be reviewed again if the change of circumstances either does not occur or occurs otherwise than on that date.

(7) Where a claimant has appealed against a decision of an adjudication officer under section 33 below and the decision is reviewed again under section 30(2), (4) or (5) above by an adjudication officer, then—

(a) if the adjudication officer considers that the decision which he has made on the review is the same as the decision that would have been made on the appeal had every ground of the appeal succeeded, then the appeal shall lapse; but

(b) in any other case, the review shall be of no effect and the appeal shall proceed accordingly.

(8) Regulations may make provision restricting the payment of any benefit, or any increase of benefit, to which a person would, but for this subsection, be entitled by reason of a review in respect of any period before or after the review (whether that period falls wholly or partly before or after the making of the regulations).

(9) Where an adjudication officer has determined that any amount paid by way of an attendance allowance, a disability living allowance or a disability working allowance is recoverable under or by virtue of section 71 below, any person from whom he has determined that it is recoverable shall have the same right of review under section 30 above as a claimant.

(10) This Act and the Contributions and Benefits Act shall have effect in relation to a review by virtue of subsection (9) above as if any reference to the claimant were a reference to the person from whom the adjudication officer has determined that the amount in question is recoverable.

DERIVATION

Social Security Act 1975, s.100C; Social Security Act 1986, s.52(3A).

AMENDMENT

1. Social Security Administration (Fraud) Act 1997, s.17(2) (July 1, 1997).

GENERAL NOTE

Subs. (1). This makes it plain that an award on a review replaces the award being reviewed. The subsection is curiously incomplete because it does not deal with reviews of individual questions as opposed to reviews of claims. However, it is fairly well settled that a review decision always replaces the decision being reviewed at least to the extent that the original decision is revised on the review. In *R(A) 5/89* it was held that a review "on any ground" (which would now be a review under s.30(1)) replaces the original decision whether or not it results in a revision of the original decision. The Commissioners left open the question whether a review under what would now be s.30(2) or (5) replaces the original decision when it does not result in a revision.

In *Chief Adjudication Officer v. Eggleton* (March 17, 1995), the Court of Appeal held that a decision reviewed and partly revised under s.25 retained an existence so that there could be an appeal against the part not revised. In so deciding, they contrasted reviews under s.25 with reviews under s.30 to which s.32(1) applies. However, in *CDLA/805/94*, the Commissioner considered the effect of a review of a decision of a tribunal under s.35(1), to which s.32(1) applies by virtue of s.35(12), upon an appeal against the tribunal's decision. He held that the extent to which s.32(1) had the effect that the whole of the reviewed decision was replaced depended on the particular circumstances of the case. In that case the tribunal's decision had been reviewed on the ground of change of circumstances but had not been revised. On the facts of that case, the Commissioner held that the review decision did not wholly replace the tribunal's decision so as to cause the appeal to the Commissioner to lapse but, on the contrary, the review decision fell with the tribunal's decision when the Commissioner set the latter aside.

Subss. (2) and (3). The care and mobility components of disability living allowance may seem to be completely separate but, formally, the allowance is just one benefit. Therefore, a review raised in respect of one component invites inquiry into entitlement to the other (see *R(A) 2/90* discussed in the notes to s.30). These subsections relieve an adjudication officer of the requirement to consider entitlement to a component already awarded to a claimant if the claimant has merely sought a review in respect of the other component. However, an adjudication *may* still consider entitlement to the first component and will presumably do so if the evidence produced in support of the claim to the second component throws clear doubt on the correctness of the award of the first component. If an adjudication officer has not considered the question of entitlement to the first component, a disability appeal tribunal dealing with an appeal concerning the second could do so although it would be necessary to give the parties the opportunity of making representations on that new point. On the other hand, if the adjudication officer *has* considered the entitlement to the first component, it would seem that a tribunal dealing with the appeal would be bound to do so as well and could not simply decide that the adjudication officer should not have considered the issue, unless the award is for life and is covered by subs. (4). A tribunal may open up new issues but it may not refuse to deal with issues placed before it.

On the other hand, where there has not been an award of either component, an appeal to a tribunal which is directed solely at entitlement to one component does not relieve the tribunal of the duty to consider entitlement to both components if there is evidence which suggests that the claimant might be entitled to the other component (*CDLA/21/94*).

Subs. (4). This is intended to give some security to claimants who have life awards. If a claimant has a life award of a component of disability living allowance, an adjudication officer is not entitled to consider the claimant's entitlement to that component unless the claimant requests it or the adjudication officer has information giving reasonable grounds for believing that entitlement ought not to continue. It is presumably intended that the Department will not initiate inquiries which might generate information to place before an adjudication officer, but the subsection does not actually prohibit such inquiries. It is foreseeable that there will be cases where a disability appeal tribunal considers that the adjudication officer did not have grounds for beginning to consider the question of entitlement to the component but acquired sufficient information subsequently. It would not appear to be open to the tribunal to ignore the latest information even if it is clear that it would not have been obtained but for the adjudication officer embarking upon an investigation he ought not to have started.

Subs. (5). This enables a person who is already entitled to attendance allowance or disability living allowance and who becomes "terminally ill" to have the original award reviewed and obtain a new award at the higher or highest rates. The application for the review must be on the express ground that the claimant is terminally ill but may be made by someone else without the claimant's knowledge or authority. This makes such applications for review subject to the same conditions as an original claim on the ground of terminal illness.

Subs. (7). This is an attempt avoid the awkward problem, illustrated by *R(A) 5/89*, which can arise when a decision may be subject to both an appeal and a review. Because a review decision replaces the decision being reviewed, an appeal pending against the original decision must lapse if the original decision is reviewed. A new appeal would have to be initiated against the review decision if the claimant had still not got all he or she wanted. This subsection provides that, if an appeal is pending against the original decision, the review is of no effect unless the claimant is given everything he or she could obtain on the appeal. This may involve an element of judgment because the scope of an appeal is not always clear. The subsection also replaces the procedural problem with another, practical, one. If the adjudication officer is happy to award the claimant part of what he or she is seeking, why should the claimant be prevented from receiving the appropriate benefit while an appeal is continued in respect of another aspect of the case? In practice, the equivalent provision relevant to most appeals to social security appeal tribunals (s.29) is sometimes ignored by adjudication officers when that is to the advantage of claimants. That approach might in some cases be justified by regarding the review and the appeal as being in respect of different questions arising from the same claim (see s.20(5) and 30(10)). Otherwise, tribunals need to be careful to record the correct decision on the appeal before them. If the tribunal agrees with the adjudication officer as to the conclusion but considers that the review should not have had any effect, it is wrong simply to dismiss the appeal. Instead, the tribunal should hold the review to have been of no effect and allow the appeal against the original decision to the extent they feel correct. Whether any benefit paid under the invalid review decision is to be treated, under reg. 5 of the Social Security (Payments on account, Overpayments and Recovery) Regulations 1988, as having been paid on account of benefit due under the tribunal's decision is a moot point since it is difficult to say that it was paid "under an award which is subsequently varied on appeal".

Subs. (8). See regs. 59 and 66 of the Social Security (Adjudication) Regulations 1995. For other limitations see s.69.

Subss. (9) and (10). S. 71(3) provides that overpayments of benefit are recoverable from any person whose misrepresentation or failure to disclose material facts led to the overpayment. Normally that person is the claimant but, where it is someone else, that person is to have the right to apply for a review of (and therefore to appeal against) the decision, just as a claimant would. The wording is wide enough to enable the person to apply for a review of the decision that the claimant was not entitled to the benefit as well as the consequential decision that the overpayment is recoverable.

Appeals following reviews

33.—(1) Where an adjudication officer has given a decision on a review under section 30(1) above, the claimant or such other person as may be prescribed may appeal—

(a) in prescribed cases, to a disability appeal tribunal; and

(b) in any other case, to a social security appeal tribunal.

(2) Regulations may make provision as to the manner in which, and the time within which, appeals are to be brought.

(3) An award on an appeal under this section replaces any award which was the subject of the appeal.

(4) Where a person who has been awarded a disability living allowance consisting of one component alleges on an appeal that he is also entitled to the other component, the tribunal need not consider the question of his entitlement to the component which he has already been awarded or the rate of that component.

(5) Where a person who has been awarded a disability living allowance consisting of both components alleges on an appeal that he is entitled to one component at a rate higher than that at which it has been awarded, the tribunal need not consider the question of his entitlement to the other component or the rate of that component.

(6) The tribunal shall not consider—

(a) a person's entitlement to a component which has been awarded for life; or

(b) the rate of a component so awarded; or

(c) the period for which a component has been so awarded,

unless—

(i) the appeal expressly raises that question; or

(ii) information is available to the tribunal which gives it reasonable grounds for believing that entitlement to the component, or entitlement to it at the rate awarded or for that period, ought not to continue.

DERIVATION

Social Security Act 1975, s.100D; Social Security Act 1986, s.52(3A).

GENERAL NOTE

This section provides for an appeal against any review decision made under s.30(1). No appeal lies against a review decision under s.30(2), (4) or (5); it is necessary for a claimant first to apply for such a review decision to be itself reviewed under s.30(1) (s.31(2)). For the constitution of disability appeal tribunals see ss.42 and 43.

Subs. (1). Some appeals are heard by disability appeal tribunals and some by social security appeal tribunals. Under reg. 27 of the Social Security (Adjudication) Regulations 1995, appeals are heard by a disability appeal tribunal if they involve a "disability question". If there is some other question as well as a disability question, both questions may be considered by a disability appeal tribunal. Otherwise, questions other than disability questions must be considered by social security appeal tribunals. "Disability question" is defined in reg. 27 to include any question as to the satisfaction of the attendance conditions for the care component for disability living allowance or attendance allowance, the mobility conditions for the mobility component of disability allowance, or the condition for disability working allowance that a claimant has a physical or mental disability which puts him at a disadvantage in getting a job. Questions as to the period throughout which a person is likely to satisfy the conditions or entitlement to attendance allowance or disability living allowance and as to the rate of payment of those allowances are also disability questions.

A disability appeal tribunal should consider not just entitlement at the date of claim but also entitlement down to the date of their decision (*CDLA/2/93*). They must also consider entitlement to both components of disability living allowance if the evidence raises the possibility of entitlement to both, even though the appeal was directed only to one component (*CDLA/21/94*). *Appeal * after 21/5/98

If a disability appeal tribunal has heard an appeal concerning both a disability question and another question, and wishes to determine the disability question and to defer consideration of the other question pending the provision of more information, it is not open to the tribunal to direct that the next hearing should be before a social security appeal tribunal. The claimant would have appealed "to a disability appeal tribunal".

Under reg. 28 of the Adjudication Regulations, a person purporting to act on behalf of a terminally ill person has the same rights of appeal as a claimant.

In *CSDLA/178/94*, the Commissioner said:

> "The whole system of claiming and appealing in disability allowance cases is dependent upon the presentation of adequate evidence to enable the tribunal to determine the case before them. Claimants, their representatives and adjudication officers have responsibilities in that regard—particularly the adjudication officers whose respective responsibilities are to decide the claim and to carry out a review of that decision following a valid request to do so. Adjudication officers have the powers to call for medical evidence and provided they select with discernment the medical enquiry forms which contain the questions appropriate to the evidence required both adjudication officers and disability appeal tribunals will be in a better position to make proper findings of fact. There are far too many cases relating to disability living allowance where adequate evidence is not presented and the findings [of] fact are in consequence inadequate."

Subs. (2). See reg. 3 of and Sched. 2 to the Adjudication Regulations.

Subs. (3). If an award is varied on appeal, the new award replaces the old one. It is not made clear whether there is an "award" when a tribunal dismisses an appeal and does not vary an award by an adjudication officer.

Subss. (4) and (5). These provisions mirror s.32(2) and (3) which provides for similar restrictions on review. The intention is plainly to limit the extent to which a claimant may put in jeopardy an award of one component of disability living allowance when appealing against a decision in respect of the other. However, both subsections provide only that the tribunal "need not" consider entitlement to the other component. There is therefore a discretionary power to consider the other component which must be exercised judicially. Since the provisions are for the purpose of protecting claimants, it would usually be appropriate to exercise the power if it appears to the tribunal that the claimant might benefit from it because it appears that he or she ought to be entitled to the other component at a higher rate (*CDLA/21/94*)—provided, of course, that the adjudication officer is given the chance to deal with the point. Equally, when there is clear evidence that the claimant ought not to be entitled to the other component a tribunal ought not to ignore it but must give the claimant the opportunity of making proper representations on the issue. What a tribunal should not do is to consider removing entitlement to the other component in a case when the evidence is not clear and it would merely be a question of substituting one tribunal's judgment for that of the adjudication officer. This therefore limits the effect of *R(A) 2/90* in which it was suggested that when entitlement was challenged, every aspect of the decision is open to scrutiny. Where a component has been awarded for life, further restrictions are imposed by subs. (6).

Subs. (6). This mirrors s.32(4). Where there is an award of a component for life, the tribunal may not consider the claimant's entitlement to it, the rate at which it is paid or the period for which it has been awarded unless *either* the appeal expressly raises that question *or* the tribunal has information giving it reasonable grounds for believing that entitlement ought not to continue as before. Under the first limb, a claimant does not put in jeopardy a life award of one component by appealing against a decision relating to the other. However, an appeal against a life award of, say, the lower rate of the mobility component by a claimant seeking the higher rate of the same component does put in jeopardy the life award of the lower rate. The value of this protection is somewhat undermined by the second limb allowing a tribunal to consider a life award if in possession of information giving reasonable grounds for believing that the life award should not continue. This requires some fairly clear evidence suggesting that the life award should not continue. The fact that a tribunal takes a different view of evidence that was before the adjudication officer is not enough, if the view of the adjudication officer was a legitimate one. Often there will be new evidence before the tribunal but the effect that this subsection has is that the life award is not to be disturbed unless the new evidence is clearly inconsistent with it. Nor may a tribunal adjourn in order to obtain such evidence. In *CSDLA/251/94* and *CDLA/7082/95* the claimants were in receipt of the mobility component at the higher rate and, on appeals relating to the care component, tribunals decided that the claimants were not entitled to the mobility component simply because they could walk 120 or 150 yards. The Commissioners set aside the decisions on the grounds that those findings were not enough to show that the claimants were not entitled to the mobility component. There had to be information showing that the claimants satisfied *none* of the different grounds for qualifying for the mobility component before it could be taken away.

Appeal from social security appeal tribunals or disability appeal tribunals to Commissioners and appeals from Commissioners

34.—(1) Subject to the provisions of this section, an appeal lies to a Commissioner from any decision of a social security appeal tribunal or disability appeal tribunal under section 33 above on the ground that the decision of the tribunal was erroneous in point of law.

(2) An appeal lies under this section at the instance of any of the following—

(a) an adjudication officer;

(b) the claimant;

(c) a trade union—

(i) where the claimant is a member of the union at the time of the appeal and was so immediately before the question at issue arose;

(ii) where that question in any way relates to a deceased person who was a member of the union at the time of his death; and

(d) a person from whom it is determined that any amount is recoverable under section 71(1) below.

(3) Subsection (2) above, as it applies to a trade union, applies also to any other association which exists to promote the interests and welfare of its members.

(4) Subsection (7) to (10) of section 23 above have effect for the purposes of this section as they have effect for the purposes of that section.

(5) Section 24 above applies to a decision of a Commissioner under this section as it applies to a decision of a Commissioner under section 23 above.

Derivation

Subss. (1)–(4): Social Security Act 1975, s.101; Social Security Act 1986, s.52(3) and (3A).
Subs. (5): Social Security Act 1980, s.14.

GENERAL NOTE

The Commissioners have two offices, at Harp House, 83 Farringdon Street, London EC4A 4DH and at 23 Melville Street, Edinburgh EH3 7PW. Most appeals to Commissioners are dealt with by way of written submissions (see regs. 10 and 11 of the Social Security Commissioners Procedure Regulations 1987) but claimants may ask for oral hearings (regs. 15–17). Oral hearings usually take place at one of the offices (cases from the far north of England being heard in Edinburgh when that is more convenient although English law is applied) but the Commissioners also regularly travel to sit at the law courts in Cardiff. If a claimant is disabled and would have great difficulty in travelling to one of those centres, it is possible to ask the Commissioners' office to arrange a hearing in a more local court building.

Commissioners are of the same standing as circuit judges. Nevertheless, they have no power to award costs to successful claimants (or adjudication officers) (see *R(FC) 2/90*). Nor is legal aid available for proceedings before Commissioners.

Subs. (1). An appeal lies only on a point of law. The Commissioners have long held there to be five ways in which a tribunal's decision may be erroneous in point of law (see in particular *R(A) 1/72* and *R(SB) 11/83*):

(1) The decision contains a false proposition of law *ex facie*, in other words the tribunal has recorded a misinterpretation of the law;
(2) The decision is unsupported by evidence;
(3) The facts found are such that no person acting judicially and properly instructed as to the relevant law could have come to the determination in question. This means that it must be implicit in the decision that either the tribunal ignored some relevant evidence or else misinterpreted the law although they have not clearly recorded the misinterpretation;
(4) There has been a breach of the rules of natural justice. These rules are concerned with procedural justice and may be summarised as the rule that every party to the proceedings should have a proper opportunity to present his or her case and the rule against bias;
(5) A failure to comply with the statutory requirements to record findings of fact and reasons for the decision (regs. 23(2), 29(5) and 38(4)) of the Social Security (Adjudication) Regulations 1995).

In *R(A) 1/72*, the Commissioner said:

> "The obligation to give reasons for the decision ... imports a requirement to do more than only to state the conclusion, and for the determining authority to state that on the evidence the authority is not satisfied that the statutory conditions are met, does no more than this. It affords no guide to the selective process by which the evidence has been accepted, rejected, weighed or considered, or the reasons for any of these things. It is not, of course, obligatory thus to deal with every piece of evidence or to over-elaborate, but in an administrative quasi-judicial decision the minimum requirement must at least be that the claimant, looking at the decision should be able to discern on the face of it the reasons why the evidence has failed to satisfy the authority."

However, in *Baron v. Secretary of State for Social Services* (reported as an appendix to *R(M) 6/86*), the Court of Appeal stressed that there are limits to the extent that it is possible to give reasons for decisions on matters of judgment such as the distance a claimant could walk without having to stop or the extent of breathlessness and pain which caused him to do so. For further consideration of the standard of reasons, see the note to reg. 29(5) of the Social Security (Adjudication) Regulations 1995.

Subs. (2). It is to be noted that not everyone who has a right to be heard before a tribunal as being "interested in the proceedings" (see reg. 4(5) of the Social Security (Adjudication) Regulations 1995 and the definition of "party to the proceedings" in reg. 1(2)) has the right to appeal. More seriously, there is no provision allowing an appeal to a Commissioner by a person acting on behalf of a terminally ill person without his or her knowledge or authority even though such a person has a right of appeal to a tribunal under reg. 28 of the Adjudication Regulations.

Reviews of decisions on appeal

35.—(1) Any decision under this Act of a social security appeal tribunal, a disability appeal tribunal or a Commissioner which relates to an attendance allowance or a disability living allowance may be reviewed at any time by an adjudication officer if—

(a) he is satisfied that the decision was given in ignorance of, or was based on a mistake as to, some material fact; or

(b) there has been any relevant change of circumstances since the decision was given; or

(c) it is anticipated that a relevant change of circumstances will so occur; or

(d) the decision was that a person is or was at any time terminally ill for the purposes of section 66(1), 72(5) or 73(12) of the Contributions and Benefits Act and there has been a change of medical opinion with respect to his condition or his reasonable expectation of life; or

(e) the decision was to make an award for a period wholly or partly after the date on which the claim was made or treated as made but subject to a condition being fulfilled and that condition has not been fulfilled,

but regulations may provide that a decision may not be reviewed on the ground mentioned in paragraph (a) above unless the officer is satisfied as mentioned in that paragraph by fresh evidence.

(2) Regulations may prescribe what are, or are not, relevant changes of circumstances for the purposes of subsection (1)(b) and (c) above.

(3) Any decision under this Act of a social security appeal tribunal, a disability appeal tribunal or a Commissioner which relates to a disability working allowance may be reviewed at any time by an adjudication officer if—

(a) he is satisfied that the decision was given in ignorance of, or was based on a mistake as to, some material fact; or

(b) subject to section 129(7) of the Contributions and Benefits Act, there has been any prescribed change of circumstances since the decision was given; or

(c) the decision was to make an award for a period wholly or partly after the date on which the claim was made or treated as made but subject to a conditon being fulfilled and that condition has not been fulfilled,

but regulations may provide that a decision may not be reviewed on the ground mentioned in paragraph (a) above unless the officer is satisfied as mentioned in that paragraph by fresh evidence.

(4) A question may be raised with a view to a review under this section by means of an application made in writing to an adjudication officer, stating the grounds of the application and supplying such information and evidence as may be prescribed.

(5) Regulations may provide for enabling or requiring, in prescribed circumstances, a review under this section notwithstanding that no application for a review has been made under subsection (4) above.

(6) Reviews under this section shall be carried out by adjudication officers.

(7) Except in prescribed circumstances, where a claim for a disability living allowance in respect of a person already awarded such an allowance on an appeal is made or treated as made during the period for which he has been awarded the allowance, it shall be treated as an application for a review under this section.

(8) Subsections (1), (2), (4) and (5) of section 30 above shall apply—

(a) to a decision on a review under this section; and

(b) to a refusal to review a decision such as is mentioned in subsection (1) above,

as they apply to a decision of an adjudication officer under section 21 above.

(9) The person whose claim was the subject of the appeal the decision on which has been reviewed under this section shall be given such notification as may be prescribed—

(a) of the decision on the review; and

(b) of his right to a further review under section 30(1) above.

(10) Regulations may make provision restricting the payment of any benefit, or any increase of benefit, to what a person would, but for this subsection, be entitled by reason of a review in respect of any period before or after the review

(whether that period falls wholly or partly before or after the making of the regulations).

(11) Where a decision is reviewed on the ground mentioned in subsection (1)(c) above, the decision given on the review—

(a) shall take effect on the day prescribed for that purpose by reference to the date on which the relevant change of circumstances is expected to occur; and

(b) shall be reviewed again if the relevant change of circumstances either does not occur or occurs otherwise than on that date.

(12) Section 30(10) above and section 32(1) to (5) above shall apply in relation to a review under this section as they apply to a review under section 30 above.

DERIVATION

Social Security Act 1975, s.104A; Social Security Act 1986, s.52(3A).

GENERAL NOTE

Under this section, adjudication officers may review decisions of social security appeal tribunals, disability appeal tribunals or Social Security Commissioners concerning attendance allowance, disability living allowance or disability working allowance. This section therefore complements s.30(2) under which decisions of adjudication officers may be reviewed.

Subs. (1). See the notes to s.30(2). No regulations have been made requiring "fresh evidence".

Subs. (2). See reg. 67A of the Social Security (Adjudication) Regulations 1995.

Subs. (3). See notes to s.30(5). No regulations have been made requiring "fresh evidence".

Subs. (4). Whereas the power to review under s.30(2) or (5) arises only on an application being made, the power to review a decision of a tribunal or Commissioner under s.35 may be exercised by an adjudication officer of his or her own initiative. In *CSB/336/87*, it was held that s.104(2) of the Social Security Act 1975, which was in similar terms to s.35(4), did not require an application to be made in writing in all cases.

Subs. (7). See the note to s.30(12).

Subs. (8). This enables a decision under this section to be further reviewed by an adjudication officer. In particular, it enables a person to apply for a review within the prescribed period under s.30A(1) so as to open the way for an appeal under s.33. For this purpose, a refusal to review under subs. (1) is treated as a decision.

Subs. (9). See reg. 18 of the Social Security (Adjudication) Regulations 1995.

Subs. (11). These provisions are concerned with the date from which the review is to be effective. See also regs. 57–59 and 66 of the Social Security (Adjudication) Regulations 1995.

Subs. (12). For the application of s.32(1) to this section, see *CDLA/805/94*.

Questions first arising on appeal

Questions first arising on appeal

36.—(1) Where a question which but for this section would fall to be determined by an adjudication officer first arises in the course of an appeal to a social security appeal tribunal, a disability appeal tribunal or a Commissioner, the tribunal, subject to subsection (2) below, or the Commissioner may, if they or he think fit, proceed to determine the question notwithstanding that it has not been considered by an adjudication officer.

(2) A social security appeal tribunal may not determine a question by virtue of subsection (1) above if an appeal in relation to such a question would have lain to a disability appeal tribunal.

DERIVATION

Social Security Act 1975, s.102; Social Security Act 1986, s.52(3) and (3A).

GENERAL NOTE

This is a useful provision that is often overlooked. It enables a tribunal to deal with any question relevant to the appeal even though the adjudication officer has not considered it first. The question must "arise in the course of appeal" and so be relevant to the determination of the appeal (*CS/101/86*) and it must "first" arise in the course of the appeal. Thus, in *CS/104/89*, it was held that a tribunal cannot consider, under what is now s.36, a question which has already been determined by an adjudication officer. Presumably, in such a case, the tribunal could invite an appeal against the adjudication officer's decision if the interests of justice demanded that the question be reconsidered. A tribunal should be careful to ensure that all parties have the opportunity of making representations concerning the new question (*R(F) 1/72*).

Reference of special questions

Reference of special questions

37.—(1) Subject to subsection (2) below—

(a) if on consideration of any claim or question an adjudication officer is of opinion that there arises any question which under or by virtue of this Act falls to be determined otherwise than by an adjudication officer, he shall refer the question for such determination; and

(b) if on consideration of any claim or question a social security appeal tribunal or Commissioner is of opinion that any such question arises, the tribunal or Commissioner shall direct it to be referred by an adjudication officer for such determination.

(2) The person or tribunal making or directing the reference shall then deal with any other question as if the referred question had not arisen.

(3) The adjudication officer, tribunal or Commissioner may—

(a) postpone the reference of, or dealing with, any question until other questions have been determined;

(b) in cases where the determination of any question disposes of a claim or any part of it, make an award or decide that an award cannot be made, as to the claim or that part of it, without referring or dealing with, or before the determination of, any other question.

DERIVATION

Social Security Act 1975, s.103; Social Security Act 1986, s.52(3) and (3A).

GENERAL NOTE

The questions which fall to be decided otherwise than by an adjudication officer are those which fall to be decided by the Secretary of State (s.17 and regulations under s.58(1)(a)) and the disablement questions which normally fall to be determined by an adjudicating medical authority (s.45(2)). Presumably the section has not been applied to disability appeal tribunals because it is not anticipated that any such question might arise before such a tribunal. It is certainly difficult to envisage any of the questions covered by s.17 or s.45 arising in a case before a disability appeal tribunal but there are several more relevant questions which fall to be determined by the Secretary of State under regulations made under s.58(1)(a) including, in particular, what can constitute a valid claim. However, even in the absence of an express provision like this section, a disability appeal tribunal would be bound to adjourn while such a question was considered by the Secretary of State, unless the claim was bound to fail for some other reason.

Adjudication officers and the Chief Adjudication Officer

Adjudication officers

38.—(1) Adjudication officers shall be appointed by the Secretary of State, subject to the consent of the Treasury as to number, and may include—
(a) officers of the Department of Employment appointed with the concurrence of the Secretary of State in charge of that Department; or
(b) officers of the Northern Ireland Department appointed with the concurrence of that Department.

(2) An adjudication officer may be appointed to perform all the functions of adjudication officers under any enactment or such functions of such officers as may be specified in his instrument of appointment.

Derivation

Social Security Act 1975, s.97(1) and (1A).

General Note

Subs. (2) Some adjudication officers are appointed just to deal with specific functions. S.20(5) provides that different aspects of the same claim or question may be dealt with by different adjudication officers.

The Chief Adjudication Officer

39.—(1) The Secretary of State shall appoint a Chief Adjudication Officer.

(2) It shall be the duty of the Chief Adjudication Officer to advise adjudication officers on the performance of their functions under this or any other Act.

(3) The Chief Adjudication Officer shall keep under review the operation of the system of adjudication by adjudication officers and matters connected with the operation of that system.

(4) The Chief Adjudication Officer shall report annually in writing to the Secretary of State on the standards of adjudication and the Secretary of State shall publish his report.

Derivation

Social Security Act 1975, s.97(1B)–(1E).

General Note

Subs. (2) The *Adjudication Officers' Guide*, a looseleaf work in 13 substantial volumes, is published by HMSO.

Social Security appeal tribunals

Panels for appointment to social security appeal tribunals

40.—(1) The President shall constitute for the whole of Great Britain, to act for such areas as he thinks fit and be composed of such persons as he thinks fit to appoint, panels of persons to act as members of social security appeal tribunals.

(2) The panel for an area shall be composed of persons appearing to the President to have knowledge or experience of conditions in the area and to be representative of persons living or working in the area.

(3) Before appointing members of a panel, the President shall take into consideration any recommendations from such organisations or persons as he considers appropriate.

(4) The members of the panels shall hold office for such period as the President may direct, but the President may at any time terminate the appointment of any member of a panel.

DERIVATION

Social Security Act 1975, Sched. 10, para. 1(1)–(6).

Constitution of social security appeal tribunals

41.—(1) A social security tribunal shall consist of a chairman and two other persons.

(2) The members other than the chairman shall be drawn from the appropriate panel constituted under section 40 above.

(3) The President shall nominate the chairman.

(4) The President may nominate as chairman—

(a) himself;

(b) one of the full-time chairmen appointed under section 51(1) below; or

(c) a person drawn from the panel appointed by the Lord Chancellor or, as the case may be, the Lord President of the Court of Session under [[1]section 6 of the Tribunals and Inquiries Act 1992].

(5) No person shall be appointed chairman of a tribunal under subsection (4)(c) above unless he has a five year general qualification or he is an advocate or solicitor in Scotland of at least five years' standing.

(6) If practicable, at least one of the members of the appeal tribunal hearing a case shall be of the same sex as the claimant.

(7) Schedule 2 to this Act shall have effect for supplementing this section.

DERIVATION

Subss. (1)–(5): Social Security Act 1975, s.97(2)–(2E).
Subs. (6): Social Security Act 1975, Sched. 10, para. 1(8).
Subs. (7): Social Security Act 1975, s.97(4).

AMENDMENT

1. Tribunals and Inquiries Act 1992, Sched. 3, para. 36 (October 1, 1992).

GENERAL NOTE

Social security appeal tribunals deal with all appeals from adjudication officers except those allocated to disability appeal tribunals (s.33(1)(a) of this Act and reg. 27 of the Social Security (Adjudication) Regulations 1995) or medical boards (reg. 48 of the Social Security (Adjudication) Regulations 1995).

Subs. (5). See the note to s.43(6).

Subs. (6). See the note to s.43(8).

Disability appeal tribunals

Panels for appointment to disability appeal tribunals

42.—(1) The President shall constitute for the whole of Great Britain, to act for such areas as he thinks fit and be composed of such persons as he thinks fit to appoint, panels of persons to act as members of disability appeal tribunals.

(2) There shall be two panels for each area.

(3) One panel shall be composed of medical practitioners.

(4) The other shall be composed of persons who are experienced in dealing with the needs of disabled persons—

(a) in a professional or voluntary capacity; or
(b) because they are themselves disabled,
but may not include medical practitioners.

(5) In considering the appointment of members of the panels the President shall have regard to the desirability of appointing disabled persons.

(6) Before appointing members of a panel, the President shall take into consideration any recommendations from such organisations or persons as he considers appropriate.

(7) The members of the panels shall hold office for such periods as the President may direct, but the President may at any time terminate the appointment of any member of a panel.

DERIVATION

Subss. (1)–(5): Social Security Act 1975, Sched. 10A, paras. 3–7.
Subss. (6)–(7): Social Security Act 1975, Sched. 10, para. 1(2A) and (6) and Sched. 10A, para. 8.

GENERAL NOTE

In *CDLA/224/94* the Commissioner held that there was no real danger of bias arising from the fact that a medical practictioner who was a member of a disability appeal tribunal was also a part-time adjudicating medical practitioner appointed by the Secretary of State under section 49.

Constitution of disability appeal tribunals

43.—(1) A disability appeal tribunal shall consist of a chairman and two other persons.

(2) Of the members of a tribunal other than the chairman, one shall be drawn from the panel mentioned in subsection (3) of section 42 above.

(3) The other shall be drawn from the panel mentioned in subsection (4) of that section.

(4) The President shall nominate the chairman.

(5) The President may nominate as chairman—
(a) himself;
(b) one of the full-time chairmen appointed under section 51(1) below; or
(c) person drawn from the panel appointed by the Lord Chancellor or, as the case may be, the Lord President of the Court of Session under [[1]section 6 of the Tribunals and Inquiries Act 1992].

(6) No person shall be appointed chairman of a tribunal under subsection (5)(c) above unless he has a five year general qualification or he is an advocate or solicitor in Scotland of at least five years' standing.

(7) In summoning members of a panel to serve on a tribunal, the clerk to the tribunal shall have regard to the desirability of at least one of the members of the tribunal being a disabled person.

(8) If practicable, at least one of the members of the tribunal shall be of the same sex as the claimant.

(9) Schedule 2 to this Act shall have effect for supplementing this section.

DERIVATION

Subss. (1)–(3): Social Security Act 1975, Sched. 10A, paras. 1, 9 and 10.
Subss. (4)–(6): Social Security Act 1975, s. 97(2C)-(2E) and Sched. 10A, para. 2.
Subss. (7) and (8): Social Security Act 1975, Sched. 10A, paras. 12 and 13.

AMENDMENT

1. Tribunals and Inquiries Act 1992, Sched. 3, para. 36 (October 1, 1992).

GENERAL NOTE

Subs.(8) in R(SB) 2/88, it was held that a requirement that at least one member of the tribunal should be of the same sex as the claimant "if practicable" is mandatory. If there is no member of the same sex as the claimant, the chairman should ask the clerk why and should record the reason on the tribunal's record of proceedings (Form AT3 or DAT 28). This is slightly unreal as the clerk present on the day is unlikely to know the answer to the question and the practical difficulties are acknowledged in the Commissioner's decision. The failure to deal with this issue on Form AT3 or DAT 28 is not fatal. However, if the tribunal is all of the opposite sex to the claimant, it will be presumed to be invalidly constituted unless the contrary is shown, should the issue arise on an appeal to the Commissioner. Should the situation arise, the chairman may think it appropriate to draw the matter to the claimant's attention and offer an adjournment.

In *CS/99/93* it was held that a claimant was entitled to waive his or her right to have at least one member of the tribunal of the same sex as him or her, notwithstanding that the requirement was mandatory.

Adjudication in relation to industrial injuries and disablement benefit

Declaration that accident is an industrial accident

44.—(1) Where, in connection with any claim for industrial injuries benefit, it is determined that the relevant accident was or was not an industrial accident, an express declaration of that fact shall be made and recorded and (subject to subsection (3) below) a claimant shall be entitled to have the question whether the relevant accident was an industrial accident determined notwithstanding that his claim is disallowed on other grounds.

(2) Subject to subsection (3) below and to section 60 below, any person suffering personal injury by accident shall be entitled, if he claims the accident was an industrial accident, to have that question determined, and a declaration made and recorded accordingly, notwithstanding that no claim for benefit has been made in connection with which the question arises; and this Part of this Act applies for that purpose as if the question had arisen in connection with a claim for benefit.

(3) The adjudication officer, social security appeal tribunal or Commissioner (as the case may be) may refuse to determine the question whether an accident was an industrial accident if satisfied that it is unlikely to be necessary to determine the question for the purposes of any claim for benefit; but any such refusal of an adjudication officer or social security appeal tribunal shall be subject to appeal to a social security appeal tribunal or Commissioner, as the case may be.

(4) Subject to the provisions of this Part of this Act as to appeal and review, any declaration under this section that an accident was or was not an industrial accident shall be conclusive for the purposes of any claim for industrial injuries benefit in respect of that accident.

(5) Where subsection (4) above applies—

(a) in relation to a death occurring before 11th April 1988; or

(b) for the purposes of section 60(2) of the Contributions and Benefits Act,

it shall have effect as if at the end there were added the words "whether or not the claimant is the person at whose instance the declaration was made."

(6) For the purposes of this section (but subject to section 60(3) below), an accident whereby a person suffers personal injury shall be deemed, in relation to him, to be an industrial accident if—

(a) it arises out of and in the course of his employment;

(b) that employment is employed earner's employment for the purposes of Part V of the Contributions and Benefits Act;

(c) payment of benefit is not under section 94(5) of that Act precluded because the accident happened while he was outside Great Britain.

(7) A decision under this section shall be final except that sections 25 to 29 above apply to a decision under this section that an accident was or was not an industrial accident as they apply to a decision under sections 21 to 23 above if, but only if, the adjudication officer or social security appeal tribunal, as the case may be, is satisfied that the decision under this section was given in consequence of any wilful non-disclosure or misrepresentation of a material fact.

DERIVATION

Social Security Act 1975, s.107.

GENERAL NOTE

This section provides for an adjudication officer to make a declaration that a person has suffered an industrial accident, whether or not there has been a claim for benefit and whether or not any claim has any prospects of success on other grounds, although, under subs. (3), the adjudication officer (or a tribunal or Commissioner) may refuse to determine that question if it is unlikely there will ever be a claim for benefit.

A determination that there was or was not an industrial accident is conclusive for the purposes of later claims for benefit. However, it is important to note that this section is expressed to be subject to s.60(3), so that a decision under this section which implies that a person has suffered personal injury as a result of an accident does not require an adjudicating medical authority to find that the claimant has suffered disablement as a result of the injury even though the two decisions may appear, in the circumstances of the case, to contradict one another.

The usual rights of appeal apply to declarations under this section, but the power to review such decisions is strictly limited, by subs. (7), to cases of *wilful* non-disclosure or mis-representation of a material fact.

Disablement questions

45.—(1) In relation to industrial injuries benefit and severe disablement allowance, the "disablement questions" are the questions—

(a) in relation to industrial injuries benefit, whether the relevant accident has resulted in a loss of faculty;

(b) in relation to both benefits, at what degree the extent of disablement resulting from a loss of faculty is to be assessed, and what period is to be taken into account by the assessment;

but questions relating to the aggregation of percentages of disablement resulting from different accidents are not disablement questions (and accordingly fall to be determined by an adjudication officer).

(2) Subject to and in accordance with regulations, the disablement questions shall be referred to and determined—

(a) by an adjudicating medical practitioner; or

(b) by two or more adjudicating medical practitioners; or

(c) by a medical appeal tribunal; or

(d) in such cases relating to severe disablement allowance as may be prescribed, by an adjudication officer.

(3) Where—

(a) the case of a claimant for disablement benefit has been referred by the adjudication officer to one or more adjudicating medical practitioners for determination of the disablement questions; and

(b) on that or any subsequent reference, the extent of the disablement is provisionally assessed,

the case shall again be referred under this section, to one or more adjudicating medical practitioners as regulations may provide for the purposes of such subsequent references, not later than the end of the period taken into account by the provisional assessment.

(4) Where, in the case of a claimant for disablement benefit, the extent of any disablement of his resulting from an aggregable accident (that is to say, an accident other than the one which is the basis of the claim in question) has been assessed in accordance with paragraph 6(3) of Schedule 6 to the Contributions and Benefits Act at less than 14 per cent., then—

(a) the adjudication officer may refer the disablement questions relating to the aggregable accident to one or more adjudicating medical practitioners for fresh determination; and

(b) on any such reference—

(i) those questions shall be determined as at the first day of the common period; and

(ii) the period to be taken into account shall be the period beginning with that day.

(5) In subsection (4) above "the first day of the common period" means whichever is the later of—

(a) the first day of the period taken into account by the assessment of the extent of the claimant's disablement resulting from the accident which is the basis of the claim in question;

(b) the first day of the period taken into account by the assessment of the extent of his disablement resulting from the aggregable accident.

(6) In the following provisions of this Act "adjudicating medical practitioner" means, in relation to any case, one such practitioner, unless regulations applicable to cases of that description provide for references to more than one.

DERIVATION

Social Security Act 1975, s.108.

GENERAL NOTE

Subs. (1). This defines the "disablement questions" for industrial injuries benefit (*i.e.* disablement benefit and reduced earnings allowance) and severe disablement allowance. Essentially there are four questions, although the second is not relevant for severe disablement allowance.

(a) Is there one or more loss of faculty?

(b) Is any loss of faculty the result of the relevant accident?

(c) What is the degree of disablement resulting from that loss of faculty?

(d) What period is to be taken into account by the assessment?

By virtue of Sched. 2 to the Social Security (Industrial Injuries) (Prescribed Diseases) Regulations 1985, this section applies in industrial disease cases with the modification that references to "relevant accident" are to be read as references to "relevant disease". Determining the date of onset of an industrial disease involves the consideration of a disablement question and is accordingly a matter for the medical authorities (*CI/774/93*).

Aggregating (under Social Security Contributions and Benefits Act 1992, s.103(2)) percentages of disablement arising from different accidents is not a disablement question and so does not fall within the province to adjudicating medical authorities. It follows from this that in a disablement benefit case, the exercise of rounding an assessment to the nearest multiple of 10, under s.103(3), is not a function for adjudicating medical authorities. On the other hand, in a severe disablement allowance case the similar exercise of rounding an assessment under (Social Security Contributions and Benefits Act 1992, Sched. 6, para. 5) *is* to be carried out by the adjudicating medical authority.

Subs. (2). The disablement questions are generally to be determined by adjudicating medical authorities. The only exceptions are those cases relating to severe disablement allowance where the Department of Social Security has an official record showing that the claimant has already had his or her disablement assessed as 80 per cent or that he or she is entitled to a relevant benefit. Such cases are determined by an adjudication officer under reg. 10(3) of the Social Security (Severe Disablement Allowance) Regulations 1984.

Regs. 34–42 of the Social Security (Adjudication) Regulations 1995 provide for medical adjudication.

Subs. (3). Where there has been a provisional assessment (under Social Security Contribution and Benefits Act 1992, Sched. 6, para. 6(2)), the case is automatically referred back to an adjudicating medical practitioner not later than the end of the period of the provisional assessment. The referral may then be to a single adjudicating medical practitioner notwithstanding that the provisional assessment was made by a review medical board (*Parker v. Secretary of State for Social Security* reported as an appendix to *R(I) 2/90*).

Subss. (4) and (5). Where an assessment falls between 1 per cent and 14 per cent, it is not generally necessary for an adjudicating medical authority to specify in any more detail what the assessment is and (under Social Security Contribution and Benefits Act 1992, Sched. 6, para. 6(3) and (7)) an adjudicating medical authority should not attempt to do so. However, it may become necessary if a person suffers another accident and there is a possibility of the aggregated disablement being 14 per cent or more. In those circumstances, the disablement questions relating to the first accident are referred back to an adjudicating medical practitioner for a more precise determination as permitted by para. 6(4) of Sched. 6.

Subs. (6). See reg. 36 of the Social Security (Adjudication) Regulations 1995.

Medical appeals and references

46.—(1) This section has effect where the case of a claimant for disablement benefit or severe disablement allowance has been referred by the adjudication officer to an adjudicating medical practitioner for determination of the disablement questions.

(2) Subject to subsection (3) below, if the claimant is dissatisfied with the decision of the adjudicating medical practitioner, he may appeal in the prescribed manner and within the prescribed time, and the case shall be referred to a medical appeal tribunal.

(3) If—

(a) the Secretary of State notifies the adjudication officer within the prescribed time that he is of the opinion that any decision of the adjudicating medical practitioner ought to be considered by a medical appeal tribunal; or

(b) the adjudication officer is of the opinion that any such decision ought to be so considered,

the adjudication officer shall refer the case to a medical appeal tribunal for their consideration, and the tribunal may confirm, reverse or vary the decision in whole or in part as on an appeal.

DERIVATION

Social Security Act 1975, s.109.

GENERAL NOTE

For the procedure in medical appeal tribunals, see regs. 2–11 and 38 of the Social Security (Adjudication) Regulations 1995. If a medical appeal tribunal decide that the decision of the adjudicating medical authority was a nullity (*e.g.* because not all the members of a medical board signed the decision), the proper course of action is for the tribunal merely to make a decision to that effect, without considering the merits of the case. The adjudication officer can then make a fresh reference to another adjudicating medical authority (*R(I) 3/92* applying the unreported decision of a Tribunal of Commissioners in *CI/141/87*). However, it is at least arguable that, if both parties are content for the tribunal to substitute their own decision on the merits of the case for the invalid decision, the tribunal may do so. Normally parties are entitled to waive their strict rights.

Subs. (1). Note that this section applies only in relation to the disablement questions defined in s.45(1). Reg. 49 of the Social Security (Adjudication) Regulations 1995 makes similar provision for appeals and references to medical appeal tribunals from decisions of medical boards dealing with diagnosis and recrudescence questions relating to prescribed diseases.

Subs. (2). This provides for a claimant to appeal to a medical appeal tribunal if dissatisfied with a decision of an adjudicating medical practitioner or, by virtue of s.45(6), a medical board. Under reg. 3 of the Social Security (Adjudication) Regulations 1995, the appeal must usually be brought by giving notice in writing within three months of notification of the decision of the adjudicating medical practitioner or the medical board, but the time may be extended. No appeal lies against an initial provisional assessment in respect of occupational deafness (reg. 32 of the Social Security (Industrial Injuries) (Prescribed Diseases) Regulations 1985), but a claimant may still ask the Secretary of State to refer such a case under subs. (3).

Subs. (3) The Secretary of State may require a case to be referred to a medical appeal tribunal. This may be done not only if the Secretary of State considers that a determination is too favourable to a claimant but also if he considers it ought to be more favourable. The same three month time limit applies to references under subs. (3) as to appeals under subs. (2).

Review of medical decisions

47.—(1) Any decision under this Act of an adjudicating medical practitioner or a medical appeal tribunal may be reviewed at any time by [[1]a medical board] if satisfied that the decision was given in ignorance of a material fact or was based on a mistake as to a material fact.

(2) Any decision under this Act of an adjudicating medical practitioner may be reviewed at any time by [[1]a medical board if it] is satisfied that the decision was erroneous in point of law.

(3) Regulations may provide that a decision may not be reviewed under subsection (1) above unless the adjudicating medical practitioner is satisfied as mentioned in that subsection by fresh evidence.

(4) Any assessment of the extent of the disablement resulting from the relevant loss of faculty may also be reviewed by an adjudicating medical practitioner if he is satisfied that since the making of the assessment there has been an unforeseen aggravation of the results of the relevant injury.

(5) Where in connection with a claim for disablement benefit made after 25th August 1953 it is decided that the relevant accident has not resulted in a loss of faculty, the decision—

(a) may be reviewed under subsection (4) above as if it were an assessment of the extent of disablement resulting from a relevant loss of faculty; but

(b) subject to any further decision on appeal or review, shall be treated as deciding the question whether the relevant accident had so resulted both for the time about which the decision was given and for any subsequent time.

(6) For the purposes of subsection (5) above, a final assessment of the extent of the disablement resulting from a loss of faculty made for a period limited by reference to a definite date shall be treated as deciding that at that date the relevant accident had not resulted in a loss of faculty.

(7) An assessment made, confirmed or varied by a medical appeal tribunal shall not be reviewed under subsection (4) above without the leave of a medical appeal tribunal, and (notwithstanding the provisions of Part V of the Contributions and Benefits Act) on a review under that subsection the period to be taken into account by any revised assessment shall only include a period before the date of the application for the review if and in so far as regulations so provide.

(8) Subject to the foregoing provisions of this section [[1]and of subsection (8A)], an adjudicating medical practitioner may deal with a case on a review in any manner in which he could deal with it on an original reference to him, and in particular may in any case relating to disablement benefit make a provisional assessment notwithstanding that the assessment under review was final.

[[1](8A) Where—

(a) a final assessment of the extent of disablement resulting from a loss of faculty has been made for a period limited by reference to a definite date, and

(b) an application for review on the ground that there has been unforseen aggravation of the results of the relevant disease is made within a period of 3 months immediately following that date, the adjudicating medical authority shall determine the extent of disablement resulting from the relevant loss of faculty both for the period mentioned in paragraph (a) and any time after that period.]

(9) Section 46 above applies to an application for a review under this section and to a decision of an adjudicating medical practitioner in connection with such an application as it applies to an original claim for disablement benefit or severe disablement allowance, as the case may be, and to a decision of an adjudicating medical practitioner in connection with such a claim.

(10) In subsection (6) above the reference to a final assessment does not include an assessment made for the purpose of section 12(1)(a) or (b) of the National Insurance (Industrial Injuries) Act 1946 as originally enacted and having the effect that benefit is not payable.

DERIVATION

Subss. (1)–(9): Social Security Act 1975, s.110.
Subs. (10): Social Security (Consequential Provisions) Act 1975, ss.2 and 4 and Sched. 3, para. 20.

AMENDMENT

1. Social Security (Adjudication) Regulations 1995 (S.I. 1995 No. 1801), regs. 32(1)(a) and 52.

GENERAL NOTE

Review under subss (1) and (2) may be carried out only by medical boards. It is odd that subs. (3) was not amended when subs. (1) was. A review under subs. (4) may also be carried out by a medical board if the Secretary of State considers it appropriate (see reg. 36(4) of the Social Security (Adjudication) Regulations 1995). The Benefits Agency issue different forms depending on whether the review is brought under either subss. (1) or (2) or else subs. (4) In *CI/307/93*, a claimant applied for a review on a form appropriate to what is now subs. (4) but his grounds of application suggested that he should have made the application under what is now subs (1). The adjudicating medical authority and the medical appeal tribunal dealt with the case under subs. (4). The Commissioner held that the tribunal should have considered the case under subs. (1). However, in *CI/11471/95*, it was suggested that the tribunal could have confined their consideration of the case to the issue considered by the adjudicating medical authority and merely have drawn attention to the need for another adjudicating medical authority to deal with the true grounds of the application. The course of action to be taken will depend on the circumstances of the case. If an application for review is made when there is no existing award of disablement benefit, it may be necessary for the Secretary of State to treat the application for review as a claim for benefit if any benefit is to be payable, because section 1 of this Act requires that there be a claim (*CI/6872/95*).

References to an adjudicating medical practitioner include references to a medical board (see s.45(6).

Subs. (1). This permits a decision to be made at any time on the ground that the adjudicating medical authority was in ignorance of, or made a mistake as to, a material fact. Although a review may be carried out at any time, regs. 57 and 60 of the Social Security (Adjudication) Regulations 1995 limit the extent to which benefit may be payable in respect of the period before the date of application for the review.

The burden of proof in review cases lies upon the person initiating the review. Furthermore, under reg. 61 of the Social Security (Adjudication) Regulations 1995, a decision may be reviewed only if there is "fresh evidence" as to the material fact of which the adjudicating medical authority was ignorant or mistaken. In *R. v. Medical Appeal Tribunal (North Midland Region), ex p. Hubble* [1959] 2 Q.B. 408, the Court of Appeal approved the approach of a tribunal who had held that "fresh evidence means some evidence which the claimant was unable to produce before the decision was given, or which he could not reasonably be expected to have produced in the circumstances of the case" and that decision was applied in the more recent case of *Saker v. Secretary of State for Social Services* (reported as an appendix to *R(I) 2/88*). Whether evidence in a particular case is "fresh" has been regarded as a question of fact *(R(I) 27/61)*, so an appeal will not lie to a Commissioner on that issue unless a tribunal has erred in its approach to the issue.

A fact is "material" if it *could* but not necessarily *would* have made a difference to the decision under consideration. In *Saker*, Nicholls L.J. said that a fact was material "if it is one which, had it been known to the medical board, would have called for serious consideration by the board and might well have affected its decision''. Hence there is a possibility of a medical board deciding that a decision should be reviewed but not revised *(R(I) 1/71)*.

The ignorance or mistake must be as to a primary fact and not merely as to an inference or conclusion of fact. Thus a decision cannot be reviewed simply on the ground that an adjudication officer is now satisfied that the original decision as to, say, the claimant's ability to walk was wrong. ''He must go further and assert and prove that the inference might not have been drawn, if the determining authority had not been ignorant of some specific fact of which it could have been aware, or had not been mistaken as to some specific fact which it took into consideration'' *(R(I) 3/75)*. A medical report may or may not give grounds for a review. It may provide evidence of facts about the claimant's disabilities as to which the adjudication officer making the earlier decision may have been ignorant or mistaken. On the other hand, a new medical opinion does not justify a review *(R(S) 4/86)*.

In *R(A) 2/90*, it was held that once grounds for a review are made out, the whole of the determination under review may be considered even if the application for review relates only to one question.

Subs. (2). This permits a review of a decision of an adjudicating medical practitioner or medical, board (but not a decision of a medical appeal tribunal) to be reviewed if it was erroneous in point of law. Again, regs. 57 and 60 of the Social Security (Adjudication) Regulations 1995 have effect to limit the amount of benefit which can be paid in respect of the period before the application for the review.

Subs. (4). This permits a review on the ground that there has been an unforeseen aggravation of the results of the relevant injury. There is no equivalent ground of review if there has been an unforeseen amelioration of a claimant's condition. In *R(I) 18/62*, the Commissioner was prepared to assume that there was unforeseen aggravation of the results of an injury not only where there has been a worsening of the original results but also where there has been the addition of further results because there has been a further accident. That must be right because otherwise there could not be a review to allow a medical board to give effect to reg. 11(4) of the Social Security (General Benefit) Regulations 1982 which provides for the ''connection factor'' to be taken into account where there has been a subsequent, non-industrial, injury. However, in the same case, the Commissioner made it clear that the mere fact that a second injury would not have occurred but for the first did not mean that the results of the second injury could be said to be an unforeseen aggravation of the results of the first injury. The first injury must have been an effective cause of the second injury rather than simply being a *causa sine qua non*. The extent to which a reviewing authority is bound to reach a decision consistent with the decision under review under subs. (4) was considered at length in *CI/437/92*. The Commissioner concluded that ''what the reviewing authority cannot do is to admit evidence or reach a conclusion from its own examination or questioning which is inconsistent with the decision of the authority which made the assessment under review that the claimant suffered from the loss of faculty identified in its decision at the date of assessment [*i.e.* the date of decision—unless there is a contrary indication—or the date of the beginning of the period of assessment]''.

The period to be taken into account on a review under subs. (4) must begin no earlier than three months before the date of the application for review (reg. 62 of the Social Security (Adjudication) Regulations 1995).

In *Parker v. Secretary of State for Social Security* (reported as an appendix to *R(I) 2/90*), the claimant had sought a review of a life assessment of 18 per cent on the ground of unforeseen aggravation. A provisional assessment of 40 per cent was made for two years and at the end of that period an adjudicating medical practitioner assessed the extent of disablement as 50 per cent for one year. The case was referred to a medical appeal tribunal who reduced the assessment to one of 10 per cent for life. Before the Commissioner and the Court of Appeal it was argued that the tribunal's decision was erroneous in point of law because the further assessment after the provisional assessment was a continuation of the review so that the minimum assessment should have been 18 per cent. That argument was rejected, it being held that, although the first assessment on a review under subs. (2) could not be lower than the assessment being reviewed, that did not apply to any subsequent assessments which could take account of any improvement in the claimant's condition. Subs. (7) provides that a decision of a medical appeal tribunal may be reviewed under subs. (4) only with the leave of a similar tribunal.

The circumstances in which an assessment in respect of occupational deafness can be reviewed on the ground of unforeseen aggravation are severely limited by regs. 30 and 31 of the Social Security (Industrial Injuries) (Prescribed Diseases) Regulations 1985.

Subss. (5) and (6). These enable a decision that a person has no loss of faculty to be reviewed if the claimant subsequently does suffer from a loss of faculty. In particular, subs. (6) makes it clear that a person with a final assessment limited to a fixed period may apply for a review on the ground of unforeseen aggravation if he or she continues to be disabled after the end of the fixed period, even if the extent of disablement has not worsened. However, these subsections do not apply to prescribed disease cases (see *CI/12673/96*).

Subs. (7). There can be no review of a decision of a medical appeal tribunal on the ground of unforeseen aggravation without the leave of a similar tribunal to whom the application for review must first be submitted under reg. 41 of the Social Security (Adjudication) Regulations 1995. A tribunal is not obliged to hold an oral hearing of such an application. If the applicant has an arguable case, then leave to apply for the review should be given because it is for the review adjudicating medical authority (and not the tribunal) to decide in the first instance whether there are grounds for a review. The requirement for leave is intended only to weed out hopeless cases. It is arguable that a tribunal are bound by s.10 of the Tribunals and Inquiries Act 1992 to give reasons for a refusal of leave.

Reg. 62 of the Social Security (Adjudication) Regulations 1995, read with the latter part of this subsection, has the effect that the period to be taken into account on any application for review on the ground of unforeseen aggravation shall not include any period more than three months before the application for the review. That is not confined to reviews of decisions of medical appeal tribunals. Presumably it is intended that the adjudication officer will consider the beginning of the period of assessment to be a date from which it is "reasonable in the circumstances" to award benefit under reg. 60 of those Regulations following a review on the ground of unforeseen aggravation.

Subs. (8). A review decision, including a refusal to review, is subject to the same rights of appeal and reference as an initial decision.

Subs. (8A) This applies only to industrial disease cases. Subs. (6) makes it unnecessary to have a similar provision in respect of industrial accidents.

Appeal etc. on question of law to Commissioner

48.—(1) Subject to this section, an appeal lies to a Commissioner from any decision of a medical appeal tribunal (if given after 27th September 1959) on the ground that the decision is erroneous in point of law, at the instance of—

(a) an adjudication officer;
(b) the claimant;
(c) a trade union of which the claimant was a member at the time of the relevant accident or, in a case relating to severe disablement allowance, at the prescribed time; or
(d) the Secretary of State.

(2) Subsection (1) above, as it applies to a trade union, applies also to any other association which exists to promote the interests and welfare of its members.

(3) No appeal lies under subsection (1) above without the leave—

(a) of the person who was the chairman of the medical appeal tribunal when the decision was given or, in a prescribed case, the leave of some other chairman of a medical appeal tribunal; or
(b) subject to and in accordance with regulations, of a Commissioner, and regulations may make provision as to the manner in which, and the time within which, appeals are to be brought and applications made for leave to appeal.

(4) On any such appeal, the question of law arising for the decision of the Commissioner and the facts on which it arises shall be submitted for his consideration in the prescribed manner.

(5) Where the Commissioner holds that the decision was erroneous in point of law, he shall set it aside and refer the case to a medical appeal tribunal with directions for its determination.

(6) Subject to any direction of the Commissioner, the tribunal on a reference under subsection (5) above shall consist of persons who were not members of the tribunal which gave the erroneous decision.

Derivation

Social Security Act 1975. s.112.

General Note

Subs. (1). The right of appeal to the Commissioner provided by this section is similar to that provided by s.34(1) which deals with appeals from disability appeal tribunals. Reference should be made to the annotations to that section.

As with other tribunals, a great many medical appeal tribunal decisions are held to be erroneous in point of law due to a failure to record adequate reasons for the decision as required by reg. 38(4) of the Social Security (Adjudication) Regulations 1995.

For the standard of reason required from a medical appeal tribunal see the note to that regulation.

Subs. (3). Before appealing to a Commissioner, a person must first obtain leave to appeal from either the chairman of the tribunal or the Commissioner. The procedure for applications for leave to appeal is laid down in reg. 39 of the Social Security (Adjudication) Regulations 1995 and regs. 4 and 5 of the Social Security Commissioners Procedure Regulations 1987. Application is made to the chairman first, unless the three month time-limit has expired in which case the application must be made straight to a Commissioner. Regulation 39(4) of the Adjudication Regulations provides that, if it would be impracticable or would cause undue delay for the person who was chairman of the tribunal giving the decision to consider the application for leave, any other chairman may do so. If a chairman refuses leave to appeal, a further application may be made to a Commissioner. No appeal lies against a refusal by a Commissioner to grant leave although such a refusal many be challenged by way of an application for judicial review (*Bland v. Chief Supplementary Benefit Officer* [1983] 1 W.L.R. 262, also reported as *R(SB) 12/83*). Regs. 6 and 7 of the Social Security Commissioners Procedure Regulations 1987 provide for the bringing of appeals, but note that if leave to appeal is granted by a Commissioner, the application for leave to appeal is usually treated as the notice of appeal, under reg. 5(2).

Subs. (4). See regs. 6 and 12(2) of the Social Security Commissioners Procedure Regulations 1987.

Subss. (5) and (6). For the procedure of the tribunal on receipt of a Commissioner's decision, see reg. 42 of the Social Security (Adjudication) Regulations 1995. Note that any tribunal rehearing a case after an appeal to a Commissioner *must* consist of people who were not members of the tribunal whose decision has been set aside unless the Commissioner directs otherwise. On an appeal from a medical appeal tribunal, a Commissioner does not have any power to give the decision he or she considers the tribunal should have given and in this respect the Commissioner's powers are more limited than they are on appeal from a social security appeal tribunal or disability appeal tribunal. In *R(I) 5/91*, it was obvious what decision the tribunal should have given and so the Commissioner referred the case to a tribunal consisting of the *same* members and gave directions as to precisely the decision they should give. When a Commissioner sets aside a decision of a tribunal on the ground that the tribunal had no jurisdiction, the case is not referred to another tribunal because there is no point in doing so (*R(I) 3/92*).

On an appeal in respect of mobility allowance, formerly paid under s.37A of the Social Security Act 1975, if the Commissioner sets aside the decision of the medical appeal tribunal, the case is referred to an adjudication officer rather than another tribunal (reg. 24(13) of the Social Security (Introduction of Disability Living Allowance) Regulations 1991).

Adjudicating medical practitioners and medical appeal tribunals

Adjudicating medical practitioners

49.—(1) Adjudicating medical practitioners shall be appointed by the Secretary of State.

(2) Subject to subsection (1) above, their appointment shall be determined by regulations.

DERIVATION

Social Security Act 1975, Sched. 12, paras. 1 and 3.

GENERAL NOTE

See reg. 35 of the Social Security (Adjudication) Regulations 1995.

Constitution of medical appeal tribunals

50.—(1) A medical appeal tribunal shall consist of a chairman and two other persons.

(2) The members other than the chairman shall be medical practitioners appointed by the President after consultation with such academic medical bodies as appear to him to be appropriate.

(3) The President shall nominate the chairman.

(4) The President may nominate as chairman—

(a) himself;

(b) one of the full-time chairmen appointed under section 51(1) below; or

(c) a person drawn from the panel appointed by the Lord Chancellor or, as the case may be, the Lord President of the Court of Session under [[1]section 6 of the Tribunals and Inquiries Act 1992].

(5) No person shall be appointed chairman of a tribunal under subsection (4)(c) above unless he has a five year general qualification, or he is an advocate or solicitor in Scotland of at least five years' standing.

(6) Subject to subsections (1) to (5) above, the constitution of medical appeal tribunals shall be determined by regulations.

(7) Schedule 2 to this Act shall have effect for supplementing this section.

Derivation

Social Security Act 1975, Sched. 12, paras. 2 and 3.

Amendment

1. Tribunals and Inquiries Act 1992, Sched. 3, para. 36 (October 1, 1992).

The President and full-time chairmen of tribunals

The President of social security appeal tribunals, medical appeal tribunals and disability appeal tribunals and regional chairmen and other full-time chairmen

51.—(1) The Lord Chancellor may, after consultation with the Lord Advocate, appoint—

(a) a President of social security appeal tribunals, medical appeal tribunals and disability appeal tribunals; and

(b) regional and other full-time chairmen of such tribunals.

(2) A person is qualified to be appointed President if he has a 10 year general qualification or he is an advocate or solicitor in Scotland of at least 10 years' standing.

(3) A person is qualified to be appointed a full-time chairman if he has a five year general qualification or he is an advocate or solicitor in Scotland of at least five years' standing.

(4) Schedule 2 to this Act shall have effect for supplementing this section.

Derivation

Social Security Act 1975, Sched. 10, para. 1A.

Social Security Commissioners

Appointment of Commissioners

52.—(1) Her Majesty may from time to time appoint, from among persons who have a 10 year general qualification or advocates or solicitors in Scotland of at least 10 years' standing—

(a) a Chief Social Security Commissioner; and

(b) such number of other Social Security Commissioners as Her Majesty thinks fit.

(2) If the Lord Chancellor considers that, in order to facilitate the disposal of the business of Social Security Commissioners, he should make an appointment in pursuance of this subsection, he may appoint—
(a) a person who has a 10 year general qualification; or
(b) an advocate or solicitor in Scotland of at least 10 years' standing; or
(c) a member of the bar of Northern Ireland or solicitor of the Supreme Court of Northern Ireland of at least 10 years' standing,
to be a Social Security Commissioner (but to be known as a deputy Commissioner) for such period or on such occasions as the Lord Chancellor thinks fit.

(3) When the Lord Chancellor proposes to exercise the power conferred on him by subsection (2) above, it shall be his duty to consult the Lord Advocate with respect to the proposal.

(4) Schedule 2 to this Act shall have effect for supplementing this section.

DERIVATION

Social Security Act 1975, s.97(3); Social Security Act 1980, s.13(5) and (6).

GENERAL NOTE

Commissioners hear appeals from social security appeal tribunals, disability appeal tribunals and medical appeal tribunals. They are of the same standing as circuit judges. At present there are 18 full-time Commissioners and nearly as many Deputy Commissioners. Three of the full-time Commissioners are based in Edinburgh. The remainder are based in London but travel regularly to Cardiff and occasionally to other places to hear appeals.

Barristers and solicitors called or admitted before 1991 are treated as having a general qualification within the meaning of the 1990 Act.

References by authorities

Power of adjudicating authorities to refer matters to experts

53.—(1) An authority to which this section applies may refer any question of special difficulty arising for decision by the authority to one or more experts for examination and report.

(2) The authorities to which this section applies are—
(a) an adjudication officer;
(b) an adjudicating medical practitioner, or two or more such practitioners acting together;
(c) a specially qualified adjudicating medical practitioner appointed by virtue of section 62 below, or two or more such practitioners acting together;
(d) a social security appeal tribunal;
(e) a disability appeal tribunal;
(f) a medical appeal tribunal;
(g) a Commissioner;
(h) the Secretary of State.

(3) Regulations may prescribe cases in which a Commissioner shall not exercise the power conferred by subsection (1) above.

(4) In this section "expert" means a person appearing to the authority to have knowledge or experience which would be relevant in determining the question of special difficulty.

DERIVATION

Social Security Act 1975, s.115A.

General Note

Given the wide definition of "expert" in subs. (4), the scope of this power to refer questions for examination and report is enormous. On the other hand, the issues arising before disability appeal tribunals and medical appeal tribunals are likely to be medical ones and both types of tribunal have medical practitioners among their members. A question must be one of "special difficulty" before the power can be exercised. Chairmen of disability appeal tribunals have additional powers under s.55(1).

Although it is a "question" which is to be referred for examination, this may include the physical examination of the claimant with his or her consent (see the note to *R(I) 14/51*). S.55(2) forbids a disability appeal tribunal from carrying out its own physical examination. The medical members of medical appeal tribunals may, and frequently do, carry out such examinations.

For additional powers given to the Secretary of State and adjudication officers in cases concerning attendance allowance, disability living allowance or disability working allowance, see s.54. In a case involving a prescribed industrial disease, an adjudication officer considering a diagnosis or recrudescence question may obtain a report under reg. 45 of the Social Security (Adjudication) Regulations 1995. A special medical board may also obtain a radiologist's report or reports on other tests under reg. 54(1) of the Adjudication Regulations.

If a question concerning attendance allowance, disability living allowance or disability working allowance is referred under this section to a medical officer who is an officer of the Secretary of State, that medical officer may refer the question to the Disability Living Allowance Advisory Board for their advice (s.54(4)).

Medical evidence may be withheld from the person concerned if disclosure would be harmful to his or her health (reg. 8 of the Adjudication Regulations).

Claims relating to attendance allowance, disability living allowance and disability working allowance

54.—(1) Before a claim for an attendance allowance, a disability living allowance or a disability working allowance or any question relating to such an allowance is submitted to an adjudication officer under section 20 above the Secretary of State may refer the person in respect of whom the claim is made or the question is raised to a medical practitioner for such examination and report as appears to him to be necessary—

(a) for the purpose of providing the adjudication officer with information for use in determining the claim or question; or

(b) for the purpose of general monitoring of claims for attendance allowances, disability living allowances and disability working allowances.

(2) An adjudication officer may refer—

(a) a person in respect of whom such a claim is made or such a question is raised;

(b) a person [[2]in respect of whom an application for a review under section 30 or 35 above has been made or is treated as having been made,]

to a medical practitioner for such examination and report as appears to the adjudication officer to be needed to enable him to reach a decision on the claim or question or the matter under review.

(3) The Secretary of State may direct adjudication officers to refer for advice to a medical practitioner who is an officer of the Secretary of State any case falling within a specified class of cases relating to attendance allowance or disability living allowance, and an adjudication officer may refer for advice any case relating to attendance allowance or disability living allowance to such a medical practitioner without such a direction.

(4) An adjudication officer may refer for advice any case relating to disability working allowance to such a medical practitioner.

(5) A medical practitioner who is an officer of the Secretary of State and to whom a case or question relating to an attendance allowance or a disability living allowance is referred under section 53 above or subsection (3) above may

refer the case or question to the Disability Living Allowance Advisory Board for advice.

(6) Such a medical practitioner may obtain information about such a case or question from another medical practitioner.

(7) A medical practitioner who is an officer of the Secretary of State and to whom a question relating to disability working allowance is referred under section 53 above may obtain information about it from another medical practitioner.

[[1](7A) Any reference in subsections (3) to (7) above to a medical practitioner who is an officer of the Secretary of State includes a reference to a medical practitioner who is provided by any person in pursuance of a contract entered into with the Secretary of State.]

(8) Where—

(a) the Secretary of State has exercised the power conferred on him by subsection (1) above or an adjudication officer has exercised the power conferred on him by subsection (2) above; and

(b) the medical practitioner requests the person referred to him to attend for or submit himself to medical examination; but

(c) he fails without good cause to do so,

the adjudication officer shall decide the claim or question or matter under review against him.

Derivation

Social Security Act 1975, s.115C; Social Security Act 1986, s.52(3A).

Amendment

1. Deregulation and Contracting Out Act 1994, Sched. 16, para. 20(1) (January 3, 1995).
2. Social Security Administration (Fraud) Act 1997, Sched. 1, para. 2 (July 1, 1997).

General Note

The claim forms for attendance allowance, disability living allowance and disability working allowance are long and complicated but the general idea is that entitlement shall be decided in most cases on the basis of self-assessment rather than by medical examination. However, this section enables the Secretary of State or an adjudication officer to refer a claimant for a medical examination.

Subs. (1). This enables the Secretary of State to refer a claimant for examination before a *claim* (which may be a continuation claim) or a Secretary of State's application for review (CDLA/14884/96) is referred to an adjudication officer.

Subs. (2). Once a *claim or a review* is before an adjudication officer, he or she may refer a claimant for examination. Where the Secretary of State has applied for a review, para. (a) applies because a "question" will have been raised (*CDLA/14884/96*).

Subs. (3). The Secretary of State may direct adjudication officers to refer classes of cases for examination.

Subss. (4)–(6. A medical practitioner to whom a case is referred may obtain information from other medical practitioners and also may refer an attendance allowance or disability living allowance case to the Disability Living Allowance Advisory Board for advice.

Subss. (7) and (7A). Para. 20(2)–(4) of Sched. 16 to the Deregulation and Contracting Out Act 1994 provides that consent given before January 3, 1995 authorising disclosure of any information to the Secretary of State or an officer of the Secretary of State has effect as though it also authorised disclosure to a medical practitioner who is provided in pursuance of a contract with the Secretary of State and, to the extent directed by the Secretary of State, to any employee of such a practitioner, including any person performing ancillary services for the practitioner and any employee of such a person.

Subs. (8). If claimants are referred for examination and fail to attend without good cause, their cases are decided against them. "Good cause" was a familiar phrase in the context of late claims. It requires there to be "some fact which, having regard to all the circumstances (including the claimant's state of health and the information which he had received and that which he had received and that which he might have obtained) would probably have caused a reasonable person of his age and experience to act (or fail to act) as the claimant did" (*R(S) 2/63*). If a claimant does not have "good cause", the case *shall* be decided against him or her. However, where the adjudication officer is considering a review, the "question or matter" under review may not be the whole entitlement to benefit but only one component or the conditions for a higher rate rather than a lower rate so the claimant may not lose all entitlement. The same could apply on a claim if the adjudication officer required the report only in respect of one question arising on the claim. If the case is determined against the claimant, the remedy is to seek a review under ss.30 or 35(8).

Medical examination etc. in relation to appeals to disability appeal tribunals

55.—(1) Where an appeal has been brought under section 33(1) (a) above, a person who may be nominated as chairman of a disability appeal tribunal may, if prescribed conditions are satisfied, refer the claimant to a medical practitioner for such examination and report as appears to him to be necessary for the purpose of providing a disability appeal tribunal with information for use in determining the appeal.

(2) At a hearing before a disability appeal tribunal, except in prescribed circumstances, the tribunal—

(a) may not carry out a physical examination of the claimant; and

(b) may not require the claimant to undergo any physical test for the purpose of determining whether he satisfies the condition mentioned in section 73(1) (a) of the Contributions and Benefits Act.

Derivation

Social Security Act 1975, s.115D; Social Security Act 1986, s.52(3A).

General Note

Subs. (1). This enables a chairman to refer a claimant for examination by a medical practitioner. The power may be exercised either before a hearing (on reading the papers) or during the hearing. Reg. 30 of the Social Security (Adjudication) Regulations 1995 provides that this power shall be exercised only if the chairman is satisfied that the appeal cannot properly be determined unless the claimant is examined and the medical practitioner has provided the tribunal with information for use in determining the appeal. There is no express sanction against a claimant who fails to attend such an examination but if the tribunal are not satisfied that there was a good cause for the failure, they are likely to draw adverse inferences against the claimant.

Subs. (2). A disability appeal tribunal is prohibited from carrying out a physical examination of a claimant or from requiring a claimant to take part in a walking or other test for the purposes of seeing whether the claimant is virtually unable to walk and so entitled to the mobility component of disability living allowance. Medical appeal tribunals considering mobility allowance claims used to do both those things. A disability appeal tribunal considering a mobility allowance appeal under reg. 24(9) (b) of the Social Security (Introduction of Disability Living Allowance) Regulations 1991 must deal with the case as though it were a claim for the mobility component of disability living allowance and so this subsection applies. Since the subsection distinguishes between examination and tests, requiring a claimant to take part in tests for purposes other than assessing ability to walk is not expressly forbidden. However, it would seem consistent with the purpose of the legislation that claimants should not be asked to give demonstrations of their abilities. The tribunal may not carry out a physical examination even if the claimant asks for one. However, a tribunal is not prohibited from watching a claimant demonstrate the extent of his or her ability to walk or perform other tasks if the claimant wishes to do so. Since the subsection applies only to physical examination and physical tests, there is no restriction on a tribunal's power to "take a history" for the purpose of assessing disability. They are also entitled to take into account their informal observation of the claimant during the hearing *(R(DLA)1/95)*.

No regulations have been made prescribing circumstances in which this subsection shall not apply.

Determination of questions of special difficulty

Assessors

56.—(1) Where it appears to an authority to which this section applies that a matter before the authority involves a question of fact of special difficulty, then, unless regulations otherwise provide, the authority may direct that in dealing with that matter they shall have the assistance of one or more assessors.

(2) The authorities to which this section applies are—

(a) two or more adjudicating medical practitioners acting together;

(b) two or more specially qualified adjudicating medical practitioners, appointed by virtue of section 62 below, acting together;

(c) a social security appeal tribunal;

(d) a disability appeal tribunal;

(e) a medical appeal tribunal;

(f) a Commissioner;

(g) the Secretary of State.

DERIVATION

Social Security Act 1975, s.115B.

GENERAL NOTE

A tribunal may sit with an assessor. No regulations have been made restricting the scope of this section. The section is not confined to medical assessors although, if the power is ever used at all, it is most likely to be used in relation to medical questions. The role of assessors was considered in *R(1) 14/51*. Their sole function is to give the tribunal information and advice on the issue involved including the effect and value of evidence. They are not witnesses and cannot be cross-examined. It is not desirable that they should question witnesses themselves. Instead, the chairman should invite the assessor to mention any question which should be put and the chairman should then ask the question if it seems sensible. The chairman should summarise briefly the effect of any advice given by the assessor so as to give the parties an opportunity to comment before the tribunal begin to deliberate on their decision. The assessor is not a member of the tribunal and it remains for the tribunal alone to decide all the issues. They must not accept any advice of the assessor unless they are satisfied that having regard to all the evidence in the case the advice is correct.

Tribunal of three Commissioners

57.—(1) If it appears to the Chief Social Security Commissioner (or, in the case of his inability to act, to such other of the Commissioners as he may have nominated to act for the purpose) that an appeal falling to be heard by one of the Commissioners involves a question of law of special difficulty, he may direct that the appeal be dealt with, not by that Commissioner alone, but by a Tribunal consisting of any three of the Commissioners.

(2) If the decision of the Tribunal is not unanimous, the decision of the majority shall be the decision of the Tribunal.

DERIVATION

Social Security Act 1975, s.116.

GENERAL NOTE

Decisions of Tribunals of Commissioners are more authoritative than decisions of single Commissioners. A single Commissioner is bound to follow a decision of a Tribunal (*R(I) 12/75*) but a Tribunal may depart from a decision of an earlier Tribunal although it will be slow to do so (*R(U) 4/88*). Tribunals are generally convened only when there has been a difference of opinion between single Commissioners.

[1Medical examinations

Medical examinations of persons awarded attendance allowance or disability living allowance

57A.—Regulations may make provision—

(a) enabling the Secretary of State to require a person to whom attendance allowance or disability living allowance has been awarded to submit to medical examination in prescribed circumstances;

(b) for withholding payments of benefit in prescribed circumstances where a person has failed to submit himself to a medical examination to which he has been required to submit in accordance with regulations under paragraph (a) above; and

(c) for the subsequent making in prescribed circumstances of payments withheld in in accordance with regulations under paragraph (b) above.]

AMENDMENT

1. Social Security Administration (Fraud) Act 1997, s.18 (July 1, 1997).

GENERAL NOTE

See regs. 8C to 8E of the Social Security (Attendance Allowance) Regulations 1991 and regs. 5A to 5C of the Social Security (Disability Living Allowance) Regulations 1991. These regulations add to the powers the Secretary of State already had by virtue of section 54(1) and regulation 37 of the Social Security (Claims and Payments) Regulations 1987.

Regulations

Regulations as to determination of questions and matters arising out of, or pending, reviews and appeals

58.—(1) Subject to the provisions of this Act, provision may be made by regulations for the determination—

(a) (a) by the Secretary of State; or

(b) by a person or tribunal appointed or constituted in accordance with the regulations,

of any question arising under or in connection with the Contributions and Benefits Act [,1the Jobseekers Act 1995] or the former legislation, including a claim for benefit.

(2) In this section "the former legislation" means the National Insurance Acts 1965 to 1974 and the National Insurance (Industrial Injuries) Acts 1965 to 1974 and the 1975 Act and Part II of the 1986 Act.

(3) Regulations under subsection (1) above may modify, add to or exclude any provisions of this Part of this Act, so far as relating to any questions to which the regulations relate.

(4) It is hereby declared for the avoidance of doubt that the power to make regulations under subsection (1) above includes power to make regulations for the determination of any question arising as to the total or partial recoupment of unemployment benefit [1or a jobseeker's allowance] in pursuance of regulations under [2section 16 of the Industrial Tribunals Act 1996] (including any decision as to the amount of benefit).

(5) Regulations under subsection (1) above may provide for the review by the Secretary of State of decisions on questions determined by him.

(6) The Lord Chancellor may by regulations provide—

(a) for officers authorised—

(i) by the Lord Chancellor; or

(ii) in Scotland, by the Secretary of State,

to determine any question which is determinable by a Commissioner and which does not involve the determination of any appeal, application for leave to appeal or reference;

(b) for the procedure to be followed by any such officer in determining any such question;

(c) for the manner in which determinations of such questions by such officers may be called in question.

(7) A determination which would have the effect of preventing an appeal, application for leave to appeal or reference being determined by a Commissioner is not a determination of the appeal, application or reference for the purposes of subsection (6) above.

(8) Regulations under subsection (1) above may provide—

(a) for the reference to the High Court or, in Scotland, the Court of Session for decision of any question of law arising in connection with the determination of a question by the Secretary of State; and

(b) for appeals to the High Court or Court of Session from the decision of the Secretary of State on any such question of law;

and subsections (5) to (7) of section 18 above shall apply to a reference or appeal under this subsection as they apply to a reference or appeal under subsections (1) to (3) of that section.

Derivation

Social Security Act 1975, s.114; Social Security Act 1986, s.52(3) and (3A).

Amendments

1. Jobseekers Act 1996, Sched. 2, para. 44 (April 22, 1996).
2. Industrial Tribunals Act 1996, Sched. 1, para. 7 (August 22, 1996).

Procedure

59.—(1) Regulations (in this section referred to as "procedure regulations") may make any such provision as is specified in Schedule 3 to this Act.

(2) Procedure regulations may deal differently with claims and questions relating to—

(a) benefit under Parts II to IV of the Contributions and Benefits Act;

(b) industrial injuries benefit;

(c) each of the other benefits to which section 20 above applies.

(3) At any inquiry held by virtue of procedure regulations the witnesses shall, if the person holding the inquiry thinks fit, be examined on oath; and the person holding the inquiry shall have power to administer oaths for that purpose.

(4) In proceedings for the determination of a question mentioned in section 17(1) (c) above (including proceedings on an inquiry)—

(a) in England and Wales, there shall be available to a witness (other than the person who is liable, or alleged to be liable, to pay the Class 1A contribution in question) any privilege against self-incrimination or incrimination of a spouse which is available to a witness in legal proceedings; and

(b) In Scotland, section 3 of the Evidence (Scotland) Act 1853 (competence and compellability of witnesses) shall apply as it applies to civil proceedings.

(5) Procedure regulations prescribing the procedure to be followed in cases before a Commissioner shall provide that any hearing shall be in public except in so far as the Commissioner for special reasons otherwise directs.

(6) It is hereby declared—

(a) that the power to prescribe procedure includes power to make provision as to the representation of one person, at any hearing of a case, by another person whether having professional qualifications or not; and

(b) that the power to provide for the manner in which questions arising for determination by the Secretary of State are to be raised includes power to make provision with respect to the formulation of any such questions, whether arising on a reference under section 117 below or otherwise.

(7) Except so far as it may be applied in relation to England and Wales by procedure regulations, [[1]Part I of the Arbitration Act 1996] shall not apply to any proceedings under this Part of this Act.

DERIVATION

Social Security Act 1975, s.115; Social Security Act 1986, s.52(3) and (3A).

AMENDMENT

1. Arbitration Act 1996, Sched. 3, para. 54.

Finality of decisions

60.—(1) Subject to the provisions of this Part of this Act, the decision of any claim or question in accordance with the foregoing provisions of this Part of this Act shall be final; and subject to the provisions of any regulations under section 58 above, the decision of any claim or question in accordance with those regulations shall be final.

(2) Subsection (1) above shall not make any finding of fact or other determination embodied in or necessary to a decision, or on which it is based, conclusive for the purpose of any further decision.

(3) A decision (given under subsection (2) of section 44 above or otherwise) that an accident was an industrial accident is to be taken as determining only that paragraphs (a), (b) and (c) of subsection (5) of that section are satisfied in relation to the accident, and neither any such decision nor the reference to an adjudicating medical practitioner or a medical appeal tribunal under section 45 above of the disablement questions in connection with any claim to or award of disablement benefit is to be taken as importing a decision as to the origin of any injury or disability suffered by the claimant, whether or not there is an event identifiable as an accident apart from any injury that may have been received; but—

(a) a decision that on a particular occasion when there was no such event a person had an industrial accident by reason of an injury shall be treated as a decision that, if the injury was suffered by accident on that occasion, the accident was an industrial accident; and

(b) a decision that an accident was an industrial accident may be given, and a declaration to that effect be made and recorded in accordance with section 44 above, without its having been found that personal injury resulted from the accident (saving always the discretion under subsection (3) of that section to refuse to determine the question if it is unlikely to be necessary for the purposes of a claim for benefit).

(4) Notwithstanding anything in subsection (2) or (3) above (but subject to the provisions of this Part of this Act as to appeal and review), where for purposes of disablement pension or disablement gratuity in respect of an accident it has been found by an adjudicating medical practitioner or a medical appeal tribunal, on the determination or last determination of the disablement questions, that an injury resulted in whole or in part from the accident, then for purposes of industrial death benefit in respect of that accident the finding shall be conclusive that the injury did so result.

(5) Subsections (2) to (4) above shall apply as regards the effect to be given in any proceedings to any decision, or to a reference under section 45 above, whether the decision was given or reference made or the proceedings were commenced before or after the passing of the National Insurance Act 1972 (section 5 of which originally contained the provisions contained in this section), except that it shall not affect the determination of any appeal under section 48 above from a decision of a medical appeal tribunal given before the passing of that Act, nor affect any proceedings consequent on such an appeal from a decision so given; and accordingly—

(a) any decision given before the passing of that Act that a claimant was not entitled to industrial death benefit may be reviewed in accordance with this Part of this Act to give effect to subsection (4) above; and

(b) the references in subsections (2) and (3) above to provisions of this Act, and the reference in this subsection to section 45 above shall (so far as necessary) include the corresponding provisions of previous Acts.

DERIVATION

Social Security Act 1975, s.117.

GENERAL NOTE

Subs. (1). Decisions are "final" subject to appeals and reviews. Therefore, it is not possible to sue an adjudication officer in negligence in respect of a decision (*Jones v. Department of Employment* [1989] Q.B. 1) although an action could lie in misfeasance. That does not prevent the Department of Social Security being sued in respect of bad advice. The finality of decisions does not prevent decisions being challenged by way of judicial review (*R. v. Medical Appeal Tribunal, ex p. Gilmore* [1957] 1 Q.B. 574, a decision made before there was a right of appeal from a medical appeal tribunal to a Commissioner) although the reluctance of the High Court to allow such challenges when there is a statutory right of appeal means that they are confined to exceptional cases.

Subs. (2). Issue estoppel does not arise in social security law.

Subs. (3). A finding by an adjudication officer or social security appeal tribunal (or a Commissioner or court) that there has been an industrial accident does not prevent an adjudicating medical authority or a medical appeal tribunal from finding that there has been no loss of faculty resulting from the accident even if the two decisions appear to be inconsistent. This is so even in a case where a person suffers a heart attack and the only "accident" found by the adjudication officer was the heart attack itself. An adjudicating medical authority is still entitled to hold that the heart attack was not the result of an accident. This provision was first introduced by the National Insurance Act 1972 to reverse the effect of *Jones v. Secretary of State for Social Services* [1972] A.C. 944 (also reported as an appendix to *R(I) 3/69*)—hence subs. (5).

Regulations about supplementary matters relating to determinations

61.—(1) Regulations may make provision as respects matters arising—

(a) pending the determination under this Act (whether in the first instance or on an appeal or reference, and whether originally or on review)—

  (i) of any claim for benefit to which this section applies; or

  (ii) of any question affecting any person's right to such benefit or its receipt; or

  (iii) of any person's liability for contributions under Part I of the Contributions and Benefits Act; or

(b) out of the revision on appeal or review of any decision under this Act on any such claim or question.

(2) Without prejudice to the generality of subsection (1) above, regulations under that subsection may include provision as to the date from which any decision on a review is to have effect or to be deemed to have had effect.

(3) Regulations under subsection (1) above as it applies to child benefit may include provision as to the date from which child benefit is to be payable to a

person in respect of a child in a case where, before the benefit was awarded to that person, child benefit in respect of the child was awarded to another person.

(4) This section applies—

(a) to benefit as defined in section 122 of the Contributions and Benefits Act;

[[1](aa) to a jobseeker's allowance]

(b) to child benefit;

(c) to statutory sick pay;

(d) to statutory maternity pay;

(e) to income support;

(f) to family credit;

(g) to disability working allowance; and

(h) to any social fund payments such as are mentioned in section 138(1) (a) or (2) of the Contributions and Benefits Act.

Derivation

Social Security Act 1975, s.119; Social Security (Miscellaneous Provisions) Act 1977, s.17(5); Social Security Act 1986, s.52(3) and (3A).

Amendment

1. Jobseekers Act 1996, Sched. 2, para. 45 (April 22, 1996).

61A. *Omitted.*

Industrial diseases

Adjudication as to industrial diseases

62.—(1) Regulations shall provide for applying, in relation—

(a) to claims for benefit under section 108 to 110 of the Contributions and Benefits Act; and

(b) to questions arising in connection with such claims or with awards of such benefit,

the provisions of this Part of this Act subject to any prescribed additions or modifications.

(2) Regulations for those purposes may in particular provide—

(a) for the appointment of specially qualified adjudicating medical practitioners and the appointment of medical officers for the purposes of the regulations (which shall be taken to include, in the case of specially qualified adjudicating medical practitioners, the purposes for which adjudicating medical practitioners are appointed and medical appeal tribunals are established); and

(b) for the payment by the prescribed persons of fees of the prescribed amount in connection with any medical examination by specially qualified adjudicating medical practitioners or any such officer and their return in any prescribed cases, and (so far as not required to be returned) their payment into the National Insurance Fund and recovery as sums due to that Fund.

Derivation

Social Security Act 1975, s.113.

63.—66. *Omitted.*

Christmas bonus

Determination of questions

67.—(1) A determination by the competent authority that a person is entitled or not entitled to payment of a qualifying benefit in respect of a period which includes a day in the relevant week shall be conclusive for the purposes of section 148 of the Contributions and Benefits Act; and in this subsection "competent authority" means, in relation to a payment of any description of a qualifying benefit, an authority that ordinarily determines whether a person is entitled to such a payment.

(2) Any question arising under that section other than one determined or falling to be determined under subsection (1) above shall be determined by the Secretary of State whose decision shall except as provided by subsection (3) below be final.

(3) The Secretary of State may reverse a decision under subsection (2) above on new facts being brought to his notice or if he is satisfied that the decision was given in ignorance of, or was based on a mistake as to, some material fact.

(4) Expressions used in this section to which a meaning is assigned by section 150 of the Contributions and Benefits Act have that meaning in this section.

DERIVATION

Social Security Act 1986, s.66 and Sched. 6, para. 4.

Restrictions on entitlement to benefit following erroneous decision

Restrictions on entitlement to benefit in certain cases of error

68.—(1) This section applies where—

(a) on the determination, whenever made, of a Commissioner or the court (the "relevant determination"), a decision made by an adjudicating authority is or was found to have been erroneous in point of law; and

(b) after both—

(i) 13th July 1990 (the date of the coming into force of section 165D of the 1975 Act, the provision of that Act corresponding to this section); and

(ii) the date of the relevant determination,

a claim which falls, or which would apart from this section fall, to be decided in accordance with the relevant determination is made or treated under section 7(1) above as made by any person for any benefit.

(2) Where this section applies, any question which arises on, or on the review of a decision which is referable to, the claim mentioned in subsection (1)(b) above and which relates to the entitlement of the claimant or any other person to any benefit—

(a) in respect of a period before the relevant date; or

(b) in the case of a widow's payment, in respect of a death occurring before that date,

shall be determined as if the decision referred to in subsection (1)(a) above had been found by the Commissioner or court in question not to have been erroneous in point of law.

(3) In determining whether a person is entitled to benefit in a case where—

(a) his entitlement depends on his having been entitled to the same or some other benefit before attaining a particular age; and

(b) he attained that age—

(i) before both the date of the relevant determination and the date of the claim referred in subsection (1)(b) above, but

(ii) not before the earliest day in respect of which benefit could, apart from this section, have been awarded on that claim,

subsection (2) above shall be disregarded for the purpose only of determining the question whether he was entitled as mentioned in paragraph (a) above.

(4) In this section—

"adjudicating authority" means—

(a) an adjudication officer or, where the original decision was given on a reference under section 21(2) or 25(1) above, a social security appeal tribunal, a disability appeal tribunal or a medical appeal tribunal;

(b) any of the following former bodies or officers, that is to say, the National Assistance Board, the Supplementary Benefits Commission, the Attendance Allowance Board, a benefit officer, an insurance officer or a supplement officer; or

(c) any of the officers who, or tribunals or other bodies which, in Northern Ireland correspond to those mentioned in paragraph (a) or (b) above;

"benefit" means—

(a) benefit as defined in section 122 of the Contributions and Benefits Act;

[[1](aa) a jobseeker's allowance]; and

(b) any income-related benefit;

"the court" means the High Court, the Court of Appeal, the Court of Session, the High Court or Court of Appeal in Northern Ireland, the House of Lords or the Court of Justice of the European Community;

"the relevant date" means whichever is the latest of—

(a) the date of the relevant determination;

(b) the date which falls 12 months before the date on which the claim referred to in subsection (1)(b) above is made or treated under section 7(1) above as made; and

(c) the earliest date in respect of which the claimant would, apart from this section, be entitled on that claim to the benefit in question.

(5) For the purposes of this section—

(a) any reference in this section to entitlement to benefit includes a reference to entitlement—

(i) to any increase in the rate of a benefit; or

(ii) to a benefit, or increase of benefit, at a particular rate; and

(b) any reference to a decision which is "referable to" a claim is a reference to—

(i) a decision on the claim,

(ii) a decision on a review of the decision on the claim, or

(iii) a decision on a subsequent review of the decision on the review, and so on.

(6) The date of the relevant determination shall, in prescribed cases, be determined for the purposes of this section in accordance with any regulations made for that purpose.

Derivation

Social Security Act 1975, s.165D.

Amendment

1. Jobseekers Act 1995, Sched. 2, para. 46 (June 11, 1996).

GENERAL NOTE

This section and s.69 are in similar terms. This section applies where there is a claim for benefit following a finding by a Commissioner or court in another case (hereinafter "the relevant finding" that a decision made by an adjudicating authority was erroneous in point of law. S.69 applies where there is a review by an adjudication officer (but not an adjudicating medical authority) on the ground of error of law following such a finding by a Commissioner or a court. In each case, entitlement to benefit in respect of any period before the date of the relevant finding is to be determined as if the decision of the adjudicating authority had been found by the Commissioner or court "not to have been erroneous in point of law".

For the meaning of that phrase, see the note to s.69. What was said by the House of Lords in *Bate v. Chief Adjudication Officer* [1996] 1 W.L.R. 814 in the contest of the precurser to s.69 applies equally to s.68 (*CS/184/94*).

It is arguable that s.68 is even more objectionable than s.69. Both sections require claimants' entitlement to benefit in respect of a past period to be determined in a way that is erroneous in point of law. That is defensible if the claimant's entitlement in respect of that period was previously assessed on that basis and he or she did not challenge the decision until after the "test case" had been determined, but it is difficult to see any adequate justification when the claimant is making an entirely new claim. The argument advanced when the predecessor of s.68 was introduced was that it would create consistency between those caught by s.69 and those making new claims. In both cases, it is hard to see why the ordinary time limits for reviews and claims should not be applied but it seems especially hard that a claimant, the timing of whose claim was wholly uninfluenced by the "test case", should not be awarded benefit when he or she satisfies all the statutory conditions, merely because an adjudication officier misapplied the law in another case.

Furthermore, the potential scope of s.68 is far wider than that of s.69. S.69 applies only when a claimant's entitlement to benefit falls to be reviewed on the ground that it was erroneous in point of law and it is unlikely that there will be such a ground arising out of a decision of a Commissioner who has found a rogue decision of an adjudication officier to be erroneous in point of law, unless, by coincidence, the award of benefit to the claimant caught by s.69 happens to be erroneous on some other ground. However, there is no such limitation in cases to which s.68 might apply and all sorts of odd errors made by local adjudication officers might have to be applied to new claims made by other claimants. It seems that the only reason why large numbers of arbitrary decisions are not made under s.68 is because no-one analyses Commissioners' decisions looking for cases which might give rise its application. Thus is total chaos averted and so it has not yet had to be determined what should happen if two adjudication officers have been found to have made different errors.

An interesting problem arises because the definition of "adjudicating authority" in s.68(4) is not the same as that contained in s.165D of the Social Security Act 1975. In subs. (4)(a) the words "where the original decision was given on a reference under ss.21(2) or 25(1) above" have been inserted. Those words can qualify only "a social security appeal tribunal" and not "a disability appeal tribunal or a medical appeal tribunal" because ss.21 and 25 provide only for a power to refer questions to a social security appeal tribunal.

This Act is basically a consolidation Act and one does not expect material alterations to the law in such a statute. This was not an amendment suggested by the Law Commission (see the long title of the Act) in the relevant report (Law. Com. 203). However, the Consolidation of Enactments (Procedure) Act 1949 permits a consolidation Act to include "corrections and minor improvements" which phrase is defined in s.2 as meaning "amendments of which the effect is confined to resolving ambiguities, removing doubts, bringing obsolete provisions into conformity with modern practice, or removing unnecessary provisions or anomalies which are not of substantial importance, and amendments designed to facilitate improvement in the form or manner in which the law is stated, and includes any transitional provisions which may be necessary in consequence of such amendments". The Bill went through the Parliamentary procedure prescribed by s.1 of the 1949 Act and the amendments were approved by a joint committee of both Houses and the Lord Chancellor and Speaker. Under s.1(7) they were therefore deemed to be part of the existing law so that the Bill could be treated as a pure consolidation Bill. The general rule is that the words of a consolidation Act must be given their plain meaning even if they do effect a change in the law and that was the rule long before corrections and minor amendments were permitted by the 1949 Act. However, it is for the courts rather than for Parliament to interpret statutes and, where the joint committee has accepted that an amendment is being proposed which can be made only under the 1949 Act, it would appear in principle to be possible for a court to hold that the committee erred in accepting that the amendment fell within the definition in s.2 of that Act with the consequence that that particular amendment would be of no effect and should be ignored. The court would doubtless be wary of trespassing on Parliament's power to legislate but if Parliament fetters its committee by statute rather than by standing order, the role of the court is not excluded altogether. It is difficult to see how the amendment can be said to resolve ambiguities or remove doubts and, since s.165D of the 1975 Act was added only in 1990, the amendment can hardly be said to have been dealing with obsolete provisions. It is unlikely to be suggested that an unnecessary provision has been removed. If an anomaly has been removed, it has been replaced by a greater one and it is difficult to see how any removed anomaly could be said to be "not of substantial importance". The amendment certainly goes beyond a mere improvement in the form or manner in which the law is stated.

The effect of the addition of the phrase "on a reference under section 21(2) or 25(1) above" would appear to be substantial because the majority of decisions of social security appeal tribunals are made on appeals rather than references. Presumably it is intended to reduce the scope for confusion that would have arisen where a tribunal had made a different error from that made by the adjudication officer. The tribunal's error might have been favourable to the claimant when the adjudication officer's error was not. However, there will still be scope for confusion where a Commissioner holds a disability appeal tribunal to have erred and, by implication, finds the adjudication officer from whom the claimant appealed to the tribunal to have erred in a different way. Which error is to be applied to the claimant subsequently caught by s.68 or s.69? Such difficulties may be overlooked in practice because a Commissioner is concerned primarily with whether the relevant tribunal has erred in law and it may not be possible to discern from his or her decision whether the adjudication officer or adjudicating medical authority also erred or, if it is clear that there was an error at that level, it may not be clear precisely what the error was.

Determination of questions on review following erroneous decisions

69.—(1) Subsection (2) below applies in any case where—

(a) on the determination, whenever made, of a Commissioner or the court (the "relevant determination"), a decision made by an adjudicating authority is or was found to have been erroneous in point of law; and

(b) in consequence of that determination, any other decision—

(i) which was made before the date of that determination; and

(ii) which is referable to a claim made or treated as made by any person for any benefit,

falls (or would, apart from subsection (2) below, fall) to be revised on a review carried out under section 25(2) above on or after 13th July 1990 (the date of the passing of the Social Security Act 1990, which added to the 1975 Act sections 104(7) to (10), corresponding to this section) or on a review under section 30 above on the ground that the decision under review was erroneous in point of law.

(2) Where this subsection applies, any question arising on the review referred to in subsection (1) (b) above, or on any subsequent review of a decision which is referable to the same claim, as to any person's entitlement to, or right to payment of, any benefit—

(a) in respect of any period before the date of the relevant determination; or

(b) in the case of widow's payment, in respect of a death occurring before that date,

shall be determined as if the decision referred to in subsection (1)(a) above had been found by the Commissioner or court in question not to have been erroneous in point of law.

(3) In determining whether a person is entitled to benefit in a case where his entitlement depends on his having been entitled to the same or some other benefit before attaining a particular age, subsection (2) above shall be disregarded for the purpose only of determining the question whether he was so entitled before attaining that age.

(4) For the purposes of this section—

(a) "adjudicating authority" and "the court" have the same meaning as they have in section 68 above;

(b) any reference to—

(i) a person's entitlement to benefit; or

(ii) a decision which is referable to a claim,

shall be construed in accordance with subsection (5) of that section; and

(c) the date of the relevant determination shall, in prescribed cases, be determined in accordance with any regulations made under subsection (6) of that section.

DERIVATION

Social Security Act 1975, ss.100C(8)(b) and 104(7) to (10); Social Security Act 1986, s.52(3) and (3A)

GENERAL NOTE

This is a complicated provision that has been much criticised. It is generally accepted that the object of the provision is to make it unnecessary retrospectively to review existing awards of benefit when a "test case" goes against the Department of Social Security. In cases to which the provision applies, the view of the law formerly held by the Department is to prevail in respect of any period before the "test case" is decided. The convoluted language is no doubt due to a feeling that Parliament might have baulked at passing a law that said bluntly that the Department of Social Security's view of the law must prevail. The provision started as a Government amendment to the Social Security Bill that subsequently became the Social Security Act 1990. Part of the justification for the amendment was that the Parliamentary Commissioner for Administration had been unhappy that, where people had applied for reviews following "test case", the arrears had been limited to 12 months before the date of application for review even if claimants had not applied for the review until more than a year had elapsed since the "test case" had been determined (HL Deb., Vol. 519, cols. 684–686). In fact, the amendment did nothing to meet that concern which required, and only required, an amendment to reg. 72 of the Social Security (Adjudication) Regulations 1986. The 1986 Regulations were amended only on August 31 1991—a year after the 1990 Act had come into force—when reg. 72 was revoked and regs. 64A and 64B (now regs. 57 and 58 of the Social Security (Adjudication) Regulations 1995) were inserted in its place.

Subs. (1). This section applies only when a decision falls to be reviewed *in consequence of* a decision of a Commissioner or court which has found an earlier determination of an adjudicating authority to be erroneous in point of law. In *Bate v. Chief Adjudication Officer* [1996] 1 W.L.R. 814, the House of Lords rejected an argument that the predeccesor of this section applied only when the "relevant determination" overruled a previous binding decision. However, if the request for review was made *before* the "relevant determination", this section does not apply because the review will not be the consequence of the "relevant determination" (*CDLA/577/94*). For the approach taken by tribunals while a "test case" is pending, see *President's Circular No. 9*. In *Bate*, it was held that a decision of an adjudication officer may be "found" to be erroneous in point of law by a Commissioner or court, notwithstanding that the question for the Commissioner or court is really whether a tribunal from whom the claimant appealed against the adjudication officer's decision erred in law. That approach did not create any practical difficulties in *Bate* itself, but it is not always clear from a decision of a Commissioner or court whether any error was made by the adjudication officier or, if an error was made, what the error was. An order made by the Court of Appeal allowing an appeal by consent without argument cannot be a "relevant determination" (*CFC/2298/95*).

Subs. (2). The practical difficulties that might arise from trying to give effect to error of the adjudicating authority, found in the "relevant determination" to have erred, are removed by regulation 58 of the Social Security (Adjudication) Regulations 1995 which provides that a review in a case where this section applies has effect from the date of the "relevant determination". In *CDLA/8170/95*, decisions were reviewed in the light of a "relevant determination", the date of which was April 21, 1994. The conditions for entitlement to the care component of disability living allowance were met only in reliance on that decision and the question that arose was whether the three-month qualifying period (s.72(2) of the Social Security Contributions and Benefits Act 1992) could run only from the date of the "relevant determination", so that there would be no entitlement to benefit until June 21, 1994, or whether the qualifying period could be before the date of the "relevant determination", so that benefit could be awarded from April 21, 1994. The Commissioner took the later approach.

Subs. (4)(c). No regulations have been made under this paragraph.

Correction of errors

Regulations as to correction of errors and setting aside of decisions

70.—(1) Regulations may make provision with respect to—
(a) the correction of accidental errors in any decision or record of a decision given with respect to a claim or question arising under or in connection with any relevant enactment by a body or person authorised to decide the claim or question; and
(b) the setting aside of any such decision in a case where it appears just to set the decision aside on the ground that—
(i) a document relating to the proceedings in which the decision was given was not sent to, or was not received at an appropriate time by, a party to the proceedings or a party's representative or was not received at an appropriate time by the body or person who gave the decision; or
(ii) a party to the proceedings or a party's representative was not present at a hearing related to the proceedings.

(2) Nothing in subsection (1) above shall be construed as derogating from any power to correct errors or set aside decisions which is exercisable apart from regulations made by virtue of that subsection.

(3) In this section "relevant enactment" means any enactment contained in—
(a) the National Insurance Acts 1965 to 1974;
(b) the National Insurance (Industrial Injuries) Acts 1965 to 1974;
(c) the Industrial Injuries and Diseases (Old Cases) Acts 1967 to 1974;
(d) the Social Security Act 1973;
(e) the Social Security Acts 1975 to 1991;
(f) the Old Cases Act;
(g) the Child Benefit Act 1975;
(h) the Family Income Supplements Act 1970;
(i) the Supplementary Benefits Act 1976; or
(j) the Contributions and Benefits Act [[2] or
(k) the Jobseekers Act 1995] [[1]or
(k) the Pensions Act.]

Derivation

National Insurance Act 1974, s.6.

Amendments

1. Pensions Schemes Act 1993, Sched. 8, para. 25 (February 7, 1994)
2. Jobseekers Act 1995, Sched. 2. para. 47 (April 22, 1996) introducing a second para. (k) by mistake.

Definitions

For "the Old Cases Act", "the Contributions and Benefits Act" and "the Pensions Act", see s.191.

General Note

See regs. 10–12 of the Social Security (Adjudication) Regulations 1995.

PART III

OVERPAYMENTS AND ADJUSTMENTS OF BENEFIT

Misrepresentation etc.

Overpayments—general

71.—(1) Where it is determined that, whether fraudulently or otherwise, any person has misrepresented, or failed to disclose, any material fact and in consequence of the misrepresentation or failure—

(a) a payment has been made in respect of a benefit to which this section applies; or

(b) any sum recoverable by or on behalf of the Secretary of State in connection with any such payment has not been recovered,

the Secretary of State shall be entitled to recover the amount of any payment which he would not have made or any sum which he would have received but for the misrepresentation or failure to disclose.

[[1]\(2) Where any such determination as is referred to in subsection (1) above is made, the person making the determination shall—

(a) determine whether any, and if so what, amount is recoverable under that subsection by the Secretary of State, and

(b) specify the period during which that amount was paid to the person concerned.]

(3) An amount recoverable under subsection (1) above is in all cases recoverable from the person who misrepresented the fact or failed to disclose it.

(4) In relation to cases where payments of benefit to which this section applies have been credited to a bank account or other account under arrangements made with the agreement of the beneficiary or a person acting for him, circumstances may be prescribed in which the Secretary of State is to be entitled to recover any amount paid in excess of entitlement; but any such regulations shall not apply in relation to any payment unless before he agreed to the arrangements such notice of the effect of the regulations as may be prescribed was given in such manner as may be prescribed to the beneficiary or to a person acting for him.

(5) Except where regulations otherwise provide, an amount shall not be recoverable under [[1]. . .] regulations under subsection (4) above unless—

(a) the determination in pursuance of which it was paid has been reversed or varied on an appeal or revised on a review; and

(b) it has been determined on the appeal or review that the amount is so recoverable.

[[1]\(5A) Except where regulations otherwise provide, an amount shall not be recoverable under subsection (1) above unless the determination in pursuance of which it was paid has been reversed or varied or an appeal or revised on a review.]

(6) Regulations may provide—

(a) that amounts recoverable under subsection (1) above or regulations under subsection (4) above shall be calculated or estimated in such manner and on such basis as may be prescribed;

(b) for treating any amount paid to any person under an award which it is subsequently determined was not payable—

  (i) as properly paid; or

  (ii) as paid on account of a payment which it is determined should be or should have been made,

  and for reducing or withholding any arrears payable by virtue of the subsequent determination;

(c) for treating any amount paid to one person in respect of another as properly paid for any period for which it is not payable in cases where in consequence of a subsequent determination—

(i) the other person is himself entitled to a payment for that period; or

(ii) a third person is entitled in priority to the payee to a payment for that period in respect of the other person,

and for reducing or withholding any arrears payable for that period by virtue of the subsequent determination.

(7) Circumstances may be prescribed in which a payment on account by virtue of section 5(1)(r) above may be recovered to the extent that it exceeds entitlement.

(8) Where any amount paid is recoverable under—

(a) subsection (1) above;

(b) regulations under subsection (4) or (7) above; or

(c) section 74 below,

it may, without prejudice to any other method of recovery, be recovered by deduction from prescribed benefits.

(9) Where any amount paid in respect of a married or unmarried couple is recoverable as mentioned in subsection (8) above, it may, without prejudice to any other method of recovery, be recovered, in such circumstances as may be prescribed, by deduction from prescribed benefits payable to either of them.

(10) Any amount recoverable under the provisions mentioned in sub-section (8) above—

(a) if the person from whom it is recoverable resides in England and Wales and the county court so orders, shall be recoverable by execution issued from the county court or otherwise as if it were payable under an order of that court; and

(b) if he resides in Scotland, shall be enforced in like manner as an extract registered decree arbitral bearing a warrant for execution issued by the sheriff court of any sheriffdom in Scotland.

[[2](10A) Where—

(a) a jobseeker's allowance is payable to a person from whom any amount is recoverable as mentioned in subsection (8) above; and

(b) that person is subject to a bankruptcy order,

a sum deducted from that benefit under that subsection shall not be treated as income of his for the purposes of the Insolvency Act 1996.

(10B) Where—

(a) a jobseeker's allowance is payable to a person from whom any amount is recoverable as mentioned in subsection (8) above; and

(b) the estate of that person is sequestrated.

a sum deducted from that benefit under that subsection shall not be treated as income of his for the purposes of the Bankruptcy (Scotland) Act 1995.]

(11) This section applies to the following benefits—

(a) benefits as defined in section 122 of the Contributions and Benefits Act;

[[2](aa) subject to section 71A below, a jobseeker's allowance;]

(b) [[2]. . .], income support;

(c) family credit;

(d) disability working allowance;

(e) any social fund payments such as are mentioned in section 138(1)(a) or (2) of the Contributions and Benefits Act; and

(f) child benefit.

Derivation

Social Security Act 1986, s.53

AMENDMENTS

1. Social Security (Overpayments) Act 1996, s.1 (July 24, 1996).
2. Jobseekers Act 1995, s.32(1) and Sched. 2, para. 48 and Sched. 3 (October 7, 1996).

GENERAL NOTE

This section provides for the recovery of overpaid benefit where the overpayment has resulted from a misrepresentation of, or a failure to disclose, a material fact. The test is rather different from that applying in the general civil law and it seems fairly clear that it is intended that overpayments of social security benefits can be recovered only where this section applies and not also under the general civil law.

What is determined under this section is the question whether an overpayment *may* be recovered. That is a decision for an adjudication officer or, on appeal, a social security appeal tribunal or disability appeal tribunal. Once a decision has been made in favour of the Secretary of State, it is then for the Secretary of State (in reality, an officer acting on his or her behalf) to decide whether to exercise that right of recovery. There is no right of appeal against such a decision of the Secretary of State. If he or she does seek recovery, the overpayment may be deducted from other social security benefits (subss. (8) and (9)) or by execution in the County Court or, in Scotland, the Sheriff Court (subs. (10)). Any challenge to the decision of the adjudication officer or tribunal must be made by way of an application for review of, or appeal against, that decision. If a warrant of execution has been obtained in the County Court, it is possible to apply for it to be stayed while an application for review or appeal is brought in the proper way.

Subs. (1). An overpayment is recoverable only if it was the consequence of a misrepresentation of, or failure to disclose, a material fact. The Court of Appeal has confirmed that the words "whether fraudulently or otherwise" mean that an innocent misrepresentation or failure to disclose is enough to make any consequent overpayment recoverable (*Page v. Chief Adjudication Officer*, reported as an appendix to *R(SB) 2/92*). It had been argued that those words implied that some dishonesty was required.

misrepresentation: Any statement of fact is a representation. It is a *mis*representation if it is not true, even if it was thought to be true and so was made quite innocently. A representation may be written, oral or merely inferred from conduct (*CS/102/93*). Where two contradictory statements are made at the same time, they have to be considered together. Thus a written representation may be qualified by an oral one, or even by a representation inferred from conduct. In *R(SB) 18/85* a claimant had signed, during an interview, a declaration to the effect that he had no income. However, he was in fact in receipt of a war pension and it was said that he had produced his pension book in the course of the interview. The Commissioner held that the production of the war pension book could amount to a qualification of the written representation.

In *R(SB) 9/85*, the claimant had signed a declaration to the effect that his wife's circumstances had not changed. In fact, unbeknown to him, her earnings had increased. It was held that there had been a misrepresentation but that there would not have been had he written "I do not know" or "Not to my knowledge".

failure to disclose: A failure to disclose which is quite innocent may be sufficient to make an overpayment recoverable. However, it has been emphasised that "failed to disclose" does not mean the same as "did not disclose". "[A] 'failure' to disclose necessarily imports some breach of obligation, moral or legal, *i.e.* the non-disclosure must have occurred in circumstances in which, at lowest, disclosure by the person in question was reasonably to be expected" (*R(SB) 21/82*). This requires that the claimant must have had knowledge of the material fact. If he or she has forgotten it, there will still be a failure to disclose, albeit an innocent one (*R(SB) 21/82*). Care needs to be exercised in this area. A very elderly person with limited mental capacity may not be aware of facts that might be apparent to other claimants (*R(SB) 40/84*, where there was some doubt as to whether an elderly person understood that there had been an increase in her superannuation) but in *R(A)/1/95* it was held that lack of mental capacity was relevant only to the question whether or not the claimant knew the material fact and not also to whether or not he understood the materiality of the fact. In such a case, there is often someone else acting on behalf of the claimant and, under subs. (3), an overpayment may be recovered from that person if he or she has failed to disclose a material fact. In *R(SB) 28/83*, an overpayment was recoverable from the estate of a claimant where his brother had been appointed receiver by the Court of Protection and had failed to disclose the claimant's capital assets. The brother knew of the assets and either knew, or ought to have known, that the claimant was in receipt of supplementary benefit. In *Chief Adjudication Officer v. Sherriff* (*The Times*, May 10, 1995), the receiver appointed by the Court of Protection to act on behalf of the claimant had died and no new receiver had been appointed when the claimant herself signed the standard declaration on a claim form which had been completed by someone else and which contained an error. The error led to an overpayment. It was argued that the claimant was incapable of making a misrepresentation but the Court of Appeal held that it was immaterial that she might have been incapable of understanding her affairs. By her signature, she made the misrepresentation and it was immaterial whether she knew she was making a misrepresentation or not. The overpayment was recoverable from her. In *CIS/734/92* it was held that an error by an appointee could not be imputed to the claimant and that therefore recovery could be only from the appointee personally. That approach was rejected in *CIS/332/93* where it was held that the overpayment could be recovered only from the claimant and not from the appointee.

The test of reasonableness suggested in *R(SB) 21/81* also requires that a reasonable person in the position of the person from whom recovery is sought would have thought it necessary to disclose the material fact. This is essentially an objective test. A failure to answer a question in a claim form is likely to be fatal as is a failure to follow instructions in an order book. However, if such instructions are contradicted by the settled practice of the Department of Social Security (*R(SB) 3/81*) or by advice from the claimant's solicitor (*CSB/510/87*), it may not be reasonable to expect a claimant to follow them. In *R(SB) 2/91*, an overpayment was held not to be recoverable when a student had given details of his course but had not described it as "full-time". The question whether it was full-time was a matter for determination by the adjudication officer and not by the student, whose view was held to be immaterial. The case is decided on the basis that disclosure by the claimant was not reasonably to be expected.

A disclosure is not usually effective if it is not made to the right part of the Department of Social Security. However, again the test of reasonableness is relevant. Claimants cannot be expected to know exactly how the Department is organised. Generally, telling the local office will be sufficient if sufficient details are given so that the claimant could reasonably expect the information to be passed on to the relevant section (*R(SB) 15/87*). If in fact the disclosure is made to the correct section, there is no further duty to disclose, even if the claimant ought to have become aware that the adjudication officer had not acted on the disclosure. On the other hand, if disclosure is to the wrong section, the duty to disclose is satisfied only until such time as the claimant ought to have realised that the information had not been passed on. After that, the duty to disclose arises again and any further overpayment made will be recoverable.

material fact: It is only a misrepresentation of, or failure to disclose, a material fact that can make an overpayment recoverable. Thus a representation of law is not relevant. This is important because it is sometimes suggested that an overpayment may be recoverable merely because a claimant has signed the standard declaration on an order from an order book which says: "I declare that I have read and understand all the instructions in this order book, that I have correctly reported any fact which could affect the amount of my payment and that I am entitled to the above sum." "I am entitled to the above sum" will generally be regarded as a representation of law (*CS/102/93*). However, in *Jones v. Chief Adjudication Officer* [1994] 1 W.L.R. 62, the Court of Appeal held the phrase "I have correctly reported any fact which could affect the amount of my payment" to be a representation of a material fact but they also held that there was only a misrepresentation if the claimant knew the facts that he had not correctly reported. That approach was confirmed in *Franklin v. Chief Adjudication Officer* (*The Times*, December 29, 1995), where the Court of Appeal held that knowledge of the relevant facts was essential if a claimant was to be found to have made a misrepresentation simply on the basis of having signed a declaration to the effect that he had reported those facts.

in consequence of: There must be a causal connection between the misrepresentation or failure to disclose and the overpayment. The fact that internal checks ought to have alerted the Department as to the relevant facts does not always prevent an overpayment being recoverable. Thus, in *R(SB) 3/90*, it was held that a disclosure of a material fact did not prevent an overpayment from being recoverable when it was due to a subsequent misrepresentation. When first claiming supplementary benefit the claimant had disclosed that he was receiving superannuation payments. That claim ended. When he next claimed, the claimant made a representation to the effect that he had no income. It was held that the overpayment was recoverable even though the Department had the means of checking the veracity of that representation. In *Duggan v. Chief Adjudication Officer* (reported as an appendix to *R(SB) 13/89*), the claimant's wife was in receipt of maternity allowance. At the end of the maternity allowance period, the adjudication officer reviewed the decision awarding supplementary benefit to the claimant so as to increase it because of the loss of maternity allowance. However, the claimant's wife had claimed unemployment benefit. The fact that the adjudication officer had made an assumption that she had no income other than child benefit, without first checking whether that assumption was justified, did not prevent the overpayment from being recoverable on the ground that the claimant had failed to disclose the fact that his wife was receiving unemployment benefit. On the other hand, if the relevant part of the Department already knows a fact but has failed to act on that knowledge, any failure by the claimant to disclose the fact is not the cause of the overpayment. In *CIS/159/90*, a claimant failed to disclose that she had received an order book for child benefit but the local office had already been informed of that fact by the Child Benefit Centre. The overpayment was not recoverable.

the amount recoverable: The general rule is that the whole of the overpayment caused by the misrepresentation or failure to disclose is recoverable. However, reg. 13 of the Social Security (Payments on account, Overpayments and Recovery) Regulations 1988 permits the deduction of any amount previously offset under reg. 5. Reg. 14 is relevant where there has been an overpayment because a claimant has misrepresented or failed to disclose the amount of his or her capital assets. In such a case, it is assumed that had the capital been properly taken into account when calculating entitlement to benefit, the amount of capital would have been reduced by the amount of benefit actually overpaid. The calculation is done at precise quarterly intervals.

Subs. (2). This subsection was substituted in order to reverse the effect of *CIS/451/95* in which it had been held that the original version had required the decision on recoverability to be made as part of the decision reviewing (or varying on appeal) the original award of benefit and thus giving rise to the finding that hrere had been an overpayment. Presumably the object of the subsection as originally enacted was to keep together the decision as to the true amount of entitlement and the decision as to the recoverability of any overpayment. It is arguable that the new subsection does not make all that much difference because the adjudication officer or tribunal reviewing (or varying on appeal) the original award is likely to be the person making the determination referred to in subsection (1). The Commissioner deciding *CIS/451/95* took the view that it would give rise to problems if the review (or appeal) decision were to be separated from the decision as to recoverability of any overpayment. However, where a review decision gives rise to an overpayment, it will generally be open to an adjudication officer, subsequently calculating the amount of the overpayment and deciding whether or not it is recoverable, to review the review decision if it appears to him or her to be wrong. Thus, inconsistent decisions can be avoided (*CIS/11037/95*), although there may be difficulties where the review decision was given by a tribunal and it appears that the decision of the tribunal was erroneous in point of law, as such a decision cannot be reviewed. The new subsection is effective in any case where a determination mentioned in subsection (1) is made after July 24, 1996 (s.1(5) of the Social Security (Overpayments) Act 1996).

Subs. (3). An overpayment may be recovered from any person who has misrepresented or failed to disclose the material fact and so caused the overpayment. If that person has died, the overpayment may be recovered from his or her estate (*Secretary of State for Social Services v. Solly* [1974] 3 All E.R. 922).

Subss. (5) and (5A). No decision as to recovery can be made until the decision under which the overpayment was made has been properly varied on appeal or revised on review. If an adjudication officer has failed to carry out a review but has made a decision to the effect that there has been an overpayment which is recoverable and the claimant has appealed, the tribunal can itself make the review decision (*CIS/35/90, CIS/287/92*). Reg. 12 of the Social Security (Payments on account, Overpayments and Recovery) Regulations 1988 provides that this subsection does not apply "where the facts and circumstances of the misrepresentation or non-disclosure do not provide a basis for reviewing and revising the determination under which payment was made". In *CIS/102/93* it was suggested that reg. 12 had effect in a case where a claimant cashed an order book *after* an adjudication officer had reviewed the award of benefit and determined that no benefit was payable.

Subss. (6)–(9). See the Social Security (Payments on account, Overpayments and Recovery) Regulations 1988.

Subs. (11). Note that this section does not apply to the Christmas bonus paid under s. 148 of the Social Security Contributions and Benefits Act 1992 or under earlier legislation. However, by virtue of subs (11)(a) and also Sched. 10 to this Act, this section also applies to other overpayments of benefit under former legislation, although, in respect of overpayments made before April 6, 1987 under the Social Security Act 1975 or its predecessors, the right to recovery depends on the claimant having failed to use due care and diligence to avoid the overpayment (*Plewa v. Chief Adjudication Officer* [1995] A.C. 249).

71A–72. *Omitted.*

Adjustments of benefits

Overlapping benefits—general

73.—(1) Regulations may provide for adjusting benefit as defined in section 122 of the Contributions and Benefits Act [[1], or a contribution—based jobseeker's allowance,] which is payable to or in respect of any person, or the conditions for [[1]receipt of that benefit], where—

(a) there is payable in his case any such pension or allowance as is described in subsection (2) below; or

(b) the person is, or is treated under the regulations as, undergoing medical or other treatment as an in-patient in a hospital or similar institution.

(2) Subsection (1)(a) above applies to any pension, allowance or benefit payable out of public funds (including any other benefit as so defined, whether it is of the same or a different description) which is payable to or in respect of—

(a) the person referred to in subsection (1);

(b) that person's wife or husband;

(c) any child or adult dependant of that person; or

(d) the wife or husband of any adult dependant of that person.

(3) Where but for regulations made by virtue of subsection (1)(a) above two persons would both be entitled to an increase of benefit in respect of a third person, regulations may make provision as to their priority.

[[1](4) Regulations may provide for adjusting

(a) benefit as defined in section 122 of the Contributions and Benefits Act; or

(b) a contribution-based jobseeker's allownce.

payable to or in respect of any person where there is payable in his case any such benefit as is described in subsection (5) below.]

(5) Subsection (4) above applies to any benefit payable under the legislation of any member State other than the United Kingdom which is payable to or in respect of—

(a) the person referred to in that subsection;

(b) that person's wife or husband;

(c) any child or adult dependant of that person; or

(d) the wife or husband of any adult dependant of that person.

Derivation

Social Security Act 1975, s.85.

Amendment

1. Jobseekers Act 1995, Sched. 2, para. 49 (June 11, 1996).

General Note

See the Social Security (Overlapping Benefits) Regulations 1979.

74.—80. *Omitted.*

Part IV

Recovery From Compensation Payments

81.—104. *Repealed by the Social Security (Recovery of Benefits) Act 1997, s.33(2) and Sched. 4, with effect from October 1, 1997, save in those cases excepted from the application of the new Act by s.2.*

105.—154. *Omitted.*

PART XI

COMPUTATION OF BENEFITS

Effect of alteration of rates of benefit under Parts II to V of Contributions and Benefits Act

155.—(1) This section has effect where the rate of any benefit to which this section applies is altered—

(a) by an Act subsequent to this Act;

(b) by an order under section 150 or 152 above; or

(c) in consequence of any such Act or order altering any maximum rate of benefit;

and in this section "the commencing date" means the date fixed for payment of benefit at an altered rate to commence.

(2) This section applies to benefit under Part II, III, IV or V of the Contributions and Benefits Act.

(3) Subject to such exceptions or conditions as may be prescribed, where—

(a) the weekly rate of a benefit to which this section applies is altered to a fixed amount higher or lower than the previous amount; and

(b) before the commencing date an award of that benefit has been made (whether before or after the passing of the relevant Act or the making of the relevant order),

except as respects any period falling before the commencing date, the benefit shall become payable at the altered rate without any claim being made for it in the case of an increase in the rate of benefit or any review of the award in the case of a decrease, and the award shall have effect accordingly.

(4) Where—

(a) the weekly rate of a benefit to which this section applies is altered; and

(b) before the commencing date (but after that date is fixed) an award is made of the benefit;

the award either may provide for the benefit to be paid as from the commencing date at the altered rate or may be expressed in terms of the rate appropriate at the date of the award.

(5) Where in consequence of the passing of an Act, or the making of an order, altering the rate of disablement pension, regulations are made varying the scale of disablement gratuities, the regulation may provide that the scale as varied shall apply only in cases where the period taken into account by the assessment of the extent of the disablement in respect of which the gratuity is awarded begins or began after such day as may be prescribed.

(6) Subject to such exceptions or conditions as may be prescribed, where—

(a) for any purpose of any Act or regulations the weekly rate at which a person contributes to the cost of providing for a child, or to the maintenance of an adult dependant, is to be calculated for a period beginning on or after the commencing date for an increase in the weekly rate of benefit; but

(b) account is to be taken of amounts referrable to the period before the commencing date,

those amounts shall be treated as increased in proportion to the increase in the weekly rate of benefit.

(7) *Omitted.*

DERIVATION

Social Security Act 1986, s.64.

GENERAL NOTE

Subs. (3) is modified by reg. 2 of the Social Security Benfits (Up-rating) Regulations 1997 so that it dos not apply until there has been determined any question as to the weekly rate at which benefit is to be payable by virtue of the Social Security Benefits Up-rating Order 1997 or whether the conditions for receipt of the benefit at the altered rate are satisfied. There were similar modifications in earlier years.

156.—169. *Omitted.*

PART XIII

ADVISORY BODIES AND CONSULTATION

The Social Security Advisory Committee and the Industrial Injuries Advisory Council

The Social Security Advisory Committee

170.—(1) The Social Security Advisory Committee (in this Act referred to as "the Committee") constituted under section 9 of the Social Security Act 1980 shall continue in being by that name—

(a) to give (whether in pursuance of a reference under this Act or otherwise) advice and assistance to the Secretary of State in connection with the discharge of his functions under the relevant enactments;

(b) to give (whether in pursuance of a reference under this Act or otherwise) advice and assistance to the Northern Ireland Department in connection with the discharge of its functions under the relevant Northern Ireland enactments; and

(c) to perform such other duties as may be assigned to the Committee under any enactment.

(2) Schedule 5 to this Act shall have effect with respect to the constitution of the Committee and the other matters there mentioned.

(3) The Secretary of State may from time to time refer to the Committee for consideration and advice such questions relating to the operation of any of the relevant enactments as he thinks fit (including questions as to the advisability of amending any of them).

(4) The Secretary of State shall furnish the Committee with such information as the Committee may reasonably require for the proper discharge of its functions.

(5) In this Act—

"the relevant enactments" means—

(a) the provisions of the Contributions and Benefits Act [[2], this Act and the Social Security (Incapacity for Work) Act 1994], except as they apply to industrial injuries benefit and Old Cases payments;

[[3](aa) the provisions of the Jobseekers Act 1995;] and

(b) the provisions of Part II of Schedule 3 to the Consequential Provisions Act, except as they apply to industrial injuries benefit; and

"the relevant Northern Ireland enactments" means—

(a) the provisions of the Northern Ireland Contributions and Benefits Act and the Northern Ireland Administration Act, except as they apply to Northern Ireland industrial injuries benefit and payments under Part I of Schedule 8 to the Northern Ireland Contributions and Benefits Act;

[[3](aa) any provisions in Northern Ireland which corresponds to provisions of the Jobseekers Act 1995; and]

(b) the provisions of Part II of Schedule 3 to the Social Security (Consequential Provisions) (Northern Ireland) Act 1992, except as they apply to Northern Ireland industrial injuries benefit; and

(c) [[1] section 32(6) of the Pension Schemes (Northern Ireland) Act 1993];

and in this definition—

(i) "Northern Ireland Contributions and Benefits Act" means the Social Security Contributions and Benefits (Northern Ireland) Act 1992;

(ii) "Northern Ireland industrial injuries benefit" means benefit under Part V of the Northern Ireland Contributions and Benefits Act other than under Schedule 8 to that Act.

DERIVATION

Social Security Act 1980, s.9.

AMENDMENTS

1. Pension Schemes (Northern Ireland) Act 1993, Sched. 7, para. 26 (February 2, 1994)
2. Social Security (Incapacity for Work) Act 1994, Sched. 1, para. 51 (April 13, 1995).
3. Jobseekers Act 1995, Sched. 2, para. 67 (April 22, 1996).

The Industrial Injuries Advisory Council

171.—(1) The Industrial Injuries Advisory Council (in this Act referred to as "the Council") constituted under section 62 of the National Insurance (Industrial Injuries) Act 1965 shall continue in being by that name.

(2) Schedule 6 to this Act shall have effect with respect to the constitution of the Council and the other matters there mentioned.

(3) The Secretary of State may from time to time refer to the Council for consideration and advice such questions as he thinks fit relating to industrial injuries benefit or its administration.

(4) The Council may also give advice to the Secretary of State on any other matter relating to such benefit or its administration.

DERIVATION

Social Security Act 1975, s.141(1) and (3).

Functions of Committee and Council in relation to regulations

172.—(1) Subject—

(a) to subsection (3) below; and

(b) to section 173 below,

where the Secretary of State proposes to make regulations under any of the relevant enactments, he shall refer the proposals, in the form of draft regulations or otherwise, to the Committee.

(2) Subject—

(a) to subsection (4) below; and

(b) to section 173 below,

where the Secretary of State proposes to make regulations relating only to industrial injuries benefit or its administration, he shall refer the proposals, in the form of draft regulations or otherwise, to the Council for consideration and advice.

(3) Subsection (1) above does not apply to the regulations specified in Part I of Schedule 7 to this Act.

(4) Subsection (2) above does not apply to the regulations specified in Part II of that Schedule.

(5) In relation to regulations required or authorised to be made by the Secretary of State in conjunction with the Treasury, the reference in subsection (1) above to the Secretary of State shall be construed as a reference to the Secretary of State and the Treasury.

DERIVATION

Social Security Act 1975, s.141(2); Social Security Act 1980, s.10(1), (2) and (9).

Cases in which consultation is not required

173.—(1) Nothing in any enactment shall require any proposals in respect of regulations to be referred to the Committee or the Council if—

(a) it appears to the Secretary of State that by reason of the urgency of the matter it is inexpedient so to refer them; or

(b) the relevant advisory body have agreed that they shall not be referred.

(2) Where by virtue only of subsection (1)(a) above the Secretary of State makes regulations without proposals in respect of them having been referred, then, unless the relevant advisory body agrees that this subsection shall not apply, he shall refer the regulations to that body as soon as practicable after making them.

(3) Where the Secretary of State has referred proposals to the Committee or the Council, he may make the proposed regulations before the Committee have made their report or, as the case may be the Council have given their advice, only if after the reference it appears to him that by reason of the urgency of the matter it is expedient to do so.

(4) Where by virtue of this section regulations are made before a report of the Committee has been made, the Committee shall consider them and make a report to the Secretary of State containing such recommendations with regard to the regulations as the Committee thinks appropriate; and a copy of any report made to the Secretary of State on the regulations shall be laid by him before each House of Parliament together, if the report contains recommendations, with a statement—

(a) of the extent (if any) to which the Secretary of State proposes to give effect to the recommendations; and

(b) in so far as he does not propose to give effect to them, of his reasons why not.

(5) Except to the extent that this subsection is excluded by an enactment passed after 25th July 1986, nothing in any enactment shall require the reference to the Committee or the Council of any regulations contained in either—

(a) a statutory instrument made before the end of the period of six months beginning with the coming into force of the enactment under which those regulations are made; or

(b) a statutory instrument—

(i) which states that it contains only regulations made by virtue of, or consequential upon, a specified enactment; and

(ii) which is made before the end of the period of six months beginning with the coming into force of that specified enactment.

(6) In relation to regulations required or authorised to be made by the Secretary of State in conjunction with the Treasury, any reference in this section to the Secretary of State shall be construed as a reference to the Secretary of State and the Treasury.

(7) In this section "regulations" means regulations under any enactment, whenever passed.

DERIVATION

Social Security Act 1980, s.10(9); Social Security Act 1986, s.61(1)–(5).

Committee's report on regulations and Secretary of State's duties

174.—(1) The Committee shall consider any proposals referred to it by the Secretary of State under section 172 above and shall make to the Secretary of State a report containing such recommendations with regard to the subject-matter of the proposals as the Committee thinks appropriate.

(2) If after receiving a report of the Committee the Secretary of State lays before Parliament any regulations or draft regulations which comprise the whole or any part of the subject-matter of the proposals referred to the Committee, he shall lay with the regulations or draft regulations a copy of the Committee's report and a statement showing—

(a) the extent (if any) to which he has, in framing the regulations, given effect to the Committee's recommendations; and

(b) in so far as effect has not been given to them, his reasons why not.

(3) In the case of any regulations laid before Parliament at a time when Parliament is not sitting, the requirements of subsection (2) above shall be satisfied as respects either House of Parliament if a copy of the report and statement there referred to are laid before that House not later than the second day on which the House sits after the laying of the regulations.

(4) In relation to regulations required or authorised to be made by the Secretary of State in conjunction with the Treasury any reference in this section to the Secretary of State shall be construed as a reference to the Secretary of State and the Treasury.

DERIVATION

Social Security Act 1980, s.10(3)–(5) and (9).

Disability Living Allowance Advisory Board

Disability Living Allowance Advisory Board

175.—(1) The Disability Living Allowance Advisory Board (in this section referred to as "the Board") constituted under section 3(1) of the Disability Living Allowance and Disability Working Allowance Act 1991 shall continue in being by that name.

(2) Regulations shall confer on the Board such functions relating to disability living allowance or attendance allowance as the Secretary of State thinks fit and shall make provision for—

(a) the Board's constitution;

(b) the qualifications of its members;

(c) the method of their appointment;

(d) the term of office and other terms of appointment of its members;

(e) their removal.

(3) Regulations may also make provision—

(a) enabling the Board to appoint persons as advisers to it on matters on which in its opinion they are specially qualified;

(b) for the appointment of officers and servants of the Board;

(c) enabling the Board to act notwithstanding any vacancy among its members;

(d) enabling the Board to make rules for regulating its procedure (including its quorum).

(4) The expenses of the Board to such an amount as may be approved by the Treasury shall be paid by the Secretary of State out of money provided by Parliament.

(5) There may be paid as part of the expenses of the Board—

(a) to all or any of the members of the Board, such salaries or other remuneration and travelling and other allowances;

(b) to advisers to the Board, such fees; and

(c) to such other persons as may be specified in regulations such travelling and other allowances (including compensation for loss of remunerative time),

as the Secretary of State may with the consent of the Treasury determine.

(6) The Secretary of State may furnish the Board with such information as he considers that it may need to enable it to discharge its functions.

DERIVATION

Disability Living Allowance and Disability Working Allowance Act 1991, s.3(1)–(6).

GENERAL NOTE

See the Disability Living Allowance Advisory Board Regulations 1991. Among functions conferred on the Board by reg. 2 of those Regulations is a duty to give advice to medical practitioners referring cases or questions under s.54(5).

176.—179. *Omitted.*

PART XV

MISCELLANEOUS

180.—182. *Omitted.*

Industrial injuries and diseases

Research on industrial injuries etc.

183.—(1) The Secretary of State may promote research into the causes and incidence of accidents arising out of and in the course of employment, or injuries and diseases which—

(a) are due to the nature of employment; or

(b) it is contemplated might be prescribed for the purposes of sections 108 to 110 of the Contributions and Benefits Act,

either by himself employing persons to conduct such research or by contributing to the expenses of, or otherwise assisting, other persons engaged in such research.

(2) The Secretary of State may pay to persons so employed by him such salaries or remuneration, and such travelling and other allowances, as he may determine with the consent of the Treasury.

DERIVATION

Social Security Act 1975, s.154.

Control of pneumoconiosis

184. As respects pneumoconiosis, regulations may provide—

(a) for requiring persons to be medically examined before, or within a prescribed period after, becoming employed in any occupation in relation to which pneumoconiosis is prescribed, and to be medically examined periodically while so employed, and to furnish information required for the purposes of any such examination;

(b) for suspending from employment in any such occupation, and in such other occupations as may be prescribed, persons found on such an examination—

(i) to be suffering from pneumoconiosis or tuberculosis, or

(ii) to be unsuitable for such employment, having regard to the risk of pneumoconiosis and such other matters affecting their susceptibility to pneumoconiosis as may be prescribed;

(c) for the disqualification for the receipt of benefit as defined in section 122 of the Contributions and Benefits Act in respect of pneumoconiosis of any person who fails without good cause to submit himself to any such examination or to furnish information required by the regulations or who engages in any employment from which he has been suspended as mentioned in paragraph (b) above;

(d) for requiring employers—

(i) to provide facilities for such examinations,

(ii) not to employ in any occupation a person who has been suspended as mentioned in paragraph (b) above from employment in that occupation or who has failed without good cause to submit himself to such an examination,

(iii) to give to such officer as may be prescribed the prescribed notice of the commencement of any prescribed industry or process;

(e) for the recovery on summary conviction of monetary penalties in respect of any contravention of or failure to comply with any such requirement as is mentioned in paragraph (d) above, so, however, that such penalties shall not exceed £5.00 for every day on which the contravention or failure occurs or continues;

(f) for such matters as appear to the Secretary of State to be incidental to or consequential on provisions included in the regulations by virtue of paragraphs (a) to (d) above or section 110 (1) of the Contributions and Benefits Act.

DERIVATION

Social Security Act 1975, s.155.

185.—188. *Omitted.*

PART XVI

GENERAL

Subordinate legislation

Regulations and orders—general

189.—(1) Subject to subsection (2) below and to any other express provision of this Act, regulations and orders under this Act shall be made by the Secretary of State.

(2) Regulations with respect to proceedings before the Commissioners (whether for the determination of any matter or for leave to appeal to or from the Commissioners) shall be made by the Lord Chancellor.

(3) Powers under this Act to make regulations or orders are exercisable by statutory instrument.

(4) Except in the case of regulations under section 24 or 175 above and in so far as this Act otherwise provides, any power conferred by this Act to make an Order in Council, regulations or an order may be exercised—

(a) either in relation to all cases to which the power extends, or in relation to those cases subject to specified exceptions, or in relation to any specified cases or classes of case;

(b) so as to make, as respect the cases in relation to which it is exercised—

(i) the full provision to which the power extends or any less provision (whether by way of exception or otherwise);

(ii) the same provision for all cases in relation to which the power is exercised, or different provision for different cases or different classes of case or different provision as respects the same case or class of case for different purposes of this Act;

(iii) any such provision either unconditionally or subject to any specified condition;

and where such a power is expressed to be exercisable for alternative purposes it may be exercised in relation to the same case for any or all of those purposes; and powers to make an Order in Council, regulations or an order for the purposes of any one provision of this Act are without prejudice to powers to make regulations or an order for the purposes of any other provision.

(5) Without prejudice to any specific provision in this Act, a power conferred by this Act to make an Order in Council, regulations or an order (other than the power conferred by section 24 above) includes power to make thereby such incidental, supplementary, consequential or transitional provision as appears to Her Majesty, or the authority making the regulations or order, as the case may be, to be expedient for the purposes of the Order in Council, regulations or order.

(6) Without prejudice to any specific provisions in this Act, a power conferred by any provision of this Act, except sections 14, 24, 130 and 175, to make an Order in Council, regulations or an order includes power to provide for a person to exercise a discretion in dealing with any matter.

(7) *Omitted.*

(8) An order under section 135, 140, 150, 152, 165(4) or 169 above and regulations prescribing relevant benefits for the purposes of Part IV of this Act or under section 85 above shall not be made without the consent of the Treasury.

(9) Any power of the Secretary of State under any provision of this Act, except under sections 80, 154, 175 and 178, to make any regulations or order, where the power is not expressed to be exercisable with the consent of the Treasury, shall if the Treasury so direct be exercisable only in conjunction with them.

(10) Where the Lord Chancellor proposes to make regulations under this Act, other than under section 24 above, it shall be his duty to consult the Lord Advocate with respect to the proposal.

(11) A power under any of sections 177 to 179 above to make provision by regulations or Order in Council for modifications or adaptations of the Contributions and Benefits Act or this Act shall be exercisable in relation to any enactment passed after this Act which is directed to be construed as one with them, except in so far as any such enactment relates to a benefit in relation to which the power is not exercisable; but this subsection applies only so far as a contrary intention is not expressed in the enactment so passed, and is without prejudice to the generality of any such direction.

(12) Any reference in this section or section 190 below to an Order in Council, or an order or regulations, under this Act includes a reference to an Order in Council, an order or regulations made under any provision of an enactment passed after this Act and directed to be construed as one with this Act; but this subsection applies only so far as a contrary intention is not expressed in the enactment so passed, and without prejudice to the generality of any such direction.

DERIVATION

Social Security Act 1975, ss.113(2)(c), 133(6), 166 and 168; Social Security Act 1986, s.83(1) and (2); and other statutes not relevant to this book.

Parliamentary control of orders and regulations

190.—(1) Subject to the provisions of this section, a statutory instrument containing (whether alone or with other provisions)—

(a) an order under section 141, 143, 145, 146, 150, 152 or 162(7) above; or

(b) regulations under section 102(2) or [[1]122B(1)(b) or] 154 above,

shall not be made unless a draft of the instrument has been laid before Parliament and been approved by a resolution of each House of Parliament.

(2) Subsection (1) above does not apply to a statutory instrument by reason only that it contains regulations under section 154 above which are to be made for the purpose of consolidating regulations to be revoked in the instrument.

(3) A statutory instrument—

(a) which contains (whether alone or with other provisions) orders or regulations made under this Act by the Secretary of State; and

(b) which is not subject to any requirement that a draft of the instrument be laid before and approved by a resolution of each House of Parliament,

shall be subject to annulment in pursuance of a resolution of either House of Parliament.

(4) A statutory instrument—

(a) which contains (whether alone or with other provisions) regulations made under this Act by the Lord Chancellor; and

(b) which is not subject to any requirement that a draft of the instrument be laid before and approved by a resolution of each House of Parliament,

shall be subject to annulment in pursuance of a resolution of either House of Parliament.

DERIVATION

Social Security Act 1975, s.167; Social Security Act 1980, s.14(8); Social Security Act 1986, s.83(3) and (4).

AMENDMENT

1. Social Security Administration (Fraud) Act 1997, Sched. 1, para. 11 (July 1, 1997).

Supplementary

Interpretation—general

191. In this Act, unless the context otherwise requires—

"the 1975 Act" means the Social Security Act 1975;

"the 1986 Act" means the Social Security Act 1986;

"benefit" means benefit under the Contributions and Benefits Act [[4]and includes a jobseeker's allowance];

[. . .]

"Christmas bonus" means a payment under Part X of the Contributions and Benefits Act;
"claim" is to be construed in accordance with "claimant";
"claimant" (in relation to contributions under Part I and to benefit under Parts II to IV of the Contributions and Benefits Act) means—
(a) a person whose right to be excepted from liability to pay, or to have his liability deferred for, or to be credited with, a contribution, is in question;
(b) a person who has claimed benefit;
and includes, in relation to an award or decision a beneficiary under the award or affected by the decision;
"claimant" (in relation to industrial injuries benefit) means a person who has claimed such a benefit and includes—
(a) an applicant for a declaration under section 44 above that an accident was or was not an industrial accident; and
(b) in relation to an award or decision, a beneficiary under the award or affected by the decision;
"Commissioner" means the Chief Social Security Commissioner or any other Social Security Commissioner and includes a tribunal of three Commissioners constituted under section 57 above;
"compensation payment" and "compensator" have the meanings assigned to them respectively by sections 81 and 82 above;
"the Consequential Provisions Act" means the Social Security (Consequential Provisions) Act 1992;
[[5]"contribution" means a contribution under Part I of the Contributions and Benefits Act;]
[[4]"contribution-based jobseeker's allowance" has the same meaning as in the Jobseekers Act 1995;]
[. . .]
"the Contributions and Benefits Act" means the Social Security Contributions and Benefits Act 1992;
"disablement benefit" is to be construed in accordance with section 94(2)(a) of the Contributions and Benefits Act;
"the disablement questions" is to be construed in accordance with section 45 above;
[. . .]
"5 year general qualification" is to be construed in accordance with section 71 of the Courts and Legal Services Act 1990;
[. . .]
[[4]"income-based jobseeker's allowance" has the same meaning as in the Jobseekers Act 1995;]
"income-related benefit" means—
(a) income support;
(b) family credit;
(c) disability working allowance;
(d) housing benefit; and
[[1](e) council tax benefit];
"industrial injuries benefit" means benefit under Part V of the Contributions and Benefits Act, other than under Schedule 8;
[. . .]
"medical examination" includes bacteriological and radiographical tests and similar investigations, and "medically examined" has a corresponding meaning;
"medical practitioner" means—
(a) a registered medical practitioner; or
(b) a person outside the United Kingdom who is not a registered medical

practitioner, but has qualifications corresponding (in the Secretary of State's opinion) to those of a registered medical practitioner;

''medical treatment'' means medical, surgical or rehabilitative treatment (including any course of diet or other regimen), and references to a person receiving or submitting himself to medical treatment are to be construed accordingly;

[. . .]

''the Northern Ireland Department'' means the Department of Health and Social Services for Northern Ireland;

''the Northern Ireland Administration Act'' means the Social Security (Northern Ireland) Administration Act 1992;

''occupational pension scheme'' has the same meaning as in [2Section 1] of the Pensions Act;

''the Old Cases Act'' means the Industrial Injuries and Diseases (Old Cases) Act 1975;

''Old Cases payments'' means payments under Part I of Schedule 8 to the Contributions and Benefits Act;

[3''pensionable age'' has the meaning given by the rules in paragraph 1 of Schedule 4 to the Pensions Act 1995];

''the Pensions Acts'' means the [2Pension Schemes Act 1993];

''personal pension scheme'' has the meaning assigned to it by [2section 1 of the Pension Act and ''appropriate'' in relation to such a scheme, shall be construed in accordance with section 7(4) of that Act;]

''prescribe'' means prescribe by regulations;

''President'' means the President of social security appeal tribunals, disability appeal tribunals and medical appeal tribunals;

[. . .]

''tax year'' means the 12 months beginning with 6th April in any year;

''10 year general qualification'' is to be construed in accordance with section 71 of the Courts and Legal Services Act 1990; and

''widow's benefit'' has the meaning assigned to it by section 20(1)(e) of the Contributions and Benefits Act.

Derivation

Social Security Act 1975, s.168(1) and Sched. 20; Social Security Act 1986, s.84(1).

Amendments

1. Local Government Finance Act 1992, Sched. 9, para. 25(c) (April 1, 1993).
2. Pension Schemes Act 1993, Sched.8, para.31 (February 7, 1994).
3. Pensions Act 1995, Sched. 4, para. 14 (July 19, 1995).
4. Jobseekers Act 1995, Sched. 2, para. 73 (April 22, 1996).
5. Social Security Administration (Fraud) Act 1997, Sched. 1, para. 12 (July 1, 1997).

Short title, commencement and extent

192.—(1) This Act may be cited as the Social Security Administration Act 1992.

(2) This Act is to be read, where appropriate, with the Contributions and Benefits Act and the Consequential Provisions Act.

(3) The enactments consolidated by this Act are repealed, in consequence of the consolidation, by the Consequential Provisions Act.

(4) Except as provided in Schedule 4 to the Consequential Provisions Act, this Act shall come into force on 1st July 1992.

(5) The following provisions extend to Northern Ireland—

section 24;

section 101;
section 170 (with Schedule 5);
section 177 (with Schedule 8); and
this section.

(6) Except as provided by this section, this Act does not extend to Northern Ireland.

SCHEDULES

SCHEDULE 1

CLAIMS FOR BENEFIT MADE OR TREATED AS MADE BEFORE 1ST OCTOBER 1990

Claims made or treated as made on or after 2nd September 1985 and before 1st October 1986

1. Section 1 above shall have effect in relation to a claim made or treated as made on or after 2nd September 1985 and before 1st October 1986 as if the following subsections were substituted for subsections (1) to (3)—

"(1) Except in such cases as may be prescribed, no person shall be entitled to any benefit unless, in addition to any other conditions relating to that benefit being satisfied—

(a) he makes a claim for it—

(i) in the prescribed manner; and

(ii) subject to subsection (2) below, within the prescribed time; or

(b) by virtue of a provision of Chapter VI of Part II of the 1975 Act or of regulations made under such a provision he would have been treated as making a claim for it.

(2) Regulations shall provide for extending, subject to any prescribed conditions, the time within which a claim may be made in cases where it is not made within the prescribed time but good cause is shown for the delay.

(3) Notwithstanding any regulations made under this section, no person shall be entitled to any benefit (except disablement benefit or industrial death benefit) in respect of any period more than 12 months before the date on which the claim is made.".

Claims made or treated as made on or after 1st October 1986 and before 6th April 1987

2. Section 1 above shall have effect in relation to a claim made or treated as made on or after 1st October 1986 and before 6th April 1987 as if the subsections set out in paragraph 1 above were substituted for subsections (1) to (3) but with the insertion in subsection (3) of the words, "reduced earnings allowance" after the words "disablement benefit".

Claims made or treated as made on or after 6th April 1987 and before 21st July 1989

3. Section 1 above shall have effect in relation to a claim made or treated as made on or after 6th April 1987 and before 21st July 1989, as if—

(a) the following subsection were substituted for subsection (1)—

"(1) Except in such cases as may be prescribed, no person shall be entitled to any benefit unless, in addition to any other conditions relating to that benefit being satisfied—

(a) he makes a claim for it in the prescribed manner and within the prescribed time; or

(b) by virtue of regulations made under section 51 of the 1986 Act he would have been treated as making a claim for it."; and

(b) there were omitted—

(i) from subsection (2), the words "except as provided by section 3 below"; and

(ii) subsection (3).

Claims made or treated as made on or after 21st July 1989 and before 13th July 1990

4. Section 1 above shall have effect in relation to a claim made or treated as made on or after 21st July 1989 and before 13th July 1990 as if there were omitted—

(a) from subsection (1), the words "and subject to the following provisions of this section and to section 3 below";

(b) from subsection (2), the words "except as provided by section 3 below"; and

(c) subsection (3).

Claims made or treated as made on or after 13th July 1990 and before 1st October 1990

5. Section 1 above shall have effect in relation to a claim made or treated as made on or after 13th July 1990 and before 1st October 1990 as if there were omitted—

(a) from subsection (1), the words "the following provisions of this section and to"; and

(b) subsection (3).

DERIVATION

Social Security Act 1975, s.165A.

SCHEDULE 2

COMMISSIONERS, TRIBUNALS ETC—SUPPLEMENTARY PROVISIONS

Tenure of offices

1.—(1) Subject to the following provisions of this paragraph, the President and the regional and other full-time chairmen of social security appeal tribunals, medical appeal tribunals and disability appeal tribunals shall hold and vacate office in accordance with the terms of their appointment.

(2) Commissioners, the President and the full-time chairmen shall vacate their offices [[1] on the day on which they attain the age of 70, but subject to section 26(4) to (6) of the Judicial Pensions and Retirement Act 1993 (power to authorise continuance in office up to the age of 75).]

(3) [[1] . . .]

(4) A Commissioner, the President and a full-time chairman may be removed from office by the Lord Chancellor on the ground of incapacity or misbehaviour.

(5) Where the Lord Chancellor proposes to exercise a power conferred on him by sub-paragraph [[1] . . .] (4) above, it shall be his duty to consult the Lord Advocate with respect to the proposal.

(6) Nothing in sub-paragraph (2) or (3) above or in section 13 or 32 of the Judicial Pensions Act 1981 (which relate to pensions for Commissioners) shall apply to a person by virtue of his appointment in pursuance of section 52(2) above.

(7) Nothing in sub-paragraph [[1] . . .] (4) above applies to a Commissioner appointed before 23rd May 1980.

Remuneration etc. for President and Chairmen

2.—(1) The Secretary of State may pay, or make such payments towards the provision of, such remuneration, pensions, allowances or gratuities to or in respect of the President and full-time chairmen as, with the consent of the Treasury, he may determine.

[[1] (2) Sub-paragraph (1) above, so far as relating to pensions, allowances and gratuities, shall not have effect in relation to persons to whom Part I of the Judicial Pensions and Retirement Act 1993 applies, except to the extent provided by or under that Act.]

Officers and staff

3. The President may appoint such officers and staff as he thinks fit—

(a) for himself;

(b) for the regional and other full-time chairmen;

(c) for social security appeal tribunals;

(d) for disability appeal tribunals; and

(e) for medical appeal tribunals,

with the consent of the Secretary of State and the Treasury as to numbers and as to remuneration and other terms and conditions of service.

Clerks to social security appeal tribunals and disability appeal tribunals

4.—(1) The President shall assign clerks to service the social security appeal tribunal for each area and the disability appeal tribunal for each area.

(2) The duty of summoning members of a panel to serve on such a tribunal shall be performed by the clerk to the tribunal.

Miscellaneous administrative duties of President

5. It shall be the duty of the President—

(a) to arrange—

  (i) such meetings of chairmen and members of social security appeal tribunals, chairmen and members of disability appeal tribunals and chairmen and members of medical appeal tribunals;

  (ii) such training for such chairmen and members,

  as he considers appropriate; and

(b) to secure that such works of reference relating to social security law as he considers appropriate are available for the use of chairmen and members of social security appeal tribunals, disability appeal tribunals and medical appeal tribunals.

Remuneration etc.

6. The Lord Chancellor shall pay to a Commissioner such salary or other remuneration, and such expenses incurred in connection with the work of a Commissioner or any tribunal presided over by a Commissioner, as may be determined by the Treasury.

7.—(1) The Secretary of State may pay—

(a) to any person specified in sub-paragraph (2) below, such remuneration and such travelling and other allowances;

(b) to any person specified in sub-paragraph (3) below, such travelling and other allowances; and

(c) subject to sub-paragraph (4) below, such other expenses in connection with the work of any person, tribunal or inquiry appointed or constituted under any provision of this Act,

as the Secretary of State with the consent of the Treasury may determine.

(2) The persons mentioned in sub-paragraph (1)(a) above are—

(a) any person (other than a Commissioner) appointed under this Act to determine questions or as a member of, or assessor to, a social security appeal tribunal, a disability appeal tribunal or a medical appeal tribunal; and

[[2](aa) a person appointed as medical assessor to a social security appeal tribunal under regulations under section 61A(4) above; and]

(b) a medical officer appointed under regulations under section 62 above.

(3) The persons mentioned in sub-paragraph (1)(b) above are—

(a) any person required to attend at any proceedings or inquiry under this Act; and

(b) any person required under this Act (whether for the purposes of this Act or otherwise) to attend for or to submit themselves to medical or other examination or treatment.

(4) Expenses are not payable under sub-paragraph (1)(c) above in connection with the work—

(a) of a tribunal presided over by a Commissioner; or

(b) of a social fund officer, a social fund inspector or the social fund Commissioner.

(5) In this paragraph references to travelling and other allowances include references to compensation for loss of remunerative time but such compensation shall not be paid to any person in respect of any time during which he is in receipt of remuneration under this paragraph.

Certificates of decisions

8. A document bearing a certificate which—

(a) is signed by a person authorised in that behalf by the Secretary of State; and

(b) states that the document, apart from the certificate, is a record of a decision—

(i) of a Commissioner;

(ii) of a social security appeal tribunal;

(iii) of a disability appeal tribunal; or

(iv) of an adjudication officer,

shall be conclusive evidence of the decision; and a certificate purporting to be so signed shall be deemed to be so signed unless the contrary is proved.

Derivation

Para. 1: Social Security Act 1975, Sched. 10, para. 1A(4), (5)–(7) and (10); Social Security Act 1980, s.13.

Para. 2: Social Security Act 1975, Sched. 10, para. 1A(10).

Para. 3: Social Security Act 1975, Sched. 10, para. 1A(11), Sched. 10A, para. 11 and Sched. 12, paras. 5A and 7.

Para. 4: Social Security Act 1975, Sched. 10, paras. 1B and 1C, Sched. 10A, para. 11.

Para. 5: Social Security Act 1975, Sched. 10, para. 1D, Sched. 10A, para. 11 and Sched. 12, para. 9.

Para. 6: Social Security Act 1975, Sched. 10, para. 4.

Para. 7: Social Security Act 1975, Sched. 10, para. 3, Sched. 10A, para. 11 and Sched. 12, paras. 4 and 7.

Para. 8: Social Security Act 1980, s.17.

Amendments

1. Judicial Pensions and Retirement Act 1993, Sched. 6, para. 21 and Sched. 8, para. 24 (April 1, 1995).

2. Social Security (Incapacity for Work) Act 1994, Sched. 1, para. 53 (April 13, 1995).

SCHEDULE 3

REGULATIONS AS TO PROCEDURE

Interpretation

1. In this Schedule "competent tribunal" means—
(a) a Commissioner;
(b) a social security appeal tribunal;
(c) a disability appeal tribunal;
(d) a medical appeal tribunal;
(e) an adjudicating medical practitioner.

Provision which may be made

2. Provision prescribing the procedure to be followed in connection with the consideration and determination of claims and questions by the Secretary of State, an adjudication officer and a competent tribunal, or in connection with the withdrawal of a claim.

3. Provision as to the striking out of proceedings for want of prosecution.

4. Provision as to the form which is to be used for any document, the evidence which is to be required and the circumstances in which any official record or certificate is to be sufficient or conclusive evidence.

5. Provision as to the time to be allowed—
(a) for producing any evidence; or
(b) for making an appeal.

6. Provision as to the manner in which, and the time within which, a question may be raised with a view to its decision by the Secretary of State under Part II of this Act or with a view to the review of a decision under that Part.

7. Provision for summoning persons to attend and give evidence or produce documents and for authorising the administration of oaths to witnesses.

8. Provision for authorising a competent tribunal consisting of two or more members to proceed with any case, with the consent of the claimant, in the absence of any member.

9. Provision for giving the chairman or acting chairman of a competent tribunal consisting of two or more members a second or casting vote where the number of members present is an even number.

10. Provision for empowering the chairman of a social security appeal tribunal, a disability appeal tribunal or a medical appeal tribunal to give directions for the disposal of any purported appeal which he is satisfied that the tribunal does not have jurisdiction to entertain.

11. Provision for the non-disclosure to a person of the particulars of any medical advice or medical evidence given or submitted for the purposes of a determination.

12. Provision for requiring or authorising the Secretary of State to hold, or to appoint a person to hold, an inquiry in connection with the consideration of any question by the Secretary of State.

DERIVATION

Social Security Act 1975, s.115 and Sched. 13; Social Security Act 1986, s.52(3) and (3A).

Schedules 4.—6. *Omitted.*

SCHEDULE 7

REGULATIONS NOT REQUIRING PRIOR SUBMISSION

PART I

SOCIAL SECURITY ADVISORY COMMITTEE

Disability living allowance

1. Regulations under section 72(3) or 73(10) of the Contributions and Benefits Act.

Industrial injuries

2. Regulations relating only to industrial injuries benefit.

Up-rating etc.

3. Regulations contained in a statutory instrument which states that it contains only provisions in consequence of an order under one or more of the following provisions—

(a) section 141, 143 or 145 above;

(b) section 150 above.

Earnings limits

4. Regulations under section 5 of the Contributions and Benefits Act or regulations contained in a statutory instrument which states that it contains only regulations to make provision consequential on regulations under that section.

Married women and widows—reduced rate contributions

5. Regulations under section 19(4)(a) of the Contributions and Benefits Act.

Child benefit

6. Regulations prescribing the rate or any of the rates of child benefit in Great Britain.

7. Regulations varying social security benefits following an increase of the rate or any of the rates of child benefit in Great Britain.

Statutory maternity pay and statutory sick pay

8. Regulations under section [2. . .] 167 of the Contributions and Benefits Act.

Procedural rules for tribunals

9. Regulations in so far as they consist only of procedural rules for a tribunal in respect of which consultation with the Council on Tribunals is required by [1section 8(1) of the Tribunals and Inquiries Act 1992].

Consolidation

10. Regulations made for the purpose only of consolidating other regulations evoked by them.

Part II

Industrial Injuries Advisory Council

11. Regulations under section 121(1)(b) of the Contributions and Benefits Act.

12. Regulations contained in a statutory instrument which states that it contains only provisions in consequence of an order under section 141, 143 or 150 above.

13. Regulations contained in a statutory instrument made within a period of six months from the date of any Act passed after this Act and directed to be construed as one with this Act, where the statutory instrument states that it contains only regulations to make provision consequential on the passing of the Act, and the Act does not exclude this paragraph in respect of the regulations.

14. Regulations in so far as they consist only of procedural rules for a tribunal in respect of which consultation with the Council on Tribunals is required by [[1]section 8(1) of the Tribunals and Inquiries Act 1992].

15. Regulations contained in a statutory instrument which states that it contains only regulations making with respect to industrial injuries benefit or its administration the same or substantially the same provision as has been, or is to be, made with respect to other benefit as defined in section 122(1) of the Contributions and Benefits Act or its administration.

16. Regulations contained in a statutory instrument which states that the only provision with respect to industrial injuries benefit or its administration that is made by the regulations is the same or substantially the same as provision made by the instrument with respect to other benefit as defined in section 122(1) of the Contributions and Benefits Act or its administration.

17. Regulations made for the purpose only of consolidating other regulations revoked by them.

Derivation

Part I: Social Security Act 1980, s.10(2) and Sched. 3.
Part II: Social Security Act 1975, s.141 and Sched. 16; Social Security Act 1980, s.11(2)(a).

Amendments

1. Tribunals and Inquiries Act 1992, Sched. 3, para. 37 (October 1, 1992)
2. Statutory Sick Pay Percentage Threshold Order 1995 (S.I. 1995 No. 512), art. 6(2)(c) (April 6, 1995).

Schedules 8.—10. *Omitted.*

Social Security (Consequential Provisions) Act 1992

(1992 c. 6)

Arrangement of Sections

3. Transitional provisions and savings (including some transitional provisions retained from previous Acts).
   Part I General and miscellaneous.
   Part II Specific transitional provisions and savings (including some derived from previous Acts).
4. Transitory modifications.
   Part I *Omitted.*
   Part II Other transitory modifications.

An Act to make provision for repeals, consequential amendments, transitional and transitory matters and savings in connection with the consolidation of enactments of the Social Security Contributions and Benefits Act 1992 and the Social Security Administration Act 1992 (including provisions to give effect to recommendations of the Law Commission and the Scottish Law Commission).

[13th February 1992]

Meaning of "the consolidating Acts"

1. In this Act—

"the consolidating Acts" means the Social Security Contributions and Benefits Act 1992 ("the Contributions and Benefits Act"), the Social Security Administration Act 1992 ("the Administration Act") and, so far as it reproduces the effect of the repealed enactments, this Act; and

"the repealed enactments" means the enactments repealed by this Act.

Continuity of the law

2.—(1) The substitution of the consolidating Acts for the repealed enactments does not affect the continuity of the law.

(2) Anything done or having effect as if done under or for the purposes of a provision of the repealed enactments has effect, if it could have been done under or for the purposes of the corresponding provision of the consolidating Acts, as if done under or for the purposes of that provision.

(3) Any reference, whether express or implied, in the consolidating Acts or any other enactment, instrument or document to a provision of the consolidating Acts shall, so far as the context permits, be construed as including, in relation to the times, circumstances and purposes in relation to which the corresponding provision of the repealed enactments has effect, a reference to that corresponding provision.

(4) Any reference, whether express or implied, in any enactment, instrument or document to a provision of the repealed enactments shall be construed, so far as is required for continuing its effect, as including a reference to the corresponding provision of the consolidating Acts.

GENERAL NOTE

This section provides for continuity between the old legislation and the new 1992 Acts. The new Acts merely consolidate the old legislation with virtually no changes although there is a lot of reorganisation and all the section numbers have been altered, some of the old sections being split into several parts. Accordingly, things which could have been done under the old legislation could also have been done under the new legislation. Subs. (2) provides that anything done or having effect as if done under the old legislation is to be treated as though it had been done under the corresponding provision of the 1992 Acts. Subs. (3) provides that references to a provision in the 1992 Acts are to be treated as references to the corresponding provision in the old legislation where the old legislation was in effect in relation to the relevant time, circumstances or purposes. Subs. (4) provides for references to the old legislation to be treated as references to the corresponding provisions of the 1992 Acts. S.5 and Sched. 3 make other transitional provisions. Note that para. 1(1)(a) of Sched. 3 provides that virtually all questions as to entitlement to benefit for any period before July 1, 1992 (when the new Acts came into force) are to be determined under the old legislation. Other issues relating to any period before July 1, 1992 (such as the recovery of an overpayment) are all to be determined under the new legislation by virtue of para. 1(2) of Sched. 3.

Repeals

3.—(1) The enactments mentioned in Schedule 1 to this Act are repealed to the extent specified in the third column of that Schedule.

(2) Those repeals include, in addition to repeals consequential on the consolidation of provisions in the consolidating Acts, repeals in accordance with Recommendations of the Law Commission and the Scottish Law Commission, of section 30(6)(b) of the Social Security Act 1975, paragraphs 2 to 8 of Schedule 9 to that Act, paragraph 2(1) of Schedule 10 to that Act and section 10 of the Social Security Act 1988.

(3) The repeals have effect subject to any relevant savings in Schedule 3 to this Act.

Consequential amendments

4. The enactments mentioned in Schedule 2 to this Act shall have effect with the amendments there specified (being amendments consequential on the consolidating Acts).

Transitional provisions and savings

5.—(1) The transitional provisions and savings in Schedule 3 to this Act shall have effect.

(2) Nothing in that Schedule affects the general operation of section 16 of the Interpretation Act 1978 (general savings implied on repeal) or of the previous provisions of this Act.

Transitory modifications

6. The transitory modifications in Schedule 4 to this Act shall have effect.

Short title, commencement and extent

7.—(1) This Act may be cited as the Social Security (Consequential Provisions) Act 1992.

(2) This Act shall come into force on 1st July 1992.

(3) Section 2 above and this section extend to Northern Ireland.

(4) Subject to subsection (5) below, where any enactment repealed or amended by this Act extends to any part of the United Kingdom, the repeal or amendment extends to that part.

(5) The repeals—

(a) of provisions of sections 10, 13 and 14 of the Social Security Act 1980 and Part II of Schedule 3 to that Act;

(b) of enactments amending those provisions;

(c) of paragraph 2 of Schedule 1 to the Capital Allowances Act 1990; and

(d) of section 17(8) and (9) of the Social Security Act 1990,

do not extend to Northern Ireland.

(6) Section 6 above and Schedule 4 to this Act extend to Northern Ireland in so far as they give effect to transitory modifications of provisions of the consolidating Acts which so extend.

(7) Except as provided by this section, this Act does not extend to Northern Ireland.

(8) Section 4 above extends to the Isle of Man so far as it relates to paragraphs 53 and 54 of Schedule 2 to this Act.

SCHEDULES

Schedule 1

Repeals

Chapter	Short title	Extent of repeal
1974 c. 14.	National Insurance Act 1974.	Section 6(1) and (3).
1975 c. 14.	Social Security Act 1975.	The whole Act
[...]	[...]	[...]
Chapter	Short title	Extent of repeal
1977 c. 5.	Social Security (Miscellaneous Provisions) Act 1977.	[...] Section 13.
[...]	[...]	[...]
1980 c. 30.	Social Security Act 1980.	[...] Section 14. Sections 17 and 18. [...]
[...]	[...]	[...]
1986 c. 50.	Social Security Act 1986.	Sections 18 to 29. Section 30(1) to (9) and (11). Sections 31 to 36. Section 37(1). Section 38. Sections 40 to 51. Section 52(3) to (10). Section 53. [...] Sections 62 to 69. Section 70(1). Sections 73 and 74. Section 79(3) and (4). In section 80(1), the words "and V". Section 81. In section 83, subsection (2), subsection (3)(b) to (e), and in subsection (5), the words from "30" to "section", in the second place where it occurs. In section 84, in subsection (1), the definition of "applicable amount", paragraphs (c) and (d) of the definition of "the benefit Acts", the definitions of "dwelling", "housing authority", "housing benefit scheme", "Housing Revenue Account dwelling", "income-related benefit", "local authority", "long-term benefit", "new town corporation", "primary class 1 contributions", "secondary

Chapter	Short title	Extent of repeal
		Class 2 contributions'', ''qualifying benefit'', ''rate rebate'', ''rent rebate'', ''rent allowance'', ''rates'', ''rating authority'', ''trade dispute'', ''war disablement pension'' and ''war widow's pension'', and subsection (3). [. . .] Schedule 3, except paragraph 17. [. . .] Schedules 6 and 7. [. . .] In Schedule 10, paragraphs 10, 34, 40, 48, 54, 62 to 67, 68(2), 69, 70, 72, 74, 77, 83 to 88, 90 to 92, 95, 97 to 100, 103(a) and (b), 104 to 107 and 108(a).
[. . .]	[. . .]	[. . .]
1988 c. 7.	Social Security Act 1988.	Sections 1 to 8. [. . .]
[. . .]	[. . .]	[. . .]
1989 c. 24.	Social Security Act 1989.	[. . .] Section 22(1) to (6) and (8). Section 27. [. . .] In Schedule 4, paragraphs 1 to 21 and 24. [. . .]
[. . .]	[. . .]	[. . .]
1991 c. 21.	Disability Living Allowance and Disability Working Allowance Act 1991.	Section 1. Section 2(1). Section 3. Section 4(1). Sections 5 and 6. Section 7(1). Sections 8 and 9. Sections 11 and 14. Schedule 1. In Schedule 2, paragraphs 2(2), 3 to 5, 8, 10 and 11, 15 to 17 and 19. In Schedule 3, Part I.
[. . .]	[. . .]	[. . .]

Schedule 2. *Omitted.*

SCHEDULE 3

TRANSITIONAL PROVISIONS AND SAVINGS (INCLUDING SOME TRANSITIONAL PROVISIONS RETAINED FROM PREVIOUS ACTS)

PART I

GENERAL AND MISCELLANEOUS

Questions relating to contributions and benefits

1.—(1) A question other than a question arising under any of sections 1 to 3 of the Administration Act—

(a) whether a person is entitled to benefit in respect of a time before 1st July 1992;

(b) whether a person is liable to pay contributions in respect of such a time,

and any other question not arising under any of those sections with respect to benefit or contributions in respect of such a time is to be determined, subject to section 68 of the Administration Act, in accordance with provisions in force or deemed to be in force at that time.

(2) Subject to sub-paragraph (1) above, the consolidating Acts apply to matters arising before their commencement as to matters arising after it.

General saving for old savings

2. The repeal by this Act of an enactment previously repealed subject to savings (whether or not in the repealing enactment) does not affect the continued operation of those savings.

Documents referring to repealed enactments

3. Any document made, served or issued after this Act comes into force which contains a reference to any of the repealed enactments shall be construed, except so far as a contrary intention appears, as referring or, as the context may require, including a reference to the corresponding provision of the consolidating Acts.

Provisions relating to the coming into force of other provisions

4. The repeal by this Act of a provision providing for or relating to the coming into force of a provision reproduced in the consolidating Acts does not affect the operation of the first provision, in so far as it remains capable of having effect, in relation to the enactment reproducing the second provision.

Continuing powers to make transitional etc. regulations

5. Where immediately before 1st July 1992 the Secretary of State has power under any provision of the Social Security Acts 1975 to 1991 not reproduced in the consolidating Acts by regulations to make provision or savings in preparation for or in connection with the coming into force of a provision repealed by this Act but reproduced in the consolidating Acts, the power shall be construed as having effect in relation to the provision reproducing the repealed provision.

Powers to make preparatory regulations

6. The repeal by this Act of a power by regulations to make provision or savings in preparation for or in connection with the coming into force of a provision reproduced in the consolidating Acts does not affect the power, in so far as it remains capable of having effect, in relation to the enactment reproducing the second provision.

Provisions contained in enactments by virtue of orders or regulations

7.—(1) Without prejudice to any express provision in the consolidating Acts, where this Act repeals any provision contained in any enactment by virtue of any order or regulations and the provision is reproduced in the consolidating Acts, the Secretary of State shall have the like power to make orders or regulations repealing or amending the provision of the consolidating Acts which reproduces the effect of the repealed provision as he had in relation to that provision.

(2) Sub-paragraph (1) above applies to a repealed provision which was amended by Schedule 7 to the Social Security Act 1989 as it applies to a provision not so amended.

Amending orders made after passing of Act

8. An order which is made under any of the repealed enactments after the passing of this Act and which amends any of the repealed enactments shall have the effect also of making a corresponding amendment of the consolidating Acts.

PART II

SPECIFIC TRANSITIONAL PROVISIONS AND SAVINGS (INCLUDING SOME DERIVED FROM PREVIOUS ACTS)

Interpretation

9. In this Part of this Schedule—

"the 1965 Act" means the National Insurance Act 1965;

"the 1973 Act" means the Social Security Act 1973;

"the 1975 Act" means the Social Security Act 1975;

"the former Consequential Provisions Act" means the Social Security (Consequential Provisions) Act 1975; and

"the 1986 Act" means the Social Security Act 1986.

10.—19. *Omitted.*

Attendance allowance—provision derived from section 1 of Social Security Act 1988

20. For the purposes—

(a) of any determination following a claim made before 15th March 1988 (the date of the passing of the Social Security Act 1988);

(b) of any review following an application made before that date; and

(c) of any review following a decision to conduct a review made before that date,

section 64 of the Contributions and Benefits Act shall have effect as if the following subsection were substituted for subsection (3)—

"(3) A person satisfies the night attendance condition if he is so severely disabled physically or mentally that, at night, he requires from another person either—

(a) prolonged or repeated attention during the night in connection with his bodily functions; or

(b) continual supervision throughout the night in order to avoid substantial danger to himself or others."

21. *Omitted.*

Substitution of disability living allowance for attendance allowance and mobility allowance and dissolution of Attendance Allowance Board—provision derived from section 5 of Disability Living Allowance and Disability Working Allowance Act 1991

22.—(1) The Secretary of State may make such regulations as appear to him necessary or expedient in relation to the substitution of disability living allowance for attendance allowance and mobility allowance and the dissolution of the Attendance Allowance Board.

(2) Without prejudice to the generality of this paragraph, regulations under this paragraph—

(a) may provide for the termination or cancellation of awards of attendance allowance and awards of mobility allowance;

(b) may direct that a person whose award of either allowance has been terminated or cancelled by virtue of the regulations or who is a child of such a person shall by virtue of the regulations be treated as having been awarded one or more disability living allowances;

(c) may direct that a disability living allowance so treated as having been awarded shall consist of such component as the regulations may specify or, if the regulations so specify, of both components, and as having been awarded either component at such weekly rate and for such period as the regulations may specify;

(d) may provide for the termination in specified circumstances of an award of disability living allowance;

(e) may direct that in specified circumstances a person whose award of disability living allowance has been terminated by virtue of the regulations shall by virtue of the regulations be treated as having been granted a further award of a disability living allowance consisting of such component as the regulations may specify or, if the regulations so specify, of both components, and as having been awarded on the further award either component at such weekly rate and for such period as the regulations may specify;

(f) may provide for the review of awards made by virtue of paragraph or (b) or (e) above and for the treatment of claims for disability living allowance in respect of beneficiaries with such awards;

(g) may direct that for specified purposes certificates issued by the Attendance Allowance Board shall be treated as evidence of such matters as may be specified in the regulations;

(h) may direct that for specified purposes the replacement of attendance allowance and mobility allowance by disability living allowance shall be disregarded;

(i) may direct that a claim for attendance allowance or mobility allowance shall be treated in specified circumstances and for specified purposes as a claim for disability living allowance or that a claim for disability living allowance shall be treated in specified circumstances and for specified purposes as a claim for attendance allowance of mobility allowance or both;

(j) may direct that in specified circumstances and for specified purposes a claim for a disability living allowance shall be treated as having been made when no such claim was in fact made;

(k) may direct that in specified circumstances a claim for attendance allowance, mobility allowance or disability living allowance shall be treated as not having been made;

(l) may direct that in specified circumstances where a person claims attendance allowance or mobility allowance or both, and also claims disability living allowance, his claims may be treated as a single claim for such allowances for such periods as the regulations may specify;

(m) may direct that cases relating to mobility allowance shall be subject to adjudication in accordance with the provisions of Part II of the Administration Act relating to disability living allowance; and

(n) may direct that, at a time before the Attendance Allowance Board is dissolved, in specified circumstances cases relating to attendance allowance shall be subject to adjudication under the system of adjudication for such cases introduced by the Disability Living Allowance and Disability Working Allowance Act 1991.

(3) Regulations under this paragraph may provide that any provision to which this sub-paragraph applies—

(a) shall have effect subject to modifications, additions or amendments; or

(b) shall not have effect.

(4) Sub-paragraph (3) above applies—

(a) to any provision of the 1975 Act which relates to mobility allowance, so far as it so relates;

(b) to any provision of Part VI of the 1986 Act which is relevant to mobility allowance;

(c) to any provision of the Contributions and Benefits Acts which relates to disability living allowance or attendance allowance, so far as it so relates; and

(d) to any provision of the Administration Act which is relevant to disability living allowance or attendance allowance.

Regulations and orders—supplementary

23.—(1) Regulations under this Part of this Schedule shall be made by the Secretary of State.

(2) Powers under this Part of this Schedule to make regulations or orders are exercisable by statutory instrument.

(3) Any power conferred by this Part of this Schedule to make regulations or orders may be exercised—

(a) either in relation to all cases to which the power extends, or in relation to those cases subject to specified exceptions, or in relation to any specified cases or classes of case;

(b) so as to make, as respects the cases in relation to which it is exercised—

(i) the full provision to which the power extends or any less provision (whether by way of exception or otherwise);

(ii) the same provision for all cases in relation to which the power is exercised, or different provision for different cases or different classes of case or different provision as respects the same case or class of case for different purposes of this Part of this Schedule;

(iii) any such provision either unconditionally or subject to any specified condition.

(4) The powers to make regulations or orders conferred by any provision of this Part of this Schedule other than paragraph 22 above include powers to make thereby such incidental, supplementary, consequential or transitional provision as appears to the Secretary of State to be expedient for the purposes of the regulations.

(5) A power conferred by this Part of this Schedule to make regulations or an order includes power to provide for a person to exercise a discretion in dealing with any matter.

(6) If the Treasury so direct, regulations or orders under this Part of this Schedule shall be made only in conjunction with them.

(7) A statutory instrument—

(a) which contains (whether alone or with other provisions) orders or regulation made under this Part of this Schedule, and

(b) which is not subject to any requirement that a draft of the instrument be laid before and approved by a resolution of each House of Parliament,

shall be subject to annulment in pursuance of a resolution of either House of Parliament.

SCHEDULE 4

PART I

TRANSITORY MODIFICATIONS

1.—20. *Omitted.*

PART II

OTHER TRANSITORY MODIFICATIONS

Transition from mobility allowance to disability living allowance

21. In the application of subsection (2) of section 129 of the Contributions and Benefits Act to claims made or treated as made before the first day in respect of which disability living allowance is payable paragraph (b) of that subsection shall have effect as if the following sub-paragraph were substituted for sub-paragraph (ii)—

"(ii) a mobility allowance under section 37A of the 1975 Act;".

GENERAL NOTE

This makes mobility allowance a qualifying benefit for the purposes of disability working allowance.

22. *Omitted.*

Social Security (Recovery of Benefits) Act 1997

(1997 c. 27)

ARRANGEMENT OF SECTIONS

Introductory

Certificates of recoverable benefits

Liability of person paying compensation

Reduction of compensation payment

Reviews and appeals

An Act to re-state, with amendments, Part IV of the Social Security Administration Act 1992. [19th March 1997]

Introductory

Cases in which this Act applies

1.—(1) This Act applies in cases where—

(a) a person makes a payment (whether on his own behalf or not) to or in respect of any other person in consequence of any accident, injury or disease suffered by the other, and

(b) any listed benefits have been, or are likely to be, paid to or for the other during the relevant period in respect of the accident, injury or disease.

(2) The reference above to a payment in consequence of any accident, injury or disease is to a payment made—

(a) by or on behalf of a person who is, or is alleged to be, liable to any extent in respect of the accident, injury or disease, or

(b) in pursuance of a compensation scheme for motor accidents;

but does not include a payment mentioned in Part I of Schedule 1.

(3) Subsection (1)(a) applies to a payment made—

(a) voluntarily, or in pursuance of a court order or an agreement, or otherwise, and

(b) in the United Kingdom or elsewhere.

(4) In a case where this Act applies—

(a) the "injured person" is the person who suffered the accident, injury or disease,

(b) the "compensation payment" is the payment within subsection (1)(a), and

(c) "recoverable benefit" is listed benefit which has been or is likely to be paid as mentioned in the subsection (1)(b).

GENERAL NOTE

As the long title says, this Act, which came into force on October 6, 1997 (see s.2 and the note thereto) re-enacts Part IV of the Social Security Administration Act 1992 with amendments. Some of the amendments are significant, albeit fairly technical, but there has also been a lot of simple redrafting to make the legislation clearer.

The broad scheme of the legislation remains as before. A person making a compensation payment (whether voluntarily or pursuant to a court order or agreement or otherwise—see s.1(3)) in respect of an accident, injury or disease must notify the Compensation Recovery Unit of the Department of Social Security at Reyrolle Building, Hebburn, Tyne and Wear NE31 1XB (Tel: 0191-489 2266) who publish a free guide to the procedures. *Before* making the payment, the compensator must apply for a "certificate of recoverable benefits" under s.4. That certificate will specify the amount of relevant benefits (listed in col. 2 of Sched. 2) paid, or expected to be paid, within the "relevant period" (defined in s.3), *in respect of* the accident injury or disease (see the definition of "recoverable benefit" in s.1(4)(c) which refers back to s.1(1)(b) and see also the note to s.12). The compensator must then pay to the Secretary of State a sum equal to the total amount of recoverable benefits (s.6) and pay to the victim a compensation payment which is reduced under s.8 to reflect the benefits the victim has received. By virtue of s.1(2) and Sched. 1, certain payments are exempted, including "small payments" not exceeding £2,500. Ss.10 to 14 provide for reviews of, and appeals from, certificates of recoverable benefits.

For the meaning of "benefit", "compensation scheme for motor accidents" and "listed benefit", see s. 29.

Compensation payments to which this Act applies

2. This Act applies in relation to compensation payments made on or after the day on which this section comes into force, unless they are made in pursuance of a court order or agreement made before that day.

GENERAL NOTE

By virtue of the Social Security (Recovery of Benefits) Act 1997 (Commencement Order) 1997, this section came into force on October 6, 1997. Where a court order or agreement was made before that date, the recovery provisions of Part IV of the Social Security Administration Act 1992 will continue to apply, unless the accident or injury occurred before January 1, 1989 (or, in the case of a disease, benefit was claimed before January 1, 1989), in which case benefits will not be recoverable by the Secretary of State at all (see s.81(7) of the 1992 Act).

"The relevant period"

3.—(1) In relation to a person ("the claimant") who has suffered any accident, injury or disease, "the relevant period" has the meaning given by the following subsections.

(2) Subject to subsection (4), if it is a case of accident or injury, the relevant period is the period of five years immediately following the day on which the accident or injury in question occurred.

(3) Subject to subsection (4), if it is a case of disease, the relevant period is the period of five years beginning with the date on which the claimant first claims a listed benefit in consequence of the disease.

(4) If at any time before the end of the period referred to in subsection (2) or (3)—

(a) a person makes a compensation payment in final discharge of any claim made by or in respect of the claimant and arising out of the accident, injury or disease, or

(b) an agreement is made under which an earlier compensation payment is treated as having been made in final discharge of any such claim,

the relevant period ends at that time.

General Note

Subs. (4) This is intended to encourage the early settlement of claims because the effect of a compensation payment being made quickly is that the standard five-year "relevant period" provided for in subss. (2) and (3) is shortened and so the amount of recoverable benefits is reduced. This has an obvious attraction from the victim's point of view which the compensator can use to encourage settlement. It has been suggested that the provision creates undue pressure to settle cases but the quality of advice available to the victim is probably a more important factor.

Certificates of recoverable benefits

Applications for certificates of recoverable benefits

4.—(1) Before a person ("the compensator") makes a compensation payment he must apply to the Secretary of State for a certificate of recoverable benefits.

(2) Where the compensator applies for a certificate of recoverable benefits, the Secretary of State must—

(a) send to him a written acknowledgement of receipt of his application, and

(b) subject to subsection (7), issue the certificate before the end of the following period.

(3) The period is—

(a) the prescribed period, or

(b) if there is no prescribed period, the period of four weeks,

which begins with the day following the day on which the application is received.

(4) The certificate is to remain in force until the date specified in it for that purpose.

(5) The compensator may apply for fresh certificates from time to time.

(6) Where a certificate of recoverable benefits ceases to be in force, the Secretary of State may issue a fresh certificate without an application for one being made.

(7) Where the compensator applies for a fresh certificate while a certificate ("the existing certificate") remains in force, the Secretary of State must issue the fresh certificate before the end of the following period.

(8) The period is—

(a) the prescribed period, or

(b) if there is no prescribed period, the period of four weeks,

which begins with the day following the day on which the existing certificate ceases to be in force.

(9) For the purposes of this Act, regulations may provide for the day on which an application for a certificate of recoverable benefits is to be treated as received.

General Note

No period has yet been prescribed for the purposes of subss. (3)(a) or (8)(a). By virtue of s.21, the consequence of the Secretary of State failing to issue a certificate of recoverable benefits within the specified period is that no benefits are recoverable and the victim is entitled to the full compensation without deduction. However, for s.21 to apply, the application for the certificate of recoverable benefits must have been accurate and it must have been acknowledged.

Information contained in certificates

5.—(1) A certificate of recoverable benefits must specify, for each recoverable benefit—

(a) the amount which has been or is likely to have been paid on or before a specified date, and

(b) if the benefit is paid or likely to be paid after the specified date, the rate and period for which, and the intervals at which, it is or is likely to be paid.

(2) In a case where the relevant period has ended before the day on which the Secretary of State receives the application for the certificate, the date specified in the certificate for the purposes of subsection (1) must be the day on which the relevant period ended.

(3) In any other case, the date specified for those purposes must not be earlier than the day on which the Secretary of State received the application.

(4) The Secretary of State may estimate, in such manner as he thinks fit, any of the amounts, rates or periods specified in the certificate.

(5) Where the Secretary of State issues a certificate of recoverable benefits, he must provide the information contained in the certificate to—

(a) the person who appears to him to be the injured person, or

(b) any person who he thinks will receive a compensation payment in respect of the injured person.

(6) A person to whom a certificate of recoverable benefits is issued or who is provided with information under subsection (5) is entitled to particulars of the manner in which any amount, rate or period specified in the certificate has been determined, if he applies to the Secretary of State for those particulars.

General Note

For reviews of, and appeals from, certificates of recoverable benefits, see ss.10 to 14.

Liability of person paying compensation

Liability to pay Secretary of State amount of benefits

6.—(1) A person who makes a compensation payment in any case is liable to pay to the Secretary of State an amount equal to the total amount of the recoverable benefits.

(2) The liability referred to in subsection (1) arises immediately before the compensation payment or, if there is more than one, the first of them is made.

(3) No amount becomes payable under this section before the end of the period of 14 days following the day on which the liability arises.

(4) Subject to subsection (3), an amount becomes payable under this section at the end of the period of 14 days beginning with the day on which a certificate of recoverable benefits is first issued showing that the amount of recoverable

benefit to which it relates has been or is likely to have been paid before a specified date.

Recovery of payments due under section 6

7.—(1) This section applies where a person has made a compensation payment but—

(a) has not applied for a certificate of recoverable benefits, or

(b) has not made a payment to the Secretary of State under section 6 before the end of the period allowed under that section.

(2) The Secretary of State may—

(a) issue the person who made the compensation payment with a certificate of recoverable benefits, if none has been issued, or

(b) issue him with a copy of the certificate of recoverable benefits or (if more than one has been issued) the most recent one,

and (in either case) issue him with a demand that payment of any amount due under section 6 be made immediately.

(3) The Secretary of State may, in accordance with subsections (4) and (5), recover the amount for which a demand for payment is made under subsection (2) from the person who made the compensation payment.

(4) If the person who made the compensation payment resides or carries on business in England and Wales and a county court so orders, any amount recoverable under subsection (3) is recoverable by execution issued from the county court or otherwise as if it were payable under an order of that court.

(5) If the person who made the payment resides or carries on business in Scotland, any amount recoverable under subsection (3) may be enforced in like manner as an extract registered decree arbitral bearing a warrant for execution issued by the sheriff court of any sheriffdom in Scotland.

(6) A document bearing a certificate which—

(a) is signed by a person authorised to do so by the Secretary of State, and

(b) states that the document, apart from the certificate, is a record of the amount recoverable under subsection (3),

is conclusive evidence that that amount is so recoverable.

(7) A certificate under subsection (6) purporting to be signed by a person authorised to do so by the Secretary of State is to be treated as so signed unless the contrary is proved.

General Note

This section provides a simple way of recovering, not only sums due under s.6 from compensators who have followed the proper procedures, but also from those who have failed to apply for a certificate of recoverable benefits at all. A certificate of recoverable benefits issued under subs. (2)(a) is not subject to the same right of appeal under s.11 as a certificate issued under s.4 but the compensator may apply for a review under s.10.

Reduction of compensation payment

Reduction of compensation payment

8.—(1) This section applies in a case where, in relation to any head of compensation listed in column 1 of Schedule 2—

(a) any of the compensation payment is attributable to that head, and

(b) any recoverable benefit is shown against that lead in column 2 of the Schedule.

(2) In such a case, any claim of a person to receive the compensation payment is to be treated for all purposes as discharged if—

(a) he is paid the amount (if any) of the compensation payment calculated in accordance with this section, and

(b) if the amount of the compensation payment so calculated is nil, he is given a statement saying so by the person who (apart from this section) would have paid the gross amount of the compensation payment.

(3) For each head of compensation listed in column 1 of the Schedule for which paragraphs (a) and (b) of subsection (1) are met, so much of the gross amount of the compensation payment as is attributable to that head is to be reduced (to nil, if necessary) by deducting the amount of the recoverable benefit or, as the case may be, the aggregate amount of the recoverable benefits shown against it.

(4) Subsection (3) is to have effect as if a requirement to reduce a payment by deducting an amount which exceeds that payment were a requirement to reduce that payment to nil.

(5) The amount of the compensation payment calculated in accordance with this section is—

(a) the gross amount of the compensation payment, and

(b) the sum of the reductions made under subsection (3),

(and, accordingly, the amount may be nil).

General Note

This is an important new provision. Under Part IV of the Social Security Administration Act 1992, the compensation payment was reduced by the amount of benefits paid within the relevant period in respect of the accident, injury or disease, even if the compensation had been awarded solely in respect of pain and suffering (*CSS/36/92*). Under this new provision, the extent to which the compensation payment may be reduced is limited by the extent to which compensation is attributable to a relevant head (*i.e.* compensation for loss of earnings, compensation for the cost of care or compensation for loss of mobility). This is likely to encourage parties to pay even closer attention to benefits than they have hitherto and will often require them to agree the proportion of the compensation attributable to each head before a claim is settled. One effect may be to encourage compensators to join with victims in challenging certificates of recoverable benefits on the ground that some of the listed benefits have not been payable "in respect of" the relevant accident, injury or disease (see the notes to s.12 and Sched. 2).

Section 8: supplementary

9.—(1) A person who makes a compensation payment calculated in accordance with section 8 must inform the person to whom the payment is made—

(a) that the payment has been so calculated, and

(b) of the date for payment by reference to which the calculation has been made.

(2) If the amount of a compensation payment calculated in accordance with section 8 is nil, a person giving a statement saying so is to be treated for the purposes of this Act as making a payment within section 1(1)(a) on the day on which he gives the statement.

(3) Where a person—

(a) makes a compensation payment calculated in accordance with section 8, and

(b) if the amount of the compensation payment so calculated is nil, gives a statement saying so,

he is to be treated, for the purpose of determining any rights and liabilities in respect of contribution or indemnity, as having paid the gross amount of the compensation payment.

(4) For the purposes of this Act—

(a) the gross amount of the compensation payment is the amount of the compensation payment apart from section 8, and

(b) the amount of any recoverable benefit is the amount determined in accordance with the certificate of recoverable benefits.

Reviews and appeals

Review of certificates of recoverable benefits

10.—(1) The Secretary of State may review any certificate of recoverable benefits if he is satisfied—

(a) that it was issued in ignorance of, or was based on a mistake as to, a material fact, or

(b) that a mistake (whether in computation or otherwise) has occurred in its preparation.

(2) On a review under this section the Secretary of State may either—

(a) confirm the certificate, or

(b) (subject to subsection (3)) issue a fresh certificate containing such variations as he considers appropriate.

(3) The Secretary of State may not vary the certificate so as to increase the total amount of the recoverable benefits unless it appears to him that the variation is required as a result of the person who applied for the certificate supplying him with incorrect or insufficient information.

General Note

The scope of subs. (1)(b) is unclear. Presumably it covers arithmetical errors, but what about errors of law? The purpose of s.10 seems primarily to allow the Secretary of State to review decisions of his own motion. It will generally be simpler for anyone else to appeal rather than apply for a review, especially as regulation 2(18) of the Social Security (Recovery of Benefits) (Appeals) Regulations 1997, made under s.11 (6), permits the Secretary of State to review a decision on any ground when an appeal is brought. However, there is no time limit for applications for review under this section, whereas there is a time limit for bringing appeals. Furthermore, Subs. (3) imposes an important limitation on the Secretary of State's power to review a certificate of recoverable benefits. There is no equivalent restriction on a tribunal's powers on appeal (*CSCR/1/95*).

Appeals against certificates of recoverable benefits

11.—(1) An appeal against a certificate of recoverable benefits may be made on the ground—

(a) that any amount, rate or period specified in the certificate is incorrect, or

(b) that listed benefits which have been, or are likely to be, paid otherwise than in respect of the accident, injury or disease in question have been brought into account.

(2) An appeal under this section may be made by—

(a) the person who applied for the certificate of recoverable benefits, or

(b) (in a case where the amount of the compensation payment has been calculated under section 8) the injured person or other person to whom the payment is made.

(3) No appeal may be made under this section until—

(a) the claim giving rise to the compensation payment has been finally disposed of, and

(b) the liability under section 6 has been discharged.

(4) For the purposes of subsection (3)(a), if an award of damages in respect of a claim has been made under or by virtue of—

(a) section 32A(2)(a) of the Supreme Court Act 1981,

(b) section 12(2)(a) of the Administration of Justice Act 1982, or

(c) section 51(2)(a) of the County Courts Act 1984,

(orders for provisional damages in personal injury cases), the claim is to be treated as having been finally disposed of.

(5) Regulations may make provision—

(a) as to the manner in which, and the time within which, appeals under this section may be made,

(b) as to the procedure to be followed where such an appeal is made, and

(c) for the purpose of enabling any such appeal to be treated as an application for review under section 10.

(6) Regulations under subsection (5)(c) may (among other things) provide that the circumstances in which a review may be carried out are not to be restricted to those specified in section 10(1).

General Note

Subs. (1) As the wording of s.12(2) has the same scope as s.11(1), all appeals under this section must be referred to medical appeal tribunals. See the notes to s.12.

Subs. (2) A compensator to whom a certificate of recoverable benefits has been issued under s.7(2)(a) (because he had not applied for a certificate) has no right of appeal.

Subs. (3) It remains the case that an appeal cannot be brought until *after* the relevant payments have been made.

Subs. (5) and (6) See the Social Security (Recovery of Benefits) (Appeals) Regulations 1997. Reg. 2(18) has been made under subs. (5)(c).

Reference of questions to medical appeal tribunal

12.—(1) The Secretary of State must refer to a medical appeal tribunal any question mentioned in subsection (2) arising for determination on an appeal under section 11.

(2) The questions are any concerning—

(a) any amount, rate or period specified in the certificate of recoverable benefits, or

(b) whether listed benefits which have been, or are likely to be, paid otherwise than in respect of the accident, injury or disease in question have been brought into account.

(3) In determining any question referred to it under subsection (1), the tribunal must take into account any decision of a court relating to the same, or any similar, issue arising in connection with the accident, injury or disease in question.

(4) On a reference under subsection (1) a medical appeal tribunal may either—

(a) confirm the amounts, rates and periods specified in the certificate of recoverable benefits, or

(b) specify any variations which are to be made on the issue of a fresh certificate under subsection (5).

(5) When the Secretary of State has received the decisions of the tribunal on the questions referred to it under subsection (1), he must in accordance with those decisions either—

(a) confirm the certificate against which the appeal was brought, or

(b) issue a fresh certificate.

(6) Regulations may make provision—

(a) as to the manner in which, and the time within which, a reference under subsection (1) is to be made, and

(b) as to the procedure to be followed where such a reference is made.

(7) Regulations under subsection (6)(b) may (among other things) provide for the non-disclosure of medical advice or medical evidence given or submitted following a reference under subsection (1).

(8) In this section "medical appeal tribunal" means a medical appeal tribunal constituted under section 50 of the Social Security Administration Act 1992.

General Note

Subs. (1) As the scope of s.12(2) is similar to that of s.11(1), *all* appeals are now referred to medical appeal tribunals. Under Part IV of the Social Security Administration Act 1992, some appeals against "certificates of total benefit" (the forerunners of certificates of recoverable benefits) were heard by social security appeal tribunals and some were heard by medical appeal tribunals. This was extremely unsatisfactory because the division of responsibility between the tribunals was unclear (*CCR/2/94*) and because many cases ended up being considered first by a medical appeal tribunal and then by a social security appeal tribunal (*CSCR/1/95*). Most cases that actually reach a tribunal raise issues of causation and it makes sense for a medical appeal tribunal to deal with both those issues and any consequential questions, even if the benefits at issue may not be those with which such tribunals are normally concerned.

Subs. (2) No appeal lies in a case where it is asserted that the provisions of the Act do not apply at all (*CSCR/3/95*). In such a case, the certificate must be challenged by way of an application for judicial review.

Benefit is paid "in respect of" an accident, injury or disease if the accident, injury or disease is *a*, but not necessarily the only, reason for it being paid. In *Hassall and Pether v. Secretary of State for Social Security* [1995] 1 W.L.R. 812, it was held that income support paid to claimants who were unemployed and already in receipt of income support when they were injured was paid in respect of their accidents. This approach could be justified in those cases on the basis that, but for the accidents, the claimants might have obtained employment. However, it appears that the same result would have been reached even if the claimants had been in receipt of income support on a different basis. The Court of Appeal relied very much on the precise language of the legislation then in force. It is not clear that the same result would be reached in all cases under the new legislation, where it may be arguable that a benefit listed in Sched. 2 as relevant to compensation for lost earnings is not payable in respect of an accident, injury or disease if it can be shown that the claimant would definitely not have been working even if the accident had not occurred. Even under the old legislation, not all benefit payable during the relevant period was recoverable. If a person was disabled due to an accident, injury or disease but would have been capable of work were it not for some unrelated medical condition which would, by itself, have rendered the victim unable to work, any benefit paid on the basis of the claimant's incapacity for work was not recoverable (*CCR/4/93, CCR/5336/95*). It should be noted that it is not only benefit in respect of incapacity or disablement that is recoverable; so too is jobseeker's allowance. Therefore, if a person becomes incapable of work due to an accident and so loses his or her job, any jobseeker's allowance payable after the claimant ceases to be incapable of work will be recoverable (but see *CCR/2/94* where the Commissioner reached the opposite conclusion). However, if the claimant then becomes incapable of work due to some condition unrelated to the accident, not only will incapacity benefit paid due to that new cause be irrecoverable, so too will any sum in respect of jobseeker's allowance that would have been payable due to the accident had the claimant not become incapable of work again (*CCR/5336/95*).

Subs. (4) In *CCR/4/93* and *CSCR/1/95*, Commissioners held that on appeals, the Secretary of State was entitled to refer to the tribunal questions which related to benefits that were not on the original "certificates of total benefit" (the forerunners of certificates of recoverable benefits). In the first case the Commissioner held that, on an appeal, all matters were at large. In the second case, the Commissioner took a narrower approach and held that a tribunal were strictly confined to the issues referred to them by the Secretary of State but that, in that case, the new benefits were within the scope of the reference. The Commissioner noted the contrast between the position on appeal and the limitation, now contained in s.10(3), with respect to reviews and warned of the perils of appealing.

Subs. (6) and (7) See the Social Security (Recovery of Benefits) (Appeals) Regulations 1997.

Appeal to Social Security Commissioner

13.—(1) An appeal may be made to a Commissioner against any decision of a medical appeal tribunal under section 12 on the ground that the decision was erroneous in point of law.

(2) An appeal under this section may be made by—

(a) the Secretary of State,

(b) the person who applied for the certificate of recoverable benefits, or

(c) (in a case where the amount of the compensation payment has been calculated in accordance with section 8) the injured person or other person to whom the payment is made.

(3) Subsections (7) to (10) of section 23 of the Social Security Administration Act 1992 apply to appeals under this section as they apply to appeals under that section.

(4) In this section "Commissioner" has the same meaning as in the Social Security Administration Act 1992 (see section 191).

GENERAL NOTE

There does not appear to be any provision for an appeal to the Court of Appeal against a decision of a Commissioner given under this section.

Reviews and appeals: supplementary

14.—(1) This section applies in cases where a fresh certificate of recoverable benefits is issued as a result of a review under section 10 or an appeal under section 11.

(2) If—

(a) a person has made one or more payments to the Secretary of State under section 6, and

(b) in consequence of the review or appeal, it appears that the total amount paid is more than the amount that ought to have been paid,

regulations may provide for the Secretary of State to pay the difference to that person, or to the person to whom the compensation payment is made, or partly to one and partly to the other.

(3) If—

(a) a person has made one or more payments to the Secretary of State under section 6, and

(b) in consequence of the review or appeal, it appears that the total amount paid is less than the amount that ought to have been paid,

regulations may provide for that person to pay the difference to the Secretary of State.

(4) Regulations under this section may provide—

(a) for the re-calculation in accordance with section 8 of the amount of any compensation payment,

(b) for giving credit for amounts already paid, and

(c) for the payment by any person of any balance or the recovery from any person of any excess,

and may provide for any matter by modifying this Act.

Courts

Court orders

15.—(1) This section applies where a court makes an order for a compensation payment to be made in any case, unless the order is made with the consent of the injured person and the person by whom the payment is to be made.

(2) The court must, in the case of each head of compensation listed in column 1 of Schedule 2 to which any of the compensation payment is attributable, specify in the order the amount of the compensation payment which is attributable to that head.

Payments into court

16.—(1) Regulations may make provision (including provision modifying this Act) for any case in which a payment into court is made.

(2) The regulations may (among other things) provide—

(a) for the making of a payment into court to be treated in prescribed circumstances as the making of a compensation payment,
(b) for application for, and issue of, certificates of recoverable benefits, and
(c) for the relevant period to be treated as ending on a date determined in accordance with the regulations.

(3) Rules of court may make provision governing practice and procedure in such cases.

(4) This section does not extend to Scotland.

General Note

In *McCafferey v. Datta* [1997] 1 W.L.R. 870, the defendant had made a payment into court. The plaintiff obtained judgement for a sum in excess of the payment into court but the whole of the sum obtained was recouped by the Secretary of State. The Court of Appeal held that she was nonetheless entitled to her costs. It was suggested that, if a defendant wishes to protect himself as to costs when he considers that the plaintiff will not recover more than the amount payable to the Compensation Recovery Unit, he must offer a specific sum not exceeding the amount certified by the certificate of total benefit, pointing out that if the offer is accepted he will pay that sum to the Compensation Recovery Unit. If the offer is not accepted and the plaintiff recovers judgement for less than the offer, the defendant will be able to rely on the offer on the question of costs.

Benefits irrelevant to assessment of damages

17. In assessing damages in respect of any accident, injury or disease, the amount of any listed benefits paid or likely to be paid is to be disregarded.

Reduction of compensation: complex cases

Lump sum and periodical payments

18.—(1) Regulations may make provision (including provision modifying this Act) for any case in which two or more compensation payments in the form of lump sums are made by the same person to or in respect of the injured person in consequence of the same accident, injury or disease.

(2) The regulations may (among other things) provide—
(a) for the re-calculation in accordance with section 8 of the amount of any compensation payment,
(b) for giving credit for amounts already paid, and
(c) for the payment by any person of any balance or the recovery from any person of any excess.

(3) For the purposes of subsection (2), the regulations may provide for the gross amounts of the compensation payments to be aggregated and for—
(a) the aggregate amount to be taken to be the gross amount of the compensation payment for the purposes of section 8,
(b) so much of the aggregate amount as is attributable to a head of compensation listed in column 1 of Schedule 2 to be taken to be the part of the gross amount which is attributable to that head;

and for the amount of any recoverable benefit shown against any head in column 2 of that Schedule to be taken to be the amount determined in accordance with the most recent certificate of recoverable benefits.

(4) Regulations may make provision (including provision modifying this Act) for any case in which, in final settlement of the injured person's claim, an agreement is entered into for the making of—
(a) periodical compensation payments (whether of an income or capital nature), or
(b) periodical compensation payments and lump sum compensation payments.

(5) Regulations made by virtue of subsection (4) may (among other things) provide—
(a) for the relevant period to be treated as ending at a prescribed time,
(b) for the person who is to make the payments under the agreement to be treated for the purposes of this Act as if he had made a single compensation payment on a prescribed date.

(6) A periodical payment may be a compensation payment for the purposes of this section even though it is a small payment (as defined in Part II of Schedule 1).

Payments by more than one person

19.—(1) Regulations may make provision (including provision modifying this Act) for any case in which two or more persons (''the compensators'') make compensation payments to or in respect of the same injured person in consequence of the same accident, injury or disease.

(2) In such a case, the sum of the liabilities of the compensators under section 6 is not to exceed the total amount of the recoverable benefits, and the regulations may provide for determining the respective liabilities under that section of each of the compensators.

(3) The regulations may (among other things) provide in the case of each compensator—
(a) for determining or re-determining the part of the recoverable benefits which may be taken into account in his case,
(b) for calculating or re-calculating in accordance with section 8 the amount of any compensation payment,
(c) for giving credit for amounts already paid, and
(d) for the payment by any person of any balance or the recovery from any person of any excess.

Miscellaneous

Amounts overpaid under section 6

20.—(1) Regulations may make provision (including provision modifying this Act) for cases where a person has paid to the Secretary of State under section 6 any amount (''the amount of the overpayment'') which he was not liable to pay.

(2) The regulations may provide—
(a) for the Secretary of State to pay the amount of the overpayment to that person, or to the person to whom the compensation payment is made, or partly to one and partly to the other, or
(b) for the receipt by the Secretary of State of the amount of the overpayment to be treated as the recovery of that amount.

(3) Regulations made by virtue of subsection (2)(b) are to have effect in spite of anything in section 71 of the Social Security Administration Act 1992 (overpayments—general).

(4) The regulations may also (among other things) provide–
(a) for the re-calculation in accordance with section 8 of the amount of any compensation payment,
(b) for giving credit for amounts already paid, and

(c) for the payment by any person of any balance or the recovery from any person of any excess.

(5) This section does not apply in a case where section 14 applies.

Compensation payments to be disregarded

21.—(1) If, when a compensation payment is made, the first and second conditions are met, the payment is to be disregarded for the purposes of sections 6 and 8.

(2) The first condition is that the person making the payment—

(a) has made an application for a certificate of recoverable benefits which complies with subsection (3), and

(b) has in his possession a written acknowledgement of the receipt of his application.

(3) An application complies with this subsection if it—

(a) accurately states the prescribed particulars relating to the injured person and the accident, injury or disease in question, and

(b) specifies the name and address of the person to whom the certificate is to be sent.

(4) The second condition is that the Secretary of State has not sent the certificate to the person, at the address, specified in the application, before the end of the period allowed under section 4.

(5) In any case where—

(a) by virtue of subsection (1), a compensation payment is disregarded for the purposes of sections 6 and 8, but

(b) the person who made the compensation payment nevertheless makes a payment to the Secretary of State for which (but for subsection (1)) he would be liable under section 6,

subsection (1) is to cease to apply in relation to the compensation payment.

(6) If, in the opinion of the Secretary of State, circumstances have arisen which adversely affect normal methods of communication—

(a) he may by order provide that subsection (1) is not to apply during a specified period not exceeding three months, and

(b) he may continue any such order in force for further periods not exceeding three months at a time.

22.—*Omitted.*

Provision of information

23.—(1) Where compensation is sought in respect of any accident, injury or disease suffered by any person ("the injured person"), the following persons must give the Secretary of State the prescribed information about the injured person—

(a) anyone who is, or is alleged to be, liable in respect of the accident, injury or disease, and

(b) anyone acting on behalf of such a person.

(2) A person who receives or claims a listed benefit which is or is likely to be paid in respect of an accident, injury or disease suffered by him, must give the Secretary of State the prescribed information about the accident, injury or disease.

(3) Where a person who has received a listed benefit dies, the duty in subsection (2) is imposed on his personal representative.

(4) Any person who makes a payment (whether on his own behalf or not)—

(a) in consequence of, or

(b) which is referable to any costs (in Scotland, expenses) incurred by reason of,

any accident, injury or disease, or any damage to property, must, if the Secretary of State requests him in writing to do so, give the Secretary of State such particulars relating to the size and composition of the payment as are specified in the request.

(5) The employer of a person who suffers or has suffered an accident, injury or disease, and anyone who has been the employer of such a person at any time during the relevant period, must give the Secretary of State the prescribed information about the payment of statutory sick pay in respect of that person.

(6) In subsection (5) ''employer'' has the same meaning as it has in Part XI of the Social Security Contributions and Benefits Act 1992.

(7) A person who is required to give information under this section must do so in the prescribed manner, at the prescribed place and within the prescribed time.

(8) Section 1 does not apply in relation to this section.

Power to amend Schedule 2

24.—(1) The Secretary of State may by regulations amend Schedule 2.

(2) A statutory instrument which contains such regulations shall not be made unless a draft of the instrument has been laid before and approved by resolution of each House of Parliament.

Provisions relating to Northern Ireland

25.–27. *Omitted.*

General

The Crown

28. This Act applies to the Crown.

General Note

This is effectively a new provision because s.104 of the Social Security Administration Act 1992 was never brought into force (see Social Security (Consequential Provisions) Act 1992, Sched. 4, para. 3).

General interpretation

29. In this Act—

''benefit'' means any benefit under the Social Security Contributions and Benefits Act 1992, a jobseeker's allowance or mobility allowance,

''compensation scheme for motor accidents'' means any scheme or arrangement under which funds are available for the payment of compensation in respect of motor accidents caused, or alleged to have been caused, by uninsured or unidentified persons,

"listed benefit" means a benefit listed in column 2 of Schedule 2,
"payment" means payment in money or money's worth, and related expressions are to be interpreted accordingly,
"prescribed" means prescribed by regulations, and
"regulations" means regulations made by the Secretary of State.

Regulations and orders

30.—(1) Any power under this Act to make regulations or an order is exercisable by statutory instrument.

(2) A statutory instrument containing regulations or an order under this Act (other than regulations under section 24 or an order under section 34) shall be subject to annulment in pursuance of a resolution of either House of Parliament.

(3) Regulations under section 20, under section 24 amending the list of benefits in column 2 of Schedule 2 or under paragraph 9 of Schedule 1 may not be made without the consent of the Treasury.

(4) Subsections (4), (5), (6) and (9) of section 189 of the Social Security Administration Act 1992 (regulations and orders—general) apply for the purposes of this Act as they apply for the purposes of that.

31. *Omitted.*

Power to make transitional, consequential etc. provisions

32.—(1) Regulations may make such transitional and consequential provisions, and such savings, as the Secretary of State considers necessary or expedient in preparation for, in connection with, or in consequence of—

(a) the coming into force of any provision of this Act, or
(b) the operation of any enactment repealed or amended by a provision of this Act during any period when the repeal or amendment is not wholly in force.

(2) Regulations under this section may (among other things) provide—

(a) for compensation payments in relation to which, by virtue of section 2, this Act does not apply to be treated as payments in relation to which this Act applies,
(b) for compensation payments in relation to which, by virtue of section 2, this Act applies to be treated as payments in relation to which this Act does not apply, and
(c) for the modification of any enactment contained in this Act or referred to in subsection (1)(b) in its application to any compensation payment.

33. *Omitted.*

Short title, commencement and extent

34.—(1) This Act may be cited as the Social Security (Recovery of Benefits) Act 1997.

(2) Sections 1 to 24, 26 to 28 and 33 are to come into force on such day as the Secretary of State may by order appoint, and different days may be appointed for different purposes.

(3) Apart from sections 25 to 27, section 33 so far as it relates to any enactment which extends to Northern Ireland, and this section this Act does not extend to Northern Ireland.

SCHEDULES

Schedule 1

Compensation Payments

Part I

Exempted payments

1. Any small payment (defined in Part II of this Schedule).

2. Any payment made to or for the injured person under section 35 of the Powers of Criminal Courts Act 1973 or section 249 of the Criminal Procedure (Scotland) Act 1995 (compensation orders against convicted persons).

3. Any payment made in the exercise of a discretion out of property held subject to a trust in a case where no more than 50 per cent. by value of the capital contributed to the trust was directly or indirectly provided by persons who are, or are alleged to be, liable in respect of—

(a) the accident, injury or disease suffered by the injured person, or

(b) the same or any connected accident, injury or disease suffered by another.

4. Any payment made out of property held for the purposes of any prescribed trust (whether the payment also falls within paragraph 3 or not).

5. Any payment made to the injured person by an insurance company within the meaning of the Insurance Companies Act 1982 under the terms of any contract of insurance entered into between the injured person and the company before—

(a) the date on which the injured person first claims a listed benefit in consequence of the disease in question, or

(b) the occurrence of the accident or injury in question.

6. Any redundancy payment falling to be taken into account in the assessment of damages in respect of an accident, injury or disease.

7. So much of any payment as is referable to costs.

8. Any prescribed payment.

Part II

Power to disregard small payments

9.—(1) Regulations may make provision for compensation payments to be disregarded for the purposes of sections 6 and 8 in prescribed cases where the amount of the compensation payment, or the aggregate amount of two or more connected compensation payments, does not exceed the prescribed sum.

(2) A compensation payment disregarded by virtue of this paragraph is referred to in paragraph 1 as a "small payment'.

(3) For the purposes of this paragraph—

(a) two or more compensation payments are "connected" if each is made to or in respect of the same injured person and in respect of the same accident, injury or disease, and

(b) any reference to a compensation payment is a reference to a payment which would be such a payment apart from paragraph 1.

SCHEDULE 2
CALCULATION OF COMPENSATION PAYMENT

(1) Head of compensation	(2) Benefit
1. Compensation for earnings lost during the relevant period	Disability working allowance Disablement pension payable under section 103 of the 1992 Act Incapacity benefit Income support Invalidity pension and allowance Jobseeker's allowance Reduced earnings allowance Severe disablement allowance Sickness benefit Statutory sick pay Unemployability supplement Unemployment benefit
2. Compensation for cost of care incurred during the relevant period	Attendance allowance Care component of disability living allowance Disablement pension increase payable under section 104 or 105 of the 1992 Act
3. Compensation for loss of mobility during the relevant period.	Mobility allowance Mobility component of disability living allowance

NOTES

1.—(1) References to incapacity benefit, invalidity pension and allowance, severe disablement allowance, sickness benefit and unemployment benefit also include any income support paid with each of those benefits on the same instrument of payment or paid concurrently with each of those benefits by means of an instrument for benefit payment.

(2) For the purpose of this Note, income support includes personal expenses addition, special transitional additions and transitional addition as defined in the Income Support (Transitional) Regulations 1987.

2. Any reference to statutory sick pay—

(a) includes only 80 per cent. of payments made between 6th April 1991 and 5th April 1994, and

(b) does not include payments made on or after 6th April 1994.

3. In this Schedule ''the 1992 Act'' means the Social Security Contributions and Benefits Act 1992.

GENERAL NOTE

It may be thought odd that disablement pension should be regarded as paid in respect of loss of earnings rather than in respect of pain and suffering.

Given the way that ss6 and 8 operate together, compensation for lost earnings presumably includes compensation for loss of *potential* earnings in the case of a person who was not employed at the time of a relevant accident or who was in temporary employment only. A benefit is recoverable only if it was paid ''in respect of'' the relevant accident, injury or disease (see the note to s.12(2)).

SCHEDULES 3 AND 4: *Omitted.*

PART II

Benefit Regulations

The Disability Working Allowance (General) Regulations 1991

(S.I. 1991 No. 2887)

Arrangement of Regulations

Part I

General

Part II

Disability Test

Part III

Presence in Great Britain and Remunerative Work

Part IV

Membership of a Family

Part V

Income and Capital

Chapter I: General

Chapter II: Normal Weekly Income

Whereas a draft of this instrument was laid before Parliament in accordance with section 12(1) of the Disability Living Allowance and Disability Working Allowance Act 1991 and approved by resolution of each House of Parliament;

Now, therefore, the Secretary of State for Social Security, in exercise of the powers conferred by section 20(1), (5)(bb), (6A)(d), (6C) to (6F), (11) and (12), section 21(3B) and (6)(aa), section 22(1) and (5) to (9), section 27B(2) and (4) and section 84(1) of the Social Security Act 1986 and section 166(1) to (3A) of the Social Security Act 1975 and of all other powers enabling him in that behalf, by this instrument, which contains only regulations made consequential upon sections 6 and 7 of the Disability Living Allowance and Disability Working Allowance Act 1991, hereby makes the following Regulations:

PART I

GENERAL

Citation and commencement

1. These Regulations may be cited as the Disability Working Allowance (General) Regulations 1991 and shall come into force on 7th April 1992.

Interpretation

2.—(1) In these Regulations, unless the context otherwise requires—

''the Act'' means the Social Security Act 1986;

''assessment period'' means such period as is prescribed in regulations 16 to 19 over which income falls to be calculated;

''attendance allowance'' means—

(a) an attendance allowance under section 35 of the Social Security Act;
(b) an increase of disablement pension under section 61 or 63 of that Act;
(c) a payment under regulations made in exercise of the power conferred by section 159(3)(b) of that Act;
(d) an increase of an allowance which is payable in respect of constant attendance under section 5 of the Industrial Injuries and Diseases (Old Cases) Act 1975;
(e) a payment by virtue of article 14, 15, 16, 43 or 44 of the Personal Injuries (Civilians) Scheme 1983 or any analogous payment; or
(f) any payment based on need for attendance which is paid as part of a war disablement pension;

[[10]the benefit Acts'' means the Contribution and Benefits Act and the Jobseekers Act 1995] "claim" means a claim for disability working allowance;

"claimant" means a person claiming disability working allowance;

"close relative" means a parent, parent-in-law, son, son-in-law, daughter, daughter-in-law, step-parent, step-son, step-daughter, brother, sister, or the spouse of any of the preceding persons or, if that person is one of an unmarried couple, the other member of that couple;

[[3]"community charge benefit" means community charge benefits under Part VII of the Contributions and Benefits Act as originally enacted;]

"concessionary payment" means a payment made under arrangements made by the Secretary of State with the consent of the Treasury which is charged either to the National Insurance Fund or to a Departmental Expenditure Vote to which payments of benefit under the Act, the Social Security Act or the Child Benefit Act 1975 are charged;

[[3]"the Contributions and Benefits Act" means the Social Security Contributions and Benefits Act 1992;]

[[7]"Crown Property" means property held by Her Majesty in right of the Crown or by a government department or which is held in trust for Her Majesty for the purposes of a government department, except (in the case of an interest held by Her Majesty in right of the Crown) where the interest is under the management of the Crown Estate Commissioners;]

"date of claim" means the date on which the claimant makes, or is treated as making, a claim for disability working allowance;

"earnings" has the meaning prescribed in regulation 21 or, as the case may be, 24;

[[11]"earnings top up" means the allowance paid by the Secretary of State under the Earnings Top-up Scheme;

"the Earnings Top-up" Scheme means the Earnings Top-up Scheme 1996;]

"employed earner" shall be construed in accordance with section 2(1)(a) of the Social Security Act;

"lone-parent" means a person who has no partner and who is responsible for, and a member of the same household as, a child or young person;

[[2]"lower rate" where it relates to rates of tax has the same meaning as in the Income and Corporation Taxes Act 1988 by virtue of section 832(1) of that Act;]

[[6]"maternity leave" means a period during which a woman is absent from work because she is pregnant or has given birth to a child, and at the end of which she has a right to return to work either under the terms of her contract of employment or under Part III of the Employment Protection (Consolidation) Act 1978;]

"mobility allowance" means an allowance under section 37A of the Social Security Act;

"mobility supplement" means any supplement under article 26A of the Naval, Military and Air Forces etc (Disablement and Death) Service Pensions Order 1983 including such a supplement by virtue of any other scheme or order or under article 25A of the Personal Injuries (Civilians) Scheme 1983;

"net earnings" means such earnings as are calculated in accordance with regulation 22;

"net profit" means such profit as is calculated in accordance with regulation 25;

"occupational pension" means any pension or other periodical payment under an occupational pension scheme but does not include any discretionary payment out of a fund established for relieving hardship in particular cases;

"partner" means, where a claimant—

(a) is a member of a married or unmarried couple, the other member of that couple,
(b) is married polygamously to two or more members of the same household, any such member;

"payment" includes a part of a payment;

[12"pay period" means the period in respect of which a claimant is, or expects to be normally paid by his employer, being a week, a fortnight, four weeks, a month or other shorter or longer period, as the case may be;]

[9"pension fund holder" means with respect to a personal pension scheme or retirement annuity contract, the trustees, managers, or scheme administrators, as the case may be of the scheme or contract concerned.]

[6"personal pension scheme" has the same meaning as in [9 section 1 of the Pension Scheme Act 1993] and, in the case of a self-employed earner, includes a scheme approved by the Inland Revenue under Chapter IV of Part XIV of the Income and Corporation Taxes Act 1988;]

"policy of life insurance" means any instrument by which the payment of money is assured on death (except death by accident only) or the happening of any contingency dependent on human life, or any instrument evidencing a contract which is subject to payment of premiums for a term dependent on human life;

[1"qualifying person" means a person in respect of whom payment has been made from the Fund [5or the Eileen Trust];]

[9"retirement annuity contract" means a contract or trust scheme approved under Chapter III of Part XIV of the Income and Corporation Taxes Act 1988;]

"self-employed earner" shall be construed in accordance with section 2(1)(b) of the Social Security Act;

"single claimant" means a claimant who neither has a partner nor is a lone parent;

"Social Security Act" means the Social Security Act 1975;

"student" has the meaning prescribed in regulation 41;

[5"the Eileen Trust" means the charitable trust of that name established on 29th March 1993 out of funds provided by the Secretary of State for the benefit of persons eligible for payment in accordance with its provisions;]

[1"the Fund" means moneys made available from time to time by the Secretary of State for the benefit of persons eligible for payment in accordance with the provisions of a scheme established by him on 24th April 1992 or, in Scotland, on 10th April 1992;]

[4"the Independent Living (Extension) Fund" means the Trust of that name established by a deed dated 25th February 1993 and made between the Secretary of State for Social Security of the one part and Robin Glover Wendt and John Fletcher Shepherd of the other part;]

"the Independent Living Fund" means the charitable trust established out of funds provided by the Secretary of State for the purpose of providing financial assistance to those persons incapacitated by or otherwise suffering from very severe disablement who are in need of such assistance to enable them to live independently;

[4"the Independent Living (1993) Fund" means the Trust of that name established by a deed dated 25th February 1993 and made between the Secretary of State for Social Security of the one part and Robin Glover Wendt and John Fletcher Shepherd of the other part;]

"the Independent Living Funds" means the Independent Living Fund, the Independence Living (Extension) Fund and the Independent Living (1993) Fund:]

"the Macfarlane (Special Payments) Trust" means the trust of that name, established on 29th January 1990 partly out of funds provided by the

Secretary of State, for the benefit of certain persons suffering from haemophilia;

"the Macfarlane (Special Payments) (No. 2) Trust" means the trust of that name, established on 3rd May 1991 partly out of funds provided by the Secretary of State, for the benefit of certain persons suffering from haemophilia and other beneficiaries;

"the Macfarlane Trust" means the charitable trust, established partly out of funds provided by the Secretary of State to the Haemophilia Society, for the relief of poverty or distress among those suffering from haemophilia;

[2"training allowance" means an allowance (whether by way of periodical grants or otherwise) payable—

(a) out of public funds by a government department or by or on behalf of the Secretary of State, Scottish Enterprise or Highlands and Islands Enterprise;

(b) to a person for his maintenance or in respect of a member of his family; and

(c) for the period, or part of the period, during which he is following a course of training or instruction provided by, or in pursuance of arrangements made with, that department or approved by that department in relation to him or so provided or approved by or on behalf of the Secretary of State, Scottish Enterprise or Highlands and Islands Enterprise,

but it does not include an allowance paid by any Government department to or in respect of a person by reason of the fact that he is following a course of full-time education, other than an allowance paid pursuant to arrangements made under section 2 of the Employment and Training Act 1973, or that he is training as a teacher;]

[8"voluntary organisation" means a body, other than a public or local authority, the activities of which are carried on otherwise than for profit;]

[3"water charges" means—

(a) as respects England and Wales, any water and sewerage charges under Chapter 1 of Part V of the Water Industry Act 1991;

(b) as respects Scotland, any water and sewerage charges under Schedule 11 to the Local Government Finance Act 1992;]

"week" means a period of seven days beginning with Sunday;

"week of claim" means the week which includes the date of claim;

"year of assessment" has the meaning prescribed in section 832(1) of the Income and Corporation Taxes Act 1988;

"young person" has the meaning prescribed in regulation 8.

(2) Unless the context otherwise requires, any reference in these Regulations to a numbered regulation, Part or Schedule is a reference to the regulation, Part or Schedule bearing that number in these Regulations and any reference in a regulation or Schedule to a numbered paragraph is a reference to the paragraph in that regulation or Schedule bearing that number.

AMENDMENTS

1. Income-related Benefits Schemes and Social Security (Recoupment) Amendment Regulations 1992 (S.I. 1992 No. 1101), reg. 3(2) (May 7, 1992).

2. Income-related Benefits Schemes (Miscellaneous) Amendments (No. 3) Regulations 1992 (S.I. 1992 No. 2155), reg. 2 (October 5, 1992).

3. Income-related Benefits Schemes (Miscellaneous Amendments) Regulations 1993 (S.I. 1993 No. 315), reg. 16 (April 13, 1993).

4. Social Security Benefits (Miscellaneous Amendments) (No. 2) Regulations 1993 (S.I. 1993 No. 963), reg. 6(2) (April 22, 1993).

5. Income-related Benefits Schemes and Social Security (Recoupment) Amendment Regulations 1993 (S.I. 1993 No. 1249), reg. 5(2)(b) (May 14, 1993).

6. Income-related Benefits Schemes (Miscellaneous Amendments) (No. 4) Regulations 1993 (S.I. 1993 No. 2119), reg. 36 (October 5, 1993).
7. Income-related Benefits Schemes (Miscellaneous Amendments) (No. 4) Regulations 1994 (S.I. 1994 No. 1924), reg. 3(2) (October 4, 1994).
8. Income-related Benefits Schemes (Miscellaneous Amendments) Regulations 1995 (S.I. 1995 No. 516), reg. 2 (April 11, 1995).
9. Income-related Benefits Schemes and Social Security (Claims and Payments) (Miscellaneous Amendments) Regulations 1995 (S.I. 1995 No. 2303), reg. 3(2) (October 3, 1995).
10. Social Security and Child Support (Jobseeker's Allowance) (Consequential Amendments) Regulations 1996 (S.I. 1996 No. 1345), reg. 7(2) (October 7, 1996).
11. Income-related Benefits Schemes and Social Fund (Miscellaneous Amendments) Regulations 1996 (S.I. 1996 No. 1944), reg. 13 and para. 1 of Sched. (October 7, 1996).
12. Disability Working Allowance and Family Credit (General) Amendment Regulations 1996 (S.I. 1996 No. 3137), reg. 2(2) (January 7, 1997).

General Note

For other definitions, see s. 137(1) of the Social Security Contributions and Benefits Act 1992.

Part II

Disability Test

Person at a disadvantage in getting a job

3.—(1) A person has a disability which puts him at a disadvantage in getting a job where—
(a) in respect of an initial claim one or more of the paragraphs in Parts I, II or III of Schedule 1 apply to him;
(b) in respect of a repeat claim one or more of the paragraphs in Part I or Part II of Schedule 1 apply to him.
(2) In this regulation and in regulation 4, the expressions "initial claim" and "repeat claim" have the same meanings as in section 27B of the Act.

General Note

S.129(3) of the Social Security Contributions and Benefits Act 1992 has the effect that a person is treated as having a disability putting him or her at a disadvantage in getting a job *only* if one of the relevant paragraphs in Sched. 1 applies to him or her. This regulation has the effect that any person to whom one of those relevant paragraphs applies is deemed to be at a disadvantage in getting a job, whether or not the disability actually has that effect. The condition in Pt. 3 of Sched. 1 (that, as a result of illness or accident, the claimant is undergoing a period of habilitation or rehabilitation) applies only to initial claims. S.27B(1) of the Social Security Act 1986 (which defined "initial claim" and "repeat claim") has now been replaced by s.11(1) of the Social Security Administration Act 1992.

Reg. 27 of the Social Security (Adjudication) Regulations 1995 provides that the question whether a claimant has a disability which puts him or her at a disadvantage in getting a job is a "disability question" falling within the jurisdiction of a disability appeal tribunal rather than a social security appeal tribunal.

Declaration by claimant

4. On an initial claim, a declaration by the claimant that he has a physical or mental disability which puts him at a disadvantage in getting a job is not conclusive that for the purposes of section 20(6A)(b) of the Act he has a disability, where—
(a) the claim itself contains contrary indications, or
(b) the adjudication officer has before him other evidence which contradicts that declaration.

GENERAL NOTE

The effect of s.11(2) of the Social Security Administration Act 1992 is that, on an initial claim (defined in s.11(1)), a claimant's statement is conclusive unless either of the conditions in this regulation is satisfied. At first glance that does little more than state the obvious since a statement which is neither inherently improbable nor contradicted should usually be accepted. However, s.11(2) appears to be intended to reinforce that position by preventing the adjudication officer from obtaining further evidence to check the claimant's account unless the existing evidence gives a clear reason for doing so. It is arguable that, if an adjudication officer does seek further evidence in breach of s.11(2), a disability appeal tribunal hearing an appeal should disregard that evidence. Otherwise, s.11(2) achieves nothing. S.20(6A)(6) of the Social Security Act 1986 has been replaced by s.129(1)(b) of the Social Security Contribution and Benefits Act 1992.

PART III

PRESENCE IN GREAT BRITAIN AND REMUNERATIVE WORK

Circumstances in which a person is treated as being or as not being in Great Britain

5.—(1) A person shall be treated as being in Great Britain if, on the date of claim—

(a) he is present and ordinarily resident in Great Britain; and

[[1](aa) subject to paragraph (1A), his right to reside or remain in Great Britain is not subject to any limitation or conditions; and]

(b) his partner, if he has one, is ordinarily resident in the United Kingdom; and

(c) his earnings derive at least in part from remunerative work in the United Kingdom; and

(d) his earnings do not wholly derive from remunerative work outside the United Kingdom nor do the earnings of his partner, if he has one.

[[1](1A) For the purposes of paragraph (1)(aa), a person's right to reside or remain in Great Britain is not to be treated as if it were subject to a limitation or condition if—

(a) he is a person recorded by the Secretary of State as a refugee within the definition in Article 1 of of the Conventions relating to the Status of Refugees done at Geneva on 28th July 1951, as extended by Article 1(2) of the Protocol relating to the Status of Refugees done at New York on 31st January 1967;

(b) he is a person who has been granted exceptional leave outside the provisions of the immigration rules within the meaning of the Immigration Act 1971 to remain in the United Kingdom by the Secretary of State;

(c) he is national, or a member of the family of a national, of a State contracting party to the Agreement on the European Economic Area signed at Oporto on 2nd May 1992 as adjusted by the Protocol signed at Brussels on 17th March 1993, or

(d) he is a person who is—

(i) lawfully working in Great Britain and is a national of a State with which the Community has concluded an Agreement under article 238 of the Treaty establishing the European Community providing, in the field of social security, for the treatment of workers who are nationals of the signatory State and their families, or

(ii) a member of the family of, and living with, such a person.]

(2) A person shall be treated as not being in Great Britain during any period for which he, or his partner, is entitled to be paid disability working allowance or family credit under the law of Northern Ireland.

AMENDMENT

1. Social Security (Persons From Abroad) Miscellaneous Amendments Regulations 1996 (S.I. 1996 No. 30), regulation 5 (February 5, 1996, subject to a saving under regulation 12(3).

GENERAL NOTE

Although it does not say so clearly, it seems to have been intended that a person shall not be treated as being in Great Britain unless the conditions in para. (1) are satisfied (see R(FC) 2/93). Note that the conditions need be satisfied only at the date of the claim.

The meaning of "ordinarily resident" was considered in *R(M) 1/85*, where the Commissioner referred to a large number of cases from other fields of law, including *R. v. Barnet L.B.C., ex p. Shah* [1983] 2 A.C. 309 in which Lord Scarman (agreeing with Lord Denning M.R.) held that "ordinarily resident" meant "that the person must be habitually and normally resident . . ., apart from temporary or occasional absences of long or short duration" and added that there must be a settled purpose. A purpose, while settled, may be for a limited period.

It will not often occur that a person will be a "partner" of the claimant at the same time as being ordinarily resident in a different country. To be a "partner" as defined in reg. 2(1), a person must be living in the same household as the claimant because otherwise they will not be a married or unmarried couple (see the annotation to s.137 of the Social Security Contribution and Benefits Act 1992).

Paras. (1)(aa) and (1A). A claimant's right to reside or remain in Great Britain must be subject to any limitation except in the cases within para. (1A). Examples of limitations are when a person has been allowed to remain as a visitor for a period of six months or is seeking asylum. Cases within para. (1A) are those where the claimant is recognised as a refugee (sub-para. (a)), or has been granted exceptional leave to remain (sub-para. (b)) or is, or is a member of a family of, a national of an E.U. country or Norway, Liechtenstein or Iceland (sub-para. (c)) or is lawfully working in Great Britain and is a national of Algeria, Morocco, Slovenia or Tunisia (sub-para. (d).

Remunerative work

6.—(1) [[1]For the purposes of Part VII of the Social Security Contributions and Benefits Act 1992 as it applies to disability working allowance and subject to paragraph (3), a person shall be treated as engaged in remunerative work;]

(a) the work he undertakes is for not less than 16 hours per week;
(b) the work is done for payment or in expectation of payment; and
(c) he is employed at the date of claim and satisfies the requirements of paragraph (5).

(2) A person who does not satisfy all the requirements of sub-paragraphs (a) to (c) of paragraph (1) shall not be treated as engaged [[1] . . .] in remunerative work.

[[3](3) A person who otherwise satisfies all the requirements of paragraph (1) shall not be treated as engaged in remunerative work insofar as—

(a) he is engaged by a charitable or voluntary organisation or is a volunteer, where the only payment received by him or due to be paid to him is a payment which is to be disregarded under regulation 27(2) and paragraph 2 of Schedule 3 (sums to be disregarded in the calculation of income other than earnings);
(b) he is engaged in caring for a person in respect of whom he receives payments to which paragraph 24 of Schedule 3 refers; or
(c) he is engaged on a scheme for which a training allowance is being paid.]

(4) [[4]Subject to paragraph (4A)] in determining for the purposes of sub-paragraph (a) of paragraph (1) whether a person has undertaken work of not less than 16 hours per week—

(a) there shall be included in the calculation any time allowed—
   (i) for meals or refreshment; or
   (ii) for visits to a hospital, clinic or other establishment for the purpose only of treating or monitoring the person's disability, but only where the person is, or expects to be, paid earnings in respect of that time; and

(b) where at the date of claim the claimant has within the previous 5 weeks—
  (i) started a new job;
  (ii) resumed work after a break of at least 13 weeks; or
  (iii) changed his hours,
  the hours worked shall be calculated by reference to the number of hours, or where these are expected to fluctuate, the average number of hours, which he is expected to work in a week; or

(c) where none of heads (i) to (iii) of sub-paragraph (b) [[1] of this paragraph]; and
  (i) a recognised cycle of working has been established at the date of claim, the hours worked shall be calculated by reference to the average number of hours worked in a week over the period of one complete cycle (including where the cycle involves periods in which the person does not work, those periods, but disregarding any other absences); or
  (ii) no recognised cycle of working has been established at that date, the hours worked shall be calculated by reference to the average number of hours worked over the 5 weeks immediately preceding the week in which the claim is made, or such other length of time preceding that week as may, in the particular case, enable the person's weekly average hours of work to be determined more accurately.

[[5](4A) Where for the purpose of paragraph (4)(c)(i), a person's recognised cycle of work at a school, other educational establishment or other place of employment is one year and includes periods of school holidays or similar vacations during which he does not work, those periods and any other periods not forming part of such holidays or vacations during which he is not required to work shall be disregarded in establishing the average hours for which he is engaged in work.]

(5) Subject to paragraph (6), the requirements of this paragraph are that the person—

(a) worked not less than 16 hours in either—
  (i) the week of claim; or
  (ii) either of the two weeks immediately preceding the week of claim; or

(b) is expected by his employer to work [[1] or, where he is a self-employed earner he expects to work,] not less than 16 hours in the week next following the week of claim; or

(c) cannot satisfy the requirements of sub-paragraph (a) or (b) above at the date of claim because he is or will be absent from work by reason of a recognised, customary or other holiday but he is expected by his employer to work not less than 16 hours in the week following his return to work,

and for the purposes of calculating the number of hours worked, sub-paragraph (a) of paragraph (4) shall apply to this paragraph as it applies to sub-paragraph (a) of paragraph (1).

[[2](6) For the purposes of paragraph (5)—

(a) work which a person does only qualifies if—
  (i) it is the work which he normally does, and
  (ii) it is likely to last for a period of 5 weeks or more beginning with the week in which the claim is made; and

(b) a person shall be treated as not on a recognised, customary or other holiday on any day on which the person is on maternity leave or is absent from work because he is ill.]

[[1](7) Where a person is treated as engaged in remunerative work in accordance with the above paragraphs, he shall also be treated as normally engaged in remunerative work.]

[[4]. . .]

AMENDMENTS

1. Income-related Benefits Schemes (Miscellaneous Amendments) (No. 3) Regulations 1992 (S.I. 1992 No. 2155), Sched., para. 2 (October 5, 1992).

2. Income-related Benefits Schemes (Miscellaneous Amendments) (No. 4) Regulations 1993 (S.I. 1993 No. 2119), reg. 37 (October 5, 1993 or later expiry of award).

3. Income-related Benefits Schemes (Miscellaneous Amendments) (No. 5) Regulations 1994 (S.I. 1994 No. 2139), reg. 2(a) (October 4, 1994 or later expiry of award).

4. Inserted by Income-related Benefits Schemes (Miscellaneous Amendments) (No. 5) Regulations 1994 (S.I. 1994 No. 2139), reg. 2(b) (October 4, 1994 or later expiry of award) and deleted by Income-related Benefits Schemes (Miscellaneous Amendments) Regulations 1995 (S.I. 1995 No. 516), reg. 3(c) (April 11, 1995 or later expiry of award).

5. Income-related Benefits Schemes (Miscellaneous Amendments) Regulations 1995 (S.I. 1995 No. 516), reg. 3 (April 11, 1995 or later expiry of award).

GENERAL NOTE

S.129(1)(a) of the Social Security Contributions and Benefits Act 1992 makes it a condition of entitlement to disability working allowance that the claimant be both "engaged" and "normally engaged" in remunerative work. However, para. (7) of this regulation now provides that a person who is engaged in remunerative work is also to be treated as normally engaged in such work. This is not as much of a concession as it looks because para. (6) provides that the claimant must, during one of the four weeks mentioned in para. (5)(a) and (b), perform work which the claimant "normally" does and which is likely to last for at least five weeks from the week in which the claim was made. It is not clear what is meant by "normally". Is it envisaged that a person starting a period of six weeks' temporary employment should not be entitled to disability working allowance? There seems to be no good reason why that should be so.

A person is treated as engaged in remunerative work if the three conditions in para. (1) are satisfied; *i.e.* (a) the work is for not less than 16 hours per week, (b) the work is done for payment or in expectation of payment and (c) the claimant is employed at the date of claim and has, or is expected to, work 16 hours in the relevant week.

Work for not less than 16 hours per week

This is concerned with the actual period worked rather than the number of hours referred to in the contract of employment. The number of hours worked must be calculated by looking at what is actually done. The fact that a claimant undertakes to work at least 36 hours for the purpose of obtaining an Enterprise Allowance is not conclusive (*CIS/514/90*). In the case of a self-employed person, the hours are not just those which are costed but can also include time spent canvassing for work, travelling to see clients and exhibitions and anything else essential to the business (*R(FIS) 6/85).* See para. (4) for the way the hours are calculated if they are not regular. Note that para. (4)(a) permits the inclusion of paid meal or refreshment breaks and also the time taken to attend hospitals, etc. if earnings are paid in respect of that time. Para. (4)(b) deals with the case of a person who has started or resumed work within the last five weeks or who has had a change of hours during that period. In such a case, the number of hours of work is calculated by reference to what is *expected.* Most cases fall to be decided under para. (4)(c). If there is a regular pattern of employment, the number of hours worked is calculated by reference to that pattern (para. (4)(c)(i)). Note that holidays are regarded as a normal part of the pattern. If a person usually works 17 hours per week but is entitled to four weeks' holiday in a year, he or she will be found to work for fewer than 16 hours per week over a 52-week period. This seems rather unfair because in most cases where there is no set pattern of work and hours fluctuate the effect of holidays is generally ignored. In such a case, an average is taken over a number of weeks preceding the week in which the claim was made (para. (4)(c)(ii)). The average is usually taken over the five weeks immediately preceding that week but, if there is something unusual about that period so that it does not really give a true picture, the average may be taken over any other period preceding (but not necessarily immediately preceding) that week.

Work done for payment or in expectation of payment

The remuneration must be derived from the work but it need not necessarily arise out of a contract (see *R(FC) 2/90* which concerned full-time officers of the Salvation Army). In the case of a self-employed craftsman or writer who tries to find a buyer for his or her efforts after the work has been done, it is necessary to distinguish between an expectation of payment and a mere hope of payment. In *R(IS)1/93*, a Commissioner held that a woman who spent well over 24 hours a week writing but who had not had much published for a long time was not working for 24 hours a week in expectation of payment (see also *CDWA/02/93*). A person may well have an expectation of payment when he or she starts a venture, but the position may have to be reviewed in the light of experience. If he or she can reasonably be expected to sell only 20 per cent of his or her work then he or she can be said to be in "remunerative" employment for only 20 per cent of the total number of hours worked.

Employed at the date of claim and para. (5)

It is not possible to make an advance claim for disability working allowance; the claimant must be employed at the date of claim. He or she must also have worked, or be expected to work, in at least one of the four weeks identified in para. (5)(a) and (b) (*i.e.* the week in which the claim was made, the two weeks preceding that week and the week following it). Sub-para. (c) prevents people from losing entitlement merely because they happen to be on holiday in one or more of the relevant weeks, provided that they are expected to work for at least 16 weeks in the week following their return to work. However, a person is not entitled to disability working allowance if absent through illness during all four relevant weeks.

Further provision as to remunerative work

[[1]**6A.** Whether, for the purposes of regulation 51(1)(bb) (determination of appropriate maximum disability working allowance) and paragraph 2A of Schedule 5, the work a person undertakes is for not less than 30 hours per week shall be determined in accordance with regulation 6(1)(b), (3), (4) and (4A) except that for the words "16 hours" in paragraph (4) there shall be substituted the words "30 hours".]

AMENDMENT

1. Income-related Benefits Schemes (Miscellaneous Amendments) (No. 2) Regulations 1995 (S.I. 1995 No. 1339), reg. 3 (July 17, 1995).

Income-related benefits

7. For the purposes of subsection (6E) of section 20 of the Act the prescribed circumstances are that the person's weekly applicable amount included a higher pensioner or disability premium in respect of him, determined—

(a) [[1] in the case of] income support, in accordance with paragraphs 10(1)(b) [[3], 10(2)(b)] or 11, and 12 of Part III of Schedule 2 to the Income Support (General) Regulations 1987 (applicable amounts);

[[4](aa) in the case of income-based jobseeker's allowance, in accordance with paragraphs 12(1)(a), (b)(ii) or (c) or 13, and 14 of Schedule 1 to the Jobseeker's Allowance Regulations 1996 (applicable amounts).]

(b) in the case of housing benefit, in accordance with paragraphs 10(1)(b) [[3], 10(2)(b)] or 11, and 12 of Part III of Schedule 2 to the Housing Benefit (General) Regulations 1987 (applicable amounts);

(c) in the case of community charge benefit, in accordance with paragraphs 11 or 12, and 13 of Part III of Schedule 1 to the Community Charge Benefits (General) Regulations 1989 (applicable amounts); [[2]. . .]

[[2] *ca*) in the case of council tax benefit, in accordance with paragraphs [[3] 11(1)(b), 11(2)(b)] or 12, and 13 of Part III of Schedule 1 to the Council Tax Benefit (General) Regulations 1992; or]

(d) in accordance with any provision equivalent to one of those specified in [[1] paragraphs [[2] (a) to (ca)] above] having effect in Northern Ireland.

AMENDMENTS

1. Income-related Benefits Schemes (Miscellaneous Amendments) (No. 3) Regulations 1992 (S.I. 1992 No. 2155), Sched. para. 3 (October 5, 1992).

2. Income-related Benefits Schemes (Miscellaneous Amendments) Regulations 1993 (S.I. 1993 No. 315), reg. 16 (April 1, 1993).

3. Income-related Benefits Schemes (Miscellaneous Amendments) Regulations 1995 (S.I. 1995 No. 516), reg. 4 (April 11, 1995 or later expiry of award).

4. Social Security and Child Support (Jobseeker's Allowance) (Consequential Amendments) Regulations 1996 (S.I. 1996 No. 1345), reg, 7(3) (October 7, 1996).

General Note

S.20(6E) of the Social Security Act 1986 has now been replaced by s.129(4) of the Social Security Contributions and Benefits Act 1992. The effect of this regulation is that income support, housing benefit and community charge benefit are only qualifying benefits for disability working allowance under s.129(2)(a)(iii) of the 1992 Act (formerly s.20(6B)(a)(iv) of the 1986 Act) if the claimant's applicable amount included either a disability premium or a higher pensioner premium.

[1 Definition of "training for work"

7A. For the purposes of section 129(2A) of the Contributions and Benefits Act (which provides that a period of training for work may count towards the period of qualification for disability working allowance) "training for work" also includes any training received on a course which a person attends for 16 hours or more a week, the primary purpose of which is the teaching of occupational or vocational skills.]

Amendment

1. Disability Working Allowance and Income Support (General) Amendment Regulations 1995 (S.I. 1995 No. 482), reg. 2 (April 13, 1995).

[1 Days to be disregarded

7B.—(1) For the purposes of section 129(2B)(c) of the Contributions and Benefits Act (days to be disregarded in determining a period of training for work) there shall be disregarded any day on which the claimant was—

(a) on holiday;

(b) attending court as a justice of the peace, a party to any proceedings, a witness or a juror;

(c) suffering from some disease or bodily or mental disablement as a result of which he was unable to attend training for work, or his attendance would have put at risk the health of other persons;

(d) unable to participate in training for work because—

(i) he was looking after a child because the person who usually looked after that child was unable to do so;

(ii) he was looking after a member of his family who was ill;

(iii) he was required to deal with some domestic emergency; or

(iv) he was arranging or attending the funeral of his partner or a relative; or

(e) authorised by the training provider to be absent from training for work.

(2) For the purposes of paragraph (1)(d)(iv), "relative" means close relative, grandparent, grandchild, uncle, aunt, nephew or niece.]

Amendment

1. Disability Working Allowance and Income Support (General) Amendment Regulations 1995 (S.I. 1995 No. 482), reg. 2 (April 13, 1995).

PART IV

MEMBERSHIP OF A FAMILY

Persons of a prescribed description

8.—(1) Subject to paragraph (2), a person of a prescribed description for the purposes of section 20(11) of the Act (meaning of the family) as it applies to disability working allowance is a person aged 16 or over but under 19 who is receiving full-time education within section 2(1)(b) of the Child Benefit Act 1975 (meaning of child), and in these Regulations such a person is referred to as "a young person".

(2) Paragraph (1) shall not apply to a person—

(a) who is entitled to income support or would, but for section 20(9) of the Act (provision against dual entitlement of members of family), be so entitled;

[[1](aa) who is entitled to income-based jobseeker's allowance or would, but for section 3(1)(d) of the Jobseekers Act 1995 (provision against dual entitlement of members of family), be so entitled;]

(b) who is receiving advanced education within the meaning of regulation 1(2) of the Child Benefit (General) Regulations 1976; or

(c) who has ceased to receive full-time education but is to continue to be treated as a child by virtue of regulation 7 of the Child Benefit (General) Regulations 1976.

AMENDMENT

1. Social Security and Child Support (Jobseeker's Allowance) (Consequential Amendments) Regulations 1996 (S.I. 1996 No. 1345), reg. 7(4) (October 7, 1996).

GENERAL NOTE

S.20(11) of the Social Security Act 1986 has been replaced by s.137(1) of the Social Security Contributions and Benefits Act 1992 and s.2(1)(b) of the Child Benefit Act 1975 has been replaced by s.142(b) of the 1992 Act.

This regulation identifies those people (other than partners and children under 16) who can be included in a person's family for the purpose of claiming disability working allowance. It is limited to people under 19 who are in full-time education. Under reg. 5 of the Child Benefit (General) Regulations 1976, full-time education is "education received by a person attending a course of education at a recognised educational establishment and in the pursuit of that course, the time spent receiving instruction or tuition, undertaking supervised study, examination or practical work or taking part in any exercise, experiment or project for which provision is made in the curriculum of the course exceeds 12 hours per week, so however that in calculating the time spent in pursuit of the course, no account shall be taken of time occupied by meal breaks or spent on unsupervised study, whether undertaken on or off the premises of the educational establishment".

Note that para. (2)(c) makes it quite clear that once a person ceases to be in full-time education, he or she ceases to be a "young person" notwithstanding that he or she would continue to be a "child" for child benefit purposes.

Circumstances in which a person is to be treated as responsible or not responsible for another

9.—(1) Subject to the following provisions of this regulation, a person shall be treated as responsible for a child or young person who is normally living with him.

(2) Where a child or young person spends equal amounts of time in different households, or where there is a question as to which household he is living in,

the child or young person shall be treated for the purposes of paragraph (1) as normally living with—

(a) the person who is receiving child benefit in respect of him; or

(b) if there is no such person—

(i) where only one claim for child benefit has been made in respect of him, the person who made that claim, or

(ii) in any other case the person who has the primary responsibility for him.

(3) For the purposes of these Regulations a child or young person shall be treated as the responsibility of only one person during the period of an award and any person other than the one treated as responsible for the child or young person under the foregoing paragraphs shall be treated as not so responsible.

General Note

Under s. 137(1) of the Social Security Contributions and Benefits Act 1992 a child or young person can be included within a family only if either the claimant or his or her partner is "responsible" for that child or young person and only if they are all members of the same household. This regulation is concerned with who is or is not responsible for a child or young person and reg. 10 is concerned with membership of the same household.

Para. (1) A child "normally" lives with a person if he or she spends more time with that person than with anyone else (*CFC/1537/95*).

Para. (2) This paragraph applies only where a person spends equal amounts of time in different households or where there is a real doubt in which household he or she spends most time because there is no established pattern. A real doubt is not raised merely because there is a dispute of fact (*CFC/1537/95*).

Membership of the same household

10.—(1) Except in a case to which paragraph (2) applies, where a claimant or any partner is treated as responsible for a child or young person by virtue of regulation 9 (circumstances where a person is treated as responsible or not responsible for another), that child or young person and any child of that child or young person shall be treated as a member of the claimant's household.

(2) A child or young person shall not be treated as a member of the claimant's household in any case where the child or young person—

(a) is a patient or in residential accommodation on account of physical or mental handicap or physical or mental illness and has been so accommodated for the 12 weeks immediately before the date of claim and is no longer in regular contact with the claimant or any member of the claimant's household; or

(b) is in a foster placement, or in Scotland boarded out, with the claimant or his partner prior to adoption; or

(c) is in a foster placement, or in Scotland boarded out, with the claimant or his partner under a relevant enactment; or

(d) has been placed for adoption with the claimant or his partner pursuant to a decision under the Adoption Agencies Regulations 1983 or the Adoption Agencies (Scotland) Regulations 1984; or

(e) is detained in custody under a sentence imposed by a court.

(3) In this regulation—

(a) "patient" means a person (other than a person who is serving a sentence imposed by a court in a prison or youth custody institution or in Scotland, young offender's institution) who is regarded as receiving free in-patient treatment within the meaning of the Social Security (Hospital In-Patients) Regulations 1975;

(b) "relevant enactment" means the Army Act 1955, the Air Force Act 1955, the Naval Discipline Act 1957, the Matrimonial Proceedings

(Children) Act 1958, the Social Work (Scotland) Act 1968, the Family Law Reform Act 1969, the Children and Young Persons Act 1969, the Matrimonial Causes Act 1973, the Guardianship Act 1973, the Children Act 1975, the Adoption Act 1976, the Domestic Proceedings and Magistrates' Courts Act 1978, the Adoption (Scotland) Act 1978, the Child Care Act 1980 and the Children Act 1989;

(c) "residential accommodation" means accommodation for a person whose stay in the accommodation has become other than temporary which is provided under—

(i) sections 21 to 24 and 26 of the National Assistance Act 1948 (provision of accommodation); or

(ii) section 21(1) of, and paragraph 1 or 2 of Schedule 8 to, the National Health Service Act 1977 (prevention, care and after-care) or, in Scotland, for the purposes of section 27 of the National Health Services (Scotland) Act 1947 (prevention of illness and after-care) or under section 59 of the Social Work (Scotland) Act 1968 (provision of residential and other establishments) or under section 7 of the Mental Health (Scotland) Act 1984 (function of local authorities).

General Note

See the note to reg. 9.

Circumstances in which a person is to be treated as being no longer a member of the same household

11.—[[1](1) Subject to the following provisions of this regulation, where the claimant and any partner of his are living apart from each other they shall be treated as members of the same household unless they do not intend to resume living together.]

(2) Where one of the members of a married or unmarried couple is a hospital patient or detained in custody he shall not be treated, on this account, as ceasing to be a member of the same household as his partner—

(a) unless he has been a patient in a hospital for 52 weeks or more; or

(b) unless he is a patient detained in a hospital provided under section 4 of the National Health Service Act 1977 (special hospitals) or section 90(1) of the Mental Health (Scotland) Act 1984 (provision of hospitals for patients requiring special security); or

(c) unless he is detained in custody whilst serving a sentence of 52 weeks or more imposed by a court,

but shall be treated as not being a member of the same household as his partner wherever the conditions in sub-paragraphs (a), (b) or (c) are fulfilled.

(3) In this regulation "patient" has the same meaning as in regulation 10(3)(a) (membership of the same household).

Amendment

1. Income-related Benefits Schemes (Miscellaneous Amendments) (No. 4) Regulations 1993 (S.I. 1993 No. 2119), reg. 38 (October 5, 1993 or later expiry of award).

General Note

Under s.137(1) of the Social Security Contributions and Benefits Act 1992 two people are treated as a married or unmarried couple only if they are living together in the same household. Para. (1) has the effect that a couple are treated as no longer treated as living together if one has entered residential accommodation (*e.g.* an old people's home) provided by the local authority unless the stay is only temporary. Para. (2)(b) and (c) have the same effect where the claimant's partner is detained in a special hospital (*e.g.* Broadmoor) or is detained in custody while serving a sentence of 52 weeks or more (even if he or she is likely to be released after a shorter period). On the other hand, para. (2)(a) has the effect that a person is an ordinary hospital is still regarded as living with his or her partner until he or she has been a patient for 52 weeks.

Part V

Income and Capital

Chapter I

General

Calculation of income and capital of members of claimant's family and of a polygamous marriage

12.—(1) The income and capital of a claimant's partner and, subject to regulation 30 (modifications in respect of children and young persons), the income of a child or young person, which by virtue of section 22(5) of the Act is to be treated as income and capital of the claimant, shall be calculated or estimated in accordance with the following provisions of this Part in like manner as for the claimant; and any reference to the "claimant" shall, except where the context otherwise requires, be construed, for the purposes of this Part, as if it included a reference to his partner or that child or young person.

(2) Where a claimant or the partner of a claimant is married polygamously to two or more members of the same household—

(a) the claimant shall be treated as possessing capital and income belonging to each such member and the income of any child or young person who is one of that member's family; and

(b) the income and capital of that member or, as the case may be, the income of that child or young person shall be calculated in accordance with the following provisions of this Part in like manner as for the claimant or, as the case may be, as for any child or young person who is a member of his family.

General Note

S.22(5) of the Social Security Act 1986 has been replaced by s.136(1) of the Social Security Contributions and Benefits Act 1992. The effect of this regulation is that all capital and income belonging to members of the "family" is treated as belonging to the claimant. However, there are very broad exceptions in respect of capital and income belonging to a child; see reg. 30 and also Sched. 2, para. 2 under which any earnings of a child or young person are disregarded.

Calculation of income and capital of students

13. The provisions of Chapters II to VI of this Part (income and capital) shall have effect in relation to students and their partners subject to the modifications set out in Chapter VII (students) thereof.

Rounding of fractions

14. Where any calculation under this Part results in a fraction of a penny that fraction shall, if it would be to the claimant's advantage, be treated as a penny, otherwise it shall be disregarded.

CHAPTER II

NORMAL WEEKLY INCOME

Calculation of income on a weekly basis

15.—(1) For the purposes of section 20(6A) of the Act (conditions of entitlement to disability working allowance), the income of a claimant shall be calculated on a weekly basis—

(a) by ascertaining in accordance with this Chapter and Chapter V of this Part (other income) the amount of his normal weekly income;

(b) by adding to that amount the weekly income calculated under regulation 40 (calculation of tariff income from capital) [[1] and

(c) by then deducting any relevant child care charges to which regulation 15A (treatment of child care charges) applies from any earnings which form part of the normal weekly income, up to a maximum deduction in respect of the claimant's family of [[2]£60] per week.]

(2) For the purposes of paragraph (1) "income" includes capital treated as income under regulation 28 (capital treated as income) and income which a person is treated as possessing under regulation 29 (notional income).

AMENDMENTS

1. Income-related Benefits Scheme (Miscellaneous Amendments) (No. 4) Regulations 1994 (S.I. 1994 No. 1924), reg. 3 (October 4, 1994).
2. Social Security Benefits Up-rating Order 1996 (S.I. 1996 No. 599), art. 17(a) (April 9, 1996).

GENERAL NOTE

This regulation provides the basic formula for calculating a claimant's income: actual normal weekly income (calculated under the regs. 16 to 20 and 27 to 30) *plus* tariff income based on the claimant's capital (calculated under reg. 40) *less* child care costs (calculated under reg. 15A). S.20(6A) of the Social Security Act 1986 has been replaced by s.129(1) of the Social Security Contributions and Benefits Act 1992.

[[1]Treatment of child care charges

15A.—(1) This regulation applies where a claimant is incurring relevant child care charges and—

(a) is a lone parent and is engaged in remunerative work;

(b) is a member of a couple both of whom are engaged in remunerative work; or

(c) is a member of a couple where one member is engaged in remunerative work and the other member is incapacitated.

(2) In this regulation—

"local authority" means, in relation to England and Wales, the council of a county or district, a metropolitan district, a London Borough, the Common Council of the City of London or the Council of the Isles of Scilly or, in relation to Scotland, a regional, islands or district council;

"relevant child care charges" means the charges paid by the claimant for care provided for any child of the claimant's family [[3]in respect of the period beginning on that child's date of birth and ending on the day preceding the first Tuesday in September following that child's eleventh birthday], other than charges paid in respect of the child's compulsory education [[2]or charges paid by a claimant to a partner or by a partner to a claimant in respect of any child for whom either or any of them is responsible in accordance with regulation 9 (circumstances in which a person is to be treated as responsible or not responsible for another),] where the care is provided—

(a) by persons registered under section 71 of the Children Act 1989 (registration of child minders and persons providing day care for young children);

(b) for children [3in respect of the period beginning on their eighth birthday and ending on the day preceding the first Tuesday in September following their eleventh birthday], out of school hours, by a school on school premises or by a local authority; or

(c) by a child care scheme operating on Crown property where registration under section 71 of the Children Act 1989 is not required, [2or

(d) in schools or establishments which are exempted from registration under section 71 of the Children Act 1989 by virtue of section 71(16) of and paragraph 3 or 4 of Schedule 9 to that Act,

and shall be calculated on a weekly basis in accordance with paragraphs (3) to (6);

"school term-time" means the school term-time applicable to the child for whom care is provided.

[3(2A) In paragraph (2)—

(a) the age of a child referred to in that paragraph shall be determined by reference to the age of the child at the date on which the period under section 129(6) of the Contributions and Benefits Act (period of award) begins;

(b) "the first Tuesday in September" means the Tuesday which first occurs in the month of September in any year.]

(3) Subject to paragraphs (4) to (6), relevant child care charges shall be calculated in accordance with the formula—

$$\frac{X+Y}{52}$$

where—

X is the average weekly charge paid for child care in the most recent 4 complete weeks which fall in school term-time in respect of the child or children concerned, multiplied by 39; and

Y is the average weekly charge paid for child care in the most recent 2 complete weeks which fall out of school term-time in respect of that child or those children, multiplied by 13.

(4) Subject to paragraph (5), where child care charges are being incurred in respect of a child who does not yet attend school, the relevant child care charges shall mean the average weekly charge paid for care provided in respect of that child in the most recent 4 complete weeks.

(5) Where in any case the charges in respect of child care are paid monthly, the average weekly charge for the purposes of paragraph (3) shall be established—

(a) where the charges are for a fixed monthly amount, by multiplying that amount by 12 and dividing the product by 52;

(b) where the charges are for variable monthly amounts, by aggregating the charges for the previous 12 months and dividing the total by 52.

(6) In a case where there is no information or insufficient information for establishing the average weekly charge paid for child care in accordance with paragraphs (3) to (5), the average weekly charge for care shall be estimated in accordance with information provided by the child minder or person providing the care or, if such information is not available, in accordance with information provided by the claimant.

(7) For the purposes of paragraph (1)(c) the other member of a couple is incapacitated where—

(a) either council tax benefit or housing benefit is payable under Part VII of the Contributions and Benefits Act to the other member or his partner and the applicable amount of the person entitled to the benefit includes—
   (i) a disability premium; or
   (ii) a higher pensioner premium by virtue of the satisfaction of—
      (aa) in the case of council tax benefit, paragraph 11(2)(b) of Schedule 1 to the Council Tax Benefit (General) Regulations 1992;
      (bb) in the case of housing benefit, paragraph 10(2)(b) of Schedule 2 to the Housing Benefit (General) Regulations 1987,
   on account of the other member's incapacity [2 or either regulation 13A(1)(c) of the Council Tax Benefit (General) Regulations 1992 (treatment of child care charges) or, as the case may be, regulation 21A(1)(c) of the Housing Benefit (General) Regulations 1987 (treatment of child care charges) applies in that person's case];
(b) there is payable in respect of him one or more of the following pensions or allowances—
   (i) invalidity pension under section 33, 40 or 41 of the Contributions and Benefits Act 1992;
   (ii) attendance allowance under section 64 of that Act;
   (iii) severe disablement allowance under section 68 of that Act;
   (iv) disability living allowance under section 71 of that Act;
   (v) increase of disablement pension under section 104 of that Act;
   (vi) a pension increase under a war pension scheme or an industrial injuries scheme which is analogous to an allowance or increase of disablement pension under head (ii), (iv) or (v) above;
(c) a pension or allowance to which head (ii), (iv), (v) or (vi) of subparagraph (b) above refers was payable on account of his incapacity but has ceased to be payable in consequence of his becoming a patient within the meaning of regulation 10(3)(a) (membership of the same household);
(d) sub-paragraph (b) or (c) above would apply to him if the legislative provisions referred to in those sub-paragraphs were provisions under any corresponding enactment having effect in Northern Ireland; or
(e) he has an invalid carriage or other vehicle provided to him by the Secretary of State under section 5(2)(a) of and Schedule 2 to the National Health Service Act 1977 or under section 46 of the National Health Service (Scotland) Act 1978 or provided by the Department of Health and Social Services for Northern Ireland under Article 30(1) of the Health and Personal Social Services (Northern Ireland) Order 1972.

AMENDMENTS

1. Income-related Schemes (Miscellaneous Amendments) (No. 4) Regulations 1994 (S.I. 1994 No. 1924), reg. 3(4) (October 4, 1994).

2. Income-related Schemes (Miscellaneous Amendments) Regulations 1995 (S.I. 1995 No. 516), reg. 5 (April 11, 1995 or later expiry of award).

3. Income-related Benefits and Jobseeker's Allowance (Personal Allowances for Children and Young Persons) (Amendment) Regulations 1996 (S.I. 1996 No. 2545), reg. 7 (October 7, 1997 or later expiry of award).

GENERAL NOTE

Para. (1). To qualify to have child care costs deducted from income under reg. 15(1)(c), a claimant must be either a lone parent, or a member of a couple where both parents are working for 16 hours or more a week or a member of a couple where one is working for 16 hours or more a week and the other is incapacitated within the terms of para. (7).

Para. (2). Only those care charges identified in the definition of "relevant care charges" may be deducted.

Normal weekly earnings of employed earners

16.—(1) Subject to regulation 19, where the claimant's income consists of earnings from employment as an employed earner, his normal weekly earnings shall be determined [2 by taking account of his earnings from that employment which are received in the assessment period relevant to his case, whether the amount so received was earned in respect of that period or not, and in accordance with the following provisions of this regulation].

(2) Subject to paragraph (7), where the claimant is paid weekly, his normal weekly earnings shall be determined by reference to his earnings over 5 consecutive weeks in the 6 weeks immediately preceding the week in which the date of claim falls.

(3) Subject to paragraph (7), where at the date of claim there is a trade dispute or period of short-time working at the claimant's place of employment, then his normal weekly earnings shall be determined by reference to his earnings over the 5 weeks immediately preceding the start of that dispute or period of short-time working.

(4) Subject to paragraph (7), where the claimant is paid monthly, his normal weekly earnings shall be determined by reference to his earnings—

(a) over a period of 2 months immediately preceding the week in which the date of claim falls; or

(b) where, at the date of claim, there is a trade dispute or a period of short-time working at his place of employment, over a period of 2 months immediately preceding the date of the start of that dispute or period of short-time working.

(5) Subject to paragraph (7), whether or not paragraph (2), (3) or (4) applies, where a claimant's earnings fluctuate or are not likely to represent his weekly earnings, his normal weekly earnings shall be determined by reference to his weekly earnings over such other period preceding the week in which the date of claim falls as may, in any particular case, enable his normal weekly earnings to be determined more accurately.

(6) Where a claimant's earnings include a bonus or commission which is paid within 52 weeks preceding the week in which the date of claim falls, and the bonus or commission is paid separately or relates to a period longer than the period relating to the other earnings with which it is paid, his normal weekly earnings shall be treated as including an amount calculated in accordance with regulation 23 (calculation of bonus or commission).

(7) Where at the date of claim—

(a) the claimant—

(i) has been in his employment, or

(ii) after a continuous period of interruption exceeding 13 weeks, has resumed his employment; or

(iii) has changed the number of hours for which he is contracted to work; and

(b) the period of his employment or the period since he resumed his employment or the period since the change in the number of hours took place, as the case may be, [1 is less than the assessment period in paragraphs (2) to (5) appropriate in his case]

his normal weekly earnings shall be determined in accordance with paragraph (8).

(8) In a case to which this paragraph applies, the Secretary of State shall require the claimant's employer to furnish an estimate of the claimant's average likely earnings for the period for which he will normally be paid and the claimant's normal weekly earnings shall be determined [2taking account of] that estimate.

(9) For the purposes of this regulation—

(a) the claimant's earnings shall be calculated in accordance with Chapter III of this Part;
(b) ''a period of short-time working'' means a continuous period not exceeding 13 weeks during which the claimant is not required by his employer to be available to work the full number of hours normal in his case under the terms of his employment.

AMENDMENTS

1. Income-related Benefits Schemes and Social Fund (Miscellaneous Amendments) Regulations 1996 (S.I. 1996 No. 1944), reg. 3(2) (October 7, 1996 or later expiry of award).
2. Disability Working Allowance and Family Credit (General) Amendment Regulations 1996 (S.I. 1996 No. 3137), reg. 2(3) (January 7, 1997).

GENERAL NOTE

This regulation is concerned only with earnings; for other forms of income, see reg. 18.
This regulation is also concerned only with employed earners; for self-employed earners, see reg. 17.
This regulation is concerned with the period over which earnings are to be calculated; see regs. 21–23 for what counts as earnings and how the ''net'' earnings are calculated.

Para. (1). The amendment, intended to reverse *CFC/6910/95*, is liable to create unfairness if holiday pay or arrears of overtime pay happen to have been paid during the relevant period. Presumably, the unfairness to some claimants is considered a worthwhile price for the greater simplicity obtained.

Para. (2). This is concerned with weekly-paid employees. The basic rule is that an employee's earnings are determined over five consecutive weeks out of the six weeks preceding the week in which the claim was made (*i.e.* either the first or the last week of the period is disregarded). This is subject to four exceptions. First, para. (3) makes a specific provision for cases where there is a trade dispute or period of short-time working at the date of claim. Secondly, paras. (7) and (8) apply in any case where the claimant has either started work or resumed work after a 13-week gap or has had a change of hours in the nine weeks before the date of claim. In such cases, the earnings cannot be determined in accordance with para. (2). Thirdly, reg. 19 permits some weeks of the five-week assessment period to be disregarded if earnings are irregular or unusual or if they include a bonus or commission relating to a longer period. Any bonus or commission is taken into account under para. (6). Fourthly, para. (5) gives a wide power to choose a different assessment period altogether.

Para. (3). This applies to weekly-paid employees where there is a trade dispute or period of short-time working at the date of claim. In those circumstances, the earnings are determined over the five weeks immediately preceding the start of the trade dispute or period of short-time. Note that that applies only if the trade dispute or short-time is still continuing at the date of claim. If it has ended by then but affected some of the weeks in the usual five-week assessment period, it may be necessary to take a different period (under para. (5)) or disregard some of the weeks (under reg. 19). ''Trade dispute'' is defined in wide terms in s.27(3)(b) of the Social Security Contributions and Benefits Act 1992 to include ''any dispute between employers and employees, or between employees and employees, which is connected with the employment or non-employment or the terms of employment or the conditions of employment of any persons, whether employees in the employment of the employer with whom the dispute arises or not''. Presumably it is intended that this sub-paragraph should apply only where the trade dispute affects earnings, *e.g.* because there is a period of working to rule. If a person is on strike or is laid off for more than 13 weeks, paras. (7) and (8) will apply. ''Period of short-time working'' is defined in para. (9)(b) so as to limit the term to periods not exceeding 13 weeks.

Para. (4). This makes provision for monthly employees similar to the provision made for weekly employees by paras. (2) and (3), except that the basic rule is that earnings are calculated over the two months before the week in which the claim was made. The same exceptions apply, trade disputes and short-time being dealt with under para. (4)(b).

Para. (5). Apart from dealing with cases where people are paid other than weekly or monthly, this introduces considerable flexibility into the calculation for weekly and monthly paid employees but also makes it much more complicated. Although the paragraph operates where either earnings fluctuate *or* are not likely to represent weekly earnings, the fact that earnings fluctuate is not really a ground for departing from the basic rules in paras. (2), (3) or (4) unless the effect is that taking the normal assessment period is likely to give a distorted picture. In any event, one cannot know whether a true representation is given by taking the normal assessment period until one has looked at longer periods. What period should be taken? Presumably, not more than 26 weeks, since that is the period for which disability working allowance will be awarded. The starting date might be the date of the last pay rise or change of hours. Where there is a peculiar feature affecting particular weeks, those weeks may be excluded under reg. 19. The assessment period must still precede the week in which the claim was made but it need not immediately precede it. However, since the idea is to assess earnings at the date of claim, it may be difficult to justify an assessment period which does not immediately precede the date of claim. If the last week or two before the week in which the claim was made were unusual in some way, it is probably best to include them in the assessment period and then disregard them under reg. 19.

Para. (6). Bonuses and commission are often paid in respect of periods rather longer than the normal wage or salary period. Therefore, they are taken into account separately. See regs. 19(a)(ii) and 23.

Paras. (7) and *(8).* If the claimant has been in employment for less than nine weeks at the date of claim, earnings are determined on the basis of the employer's estimate rather than on the basis of such past history as there is. Where overtime fluctuates, this may cause problems but the adjudication officer is bound either to accept the estimate or else to obtain another (notionally through the Secretary of State). The same rule applies where a person has resumed employment after a period of absence from work for over 13 weeks (*e.g.* due to sickness) or there has been a change in the number of hours for which the claimant is contracted to work. A change in the amount of voluntary overtime does not bring these paragraphs into play.

Normal weekly earnings of self-employed earners

17.—(1) Subject to regulation 19 (periods to be disregarded), where a claimant's income consists of earnings from employment as a self-employed earner, his normal weekly earnings shall be determined, subject to paragraph (2), by reference to his weekly earnings from that employment—

(a) except where sub-paragraph (b) applies, over a period of 26 weeks immediately preceding the week in which the date of claim falls; or

(b) where the claimant provides in respect of the employment a profit and loss account and, where appropriate, a trading account or a balance sheet or both, and the profit and loss account is in respect of a period of at least 6 months but not exceeding 15 months and that period terminates within the 12 months preceding the date of claim, over that period; or

(c) over such other period of weeks [1 or months] preceding the week in which the date of claim falls as may, in any particular case, enable his normal weekly earnings to be determined more accurately.

(2) In paragraph (1)(b)—

(a) "balance sheet" means a statement of the financial position of the employment disclosing its assets, liabilities and capital at the end of the period in question;

(b) "profit and loss account" means a financial statement showing the net profit or loss of the employment for the period in question; and

(c) "trading account" means a financial statement showing the revenue from sales, the cost of those sales and the gross profit arising during the period in question.

(3) Subject to regulation 19, where the claimant has been in employment as a self-employed earner for less than the period specified in paragraph (1) (a), his normal weekly earnings shall be determined by reference to an estimate of his likely weekly earnings over the 26 weeks next following the date of claim.

(4) For the purposes of this regulation, the claimant's earnings shall be calculated in accordance with Chapter IV of this Part.

AMENDMENT

1. Income-related Benefits Schemes (Miscellaneous Amendments) (No. 5) Regulations 1994 (S.I. 1994 No. 2139), reg. 3 (October 4, 1994 or later expiry of award).

General Note

This regulation is concerned with earnings; for other forms of income, see reg. 18.

This regulation is also concerned with self-employed earners; for other earners, see reg. 16.

This regulation is concerned with the period over which earnings are calculated; see regs. 25–26 for what counts as earnings and how the "net" earnings are calculated. There are three choices set out in para. (1). The first question to be asked is whether there are available the accounts referred to in sub-para. (b) If so, the assessment period is the period covered by those accounts, unless sub-para. (c) applies. If those accounts are not available, sub-para. (a) provides that the assessment period is the 26 weeks immediately preceding the week in which the claim was made, unless sub-para. (c) applies. Sub-para (c) applies where the other sub-paragraphs would not produce an accurate figure because, say there has been a change of circumstances. Difficulties arise when a claimant says that his earnings have fallen recently because of the recession. Fairly good evidence would have to be provided before it could be said that departing from the normal rule would "enable his normal weekly earnings to be determined more accurately". Para. (3) provides that, if a person has been in employment as a self-employed earner for less than 26 weeks, the assessment period is the 26 weeks following the week in which the claim was made (*not* the week in which the employment started). That necessarily involves an estimate which may be highly speculative. Reg. 19 (b) requires weeks to be excluded from the assessment period if no business activities are performed in them. This means that earnings are spread only over the weeks when work is done and not over holidays.

Normal weekly income other than earnings

18.—(1) Subject to [1paragraphs (2) and (2A)]. [2where a claimant's normal weekly income does not consist of earnings, or includes income that does not consist of earnings, that income] shall be determined [3taking account of] his weekly income over a period of 26 weeks immediately preceding the week in which the date of claim falls or over such period immediately preceding that week as may, in any particular case, enable his normal weekly income to be determined more accurately.

(2) Where a claimant's income consists of any payments made by a person, whether under a court order or not, for the maintenance of any member of [1the claimant's family], and those payments are made or due to be made at regular intervals, his normal weekly income shall [1except where paragraph (2A) applies,] be determined—

(a) if before the date of claim those payments are made at regular intervals [2and of regular amounts], [3taking account of] the normal weekly amount;

(b) if they are not so made, [3taking account of] the average of such payments received in the 13 weeks immediately preceding the week in which the date of claim falls.

[1(2A) Where a claimant's income consists of child support maintenance, his normal weekly income in respect of that maintenance shall be determined—

(a) if before the date of claim those maintenance payments are made at regular intervals [2and of regular amounts], [3taking account of] the normal weekly amount;

(b) if they are not so made, [2except in a case to which sub-paragraph (c) applies,] [3taking account of] the average of such payments received in the 13 weeks immediately preceding the week in which the date of claim falls.

[2(c) where the maintenance assessment has been notified to the claimant under regulation 10 of the Child Support (Maintenance Assessment Procedure) Regulations 1992, during the 13 weeks immediately preceding the week of claim, [3taking account of] the average of such payments, calculated on a weekly basis, received in the interim period.]

and if the resulting sum exceeds the amount of child support maintenance due under the maintenance assessment, the normal weekly income shall be the amount due under the maintenance assessment.]

(3) For the purposes of this regulation, income other than earnings shall be calculated in accordance with Chapter V of this Part.

[[1](4) In this regulation—

(a) "child support maintenance" means such periodical payments as are referred to in section 3(6) of the Child Support Act 1991;

(b) "maintenance assessment" has the same meaning as in the Child Support Act 1991 by virtue of section 54(a) of that Act.]

[[2](c) "the interim period" means the week in which the date of notification of the maintenance assessment falls and the subsequent period up to and including the week immediately preceding the week of claim.]

AMENDMENTS

1. Income-related Benefits Schemes (Miscellaneous Amendments) Regulations 1993 (S.I. 1993 No. 315), reg. 17 (April 13, 1993).

2. Income-related Benefits Schemes (Miscellaneous Amendments) (No. 4) Regulations 1993 (S.I. 1993 No. 2119), reg. 39 (October 5, 1993 or later expiry of award).

3. Disability Working Allowance and Family Credit (General) Amendment Regulations 1996 (S.I. 1996 No. 3137), reg. 2(4) (January 7, 1997).

GENERAL NOTE

Para. (1). The assessment period for income other than earnings is generally the 26 weeks preceding the week in which the claim was made, although a different period may be taken if appropriate.

Para. (2). If maintenance payments are received regularly, the normal weekly amount is calculated, based on the current rate of payment. On the other hand, if they are not received regularly, the average of the actual receipts over the 13 weeks immediately preceding the date of claim is taken into account. Note that, under Sched. 3, para. 13, if the claimant is responsible for a child or young person, £15pw of any maintenance payment (whether for the child or young person or for the claimant or claimant's partner) is disregarded.

Periods to be disregarded

19. For the purposes of ascertaining a claimant's normal weekly earnings there shall be disregarded—

(a) for the purposes of regulation 16(1) (normal weekly earnings of employed earners), in the case of an employed earner—

(i) any period in the assessment period where the earnings of the claimant are irregular or unusual;

(ii) any period in the assessment period in which a bonus or commission to which regulation 16(6) applies is paid where that bonus or commission is in respect of a period longer than the period relating to the other earnings with which it is paid;

(b) in the case of a self-employed earner, any week or period of weeks in the assessment period during which no activities have been carried out for the purposes of the business,

and his normal weekly earnings shall be determined by reference to his weekly earnings in the remainder of that period and in such a case any reference in these Regulations to a claimant's assessment period shall be construed as a reference to the latter period.

GENERAL NOTE

This provides for weeks falling within assessment periods prescribed by regs. 16 and 17 to be disregarded. Para. (a) applies in the case of an employed earner (see the note to reg. 16) and para. (b) applies in the case of a self-employed earner (see the note to reg. 17).

Calculation of weekly amount of income

20.—(1) [[1]For the purposes of regulations 16 (normal weekly earnings of employed earners) and 18 (normal weekly income other than earnings), where the claimant's pay period or, as the case may be, the period in respect of which a payment is made—]

(a) does not exceed a week, the weekly amount shall be the amount of that payment;

(b) exceeds a week, the weekly amount shall be determined—

(i) in a case where that period is a month, by multiplying the amount of the payment by 12 and dividing the product by 52;

(ii) in a case where that period is 3 months, by multiplying the amount of the payment by 4 and dividing the product by 52;

(iii) in a case where that period is a year, by dividing the amount of the payment by 52;

(iv) in any other case, by multiplying the amount of the payment by 7 and dividing the product by the number equal to the number of days in the period in respect of which it is made.

(2) For the purposes of regulation 17 (normal weekly earnings of self-employed earners) the weekly amount of earnings of a claimant shall be determined—

(a) except where sub-paragraph (b) applies, by dividing his earnings received in the assessment period or, as the case may be, estimated for that period by the number equal to the number of weeks in that period;

(b) in a case where regulation 17(1)(b) applies, by multiplying his earnings relcvant to the assessment period (whether or not received in that period) by 7 and dividing the product by the number equal to the number of days in that period.

AMENDMENT

1. Disability Working Allowance and Family Credit (General) Amendment Regulations 1996 (S.I. 1996 No. 3137), reg. 2(5) (January 7, 1997).

GENERAL NOTE

Entitlement to disability working allowance is calculated on the basis of weekly income, so income paid at other intervals has to be converted into weekly sums. Para. (1) applies to earnings from employed earners' employment and also to income other than earnings. Para. (2) applies to earnings from self-employed earners' employment.

CHAPTER III

EMPLOYED EARNERS

Earnings of employed earners

21.—(1) Subject to paragraph (2), "earnings" means in the case of employment as an employed earner, any remuneration or profit derived from that employment and includes—

(a) any bonus or commission;

(b) any holiday pay except any payable more than 4 weeks after termination of the employment;

(c) any payment by way of a retainer;

(d) any payment made by the claimant's employer in respect of any expenses not wholly, exclusively and necessarily incurred in the performance of the duties of the employment, including any payment made by the claimant's employer in respect of—

(i) travelling expenses incurred by the claimant between his home and place of employment;

(ii) expenses incurred by the claimant under arrangements made for the care of a member of his family owing to the claimant's absence from home;

(e) any award of compensation made under section 68(2) or 71(2)(a) of the Employment Protection (Consolidation) Act 1978 (remedies and compensation for unfair dismissal);

(f) any such sum as is referred to in section 18(2) of the Social Security (Miscellaneous Provisions) Act 1977 (certain sums to be earnings for social security purposes);

(g) any statutory sick pay under Part I of the Social Security and Housing Benefits Act 1982;

(h) any statutory sick pay under Part II of the Social Security (Northern Ireland) Order 1982;

(i) any payment made by the claimant's employer in respect of any Community Charge [[1]or council tax] to which the claimant is subject.

(2) Earnings shall not include—

(a) subject to paragraph (3), any payment in kind;

(b) any payment in respect of expenses wholly, exclusively and necessarily incurred in the performance of the duties of the employment;

(c) any occupational pension;

[[2](d) any statutory maternity pay or a corresponding benefit under any enactment having effect in Northern Ireland.]

(3) Where living accommodation is provided for a claimant by reason of his employment, the claimant shall be treated as being in receipt of weekly earnings of an amount equal to—

(a) where no charge is made in respect of the provision of that accommodation, £12;

(b) where a charge is made and that weekly charge is less than £12, the amount of the difference,

except that where the claimant satisfies the adjudication officer that the weekly value to him of the provision of that accommodation is an amount less than the amount in sub-paragraph (a) or (b), as the case may be, he shall be treated as being in receipt of that lesser value.

AMENDMENTS

1. Income-related Benefits Schemes (Miscellaneous Amendments) Regulations 1993 (S.I. 1993 No. 315), Sched., para. 13 (April 1, 1993).

2. Income-related Benefits Schemes (Miscellaneous Amendments) Regulations 1993 (S.I. 1993 No. 315), reg. 18 (April 13, 1993).

GENERAL NOTE

Para. (1). This identifies sums which are to be treated as earnings. Other income is dealt with under regs. 27–30.

Note that, under sub-para (d) the reimbursement of expenses incurred counts as earnings only if the expenses were *not* wholly, exclusively and necessarily incurred in the performance of the duties of employment. This is made plainer still by para. (2)(b). There is no specific provision for allowing a claimant to deduct expenses wholly, exclusively and necessarily incurred in the performance of the duties of employment but not refunded by the employer. However, that would plainly place those who did not receive reimbursement in an unfavourable position by comparison with those who do as well as creating inequity between the employed and the self-employed and, in *R(FC) 1/90*, it has been held that a claimant *can* effectively deduct those expenses. The Commissioner reached what might be thought to be a surprising decision by relying on the decision of the Court of Appeal in *Chief Adjudication Officer v. Hogg* [1985] 1 W.L.R. 1100 (also reported as an appendix to *R(FIS) 4/85*). In that case, it was held that, depending on its context, "earnings" could mean either "earnings before deduction of expenses" or "earnings after deduction of expenses" and the construction which did justice between claimants was to be preferred.

Para. (2). This identifies payments by employers which are not to be treated as earnings. *Prima facie*, they fall to be treated as other income. However, "any income in kind" is disregarded under

Sched. 3, para. 20 and "any payment in respect of expenses to which regulation 21(2) (earnings of employed earners) applies" is disregarded under Sched. 3, para. 32. Accordingly, only occupational pensions remain to be taken into account as other income.

Para. (3). In *R(FC) 2/90*, the claimant and her husband both worked for the Salvation Army and were provided with accommodation. Since only one house was provided, only one sum of £12 was deemed to be part of their earnings.

Calculation of net earnings of employed earners

22.—(1) For the purposes of regulation 16 (normal weekly earnings of employed earners), the earnings of a claimant derived or likely to be derived from employment as an employed earner to be taken into account shall, subject to paragraph (2), be his net earnings.

(2) There shall be disregarded from a claimant's net earnings, any sum, where applicable, specified in Schedule 2.

(3) For the purposes of paragraph (1), net earnings shall, except where paragraph (4) applies, be calculated by taking into account the gross earnings of the claimant from that employment over the assessment period, less—

(a) any amount deducted from those earnings by way of—

(i) income tax;

(ii) primary Class 1 contributions under the Social Security Act; and one-half of any sum paid by the claimant [[3]in respect of a pay period] by way of a contribution towards an occupational or personal pension scheme.

(4) Where the earnings of a claimant are estimated under paragraph (8) of regulation 16 (normal weekly earnings of employed earners), his net earnings shall be calculated by taking into account those earnings over the assessment period, less—

(a) an amount in respect of income tax equivalent to an amount calculated by applying to those earnings [[1]the lower rate or, as the case may be, the lower rate and the basic rate of tax] in the year of assessment in which the claim was made less only the personal relief to which the claimant is entitled under sections 257(1), (6) and (7) and 259 of the Income and Corporation Taxes Act 1988 (personal relief) as is appropriate to his circumstances; but, if the assessment period is less than a year [[1] the earnings to which the lower rate [[3]. . .] of tax is to be applied and], the amount of the personal relief deductible under this sub-paragraph shall be calculated on a pro rata basis;

[[2](b) where the weekly amount of those earnings equals or exceeds the lower earnings limit, an amount representing primary Class 1 contributions under the Contributions and Benefits Act, calculated by applying to those earnings the initial and main primary percentages applicable at the date of claim in accordance with section 8(1)(a) and (b) of that Act; and]

[[3](c) one half of any sum which would be payable by the claimant by way of a contribution towards an occupational or personal pension scheme, if the earnings so estimated were actual earnings.]

Amendments

1. Income-related Benefit Schemes (Miscellaneous Amendments) (No. 3) Regulations 1992 (S.I. 1992 No. 2155), Sched. para. 4 (October 5, 1992).

2. Income-related Benefits Schemes (Miscellaneous Amendments) Regulations 1994 (S.I. 1994 No. 527), reg. 23 (April 12, 1994).

3. Income-related Benefits Schemes (Miscellaneous Amendments) (No. 5) Regulations 1994 (S.I. 1994 No. 2139), regs. 4 and 5 (October 4, 1994 or later expiry of award).

General Note

Para. (1). For disability living allowance, only "net" earnings are taken into account.

Para. (2). Earnings of a child or young person are disregarded and so are earnings from abroad, if there is a prohibition against their transfer to the United Kingdom. If earnings are paid in a foreign currency, any banking charge or commission payable in converting the payment to sterling is deducted.

Paras. (3) and *(4).* "Net" earnings are "gross" earnings less tax, National Insurance contributions and one half of occupational or personal pension contributions. Gross earnings means earnings after the deduction of expenses wholly, exclusively and necessarily incurred in the performance of the duties of employment (see the note to reg. 21). If the gross earnings were calculated on the basis of actual earnings, the actual amounts of tax, etc., are deducted under para. (3). If the gross earnings were estimated, notional amounts of tax, etc., are deducted under para. (4).

Calculation of bonus or commission

23. Where a claimant's earnings include a bonus or commission to which paragraph (6) of regulation 16 (normal weekly earnings of employed earners) applies that part of his earnings shall be calculated by aggregating any payments of bonus or commission [[1]deducting from it—]

(a) an amount in respect of income tax equivalent to an amount calculated by applying to that part of the earnings the basic rate of tax in the year of assessment in which the claim is made; and

(b) an amount [[2] representing primary Class 1 contributions under the Contributions and Benefits Act, calculated by applying to that part of the earnings the main primary percentage applicable at the date of claim; and] . . .

(c) one-half of any sum payable by the claimant in respect of that part of the earnings by way of contribution towards an occupational or personal pension [[1]scheme;]

and dividing the resulting sum by 52.

Amendments

1. Income-related Benefits Schemes (Miscellaneous Amendments) (No. 3) Regulations 1992 (S.I. 1992 No. 2155), Sched. para. 5 (October 5, 1992).

2. Income-related Benefits Schemes (Miscellaneous Amendments) Regulations 1994 (S.I. 1994 No. 527), reg. 24 (April 12, 1994).

General Note

Any bonus or commission received during the previous 52 weeks is taken into account separately, with notional tax, etc., being deducted from it.

Chapter IV

Self-Employed Earners

Earnings of self-employed earners

24.—(1) Subject to [[1]paragraphs (2) and (3)], "earnings", in the case of employment as a self-employed earner, means the gross receipts of the employment and shall include any allowance paid under section 2 of the Employment and Training Act 1973 or section 2 of the Enterprise and New Towns (Scotland) Act 1990 to the claimant for the purpose of assisting him in carrying on his business unless at the date of claim the allowance has been terminated.

(2) Where a claimant is employed in providing board and lodging accommodation for which a charge is payable, any income consisting of payments of

such a charge shall only be taken into account under this Chapter as earnings if it forms a major part of the total of the claimant's weekly income less any sums disregarded under Schedule 3 other than under paragraph 38 of that Schedule.

[[1](3) ''Earnings'' shall not include any payments to which paragraph 24 of Schedule 3 refers (sums to be disregarded in the calculation of income other than earnings.]

AMENDMENT

1. Income-related Benefits Schemes (Miscellaneous Amendments) (No. 5) Regulations 1994 (S.I. 1994 No. 2139), reg. 6 (October 4, 1994 or later expiry of award).

GENERAL NOTE

Para. (1). An Enterprise Allowance counts as earnings, but only if it was in payment at the date of claim. If payment had ceased before then, the Allowance is not taken into account, even if it was payable in some of the weeks of the assessment period. That is fair because it will not be paid again during the period of the claim.

Para. (2). Receipts from board and lodging count as ''other income'' rather than earnings, unless they form *a* major (not, *the* major) part of the claimant's total assessable income (ignoring, for this purpose, the disregard in respect of board and lodging receipts allowed by Sched. 3, para. 38).

Calculation of net profit of self-employed earners

25.—(1) For the purposes of regulation 17 (normal weekly earnings of self-employed earners), the earnings of a claimant to be taken into account shall be—

- (a) in the case of a self-employed earner who is engaged in employment on his own account, the net profit derived from that employment;
- (b) in the case of a self-employed earner whose employment is carried on in partnership or is that of a share fisherman within the meaning of the Social Security (Mariners' Benefits) Regulations 1975, his share of the net profit derived from that employment less—
  - (i) an amount in respect of income tax and social security contributions payable under the Social Security Act calculated in accordance with [[1]regulation 26] (deduction of tax and contributions for self-employed earners); and
  - (ii) [[3]one-half of the amount in respect of any qualifying premium calculated in accordance with paragraph (15)].

(2) There shall be disregarded from a claimant's net profit any sum, where applicable, specified in Schedule 2.

(3) For the purposes of paragraph (1)(a) the net profit of the employment shall, except where paragraph (4), (11) or (12) applies, be calculated by taking into account the earnings of the employment received in the assessment period less—

- (a) subject to paragraphs (7) to (9), any expenses wholly and exclusively defrayed in that period for the purposes of that employment;
- (b) an amount in respect of—
  - (i) income tax; and
  - (ii) social security contributions payable under the Social Security Act, calculated in accordance with regulation 26 (deduction of tax and contributions for self-employed earners); and
- (c) [[3]one-half of the amount in respect of any qualifying premium calculated in accordance with paragraph (15)].

(4) For the purposes of paragraph (1)(a), in a case where the assessment period is determined under regulation 17(1)(b), the net profit of the employment

shall, except where paragraph (11) applies, be calculated by taking into account the earnings of the employment relevant to that period (whether or not received in that period), less—

(a) [1 subject to paragraphs (7) to (10)], any expenses relevant to that period (whether or not defrayed in that period) and which were wholly and exclusively incurred for the purposes of that employment;

(b) an amount in respect of—

(i) income tax; and

(ii) social security contributions payable under the Social Security Act, calculated in accordance with regulation 26; and

(c) [3one-half of the amount in respect of any qualifying premium calculated in accordance with paragraph (15)]

(5) For the purposes of [1paragraph] (1)(b) the net profit of the employment shall, except where [1paragraph] (6), (11) or (12) applies, be calculated by taking into account the earnings of the employment received in the assessment period less, subject to paragraphs (7) to (9), any expenses wholly and exclusively defrayed in that period for the purposes of that employment.

(6) For the purposes of paragraph (1)(b) in a case where the assessment period is determined [1under regulation 17(1)(b) (normal weekly earnings of self-employed earners)], the net profit of the employment shall, except where paragraph (11) applies, be calculated by taking into account the earnings of the employment relevant to that period (whether or not received in that period) less, subject to paragraphs (7) to (9), any expenses relevant to that period (whether or not defrayed in that period) and which were wholly and exclusively incurred for the purposes of that employment.

(7) Subject to paragraph (8), no deduction shall be made under paragraphs (3)(a), (4)(a), (5) or (6), as the case may be, in respect of—

(a) any capital expenditure;

(b) the depreciation of any capital asset;

(c) any sum employed, or intended to be employed, in the setting up or expansion of the employment;

(d) any loss incurred before the beginning of the assessment period;

(e) the repayment of capital on any loan taken out for the purposes of the employment;

(f) any expenses incurred in providing business entertainment.

(8) A deduction shall be made under paragraphs (3)(a), (4)(a), (5) or (6), as the case may be, in respect of the repayment of capital on any loan used for—

(a) the replacement in the course of business of equipment or machinery; and

(b) the repair of an existing business asset except to the extent that any sum is payable under an insurance policy for its repair.

(9) An adjudication officer shall refuse to make a deduction in respect of any expenses under paragraphs (3)(a), (4)(a), (5) or (6), as the case may be, where he is not satisfied that the expense has been defrayed or given the nature and the amount of the expense that it has been reasonably incurred.

(10) For the avoidance of doubt—

(a) a deduction shall not be made under paragraphs (3)(a), (4)(a), (5) or (6), as the case may be, in respect of any sum unless it has been expended for the purposes of the business;

(b) a deduction shall be made thereunder in respect of—

(i) the excess of any VAT paid over VAT received in the assessment period;

(ii) any income expended in the repair of an existing business asset except to the extent that any sum is payable under an insurance policy for its repair;

(iii) any payment of interest on a loan taken out for the purposes of the employment.

(11) Where a claimant is engaged in employment as a child-minder the net profit of the employment shall be one-third of the earnings of that employment, less—

(a) an amount in respect of—

(i) income tax; and

(ii) social security contributions payable under the Social Security Act, calculated in accordance with regulation 26 (deduction of tax and contributions for self-employed earners); and

(b) [[3]one-half of the amount in respect of any qualifying premium calculated in accordance with paragraph (15)].

(12) Where regulation 17(3) (normal weekly earnings of self-employed earners) applies—

(a) for the purposes of paragraph (1)(a), the net profit derived from the employment shall be calculated by taking into account the claimant's estimated and, where appropriate, actual earnings from the employment, less the amount of the deductions likely to be made and, where appropriate, made under sub-paragraphs (a) to (c) of paragraph (3); or

(b) for the purposes of paragraph (1)(b) his share of the net profit of the employment shall be calculated by taking into account the claimant's estimated and, where appropriate, his share of the actual earnings from the employment, less the amount of his share of the expenses likely to be deducted and, where appropriate, deducted under paragraph (5); or

(c) in the case of employment as a child-minder, the net profit of the employment shall be calculated by taking into account one-third of the claimant's estimated earnings and, where appropriate, actual earnings from that employment, less the amount of the deductions likely to be made and, where appropriate, made under sub-paragraphs (a) and (b) of paragraph (11).

(13) For the avoidance of doubt where a claimant is engaged in employment as a self-employed earner and he is also engaged in one or more other employments as a self-employed or employed earner any loss incurred in any one of his employments shall not be offset against his earnings in any other of his employments.

[[2](14) [[3]In this regulation—

(a) "qualifying premium" means any premium which at the date of claim is payable periodically in respect of a retirement annuity contract or a personal pension scheme;

(b) [[4]. . .]

[[3](15) The amount in respect of any qualifying premium shall be calculated by multiplying the daily amount of the qualifying premium by the number equal to the number of days in the assessment period; and for the purposes of this regulation the daily amount of the qualifying premium shall be determined—

(a) where the qualifying premium is payable monthly, by multiplying the amount of the qualifying premium by 12 and dividing the product by 365;

(b) in any other case, by dividing the amount of the qualifying premium by the number equal to the number of days in the period to which the qualifying premium relates.]

AMENDMENTS

1. Income-related Benefits Schemes (Miscellaneous Amendments) (No. 3) Regulations 1992 (S.I. 1992 No. 2155), Sched. para. 6 (October 5, 1992).

2. Income-related Benefits Schemes (Miscellaneous Amendments) (No. 4) Regulations 1993 (S.I. 1993 No. 2119), reg. 40(3) (October 5, 1993 or later expiry of award).

3. Income-related Benefits Schemes (Miscellaneous Amendments) Regulations 1994 (S.I. 1994 No. 527), reg. 25 (April 12, 1994 or later expiry of award).

4. Income-related Benefits Schemes and Social Security (Claims and Payments) (Miscellaneous Amendments) Regulations 1995 (S.I. 1995 No. 2303), reg. 3(3) (October 3, 1995).

General Note

Para. (1). Only the "net profit" is taken into account as earnings.

Para. (2). Earnings of a child or young person are disregarded as are earnings from abroad if there is a prohibition against their transfer to the United Kingdom. A deduction in respect of bank charges or commission is made from earnings paid in a foreign currency which need to be converted into sterling.

Para. (3). This paragraph applies in any case where the earnings are neither determined by reference to a profit and loss account (see para. (4)) nor derived from child-minding (see para. (11)) nor based on an estimate over the 26 weeks following the date of claim (see para. (12)). Expenses wholly and exclusively *defrayed* in the assessment period may be deducted. In *R(FC) 1/91*, it was held that where expenditure was incurred for an item (*e.g.* telephone rental charges or motor insurance) which was partly for business use and partly for private use, it was possible to apportion expenditure on a time basis to determine the amount wholly and exclusively defrayed for business purposes. In the absence of other evidence, the fact that an Inspector of Taxes has accepted an apportionment should generally be regarded as a good reason for an adjudication officer accepting the same apportionment. Tax and social security contributions are also deductable (see reg. 26), as is half of any qualifying premium (defined in para. 14).

Para. (4). Where earnings are determined by reference to a profit and loss account, any expenses relevant to the accounting period are deductable, whether or not they were defrayed in that period. They must have been defrayed at some time (see para. (9)).

Paras. (5) and *(6).* These apply to share fishermen.

Paras. (7) and *(8).* The restrictions imposed by para. (7) are partly mitigated by para. (8).

Para. (9). An expense must have been defrayed before it can be deducted and there is no deduction if the expenditure was unreasonable.

Para. (11). The net profit of a child-minder is assumed to be one-third of the earnings.

Para. (12). This applies where earnings are estimated over the 26 weeks following the date of claim. Sub-para (a) provides the general rule, sub-para (b) is concerned with share fishermen and sub-para. (c) is concerned with child-minders.

Deduction of tax and contributions for self-employed earners

26.—(1) The amount to be deducted in respect of income tax under regulation 25(1)(b)(i), (3)(b)(i), (4)(b)(i) or (11)(a)(i) (calculation of net profit of self-employed earners) shall be calculated on the basis of the amount of chargeable income, and as if that income were assessable to income tax at [[1]the lower rate or, as the case may be, the lower rate and the basic rate of tax] in the year of assessment in which the claim was made, less only the personal relief to which the claimant is entitled under [[1]sections 257(1), (6) and (7) and 259] of the Income and Corporation Taxes Act 1988 (personal relief) as is appropriate to his circumstances; but, if the assessment period is less than a year [[1], the earnings to which the lower rate [[2]. . .] of tax is to be applied and] the amount of the personal relief deductible under this paragraph shall be calculated on a pro rata basis.

(2) The amount to be deducted in respect of social security contributions under regulation 25(1)(b)(i), (3)(b)(ii), (4)(b)(ii) or (4)(a)(ii) shall be the total of—

(a) the amount of Class 2 contributions payable under section 7(1) or, as the case may be, (4) of the Social Security Act at the rate applicable at the date of claim except where a claimant's chargeable income is less than the amount specified in section 7(5) of that Act (small earnings exception) for the tax year in which the date of claim falls; but if the assessment period is less than a year, the amount specified for that tax year shall be calculated on a pro rata basis; and

(b) the amount of Class 4 contributions (if any) which would be payable under section 9(2) of that Act (Class 4 contributions) at the percentage rate applicable at the date of claim on so much of the chargeable income as exceeds the lower limit but does not exceed the upper limit of profits and gains applicable for the tax year in which the date of claim falls; but, if the assessment period is less than a year, those limits shall be calculated on a pro rata basis.

(3) In this regulation "chargeable income" means—

(a) except where sub-paragraph (b) or (c) applies, the earnings derived from the employment, less any expenses deducted under paragraph (3)(a), (4)(a), (5) or (6), as the case may be, of regulation 25;

(b) except where sub-paragraph (c) (iii) applies, in the case of employment as a child minder one-third of the earnings of that employment; or

(c) where regulation 17(3) applies (normal weekly earnings of self-employed earners)—

(i) in the case of a self-employed earner who is engaged in employment on his own account, the claimant's estimated earnings from the employment, less the amount of the deductions likely to be made and, where appropriate, made under sub-paragraph (a) of paragraph (3) of regulation 25;

(ii) in the case of a self-employed earner whose employment is carried on in partnership or is that of a share fisherman within the meaning of the Social Security (Mariners' Benefits) Regulations 1975, the claimant's estimated and, where appropriate, his share of the actual earnings from the employment, less the amount of his share of the expenses likely to be deducted and, where appropriate, deducted [[1]under paragraph (5)] of regulation 25;

(iii) in the case of employment as a child minder, one-third of the claimant's estimated and, where appropriate, actual earnings from that employment.

AMENDMENTS

1. Income-related Benefits Schemes (Miscellaneous Amendments) (No. 3) Regulations 1992 (S.I. 1992 No. 2155), Sched., para. 7 (October 5, 1992).

2. Income-related Benefits Schemes (Miscellaneous Amendments) (No. 5) Regulations 1994 (S.I. 1994 No. 2139), reg. 4 (October 4, 1994 or later expiry of award).

GENERAL NOTE

Para. (3)(c) applies where the assessment period is the period of 26 weeks following the date of claim and so earnings have to be estimated.

CHAPTER V

OTHER INCOME

Calculation of income other than earnings

27.—(1) For the purposes of regulation 18 (normal weekly income other than earnings), the income of a claimant which does not consist of earnings to be taken into account shall, subject to paragraphs (2) to (5), be his gross income and any capital treated as income under [[1]regulations 28 and 30 (capital treated as income and modifications in respect of children and young persons)].

(2) There shall be disregarded from the calculation of a claimant's gross income under paragraph (1) any sum, where applicable, specified in Schedule 3.

(3) Where the payment of any benefit under the benefit Acts is subject to any deduction by way of recovery the amount to be taken into account under paragraph (1) shall be the gross amount payable.

(4) Any payment to which regulation 21(2) applies (payments not earnings) shall be taken into account as income for the purposes of paragraph (1).

(5) Where a loan is made to a person pursuant to arrangements made under section 1 of the Education (Student Loans) Act 1990, or article 3 of the Education (Student Loans) (Northern Ireland) Order 1990 and that person ceases to be a student before the end of the academic year in respect of which the loan is payable, or, as the case may be, before the end of his course, a sum equal to the weekly amount apportionable under paragraph (2) of regulation 47 shall be taken into account under paragraph (1) for each week, in the period over which the loan fell to be apportioned, following the date on which that person ceases to be a student; but in determining the weekly amount apportionable under paragraph (2) of regulation 47 (treatment of student loans) so much of that paragraph as provides for a disregard shall not have effect.

Amendment

1. Income-related Benefits Schemes (Miscellaneous Amendments) (No. 4) Regulations 1993 (S.I. 1993 No. 2119), reg. 41 (October 5, 1993 or later expiry of award).

General Note

This regulation indicates what should be taken into account as income other than earnings. All such income is to be taken into account except for items identified in Sched. 3. Although para. (1) refers to "gross income", in *CIS/25/89* the Commissioner applied *Chief Adjudication Officer v. Hogg* [1985] 1 W.L.R. 1100 (also reported as an appendix to *R(FIS) 4/85*) and held that "gross income" means income after the deduction of expenses which are necessarily incurred in obtaining it.

Capital treated as income

28.—(1) Any capital payable by instalments which are outstanding at the date of the claim shall, if the aggregate of the instalments outstanding and the amount of the claimant's capital otherwise calculated in accordance with Chapter VI of this Part exceeds £16,000, be treated as income.

(2) Any payment received under an annuity shall be treated as income.

[[1](3) Any Career Development Loan paid pursuant to section 2 of the Employment and Training Act 1973 shall be treated as income.]

Amendment

1. Income-related Benefits and Jobseeker's Allowance (Miscellaneous Amendments) Regulations 1997 (S.I. 1997 No. 65), reg. 3(3)(b) (April 8, 1997 or later expiry of award).

Notional income

29.—(1) A claimant shall be treated as possessing income of which he has deprived himself for the purpose of securing entitlement to disability working allowance or increasing the amount of that benefit.

(2) [[9]Except in the case of—

(a) a discretionary trust;

(b) a trust derived from a payment made in consequence of a personal injury; or

(c) a personal pension scheme or retirement annuity contract where the claimant is aged under 60,] [10or
(d) any sum to which paragraph 45(a) or 46(a) of Schedule 4 (disregard of compensation for personal injuries which is administered by the Court refers,]

any income which would become available to the claimant upon application being made, but which has not been acquired by him, shall be treated as possessed by the claimant.

[8(2A) Where a person, aged not less than 60, is a member of, or a person deriving entitlement to a pension under, a personal pension scheme, or is a party to, or a person deriving entitlement to a pension under, a retirement annuity contract, and—

(a) in the case of a personal pension scheme, he fails to purchase an annuity with the funds available in that scheme where—
  (i) he defers, in whole or in part, the payment of any income which would have been payable to him by his pension fund holder;
  (ii) he fails to take any necessary action to secure that the whole of any income which would be payable to him by his pension fund holder upon his applying for it, is so paid; or
  (iii) income withdrawal is not available to him under that scheme; or
(b) in the case of a retirement annuity contract, he fails to purchase an annuity with funds available under that contract,

the amount of any income foregone shall be treated as possessed by him, but only from the date on which it could be expected to be acquired were an application for it to be made.

(2B) The amount of any income foregone in a case to which either head (2A)(a)(i) or (ii) applies shall be the maximum amount of income which may be withdrawn from the fund and shall be determined by the adjudication officer who shall take account of information provided by the pension fund holder in accordance with regulation 7(5) of the Social Security (Claims and Payments) Regulations 1987 (evidence and information).

(2C) The amount of any income foregone in a case to which either held (2A)(a)(iii) or subparagraph (2A)(b) applies shall be the income that the claimant could have received without purchasing an annuity had the funds held under the relevant personal pension scheme or retirement annuity contract been held under a personal pension scheme where income withdrawal was available and shall be determined in the manner specified in paragraph (2B).]

(3) Any payment of income, other than a payment of income made under the Macfarlane Trust, the Macfarlane (Special Payments) Trust, the Macfarlane (Special Payments) (No. 2) Trust [1, the Fund] [5, the Eileen Trust] or [4 the Independent Living Funds], [10or payments made pursuant to section 19(1)(a) of the Coal Industry Act 1994 (concessionary coal)] made—

(a) to a third party in respect of a single claimant or a member of the family (but not a member of the third party's family) shall be treated as possessed by [2 that single claimant or] that member of the family to the extent that it is used for his food, ordinary clothing or footwear, household fuel, or housing costs or is used for any personal community [3charge,] collective community charge contribution [3or council tax] for which that member is liable; and in this sub-paragraph the expression "ordinary clothing or footwear" means clothing or footwear for normal daily use, but does not include school uniforms, or clothing or footwear used solely for sporting activities;
[2(b) to a single claimant or a member of the family in respect of a third party (but not in respect of another member of the family) shall be treated as

possessed by that single claimant or, as the case may be, that member of the family to the extent that it is kept or used by him or used by or on behalf of any member of the family.]

(4) Where—

(a) a claimant performs a service for another person; and

(b) that person makes no payment of earnings or pays less than that paid for a comparable employment in the area;

the adjudication officer shall treat the claimant as possessing such earnings (if any) as is reasonable for that employment unless the claimant satisfies him that the means of that person are insufficient for him to pay or to pay more for the service, but this paragraph shall not apply to a claimant who is engaged by a charitable or [8voluntary organisation] or is a volunteer if the adjudication officer is satisfied [8in any of those cases] that it is reasonable for him to provide his services free of charge.

(5) Where a claimant is treated as possessing any income under any of paragraphs (1) to (3), the foregoing provisions of this Part shall apply for the purposes of calculating the amount of that income as if a payment had actually been made and as if it were actual income which he does possess.

(6) Where a claimant is treated as possessing any earnings under paragraph (4), the foregoing provisions of this Part shall apply for the purposes of calculating the amount of those earnings as if a payment had actually been made and as if they were actual earnings which he does possess, except that paragraph (3) of regulation 22 (calculation of net earnings of employed earners) shall not apply and his net earnings shall be calculated by taking into account those earnings which he is treated as possessing, less—

(a) an amount in respect of income tax equivalent to an amount calculated by applying to those earnings [2the lower rate, or as the case may be, the lower rate and the basic rate of tax] in the year of assessment in which the claim was made less only the personal relief to which the claimant is entitled under sections 257(1), (6) and (7) and 259 of the Income and Corporation Taxes Act 1988 (personal relief) as is appropriate to his circumstances; but, if the assessment period is less than a year [2 the earnings to which the lower rate [7. . .] of tax is to be applied and], the amount of the personal relief deductible under this sub-paragraph shall be calculated on a pro rata basis;

[6(b) where the weekly amount of those earnings equals or exceeds the lower earnings limit, an amount representing primary Class 1 contributions under the Contributions and Benefits Act, calculated by applying to those earnings the initial and main primary percentages applicable at the date of claim in accordance with section 8(1)(a) and (b) of that Act; and]

(c) one-half of any sum payable by the claimant by way of a contribution towards an occupational or personal pension scheme.

Amendments

1. Income-related Benefits Schemes and Social Security (Recoupment) Amendment Regulations 1992 (S.I. 1992 No. 1101), reg. 3(3) (May 7, 1992).

2. Income-related Benefits Schemes (Miscellaneous Amendments) (No. 3) Regulations 1992 (S.I. 1992 No. 2155), Sched., para. 7 (October 5, 1992).

3. Income-related Benefits Schemes (Miscellaneous Amendments) Regulations 1993 (S.I. 1993 No. 315), Sched., para. 14 (April 1, 1993).

4. Social Security Benefits (Miscellaneous Amendments) (No. 2) Regulations 1993 (S.I. 1993 No. 963), reg. 6 (April 22, 1993).

5. Income-related Benefits Schemes and Social Security (Recoupment) Amendment Regulations 1993 (S.I. 1993 No. 1249), reg. 5(3)(a) (May 14, 1993).

6. Income-related Benefits Schemes (Miscellaneous Amendments) Regulations 1994 (S.I. 1994 No. 527), reg. 26 (April 12, 1994 or later expiry of award).

7. Income-related Benefits Schemes (Miscellaneous Amendments) (No. 5) Regulations 1994 (S.I. 1994 No. 2139), reg. 4 (October 4, 1994).
8. Income-related Benefits Schemes (Miscellaneous Amendments) Regulations 1995 (S.I. 1995 No. 516), reg. 6 (April 11, 1995 or later expiry of award).
9. Income-related Benefits Schemes and Social Security (Claims and Payments) (Miscellaneous Amendments) Regulations 1995 (S.I. 1995 No. 2303), reg.3(4) (October 3, 1995).
10. Income-related Benefits and Jobseeker's Allowance (Amendment) (No. 2) Regulations 1997 (S.I. 1997 No. 2197), regs. 2 and 7(3) (October 7, 1997).

General Note

Para. (1). The purpose of the deprivation must be the securing of entitlement to, or an increase in the amount of, disability working allowance (and not any other income-related benefit). That need not have been the predominant purpose behind the deprivation but it must have been a "significant operative purpose" (*R(SB) 40/85*). That will often be inferred from the surrounding circumstances (*R(SB) 9/91*) although it is not enough for the adjudication officer to show that the deprivation would inevitably have an effect on entitlement to disability working allowance. There must be a positive finding of fact that the claimant (or member of the family) knew that the deprivation would affect entitlement to disability working allowance, because otherwise it cannot be said that the result was intended (*R(SB) 12/91*).

See further the detailed annotation to reg. 51 of the Income Support (General) Regulations 1987 in Mesher and Wood, *Income Related Benefits: The Legislation.*

Para. (4). Although *Sharrock v. Chief Adjudication Officer* (reported as an appendix to *R(SB) 3/92*) was decided under differently worded legislation, *CIS/93/91* confirms that this wording also potentially catches a person who is caring for a disabled relative, if that relative has the means to pay. However, *CIS/93/1991* stresses that such a carer can be classed as a volunteer so that there is a discretion not to apply the rule if it seems inappropriate to do so, having regard to all the surrounding circumstances. Note that the amount of any notional net earnings is calculated under para. (6) rather than under reg. 22.

Modifications in respect of children and young persons

30.—(1) Any capital of a child or young person payable by instalments which are outstanding at the date of claim shall, if the aggregate of the instalments outstanding and the amount of that child's or young person's other capital calculated in accordance with Chapter VI of this Part in like manner as for the claimant [2. . .] would exceed £3,000, be treated as income.

(2) Where the income of a child or young person, other than income consisting of any payment of maintenance whether under a court order or not, calculated in accordance with [2Chapters I to V] of this Part exceeds the sum specified as an allowance for that child or young person in Schedule 5 and regulation 51(5) (sum for child or young person who has income in excess to be nil) applies, that income shall not be treated as income of the claimant.

(3) Where the capital of a child or young person, if calculated in accordance with Chapter VI of this Part in like manner as for the claimant, [2except as provided in paragraph (1)], would exceed £3,000, any income of that child or young person [1, other than income consisting of any payment of maintenance whether under a court order or not,] shall not be treated as income of the claimant.

(4) Any income of a child or young person which is to be disregarded under Schedule 3 shall be disregarded in such manner as to produce the result most favourable to the claimant.

Amendments

1. Income-related Benefits Schemes (Miscellaneous Amendments) Regulations 1993 (S.I. 1993 No. 315), reg. 19 (April 13, 1993).
2. Income-related Benefits Schemes (Miscellaneous Amendments) (No. 4) Regulations 1993 (S.I. 1993 No. 2119), reg. 42 (October 5, 1993 or later expiry of award).

General Note

Under Sched. 2, para. (2), earnings of a child or young person are disregarded. Other income amounting to no more than the amount of the relevant allowance specified in Sched. 5 is taken into account in the normal way, being treated as the claimant's. However, this regulation and reg. 33 together have the effect that other income (other than maintenance payments) in excess of the specified allowance, or capital, belonging to a child or young person is not treated as the claimant's. Reg. 51(4) and (5) then provides that if a child or young person has income (other than maintenance payments) exceeding the amount of the relevant allowance, or if the child or young person has capital exceeding £3,000, that child or young person is left out of the benefit calculation altogether. (Technically, the allowance for the child or young person is then said to be nil).

Chapter VI

Capital

Capital limit

31. For the purposes of section 22(6) of the Act as it applies to disability working allowance (no entitlement to benefit if capital exceeds prescribed amount), the prescribed amount is £16,000.

General Note

S.22(6) of the Social Security Act 1986 has now been replaced by s.134(1) of the Social Security Contributions and Benefits Act 1992.

Calculation of capital

32.—(1) For the purposes of Part II of the Act as it applies to disability working allowance, the capital of a claimant to be taken into account shall, subject to paragraph (2), be the whole of his capital calculated in accordance with this Part and any income treated as capital [[1]under regulation 34] (income treated as capital).

(2) There shall be disregarded from the calculation of a claimant's capital under paragraph (1) any capital, where applicable, specified in Schedule 4.

Amendment

1. Income-related Benefits Schemes (Miscellaneous Amendments) (No. 3) Regulations 1992 (S.I. 1992 No. 2155), Sched, para. 9 (October 5, 1992).

General Note

Pt. II of the Social Security Act 1986 has now been replaced by Pt. IV of the Social Security Contributions and Benefits Act 1992.

Disregard of capital of child or young person

33. The capital of a child or young person who is a member of the claimant's family shall not be treated as capital of the claimant.

GENERAL NOTE

See the note to reg. 30.

Income treated as capital

34.—(1) Any amount by way of a refund of income tax deducted from profits or emoluments chargeable to income tax under Schedule D or E shall be treated as capital.

(2) Any holiday pay which is not earnings under regulation 21(1)(b) (earnings of employed earners) shall be treated as capital.

(3) Any charitable or voluntary payment which is not made or is not due to be made at regular intervals, other than a payment which is made under the Macfarlane Trust, the Macfarlane (Special Payments) Trust, the Macfarlane (Special Payments) (No. 2) Trust [1, the Fund] [3, the Eileen Trust] or [2the Independent Living Funds] shall be treated as capital.

(4) Except any income derived from capital disregarded under paragraphs 1, 2, 4, 6, 13 or 26 to 30 of Schedule 4, any income derived from capital shall be treated as capital but only from the date it is normally due to be credited to the claimant's account.

(5) In the case of employment as an employed earner, any advance of earnings or any loan made by the claimant's employer shall be treated as capital.

(6) Any maintenance payment other than one to which regulation 18(2) [4 or (2A)] (normal weekly income other than earnings) applies shall be treated as capital.

AMENDMENTS

1. Income-related Benefits Schemes and Social Security (Recoupment) Amendment Regulations 1992 (S.I. 1992 No. 1101), reg. 3(4) (May 7, 1992).
2. Social Security Benefits (Miscellaneous Amendments) (No. 2) Regulations 1993 (S.I. 1993 No. 963), reg. 6 (April 22, 1993).
3. Income-related Benefits Schemes and Social Security (Recoupment) Amendment Regulations 1993 (S.I. 1993 No. 1249), reg. 5(3)(b) (May 14, 1993).
4. Income-related Benefits Schemes (Miscellaneous Amendment) (No. 5) Regulations 1994 (S.I. 1994 No. 2139), reg. 7 (October 4, 1994 or later expiry of award).

GENERAL NOTE

Sched. 3, para. 26 makes it quite clear that income treated as capital under this regulation is to be disregarded as income.

Calculation of capital in the United Kingdom

35. Capital which a claimant possesses in the United Kingdom shall be calculated—

(a) except in a case to which [1paragraph] (b) applies, at its current market or surrender value less—
   (i) where there would be expenses attributable to sale, 10 per cent.; and
   (ii) the amount of any incumbrance secured on it;
(b) in the case of a National Savings Certificate—
   (i) if purchased from an issue the sale of which ceased before 1st July last preceding the date of claim, at the price which it would have realised on that 1st July had it been purchased on the last day of that issue;
   (ii) in any other case, at its purchase price.

AMENDMENT

1. Income-related Benefits Schemes (Miscellaneous Amendments) (No. 3) Regulations 1992 (S.I. 1992 No. 2155), Sched., para. 10 (October 5, 1992).

GENERAL NOTE

Commissioners have from time to time emphasised that an asset's value is what it could realistically be sold for, assuming that there was a willing seller and a willing buyer (*R(SB) 57/83 R(SB) 6/84, R(SB) 12/89* and *R(IS) 2/90*). If there are restrictions on the claimant's right to sell an asset (*e.g* shares in a small company) the value of the asset may be reduced and may even be nil (*R(SB) 25/83, R(SB) 12/89*).

Calculation of capital outside the United Kingdom

36. Capital which a claimant possesses in a country outside the United Kingdom shall be calculated—

(a) in a case where there is no prohibition in that country against the transfer to the United Kingdom of an amount equal to its current market or surrender value in that country, at that value;

(b) in a case where there is such a prohibition, at the price which it would realise if sold in the United Kingdom to a willing buyer,

less, where there would be expenses attributable to sale, 10 per cent. and the amount of any incumbrance secured on it.

Notional capital

37.—(1) [2. . .] a claimant shall be treated as possessing capital of which he has deprived himself for the purpose of securing entitlement to disability working allowance or increasing the amount of that benefit except—

(a) where that capital is derived from a payment made in consequence of any personal injury and is placed on trust for the benefit of the claimant; or

(b) to the extent that the capital which he is treated as possessing is reduced in accordance with regulation 38 (diminishing notional capital rule); [7or

(c) any sum to which paragraph 45(a) or 46(a) of Schedule 4 (disregard of compensation for personal injuries which is administered by the Court refers,]

(2) Except in the case of—

(a) a discretionary trust;

(b) a trust derived from a payment made in consequence of a personal injury; or

(c) any loan which would be obtainable only if secured against capital disregarded under Schedule 4; [6 or

(d) a personal pension scheme or retirement annuity contract,] [7or

(e) any sum to which paragraph 45(a) or 46(a) of Schedule 4 (disregard of compensation for personal injuries which is administered by the Court refers,]

any capital which would become available to the claimant upon application being made but which has not been acquired by him shall be treated as possessed by him.

(3) Any payment of capital, other than a payment of capital made under the Macfarlane Trust, the Macfarlane (Special Payments) Trust, the Macfarlane (Special Payments) (No. 2) Trust [1, the Fund] [5, the Eileen Trust] or [4 the Independent Living Funds], made—

(a) to a third party in respect of a single claimant or a member of the family (but not a member of the third party's family) shall be treated as possessed by that single claimant or member of the family to the extent that it is used for his food, ordinary clothing or footwear, household fuel, or housing costs or is used for any personal community [3charge,] collective community charge contribution [3or council tax] for which that member is liable; and in this sub-paragraph the expression "ordinary clothing or footwear" means clothing or footwear for normal daily use, but does not include school uniforms, or clothing or footwear used solely for sporting activities;

(b) to a single claimant or a member of the family in respect of a third party (but not in respect of another member of the family) shall be treated as possessed by that single claimant or member to the extent that it is kept by him or used on behalf of any member of the family.

(4) Where a claimant stands in relation to a company in a position analogous to that of a sole owner or partner in the business of that company, he shall be treated as if he were such sole owner or partner and in such a case—

(a) the value of his holding in that company shall, notwithstanding regulation 32 (calculation of capital), be disregarded; and

(b) he shall, subject to paragraph (5), be treated as possessing an amount of capital equal to the value or, as the case may be, his share of the value of the capital of that company and the foregoing provisions of this Chapter shall apply for the purposes of calculating that amount as if it were actual capital which he does possess.

(5) For so long as the claimant undertakes activities in the course of the business of the company, the amount he is treated as possessing under paragraph (4) shall be disregarded.

(6) Where a claimant is treated as possessing capital under any of paragraphs (1) to (4) the foregoing provisions of this Chapter shall apply for the purposes of calculating its amount as if it were actual capital which he does possess.

(7) For the avoidance of doubt a claimant is to be treated as possessing capital under paragraph (1) only if the capital of which he has deprived himself is actual capital and not capital which he is treated as possessing under regulation 39.

AMENDMENTS

1. Income-related Benefits Schemes and Social Security (Recoupment) Amendment Regulations 1992 (S.I. 1992 No. 1101), reg. 3(5) (October 5, 1992).

2. Income-related Benefits Schemes (Miscellaneous Amendments) (No. 3) Regulations 1992 (S.I. 1992 No. 2155), Sched., para. 11 (October 5, 1992).

3. Income-related Benefits Schemes (Miscellaneous Amendments) Regulations 1993 (S.I. 1993 No. 315), Sched., para. 15 (April 1, 1993).

4. Social Security Benefits (Miscellaneous Amendments) (No. 2) Regulations 1993 (S.I. 1993 No. 963), reg. 6 (April 22, 1993).

5. Income-related Benefits Schemes and Social Security (Recoupment) Amendment Regulations 1993 (S.I. 1993 No. 1249), reg. 5(3)(c) (May 14, 1993).

6. Income-related Benefits Schemes and Social Security (Claims and Payments) (Miscellaneous Amendments) Regulations 1995 (S.I. 1995 No. 2303), reg. 3(5) (October 3, 1995).

7. Income-related Benefits and Jobseeker's Allowance (Amendment) (No. 2) Regulations 1997 (S.I. 1997 No. 2197), reg. 2 (October 7, 1997).

GENERAL NOTE

Para. (1). See the note to reg. 29(1) and also the much more extensive note to reg. 51 of the Income Support (General) Regulations 1987 in Mesher and Wood, *Income Related Benefits: The Legislation.* The amount of capital to be taken into account diminishes in accordance with reg. 38.

Diminishing notional capital rule

38.—(1) Where a claimant is treated as possessing capital under regulation 37(1) (notional capital), the amount which he is treated as possessing—

(a) in the case of a benefit week which is subsequent to—
   (i) the relevant week in respect of which the conditions set out in paragraph (2) are satisfied; or
   (ii) a week which follows that relevant week and which satisfies those conditions,
   shall be reduced by an amount determined under paragraph (3);
(b) in the case of a benefit week in respect of which paragraph (1)(a) does not apply but where—
   (i) that week is a week subsequent to the relevant week; and
   (ii) that relevant week is a week in which the condition in paragraph (4) is satisfied,
   shall be reduced by the amount determined under paragraph (4).

(2) This paragraph applies to a benefit week where the claimant satisfies the conditions that—
(a) he is entitled to disability working allowance; and
(b) but for regulation 37, he would have been entitled to an additional amount of disability working allowance in that benefit week.

(3) In a case to which paragraph (2) applies, the amount of the reduction for the purposes of paragraph (1) (a) shall be equal to the aggregate of—
(a) the additional amount of disability working allowance to which the claimant would have been entitled; and
(b) if the claimant would, but for regulation 43(1) of the Housing Benefit (General) Regulations 1987 (notional capital), have been entitled to housing benefit or to an additional amount of housing benefit in respect of the benefit week in which the date of the last claim for disability working allowance falls, the amount (if any) which is equal to—
   (i) in a case where no housing benefit is payable the amount to which he would have been entitled, or
   (ii) in any other case, the amount equal to the additional amount of housing benefit to which he would have been entitled; and
(c) if the claimant would, but for regulation 33(1) of the Community Charge Benefit (General) Regulations 1989 (notional capital) have been entitled to community charge benefit or to an additional amount of community charge benefit in respect of the benefit week in which the date of the last claim for disability working allowance falls, the amount (if any) which is equal to—
   (i) in a case where no community charge benefit is payable the amount to which he would have been entitled, or
   (ii) in any other case, the amount equal to the additional amount of community charge benefit to which he would have been [[1]entitled; and
(d) if the claimant would, but for regulation 34(1) of the Council Tax Benefit (General) Regulations 1992 (notional capital), have been entitled to council tax benefit or to an additional amount of council tax benefit in respect of the benefit week in which the date of the last claim for disability working allowance falls, the amount (if any) which is equal to—
   (i) in a case where no council tax benefit is payable, the amount to which he would have been entitled, or
   (ii) in any other case, the amount equal to the additional amount of council tax benefit to which he would have been entitled.]

(4) Subject to paragraph (5), for the purposes of paragraph (1) (b) the condition is that the claimant would have been entitled to disability working allowance in the relevant week but for regulation 37(1) and in such a case the amount shall be equal to the aggregate of—
(a) the amount of disability working allowance to which the claimant would have been entitled in the relevant week but for regulation 37(1); and
(b) if the claimant would, but for regulation 43(1) of the Housing Benefit

(General) Regulations 1987 (notional capital), have been entitled to housing benefit or to an additional amount of housing benefit in respect of the benefit week in which the first day of the relevant week falls, the amount (if any) which is equal to—

(i) in a case where no housing benefit is payable the amount to which he would have been entitled; or

(ii) in any other case, the amount equal to the additional amount of housing benefit to which he would have been entitled; and

(c) if the claimant would, but for regulation 33(1) of the Community Charge Benefits (General) Regulations 1989 (notional capital) have been entitled to community charge benefit or to an additional amount of community charge benefit in respect of the benefit week in which the first day of the relevant week falls, the amount (if any) which is equal to—

(i) in a case where no community charge benefit is payable the amount to which he would have been entitled, or

(ii) in any other case, the amount equal to the additional amount of community charge benefit to which he would have been [[1]entitled; and

(d) if the claimant would, but for regulation 34(1) of the Council Tax Benefit (General) Regulations 1992 (notional capital), have been entitled to council tax benefit or to an additional amount of council tax benefit in respect of the benefit week in which the first day of the relevant week falls, the amount (if any) which is equal to—

(i) in a case where no council tax benefit is payable, the amount to which he would have been entitled, or

(ii) in any other case, the amount equal to the additional amount of council tax benefit to which he would have been entitled.]

(5) The amount determined under paragraph (4) shall be re-determined under that paragraph if the claimant makes a further claim for disability working allowance and the conditions in paragraph (6) are satisfied, and in such a case—

(a) sub-paragraphs (a), (b) and (c) of paragraph (4) shall apply as if for the words "relevant week" there were substituted the words "relevant subsequent week",

(b) subject to paragraph (7), the amount as re-determined shall have effect from the first week following the relevant subsequent week in question.

(6) The conditions are that—

(a) a further claim is made 20 or more weeks after—

(i) the first day of the relevant week;

(ii) in a case where there has been at least one re-determination in accordance with paragraph (5), the first day of the relevant subsequent week which last occurred;

whichever last occurred; and

(b) the claimant would have been entitled to disability working allowance but for regulation 37(1).

(7) The amount as re-determined pursuant to paragraph (5) shall not have effect if it is less than the amount which applied in that case immediately before the re-determination and in such a case the higher amount shall continue to have effect.

(8) For the purposes of this regulation—

(a) "benefit week" has the meaning prescribed in regulations 16 (date of entitlement under an award) and 27 (family credit and disability working allowance) of the Social Security (Claims and Payments) Regulations 1987 except where it appears in paragraphs [[1]3(b), (c) and (d) and 4(b), (c) and (d)] where it has the meaning prescribed in regulation 2(1) of the Housing Benefit (General) Regulations [[1]1987 (interpretation),] regulation 2(1) of the Community Charge Benefits (General) Regulations

1989 (interpretation) [1 or regulation 2(1) of the Council Tax Benefit (General) Regulations 1992 (interpretation)] as the case may be;

(b) "relevant week" means the benefit week in which the capital in question of which the claimant has deprived himself within the meaning of regulation 37(1)—

(i) was for the first time taken into account for the purpose of determining his entitlement to disability working allowance; or

(ii) was taken into account on a subsequent occasion for that purpose other than in respect of either a benefit week to which paragraph (2) applies or a further claim to which paragraph (5) applies;

and, where more than one benefit week is identified by reference to heads (i) and (ii) of this sub-paragraph, the later or latest such benefit week;

(c) "relevant subsequent week" means the benefit week in which any award of disability working allowance in respect of the further claim referred to in paragraph (6)(a) would, but for regulation 37(1), have commenced, but it shall not be earlier than the twenty-seventh week after the week in which the existing amount took effect.

Amendment

1. Income-related Benefits Schemes (Miscellaneous Amendments) Regulations 1993 (S.I. 1993 No. 315), Sched., para. 16 (April 1, 1993).

Capital jointly held

39. Except where a claimant possesses capital which is disregarded under regulation 37(4) (notional capital), where a claimant and one or more persons are beneficially entitled in possession to any capital asset they shall be treated as if each of them were entitled in possession [1to an equal share of the whole beneficial interest therein; and the value of that equal share shall be calculated by taking the value of the whole beneficial interest calculated in accordance with the foregoing provisions of this Chapter, as though—

(a) that interest is solely owned by the claimant; and

(b) in the case of a dwelling, none of the other joint owners occupies the dwelling concerned,

and dividing the same by the number of persons who have a beneficial interest in the capital in question.]

Amendment

1. Income-related Benefits Schemes and Social Security (Claims and Payments) (Miscellaneous Amendments) Regulations 1995 (S.I. 1995 No. 2303), reg. 3(6) (October 3, 1995).

General Note

The amendment reverses the effect of the decision of the Court of Appeal in *Chief Adjudication Officer v. Palfrey* (*The Times*, February 17, 1995) but see CIS/7097/95.

Calculation of tariff income from capital

40.—(1) Where the claimant's capital calculated in accordance with this Chapter exceeds £3,000, it shall be treated as equivalent to a weekly income of £1 for each complete £250 in excess of £3,000 but not exceeding £16,000.

(2) Notwithstanding paragraph (1), where any part of the excess is not a complete £250 that part shall be treated as equivalent to a weekly income of £1.

(3) For the purposes of paragraph (1), capital includes any income treated as capital under regulation 34 (income treated as capital).

CHAPTER VII

STUDENTS

Interpretation

41. In this Chapter, unless the context otherwise requires—

"a course of advanced education" means

(a) a full-time course leading to a postgraduate degree or comparable qualification, a first degree or comparable qualification, a diploma of higher education, a higher national diploma, [[1]a higher national diploma or higher national certificate of either the Business & [[2]Technology] Education Council] or the Scottish Vocational Education Council or a teaching qualification; or

(b) any other full-time course which is a course of a standard above ordinary national diploma, [[1]a national diploma of higher national certificate of either Business & [[2]Technology] Education Council] or a national certificate of the Scottish Vocational Education Council, a general certificate of education (advanced level), a Scottish certificate of education (higher level) or a Scottish certificate of sixth year studies;

"contribution" means any contribution in respect of the income of any other person which a Minister of the Crown or an education authority takes into account in assessing the amount of the student's grant and by which that amount is, as a consequence, reduced;

"course of study" means any full-time course of study or sandwich course whether or not a grant is made for attending it;

"covenant income" means the gross income payable to a student under a Deed of Covenant by a person whose income is, or is likely to be taken, into account in assessing the student's grant or award;

"education authority" means a government department, a local education authority as defined in section 114(1) of the Education Act 1944 (interpretation), an education authority as defined in section 135(1) of the Education (Scotland) Act 1980 (interpretation), an education and library board established under Article 3 of the Education and Libraries (Northern Ireland) Order 1986, any body which is a research council for the purposes of the Science and Technology Act 1965 or any analogous government department, authority, board or body of the Channel Islands, Isle of Man or any other country outside Great Britain;

"grant" means any kind of educational grant or award and includes any scholarship, studentship, exhibition, allowance or bursary but does not include a payment derived from funds made available by the Secretary of State for the purpose of assisting students in financial difficulties under section 100 of the Education Act 1944, sections 131 and 132 of the Education Reform Act 1988 or section 73 of the Education (Scotland) Act 1980;

"grant income" means—

(a) any income by way of a grant;

(b) any contribution which has been assessed whether or not it has been paid,

and any such contribution which is paid by way of a covenant shall be treated as part of the student's grant income;

"last day of the course" means the date on which the last day of the final academic term falls in respect of the course in which the student is enrolled;

"period of study" means—

(a) in the case of a course of study for one year or less, the period beginning with the start of the course and ending with the last day of the course;

(b) in the case of a course of study for more than one year, in the first or, as the case may be, any subsequent year of the course, other than the final year of the course, the period beginning with the start of the course or, as the case may be, that year's start and ending with either—

(i) the day before the start of the next year of the course in a case where the student's grant is assessed at a rate appropriate to his studying throughout the year, or, if he does not have a grant, where it would have been assessed at such a rate had he had one; or

(ii) in any other case the day before the start of the normal summer vacation appropriate to his course;

(c) in the final year of a course of study of more than one year, the period beginning with that year's start and ending with the last day of the course;

"period of experience" has the meaning prescribed in paragraph 1(1) of Schedule 5 to the Education (Mandatory Awards) Regulations 1991;

"sandwich course" has the meaning prescribed in paragraph 1(1) of Schedule 5 to the Education (Mandatory Awards) Regulations 1991;

"standard maintenance grant" means—

(a) except where paragraph (b) applies, in the case of a student attending a course of study at the University of London or an establishment within the area comprising the City of London and the Metropolitan Police District, the amount specified for the time being in paragraph 2(2)(a) of Schedule 2 to the Education (Mandatory Awards) Regulations 1991 for such a student;

(b) in the case of a student residing at his parent's home, the amount specified in paragraph 3(2) thereof; and

(c) in any other case, the amount specified in paragraph 2(2) other than in sub-paragraph (a) or (b) thereof;

[[1]"student" means a person, other than a person in receipt of a training allowance, who is aged less than 19 and attending a full-time course of advanced education or, as the case may be, who is aged 19 or over and attending a full-time course of study] at an educational establishment, and for the purposes of this definition—

(a) a person who has started on such a course shall be treated as attending it [[3]. . .] until the last day of the course or such earlier date as he abandons it or is dismissed from it;

(b) a person on a sandwich course shall be treated as attending a full-time course of advanced education or, as the case may be, of study;

"year" in relation to a course, means the period of 12 months beginning on 1st January, 1st April or 1st September according to whether the academic year of the course in question begins in the spring, the summer or the autumn respectively.

AMENDMENTS

1. Income-related Benefits Schemes (Miscellaneous Amendments) (No. 3) Regulations 1992 (S.I. 1992 No. 2155), Sched., para. 12 (October 5, 1992).

2. Income-related Benefits Schemes (Miscellaneous Amendments) (No. 4) Regulations 1993 (S.I. 1993 No. 2119), reg. 43 (October 5, 1993).

3. Social Security Benefits (Miscellaneous Amendments) Regulations 1995 (S.I. 1995 No. 1742), reg. 2 (August 1, 1995).

Calculation of grant income

42.—(1) The amount of a student's grant income to be taken into account shall, subject to [[1]paragraphs (2) and (2A)], be the whole of his grant income.

(2) There shall be disregarded from a student's grant income any payment—

(a) intended to meet tuition fees or examination fees;

(b) intended to meet additional expenditure incurred by a disabled student in respect of his attendance on a course;

(c) intended to meet additional expenditure connected with term time residential study away from the student's educational establishment;

(d) on account of the student maintaining a home at a place other than that at which he resides during his course;

(e) intended to meet the cost of books and equipment or, if not so intended, an amount equal to [[2]£287];

(f) intended to meet travel expenses incurred as a result of his attendance on the course.

[[1](2A) Where in pursuance of an award a student is in receipt of a grant in respect of maintenance under regulation 17(b) of the Education (Mandatory Awards) Regulations 1991 (payments), there shall be excluded from his grant income a sum equal to the amount specified in paragraph 7(4) of Schedule 2 to those Regulations (disregard of travel costs), being the amount to be disregarded in respect of travel costs in the particular circumstances of his case.]

(3) A student's grant income, except any amount intended for the maintenance of dependants under Part 3 of Schedule 2 to the Education (Mandatory Awards) Regulations 1991 or intended for an older student under Part 4 of that Schedule, shall be apportioned—

(a) subject to paragraph (5), in a case where it is attributable to the period of study, equally between the weeks in that period;

(b) in any other case, equally between the weeks in the period in respect of which it is payable.

(4) Any amount intended for the maintenance of dependants or for an older student under the provisions referred to in paragraph (3) shall be apportioned equally over a period of 52 weeks commencing with the week in which the period of study begins.

(5) In the case of a student on a sandwich course, any periods of experience within the period of study shall be excluded and the student's grant income shall be apportioned equally between the remaining weeks in that period.

AMENDMENTS

1. Income-related Benefits Schemes (Miscellaneous Amendments) (No. 3) Regulations 1992 (S.I. 1992 No. 2155), Sched., para. 13 (October 5, 1992).

2. Social Security (Miscellaneous Amendments) (No. 3) Regulations 1997 (S.I. 1997 No. 1671), reg. 2(2) (September 2, 1997), except where the student's period of study began between August 1, 1997 and September 1, 1997, in which case the amendment came into force on the first Tuesday of the period of study).

Calculation of covenant income where a contribution is assessed

43.—(1) Where a student is in receipt of income by way of a grant during a period of study and a contribution has been assessed, the amount of his covenant income to be taken into account shall be the whole amount of his covenant income less, subject to paragraph (3), the amount of the contribution.

(2) The weekly amount of the student's covenant income shall be determined—

(a) by dividing the amount of income which falls to be taken into account under paragraph (1) by 52; and

(b) by disregarding from the resulting amount, £5.

(3) For the purposes of paragraph (1), the contribution shall be treated as increased by the amount, if any, by which the amount excluded under [1 regulation 42(2)(f) (calculation of grant income) falls short of the amount specified in paragraph 7(4)(i) of Schedule 2 to the Education (Mandatory Awards) Regulation 1991 (travel expenditure)]

AMENDMENT

1. Income-related Benefits Schemes (Miscellaneous Amendments) (No. 3) Regulations 1992 (S.I. 1992 No. 2155), Sched., para. 14 (October 5, 1992).

Covenant income where no grant income or no contribution is assessed

44.—(1) Where a student is not in receipt of income by way of grant the amount of his covenant income shall be calculated as follows—

(a) any sums intended for any expenditure specified in regulation 42(2) (a) to (d) (calculation of grant income), necessary as a result of his attendance on the course, shall be disregarded.

(b) any covenant income, up to the amount of the standard maintenance grant, which is not so disregarded shall be apportioned equally between the weeks of the period of study and there shall be disregarded from the covenant income to be so apportioned the amount which would have been disregarded [1under regulation 42(2)(e) and (f) and (2A)] had the student been in receipt of the standard maintenance grant; and

(c) the balance, if any, shall be divided by 52 and treated as weekly income of which £5 shall be disregarded.

(2) Where a student is in receipt of income by way of a grant and no contribution has been assessed, the amount of his covenant income shall be calculated in accordance with sub-paragraphs (a) to (c) of paragraph (1), except that—

(a) the value of the standard maintenance grant shall be abated by the amount of his grant income less an amount equal to the amount of any sums disregarded under regulation 42(2)(a) to (d) and

(b) the amount to be disregarded under paragraph (1)(b) shall be abated by an amount equal to the amount of any sums disregarded [1under regulation 42(2)(e) and (f) and (2A)].

AMENDMENT

1. Income-related Benefits Schemes (Miscellaneous Amendments) (No. 3) Regulations 1992 (S.I. 1992 No. 2155), Sched., para. 15 (October 5, 1992).

Relationship with amounts to be disregarded under Schedule 3

45. No part of a student's covenant income or grant income shall be disregarded under paragraph 12 of Schedule 3 and any other income to which sub-paragraph (1) of that paragraph applies shall be disregarded thereunder only to the extent that the amount disregarded under regulation 43(2)(b) (calculation of covenant income where a contribution is assessed) or, as the case may be, regulation 44(1)(c) (covenant income where no grant income or no contribution is assessed) is less than [1£20].

AMENDMENT

1. Income-related Benefits Schemes (Miscellaneous Amendments) Regulations 1996 (S.I. 1996 No. 462), reg. 8 (April 9, 1996).

Other amounts to be disregarded

46. For the purposes of ascertaining income other than [[1]grant income covenant income and loans treated as income in accordance with regulation 47], any amounts intended for any expenditure specified in regulation 42(2) (calculation of grant income) necessary as a result of his attendance on the course shall be disregarded but only if, and to the extent that, the necessary expenditure exceeds or is likely to exceed the amount of the sums disregarded under regulation 42(2) [[1]and (2A)], 43(3) and 44(1)(a) or (b) (calculation of grant income and covenant income) on like expenditure.

AMENDMENT

1. Income-related Benefits Schemes (Miscellaneous Amendments) Regulations 1994 (S.I. 1994 No. 527), reg. 27 (April 12, 1994 or later expiry of award).

Treatment of student loans

47.—(1) A loan which is made to a student pursuant to arrangements made under section 1 of the Education (Student Loans) Act 1990 or article 3 of the Education (Student Loans) (Northern Ireland) Order 1990 shall be treated as income.

(2) In calculating the weekly amount of the loan to be taken into account as income—

(a) except where sub-paragraph (b) applies, the loan shall be apportioned equally between the weeks in the academic year in respect of which the loan is payable;

(b) in the case of a loan which is payable in respect of the final academic year of the course or, if the course is only of one academic year's duration, in respect of that year, the loan shall be apportioned equally between the weeks in the period beginning with the start of the final academic year or, as the case may be, the single academic year and ending with the last day of the course,

and from the weekly amount so apportioned there shall be disregarded £10.

[[1](3) For the purposes of this regulation a student shall be treated as possessing the maximum amount of any loan referred to in paragraph (1) which he will be able to acquire in respect of an academic year by taking reasonable steps to do so.]

AMENDMENT

1. Income-related Benefits Schemes (Miscellaneous Amendments) Regulations 1996 (S.I. 1996 No. 462), regulation 9 (April 9, 1996 or later expiry of award).

Disregard of contribution

48. Where the claimant or his partner is a student and [,[1] for the purposes of assessing a contribution to the student's grant, the other partner's income has been taken into account, an amount equal to that contribution shall be disregarded for the purposes of assessing that other partner's income.]

AMENDMENT

1. Income-related Benefits Schemes (Miscellaneus Amendments) Regulations 1996 (S.I. 1996 No. 462), regulation 10 (April 9, 1996 or later expiry of award).

Disregard of tax refund

49. Any amount by way of a refund of tax deducted from a student's covenant income shall be disregarded in calculating the student's income or capital.

Disregard of changes occurring during summer vacation

50. In calculating a student's income there shall be disregarded any change in the standard maintenance grant occurring in the recognised summer vacation appropriate to the student's course, if that vacation does not form part of his [1period of study,] from the date on which the change occurred to the end of that vacation.

AMENDMENT

1. Income-related Benefits Schemes (Miscellaneous Amendments) (No. 3) Regulations 1992 (S.I. 1992 No. 2155), Sched., para. 16 (October 5, 1992).

PART VI

CALCULATION OF ENTITLEMENT

Determination of appropriate maximum disability working allowance

51.—(1) Subject to paragraphs (2) to (7), the appropriate maximum disability working allowance shall be the aggregate of the following allowances—

(a) in respect of a single claimant, the allowance specified in column (2) of Schedule 5 at paragraph 1;

(b) in respect of a claimant who is a member of a married or unmarried couple, or who is a lone parent who is treated as responsible for a child or young person by virtue of regulation 9 (circumstances in which a person is treated as responsible or not responsible for another), the allowance specified in column (2) of Schedule 5 at paragraph 2;

[5(bb) in respect of a claimant who is—

(i) a single claimant or lone parent who works, or

(ii) a member of a married or unmarried couple either or both of whom work, for not less than 30 hours per week, the allowance specified in column (2) of Schedule 5 at paragraph 2A.]

(c) in respect of any child or young person for whom the claimant or his partner is treated as responsible by virtue of regulation 9 (circumstances in which a person is treated as responsible or not responsible for another), the allowance specified in column (2) of Schedule 5 [6 in respect of the period specified in either paragraph 3 or 4 of column (1) as appropriate to] the child or young person concerned [6 and in those paragraphs, the "first Tuesday in September" means the Tuesday which first occurs in the month of September in any year"]

[3(d) in respect of any child or young person to whom paragraph (1A) applies, the allowance specified in paragraph 5 of column (2) of Schedule 5.

(1A) This paragraph applies to a child or young person for whom the claimant or his partner is responsible and who is a member of the claimant's household, and—

(a) in respect of whom disability living allowance is payable, or has ceased to be payable solely because he is a patient; or
(b) who is registered as blind in a register compiled by a local authority under section 29 of the National Assistance Act 1948 (welfare services) or, in Scotland, has been certified as blind and in consequence he is registered as blind in a register maintained by or on behalf of a regional or islands council; or
(c) who ceased to be registered as blind in such a register within the 28 weeks immediately preceding the date of claim.

(1B) For the purposes of paragraph (1A)(a), "patient" has the same meaning it has in regulation 10.]

(2) Where a claimant or, as the case may be, the partner of a claimant is married polygamously to two or more members of the same household, the maximum amount shall include, in respect of every such member but the first, an additional allowance which [6 equals the allowance specified in column (2) of Schedule 5 against paragraph 4 in column (1).]

(3) For the purposes of paragraph (2), a person shall not be treated as a member of the same household as someone to whom he is married polygamously if he would not be so treated in the case of a monogamous marriage.

(4) Where the capital of a child or young person, if calculated in accordance with Part V (income and capital) in like manner as for the claimant, [2 except as provided in regulation 30(1) (modifications in respect of children and young persons], would exceed £3,000, the allowance in respect of that child or young person shall be nil.

(5) Where the weekly income of a child or young person, other than income consisting of any payment of maintenance whether under a court order or not, calculated [1in accordance with Part V], exceeds the amount specified for that child or young person in Schedule 5, the allowance in respect of that child or young person shall be nil.

(6) Where a child or young person is, for the purposes of regulation 10(2)(a) (membership of the same household), a patient or in residential accommodation on account of physical or mental handicap or physical or mental illness and has been so accommodated for the 52 weeks immediately before the date of claim, the allowance in respect of that child or young person shall be nil.

(7) For the purposes of this regulation the amount of any disability working allowance and the [6 period during which that amount is appropriate in respect] of any child or young person shall be determined by reference to the allowance specified in Schedule 5 and the [6 relevant period which includes] the date on which the period under [4 section 129(6) of the Contributions and Benefits Act] (period of award) begins.

AMENDMENTS

1. Income-related Benefits Schemes (Miscellaneous Amendments) (No. 3) Regulations 1992 (S.I. 1992 No. 2155), Sched., para. 17 (October 5, 1992).

2. Income-related Benefits Schemes (Miscellaneous Amendments) (No. 4) Regulations 1993 (S.I. 1993 No. 2119), reg. 44 (October 5, 1993 or later expiry of award).

3. Disability Working Allowance and Income Support (General) Amendment Regulations 1995 (S.I. 1995 No. 482), reg. 3 (April 13, 1995).

4. Income-related Benefits Schemes (Miscellaneous Amendments) Regulations 1995 (S.I. 1995 No. 516), reg. 7 (April 11, 1995 or later expiry of award).

5. Income-related Benefits Schemes (Miscellaneous Amendments) (No. 2) Regulations 1995 (S.I. 1995 No. 1339), reg. 4 (July 18, 1995 or later expiry of award).

6. Income-related Benefits and Jobseeker's Allowance (Personal Allowances for Children and Young Persons) (Amendment) Regulations 1996 (S.I. 1996 No. 2545), reg. 8 (October 7, 1997 or later expiry of award subject to a saving in reg. 10(3)).

General Note

Calculating the maximum disability working allowance is the first stage in working out the amount of benefit payable in any particular case. If the claimant's income does not exceed the applicable amount (which is prescribed in reg. 52), the amount of benefit payable is the maximum disability working allowance calculated under this regulation (s.129(5)(a) of the Social Security Contributions and Benefits Act 1992). On the other hand, if the claimant's income does exceed the applicable amount, the amount of benefit payable is what remains of the maximum disability working allowance after the deduction of the prescribed percentage (70 per cent, see reg. 53) of the excess of the income over the applicable amount (s.129(5)(b) of the Social Security Contributions and Benefits Act 1992).

Para. (1). Subject to the other paragraphs of this regulation, the maximum disability working allowance is calculated simply by adding together the appropriate allowances set out in Sched. 5.

Paras. (4) and *(5).* These paragraphs should be read with regs. 30 and 33. The overall effect is that a child or young person whose income (other than maintenance payments) exceeds the amount of the relevant allowance under Sched. 5, or whose capital exceeds £3,000, is left out of the benefit calculation altogether. Note, however, that earnings of a child or young person are disregarded (Sched. 2, para. 2) so it is only income other than earnings which can lead to a child or young person being excluded from the calculation under para. (5).

Para. (6). A nil allowance is prescribed for a child or young person who has been in hospital or residential accommodation for 52 weeks. ''Patient'' and ''residential accommodation'' are defined in reg. 10(3).

Para. (7). Entitlement to disability working allowance is calculated on the basis of the rates of allowance in force, and the age of any child or young person, at the date on which the period of the award begins (which is not necessarily the same as the date of claim). S.20(6F) of the 1986 Act has been replaced by s.129(6) of the 1992 Act.

[[1]Applicable amount

52.—(1) The applicable amount] for the purposes of section 20(6A) of the Act (conditions of entitlement to disability working allowance) shall, in the case of a claimant who is—

(a) single, be [[2]£57.85] per week;

(b) a member of a married or unmarried couple, or a lone parent, be [[2]£77.15] per week.

(2) For the purposes of section 20(6D) of the Act (date on which applicable amount is to be determined) the prescribed date is the date on which the period under section 20(6F) of the Act (period of award) begins.

Amendments

1. Income-related Benefits Schemes (Miscellaneous Amendments) (No. 3) Regulations 1992 (S.I. 1992 No. 2155), Sched., para. 18 (October 5, 1992).

2. Social Security Benefits Up-rating Order 1997 (S.I. 1995, No. 543), art. 17(c) (April 8, 1997).

General Note

Note that the higher amount is applicable to a lone parent, the term ''single claimant'' not applying to lone parents (reg. 2(1)). Entitlement to disability working allowance is calculated on the basis of the applicable amount in force at the date on which the period of the award begins (which is not necessarily the same as the date of claim). S.20(6A), (6D) and (6F) of the Social Security Act 1986 has been replaced by s.129(1), (1)(c) and (6) of the Social Security Contributions and Benefits Act 1992.

Entitlement to disability working allowance where income exceeds the applicable amount

53. The prescribed percentage for the purpose of section 21(3B) of the Act (percentage of excess of income over applicable amount which is deducted from maximum disability working allowance) shall be 70 per cent.

General Note

See the note to reg. 51. S.21(3B) of the Social Security Act 1986 has been replaced by s.129(5)(b) of the Social Security Contributions and Benefits Act 1992.

Part VII

Changes of Circumstances

Death of claimant

54.—(1) Except as provided in paragraph (2), an award of disability working allowance shall cease to have effect upon the death of the claimant.

(2) Where a claimant dies and is survived by a partner who was the claimant's partner at the date of claim, an award of disability working allowance made in the claimant's favour shall have effect for its unexpired period as if originally made in favour of the partner.

General Note

This provides an exception to the general rule that an award continues for 26 weeks irrespective of changes of circumstances. An award stops if a single claimant dies. However, if the claimant had a partner at the date of claim (*not* the date of death), that partner (even if not disabled) becomes entitled to the balance of the award.

Prevention of duplication of awards of family credit, disability working allowance and income support

55. Where provision is made for the same child or young person in awards for overlapping periods, the first being an award of disability working allowance and the second an award of disability working allowance, family credit [[1], income-based jobseeker's allowance] or income support, and at the start of the period of overlap that child or young person is no longer a member of the household of the claimant under the first award, the first award shall terminate with effect from the start of the period of overlap.

Amendment

1. Social Security and Child Support (Jobseeker's Allowance) (Consequential Amendments) Regulations 1996 (S.I. 1996 No. 1345), reg. 7(5) (October 7, 1996).

General Note

Note that the first award is terminated only if the child or young person has ceased to be a member of that claimant's household. It is quite possible to be a member of more than one household at a time, as is recognised in reg. 9(2). On the other hand, under reg. 9(3) it is possible only for one person at a time to be responsible for a child or young person during the period of an award of disability working allowance. Since the first award only terminates upon the second award being made (rather than before it is made), it seems doubtful that one person can claim disability working allowance so as to include a child or young person during the period covered by an existing award of disability working allowance including the same child or young person. On the other hand, since reg. 9(3) is limited to "the purposes of these Regulations", it would be possible for an award of disability working allowance in respect of a child or young person to be made during the period of an award of family credit or income support or *vice versa*. It is therefore in those circumstances that this regulation applies. Since the first award is terminated (rather than merely being the subject of a review), a new claim will be required if the first claimant still satisfies the conditions of entitlement to the relevant benefit.

[1Overlapping awards

[**56.**—(1) An award of disability working allowance (the new award) which is made in consequence of a claim in respect of a period beginning before the commencement of an existing award of disability working allowance (the existing award) and which overlaps with the period of the existing award, shall be treated as a relevant change of circumstances affecting the existing award and the existing award shall be reviewed and shall terminate with effect from the date on which the decision of the adjudication officer making the new award is notified to the claimant.

(2) An award of family credit which is made in consequence of a claim in respect of a period beginning [2on or] before the commencement of an existing award of disability working allowance (the existing award) and which overlaps with the period of the existing award, shall be treated as a change of circumstances affecting the existing award and the existing award shall be reviewed and shall terminate with effect from the date on which the decision of the adjudication officer awarding family credit is notified to the claimant.]

Amendments

1. Income-related Benefits Schemes (Miscellaneous Amendment) (No. 5) Regulations 1994 (S.I. 1994 No. 2139), reg. 8 (October 4, 1994 or later expiry of award).

2. Income-related Benefits Schemes and Social Fund (Miscellaneous Amendments) Regulations 1996 (S.I. 1996 No. 1944), reg. 3(3) (October 7, 1996).

[1Reduced benefit direction

56A.—(1) The following occurrences shall be changes of circumstances which affect an award of disability working allowance and the rate at which it is payable—

(a) a reduced benefit direction given by a child support officer under section 46(5) of the Child Support Act 1991;

(b) the cessation or cancellation of a reduced benefit direction under Part IX of the maintenance regulations;

(c) the suspension of a reduced benefit direction under regulation 48(1) of the maintenance regulations;

(d) the removal of a suspension imposed under paragraph (1) of regulation 48 of the maintenance regulations in accordance with paragraph (3) of that regulation.

(2) in this regulation—

(a) "child support officer" means a person appointed in accordance with section 13 of the Child Support Act 1991;

(b) "the maintenance regulations" means the Child Support (Maintenance Assessment Procedure) Regulations 1992.]

Amendment

1. Income-related Benefits Schemes (Miscellaneous Amendments) Regulations 1993 (S.I. 1993 No. 315), reg. 20 (April 13, 1993).

Part VIII

Entitlement to Family Credit and Disability Working Allowance

Prescribed circumstances for entitlement to disability working allowance

57. For the purposes of section 20(6A)(d) of the Act (prescribed circumstances) where a claimant or a member of his family is entitled to family credit, he is entitled to disability working allowance, if—

(a) at the date of the claim for disability working allowance the award of family credit for him or a member of his family will expire within 28 days; and

(b) the claimant is or would be otherwise entitled to disability working allowance by virtue of these Regulations; and

(c) the claim for disability working allowance is made in respect of a period which commences immediately after the expiry of the award of family credit.

General Note

S.20(6A)(d) of the Social Security Act 1986 has been replaced by s.129(1)(d) of the Social Security Contributions and Benefits Act 1992.

58. *Omitted.*

SCHEDULES

Schedule 1 **Regulation 3**

Disability Which puts a Person at a Disadvantage in Getting a Job

Part I

1. When standing he cannot keep his balance unless he continually holds onto something.

2. Using any crutches, walking frame, walking stick, prosthesis or similar walking aid which he habitually uses, he cannot walk a continuous distance of 100 metres along level ground without stopping or without suffering severe pain.

3. He can use neither of his hands behind his back as in the process of putting on a jacket or of tucking a shirt into trousers.

4. He can extend neither of his arms in front of him so as to shake hands with another person without difficulty.

5. He can put neither of his hands up to his head without difficulty so as to put on a hat.

6. Due to lack of manual dexterity he cannot [1 with one hand, pick up] a coin which is not more than $2\frac{1}{2}$ centimetres in diameter.

7. He is not able to use his hands or arms to pick up a full jug of 1 litre capacity and pour from it into a cup, without difficulty.

8. He can turn neither of his hands sideways through 180°.

9. He is registered as blind or registered as partially sighted in a register compiled by a local authority under section 29(4)(g) of the National Assistance Act 1948 (welfare services) or, in Scotland, has been certified as blind or as partially sighted and in consequence registered as blind or partially sighted in a register maintained by or on behalf of a regional or island council.

10. He cannot see to read 16 point print at a distance greater than 20 centimetres, if appropriate, wearing the glasses he normally uses.

11. He cannot hear a telephone ring when he is in the same room as the telephone, if appropriate, using a hearing aid he normally uses.

12. In a quiet room he has difficulty in hearing what someone talking in a loud voice at a distance of 2 metres says, if appropriate, using a hearing aid he normally uses.

13. People who know him well have difficulty in understanding what he says.

14. When a person he knows well speaks to him, he has difficulty in understanding what that person says.

15. At least once a year during waking hours he is in a coma or has a fit in which he loses consciousness.

16. He has a mental illness for which he receives regular treatment under the supervision of a medically qualified person.

17. Due to mental disability he is often confused or forgetful.

18. He cannot do the simplest addition and subtraction.

19. Due to mental disability he strikes people or damages property or is unable to form normal social relationships.

20. He cannot normally sustain an 8 hour working day or a 5 day working week due to a medical condition or intermittent or continuous severe pain.

PART II

21. Subject to paragraph 24, there is payable to him—

(a) the highest or middle rate of the care component of disability living allowance,

(b) the higher rate of the mobility component of disability living allowance,

(c) an attendance allowance under section 35 of the Social Security Act,

(d) disablement benefit where the extent of the disablement is assessed at not less than 80 per cent. in accordance with section 57 of and Schedule 8 to the Social Security Act,

(e) a war pension in respect of which the degree of disablement is certified at not less than 80 per cent.; and for the purposes of this sub-paragraph "war pension" means a war pension in accordance with section 25(4) of the Social Security Act 1989,

(f) mobility supplement, or

(g) a benefit corresponding to a benefit mentioned in sub-paragraphs (a)-(f), under any enactment having effect in Northern Ireland.

22. Subject to paragraph 24, for one or more of the 56 days immediately preceding the date when the initial claim for disability working allowance was made or treated as made, there was payable to him severe disablement allowance or a corresponding benefit under any enactment having effect in Northern Ireland.

23. Subject to paragraph 24, he has an invalid carriage or other vehicle provided by the Secretary of State under section 5(2)(a) of the National Health Service Act 1977 and Schedule 2 to that Act or under section 46 of the National Health Service (Scotland) Act 1978 or provided under Article 30(1) of the Health and Personal Social Services (Northern Ireland) Order 1972.

24. Paragraphs 21–23 are subject to the condition that no evidence is before the adjudication officer which gives him reasonable grounds for believing that in respect of an initial claim, none of the paragraphs in Part I or Part III of this Schedule apply to the claimant and in respect of a repeat claim, none of the paragraphs in Part I apply to the claimant.

PART III

25. As a result of an illness or accident he is undergoing a period of habilitation or rehabilitation.

AMENDMENT

1. Income-related Benefits Schemes and Social Security (Claims and Payments) (Miscellaneous Amendments) Regulations 1995 (S.I. 1995 No. 2303), reg. 3(7) (October 3, 1995).

GENERAL NOTE

Under s.129(3) of the Social Security Contributions and Benefits Act 1992, a person is treated as having a disability which puts him or her at a disadvantage in getting a job only if one of the paragraphs of this Schedule applies to him or her. If a paragraph does apply, reg. 3 deems the claimant to be at a disadvantage in getting a job, whether or not the disability actually has that effect.

The Schedule requires the exercise of a considerable amount of judgment. For instance, the words "without difficulty" frequently appear. The difficulty need not be severe and plainly a person may have difficulty with an action without necessarily suffering pain when performing it. Slowness may well be sufficient. On an initial claim (but not a repeat claim), a declaration by the claimant is normally conclusive (see reg. 4).

Para. 2. Note that this test is not the same as the test prescribed in reg. 12(1)(a)(ii) of the Social Security (Disability Living Allowance) Regulations 1991 in respect of the mobility component of disability living allowance. Not only is the distance of 100 metres prescribed, but the question is whether that distance can be walked "without stopping" or without "severe pain" (rather than "severe discomfort"). It should also be noted that only artificial aids which are habitually used are to be taken into account, so there is no need to consider whether an aid which is not used might be suitable. In *R(M) 2/89*, the Commissioner held that a person walks only when putting one foot in front of the other, so that a person who has to swing through crutches, rather than using them to help him or her move both legs separately, cannot walk.

Para. 6. $2\frac{1}{2}$ centimetres is the diameter of a 10 pence coin. 2 pence and 50 pence coins are bigger. £1 coins are smaller in diameter. Note that the claimant satisfies the test (and so may qualify for benefit) if he or she can pick up a 10 pence coin in one hand but not the other. The amendment simply clarifies the position.

Para. 7. This is a test of both steadiness and strength, using both hands or arms at once if necessary.

Para. 8. Presumably this is a test of wrist movements and is intended to be performed with the elbows kept still.

Para. 10. 16 point print is approximately 4mm high.

Paras. 12–14. If hearing or understanding is possible, but only with difficulty (perhaps after repetition), the claimant still qualifies. The precise relationship between paras. 12 and 14 is unclear. Clearly difficulty in understanding may arise for reasons other than loss of hearing and, indeed, a person without hearing may be able to understand through lip-reading. Can a person who can hear a loud voice, but not an ordinary conversational voice, at a distance of 2 metres qualify under para. 14 if he or she cannot lip-read? In principle the answer would seem to be "yes". That would not mean that para. 12 had no effect because the person would only be able to qualify under para. 14 if he or she was further handicapped by an inability to make use of other methods of comprehending speech.

Para. 16. Medication taken on prescription will be enough, provided that it is regular. Mental illness is not defined, but, if a person is receiving treatment there is likely to be a diagnosis of an illness and if it is an illness of the mind it will be mental illness.

Para. 17. Mental disability is not defined and neither is the extent of confusion or forgetfulness required. On one view, any confusion or forgetfulness suggests some disability of the mind and the question is whether the degree of confusion or forgetfulness is sufficient to warrant the view that the legislator intended such a claimant to qualify (see the approach of the Court Appeal in *W v. L* [1974] Q.B. 711). On the other hand, in *R(A) 2/92*, a Commissioner considered that a specific diagnosis was required and that suggests that the first question is whether there is such a diagnosis. Only after that has been answered does one go on to consider whether there is any resulting confusion or forgetfulness.

Para. 18. Presumably the words "the simplest" are not to be taken too literally.

Para. 19. See the note to para. 17. The approach taken in *R(A) 2/92* would create real difficulties here given the view expressed there that "personality disorder" can be distinguished from "mental disability".

Para. 20. Following *R(S) 11/51* (which was decided in the context of incapacity for work) the question is whether the claimant can reasonably be expected to be able normally to sustain an 8-hour working day of a 5-day working week in the sort of employment which he might reasonably be expected to do having regard to his or her age, education, training and other personal factors. In other words, given that the claimant is capable of work, is he or she capable of full-time work?

Para. 21. Note para. 24. Mobility supplement is defined in reg. 2(1); it is an increase of war pension. Ss.35 and 57 of, and Sched. 8 to, the Social Security Act 1975 have been replaced by ss.64 and 103 of, and Sched. 6 to, the Social Security Contributions and Benefits Act 1992.

Para. 25. Reg. 3 provides that this paragraph can apply only on an initial claim (not on a repeat claim).

SCHEDULE 2 **Regulations 19(2) and 21(2)**

SUMS TO BE DISREGARDED IN THE CALCULATION OF EARNINGS

1. Any earnings derived from employment which are payable in a country outside the United Kingdom where there is a prohibition against the transfer to the United Kingdom of those earnings.

2. Any earnings of a child or young person.

3. Where a payment of earnings is made in a currency other than sterling, any banking charge or commission payable in converting that payment to sterling.

SCHEDULE 3 **Regulation 27(2)**

SUMS TO BE DISREGARDED IN THE CALCULATION OF INCOME OTHER THAN EARNINGS

1. Any amount paid by way of tax on income which is taken into account under regulation 27 (calculation of income other than earnings).

2. Any payment in respect of any expenses incurred by a claimant who is—

(a) engaged by a charitable or [[9] voluntary organisation]; or

(b) a volunteer,

if he otherwise derives no remuneration or profit from the employment and is not to be treated as possessing any earnings under regulation 29(4) (notional income).

3. Any housing benefit [[15], income-based jobseeker's allowance] or income support.

4. Any mobility allowance or disability living allowance.

5. Any concessionary payment made to compensate for the non-payment of—

(a) any payment specified in paragraph 4 or 7;

(b) income support [[15]or income-based jobseeker's allowance].

6. Any mobility supplement or any payment intended to compensate for the non-payment of such a supplement.

7. Any attendance allowance.

8. Any payment to the claimant as holder of the Victoria Cross or of the George Cross or any analogous payment.

9. Any sum in respect of a course of study attended by a child or young person payable by virtue of regulations made under section 81 of the Education Act 1944 (assistance by means of scholarship or otherwise), or by virtue of section 2(1) of the Education Act 1962 (awards for courses of further education) or section 49 of the Education (Scotland) Act 1980 (power to assist persons to take advantage of educational facilities) [[18]or section 12(2)(c) of the Further and Higher Education (Scotland) Act 1992 (provision of financial assistance to students)].

10. In the case of a student, any sums intended for any expenditure specified in paragraph (2) of regulation 42 (calculation of grant income) necessary as a result of his attendance on his course.

11. In the case of a claimant participating in arrangements for training made under section 2 of the Employment and Training Act 1973 or section 2 of the Enterprise and

New Towns (Scotland) Act 1990 or attending a course at an employment rehabilitation centre established under section 2 of the 1973 Act—

(a) any travelling expenses reimbursed to the claimant;

(b) any living away from home allowance under section 2(2)(d) of the 1973 Act or section 2(4)(c) of the 1990 Act;

(c) any training premium,

but this paragraph, except insofar as it relates to a payment under sub-paragraph (a), (b) or (c), does not apply to any part of any allowance under section 2(2)(d) of the 1973 Act or section 2(4)(c) of the 1990 Act.

[[10]**11A.** Any Jobmatch Allowance payable pursuant to arrangements made under section 2(1) of the Employment and Training Act 1973 where the payments will cease by the date on which the period under section 129(6) of the Contributions and Benefits Act 1922 (period of award) is to begin.]

12.—(1) Except where sub-paragraph (2) applies and subject to sub-paragraph (3) and paragraphs 29 and 33, [[13]£20] of any charitable payment or of any voluntary payment made or due to be made at regular intervals.

(2) Subject to sub-paragraph (3) and paragraph 33, any charitable payment or voluntary payment made or due to be made at regular intervals which is intended and used for an item other than food, ordinary clothing or footwear, household fuel, or housing costs of any member of the family, or is used for any personal community [[2] charge,] collective community charge contribution [[2]or council tax] for which any member of the family is liable.

(3) Sub-paragraphs (1) and (2) shall not apply to a payment which is made or due to be made by—

(a) a former partner of the claimant, or former partner of any member of the claimant's family; or

(b) the parent of a child or young person where that child or young person is a member of the claimant's family.

(4) For the purposes of sub-paragraph (1) where a number of charitable or voluntary payments fall to be taken into account they shall be treated as though they were one such payment.

(5) For the purposes of sub-paragraph (2) the expression ''ordinary clothing or footwear'' means clothing or footwear for normal daily use, but does not include school uniforms, or clothing or footwear used solely for sporting activities.

13.—(1) Where the claimant or his partner is treated as responsible for a child or young person by virtue of regulation 9 (circumstances in which a person is to be treated as responsible or not responsible for another), £15 of any payment of maintenance, whether under a court order or not, which is made or due to be made by—

(a) the claimant's former partner, or the claimant's partner's former partner; or

(b) the parent of a child or young person where that child or young person is a member of the claimant's family except where that parent is the claimant or the claimant's partner.

(2) For the purposes of sub-paragraph (1) where more than one maintenance payment falls to be taken into account in any week, all such payments shall be aggregated and treated as if they were a single payment.

[[11]**14.**—Subject to paragraph 29, £10 of any of the following, namely—

(a) a war disablement pension (except insofar as such a pension falls to be disregarded under paragraph [[13] 6 or 7];

(b) a war widow's pension;

(c) a pension payable to a person as a widow under the Naval, Military and Air Forces, etc., (Disablement and Death) Service Pensions Order 1983 insofar as that Order is made under the Naval and Marine Pay and Pensions Act 1865 [[12] or the Pensions and Yeomanry Pay Act 1884], or is made only under section 12(1) of the Social Security (Miscellaneous Provisions) Act 1977 and any power of Her Majesty otherwise than under an enactment to make provision about pensions for or in respect of persons who have been disabled or have died in consequence of service as members of the armed forces of the Crown;

(d) a payment made to compensate for the non-payment of such a pension as is mentioned in any of the preceding sub-paragraphs;

(e) a pension paid by the government of a country outside Great Britain which is analogous to any of the pensions mentioned in sub-paragraphs (a) to (c) above;

(f) a pension paid to victims of National Socialist persecution under any special provision made by the law of the Federal Republic of Germany, or any part of it, or of the Republic of Austria.]

15. Any child benefit under Part I of the Child Benefit Act 1975.

16.—(1) Any income derived from capital to which the claimant is, or is treated under regulation 39 (capital jointly held) as, beneficially entitled but, subject to sub-paragraph (2), not income derived from capital disregarded under paragraphs 1, 2, 4, 6, 13 or 26 to 30 of Schedule 4.

(2) Income derived from capital disregarded under paragraphs 2, 4 or 26 to 30 of Schedule 4 but [[3]only to the extent of—

(a) any mortgage repayments made in respect of the dwelling or premises in the period during which that income accrued; or

(b) any council tax or water charges which the claimant is liable to pay in respect of the dwelling or premises and which are paid in the period during which that income accrued.]

17. Where a person receives income under an annuity purchased with a loan which satisfies the following conditions—

(a) that the loan was made as part of a scheme under which not less than 90 per cent. of the proceeds of the loan were applied to the purchase by the person to whom it was made of an annuity ending with his life or with the life of the survivor of two or more persons (in this paragraph referred to as "the annuitants") who include the person to whom the loan was made;

(b) that the interest on the loan is payable by the person to whom it was made or by one of the annuitants;

(c) that at the time the loan was made the person to whom it was made or each of the annuitants had attained the age of 65;

(d) that the loan was secured on a dwelling in Great Britain and the person to whom the loan was made or one of the annuitants owns an estate or interest in that dwelling; and

(e) that the person to whom the loan was made or one of the annuitants occupies the dwelling on which it was secured as his home at the time the interest is paid,

the amount, calculated on a weekly basis equal to—

[[8](i) where, or insofar as, section 369 of the Income and Corporation Taxes Act 1988 (mortgage interest payable under deduction of tax) applies to the payments of interest on the loan, the interest which is payable after deduction of a sum equal to income tax on such payments at the applicable percentage of income tax within the meaning of section 369(1A) of that Act;]

(ii) in any other case the interest which is payable on the loan without deduction of such a sum.

[[9]**18.** Any payment made to the claimant by a person who normally resides with the claimant, which is a contribution towards that person's living and accommodation costs, except where that person is residing with the claimant in circumstances to which paragraph 19 or 38 or regulation 24(2) (earnings of self-employed earners) refers.]

[[7]**19.** Where the claimant occupies a dwelling as his home and the dwelling is also occupied by [[9]another person], and there is a contractual liability to make payments to the claimant in respect of the occupation of the dwelling by that person or a member of his family—

(a) £4 of the aggregate of any payments made in respect of any one week in respect of the occupation of the dwelling by that person or a member of his family, or by that person and a member of his family; and

(b) a further [14£9.25], where the aggregate of any such payments is inclusive of an amount for heating.]

20. Any income in kind.

21. Any income which is payable in a country outside the United Kingdom where there is a prohibition against the transfer to the United Kingdom of that income.

22.—(1) Any payment made to the claimant in respect of a child or young person who is a member of his family—

(a) in accordance with regulations made by the Secretary of State under section 57A of the Adoption Act 1976, or as the case may be, section 51 of the Adoption (Scotland) Act 1978 (schemes for payments of allowances to adopters);

(b) which is a payment made by a local authority in pursuance of paragraph 15(1) of Schedule 1 to the Children Act 1989 (local authority contribution to child's maintenance),

to the extent specified in sub-paragraph (2).

(2) In the case of a child or young person—

(a) to whom regulation 30 applies (capital in excess of £3,000), the whole payment;

(b) to whom that regulation does not apply, so much of the weekly amount of the payment as exceeds the allowance in respect of that child or young person under Schedule 5.

23. Any payment made by a local authority to the claimant with whom a person is accommodated and maintained by virtue of arrangements made under section 23(2)(a) of the Children Act 1989 or, as the case may be, section 21 of the Social Work (Scotland) Act 1968 or by a voluntary organisation under section 59(1)(a) of the Children Act 1989 or by a care authority under regulation 9 of the Boarding Out and Fostering of Children (Scotland) Regulations 1985 (provision of accommodation and maintenance for children by local authorities and voluntary organisations).

24. Any payment made by a health authority, local authority or voluntary organisation to the claimant in respect of a person who is not normally a member of the claimant's household but is temporarily in his care.

25. Any payment made by a local authority under section 17 or 24 of the Children Act 1989 or, as the case may be, section 12, 24 or 26 of the Social Work (Scotland) Act 1968 (provision of services for children and their families and advice and assistance to certain children).

26. Any payment of income which under regulation 34 (income treated as capital) is to be treated as capital.

27. Any statutory maternity pay under Part V of the Act or maternity allowance under section 22 of the Social Security Act.

28. Any payment under paragraph 2 of Schedule 6 to the Act (pensioners' Christmas bonus).

29. The total of a claimant's income or, if he is a member of a family, the family's income and the income of any person which he is treated as possessing under regulation 12(2) (calculation of income and capital of members of claimant's family and of a polygamous marriage) to be disregarded under regulation 43(2)(b) (calculation of covenant income where a contribution is assessed), regulation 44(1)(c) (covenant income where no grant income or no contribution is assessed), regulation 47(2) (treatment of student loans) and paragraphs 12(1) and 14, shall in no case exceed [13£20] per week.

30. Where a payment of income is made in a currency other than sterling, any banking charge or commission payable in converting that payment into sterling.

31. Any statutory maternity pay under Part VI of the Social Security (Northern Ireland) Order 1986 or maternity allowance under section 22 of the Social Security (Northern Ireland) Act 1975.

32. Any payment in respect of expenses to which regulation 21(2) (earnings of employed earners) applies.

33.—(1) Any payment made under the Macfarlane Trust, the Macfarlane (Special Payments) Trust, the Macfarlane (Special Payments) (No. 2) Trust ("the Trusts"), [[1]the Fund] [[5], the Eileen Trust] or [[4] the Independent Living Funds].

(2) Any payment by or on behalf of a person who suffered or is suffering from haemophilia [[1]or who was or is a qualifying person], or by or on behalf of his partner or former partner from whom he is not, or, where either that person or his former partner has died, was not, estranged or divorced, which derives from a payment under any of the Trusts to which sub-paragraph (1) refers and which is made to or for the benefit of—

(a) that person or that person's partner or former partner to whom this sub-paragraph refers;

(b) any child who is a member of that person's family or who was such a member and who is a member of the claimant's family; or

(c) any young person who is a member of that person's family or who was such a member and who is a member of the claimant's family.

(3) Any payment by a person who is suffering from haemophilia [[1]or who is a qualifying person], which derives from a payment under any of the Trusts to which sub-paragraph (1) refers, where—

(a) that person has no partner or former partner from whom he is not estranged or divorced, nor any child or young person who is or had been a member of that person's family; and

(b) the payment is made either—

(i) to that person's parent or step-parent, or

(ii) where that person at the date of the payment is a child, or young person or a student who has not completed his full-time education and has no parent or step-parent, to his guardian,

but only for a period from the date of the payment until the end of two years from that person's death.

(4) Any payment out of the estate of a person who suffered from haemophilia [[1]or who was a qualifying person], which derives from a payment under any of the Trusts to which sub-paragraph (1) refers, where—

(a) that person at the date of his death (the relevant date) had no partner or former partner from whom he was not estranged or divorced, nor any child or young person who was or had been a member of his family; and

(b) the payment is made either—

(i) to that person's parent or step-parent, or

(ii) where that person at the relevant date was a child, a young person or a student who had not completed his full-time education and had no parent or step-parent, to his guardian,

but only for a period of two years from the relevant date.

(5) In the case of a person to whom or for whose benefit a payment under sub-paragraph (1), (2), (3) or (4) is made, any income which derives from any payment of income or capital made under or deriving from any of the Trusts.

[[1](6) For the purposes of sub-paragraphs (2) to (5), any reference to the Trusts shall be construed as including a reference to the Fund.] [[5] and the Eileen Trust]

34. Any payment made by the Secretary of State to compensate for the loss (in whole or in part) of entitlement to housing benefit.

35. Any payment made by the Secretary of State to compensate a person who was entitled to supplementary benefit in respect of a period ending immediately before 11th April 1988 but who did not become entitled to income support in respect of a period beginning with that day.

36. Any payment made by the Secretary of State to compensate for the loss of housing benefit supplement under regulation 19 of the Supplementary Benefit (Requirements) Regulations 1983.

37. Any payment made to a juror or witness in respect of attendance at court other than compensation for loss of earnings or for the loss of a benefit payable under the benefit Acts.

[7**38.** Where the claimant occupies a dwelling as his home and he provides in that dwelling board and lodging accommodation, an amount, in respect of each person for whom such accommodation is provided for the whole or any part of a week, equal to—

(a) where the aggregate of any payments made in respect of any one week in respect of such accommodation provided to such person does not exceed £20.00, 100 per cent. of such payments; or

(b) where the aggregate of any such payments exceeds £20.00, £20.00 and 50 per cent. of the excess over £20.00.]

39. Any community charge benefit.

40. Any payment in consequence of a reduction of a personal community charge pursuant to regulations under section 13A of the Local Government Finance Act 1988 or section 9A of the Abolition of Domestic Rates Etc (Scotland) Act 1987 (reduction of liability for personal community charge) [2or reduction of council tax under section 13 or, as the case may be, section 80 of the Local Government Finance Act 1992 (reduction of liability for council tax)].

41. Any special war widows payment made under—

(a) the Naval and Marine Pay and Pensions (Special War Widows Payment) Order 1990 made under section 3 of the Naval and Marine Pay and Pensions Act 1865;

(b) the Royal Warrant dated 19th February 1990 amending the Schedule to the Army Pensions Warrant 1977;

(c) the Queen's Order dated 26th February 1990 made under section 2 of the Air Force (Constitution) Act 1917;

(d) the Home Guard War Widows Special Payments Regulations 1990 made under section 151 of the Reserve Forces Act 1980;

(e) the Orders dated 19th February 1990 amending Orders made on 12th December 1980 concerning the Ulster Defence Regiment made in each case under section 140 of the Reserve Forces Act 1980;

and any analogous payment by the Secretary of State for Defence to any person who is not a person entitled under the provisions mentioned in sub-paragraphs (a) to (e) of this paragraph.

42.—(1) Any payment or repayment made—

(a) as respects England and Wales, under regulation 3, 5 or 8 of the National Health Service (Travelling Expenses and Remission of Charges) Regulations 1988 (travelling expenses and health service supplies);

(b) as respects Scotland, under regulation 3, 5 or 8 of the National Health Service (Travelling Expenses and Remission of Charges) (Scotland) Regulations 1988 (travelling expenses and health service supplies).

(2) Any payment or repayment made by the Secretary of State for Health, the Secretary of State for Scotland or the Secretary of State for Wales which is analogous to a payment or repayment mentioned in sub-paragraph (1).

43. Any payment made under regulation 9 to 11 or 13 of the Welfare Food Regulations 1988 (payments made in place of milk tokens or the supply of vitamins).

44. Any payment made either by the Secretary of State for the Home Department or by the Secretary of State for Scotland under a scheme established to assist relatives and other persons to visit persons in custody.

45. Any payment made, whether by the Secretary of State or any other person, under the Disabled Persons Employment Act 1944 or in accordance with arrangements made under section 2 of the Employment and Training Act 1973 to assist disabled persons to obtain or retain employment despite their disability.

46. Any family credit.

[3**47.** Any council tax benefit.

48. Any guardian's allowance.]

[7**49.** Where the claimant is in receipt of any benefit under Parts II, III or V of the Contributions and Benefits Act [10 or pension under the Naval, Military and Air Forces Etc. (Disablement and Death) Service Pensions Order 1983], any increase in the rate of that benefit arising under Part IV (increases for dependants) or section 106(a) (unemployability supplement) of that Act [[10]or the rate of that pension under that order] where the dependant in respect of whom the increase is paid is not a member of the claimant's family.]

[[8]**50.** Any supplementary pension under article 29(1A) of the Naval, Military and Air Forces etc. (Disablement and Death) Service Pensions Order 1983 (pensions to widows).

51. In the case of a pension awarded at the supplementary rate under article 27(3) of the Personal Injuries (Civilians) Scheme 1983 (pensions to widows), the sum specified in paragraph 1(c) of Schedule 4 to that Scheme.

52.—(1) Any payment which is—

(a) made under any of the Dispensing Instruments to a widow of a person—

    (i) whose death was attributable to service in a capacity analogous to service as a member of the armed forces of the Crown; and

    (ii) whose service in such capacity terminated before 31st March 1973; and

(b) equal to the amount specified in article 29(1A) of the Naval, Military and Air Forces etc. (Disablement and Death) Service Pensions Order 1983 (pensions to widows).

(2) In this paragraph "the Dispensing Instruments" means the Order in Council of 19th December 1881, the Royal Warrant of 27th October 1884 and the Order by His Majesty of 14th January 1922 (exceptional grants of pay, non-effective pay and allowances).]

[[9]**53.** Any payment made by the Secretary of State to compensate for a reduction in a maintenance assessment made under the Child Support Act 1991.]

[[16]**54.** Any payment made by the Secretary of State under the Earnings Top-up Scheme.]

[[17]**55.** Any payment made under the Community Care (Direct Payments) Act 1996 or under section 12B of the Social Work (Scotland) Act 1968.

56. (1) Any Career Development Loan paid to the Claimant pursuant to section 2 of the Employment and Training Act 1973 except to the extent that the loan has been applied for and paid in respect of living expenses for the period of education and training supported by that loan and those expenses relate to any one or more of the items specified in sub-paragraph (2).

(2) The itmes specified for the purposes of sub-paragraph (1) are food, ordinary clothing or footwear, household fuel or housing costs of any member of the family or any personal community charge, collective community charge contribution or any council tax for which any member of the family is liable.

(3) For the purposes of this paragraph, "ordinary clothing and footwear" means clothing or footwear for normal daily use, but does not include school uniforms, or clothing and footwear used solely for sporting activities.]

AMENDMENTS

1. Income-related Benefits Schemes and Social Security (Recoupment) Amendment Regulations 1992 (S.I. 1992 No. 1101), reg. 3(6) (May 7, 1992).

2. Income-related Benefits Schemes (Miscellaneous Amendments) Regulations 1993 (S.I. 1993 No. 315), Sched., para. 17 (April 1, 1993).

3. Income-related Benefits Schemes (Miscellaneous Amendments) Regulations 1993 (S.I. 1993 No. 315), reg. 21 (April 13, 1993).

4. Social Security Benefits (Miscellaneous Amendments) (No. 2) Regulations 1993 (S.I. 1993 No. 963), reg. 6 (April 22, 1993).

5. Income-related Benefits Schemes and Social Security (Recoupment) Amendment Regulations 1993 (S.I. 1993 No. 1249), reg. 5 (May 14, 1993).

6. Income-related Benefits Schemes (Miscellaneous Amendments) (No. 4) Regulations 1993 (S.I. 1993 No. 2119), reg. 45 (October 5, 1993 or later expiry of award).

7. Income-related Benefits Schemes (Miscellaneous Amendments) Regulations 1994 (S.I. 1994 No. 527), reg. 28 (April 12, 1994 or later expiry of award).

8. Income-related Benefits Schemes (Miscellaneous Amendment) (No. 5) Regulations 1994 (S.I. 1994 No. 2139), reg. 8 (October 4, 1994 or later expiry of award).

9. Income-related Benefits Schemes (Miscellaneous Amendments) Regulations 1995 (S.I. 1995 No. 516), reg. 8 (April 11, 1995 or later expiry of award).

10. Income-related Benefits Schemes and Social Security (Claims and Payments) (Miscellaneous Amendments) Regulations 1995 (S.I. 1995 No. 2303), reg. 3(8) (October 3, 1995).

11. Income-related Benefits Schemes Amendment (No. 2) Regulations 1995 (S.I. 1995 No. 2792), regulation 3 (October 28, 1995).

12. Income-related Benefits Schemes (Widows', etc., Pensions Disregards) Amendment Regulations 1995 (S.I. 1995 No. 3282), regulation 3 (December 20, 1995)

13. Income-related Benefits Schemes (Miscellaneous Amendments) Regulations 1996 (S.I. 1996 No. 462), reg. 8 (April 9, 1996 or later expiry of award).

14. Social Security Benefits Up-rating Order 1996 (S.I. 1996 No. 599), art. 17(d) (April 9, 1996 or later expiry of award).

15. Social Security and Child Support (Jobseeker's Allowance) (Consequential Amendments) Regulations 1996 (S.I. 1996 No. 1345), reg. 7(6) (October 7, 1996).

16. Income-related Benefits Schemes and Social Fund (Miscellaneous Amendments) Regulations 1996 (S.I. 1996 No. 1944), reg. 13 and para. 5 of Sched. (October 7, 1996).

17. Income-related Benefits and Jobseeker's Allowance (Miscellaneous Amendments) Regulations 1997 (S.I. 1997 No. 65), reg. 2(5) and (6) (April 8, 1997 or later expiry of award).

18. Income-related Benefits and Jobseeker's Allowance (Amendment) (No. 2) Regulations 1997 (S.I. 1997 No. 2197), reg. 7(7) (October 7, 1997 or later expiry of award).

SCHEDULE 4 **Regulation 32(2)**

CAPITAL TO BE DISREGARDED

1. The dwelling, together with any garage, garden and outbuildings, normally occupied by the claimant as his home including any premises not so occupied which it is impracticable or unreasonable to sell separately, in particular, in Scotland, any croft land on which the dwelling is situated; but, notwithstanding regulation 12 (calculation of income and capital of members of claimant's family and of a polygamous marriage), only one dwelling shall be disregarded under this paragraph.

2. Any premises acquired for occupation by the claimant which he intends to occupy as his home within 26 weeks of the date of acquisition or such longer period as is reasonable in the circumstances to enable the claimant to obtain possession and commence occupation of the premises.

3. Any sum directly attributable to the proceeds of sale of any premises formerly occupied by the claimant as his home which is to be used for the purchase of other premises intended for such occupation within 26 weeks of the date of sale or such longer period as is reasonable in the circumstances to enable the claimant to complete the purchase.

4. Any premises occupied in whole or in part by a partner or relative (that is to say any close relative, grandparent, grandchild, uncle, aunt, nephew or niece) of any member of the family as his home, where that person is aged 60 or over or has been incapacitated for a continuous period of at least 13 weeks immediately preceding the date of the claim.

[9**5.** Any future interest in property of any kind, other than land or premises in respect of which the claimant has granted a subsisting lease or tenancy including sub-leases or sub-tenancies.]

6.—(1) The assets of any business owned in whole or in part by the claimant and for the purposes of which he is engaged as a self-employed earner or, if he has ceased to be so engaged, for such period as may be reasonable in the circumstances to allow for disposal of any such asset.

(2) The assets of any business owned in whole or in part by the claimant where—

(a) he has ceased to be engaged as a self-employed earner in that business by reason of some disease or bodily or mental disablement; and

(b) he intends to become re-engaged as a self-employed earner in that business as soon as he recovers or is able to be re-engaged in that business,

for a period of 26 weeks from the date on which the claimant last ceased to be engaged in that business, or, if it is unreasonable to expect him to become re-engaged in that business within that period, for such longer period as is reasonable in the circumstances to enable him to become so re-engaged.

7. Any sum attributable to the proceeds of sale of any asset of such a business which is re-invested or to be re-invested in the business within 13 weeks of the date of sale or such longer period as may be reasonable to allow for the re-investment.

8. Any arrears of, or any concessionary payment made to compensate for arrears due to non-payment of—

(a) any payment specified in paragraphs 4, 6 or 7 of Schedule 3;

(b) an income-related benefit [[11] or income-based jobseeker's allowance] or supplementary benefit under the Supplementary Benefits Act 1976, family income supplement under the Family Income Supplements Act 1970 or housing benefit under Part II of the Social Security and Housing Benefits Act 1982 [[12] (c) any earnings top-up]

but only for a period of 52 weeks from the date of the receipt of the arrears or of the concessionary payment.

9. Any sum—

(a) paid to the claimant in consequence of damage to, or loss of, the home or any personal possession and intended for its repair or replacement; or

(b) acquired by the claimant (whether as a loan or otherwise) on the express condition that it is to be used for effecting essential repairs or improvements to the home,

which is to be used for the intended purpose, for a period of 26 weeks from the date on which it was so paid or acquired or such longer period as is reasonable in the circumstances to enable the claimant to effect the repairs, replacement or improvements.

10. Any sum—

(a) deposited with a housing association as defined in section 1(1) of the Housing Associations Act 1985 or section 338(1) of the Housing (Scotland) Act 1987 as a condition of occupying the home;

(b) which was so deposited and which is to be used for the purchase of another home, for the period of 26 weeks or such longer period as is reasonable in the circumstances to complete the purchase.

11. Any personal possessions except those which have been acquired by the claimant with the intention of reducing his capital in order to secure entitlement to disability working allowance or to increase the amount of that benefit.

12. The value of the right to receive any income under an annuity and the surrender value (if any) of such an annuity.

13. Where the funds of a trust are derived from a payment made in consequence of any personal injury to the claimant, the value of the trust fund and the value of the right to receive any payment under that trust.

14. The value of the right to receive any income under a life interest or from a liferent.

15. The value of the right to receive any income which is disregarded under paragraph 1 of Schedule 2 or 21 of Schedule 3.

16. The surrender value of any policy of life insurance.

17. Where any payment of capital falls to be made by instalments, the value of the right to receive any outstanding instalments.

18. Any payment made by a local authority under [[2]section 17 or 24] of the Children Act 1989 or, as the case may be, section 12, 24 or 26 of the Social Work (Scotland) Act 1968 (provision of services for children and their families and advice and assistance for certain children).

19. Any social fund payment under Part III of the Act.

20. Any refund of tax which falls to be deducted under section 26 of the Finance Act 1982 (deductions of tax from certain loan interest) on a payment of relevant loan interest for the purpose of acquiring an interest in the home or carrying out repairs or improvements to the home.

21. Any capital which by virtue of regulations 28 (capital treated as income) [[6]30(1) (modifications in respect of children and young persons)] or 47 (treatment of student loans) is to be treated as income.

22. Where a payment of capital is made in currency other than sterling, any banking charge or commission payable in converting that payment to sterling.

23.—(1) Any payment made under the Macfarlane Trust, the Macfarlane (Special Payments) Trust, the Macfarlane (Special Payments) (No. 2) Trust ("the Trusts") [[1], the Fund] [[5], the Eileen Trust] or [[4] the Independent Living Funds].

(2) Any payment by or on behalf of a person who suffered or is suffering from haemophilia [[1]or who was or is a qualifying person], or by or on behalf of his partner or former partner from whom he is not or, where either that person or his former partner has died, was not estranged or divorced, which derives from a payment under any of the Trusts to which sub-paragraph (1) refers and which is made to or for the benefit of—

(a) that person or that person's partner or former partner to whom this sub-paragraph refers;

(b) any child who is a member of that person's family or who was such a member and who is a member of the claimant's family; or

(c) any young person who is a member of that person's family or who was such a member and who is a member of the claimant's family.

(3) Any payment by a person who is suffering from haemophilia, [[1]or who is a qualifying person], which derives from a payment under any of the Trusts to which sub-paragraph (1) refers, where—

(a) that person has no partner or former partner from whom he is not estranged or divorced, nor any child or young person who is or had been a member of that person's family; and

(b) the payment is made either—

(i) to that person's parent or step-parent; or

(ii) where that person at the date of the payment is a child, a young person or a student who has not completed his full-time education and has no parent or step-parent, to his guardian,

but only for a period from the date of the payment until the end of two years from that person's death.

(4) Any payment out of the estate of a person who suffered from haemophilia [[1]or who was a qualifying person], which derives from a payment under any of the Trusts to which sub-paragraph (1) refers, where—

(a) that person at the date of his death (the relevant date) had no partner or former partner from whom he was not estranged or divorced, nor any child or young person who was or had been a member of his family; and

(b) the payment is made either—

(i) to that person's parent or step-parent; or

(ii) where that person at the relevant date was a child, a young person or a student who had not completed his full-time education and had no parent or step-parent, to his guardian,

but only for a period of two years from the relevant date.

(5) In the case of a person to whom or for whose benefit a payment under sub-paragraph (1), (2), (3) or (4) is made, any capital resource which derives from any payment of income or capital made under or deriving from any of the Trusts.

[[1](6) For the purposes of sub-paragraphs (2) to (5), any reference to the Trusts shall be construed as including a reference to the Fund [[5] and the Eileen Trust].]

24. The value of the right to receive an occupational or personal pension.

[[9]**24A.** The value of any funds held under a personal pension scheme or retirement annuity contract.]

25. The value of the right to receive any rent, [9 except where the claimant has a reversionary interest in the property in respect of which rent is due].

26.—(1) Where a claimant has ceased to occupy what was formerly the dwelling occupied as the home following his estrangement or divorce from his former partner, that dwelling for a period of 26 weeks from the date on which he ceased to occupy that dwelling.

(2) In this paragraph "dwelling" includes any garage, garden and outbuildings which were formerly occupied by the claimant as his home and any premises not so occupied which it is impracticable or unreasonable to sell separately, in particular, in Scotland, any croft land on which the dwelling is situated.

27. Any premises where the claimant is taking reasonable steps to dispose of those premises, for a period of 26 weeks from the date on which he first took such steps, or such longer period as is reasonable in the circumstances to enable him to dispose of those premises.

28. Any premises which the claimant intends to occupy as his home, and in respect of which he is taking steps to obtain possession and has sought legal advice, or has commenced legal proceedings, with a view to obtaining possession, for a period of 26 weeks from the date on which he first sought such advice or first commenced such proceedings whichever is the earlier, or such longer period as is reasonable in the circumstances to enable him to obtain possession and commence occupation of those premises.

29. Any premises which the claimant intends to occupy as his home to which essential repairs or alterations are required in order to render them fit for such occupation, for a period of 26 weeks from the date on which the claimant first takes steps to effect those repairs or alterations, or such longer period as is reasonable in the circumstances to enable those repairs or alterations to be carried out and the claimant to commence occupation of the premises.

30. Any premises occupied in whole or in part by the former partner of a claimant as his home; but this provision shall not apply where the former partner is a person from whom the claimant is estranged or divorced.

31. Any payment in kind made by a charity or under the Macfarlane (Special Payments) Trust [1, the Macfarlane (Special Payments) (No. 2) Trust or [4the Fund or the Independent Living (1993) Fund]].

32. [6 £200 of any payment or, if the payment is less than £200, the whole of any payment] made under section 2 of the Employment and Training Act 1973 (functions of the Secretary of State) or section 2 of the Enterprise and New Towns (Scotland) Act 1990 as a training bonus to a person participating in arrangements for training made under either of those sections but only for a period of 52 weeks from the date of the receipt of that payment.

33. Any payment made by the Secretary of State to compensate for the loss (in whole or in part) of entitlement to housing benefit.

34. Any payment made by the Secretary of State to compensate a person who was entitled to supplementary benefit in respect of a period ending immediately before 11th April 1988 but who did not become entitled to income support in respect of a period beginning with that day.

35. Any payment made by the Secretary of State to compensate for the loss of housing benefit supplement under regulation 19 of the Supplementary Benefit (Requirements) Regulations 1983.

36. Any payment made to a juror or witness in respect of attendance at court other than compensation for loss of earnings or for the loss of a benefit payable under the benefit Acts.

37. Any payment in consequence of a reduction of a personal community charge pursuant to regulations under section 13A of the Local Government Finance Act 1988 or section 9A of the Abolition of Domestic Rates Etc. (Scotland) Act 1987 (reduction of liability for personal community charge) [3 or reduction of council tax under section 13 or, as the case may be, section 80 of the Local Government Finance Act 1992 (reduction of liability for council tax),] but only for a period of 52 weeks from the date of receipt of the payment.

38. Any grant made to the claimant in accordance with a scheme made under section 129 of the Housing Act 1988 or section 66 of the Housing (Scotland) Act 1988 (schemes for payments to assist local housing authority and local authority tenants to obtain other accommodation) which is to be used—

(a) to purchase premises intended for occupation as his home; or

(b) to carry out repairs or alterations which are required to render premises fit for occupation as his home,

for a period of 26 weeks from the date on which he received such a grant or such longer period as is reasonable in the circumstances to enable the purchase, repairs or alterations to be completed and the claimant to commence occupation of those premises as his home.

39.—(1) Any payment or repayment made—

(a) as respects England and Wales, under regulation 3, 5 or 8 of the National Health Service (Travelling Expenses and Remission of Charges) Regulations 1988 (travelling expenses and health service supplies);

(b) as respects Scotland, under regulation 3, 5 or 8 of the National Health Service (Travelling Expenses and Remission of Charges) (Scotland) Regulations 1988 (travelling expenses and health service supplies);

but only for a period of 52 weeks from the date of receipt of the payment or repayment.

(2) Any payment or repayment made by the Secretary of State for Health, the Secretary of State for Scotland or the Secretary of State for Wales which is analogous to a payment or repayment mentioned in sub-paragraph (1); but only for a period of 52 weeks from the date of receipt of the payment or repayment.

40. Any payment made under regulations 9 to 11 or 13 of the Welfare Food Regulations 1988 (payments made in place of milk tokens or the supply of vitamins), but only for a period of 52 weeks from the date of receipt of the payment.

41. Any payment made either by the Secretary of State for the Home Department or by the Secretary of State for Scotland under a scheme established to assist relatives and other persons to visit persons in custody, but only for a period of 52 weeks from the date of receipt of the payment.

42. Any arrears of special war widows payment which is disregarded under paragraph 42 of Schedule 3 (sums to be disregarded in the calculation of income other than earnings) [[7]or of any amount which is disregarded under paragraph 50, 51 or 52 of that Schedule], but only for a period of 52 weeks from the date of receipt of the arrears.

43. Any payment made, whether by the Secretary of State or any other person, under the Disabled Persons Employment Act 1944 or in accordance with arrangements made under section 2 of the Employment and Training Act 1973 to assist disabled persons to obtain or retain employment despite their disability.

44. Any payment made by a local authority under section 3 of the Disabled Persons (Employment) Act 1958 to homeworkers assisted under the Blind Homeworkers' Scheme.

[[7]**45.** Any sum of capital administered on behalf of a person [[15]. . .] by the High Court under the provisions of Order 80 of the Rules of the Supreme Court, the County Court under Order 10 of the County Court Rules 1981, or the Court of Protection, where such sum derives from—

(a) an award of damages for a personal injury to that person; or

(b) compensation for the death of one or both parents [[15]where the person concerned is under the age of 18].

46. Any sum of capital administered on behalf of a person [[15]. . .] in accordance with an order made under Rule 43.15 of the Act of Sederunt (Rules of the Court of Session 1994) 1994 or under Rule 131 of the Act of Sederunt (Rules of the Court, consolidation and amendment) 1965, or under Rule 36.14 of the Ordinary Cause Rules 1993, or under Rule 128 of the Ordinary Cause Rules, where such sum derives from—

(a) an award of damages for a personal injury to that person; or

(b) compensation for the death of one or both parents [[15]where the person concerned is under the age of 18].

[[8]**47.** Any payment made by the Secretary of State to compensate for a reduction in a maintenance assessment made under the Child Support Act 1991, but only for a period of 52 weeks from the date of receipt of that payment.]

[[10]**48.** Any payment to the claimant as the holder of the Victoria Cross or George Cross.]

[[11]**49.** The amount of any back to work bonus payable by way of a jobseeker's allowance or income support in accordance with section 26 of the Jobseekers Act 1995, or a corresponding payment under article 28 of the Jobseekers (Northern Ireland) (Order 1995(d), but only for a period of 52 weeks from the date of receipt.]

[[13] [[14]**50**] The amount of any child maintenance bonus payable by way of a jobseeker's allowance or income support in accordance with section 10 of the Child Support Act 1995, or a corresponding payment under Article 4 of the Child Support (Northern Ireland) Order 1995, but only for a period of 52 weeks from the date of receipt.]

AMENDMENTS

1. Income-related Benefits Schemes and Social Security (Recoupment) Amendment Regulations 1992 (S.I. 1992 No. 1101), reg. 3(7) (May 7, 1992).

2. Income-related Benefits Schemes (Miscellaneous Amendments) (No. 3) Regulations 1992 (S.I. 1992 No. 2155), Sched. para. 19 (October 5, 1992).

3. Income-related Benefits Schemes (Miscellaneous Amendments) Regulations 1993 (S.I. 1993 No. 315), Sched. para. 18 (April 1, 1993).

4. Social Security Benefits (Miscellaneous Amendments) (No. 2) Regulations 1993 (S.I. 1993 No. 963), reg. 6 (April 22, 1993).

5. Income-related Benefits Schemes and Social Security (Recoupment) Amendment Regulations 1993 (S.I. 1993 No. 1249), reg. 5(5) (May 14, 1993).

6. Income-related Benefits Schemes (Miscellaneous Amendments) (No. 4) Regulations 1993 (S.I. 1993 No. 2119), reg. 46 (October 5, 1993 or later expiry of award).

7. Income-related Benefits Schemes (Miscellaneous Amendment) (No. 5) Regulations 1994 (S.I. 1994 No. 2139), reg. 10 (October 4, 1994 or later expiry of award).

8. Income-related Benefits Schemes (Miscellaneous Amendments) Regulations 1995 (S.I. 1995 No. 516), reg. 9 (April 11, 1995 or later expiry of award).

9. Income-related Benefits Schemes and Social Security (Claims and Payments) (Miscellaneous Amendments) Regulations 1995 (S.I. 1995 No. 2303), reg. 3(9) (October 3, 1995).

10. Income-related Benefits Schemes 1996 (S.I. 1996 No. 462), reg. 11(2) (April 9, 1996 or later expiry of award).

11. Social Security and Child Support (Jobseeker's Allowance) (Consequential Amendments) Regulations 1996 (S.I. 1996 No. 1345), reg. 7(7) (October 7, 1996).

12. Income-related Benefits Schemes and Social Fund (Miscellaneous Amendments) Regulations 1996 (S.I. 1996 No. 1944), reg. 13 and para, 7 of Sched. (October 7, 1996).

13. Social Security (Child Maintenance Bonus) Regulations 1996 (S.I. 1996 No. 3195), reg. 15 (April 7, 1996).

14. Social Security (Miscellaneous Amendments) Regulations 1997 (S.I. 1997 No. 454), reg. 8(9) (April 6, 1997).

15. Income-related Benefits and Jobseeker's Allowance (Amendment) (No. 2) Regulations 1997 (S.I. 1997 No. 2197), reg. 7(9) (October 7, 1997 or later expiry of award).

[SCHEDULE 5 **Regulation 51**

DETERMINATION OF APPROPRIATE MAXIMUM AMOUNT OF DISABILITY WORKING ALLOWANCE

(1) *Claimant, child or young person*	(2) *Amount of allowance*
1. Single claimant.	1. £49.55
2. Claimant who is a member of a married or unmarried couple, or is a lone parent.	2. £77.55
2A. In the case of a claimant to whom regulation 51(1)(bb) applies.	2A. £10.55
[3. Person in respect of the period—	3.
(a) beginning on that person's date of birth and ending on the day preceding the first Tuesday in September following that person's eleventh birthday;	(a) £12.05;
(b) beginning on the first Tuesday in September following that person's eleventh birthday and ending on the day preceding the first Tuesday in September following that person's sixteenth birthday.	(b) £19.95
4. Person in respect of the period beginning on the first Tuesday in September following that person's sixteenth birthday and ending on the day preceding the first Tuesday in September following that person's nineteenth birthday.]	[[3]4. £24.80
5. Child or young person to whom regulation 51(1A) applies (disabled child or young person).	5. £20.95

AMENDMENTS

1. Social Security Benefits Up-rating Order 1997 (S.I. 1997 No. 543), art. 17(D) and Sched. 3 (April 8, 1997).

2. Income-related Benefits and Jobseeker's Allowance (Personal Allowances for Children and Young Persons) (Amendment) Regulations 1996 (S.I. 1996 No. 2545), reg. 9 (October 7, 1997 or later expiry of award).

3. Family Credit and Disability Working Allowance (General) Amendment Regulations 1997 (S.I. 1997 No. 806), reg. 4 (October 7, 1997 or later expiry of award).

DEFINITIONS

For "child", "married couple" and "unmarried couple", see s. 137(1) of the Social Security Contributions and Benefits Act 1992. For "lone parent" and "young person", see reg. 2(1).

The Social Security (Attendance Allowance) Regulations 1991

(S.I. 1991 No. 2740)

ARRANGEMENT OF REGULATIONS

The Secretary of State for Social Security, in exercise of the powers conferred upon him by sections 35(1), (2)(b), (2A), (4A) and (6), 85(1)(b) and 166(2) and (3) of, and Schedule 20 to, the Social Security Act 1975 and of all other powers enabling him in that behalf, by this instrument, which contains regulations which relate to matters which, in accordance with section 140 of that Act, have been referred to the Attendance Allowance Board, hereby makes the following Regulations:

Citation, commencement and interpretation

1.—(1) These Regulations may be cited as the Social Security (Attendance Allowance) Regulations 1991 and shall come into force on 6th April 1992.

(2) In these Regulations—

"the Act" means the Social Security Act 1975;

"the NHS Act of 1977" means the National Health Service Act 1977;

"the NHS Act of 1978" means the National Health Service (Scotland) Act 1978;

"the NHS Act of 1990" means the National Health Service and Community Care Act 1990;

"terminally ill" shall be construed in accordance with section 35(2C) of the Act.

(3) Unless the context otherwise requires, any reference in these Regulations to a numbered regulation is a reference to the regulation bearing that number in these Regulations and any reference in a regulation to a numbered paragraph is a reference to the paragraph of that regulation bearing that number.

Conditions as to residence and presence in Great Britain

2.—(1) Subject to the following provisions of this regulation, the prescribed conditions for the purposes of section 35(1) of the Act as to residence and presence in Great Britain in relation to any person on any day shall be that—

(a) on that day—
(i) he is ordinarily resident in Great Britain, and
[[1](ia) Subject to paragraph (1A), his right to remain in Great Britain is not subject to any limitation or condition, and]
(ii) he is present in Great Britain, and
(iii) he has been present in Great Britain for a period of, or for periods amounting in the aggregate to, not less than 26 weeks in the 52 weeks immediately preceding that day; and
(b) where that day falls within a period in which that person—
(i) receives tax free emoluments, or
(ii) is the spouse of a person who receives tax free emoluments, that period is immediately preceded by a period of 4 years during which the person first mentioned in this sub-paragraph was present in Great Britain for not less than 156 weeks in aggregate.

[[1](1A) For the purposes of paragraph (1)(a)(ia), a person's right to reside or remain in Great Britain is not to be treated as if it were subject to a limitation or condition if—
(a) he is a person recorded by the Secretary of State as a refugee within the definition in Article 1 of the Convention relating to the Status of Refugees done at Geneva on 28th July 1951, as extended by Article 1(2) of the Protocol relating to the Status of Refugees done at New York on 31st January 1967;
(b) he is a person who has been granted exceptional leave outside the provsions of the immigration rules within the meaning of the Immigration Act 1971 to remain in the United Kingdom by the Secretary of State;
(c) he is a national, or a member of the family of a national, of a State contracting party to the Agreement on the European Economic Area signed at Oporto on 2nd May 1992 as adjusted by the Protocol signed at Brussels on 17th March 1993:
(d) he is a person who is—
(i) lawfully working in Great Britain and is a national of a State with which the Community has concluded an Agreement under article 238 of the Treaty establishing the European Community providing, in the field of social security, for the equal treatment of workers who are nationals of the signatory State and their families, or
(ii) a member of the family of, and living with, such a person; or
(e) he is a person in respect of whom there is an Order in Council under section 179 of the Social Security Administration Act 1992 giving effect to a reciprocal agreement which, for the purposes of attendance allowance, has the effect that periods of presence or residence in another country are to be treated as periods of presence or residence in Great Britain.]

(2) For the purposes of paragraph (1)(a)(ii) and (iii), notwithstanding that on any day a person is absent from Great Britain, he shall be treated as though he were present in Great Britain if his absence is by reason only of the fact that on that day—
(a) he is abroad in his capacity as—
(i) a serving member of the forces,
(ii) an airman or mariner within the meaning of regulations 81 and 86 respectively of the Social Security (Contributions) Regulations 1979,
and for the purpose of this provision, the expression "serving members of the forces" has the same meaning as in regulation 1(2) of the Regulations of 1979; or
(b) he is in employment prescribed for the purposes of section 132 of the Act in connection with continental shelf operations; or
(c) he is living with a person mentioned in sub-paragraph (a)(i) and is the

spouse, son, daughter, step-son, step-daughter, father, father-in-law, step-father, mother, mother-in-law or step-mother of that person; or

(d) his absence from Great Britain is, and when it began was, for a temporary purpose and has not lasted for a continuous period exceeding 26 weeks; or

(e) his absence from Great Britain is temporary and for the specific purpose of his being treated for incapacity, or a disabling condition, which commenced before he left Great Britain, and the Secretary of State has certified that it is consistent with the proper administration of the Act that, subject to the satisfaction of the foregoing condition in this sub-paragraph, he should be treated as though he were present in Great Britain.

(3) Where a person is terminally ill and makes a claim for attendance allowance expressly on the ground that he is such a person, paragraph (1) shall apply to him as if head (iii) of sub-paragraph (a) was omitted.

(4) In paragraph (1)(b), the expression "tax free emoluments" means emoluments which are exempt from tax under any of the provisions listed in paragraph (1) of regulation 9 of the Child Benefit (General) Regulations 1976.

AMENDMENT

1. Social Security (Persons From Abroad) Miscellaneous Amendments Regulations 1996 (S.I. 1996 No. 30), regulation 2 (February 5, 1996, subject to a saving under regulation 12(3)).

GENERAL NOTE

S.35(1) of the 1975 Act has now been replaced by s.64(1) of the Social Security Contributions and Benefits Act 1992.

Extension of qualifying period

3. The period prescribed for the purposes of section 35(2)(b) of the Act (claimant to satisfy one or both of the conditions in section 35(1) of the Act for 6 months immediately preceeding the date from which attendance allowance is to be awarded) shall be 2 years.

GENERAL NOTE

S.35(2)(b) of the 1975 Act has now been replaced by s.65(1)(b) of the Social Security Contributions and Benefits Act 1992.

Allowance payable before the date of claim in renewal cases

4. *Revoked by Social Security (Miscellaneous Amendments) (No. 2) Regulations 1997 (S.I. 1997 No. 793), reg. 19(b) with effect from September 1, 1997.*

GENERAL NOTE

This regulation had allowed a renewal claim made within six months of the date of termination of an earlier award to be backdated to that date.

Renal dialysis

5.—(1) Subject to paragraph (3), a person who suffers from renal failure and who is undergoing the treatment specified in paragraph (2) shall be deemed to satisfy the conditions—

(a) in section 35(1)(a) of the Act (severe physical and mental disability) if he undergoes renal dialysis by day;

(b) in section 35(1)(b) of the Act if he undergoes renal dialysis by night;
(c) in either paragraph (a) or paragraph (b) of section 35(1) of the Act, but not both, if he undergoes renal dialysis by day and by night.

(2) The treatment referred to in paragraph (1) is the undergoing of renal dialysis—
(a) two or more times a week; and
(b) which either—
(i) is of a type which normally requires the attendance of or supervision by another person during the period of dialysis, or
(ii) which, because of the particular circumstances of his case, in fact requires another person, during the period of dialysis, to attend in connection with the bodily functions of the person undergoing renal dialysis or to supervise that person in order that he avoids substantial danger to himself.

(3) Except as provided in paragraph (4), paragraph (1) does not apply to a person undergoing the treatment specified in paragraph (2) where the treatment—
(a) is provided under the NHS Act of 1977 or the NHS Act of 1978;
(b) is in a hospital or similar institution;
(c) is out-patient treatment; and
(d) takes placc with the assistance or supervision of any member of staff of the hospital or similar institution.

(4) Paragraph (3) does not apply for the purposes of determining whether a person is to be taken to satisfy either of the conditions specified in paragraph (1) during the period of 6 months referred to in section 35(2)(b) of the 1975 Act (qualifying period for attendance allowance).

General Note

Under this regulation, a person undergoing renal dialysis at least twice a week may be deemed to satisfy *either* the day *or* the night attendance condition, but not both. Some degree of attention or supervision must be required. This regulation is in slightly different terms from regs. 5B and 5C of the Social Security (Attendance Allowance) (No. 2) Regulations 1975 which governed entitlement before April 6, 1992.

Para. (1). The conditions previously to be found in s.35(1)(a) and (b) of the 1975 Act are now to be found in s.64(2) and (3) of the Social Security Contributions and Benefits Act 1992.

Para. (2)(b). The dialysis must be *either* of a type which *normally* requires the attendance of or supervision by another person (in which case the actual purpose of the attention or supervision is irrelevant) *or* the dialysis must *in the particular case* require the attention or supervision of the claimant (for the purpose specified in para. (2)(b)(ii)).

Para. (3). This excludes from the scope of the regulation claimants whose treatment satisfies all four conditions in sub-paras. (a)–(d). It is not entirely clear what assistance or supervision actually falls within sub-para. (d) but presumably it is the attention or supervision falling within para. (2)(b) so that only assistance and supervision *during the period of dialysis* is relevant and not any assistance at the beginning or end of the treatment. By virtue of para. (4), para. (3) does not apply in respect of the six-month qualifying period for attendance allowance. This means that a person previously excluded under para. (3) can qualify for attendance allowance under this reg. as soon as one of the excluding conditions of para. (3) ceases to be satisfied. S.35(2)(b) of the 1975 Act has been replaced by s.65(1)(b) of the Social Security Contributions and Benefits Act 1992.

Hospitalisation

6.—[[1](1) Subject to regulation 8, it shall be a condition for the receipt of an attendance allowance for any period in respect of any person that during that period he is not maintained free of charge while undergoing medical or other treatment as an in-patient—
(a) in a hospital or similar institution under the NHS Act of 1977, the NHS Act of 1978 or the NHS Act of 1990; or

(b) in a hospital or similar institution maintained or administered by the Defence Council.]

(2) For the purposes of [[1]paragraph (1)(a)], a person shall only be regarded as not being maintained free of charge in a hospital or similar institution for any period where his accommodation and services are provided under section 65 of the NHS Act of 1977 or section 58 of, or paragraph 14 of Schedule 7A to, the NHS Act of 1978 or paragraph 14 of Schedule 2 to the NHS Act of 1990.

(3)[[1]. . .].

Amendment

1. Social Security (Disability Living Allowance and Attendance Allowance) (Amendment) Regulation 1992 (S.I. 1992 No. 2869), reg. 2 (December 15, 1992).

General Note

By virtue of reg. 8, this regulation applies only after a person has been in hospital (or in accommodation to which reg. 7 applies) for 28 days although periods separated by intervals not exceeding 28 days may be linked.

If a person is receiving treatment as an in-patient in one of the hospitals or institutions specified in para. (1), he or she is deemed to be being maintained free of charge unless a private patient (in which case para. (2) will apply). Although the wording of this regulation is different from that considered in *R(S) 4/84*, the overall conclusion reached by the Commissioner appears to be relevant here. The claimant was able to attend college during the day but received treatment from the hospital at night. The Commissioner held that she was not receiving free in-patient treatment because "any period" and "period" must relate to a period of not less than one day.

Persons in certain accommodation other than hospitals

7.—(1) Except in the cases specified in [[1]paragraphs (2) and (3)] and subject to [[4]regulations 7A and 8], a person shall not be paid any amount in respect of an attendance allowance for any period where throughout that period he is a person for whom accommodation is provided—

(a) in pursuance of—
 (i) Part III of the National Assistance Act 1948 [[3]. . .], or
 (ii) Part IV of the Social Work (Scotland) Act 1968 or section 7 of the Mental Health (Scotland) Act 1984;

(b) in circumstances where the cost of accommodation is borne wholly or partly out of public or local funds in pursuance of those enactments or of any other enactment relating to persons under disability [[1]. . .]; or

(c) in circumstances where the cost of the accommodation may be borne wholly or partly out of public or local funds in pursuance of those enactments or of any other enactment relating to persons under disability [[2]. . .].

(2) [[3]. . .]

(3) Paragraph (1)(c) shall also not apply—

(a) where he is a person for whom accommodation is made available for his occupation in accordance with section 65 of the Housing Act 1985 [[5] or section 31 of the Housing (Scotland) Act 1987] (duties of local housing authorities to persons found to be homeless);

(b) where the person himself pays the whole cost, and always has paid the whole cost, of the [[3]accommodation [[4], and is a person to whom regulation 7A applies]];

(c) except in a case to which paragraph (4) applies, where the accommodation the person is living in is a private dwelling.

(4) [[3]Subject to paragraph (4A), this paragraph applies where—

(a) the cost of the accommodation the person previously occupied was borne in whole or in part out of public or local funds and where he was moved out of that accommodation at the instigation of the body which bore the cost into a residential care home; or

(b) the person is living in a residential care home and at least 4 other persons in that house are provided with board and personal care, excluding persons carrying on the home or employed there or their relatives,

and in this paragraph "residential care home" means an establishment in respect of which registration is required under [5Part IV of the Social Work (Scotland) Act 1968 or] Part I of the Registered Homes Act 1984 or would be so required but for section 1(4) of that Act.

[3(4A) Paragraph (4)(b) shall apply in the case of a person [4to whom regulation 7A does not apply] as if the words "and at least 4 other persons" to the end of sub-paragraph (b) were omitted.]

(a) the cost of the accommodation the person previously occupied was borne in whole or in part out of public or local funds and where he was moved out of that accommodation at the instigation of the body which bore the cost into a residential care home; or

(b) the person is living in a residential care home and at least 4 other persons in that house are provided with board and personal care, excluding persons carrying on the home or employed there or their relatives,

and in this paragraph "residential care home" means an establishment in respect of which registration is required under Part I of the Registered Homes Act 1984 or would be so required but for section 1(4) of that Act.

(5) In this regulation, references to the cost of the accommodation shall not include the cost of—

(a) domiciliary services provided in respect of a person in a private dwelling; or

(b) improvements made to, or furniture or equipment provided for, a private dwelling on account of the needs of a person under disability; or

(c) improvements made to, or furniture or equipment provided for, residential homes or other homes or premises in respect of which a grant or payment has been made out of public or local funds except where the grant or payment is of a regular or repeated nature; or

(d) social and recreational activities provided outside the accommodation in respect of which grants or payments are made out of public or local funds; or

(e) the purchase or running of a motor vehicle to be used in connection with the accommodation in respect of which grants or payments are made out of public or local funds.

AMENDMENTS

1. Social Security (Disability Living Allowance and Attendance Allowance) (Amendment) Regulations 1992 (S.I. 1992 No. 2869), reg. 3 (December 15, 1992).

2. Social Security Benefits (Amendments Consequential Upon the Introduction of Community Care) Regulations 1992 (S.I. 1992 No. 3147), reg. 8 (April 1, 1993 with saving).

3. Social Security Benefits (Miscellaneous Amendments) Regulations 1993 (S.I. 1993 No. 518), reg. 2(2) (April 1, 1993).

4. Social Security (Attendance Allowance and Disability Living Allowance) (Amendment) Regulations 1994 (S.I. 1994 No. 1779), reg. 2(2) (August 1, 1994).

5. Social Security (Attendance and Disability Living Allowances) Amendment Regulations 1995 (S.I. 1995 No. 2162), reg. 2 (September 14, 1995).

GENERAL NOTE

By virtue of reg. 8, this regulation applies only after a person has been in the relevant accommodation or in hospital for 28 days although periods separated by intervals not exceeding 28 days may be linked.

The difference between paras. (1)(b) and (1)(c) is that the former applies if the cost of the accommodation *is* being borne out of public funds and para. (1)(c) applies if the cost *may* be borne out of public funds. Note reg. 7A in cases where a claimant is terminally ill within the meaning of s.66(2) of the Social Security Contributions and Benefits Act 1992. In *R(A) 3/83*, the claimant was not entitled to attendance allowance under the precursor of para. (1)(c) even though the local authority was not making any contributions to the cost of the accommodation. It was enough that they could have done had they wished to do so. However, note the important exceptions to this rule provided for in para. (3).

[1Persons to whom regulations 7 and 8 apply with modifications

7A.—(1) This regulation applies where a person satisfies paragraph 1 or paragraph 2 of the Schedule to these Regulations.

(2) Where this regulation applies—

(a) regulation 7 shall have effect as if after paragraph (1) there were inserted the following paragraph—

"(1A) Paragraph (1)(b), in so far as it relates to enactments relating to persons under a disability not referred to in sub-paragraph (a), and paragraph (1)(c) shall not apply in the case of a person who is terminally ill where the Secretary of State has been informed of that fact—

(a) on a claim for an attendance allowance;

(b) on an application for review of an award of attendance allowance; or

(c) in writing in connection with an award of, or a claim for, or an application for a review of an award of, attendance allowance."; and

(b) regulation 8 shall have effect as if—

(i) in paragraph (1) for the words "subject to the following provisions of this regulation" there were substituted the words "subject to paragraph (3)"; and

(ii) paragraphs (4) to (7) were omitted.]

Amendment

1. Social Security (Attendance Allowance and Disability Living Allowance) (Amendment) Regulations 1994 (S.I. 1994 No. 1779), reg. 2(3) (August 1, 1994).

Exemption from regulations 6 and 7

8. [1(1) Regulation 6, or as the case may be, regulation 7, shall not, [2subject to the following provisions of this regulation], apply to a person in respect of the first 28 days of any period during which he—

(a) is undergoing medical or other treatment in a hospital or other institution in any of the circumstances mentioned in regulation 6; or

(b) would, but for this regulation, be prevented from receiving an attendance allowance by reason of regulation 7(1).]

(2) For the purposes of paragraph (1)—

(a) two or more distinct periods separated by an interval not exceeding 28 days, or by two or more such intervals, shall be treated as a continuous period equal in duration to the total of such distinct periods and ending on the last day of the later or last such period;

(b) any period or periods to which either regulation 6 or regulation 7 refers shall be taken into account and aggregated with any period to which the other of them refers.

(3) Where, on the day a person's entitlement to an attendance allowance commences, he is in accommodation in the circumstances mentioned in regulation 6 or regulation 7, paragraph (1) shall not apply to him for any period of

consecutive days, beginning with that day, on which he remains in that accommodation.

[[2](4) Regulation 6 or, as the case may be, regulation 7 shall not apply [[3]except in a case to which paragraph (7) applies] in the case of a person who is residing in a hospice and is terminally ill where the Secretary of State has been informed that he is terminally ill—

(a) on a claim for attendance allowance,
(b) on an application for a review of an award of attendance allowance, or
(c) in writing in connection with an award of, or a claim for, or an application for a review of an award of, attendance allowance.

(5) In paragraph (4) "hospice" means a hospital or other institution [[3]whose primary function is to provide palliative care for persons resident there who are suffering from a progressive disease in its final stages] other than—

(a) a health service hospital (within the meaning of section 128 of the NHS Act of 1977) in England or Wales;
(b) a health service hospital (within the meaning of section 108(1) of the NHS Act of 1978) in Scotland;
(c) a hospital maintained or administered by the Defence Council; or
(d) an institution similar to a hospital mentioned in any of the preceding sub-paragraphs of this paragraph.

(6) Regulation 7 shall not apply [[3]expect in a case to which paragraph (7) applies] in any particular case of any period during which—

(a) the person for whom the accommodation is provided—
  (i) is not entitled to income support [[4]or income-based jobseeker's allowance];
  (ii) is not entitled to housing benefit; or
  (iii) is not a member of a married or unmarried couple for whom an amount is included for income support [[4]or income-based jobseeker's allowance] purposes in the weekly applicable amount of the other member; and
(b) the whole of the cost of the accommodation is met—
  (i) out of his own resources, or partly out of his own resources and partly with assistance from another person or a charity;
  (ii) on his behalf by another person or a charity.]

(7)[[3] This paragraph applies in the case of a person who is residing in a home owned or managed, or owned and managed, by a local authority.]

AMENDMENTS

1. Social Security (Attendance Allowance) Amendment Regulations 1992 (S.I. 1992 No. 703), reg. 5 (April 6, 1992).
2. Social Security Benefits (Amendments Consequential Upon the Introduction of Community Care) Regulations 1992 (S.I. 1992 No. 3147), reg. 8 (April 1, 1993 with saving).
3. Social Security Benefits (Miscellaneous Amendments) Regulations 1993 (S.I. 1993 No. 518), reg. 2(3) (April 1, 1993).
4. Social Security and Child Support (Jobseeker's Allowance) (Consequential Amendments) Regulations 1996 (S.I. 1996 No. 1345), reg. 10 (October 7, 1996).

[[1]Adjustment of allowance where medical expenses are paid from public funds under war pensions instruments

8A.—(1) In this regulation—

"article 25B" means article 25B of the Personal Injuries (Civilians) Scheme 1983 (medical expenses) and includes that article as applied by article 48B of that Scheme; "article 26" means article 26 of the Naval, Military and Air Forces etc. (Disablement and Death) Service Pensions Order 1983 (medical expenses); and in this regulation and regulation 8B "relevant accommodation" means accommodation provided as a necessary ancillary to nursing care where the medical expenses involved are wholly borne by the Secretary of State pursuant to article 25B or article 26.

(2) This regulation applies where a person is provided with relevant accommodation.

(3) Subject to regulation 8B, where this regulation applies and there are payable in respect of a person both a payment under either article 25B or article 26 and an attendance allowance, the allowance shall be adjusted by deducting from it the amount of the payment under article 25B or article 26, as the case may be, and only the balance shall be payable.]

Amendment

1. Social Security (Attendance Allowance and Disability Living Allowance) (Amendment) Regulations 1994 (S.I. 1994 No. 1779), reg. 2(4) (August 1, 1994).

[[1]Exemption from regulation 8A

8B.—(1) Regulation 8A shall not, subject to the following provisions of this regulation, apply to a person in respect of the first 28 days of any period during which the amount of any attendance allowance would be liable to be adjusted by virtue of regulation 8A(3).

(2) For the purposes of paragraph (1) two or more distinct periods separated by an interval not exceeding 28 days, or by two or more such intervals, shall be treated as a continuous period equal in duration to the aggregate of such distinct periods and ending on the last day of the later or last such period.

(3) For the purposes of this paragraph a day is a relevant day in relation to a person if it fell not earlier than 28 days before the first day on which he was provided with relevant accommodation; and either—

(a) was a day when he was undergoing medical treatment in a hospital or similar institution in any of the circumstances mentioned in regulation 6; or

(b) was a day when he was, or would but for regulation 8 have been, prevented from receiving an attendance allowance by virtue of regulation 7(1);

and where there is in relation to a person a relevant day, paragraph (1) shall have effect as if for "28 days" there were substituted such lesser number of days as is produced by subtracting from 28 the number of relevant days in his case.]

Amendment

1. Social Security (Attendance Allowance and Disability Living Allowance) (Amendment) Regulations 1994 (S.I. 1994 No. 1779), reg. 2(4) (August 1, 1994).

[[1]Medical examination in prescribed circumstances

8C.—(1) The prescribed circumstances in which a person who is awarded attendance allowance shall be required to attend for, or submit himself to, a medical examination, are where the Secretary of State is undertaking an investigation under section 30(7A) of the Social Security Administration Act 1992.

(2) An examination under paragraph (1) shall be conducted by a medical practitioner who is—
(a) approved by the Secretary of State; or
(b) engaged by an organisation approved by the Secretary of State.]

AMENDMENT

1. Social Security (Attendance Allowance and Disability Living Allowance) (Miscellaneous Amendments) Regulations 1997 (S.I. 1997 No. 1839), reg. 2 (August 25, 1997).

GENERAL NOTE

See the note to reg. 5A of the Social Security (Disability Living Allowance) Regulations 1991 which is in the same terms.

[[1]Withholding of benefit in prescribed circumstances

8D.—(1) Subject to paragraph (2), where a person who is receiving attendance allowance is required by the Secretary of State to attend for, or submit to, a medical examination under regulation 8C and fails to comply with that requirement on more than one occasion, that allowance may be withheld, in whole or in part, from a date, not earlier than the second occasion, as the Secretary of State shall determine.

(2) Paragraph (1) shall not apply where—
(a) a person who is required to attend for, or submit to, a medical examination proves to the satisfaction of the Secretary of State that he has good cause for failing to comply with the requirement to attend for, or submit himself to, medical examination;
(b) a person who is required to attend for, or submit to, a medical examination produces such evidence as is acceptable to the Secretary of State in place of a medical examination; or
(c) the Secretary of State otherwise has available to him such evidence as is acceptable to him.

(3) For the purposes of paragraph (2)(a), the matters which are to be taken into account in determining whether a person has good cause shall include—
(a) whether he was outside Great Britain at the relevant time;
(b) his state of health at the relevant time; and
(c) the nature of any disability from which he suffers.]

AMENDMENT

1. Social Security (Attendance Allowance and Disability Living Allowance) (Miscellaneous Amendments) Regulations 1997 (S.I. 1997 No. 1839), reg. 2 (August 25, 1997).

GENERAL NOTE

See the note to reg. 5B of the Social Security (Disability Living Allowance) Regulations 1991 which is in the same terms.

[[1]Payment of withheld benefit

8E.—(1) Where the Secretary of State is satisfied that no question arises in connection with his investigation referred to in regulation 8C(1), payment of the amount withheld and the attendance allowance shall be made forthwith.

(2) Where a question arose in connection with an investigation referred to in regulation 8C(1) in respect of which—

(a) the Secretary of State made an application for the review of a person's entitlement to attendance allowance under section 30 of the Social Security Administration Act 1992(c); and

(b) an adjudication officer has made a determination;

payment of the attendance allowance shall be made in accordance with the adjudication officer's determination, on review, of the person's entitlement.

(3) Where paragraph (1) or (2) does not apply the attendance allowance is withheld under regulation 8D for a period of more than 3 months, the Secretary of State shall—

(a) make, with a view to review, an application to the adjudication officer on the ground that the person failed to attend for, or submit himself to, medical examination; and

(b) make such payments as are determined, on review, by the adjudication officer.]

AMENDMENT

1. Social Security (Attendance Allowance and Disability Living Allowance) (Miscellaneous Amendments) Regulations 1997 (S.I. 1997 No. 1839), reg. 2 (August 25, 1997).

GENERAL NOTE

See the note to reg. 5C of the Social Security (Disability Living Allowance) Regulations 1991 which is in the same terms.

9. *Omitted.*

[[1]SCHEDULE **Regulation 7A(1)**

PERSONS TO WHOM REGULATIONS 7 AND 8 APPLY WITH MODIFICATIONS

1. Subject to paragraph 3, this paragraph is satisfied in relation to a person if—

(a) on 31st March 1993, he was living in a home registered under the [[2] Social Work (Scotland) Act 1968 or the] Registered Homes Act 1984 as a residential care home or a nursing home; or

(b) on 31st March 1993, he was—

(i) entitled either to—

(aa) an attendance allowance, or

(bb) income support and his applicable amount was calculated in accordance with regulation 19 of the Income Support (General) Regulations 1987 (persons in residential care and nursing homes); and

(ii) living in a home which was not registered under the Registered Homes Act 1984 but which on 1st April 1993 was required to be registered under that Act as a residential care home by virtue of the amendments made to it by the Registered Homes (Amendment) Act 1991 (which extends registration to small homes); or

(c) he would have been living in a home such as is mentioned in either of the preceding sub-paragraphs on that date but for an absence which, including that day, does not exceed—

(i) except in a case to which head (ii) applies—

(aa) where the person was before his absence a temporary resident in the home, 4 weeks, or (bb) where the person was before his absence a permanent resident in the home, 13 weeks, or

(ii) where throughout the period of his absence he was receiving free in-patient treatment within the meaning of the Social Security (Hospital In-Patients) Regulations 1975, 52 weeks.

2. Subject to paragraph 3, this paragraph is satisfied in relation to a person if—

(a) on 31st March 1993 he was—

(i) entitled to—

(aa) an attendance allowance or the care component of a disability living allowance; or

(bb) income support and his applicable amount was calculated in accordance with regulation 19 of the Income Support (General) Regulations 1987 (persons in residential care and nursing homes); and

(ii) living in a home which was not registered under the Registered Homes Act 1984 and which would on 1st April 1993 have become registrable under that Act but for the provisions of section 1(4) of that Act as substituted by the Registered Homes (Amendment) Act 1991 (which provides that small homes need not be registered if all of the residents are, or are treated for the purposes of the Act as being, relatives of the proprietor); or

(b) he would have been living in such a home on 31st March 1993 but for an absence which, including that day, does not exceed—

(i) except in a case to which head (ii) applies—

(aa) where the person was before his absence a temporary resident in the home, 4 weeks, or

(bb) where the person was before his absence a permanent resident in the home, 13 weeks, or

(ii) where throughout the period of his absence the person was receiving free in-patient treatment within the meaning of the Social Security (Hospital In-Patients) Regulations 1975, 52 weeks,

and in either case he is either resident in the home on 1st August 1994 or would be so resident but for such an absence as is mentioned in paragraph (b), or has been continuously resident, disregarding any such absence, in residential accommodation to which the Registered Homes Act 1984 applies, or would apply but for section 1(4) of that Act, since 1st April 1993.

3. Paragraphs 1 and 2 shall cease to apply to a person where he is absent from a home such as is mentioned in paragraph 1(a) or (b), or 2(a) and that absence exceeds a period of—

(a) except in a case to which sub-paragraph (b) applies—

(i) 4 weeks, where the person was before his absence a temporary resident in the home, or

(ii) 13 weeks, where the person was before his absence a permanent resident in the home; or

(b) 52 weeks, where throughout the period of absence the person was receiving free in-patient treatment within the meaning of the Social Security (Hospital In-Patients) Regulations 1975.

4. For the purposes of this Schedule a person is a permanent resident where the home in which he resides is his principal place of abode, and a temporary resident where it is not.]

AMENDMENTS

1. Social Security (Attendance Allowance and Disability Living Allowance) (Amendment) Regulations 1994 (S.I. 1994 No. 1779), reg. 2(5) and Sched. 1 (August 1, 1994).

2. Social Security (Attendance and Disability Living Allowances) Amendment Regulations 1995 (S.I. 1995 No. 2162), reg. 2(4) (September 14, 1995).

The Social Security (Disability Living Allowance) Regulations 1991

(S.I. 1991 No. 2890)

Arrangement of Regulations

Whereas a draft of this instrument was laid before Parliament in accordance with section 12(1) of the Disability Living Allowance and Disability Working Allowance Act 1991 and approved by resolution of each House of Parliament;

Now therefore the Secretary of State for Social Security, in exercise of the powers conferred by sections 37ZA(6), 37ZB(2), (3), (7) and (8), 37ZC, 37ZD, 37ZE(2), 85(1), 114(1) and 166(2) to (3A) of and Schedule 20 to the Social Security Act 1975, section 13 of the Social Security (Miscellaneous Provisions) Act 1977 and section 5(1) of the Disability Living Allowance and Disability

Working Allowance Act 1991, and of all other powers enabling him in that behalf, by this instrument, which contains only regulations made consequential upon section 1 of the Disability Living Allowance and Disability Working Allowance Act 1991, hereby makes the following Regulations:

PART I

INTRODUCTION

Citation, commencement and interpretation

1.—(1) These Regulations may be cited as the Social Security (Disability Living Allowance) Regulations 1991 and shall come into force on 6th April 1992.

(2) In these Regulations—

[[1] "the Act" means the Social Security Contributions and Benefits Act 1992;

"the Administration Act" means the Social Security Administration Act 1992];

"the NHS Act of 1977" means the National Health Service Act 1977;

"the NHS Act of 1978" means the National Health Service (Scotland) Act 1978;

"the NHS Act of 1990" means the National Health Service and Community Care Act 1990;

"adjudicating authority" means, as the case may be, the chief or any other adjudication officer, an appeal tribunal or a disability appeal tribunal;

"care component" means the care component of a disability living allowance;

"mobility component" means the mobility component of a disability living allowance;

"terminally ill" shall be construed in accordance with [[1] section 66(2) of the Act].

(3) Unless the context otherwise requires, any reference in these Regulations to a numbered regulation or Schedule is a reference to the regulation or Schedule bearing that number in these Regulations and any reference in a regulation or Schedule to a numbered paragraph is a reference to the paragraph of that regulation or Schedule bearing that number.

AMENDMENT

1. Social Security (Disability Living Allowance) (Amendment) Regulations 1993 (S.I. 1993 No. 1939), reg. 2(2) (August 26, 1993).

PART II

GENERAL

Conditions as to residence and presence in Great Britain

2.—(1) Subject to the following provisions of this regulation, the prescribed conditions for the purposes of [[1] section 71] (6) of the Act as to residence and presence in Great Britain in relation to any person on any day shall be that—

(a) on that day—

(i) he is ordinarily resident in Great Britain; and

[[2](ia) Subject to paragraph (1A), his right to remain in Great Britain is not subject to any limitation or condition, and]

(ii) he is present in Great Britain; and
(iii) he has been present in Great Britain for a period of, or for periods amounting in the aggregate to, not less than 26 weeks in the 52 weeks immediately preceding that day; and

(b) where that day falls within a period in which that person—
(i) receives tax free emoluments, or
(ii) is the spouse of a person who receives tax free emoluments, or
(iii) is aged under 16 and is the son, daughter, step-son or step-daughter of a person who receives tax free emoluments,

that period is immediately preceded by a period of 4 years during which the person first mentioned in this sub-paragraph was present in Great Britain for not less than 156 weeks in aggregate.

[[2](1A) For the purposes of paragraph (1)(a)(ia), a person's right to reside or remain in Great Britain is not to be treated as if it were subject to a limitation or condition if—

(a) he is a person recorded by the Secretary of State as a refugee within the definition in Article 1 of the Convention relating to the Status of Refugees done at Geneva on 28th July 1951, as extended by Article 1(2) of the Protocol relating to the Status of Refugees done at New York on 31st Janauary 1967;
(b) he is a person who has been granted exceptional leave outside the provsions of the immigration rules within the meaning of the Immigration Act 1971 to remain in the United Kingdom by the Secretary of State;
(c) he is a national, or a member of the family of a national, of a State contracting party to the Agreement on the European Economic Area signed at Oporto on 2nd May 1992 as adjusted by the Protocol signed at Brussels on 17th March 1993;
(d) he is a person who is—
(i) lawfully working in Great Britain and is a national of a State with which the Community has concluded an Agreement under article 238(i) of the Treaty establishing the European Community providing, in the field of social security, for the equal treatment of workers who are nationals of the signatory State and their families, or
(ii) a member of the family of, and living with, such a person; or
(e) he is a person in respect of whom there is an Order in Council under section 179 of the Administration Act 1992 giving effect to a reciprocal agreement which, for the purposes of disability living allowance, has the effect that periods of presence or residence in another country are to be treated as periods of presence or residence in Great Britain.]

(2) For the purposes of paragraph (1)(a)(ii) and (iii), notwithstanding that on any day a person is absent from Great Britain, he shall be treated as though he was present in Great Britain if his absence is by reason only of the fact that on that day—

(a) he is abroad in his capacity as—
(i) a serving member of the forces,
(ii) an airman or mariner within the meaning of regulations 81 and 86 respectively of the Social Security (Contributions) Regulations 1979,

and for the purpose of this provision, the expression "serving members of the forces" has the same meaning as in regulation 1(2) of the Regulations of 1979; or

(b) he is in employment prescribed for the purposes of [[1] section 120] of the Act in connection with continental shelf operations; or
(c) he is living with a person mentioned in sub-paragraph (a)(i) and is the spouse, son, daughter, step-son, step-daughter, father, father-in-law, step-father, mother, mother-in-law or step-mother of that person; or
(d) his absence from Great Britain is, and when it began was, for a temporary

purpose and has not lasted for a continuous period exceeding 26 weeks; or

(e) his absence from Great Britain is temporary and for the specific purpose of his being treated for incapacity, or a disabling condition, which commenced before he left Great Britain, and the Secretary of State has certified that it is consistent with the proper administration of the Act that, subject to the satisfaction of the foregoing condition in this sub-paragraph, he should be treated as though he were present in Great Britain.

(3) In paragraph (1)(b), the expression "tax free emoluments" means emoluments which are exempt from tax under any of the provisions listed in paragraph (1) of regulation 9 of the Child Benefit (General) Regulations 1976.

(4) Where a person is terminally ill and—

(a) makes a claim for disability allowance; or

(b) an application is made for a review of his award of disability living allowance, expressly on the ground that he is such a person, paragraph (1) shall apply to him as if head (iii) of sub-paragraph (a) was omitted.

(5) Paragraph (1) shall apply in the case of a child under the age of 6 months as if in head (iii) of sub-paragraph (a) for the reference to 26 weeks there was substituted a reference to 13 weeks.

(6) Where in any particular case a child has by virtue of paragraph (5), entitlement to the care component immediately before the day he attains the age of 6 months, then until the child attains the age of 12 months, head (iii) of sub-paragraph (a) of paragraph (1) shall continue to apply in his case as if for the reference to 26 weeks there was substituted a reference to 13 weeks.

AMENDMENTS

1. Social Security (Disability Living Allowance) (Amendment) Regulations 1993 (S.I. 1993 No. 1939), reg. 2 (August 26, 1993).

2. Social Security (Persons From Abroad) Miscellaneous Amendments Regulations 1996 (S.I. 1996 No. 30), regulation 4 (February 5, 1996, subject to a saving under regulation 12(3)).

Age 65 or over

3.—(1) A person shall not be precluded from entitlement to either component of disability living allowance by reason only that he has attained the age of 65 years [[2]if he is a person to whom paragraphs (2) and (3) apply]

(2) Paragraph (3) applies to a person who—

(a) made a claim for disability living allowance before he attained the age of 65, which was not determined before he attained that age, and

(b) did not at the time he made the claim have an award of disability living allowance for a period ending on or after the day he attained the age of 65.

(3) In determining the claim of a person to whom this paragraph applies, where the person otherwise satisfies the conditions of entitlement to either or both components of disability living allowance for a period commencing before his 65th birthday (other than the requirements of [[1]section 72](2)(a), or, as the case may be, [[1]section 73](9)(a) of the Act (3 months qualifying period)), the determination shall be made without regard to the fact that he is aged 65 or over at the time the claim is determined.

(4) Schedule 1, which makes further provision for persons aged 65 or over shall have effect.

AMENDMENTS

1. Social Security (Disability Living Allowance) (Amendment) Regulations 1993 (S.I. 1993 No. 1939), reg. 2 (August 26, 1993).

2. Social Security (Disability Living Allowance) Amendments Regulations 1997 (S.I. 1997 No. 349), reg. 2 (October 6, 1997).

GENERAL NOTE

Para. (1). S.75(1) of the Social Security Contributions and Benefits Act 1992 has the effect that normally a person cannot be entitled to disability living allowance after he or she has attained the age of 65 unless awarded it before that age. Before its amendment, this paragraph enabled a person who would have satisfied the conditions of entitlement continuously since the age of 65 to qualify provided he or she made a claim before reaching the age of 66. The amendment means that it is now necessary for the claimant to have made a claim before reaching the age of 65. An earlier unsuccessful claim is irrelevant (*R(M) 4/86*). Where a claim has been determined in the claimant's favour before his or her 65th birthday, para. (4) and Sched. 1 apply and make provision for reviews and renewal claims. Where a claim has not been determined before the claimant's 65th birthday, paras. (2) and (3) apply. Those who are too old to be entitled to disability living allowance but who would otherwise qualify for the highest or middle rate of the care component will be entitled to attendance allowance instead, subject to satisfying the longer six-month qualifying condition.

Paras. (2) and (3). S. 75(1) of the 1992 Act specifically provides that a claimant cannot be entitled to disability living allowance unless the *award* has been made before his or her 65th birthday. These paragraphs make provision for a person whose *claim* was made before the 65th birthday and who is not making an advance claim to follow an existing award ending on or after that birthday. In such a case, provided that the conditions of entitlement are satisfied for a period commencing before the claimant's 65th birthday, entitlement is to be determined without regard to the fact that he or she is aged 65 or over at the time of the determination. Note that it is not necessary for the three-month qualifying condition to be satisfied before the claimant reaches the age of 65. Thus a person who becomes seriously disabled, say, a month before his or her birthday, can become entitled to disability living allowance two months after the birthday.

Para. (4). See the notes to Sched. 1 which deals with the determination of reviews and renewal claims after a person's 65th birthday and with the position of former beneficiaries under the invalid vehicle scheme.

Rate of Benefit

4.—(1) The three weekly rates of the care component are—

(a) the highest rate, payable in accordance with [[1]section 72](4)(a) of the Act, [[2]£49.50];

(b) the middle rate, payable in accordance with [[1]section 72](4)(b) of the Act, [[2]£33.10]; and

(c) the lowest rate, payable in accordance with [[1]section 72](4)(c) of the Act, [[2]£13.15].

(2) The two weekly rates of the mobility component are—

(a) the higher rate, payable in accordance with [[1]section 73] (11)(a) of the Act, [[2]£34.60]; and

(b) the lower rate, payable in accordance with [[1]section 73] (11)(b) of the Act, [[2]£13.15].

AMENDMENTS

1. Social Security (Disability Living Allowance) (Amendment) Regulations 1993 (S.I. 1993 No. 1939), reg. 2 (August 26, 1993).

2. Social Security Benefits Up-rating Order 1997 (S.I. 1997 No. 543), art. 12 (April 7, 1997).

Late claim by a person previously entitled

5.—*Revoked by Social Security (Miscellaneous Amendments) (No. 2) Regulations 1997 (S.I. 1997 No. 793), reg. 19(c) with effect from September 1, 1997.*

General Note

This regulation had allowed a renewal claim made within six months of date of termination of an earlier award to be backdated to that date.

[[1]Medical examination in prescribed circumstances

5A.—(1) The prescribed circumstances in which a person who is awarded disability living allowance shall be required to attend for, or submit himself to, a medical examination, are where the Secretary of State is undertaking an investigation under section 30(7A) of the Administration Act.

(2) An examination under paragraph (1) shall be conducted by a medical practitioner who is—

(a) approved by the Secretary of State; or

(b) engaged by an organisation approved by the Secretary of State.]

Amendment

1. Social Security (Attendance Allowance and Disability Living Allowance) (Miscellaneous Amendments) Regulations 1997 (S.I. 1997 No. 1839), reg. 3 (August 25, 1997).

General Note

This is in the same terms are reg. 8C of the Social Security (Attendance Allowance) Regulations 1991. It is made under s.57A of the Social Security Administration Act 1992 (inserted by s.18 of the Social Security Administration (Fraud) Act 1997) and is limited to circumstances where there is already an award of benefit and the Secretary of State is contemplating applying for a review. Apart from this provision, a claimant cannot be *required* to attend, or submit to, a medical examination for the purposes of a claim for disability living allowance. The next two regulations deal with the consequences of a failure to comply with such a requirement.

[[1]Withholding of benefit in prescribed circumstances

5B.—(1) Subject to paragraph (2), where a person who is receiving disability living allowance is required by the Secretary of State, to attend for, or submit to, a medical examination under regulation 5A and fails to comply with that requirement on more than one occasion, that allowance may be withheld, in whole or in part, from a date, not earlier than the second occasion, as the Secretary of State shall determine.

(2) Paragraph (1) shall not apply where—

(a) a person who is required to attend for, or submit to, a medical examination proves to the satisfaction of the Secretary of State that he has good cause for failing to comply with the requirement to attend for, or submit himself to, medical examination;

(b) a person who is required to attend for, or submit to, a medical examination produces such evidence as is acceptable to the Secretary of State in place of a medical examination; or

(c) the Secretary of State otherwise has available to him such evidence as is acceptable to him.

(3) For the purposes of paragraph (2)(a), the matters which are to be taken into account in determining whether a person has good cause shall include—

(a) whether he was outside Great Britain at the relevant time;

(b) his state of health at the relevant time; and

(c) the nature of any disability from which he suffers.]

Amendment

1. Social Security (Attendance Allowance and Disability Living Allowance) (Miscellaneous Amendments) Regulations 1997 (S.I. 1997 No. 1839), reg. 3 (August 25, 1997).

General Note

This is in the same terms as reg. 8D of the Social Security (Attendance Allowance) Regulations 1991. It is to be noted that all the questions arising under this regulation are to be determined by the Secretary of State.

Para. (1). Benefit may be withheld only after the second failure to attend or submit to a medical examination. The Secretary of State has a discretion as to whether benefit is withheld, what proportion of benefit is to be withheld and from what date (not earlier than the second refusal) it is to be withheld. Reg. 5C provides for the payment of withheld benefit.

Paras. (2) and (3). Benefit cannot be withheld once the Secretary of State has acceptable alternative medical evidence but it is for her to decide what is acceptable. Nor can benefit be withheld if the claimant has good cause for failing to attend or submit to an examination. The claimant must show good cause for both failures to attend but a subsequent willingness to attend or submit is likely to lead to withheld benefit being repaid, subject to reg. 5C(2). The matters set out in para. (3) are not exhaustive so other causes can be advanced (*e.g.* cancelled public transport).

[[1]Payment of withheld benefit

5C.—(1) Where the Secretary of State is satisfied that no question arises in connection with his investigation referred to in regulation 5A(1), payment of the amount withheld and the disability living allowance shall be made forthwith.

(2) Where a question arose in connection with an investigation referred to in regulation 5A(1) in respect of which—

(a) the Secretary of State made an application for the review of a peroson's entitlement to disability living allowance under section 30 of the Administration Act; and

(b) an adjudication officer has made a determination;

payment of the disability living allowance shall be made in accordance with the adjudication officer's determination, on review, of the person's entitlement.

(3) Where paragraph (1) or (2) does not apply and disability living allowance is withheld under regulation 5B for a period of more than 3 months, the Secretary of State shall—

(a) make, with a view to review, an application to the adjudication officer on the ground that the person failed to attend for, or submit himself to, medical examination; and

(b) make such payments as are determined, on review, by the adjudication officer.]

Amendment

1. Social Security (Attendance Allowance and Disability Living Allowance) (Miscellaneous Amendments) Regulations 1977 (S.I. 1997 No. 1839), reg. 3 (August 25, 1997).

General Note

This is in the same terms as reg. 8E of the Social Security (Attendance Allowance) Regulations 1991.

Para. (1). Where the Secretary of State decides not to apply for a review of the award of benefit, all the withheld benefit must be paid forthwith.

Para. (2). Where the Secretary of State applies for a review of the award of benefit, the amount of withheld benefit paid depends on the adjudication officer's decision on the review.

Para. (3). Reg. 67A of the Social Security (Adjudication) Regulations 1995 permits the Secretary of State to apply for a review on the simple ground that the claimant has failed to comply with a requirement to attend, or submit to, a medical examination. Once benefit has been withheld for three months, the Secretary of State *must* apply for such a review so that an adjudication officer may determine whether some or all of the withheld benefit should be paid. Note that this applies even if the Secretary of State has applied for a review on more conventional grounds but the adjudication officer has not yet made a determination. It is suggested that, before applying this paragraph, an adjudication officer should consider whether there is sufficient evidence to justify a review of the award of benefit which deals with the merits of the case, drawing such inferences as may be appropriate from the failures to attend or submit to the examinations. Once an adjudication officer or tribunal has reviewed an award on the simple ground of failure to comply with a requirement to attend or submit to an examination and has decided under this paragraph that not all the withheld benefit should be paid, it may be difficult for the claimant to recover the balance as that will require a further review and time-limits may operate to prevent the recovery.

Part III

Care Component

Qualifying period for care component after an interval

6.—(1) The period prescribed for the purposes of [[1]section 72] (2)(a)(ii) of the Act is a period of 3 months ending on the day on which the person was last entitled to the care component or to attendance allowance where that day falls not more than 2 years before the date on which entitlement to the care component would begin, or would have begun but for any regulations made under [[1]section 5(1)(k) of the Administration Act] (which enables regulations to provide for the day on which entitlement to benefit is to begin or end).

(2) Except in a case to which paragraph (3) applies, this regulation shall apply to a person to whom paragraph 3 or 7 of Schedule 1 refers as if for the reference to 3 months there was substituted a reference to 6 months.

(3) Paragraph (1) and not paragraph (2), shall apply to those persons referred to in paragraph (2) who, on the day before they attained the age of 65, had already completed the period of three months referred to in paragraph (1).

(4) For the purposes of paragraph (3), the modification made in Schedule 1—

(a) in paragraph 3(2) and 7(2), to [[1]section 72] (2)(a) of the Act, and

(b) in paragraph 5(2), to [[1]section 73] (9)(a) of the Act,

shall be treated as not having been made.

Amendment

1. Social Security (Disability Living Allowance) (Amendment) Regulations 1993 (S.I. 1993 No. 1939), reg. 2 (August 26, 1993).

General Note

The general effect of this provision is that the three month qualifying period (six months for people aged 65 or over) for the care component is deemed to be satisfied if the new claim is within two years of a previous period of entitlement to the care component (or attendance allowance) at the relevant rate.

Renal Dialysis

7.—(1) A person who suffers from renal failure and falls within the provisions in paragraph (2) shall be taken to satisfy—

(a) where he undergoes renal dialysis by day, the conditions in paragraph (b) of subsection (1) of [[1]section 72] of the Act (severe physical or mental disability);

(b) where he undergoes renal dialysis by night, the conditions in paragraph (c) of that subsection; or

(c) where he undergoes renal dialysis by day and by night, the conditions in either paragraph (b) or paragraph (c) of subsection (1), but not both.

(2) Subject to paragraph (3), a person falls within this paragraph—

(a) if—

(i) he undergoes renal dialysis two or more times a week; and

(ii) the renal dialysis he undergoes is of a type which normally requires the attendance or supervision of another person during the period of the dialysis; or

(iii) because of the particular circumstances of his case he in fact requires another person, during the period of the dialysis, to attend in connection with his bodily functions or to supervise him in order to avoid substantial danger to himself; and

(b) if, where he undergoes dialysis as an out-patient in a hospital or similar institution, being treatment provided under the NHS Act of 1977 or the NHS Act of 1978, no member of the staff of the hospital or institution assists with or supervises the dialysis.

[[1]](3) Paragraph (2)(b) does not apply for the purpose of determining whether a person is to be taken to satisfy any of the conditions mentioned, in paragraph (1) during the periods mentioned in section 72(2)(a)(i) and (b)(i) of the Act.]

(4) Except to the extent that provision is made in paragraph (2)(b), a person who undergoes treatment by way of renal dialysis as an out-patient in a hospital or similar institution, being treatment provided under the NHS Act of 1977 or the NHS Act of 1978, shall not be taken solely by reason of the fact that he undergoes such dialysis, as satisfying any of the conditions mentioned in subsection (1)(a) to (c) of [[1]section 72] of the Act.

AMENDMENT

1. Social Security (Disability Living Allowance) (Amendment) Regulations 1993 (S.I. 1993 No. 1939), reg. 2 (August 26, 1993).

GENERAL NOTE

Under this regulation, a person undergoing renal dialysis at least twice a week may be deemed to satisfy *either* the "day" *or* the "night" attendance conditions of s.72(1)(b) and (c) of the Social Security Contributions and Benefits Act 1992, but not both. Some degree of attention or supervision must be required. This regulation is in slightly different terms from reg. 5 of the Social Security (Attendance Allowance) Regulations 1991.

Para. (2)(a). The dialysis must be *either* of a type which *normally* requires the attendance of or supervision by another person (in which case the actual purpose of the attention or supervision is irrelevant) *or* the dialysis must *in the particular case* require the attention or supervision of the claimant (for the purpose specified in para. (2)(a)(iii)).

Paras. (2)(b), (3) *and* (4). Under paras. (2)(b) and (4), a person receiving treatment under the National Health Service cannot qualify for the care component under this regulation if he or she receives assistance or supervision during the dialysis from a member of staff of the hospital or other relevant institution, although there is nothing in para. (4) to prevent the need for any such assistance or supervision from being taken into account when considering whether the ordinary "day" or "night" conditions are satisfied. Para. (3) has the effect that, where a person has been undergoing dialysis falling within para. (2)(a) but para. (2)(b) was not satisfied because, say, supervision was provided in a National Health Service hospital, he or she can qualify under this regulation as soon as that supervision ceases, as long as he or she had been undergoing the dialysis for the usual three-month qualifying period. Presumably para. (3) applies equally to the six-month qualifying period substituted under para. 3 of Sched. 1 for claimants aged 65 or over.

Hospitalisation

8.—[[1]](1) Subject to regulation 10, it shall be a condition for the receipt of a disability living allowance which is attributable to entitlement to the care component for any period in respect of any person that during that period he is not maintained free of charge while undergoing medical or other treatment as an in-patient—

(a) in a hospital or similar institution under the NHS Act of 1977, the NHS Act of 1978 or the NHS Act of 1990; or

(b) in a hospital or other similar institution maintained or administered by the Defence Council.]

(2) For the purposes of [1 paragraph (1)(a)] a person shall only be regarded as not being maintained free of charge in a hospital or similar institution during any period when his accommodation and services are provided under section 65 of the NHS Act of 1977 or section 58 of, or paragraph 14 of Schedule 7A to, the NHS Act of 1978, or paragraph 14 of Schedule 2 to the NHS Act of 1990.

(3) [1. . .].

AMENDMENT

1. Social Security (Disability Living Allowance and Attendance Allowance) (Amendment) Regulations 1992 (S.I. 1992 No. 2869), reg. 4 (December 15, 1992).

GENERAL NOTE

See the annotations to reg. 6 of the Social Security (Attendance Allowance) Regulations 1991 which is in identical terms.

Note that, by virtue of reg. 10, a person may remain entitled to the care component for up to 28 days (84 days in the case of a person under the age of 16) in hospital or accommodation covered by reg. 9, but that separate periods in hospital or such accommodation are aggregated unless they are more than 28 days apart.

Persons in certain accommodation other than hospitals

9.—(1) Except in the cases specified in [2paragraphs (1A) to (4)], and subject to [6regulations 9A and 10], a person shall not be paid any amount in respect of a disability living allowance which is attributable to entitlement to the care component for any period where throughout that period he is a person for whom accommodation is provided—

(a) in pursuance—

(i) of Part III of the National Assistance Act 1948; [4. . .] or

(ii) of Part IV of the Social Work (Scotland) Act 1968 or section 7 of the Mental Health (Scotland) Act 1984;

(b) in circumstances where the cost of the accommodation is borne wholly or partly out of public or local funds in pursuance of those enactments or of any other enactment relating to persons under disability or to young persons or to education or training; or

(c) in circumstances where the cost of the accommodation may be borne wholly or partly out of public or local funds in pursuance of those enactments or of any other enactment relating to persons under disability or to young persons or to education or training.

[2(1A) Paragraph (1)(b) and (c) shall not apply in circumstances where the cost of the accommodation is or may be borne wholly or partly out of public or local funds by virtue of—

(a) section 100 of the Education Act 1944 [7 or section 73 of the Education (Scotland) Act 1980] (grants in aid of educational services);

(b) sections 1, 2 or 3 of the Education Act 1962 (which relate respectively to awards by local education authorities in respect of degree courses and further education and awards by the Secretary of State to persons undergoing teacher training or postgraduate courses) [7 or sections 49 or 73 of the Education (Scotland) Act 1980 (which relate respectively to the power of local authorities to assist persons to take advantage of educational facilities and the powers of the Secretary of State to make grants to education authorities and others)];

(c) sections 131(6) or 132(7) of the Education Reform Act 1988 (which respectively relate to the payment of grants to institutions by the Universities Funding Council and the Polytechnics and Colleges Funding Council) [7 or sections 4 or 40 of the Further and Higher Education (Scotland) Act 1992 (which relate respectively to the funding of further education and the administration of funds)]; or

(d) section 1 of the Education (Student Loans) Act 1990 (student loans).]

[1(2) Subject to paragraph (2A), paragraph (1) shall not apply in the case of a child who—

(a) has not attained the age of 16 and is being looked after by a local authority; or

(b) has not attained the age of 18 and to whom—

(i) section 17(10)(b) of the Children Act 1989 (impairment of health and development) applies because his health is likely to be significantly impaired, or further impaired, without the provision of services for him, or [7 to whom section 12 of the Social Work (Scotland) Act 1968 applies, or]

(ii) section 17(10)(c) of the Act of 1989 (disability) [7 or section 12 of the Social Work (Scotland) Act 1968] applies; or

(c) who is accommodated outside the United Kingdom and the cost of the accommodation is or may be borne wholly or partly by a local authority pursuant to their powers under section 3A of the Education Act 1981 [7 or section 65G of the Education (Scotland) Act 1980].

(2A) Sub-paragraphs (a) and (b) of paragraph (2) shall only apply during any period during which the local authority looking after the child place him in a private dwelling with a family, or a relative of his, or some other suitable person].

(3)[3. . .].

(4) Paragraph (1)(c) shall also not apply—

(a) where the person is living in accommodation as a privately fostered child;

(b) where he is a person for whom accommodation is made available for his occupation in accordance with section 65 of the Housing Act 1985 [7 or section 31 of the Housing (Scotland) Act 1987] (duties of local housing authorities to persons found to be homeless);

(c) where the person himself pays the whole cost, and always has paid the whole cost, of the [4 accommodation [6, and is a person to whom regulation 9A applies];]

(d) except in a case to which paragraph (5) applies, where the accommodation the person is living in is a private dwelling.

(5)[4 Subject to paragraph (5A), this paragraph] applies where—

(a) the cost of the accommodation the person previously occupied was borne in whole or in part out of public or local funds and where he was moved out of that accommodation at the instigation of the body which bore the cost into a residential care home; or

(b) the person is living in a residential care home and at least 4 other persons in that home are provided with board and personal care, excluding persons carrying on the home or employed there or their relatives.

[3(5A) Paragraph (5)(b) shall apply in the case of a person [6 to whom regulation 9A does not apply] as if the words "and at least 4 other persons" to the end of sub-paragraph (b) were omitted.]

(6) In this regulation, references to the cost of the accommodation shall not include the cost of—

(a) domiciliary services provided in respect of a person in a private dwelling; or

(b) improvements made to, or furniture or equipment provided for, a private dwelling on account of the needs of a person under disability; or

(c) improvements made to, or furniture or equipment provided for, residential homes or other homes or premises in respect of which a grant or payment has been made out of public or local funds except where the grant or payment is of a regular or repeated nature; or

(d) social and recreational activities provided outside the accommodation in respect of which grants or payments are made out of public or local funds; or

(e) the purchase or running of a motor vehicle to be used in connection with the accommodation in respect of which grants or payments are made out of public or local funds.

(7) In [5 this regulation] the expression—

''privately fostered child'' has the meaning it bears in Part IV of the Children Act 1989 by virtue of section 66(1) of that Act.

''residential care home'' means an establishment in respect of which registration is required under [7Part IV of the Social Work (Scotland) Act 1968] Part I of the Registered Homes Act 1984 or would be so required but for section 1(4) of that Act.

AMENDMENTS

1. Social Security (Disability Living Allowance) Amendment Regulations 1992 (S.I. 1992 No. 633) (April 6, 1992).

2. Social Security (Disability Living Allowance and Attendance Allowance) (Amendment) Regulations 1992 (S.I. 1992 No. 2869), reg. 5 (December 15, 1992).

3. Social Security Benefits (Amendments Consequential Upon the Introduction of Community Care) Regulations 1992 (S.I. 1992 No. 3147), reg. 7 (April 1, 1993 with saving).

4. Social Security Benefits (Miscellaneous Amendments) Regulations 1993 (S.I. 1993 No. 518), reg. 3(2) (April 1, 1993).

5. Social Security (Disability Living Allowance) (Amendment) Regulations 1993 (S.I. 1993 No. 1939), reg. 2(9) (August 26, 1993).

6. Social Security (Attendance Allowance and Disability Living Allowance) (Amendment) Regulations 1994 (S.I. 1994 No. 1779), reg. 3(2) (August 1, 1994).

7. Social Security (Attendance and Disability Living Allowances) Amendment Regulations 1995 (S.I. 1995 No. 2162), reg. 3 (September 14, 1995).

GENERAL NOTE

Paras. (1) and (3)-(6) are in identical terms to reg. 7(1)-(5) of the Social Security (Attendance Allowance) Regulations 1991 (save that the definition of ''residential care home'' is in para. (7) of these regulations). For further annotations, see those Regulations.

Note that, by virtue of reg. 10, a person may remain entitled to the care component for up to 28 days (84 days in the case of a person under the age of 16) in accommodation covered by reg. 9 or in a hospital, but that separate periods in such accommodation or hospital are aggregated unless they are more than 28 days apart.

Para. (2) makes specific provision enabling certain children to qualify for the care component even though they would otherwise fall within the provisions of para. (1).

[1Persons to whom regulations 9 and 10 apply with modifications

9A.—(1) This regulation applies where a person satisfies paragraph 1 or paragraph 2 of Schedule 3 to these Regulations.

(2) Where this regulation applies—

(a) regulation 9 shall have effect as if after paragraph (2A) there were inserted the following paragraph—

''(2B) Paragraph (1)(b), in so far as it relates to enactments relating to persons under a disability or to education or training not referred to in subparagraph (a), and paragraph (1)(c) shall not apply in the case of a person who is terminally ill where the Secretary of State has been informed of that fact—

(a) on a claim for a disability living allowance which is attributable to the care component;
(b) on an application for a review of an award of disability living allowance which is attributable to the care component; or
(c) in writing in connection with an award of, or a claim for, or an application for a review of an award of, the care component of a disability living allowance.''; and

(b) regulation 10 (exemption from regulations 8 and 9) shall have effect as if—
(i) in paragraph (1) for the words ''subject to the following provisions of this regulation'' there were substituted the words ''subject to paragraphs (2) and (3)''; and
(ii) paragraphs (6) to (9) were omitted.]

AMENDMENT

1. Social Security (Attendance Allowance and Disability Living Allowance) (Amendment) Regulations 1994 (S.I. 1994 No. 1779), reg. 3(3) (August 1, 1994).

Exemption from regulation 8 and 9

10.—(1) Regulation 8, or as the case may be, regulation 9, shall not, [[2]subject to the following provisions of this regulation], apply to a person for the first 28 days of any period throughout which he is someone to whom paragraph (4) applies.

(2) Regulation 8 shall not, subject to paragraph (3), apply to a person who has not attained the age of 16 for the first 84 days of any period throughout which he is someone to whom paragraph (4) refers.

(3) Where on the day the person's entitlement to the care component commenced, he is a person to whom paragraph (4) refers, then paragraph (1) or, as the case may be, paragraph (2) shall not apply to him for any period of consecutive days, beginning with that day, in which he continues to be a person to whom paragraph (4) refers.

(4) This paragraph refers to a person who—
(a) is undergoing medical or other treatment in a hospital or other institution in any of the circumstances mentioned in regulation 8; or
[[1](b) would, but for this regulation, be prevented from receiving the care component of a disability working allowance by reason of regulation 9.]

(5) For the purposes of paragraphs (1) and (2)—
(a) 2 or more distinct periods separated by an interval not exceeding 28 days, or by 2 or more such intervals shall be treated as a continuous period equal in duration to the total of such distinct periods and ending on the last day of the later or last such period;
(b) any period or periods to which regulations 8(1) or 9(1) refers shall be taken into account and aggregated with any period to which the other of them refers.

[[2](6) Regulation 8 or as the case may be regulation 9 shall not apply [[3]except in a case to which paragraph (9) applies] in the case of a person who is residing in a hospice and is terminally ill where the Secretary of State has been informed that he is terminally ill—
(a) on a claim for the care component,
(b) on an application for a review of an award of disability living allowance, or
(c) in writing in connection with an award of, or a claim for, or an application for a review of an award of, disability living allowance.

(7) In paragraph (6) "hospice" means a hospital or other institution [3whose primary function is to provide palliative care for persons resident there who are suffering from a progressive disease in its final stages] other than—

(a) a health service hospital (within the meaning of section 128 of the NHS Act of 1977) in England or Wales;

(b) a health service hospital (within the meaning of section 108(1) of the NHS Act of 1978) in Scotland;

(c) a hospital maintained or administered by the Defence Council; or

(d) an institution similar to a hospital mentioned in any of the preceding sub-paragraphs of this paragraph.

(8) Regulation 9 shall not apply [3except in a case to which paragraph (9) applies] in any particular case for any period during which—

(a) the person for whom the accommodation is provided—

(i) is not entitled to income support or income-based jobseeker's allowance],

(ii) is not entitled to housing benefit, or

(iii) is not a member of a married or unmarried couple for whom an amount is included for income support [or income-based jobseeker's allowance] purposes in the weekly applicable amount of the other member, and

(b) the whole of the cost of that accommodation is met—

(i) out of the person's own resources, or partly out of his own resources and partly with assistance from another person or a charity; or

(ii) on his behalf by another person or a charity.]

[3(9) This paragraph applies in the case of a person who is residing in a home owned or managed, or owned and managed, by a local authority.]

AMENDMENTS

1. Social Security (Disability Living Allowance) Amendment Regulations 1992 (S.I. 1992 No. 633) (April 6, 1992).

2. Social Security Benefits (Amendments Consequential Upon the Introduction of Community Care) Regulations 1992 (S.I. 1992 No. 3147), reg. 7 (April 1, 1993).

3. Social Security Benefits (Miscellaneous Amendments) Regulations 1993 (S.I. 1993 No. 518), reg. 3(3) (April 1, 1993).

4. Social Security and Child Support (Jobseeker's Allowance) (Consequential Amendments) Regulations 1996 (S.I. 1996 No. 1345), reg. (October 7, 1996).

GENERAL NOTE

A person may remain entitled to the care component for up to 28 days (84 days in the case of a person under the age of 16) in a hospital covered by reg. 8 or accommodation covered by reg. 9. However, separate periods in such a hospital or such accommodation are aggregated unless they are more than 28 days apart. Furthermore, under para. (3), a person cannot first qualify for the care component while in hospital or the relevant accommodation.

[1Adjustment of allowance where medical expenses are paid from public funds under war pensions instruments

10A.—(1) In this regulation—

"article 25B" means article 25B of the Personal Injuries (Civilians) Scheme 1983 (medical expenses) and includes that article as applied by article 48B of that Scheme;

"article 26" means article 26 of the Naval, Military and Air Forces etc. (Disablement and Death) Service Pensions Order 1983 (medical expenses);

and in this regulation and regulation 10B "relevant accommodation" means accommodation provided as a necessary ancillary to nursing care where the medical expenses involved are wholly borne by the Secretary of State pursuant to article 25B or article 26.

(2) This regulation applies where a person is provided with relevant accommodation.

(3) Subject to regulation 10B, where this regulation applies and there are payable in respect of a person both a payment under article 25B or article 26 and a disability living allowance which is attributable to the care component, the allowance, in so far as it is so attributable, shall be adjusted by deducting from it the amount of the payment under article 25B or article 26, as the case may be, and only the balance shall be payable.]

AMENDMENT

1. Social Security (Attendance Allowance and Disability Living Allowance) (Amendment) Regulations 1994 (S.I. 1994 No. 1779), reg. 3(4) (August 1, 1994).

[1Exemption from regulation 10A

10B.—(1) Regulation 10A shall not, subject to the following provisions of this regulation, apply to a person in respect of the first 28 days of any period during which the amount of any disability living allowance attributable to the care component would be liable to be adjusted by virtue of regulation 10A(3).

(2) For the purposes of paragraph (1) two or more distinct periods separated by an interval not exceeding 28 days, or by two or more such intervals, shall be treated as a continuous period equal in duration to the aggregate of such distinct periods and ending on the last day of the later or last such period.

(3) For the purposes of this paragraph a day is a relevant day in relation to a person if it fell not earlier than 28 days before the first day on which he was provided with relevant accommodation; and either—

(a) was a day when he was undergoing medical treatment in a hospital or similar institution in any of the circumstances mentioned in regulation 8; or

(b) was a day when he was, or would but for regulation 10 have been, prevented from receiving a disability living allowance attributable to the care component by virtue of regulation 9(1);

and where there is in relation to a person a relevant day, paragraph (1) shall have effect as if for "28 days" there were substituted such lesser number of days as is produced by subtracting from 28 the number of relevant days in his case.]

AMENDMENT

1. Social Security (Attendance Allowance and Disability Living Allowance) (Amendment) Regulations 1994 (S.I. 1994 No. 1779), reg. 3(4) (August 1, 1994).

PART IV

MOBILITY COMPONENT

Qualifying period for mobility component after an interval

11. The period prescribed for the purposes of [1section 73] (9)(a)(ii) of the Act is a period of 3 months ending on the day which the person was last entitled to the mobility component or to mobility allowance, where that day falls not more than 2 years before the date on which entitlement to the mobility component would begin or would have begun but for any regulations made under [1section 5(1)(k) of the Administration Act] (which enables regulations to provide for the day on which entitlement to benefit is to begin or end).

AMENDMENT

1. Social Security (Disability Living Allowance) (Amendment) Regulations 1993 (S.I. 1993 No. 1939), reg. 2 (August 26, 1993).

GENERAL NOTE

The general effect of this provision is that the three-month qualifying period for the mobility component is deemed to be satisfied if the new claim is within two years of a previous period of entitlement to the mobility component (or mobility allowance) at the relevant rate.

Entitlement to the mobility component

12.—(1) A person is to be taken to satisfy the conditions mentioned in [[1]section 73] (1)(a) of the Act (unable or virtually unable to walk) only in the following circumstances—

(a) his physical condition as a whole is such that, without having regard to circumstances peculiar to that person as to the place of residence or as to place of, or nature of, employment—

(i) he is unable to walk; or

(ii) his ability to walk out of doors is so limited, as regard the distance over which or the speed at which or the length of time for which or the manner in which he can make progress on foot without severe discomfort, that he is virtually unable to walk; or

(iii) the exertion required to walk would constitute a danger to his life or would be likely to lead to a serious deterioration in his health; or

(b) he has both legs amputated at levels which are either through or above the ankle, or he has one leg so amputated and is without the other leg, or is without both legs to the same extent as if it, or they, had been so amputated.

(2) For the purposes of [[1] section 73](2)(a) of the Act (mobility component for the blind and deaf) a person is to be taken to satisfy—

(a) the condition that he is blind only where the degree of disablement resulting from the loss of vision amounts to 100 per cent; and

(b) the condition that he is deaf only where the degree of disablement resulting from loss of hearing [[2] when using any artificial aid which he habitually uses or which is suitable in his case] amounts to not less than 80 per cent on a scale where 100 per cent represents absolute deafness.

(3) For the purposes of [[1] section 73](2)(b) of the Act, the conditions are that by reason of the combined effects of the person's blindness and deafness, he is unable, without the assistance of another person, to walk to any intended or required destination while out of doors.

(4) Except in a case to which paragraph (1)(b) applies, a person is to be taken not to satisfy the conditions mentioned in [[1] section 73](1)(a) of the Act if he—

(a) is not unable or virtually unable to walk with a prosthesis or artificial aid which he habitually wears or uses, or

(b) would not be unable or virtually unable to walk if he wore or used a prosthesis or an artificial aid which is suitable in his case.

(5) A person falls within subsection (3)(a) of [[1] section 73] of the Act (severely mentally impaired) if he suffers from a state of arrested development or incomplete physical development of the brain, which results in severe impairment of intelligence and social functioning.

(6) A person falls within subsection (3)(b) of [[1] section 73] of the Act (severe behavioural problems) if he exhibits disruptive behaviour which—

(a) is extreme,
(b) regularly requires another person to intervene and physically restrain him in order to prevent him causing physical injury to himself or another, or damage to property, and
(c) is so unpredictable that he requires another person to be present and watching over him whenever he is awake.

AMENDMENTS

1. Social Security (Disability Living Allowance) (Amendment) Regulations 1993 (S.I 1993 No 1939), reg. 2 (August 26, 1993).
2. Social Security (Attendance Allowance and Disability Living Allowance) (Amendment) Regulations 1994 (S.I. 1994 No. 1779), reg. 3(5)(August 1, 1994).

GENERAL NOTE

Sub-para. (1)(a). This re-enacts reg. 3(1)(a) of the Mobility Allowance Regulations 1975 and some of the words and phrases used have been considered by the Commissioners.

''*Physical disablement*'' ''*physical condition*''. It seems fairly clear that the use of the word ''physical'' is intended to be limiting so that the scope of s.73(1)(a) of the Social Security Contributions and Benefits Act 1992 does not extend to those suffering from purely psychiatric conditions although such people may qualify under s.73(1)(c) or (d). Whether or not a person is suffering from ''physical'' disablement is regarded as primarily a medical question although, in principle, the process of reasoning used by a disability appeal tribunal to reach the conclusion is challengeable on the ground that it is erroneous in point of law. In a fairly uncontroversial case, a medical appeal tribunal did not err in law in holding that, because agoraphobia was not a physical condition, the claimant could not succeed (*R(M) 1/80*). More famously, in *R(M)* 2/78, a Commissioner held that a medical appeal tribunal had not erred in law in deciding that a child (Robert) suffering from Down's syndrome was suffering from a physical condition. The tribunal had said: ''We agree that the boy is suffering from mongolism, a condition which is due to faulty genetic inheritance and can therefore be classified as a physical disorder. We accept the evidence that while he walks for some yards he is liable to run, stop, lie down and refuse to go further; this reaction which severely impairs mobility is directly due to the physical condition of mongolism''. In refusing leave to appeal, the Chairman added: ''The submission of the Secretary of State seeks to separate the claimant's mental state from the physical condition to which that mental state is directly due. This cannot be accepted because the mental state is the direct consequence of the physical malformation of a particular chromosome (No. 21).'' The Chief Commissioner said: ''I think it is plain that the medical appeal tribunal regarded Robert's physical condition as a whole as being a disabling condition, preventing him from doing the particular action of walking. The weight to be attached to physical and mental disablement in cases where both factors may be present is for the medical authorities to decide, and the answer to the question whether the one or the other is, or both are responsible for an inability or virtual inability to walk is for their decision as a medical question. I do not consider that the medical appeal tribunal misapprehended what physical disablement means, or that it can be said that they were wrong in law in concluding from their findings that it was physical disablement which was responsible for his virtual inability to walk.'' He stressed that not all Down's cases would have the same result, although it is not entirely clear whether that was because he thought that different conclusions might be reached as to whether the condition was a physical one or whether it was because not all people suffering from Down's syndrome are disabled to the same extent. The Mobility Allowance Regulations 1975 were amended in 1979 following *R(M) 2/78* but, in *R(M) 1/83*, a Tribunal of Commissioners held that the amendments did not affect the reasoning of the Commissioner in *R(M) 2/78. R(M) 3/86* concerned a child who had suffered brain damage at birth leading to severe mental subnormality. While capable of the physical movements of walking, his behaviour while doing so was erratic and unpredictable. In setting aside the decision of a medical appeal tribunal who had disregarded the behavioural problems, the Tribunal of Commissioners held that *R(M) 2/78* is still good law despite what was said in *Lees v. Secretary of State for Social Services* (see below) and that behavioural problems arising out of a physical disability were relevant. It should be noted that in *Harrison v. Secretary of State for Social Services*, reported as an appendix to *R(M) 1/88*, Lloyd L.J. suggested that *R(M) 2/78* should be regarded with caution in the light of *Lees*, but it is not clear which part of the Commissioner's decision he had in mind.

In *R(M) 1/88*, the claimant had injured his back in an accident in 1979. He was awarded mobility allowance up to 1983 but, on a renewal claim, a medical appeal tribunal held that his inability to walk was not due to a physical cause but was hysterical in origin. In the course of his decision, the Commissioner said: "It may be that in the last analysis all mental disablement may be ascribed to physical causes. But, if so, it is obvious that the Act on drawing the distinction between physical and mental disablement did not mean this last analysis to be resorted to." He held that the question what was and what was not a physical inability to walk was a medical question for the tribunal to determine but he added: "This does not mean that in every case of hysteria the medical authorities are bound to hold that a claimant's hysteria is not a manifestation of his physical condition as a whole; but it does mean that if they do so find it will be impossible to disturb their decision on the ground that they ought to have found it to be a manifestation of the claimant's physical condition." An appeal to the Court of Appeal was dismissed (*Harrison v. Secretary of State for Social Services*, reported as an appendix to *R(M) 1/88*). The Court effectively adopted the Commissioner's reasoning. Stocker L.J. said: "Hysteria is not itself a physical condition, since physical and hysterical conditions are often used in constrasting terms, and in my view correctly so. The Commissioner points out, however, that where hysteria is itself a consequence of a physical condition, it is open to a Tribunal or medical board, as a matter of medical opinion, to find that where hysteria is caused by a physical condition, for example due to pain due to some spinal condition, the inability to walk may itself be caused by that same physical condition." He drew attention, without apparent criticism, to the fact that the claimant has since been awarded mobility allowance on a further claim.

In *CDLA/15106/96*, it was argued that there was "physical disablement" where a tribunal found a claimant to be suffering from genuine pain due to a psychological condition. However, the Commissioner said; "it is important to note that 'physical disablement' is a phrase that appears only in section 73(1)(a) of the Act. Regulation 12(1) of the Regulations provides that a person shall be taken to satisfy the conditions mentioned in section 73(1)(a) *only* in the circumstances prescribed in that paragraph and the phrase that appears in that paragraph is 'physical condition as a whole'. Pain is a physical symptom and it may be said that in one sense disablement due to pain is 'physical disablement'. However, it may be a symptom of either a physical condition or a psychological condition. In this case, the tribunal found it to be a symptom of a psychological condition and therefore the claimant's circumstances did not fall within the terms of regulation 12(1)(a) of the Regulations. They were entitled to make that finding."

"*without having regard to circumstances peculiar to that person as to place of residence or as to place of, or nature of, employment*". Note that it is simply the claimant's physical condition which is relevant. The distance to his or her local shops is not relevant although it is often helpful for a tribunal to know whether, and if so how, a claimant manages to get to the local shops and then, having ascertained how far that is, to consider ability to walk in the light of that evidence.

(i) "unable to walk"

In *R(M) 3/78*, the Commissioner said: "The word 'walk' is an ordinary English word in common usage and, in the context of regulation 3 [of the Mobility Allowance Regulations 1975], means to move by means of a person's legs and feet or a combination of them." In *R(M) 1/83*, no definition was attempted but the Tribunal of Commissioners said: "We consider that a person who cannot walk at all ought not to be regarded as unable to walk, though he may well be regarded as virtually unable to walk. This does not of course preclude the medical authorities from finding that a claimant's method of moving about does not amount to walking at all." In the course of the litigation in *Lees* (see below) O'Connor L.J., in the Court of Appeal, said: "A person is unable to walk if he cannot use his legs for walking, so a person who is bedridden, a person who is a paraplegic and indeed a person who has a leg amputated is unable to walk. The last category can be enabled to walk by artificial aids such as a false limb or crutches and for that reason we find regulation 3(2) [now regulation 12(4)] applies" (see the appendix to *R(M) 1/84*). In *R(M) 2/89*, it was made clear that a person with only one foot cannot "walk" in the absence of an artificial limb. Where a person uses crutches, it is necessary to consider the way in which they are used. Unless they are used so that the claimant can walk, as opposed to simply swinging through the crutches, the claimant will satisfy the condition of reg. 12(1)(a)(i) even if the distance he or she can travel is such that reg. 12(1)(a)(ii) would not be satisfied.

(ii) "virtually unable to walk"

In *R(M) 1/91* the Commissioner said that "the base point is total inability to walk, which is extended [by reg. 12(1)(a)(ii)] to take in people who can technically walk but only to an insignificant extent". There is clearly some scope for disagreement as to what is meant by "virtually" or "insignificant".

It is to be noted that the virtual inability to walk must be a virtual inability to do so "out of doors". A medical appeal tribunal, conducting a walking test indoors can infer from that that the claimant is not virtually unable to walk out of doors although it is desirable that they should indicate that they have addressed their minds to the different conditions pertaining out of doors (*CM/103/1984*). In *R(M) 1/91*, the Commissioner held that the test envisaged walking on the kind of pavement or road which one would normally expect to find in the course of walking out of doors, any unusual hazards peculiar to the claimant's situation being ignored. He also pointed out that some degree of incline must be contemplated but that the question is not whether the claimant is unable or virtually unable to *climb* and any inability to surmount hills or mountains is irrelevant.

The distance a person can walk is important but it should not be considered without reference to the other relevant factors of speed, length of time and manner of walking. In *R(M) 1/78*, it was held that a medical appeal tribunal had erred in law in holding that a claimant was virtually unable to walk when she could walk a mile. However, whether the distance a person can walk means that he or she is virtually unable to walk is generally regarded as a matter of judgment for a tribunal and Commissioner's have shown no inclination to interfere. Thus, medical appeal tribunals have not been held to have erred *in law* in holding that claimants were not virtually unable to walk where their walking ability has been very limited. In *CM/39/84*, the claimant could manage 100 yards at 2 mph and, in *CM/47/86*, the claimant could manage only 50 yards. On the other hand, in *R(M) 5/86*, it seems to have been accepted that a claimant who could walk only 50 yards should qualify. Apart from speed, a tribunal should probably consider how long it takes a person to recover after walking a short distance. A claimant who can walk a substantial distance provided that he or she stands still for a couple of minutes every hundred yards has a greater ability to walk than a person who has to rest for an hour after walking a hundred yards. In *CDLA/805/94* the Commissioner suggested that this factor should be taken into account when considering "the length of time for which" the claimant could walk. He pointed out that, as speed is a function of time and distance, consideration of the length of time for which the claimant can walk must involve consideration of something beyond the mere time it necessarily takes the claimant to walk the distance he can manage at the speed he can manage.

Consideration of the manner of walking involves consideration of behaviour while walking as well as the steadiness of the claimant's gait. However, a need for supervision or attendance while walking is not, of itself, relevant. In *R(M) 1/78*, it was not material that the claimant was always accompanied because she suffered from fits. Thus a person who suffers from fits only occasionally is unlikely to qualify on that ground alone but, in *CM/125/1983*, a Commissioner held that the fact that a claimant was liable to suffer from three fits in half a mile might lead to the conclusion that the quality of walking was so poor as to amount to a virtual inability to walk. Similarly, a "propensity to trip . . . would have to be extremely marked before it became relevant to the manner of a claimant's walking" (*CM/364/92*).

While in *R(M) 1/83* it was pointed out that the need for attendance and supervision was met through the social security system by entitlement to attendance allowance (see now the care component of disability living allowance and also the lower rate of the mobility component), the Tribunal of Commissioners did consider that the need for such assistance was a facet of the manner in which a person can make progress on foot and was to be taken into account by the medical authorities in conjunction with any other matters in determining whether the person concerned was virtually unable to walk. They said: "The main question in each case will be whether the child is so incapable inasmuch as his ability to walk out of doors is so limited as regards the manner in which he is able to make progress on foot, since behavioural limitations on a person's walking generally affect the manner of walking. It is possible also that speed of walking from place to place may enter into it. It will clearly be relevant that tantrums or refusals to walk are of frequent occurrence or not. We accept the submission made to us that the reference in reg. 3(1)(b) [now reg. 12(1)(a)(ii)] to the making of progress on foot means that it is proper to take account of the fact that a major purpose of walking is to get to a designated place. It follows that if a person can be caused to move himself to a designated place only with the benefit of guidance and supervision and possibly after much cajoling *the point may be reached at which he may be found to be virtually unable to walk.* There may be other factors such as blindness and deafness . . . to be taken into account in addition." That passage needs to be treated with some caution in the light of the decision of the House of Lords in *Lees v. Secretary of State for Social Services* (reported as an appendix to *R(M) 1/84*) but it is not inconsistent with it. Christine Lees was blind and suffered from some hydrocephalus with symptoms including some impairment of balance and marked impairment of capacity for spatial orientation. She needed an intelligent adult as a "pilot". Lord Scarman rejected the argument that she was virtually unable to walk because the legislation points to consideration of the physical ability to get about on foot. In effect, he said that her position was no different from that of any other blind person who would need a guide of some sort. He also said that some Commissioners' decisions cited to the House and which differ must be regarded as erroneous in law. But it is not clear from his speech which decisions he had in mind or to what extent they are erroneous.

As already noted, in *Harrison*, Lloyd L.J. suggested that *R(M) 2/78* must be treated with caution but in *R(M) 3/86* a Tribunal of Commissioners said that it was correctly stating the law in that a claimant's behavioural problems, including a failure on occasion to exercise his walking powers (stemming from a physical disability) were necessarily relevant. "What is relevant is whether or not they suffer from temporary paralysis (as far as walking is concerned) and, if so, to what extent." In *CM/186/1985*, the Commissioner, relying on *R(M) 3/86*, drew a distinction between, on one hand, a child who suffered from "temperamental refusal episodes, these episodes occurring at distances varying between 20 and several hundred yards and on occasion [made] progress impossible by sitting down" as a result of his physical condition (autism) and, on the other hand, the hypothetical "case of a child who is open to coaxing". Thus once it is established that, due to physical disablement, a person cannot be persuaded to walk in a desired direction, that person may be regarded as virtually unable to walk and so be entitled to the higher rate of the mobility component of disability living allowance and not just to the lower rate under s.73(1)(d) of the Social Security Contributions and Benefits Act 1992.

R(M) 2/81 concerned a blind person who could get around perfectly well with a guide dog until some scaffolding fell on his head and caused a physical injury. The medical appeal tribunal found: "The claimant's legs are capable of making the movements required in the activity of walking but he is blind and has a physical disablement in his balance mechanism and sense of direction which makes it impossible for him to control the direction in which he wishes to move . . . With human guidance he can be steered and can with much help progress in a straight line in a desired direction." In *R(M) 3/86* it was held that that case did not survive *Lees* but it is interesting that the Court of Appeal in *Lees* would have distinguished it on the facts. O'Connor L.J. said: "I repeat it is a medical question as to whether physical disablement including a disturbance of directional mechanism, if the doctors decide that that is a physical disablement, renders a person unable to walk or virtually unable to walk." The House of Lords suggested that they were not disagreeing with the Court of Appeal at all. The extent to which assistance can be of use would appear to be relevant but some of the sweeping *dicta* in *R(M) 2/81* clearly go.

The distance over which, the speed at which, the length of time for which and the manner in which the claiamnts can make progress are all relevant. However, the need to make findings on each of the factors only applies where the factors are all in issue (*CDLA/8462/95*). Whether a tribunal errs in law in failing to deal with some factors depends very much on the evidence in the particular case.

Any ability to make progress on foot must, to be relevant, be without severe discomfort. In *R(M) 1/81*, it was held that a tribunal must ignore any walking which can be managed only with severe discomfort. In *R(M) 1/83*, the claimant's representative submitted that the words "without severe discomfort" must be interpreted as meaning "without risk of severe discomfort" and that a person who could not be allowed to go out of doors unattended for fear of his being injured in a street accident could not do so without risk of severe discomfort. The Commissioners said "this submission involves imputing to the draftsman the rather heavy humour of describing the risk of being run over as a risk of severe discomfort and we do not think that the words used are appropriate to carry the meaning suggested. In our view the words 'severe discomfort' relate to matters like pain and breathlessness that may be brought on by walking. . . . [They do] not extend to the screaming attack of an autistic child or the refusal to walk of the child suffering from Down's syndrome. . . . These are the consequence of resistence to the idea of walking and [*sic*] rather than of the walking itself."

In *Cassinelli v. Secretary of State for Social Services* (misreported in *The Times*, December 6, 1991), the Court of Appeal held that a medical appeal tribunal had erred in law when holding that a person was not virtually unable to walk because the exertion of walking did not cause "severe pain or distress". Glidewell L.J. said that that phrase seemed "to be drawing a distinction between the factor of pain, of which discomfort is a lesser concomitant, and the factor of distress which may arise for other reasons than pain; distress may result of course from pain or discomfort, but may also result from breathlessness, which is another matter to which the tribunal referred." He rejected the argument put on behalf of the Secretary of State that the tribunal had, inferentially at least, applied the right test and answered the right question. It is difficult to follow the logic of the decision but it is clear that tribunals depart from the statutory language at their peril. It remains arguable that breathlessness can give rise to severe discomfort.

In *CDLA/12653/96* and *CDLA/15997/96*, the claimants suffered from porphyria which caused severe discomfort when they went out of doors due to the extreme sensitivity of their skin. However, as the physical act of walking was not impaired and that physical act did not itself cause any discomfort, the Commissioner held that the claimants could not be said to be virtually unable to walk. The claimant in *CDLA/15997/96* has been granted leave to appeal to the Court of Appeal.

(iii) exertion

In *R(M) 3/78*, the claimant needed oxygen to be available in case of a drop attack (which might also have occurred while she was asleep). The Commissioner held that what is now reg. 12(1)(a)(iii) "does not extend to conditions or symptoms which might intervene during the course of walking without there being any connection or relationship to or with walking or being precipitated by the exertion of walking." The deterioration in health need not be permanent or last for any great length of time (*CM/23/1985*) but it must be serious. In *CM/158/94*, the tribunal had found that, although exertion left the claimant exhausted, "it did not result in a serious deterioration in his health since, having rested, he would improve." The Commissioner dismissed the claimant's appeal and suggested that a serious deterioration in a claimant's health would only be shown where:

"(a) there was a worsening of his condition from which he never recovered, or

(b) there was a worsening from which he only recovered after a significant period of time, eg 12 months, or

(c) there was a worsening from which recovery could only be effected by some form of medical intervention."

Sub-para. (1)(b). Double amputees may qualify under this provision even if they have recovered sufficiently to have artificial limbs fitted and are no longer either unable to walk or virtually unable to walk.

Para. (2). There is no indication given as to how the degree of disablement is to be assessed. However, Sched. 2 to the Social Security (General Benefit) Regulations 1982 provides that 100 per cent disablement is appropriate for "loss of sight to such an extent as to render the claimant unable to perform any work for which eyesight is essential". Sched. 3 to the Social Security (Industrial Injuries) (Prescribed Diseases) Regulations 1985 sets out a test for establishing an assessment of 80 per cent for occupational deafness. In *R(DLA)/3/95* the Commissioner said that these tests should be used for the purposes of reg. 12(2). When the 1982 Regulations are being applied in industrial accident cases, an assessment of 100 per cent for loss of vision is regarded as appropriate where the vision is found to be less than 6/60, using both eyes whilst glasses are used; or where finger counting is not possible beyond one foot. Before *R(DLA)/3/95* was decided, an assessment of 80 per cent for deafness was regarded as appropriate where the claimant was unable to hear a shout beyond one metre using both ears (with aids). This was tested by shouting an instruction or question from just beyond one metre behind the claimant.

Para. (3). Note that it is only an inability to walk in the right direction due to the *combined* effects of blindness and deafness which can be relevant.

Para. (4). An ability to wear an artificial prosthesis or to use an artificial aid (such as a pair of crutches) must be taken into account and the claimant's ability to get about must usually be assessed on the basis that a prosthesis or aid is used. However, if the claimant does not in fact habitually wear or use such a prosthesis or aid, it is necessary to consider whether one would be suitable for him or her (*R(M) 2/89*). If a prosthesis is habitually, or could be, worn but any walking is, or would be, achieved only with severe discomfort, such ability to walk would not fall within para. (1)(a)(ii) anyway. But a prosthesis might not be suitable even if the discomfort were not severe. It is arguable that a prosthesis or aid cannot be "suitable" until it is actually available to the claimant. Reg. 12(4) cannot be read as requiring a person to undergo surgery to improve his or her medical condition (*R(M)1/95*).

Para. (5). Only those suffering from a state of arrested development or incomplete physical development of the brain can qualify under those provisions. If someone becomes disabled as a result of an injury after the brain has reached full development, he or she will probably have to rely on para. (1)(a) instead. In *CDLA/156/94*, the Commissioner, having heard expert medical evidence, held that sufferers from Alzheimer's disease do not satisfy the condition mentioned in reg. 12(5). He found that the disease resulted in a deterioration of a developed brain rather than an arrest of development, rejecting the idea that the brain develops throughout life which, he pointed out, would render otiose the restriction implied by reg. 12(5). In that case, the expert evidence suggested that the brain had reached maturity by the time a perosn was aged 30. In *CDLA/393/94*, the claimant was in her early 20s when she became ill and it was held to be arguable that her brain had not fully developed and that she suffered from a state of arrested development or incomplete physical development. The burden of proof rested on the claimant. In *CDLA/8353/95*, the Commissioner heard evidence in respect of a claimant suffering from schizophrenia and concluded that she suffered from arrested development of the brain but that that did not result in severe impairment of intelligence in her case.

Para. (6). Physical restraint must be *regularly* required and the behaviour must be *disruptive* and *unpredictable*. Indeed, since "extremes" describes "disruptive behaviour", it is probably right to say that the behaviour must be extremely disruptive. A person who satisfies the conditions of sub-paras. (b) and (c) but who does not exhibit extremely disruptive behaviour may qualify for the mobility component at the lower rate (under s.73(1)(d) of the 1992 Act).

[[1]Hospitalisation in mobility component cases

12A.—(1) Subject to regulation 12B (exemption), it shall be a condition for the receipt of a disability living allowance which is attributable to entitlement to the mobility component for any period in respect of any person that during that period he is not maintained free of charge while undergoing medical or other treatment as an in-patient—

(a) in a hospital or similar institution under the NHS Act of 1977, the NHS Act of 1978 or the NHS Act of 1990; or

(b) in a hospital or other similar institution maintained or administered by the Defence Council.

(2) For the purposes of paragraph (1)(a) a person shall only be regarded as not being maintained free of charge in a hospital or similar institution during any period when his accommodation and services are provided under section 65 of the NHS Act of 1977, section 58 of, or paragraph 14 of Schedule 7A to, the NHS Act of 1978 or paragraph 14 of Schedule 2 to the NHS Act of 1990.]

Amendment

1. Social Security (Disability Living Allowance and Claims and Payments) Amendment Regulations 1996 (S.I. 1996 No. 1436), reg. 2 (July 31, 1996).

General Note

Until this regulation was introduced in 1996, the mobility component of disability living allowance, like mobility allowance before it, was payable however long the claimant was in hospital. It was only if a claiamnt ceased to be able to benefit at all from enhanced facilities for locomotion (see s.73(8) of the Social Security Contributions and Benefits Act 1992) that he might lose entitlement. Regs. 12B and 12C set out a large number of exemptions and adjustments to the basic rule.

[[1]Exemption from regulation 12A

12B.—(1) Subject to paragraph (2), regulation 12A shall not apply to a person—

(a) for the first 28 days; or

(b) where he has not attained the age of 16, for the first 84 days,

of any period throughout which he is a person to whom paragraph (10) applies.

(2) Where, on the day on which a person's entitlement to the mobility component commences, he is a person to whom paragraph (10) applies, paragraph (1) shall not apply to him for any period of consecutive days, beginning with that day, in which he continues to be a person to whom paragraph (10) applies.

(3) For the purposes of paragraphs (1) and (4), two or more distinct periods separated by an interval not exceeding 28 days, or by two or more such intervals, shall be treated as a continuous period equal in duration to the total of such distinct periods and ending on the last day of the later such period.

(4) Subject to paragraph (5) and regulation 12C, where—

(a) immediately before 31st July 1996, a person has, for a continuous period of not less than 365 days, been a person to whom paragraph (10) applies and in receipt of the mobility component and on 31st July 1996 is a person to whom that paragraph applies; or

(b) on a day not more than 28 days prior to 31st July 1996, a person has, for a continuous period of not less than 365 days, been a person to whom paragraph (10) applies and in receipt of the mobility component, and on or after 31st July 1996 and not more than 28 days after the last day of the previous distinct period during which that paragraph applies, becomes a person to whom that paragraph again applies,

regulation 12A shall not apply until such time as paragraph (10) first ceases to apply to him for more than 28 consecutive days.

(5) Paragraph (4) shall not apply where on 31st July 1996 a person is detained under Part II or III of the Mental Health Act 1983 or Part V or VI of the Mental Health (Scotland) Act 1984.

(6) Where, on a day after 31st July 1996, a person—

(a) becomes detained under Part II or III of the Mental Health Act 1983 or Part V or VI of the Mental Health (Scotland) Act 1984; or

(b) ceases to be entitled to the mobility component,

paragraph (4) shall cease to be applicable to that person and shall not again become applicable to him.

(7) Subject to regulation 12C, where—

(a) on 31st July 1996, a person is a person to whom paragraph (10) applies and a Motability agreement entered into by or on behalf of that person is in force; or

(b) a person becomes a person to whom paragraph (10) applies on a day after 31st July 1996 and on that day there is in force a Motability agreement entered into by or on behalf of that person,

regulation 12A shall, for the period following that referred to in paragraph (1)(a) or, as the case may be, paragraph (1)(b), continue not to apply to that person for the period referred to in paragraph (8) or, as the case may be, paragraph (9).

(8) Subject to paragraph (9), the period referred to in paragraph (7) shall terminate at the end of the period specified in regulation 44(3) or, as the case may be, regulation 44(4) of the Social Security (Claims and Payments) Regulations 1987 that is relevant to that Motability agreement.

(9) Where—

(a) the Motability agreement was made under the scheme run by Motability for wheelchairs;

(b) on the day immediately following the day that agreement ceases to be in force, a subsequent agreement of the same type is entered into by or on behalf of that person; and

(c) on the day referred to in sub-paragraph (b), the person is a person to whom paragraph (10) applies,

the period referred to in paragraph (7) shall terminate at the end of the period specified in regulation 44(3) or, as the case may be regulation 44(4) of the Social Security (Claims and Payments) Regulations 1987 that is relevant to the last such Motability agreement.

[[2](9A) Regulation 12A shall not apply in the case of a person who is residing in a hospice and is terminally ill where the Secretary has been informed that he is terminally ill—

(a) on a claim for disability living allowance;

(b) on an application for a review of an award of disability living allowance; or

(c) in writing in connection with an award of, or a claim for, or an application for review of an award of, disability living allowance.]

(10) This paragraph refers to a person who is undergoing medical or other treatment in a hospital or other institution in any of the circumstances referred to in regulation 12A.

(11) For the purposes of paragraph (4), receipt of mobility allowance prior to 6th April 1992 shall be treated as receipt of the mobility component.

(12) In this regulation—

[[2]ia) "hospice" has the same meaning as that given in paragraph (7) of regulation 10;]

(a) "motability agreement" means an agreement such as is referred to in regulation 44(1) of the Social Security (Claims and Payments) Regulations 1987 (payment of disability living allowance on behalf of a beneficiary in settlement of liability for payments under an agreement for the hire or hire-purchase of a vehicle);

(b) "Motability" means the company, set up under that name as a charity and originally incorporated under the Companies Act 1985 and subsequently incorporated by Royal Charter.]

AMENDMENTS

1. Social Security (Disability Living Allowance and Claims, and Payments) Amendment Regulations 1996 (S.I. 1996 No. 1436), reg. 2 (July 31, 1996).

2. Social Security (Disability Living Allowance) Amendment Regulations 1996 (S.I. 1996 No. 1767), reg. 2 (July 31, 1996).

[[1]Adjustment of benefit to certain persons exempted from regulation 12A

12C.—(1) Subject to paragraph (3), where a person is a person to whom regulation 12B(4) applies and the mobility component would otherwise be payable at the higher rate prescribed by regulation 4(2)(a), the benefit shall be adjusted so that it is payable at the lower rate prescribed by regulation 4(2)(b).

(2) Subject to paragraph (3), where regulation 12B(7) applies, the benefit shall be adjusted so that it is payable at a rate equal to the weekly amount payable under the relevant agreement for the period referred to in that regulation.

(3) Where paragraphs (4) and (7) of regulation 12B both apply, the benefit shall be adjusted so that it is payable either at the lower rate prescribed by regulation 4(2)(b) or at a rate equal to the weekly amount payable under the relevant agreement referred to in regulation 12B(7), whichever is the greater.]

AMENDMENT

1. Social Security (Disability Living Allowance and Claims and Payments) Amendment Regulations 1996 (S.I. 1996 No. 1436), reg. 2 (July 31, 1996).

Invalid Vehicle Scheme

13. Schedule 2, which relates to the entitlement to mobility component of certain persons eligible for invalid carriages shall have effect.

SCHEDULES

SCHEDULE 1 **Regulation 3(4)**

PERSONS AGED 65 AND OVER

Review of an award made before person attained 65

1.—(1) This paragraph applies where—

(a) a person is aged 65 or over;

(b) the person has an award of disability living allowance made before he attained the age of 65;

(c) an application in writing is made in accordance with [[1] section 30(7) or 35(4) of the Administration Act] for that award to be reviewed; and

(d) an ajudicating authority is satisfied that the decision awarding disability living allowance ought to be both reviewed and revised.

(2) Where paragraph (1) applies, the person to whom the award relates shall not, subject to paragraph (3), be precluded from entitlement to either component of disability living allowance solely by reason of the fact that he is aged 65 or over when the revised award is made.

(3) Where the adjudicating authority determining the application for review is satisfied that the decision ought to be reviewed on the ground that there has been a relevant change of circumstances since the decision was given, paragraph (2) shall apply only where the relevant change of circumstances occurred before the person attained the age of 65.

Reviews of an award other than a review to which paragraph 1 refers

2. References in the following paragraphs of this Schedule to a review of an award refer only to those reviews where the awards which are being reviewed were made—

(a) on or after the date the person to whom the award relates attained the age of 65; or

(b) before the person to whom the award relates attained the age of 65 where the award is reviewed and revised by reference to a change in the person's circumstances which occurred on or after the day he attained the age of 65.

Age 65 and over and entitled to the care component

3.—(1) This paragraph applies where a person on or after attaining the age of 65—

(a) is entitled to the care component and an adjudicating authority is satisfied that the decision awarding it ought to be revised on a review under [[1]section 30, 31 or 35 of the Administration Act]; or

(b) makes a renewal claim for disability living allowance.

(2) Where a person was entitled on the previous award or on the award under review to the care component payable—

(a) at the lowest rate, that person shall not be precluded, solely by reason of the fact that he is aged 65 or over, from entitlement to the care component; or

(b) at the middle or highest rate, that person shall not be precluded, solely by reason of the fact that he has attained the age of 65, from entitlement to the care component payable at the middle or highest rate,

but in determining that person's entitlement, [[1] section 72] of the Act shall have effect as if in paragraph (a) of subsection (2) of that section for the reference to 3 months there was substituted a reference to 6 months and paragraph (b) of that subsection was omitted.

(3) In this paragraph, a renewal claim is a claim made for a disability living allowance where the person making the claim had—

(a) within the period of 12 months immediately preceding the date the claim was made, been entitled under an earlier award to the care component or to attendance allowance (referred to in this paragraph as "the previous award"); and

(b) attained the age of 65 before that entitlement ended.

Invalid Vehicle Scheme

4.—(1) Where—

(a) a certificate issued in respect of a person under section 13(1) of the Social Security (Miscellaneous Provisions) Act 1977 is in force, or

(b) an invalid carriage or other vehicle is or was on or after January 1, 1976 made available to a person by the Secretary of State under section 5(2)(a) of the NHS Act of 1977 or section 46(1) of the NHS Act of 1978, being a carriage or other vehicle which is—

(i) propelled by a petrol engine or an electric motor;

(ii) provided for use on a public road; and

(iii) controlled by the occupant,

that person shall not be precluded from entitlement to mobility component payable at the higher rate specified in regulation 4(2)(a), or a care component payable at the highest or middle rate specified in regulation 4(1)(a) or (b) by reason only that he has attained the age of 65.

(2) In determining a person's entitlement where paragraph (1) applies, [[1]section 72] of the Act shall have effect as if in paragraph (a) of subsection (2) of that section for the reference to 3 months there was substituted a reference to 6 months and paragraph (b) of that subsection was omitted.

Age 65 or over and entitled to mobility component

5.—(1) This paragraph applies where a person on or after attaining the age of 65 is entitled to the mobility component payable at the higher rate specified in regulation 4(2)(a), and—

(a) an adjudicating authority is satisfied that the decision giving effect to that entitlement ought to be revised on a review under [[1]section 30, 31 or 35 of the Administration Act], or

(b) the person makes a renewal claim for disability living allowance.

(2) A person to whom this paragraph applies shall not be precluded, solely by reason of the fact that he has attained the age of 65, from entitlement to the mobility component by virtue of having satisfied or being likely to satisfy one or other of the conditions mentioned in subsection (1)(a), (b) or (c) of [[1]section 73] of the Act.

(3) In this paragraph and paragraph 6 and 7 a renewal claim is a claim made for a disability living allowance where the person making the claim had—

(a) within the period of 12 months immediately preceding the date the claim was made been entitled under an earlier award to the mobility component (referred to in these paragraphs as "the previous award"); and

(b) attained the age of 65 before that entitlement ended.

Aged 65 or over and award of lower rate mobility component

6.—(1) This paragraph applies where a person on or after attaining the age of 65 is entitled to the mobility component payable at the lower rate specified in regulation 4(2) and—

(a) an adjudicating authority is satisfied that the decision giving effect to that entitlement ought to be revised on a review under [[1]section 30, 31 or 35 of the Administration Act], or

(b) the person makes a renewal claim for disability living allowance.

(2) A person to whom this paragraph applies shall not be precluded, solely by reason of the fact that he has attained the age of 65, from entitlement to the mobility component, but in determining the person's entitlement to that component [[1]section 73] (11) of the Act shall have effect in his case as if paragraph (a), and the words "in any other case" in paragraph (b), were omitted.

Award of care component where person entitled to mobility component

7.—(1) This paragraph applies where a person on or after attaining the age of 65 is entitled to the mobility component and—

(a) an adjudicating authority is satisfied that the decision giving effect to that entitlement ought to be revised on a review under [[1]section 30, 31 or 35 of the Administration Act], or

(b) the person makes a renewal claim for disability living allowance.

(2) A person to whom this paragraph applies shall not be precluded solely by reason of the fact that he has attained the age of 65 from entitlement under [[1]section 72] (1) of the Act by virtue of having satisfied either the conditions mentioned in subsection (1)(b) or in subsection (1)(c), or in both those subsections, but in determining a person's entitlement, [[1]section 72] of the Act shall have effect as if in paragraph (a) of subsection (2)

of that section, for the reference to 3 months there was substituted a reference to 6 months and paragraph (b) of that subsection were omitted.

AMENDMENT

1. Social Security (Disability Living Allowance) (Amendment) Regulations 1993 (S.I. 1993 No. 1939), reg. 2(2) (August 26, 1993).

GENERAL NOTE

Para. 1. This is concerned with reviews of awards which partly cover a period before the claimant's 65th birthday and partly cover a later period. On a review, entitlement in respect of the latter period is to be determined as though the claimant was under the age of 65 unless the review is on the ground of a change of circumstances which occurred on or after the claimant's 65th birthday (in which case see *Para. 2*).

Para. 2. This is concerned with reviews of awards relating solely to a period no earlier than the claimant's 65th birthday or to an award beginning before that birthday but reviewed on the ground of a change of circumstances which occurred on or after that birthday. In such cases, paras. 3–7 have the effect that the conditions of entitlement may be different from those applying to younger claimants and are the same as those governing certain renewal claims made at or after the age of 65.

Para. 3. On a review (within para. 2) or a renewal claim (within sub-para. (3)), a person of or over 65 can continue to be entitled to the care component at the same rate as before or at a higher rate. A person who was previously entitled to the highest rate but no longer satisfies both the "day" and "night" conditions can also become entitled at the middle rate. However, a person previously entitled to either the highest or the middle rate and who no longer satisfies either of the "day" or "night" conditions cannot become entitled to the component at the lowest rate and so will cease to be entitled to any care component. Furthermore, the qualifying period required of those hoping for entitlement to the component at a higher rate than before, is six months rather than three months as it would be for younger claimants. The overall effect of this paragraph is to make the conditions for entitlement to the care component the same as those for entitlement to attendance allowance under s. 64 of the Social Security Contributions and Benefits Act 1992 which is the benefit which a person would be required to claim if the claim were an entirely fresh one or a repeat claim too late to be included as a renewal claim within sub-para. (3).

Para. 4. Former vehicle scheme beneficiaries who have attained the age of 65 are eligible for the middle or highest rates of the care component or the higher rate of the mobility component. The three-month qualifying period is increased to six-months in respect of the care component but is removed altogether in the case of the mobility component. This effectively recreates the position as it was before disability living allowance replaced attendance allowance and mobility allowance on April 6, 1992. Under s.74(1) of the Social Security Contributions and Benefits Act 1992, a person issued with a certificate under Sched. 2 to these Regulations is deemed to satisfy the conditions for the mobility component at the higher rate.

Para. 5. On a review (within para. 2) or a renewal claim (within sub-para. (3)), a person of or over 65 previously entitled to the higher rate of the mobility component can continue to be entitled to the higher rate even if the ground of entitlement is different. However, if he or she no longer satisfies one of the conditions for entitlement to the higher rate, he or she cannot qualify for the lower rate instead.

Para. 6. On a review (within para. 2) or a renewal claim (within para. 5(3)), a person of or over 65 previously entitled to the lower rate of the mobility component can still be awarded the lower rate but cannot qualify for the higher rate. However, if he or she does not qualify for the lower rate on the usual ground (by satisfying the condition of s.73(1)(d) of the Social Security Contributions and Benefits Act 1992, the claimant may qualify by satisfying one of the conditions of s.73(1)(a), (b) or (c) which are usually the grounds for qualifying for the higher rate.

Para. 7. On a review (within para. 2) or a renewal claim (within para. 5(3)), a person of or over 65 previously entitled to the mobility component can be awarded the care component at the higher or middle rates but the qualifying period for the care component is six months rather than the usual three months for younger claimants. Effectively, the conditions are then the same as for attendance allowance which is what a claimant of that age would claim if he or she were not entitled to the mobility component.

SCHEDULE 2 **Regulation 13**

INVALID VEHICLE SCHEME

Interpretation

1. In this Schedule, unless the context otherwise requires,—

"the 1977 Act" means the Social Security (Miscellaneous Provisions) Act 1977;

"vehicle scheme beneficiary" means any person of a class specified in section 13(3)(a), (c) or (d) of the 1977 Act or any person of the class specified in section 13(3)(b) of the 1977 Act whose application was approved on or after 1st January 1976 and, where an invalid carriage or other vehicle was provided or as the case may be applied for, is a person of any such class in respect of whom the invalid carriage or other vehicle provided or applied for was a vehicle—

(a) propelled by a petrol engine or by an electric motor,

(b) supplied for use on a public road, and

(c) to be controlled by the occupant;

"certificate" means a certificate issued in accordance with paragraph 3.

Prescribed periods for purposes of section 13(3)(c) of the 1977 Act

2. For the purposes of section 13(3)(c) of the 1977 Act—

(a) the prescribed period before 1 January 1976 shall be that commencing with 31st January 1970 and ending with 31st December 1975; and

(b) the prescribed period after 1st January 1976 shall be that commencing with 2nd January 1976 and ending with 31st March 1978.

Issue of certificates

3.—(1) The Secretary of State shall issue a certificate in the form approved by him in respect of any person—

(a) who has made an application for a certificate in the form approved by the Secretary of State; and

(b) whom the Secretary of State considers satisfies the conditions specified in sub-paragraph (2).

(2) The conditions specified in this sub-paragraph are that—

(a) the person is a vehicle scheme beneficiary; and

(b) his physical condition has not improved to such an extent that he no longer satisfies the conditions which it was necessary for him to satisfy in order to become a vehicle scheme beneficiary.

Duration and cancellation of certificates

4.—(1) Subject to sub-paragraph (2) the period during which a certificate is in force shall commence on the day specified in the certificate as being the date on which it comes into force and shall continue for the life of the person concerned.

(2) If in any case the Secretary of State determines that the condition specified in paragraph 3(2)(b) is not satisfied, the certificate shall cease to be in force from the date of such non-satisfaction as determined by the Secretary of State (or such later date as appears to the Secretary of State to be reasonable in the circumstances).

Application of these Regulations in relation to vehicle scheme beneficiaries

5. In relation to a person in respect of whom a certificate is in force these Regulations shall have effect as though regulation 2(1)(a)(iii) were omitted.

General Note

These provisions replace the Mobility Allowance (Vehicle Scheme Beneficiaries) Regulations 1977 (S.I. 1977 No. 1229). A person issued with a certificate under this Schedule is deemed, by s.74(1) of the Social Security Contributions and Benefits Act 1992, to satisfy the condition of s.73(1)(a) so that he or she can qualify for the mobility component at the higher rate. He or she is also deemed to have satisfied that condition during the three-month qualifying period. Para. 1 of Sched. 1 to these Regulations entitles such a person to the mobility component notwithstanding that he or she has attained the age of 65. Note that, under reg. 7 of the 1977 Regulations a person could be entitled to mobility allowance for a period *before* the date of claim for the allowance as long as it was after the certificate came into force. No equivalent provision appears in respect of the mobility component of disability living allowance.

[[1]Schedule 3 **Regulation 9A(1)**

Persons to Whom Regulations 9 and 10 Apply With Modifications

1. Subject to paragraph 3, this paragraph is satisfied in relation to a person if—
(a) on 31st March 1993, he was living in a home registered under the [[2] Social Work (Scotland) Act 1968 or the] Registered Homes Act 1984 as a residential care home or a nursing home; or
(b) on 31st March 1993, he was—
(i) entitled either to—
(aa) the care component of a disability living allowance, or
(bb) income support and his applicable amount was calculated in accordance with regulation 19 of the Income Support (General) Regulations 1987 (persons in residential care and nursing homes); and
(ii) living in a home which was not registered under the Registered Homes Act 1984 but which on 1st April 1993 was required to be registered under that Act as a residential care home by virtue of the amendments made to it by the Registered Homes (Amendment) Act 1991 (which extends registration to small homes); or
(c) he would have been living in a home such as is mentioned in either of the preceding sub-paragraphs on that date but for an absence which, including that day, does not exceed—
(i) except in a case to which head (ii) applies—
(aa) where the person was before his absence a temporary resident in the home, 4 weeks, or
(bb) where the person was before his absence a permanent resident in the home, 13 weeks, or
(ii) where throughout the period of his absence the person was receiving free in-patient treatment within the meaning of the Social Security (Hospital In-Patients) Regulations 1975, 52 weeks.

2. Subject to paragraph 3, this paragraph is satisfied in relation to a person if—
(a) on 31st March 1993 he was—
(i) entitled to—
(aa) the care component of a disability living allowance; or
(bb) income support and his applicable amount was calculated in accordance with regulation 19 of the Income Support (General) Regulations 1987 (persons in residential care and nursing homes); and
(ii) living in a home which was not registered under the Registered Homes Act 1984 and which would on 1st April 1993 have become registrable under that Act but for the provisions of section 1(4) of that Act as substituted by the Registered Homes (Amendment) Act 1991 (which provides that small homes need not be registered if all of the residents are, or are treated for the purposes of the Act as being, relatives of the proprietor); or

(b) he would have been living in such a home on 31st March 1993 but for an absence which, including that day, does not exceed—
  (i) except in a case to which head (ii) applies—
    (aa) where the person was before his absence a temporary resident in the home, 4 weeks, or
    (bb) where the person was before his absence a permanent resident in the home, 13 weeks, or
  (ii) where throughout the period of his absence the person was receiving free in-patient treatment within the meaning of the Social Security (Hospital In-Patients) Regulations 1975, 52 weeks,

and in either case he is either resident in the home on 1st August 1994 or would be so resident but for such an absence as is mentioned in paragraph (b), or has been continuously resident, disregarding any such absence, in residential accommodation to which the Registered Homes Act 1984 applies, or would apply but for section 1(4) of that Act, since 1st April 1993.

3. Paragraphs 1 and 2 shall cease to apply to a person where he is absent from a home such as is mentioned in paragraph 1(a) or (b), or 2(a) and that absence exceeds a period of—

(a) except in a case to which sub-paragraph (b) applies—
  (i) 4 weeks, where the person was before his absence a temporary resident in the home, or
  (ii) 13 weeks, where the person was before his absence a permanent resident in the home; or
(b) 52 weeks, where throughout the period of absence the person was receiving free in-patient treatment within the meaning of the Social Security (Hospital In-Patients) Regulations 1975.

4. For the purposes of this Schedule a person is a permanent resident where the home in which he resides is his principal place of abode, and a temporary resident where it is not.]

Amendments

1. Social Security (Attendance Allowance and Disability Living Allowance) (Amendment) Regulations 1994 (S.I. 1994 No. 1779), reg. 3(6) and Sched. 2 (August 1, 1994).

2. Social Security (Attendance and Disability Living Allowances) Amendment Regulations 1995 (S.I. 1995 No. 2162), reg. 3(6) (September 14, 1995).

The Social Security (General Benefit) Regulations 1982

(S.I. 1982 No. 1408)

Arrangement of Regulations

Part I

General

PART III

PROVISIONS RELATING TO INDUSTRIAL INJURIES BENEFIT ONLY

Principles of assessment

Disablement benefit

Increase of disablement benefit

Adjustment of benefit for successive accidents

Disqualification for receipt of benefit and suspension of benefit pending appeals etc.

SCHEDULES

The Secretary of State for Social Services, in exercise of the powers conferred upon him by sections 50(4), 56(7), 58(3), 60(4) and (7), 61(1), 62(2), 67(1), 68(2), 70(2), 72(1) and (8), 74(1), 81(6), 82(5) and (6), 83(1), 85(1), 86(2) and (5), 90(2), 91(1), 119(3) and (4) and 159(3) of, and paragraphs 2, 3 and 6 of Schedule 8, paragraphs 1 and 8 of Schedule 9 and Schedule 14 of the Social Security Act 1975 and of all other powers enabling him in that behalf, hereby makes the following regulations, which only consolidate the regulations hereby revoked, and which accordingly, by virtue of paragraph 20 of Schedule 3 to the Social Security Act 1980, are not subject to the requirements of section 10 of that Act for prior reference to the Social Security Advisory Committee and, by virtue of section 141(2) and paragraph 12 of Schedule 16 of the Social Security Act 1975, do not require prior reference to the Industrial Injuries Advisory Council:

PART I

GENERAL

Citation, commencement and interpretation

1.—(1) These regulations may be cited as the Social Security (General Benefit) Regulations 1982 and shall come into operation 4th November 1982.

(2) In these regulations, unless the context otherwise requires—

"the Act" means the Social Security Act 1975;

"the Child Benefit Act" means the Child Benefit Act 1975;

"child benefit" means benefit under Part I of the Child Benefit Act;

"determining authority" means, as the case may require, an [[2]adjudication officer] appointed under section 97(1) of the Act [[3]or a disability appeal tribunal constituted under Schedule 10A to the Act], a [[2]social security appeal tribunal] constituted under section 97(2) of the Act, or the Chief Social Security Commissioner appointed under section 97(3) of the Act or any other Social Security Commissioner so appointed, or any Tribunal of Commissioners constituted under section 116(1) of the Act;

"entitled to child benefit" includes treated as so entitled;

"industrial injuries benefit" means [[1]. . .] disablement benefit and industrial death benefit payable under section 50 of the Act;

"parent" has the meaning assigned to it by section 24(3) of the Child Benefit Act;

"standard rate of increase" means the amount specified in Part IV or Part V of Schedule 4 to the Act as the amount of an increase of the benefit in question for an adult dependant;

"the Workmen's Compensation Act" means the Workmen's Compensation Acts 1925 to 1945, or the enactments repealed by the Workmen's Compensation Act 1925 or the enactments repealed by the Workmen's Compensation Act 1906;

and other expressions have the same meanings as in the Act.

(3) Unless the context otherwise require, any reference in these regulations—

(a) to a numbered section is to the section of the Act bearing that number;

(b) to a numbered regulation is a reference to the regulation bearing that number in these regulations and any reference in a regulation to a numbered paragraph is a reference to the paragraph of that regulation bearing that number.

AMENDMENTS

1. Social Security (Abolition of Injury Benefit) (Consequential) Regulations 1983 (S.I. 1983 No. 186), reg. 13(2) (April 6, 1983).

2. Health and Social Services and Social Security Adjudications Act 1983, Sched. 8, para. 1(3)(a) (April 23, 1984).

3. Disability Living Allowance and Disability Working Allowance (Consequential Provisions) Regulations 1991 (S.I. 1991 No. 2742), reg. 8 (April 6, 1992).

Exceptions from disqualification for imprisonment etc.

2.—(1) The following provisions of this regulation shall have effect to except benefit from the operation of section 82(5)(b) of the Act which provides that (except where regulations otherwise provide) a person shall be disqualified for receiving any benefit and an increase of benefit shall not be payable in respect of any person as the beneficiary's wife or husband, for any period during which that person is undergoing imprisonment or detention in legal custody (hereinafter in this regulation referred to as "the said provisions").

(2) The said provisions shall not operate to disqualify a person for receiving [[5]incapacity benefit], [[4]attendance allowance, disability living allowance,] [[4]. . .] widow's benefit, child's special allowance, maternity allowance, retirement pension of any category, age addition, [[2]severe disablement allowance], [[1]. . .] disablement benefit [[3], [[6]reduced earnings allowance, retirement allowance] or industrial death benefit or to make an increase of benefit not payable in respect of a person as the beneficiary's wife or husband, for any period during which that person is undergoing imprisonment or detention in legal custody in connection with a charge brought or intended to be brought against him in criminal proceedings, or pursuant to any sentence or order for detention made by a court in such proceedings, unless, in relation to him, a penalty is imposed at the conclusion of those proceedings or, in the case of default of payment of a sum adjudged to be paid on conviction, a penalty is imposed in respect of such default.

(3) The said provisions shall not operate to disqualify a person for receiving any benefit (not being a guardian's allowance or death grant), or to make an increase of benefit not payable in respect of a person as the beneficiary's wife or husband, for any period during which the person is undergoing detention in legal custody after the conclusion of criminal proceedings if it is a period during which he is liable to be detained in a hospital or similar institution in Great Britain as a person suffering from mental disorder unless—

(a) pursuant to any sentence or order for detention made by the court at the conclusion of those proceedings, he has undergone detention by way of penalty in a prison, a detention centre, a Borstal institution or a young offenders institution; and

(b) he was removed to the hospital or similar institution while liable to be detained as a result of that sentence or order, and, in the case of a person who is liable to be detained in the hospital or similar institution by virtue of any provision of the Mental Health Act 1959 or the Mental Health (Scotland) Act 1960, a direction restricting his discharge has been given under either of those Acts and is still in force.

(4) Where, as respects a person in relation to whom each of the conditions specified in paragraph (3)(a) and (b) is satisfied, a certificate given by or on behalf of the Secretary of State for the Home Department or the Secretary of State for Scotland and furnished to the Secretary of State for Social Services shows the earliest date on which that person would have been expected to be discharged from detention pursuant to the said sentence or order if he had not been transferred to a hospital or similar institution, the said conditions, shall be deemed not to be satisfied in relation to that person as from the day next following that date.

(5) The said provisions shall not operate to disqualify a person for receiving a guardian's allowance or death grant.

[[6](6) Subject to paragraph (7), the said provisions shall not operate to disqualify a person for receiving disablement benefit, other than any increase of that benefit, for any period during which he is undergoing imprisonment or detention in legal custody.]

(7) The amount payable by virtue of the last preceding paragraph by way of any disablement pension or pensions in respect of any period, other than a period in respect of which that person is excepted from disqualification by virtue of the provisions of paragraph (3) of this regulation, during which that person is and has continuously been undergoing imprisonment or detention in legal custody, shall not exceed the total amount payable by way of such pension or all such pensions for a period of one year.

(8) For the purposes of this regulation—

(a) "court" means any court in the United Kingdom, the Channel Islands or the Isle of Man or in any place to which the Colonial Prisoners

Removal Act 1884 applies or any naval court-martial, army court-martial or air force court-martial within the meaning of the Courts-Martial (Appeals) Act 1968, or the Courts-Martial Appeal Court;

(b) "hospital or similar institution" means any place (not being a prison, a detention centre, a Borstal institution, a young offenders institution or a remand centre, and not being at or in any such place) in which persons suffering from mental disorder are or may be received for care or treatment;

(c) "penalty" means a sentence of imprisonment, Borstal training or detention under section 53 of the Children and Young Persons Act 1933 or under section 57(3) of the Children and Young Persons (Scotland) Act 1937 or under section 208(3) and 416(4) of the Criminal Proceedings (Scotland) Act 1975 or an order for detention in a detention centre;

(d) in relation to a person who is liable to be detained in Great Britain as a result of any order made under the Colonial Prisoners Removal Act 1884, references to a prison shall be construed as including references to a prison within the meaning of that Act;

(e) a person who is liable to be detained by virtue of any provision of the Mental Health Act 1959 or the Mental Health (Scotland) Act 1960 shall be treated as if a direction restricting his discharge had been given under one or other of those Acts if for the purposes thereof he is to be so treated;

(f) references to mental disorder shall be construed as including references to any mental disorder within the meaning of the Mental Health Act 1959 or the Mental Health (Scotland) Act 1960;

(g) criminal proceedings against any person shall be deemed to be concluded upon his being found insane in those proceedings so that he cannot be tried or his trial cannot proceed.

(9) Where a person outside Great Britain is undergoing imprisonment or detention in legal custody and, in similar circumstances in Great Britain, he would have been excepted, by the operation of any of the preceding paragraphs of this regulation, from disqualification under the said provisions (referred to in paragraph (1)) for receiving the benefit claimed, he shall not be disqualified for receiving the benefit by reason only of his said imprisonment or detention.

(10) Paragraph (9) applies to increases of benefit not payable under the said provisions as it applies to disqualification for receiving benefit.

AMENDMENTS

1. Social Security (Abolition of Injury Benefit) (Consequential) Regulations 1983 (S.I. 1983 No. 186), reg. 13(2) (April 6, 1983).

2. Social Security (Severe Disablement Allowance) Regulations 1984 (S.I. 1984 No. 1303), reg. 11 and Sched. 2 (November 29, 1984).

3. Social Security (Industrial Injuries and Diseases) Miscellaneous Provisions Regulations 1986 (S.I. 1986 No. 1561), reg. 7(2) (October 1, 1986).

4. Disability Living Allowance and Disability Working Allowance (Consequential Provisions) Regulations 1991 (S.I. 1991 No. 2742), reg. 8 (April 6, 1992).

5. Social Security (Incapacity Benefit) (Consequential and Transitional Amendments and Savings) Regulations 1995 (S.I. 1995 No. 829), reg.16 (April 13, 1995).

6. Social Security (Industrial Injuries and Diseases) (Miscellaneous Amendments) Regulations 1996 (S.I. 1996 No. 425), regulation 4 (March 24, 1996).

GENERAL NOTE

S.82(5)(b) of the Social Security Act 1975 has been replaced by s.113(1)(b) of the Social Security Contributions and Benefits Act 1992.

Suspensions of payment of benefit during imprisonment etc.

3.—(1) Subject to the following provisions of this regulation, the payment to any person of any benefit—

(a) which is excepted from the operation of section 82(5)(b) of the Act by virtue of the provisions of regulation 2(2), (5) or (6) or by any of those paragraphs as applied by regulation 2(9); or

(b) which is payable otherwise than in respect of a period during which he is undergoing imprisonment or detention in legal custody;

shall be suspended while that person is undergoing imprisonment or detention in legal custody.

(2) Paragraph (1) shall not operate to require the payment of any benefit to be suspended while the beneficiary is liable to be detained in a hospital or similar institution as defined in regulation 2(8)(b) during a period for which in his case, benefit to which regulation 2(3) applies is or would be excepted from the operation of the said section 82(5) by virtue of the provision of regulation 2(3).

(3) A guardian's allowance or death grant, or any benefit to which paragraph (1)(b) applies may nevertheless be paid while the beneficiary is undergoing imprisonment or detention in legal custody to any person appointed for the purpose by the Secretary of State to receive and deal with any sums payable on behalf of the beneficiary on account of that benefit, and the receipt of any person so appointed shall be a good discharge to the Secretary of State and the National Insurance Fund for any sum so paid.

(4) Where, by virtue of this regulation, payment of benefit under Chapter IV or V of Part II of the Act is suspended for any period, the period of suspension shall not be taken into account in calculating any period under the provisions of regulation 22 of the Social Security (Claims and Payments) Regulations 1979 (extinguishment of right to sums payable by way of benefit which are not obtained within the prescribed time).

Interim payments by way of benefit under the Act

4.—(1) Where, under arrangements made by the Secretary of State with the consent of the Treasury, payment by way of benefit has been made pending determination of a claim for it without due proof of the fulfilment of the relevant conditions or otherwise than in accordance with the provisions of the Act and orders and regulations made under it, the payment so made shall, for the purposes of those provisions, but subject to the following provisions of this regulation, be deemed to be a payment of benefit duly made.

(2) When a claim for benefit in connection with which a payment has been made under arrangements such as are referred to in paragraph (1) above is determined by a determining authority—

(a) if that authority decides that nothing was properly payable by way of the benefit in respect of which the payment was made or that the amount properly payable by way of that benefit was less than the amount of the payment, it may, if appropriate, direct that the whole or part of the overpayment be treated as paid on account of benefit (whether benefit under the Act or the Supplementary Benefits Act 1976) which is properly payable, but subject as aforesaid shall require repayment of the overpayment; and

(b) if that authority decides that the amount properly payable by way of the benefit in respect of which the payment was made equals or exceeds the amount of that payment, it shall treat that payment as paid on account of the benefit properly payable.

(3) Unless before a payment made under arrangements such as are mentioned in paragraph (1) above has been made to a person that person had been informed of the effect of sub-paragraph (a) of paragraph (2) above as it relates to repayment of an overpayment, repayment of an overpayment shall not be required except where the determining authority is satisfied that [[1]he, or any person acting for him has, whether fraudulently or otherwise, misrepresented or failed to dis-

close any material fact and that the interim payment has been made in consequence of the misrepresentation or failure].

(4) An overpayment required to be repaid under the provisions of this regulation shall, without prejudice to any other method of recovery, be recoverable by deduction from any benefit then or thereafter payable to the person by whom it is to be repaid or any person entitled to receive his benefit on his death.

AMENDMENT

1. Social Security (Payments on Account, Overpayments and Recovery) Regulations 1987 (S.I. 1987 No. 491), reg. 19 (April 6, 1987, with savings).

GENERAL NOTE

S.82(5) of the Social Security Act 1975 has been replaced by s.113(1) of the Social Security Contributions and Benefits Act 1992.

5.—8. *Revoked.*
9. and **10.** *Omitted.*

PART III

PROVISIONS RELATING TO INDUSTRIAL INJURIES BENEFIT ONLY

Principles of assessment

Further definition of the principles of assessment of disablement and prescribed degrees of disablement

11.—(1) Schedule 8 to the Act (general principles relating to the assessment of the extent of disablement) shall have effect subject to the provisions of this regulation.

(2) When the extent of disablement is being assessed for the purposes of section 57, any disabilities which, though resulting from the relevant loss of faculty, also result, or without the relevant accident might have been expected to result, from a cause other than the relevant accident (hereafter in this regulation referred to as "the other effective cause") shall only be taken into account subject to and in accordance with the following provisions of this regulation.

(3) [1Subject to paragraphs (5A) and (5B)] an assessment of the extent of disablement made by reference to any disability to which paragraph (2) applies, in a case where the other effective cause is a congenital defect or is an injury or disease received or contracted before the relevant accident, shall take account of all such disablement except to the extent to which the claimant would have been subject thereto during the period taken into account by the assessment if the relevant accident had not occurred.

(4) [1Subject to paragraphs (5A) and (5B)] any assessment of the extent of disablement made by reference to any disability to which paragraph (2) applies, in a case where the other effective cause is an injury or disease received or contracted after and not directly attributable to the relevant accident, shall take account of all such disablement to the extent to which the claimant would have been subject thereto during the period taken into account by the assessment if that other effective cause had not arisen and where, in any such case, the extent of a disablement would be assessed at not less than 11 per cent. if that other effective cause had not arisen, the assessment shall also take account of any disablement to which the claimant may be subject as a result of that other effect-

ive cause except to the extent to which he would have been subject thereto if the relevant accident had not occurred.

(5) [[1]Subject to paragraphs (5A) and (5B)] any disablement to the extent to which the claimant is subject thereto as a result both of an accident and a disease or two or more accidents or diseases (as the case may be), being accidents arising out and in the course of, or diseases due to the nature of, employed earners' employment, shall only be taken into account in assessing the extent of disablement resulting from one such accident or disease being the one which occurred or developed last in point of time.

[[1](5A) Where—

(a) a person has an award of industrial injuries disablement benefit in respect of the disease specified in paragraph D1 of Part I of Schedule 1 to the Social Security (Industrial Injuries) (Prescribed Diseases) Regulations 1985 (in this paragraph and in paragraph (5B) referred to as "disease D1"); and

(b) by virtue of either paragraph (3) or (4) that award takes account of disablement resulting from the effects of chronic bronchitis or emphysema, not being chronic bronchitis or emphysema prescribed in paragraph D12 of Part I of Schedule 1 to the Social Security (Industrial Injuries) (Prescribed Diseases) Regulations 1985 (in this paragraph and paragraph (5B) referred to as "disease D12"); and

(c) after the date on which the award referred to in sub-paragraph (a) of this paragraph was made the person becomes entitled to industrial injuries disablement benefit in respect of disease D12,

then, during any period when such disablement benefit is payable in respect of disease D12, paragraphs (3), (4) and (5) shall not apply to the assessment in respect of disease D1 for the purpose of assessing the extent of disablement resulting from disease D12.

(5B) Where—

(a) a person has an award of industrial injuries disablement benefit in respect of the disease D12; and

(b) by virtue of either paragraph (3) or (4) that award takes account of disablement resulting from the effects of pneumoconiosis, not being disease D1; and

(c) after the date on which the award referred to in sub-paragraph (a) of this paragraph was made the person becomes entitled to industrial injuries disablement benefit in respect of disease D1,

then, during any period when such disablement benefit is payable in respect of disease D1, paragraphs (3), (4) and (5) shall not apply to the assessment in respect of disease D12 for the purpose of assessing the extent of disablement resulting from disease D1.]

(6) Where the sole injury which a claimant suffers as a result of the relevant accident is one specified in column 1 of Schedule 2 to these regulations, whether or not such injury incorporates one or more other injuries so specified, the loss of faculty suffered by the claimant as a result of that injury shall be treated for the purposes of section 57 of, and Schedule 8 to, the Act as resulting in the degree of disablement set against such injury in column 2 of the said Schedule 2 subject to such increase or reduction of that degree of disablement as may be reasonable in the circumstances of the case where, having regard to the provisions of the said Schedule 8 to the Act and to the foregoing paragraphs of this regulation, that degree of disablement does not provide a reasonable assessment of the extent of disablement resulting from the relevant loss of faculty.

(7) For the purposes of paragraph (6) where the relevant injury is one so specified in the said column 1 against which there is set in the said column 2 the degree of disablement of 100 per cent. and the claimant suffers some disablement to which he would have been subject whether or not the relevant accident

had occurred, no reduction of that degree of disablement shall be required if the medical appeal tribunal, the medical board or single medical practitioner acting instead of a medical board (as the case may be) is satisfied that, in the circumstances of the case, 100 per cent is a reasonable assessment of the extent of disablement from the relevant loss of faculty.

(8) For the purposes of assessing, in accordance with the provisions of Schedule 8 to the Act, the extent of disablement resulting from the relevant injury in any case which does not fall to be determined under paragraph (6) or (7), the medical appeal tribunal, the medical board or single medical practitioner acting instead of a medical board (as the case may be) may have such regard as may be appropriate to the prescribed degrees of disablement set against the injuries specified in the said Schedule 2.

AMENDMENT

1. Social Security (Industrial Injuries) (Prescribed Diseases) Amendment (No. 2) Regulations 1993 (S.I. 1993 No. 1985), reg. 7 (September 13, 1993).

GENERAL NOTE

This regulation provides for the assessment of the extent of disablement in cases where a disability is due both to the relevant accident and another cause and it also introduces Sched. 2 to the Regulations which sets out the prescribed degrees of disablement. S.57 of, and Sched. 8 to, the Social Security Act 1975 have been replaced by s.103 of, and Sched. 6 to, the Social Security Contributions and Benefits Act 1992.

Para. (2). Adjudicating medical authorities used to distinguish between conditions that were regarded as "partly relevant" ("O pre" or "O post") and those that were regarded as merely "connected" ("C"). The former were those conditions considered to have more than one cause and the latter were those conditions considered to be quite separate from the one arising from the relevant accident but which were nonetheless thought to have some effect on the disability arising from the condition caused by the relevant accident. That approach (and Form BI 113(Accident) which reflected it) has been criticised in *R(I) 4/94* and *R(I) 1/95.* Any contributory factor is either to be included in the relevant loss of faculty or else is an "other effective cause" within para. (2), in which case it is taken into account under paras. (3), (4) or (5).

Para. (3). This makes provision for a case where the "other effective cause" is either a congenital defect or is an injury or disease received or contracted *before* the relevant accident. In *R(I) 13/75*, the Commissioner said:

> "In the context of regulation [11(3)] I do not think that 'congenital' should receive its primary meaning, which is 'begotten' or 'born with'; see Shorter Oxford English Dictionary. In my view, the word is used in this regulation in a rather wider sense. I think that it must be taken to mean 'inherent' or 'constitutional,' this is to say that it refers to a defect which is a natural constituent of the person's make-up whether physical or mental. Since Dr. Wright [a principal medical officer of the Department of Health and Social Security] stated that a functional overlay is 'a manifestation of constitutional mental make-up,' I cannot hold that it is not covered by the phrase 'congenital defect' in regulation [11(3)]."

Disablement due to the "other effective cause" must be taken into account except to the extent to which the claimant would have been disabled if the relevant accident had not occurred. Usually this is done by making an assessment of the full extent of disablement resulting from the condition and then applying an "offset" in respect of disablement which would have been present even if the relevant accident had not occurred. There should be no offset in respect of a mere *predisposition* to hysteria (*R(I) 2/74*), functional overlay (*R(I) 13/75*), detachment of retina (*R(I) 3/76*) or development of multiple sclerosis (*R(I) 1/81*). In *R(I) 1/81*, it was held that "constitutional liability to develop the disease cannot have been a 'disability' because it was wholly symptomless. Such liability corresponds with the statutory concept of 'loss of faculty,' that is to say it is a potential cause of disability but not itself a disability." The Commissioner emphasised that the assessment was an assessment of disablement and not an assessment of loss of faculty. However, it does not follow that there can never be an offset in respect of a condition which was symptomless before the relevant accident. An adjudicating medical authority might legitimately apply an offset if a pre-existing, and previously symptomless, condition could have been expected to produced disability at some time even if the accident had not occurred. Nevertheless, such reasoning must be clear, and a medical appeal tribunal which fails to record good reasons for applying an offset in a case where a claimant has asserted that he or she had no symptoms before the relevant accident is liable to find its decision set aside on appeal (*CI/34/93*). On the other hand, there are some conditions, such as arthritis, from which many older people suffer. That is not a ground for an offset. Rather, it is a ground for not including the effects of the arthritis, to the extent to which other people of the same age would suffer from them, in the assessment of total disability at all. That is because that assessment should be made by comparing the claimant "with a person of the same age and sex whose physical and mental condition is normal" (Social Security Contributions and Benefits Act 1992, Sched. 6, para. 1(a)). There is no reason why an adjudicating medical authority should not make an assessment which is tapered to take account of the fact that the claimant would have become increasingly disabled even if the accident had not occurred. Whether that is done by increasing an offset over the period of assessment or by simply reducing the total assessment of disablement depends on whether or not the increasing disability is something from which the "normal" person would suffer. In a case where the assessment of total disablement is 100 per cent, see para. (7).

Where the "other effective cause" is a different type of condition or an injury to a different part of the body, it is conventional to talk of a "connection factor" which is expressed as an increase of the disablement resulting from the relevant accident. Like an "offset", a "connection factor" is not a statutory concept, but both concepts are useful ways of explaining decisions. Use of the concepts enables a claimant to be told the proportion of his or her total disablement that is attributable to the relevant accident (*R(I) 2/74*, *R(I) 1/95*). A claimant ought to know the assessment of the total disablement to which he or she is thought to be subject, as well as the assessment of the disablement attributed to the relevant accident. In *R(I) 1/95*, it was observed that "[a]n inability to lift moderate weights with one hand may not be particularly significant when the claimant can use the other hand instead, but it is obviously a substantial handicap if the claimant has only the one hand and cannot be provided with a functional artificial limb". The "connection factor" represented that additional degree of disablement from which the claimant would not have suffered but for the relevant accident, over and above the degree of disablement suffered by a person who had a fully functional second hand. The same result is reached if the claimant's total disablement is assessed and there is an "offset" in respect of the disablement from which he would have suffered had the relevant accident not occurred. Ideally, both the "connection factor" and the "offset" should be assessed so that it is quite clear that reg. 11(3) has been applied correctly (*R(I) 1/95*). In *R(I) 23/61*, the claimant had a pre-existing disability arising from a defective forefinger and then lost a thumb in the relevant accident. The Commissioner said that:

> "where the medical authorities are dealing with an injury to a hand, the possibility of a connection factor is so obvious, or at any rate will seem so obvious to the claimant, that it is essential that they should satisfy themselves specifically whether or not there is any other defect in the hand which might bring the case within regulation [11(3)] and should give a clear decision on it one way or the other."

In *Murrell v. Secretary of State for Social Services* (reported as an appendix to *R(I) 3/84*), a blind man who suffered an injury to his elbow, which resulted in a loss of sensation in his hand rendering him unable to read braille, had the 15 per cent assessment in respect of the elbow injury increased by a further 15 per cent to take account of the extra disability arising from that injury because of his pre-existing blindness. The Court of Appeal thought that the increase was rather on the low side.

The fact that the claimant is entitled to a disablement pension under the war pensions scheme in respect of the previous injury is not a ground for reducing the assessment in respect of the later one (*R(I) 1/79*).

Para. (4). This applies where the "other effective cause" arises *after* the relevant accident. The paragraph is in two parts. First, account must be taken of all disablement "to the extent to which the claimant would have been subject thereto . . . if *that other effective cause* had not arisen". Thus, a claimant who has lost his right forefinger in an industrial accident and then loses his right hand in a non-industrial accident continues to be entitled to an assessment based on the loss of the forefinger, notwithstanding that he or she would have lost it in the second accident even if the first had not occurred. Secondly, effect is given to the "connection factor", but only in a case where the disablement from which the claimant would have suffered would have been at least 11 per cent without the "other effective cause" arising. In such a case, account must be taken of all disablement to which the claimant is subject "*except* to the extent to which he would have been subject thereto if *the relevant accident* had not occurred". In the example given above concerning the loss of a forefinger followed by the loss of the rest of the hand, no increase would be awarded under the second part of the paragraph because the claimant would have been just as disabled after the second accident even if the first had never occurred. However, an assessment may be increased where a subsequent injury results in greater disablement than it normally would because of the effects of the relevant accident. In *R. v. Medical Appeal Tribunal, ex p. Cable* (reported as an appendix to

R(I) 11/66 and decided under earlier legislation) a man who had lost the sight of one eye in an industrial accident was held by the Court of Appeal to be entitled to the benefit of the "connection factor" when he lost the sight of the other as the result of a non-industrial disease. If the assessment of total disablement is 100 per cent, adjudicating medical authorities must bear in mind paras. (7) and (8) when considering the "connection factor" under this para. To obtain an increase in the assessment of disablement under this paragraph, it is usually necessary for the claimant to apply for a review of the original assessment on the ground of unforeseen aggravation under s.47(4) of the Social Security Administration Act 1992.

Para. (5). Where a person suffers disablement as a result of two or more industrial accidents or prescribed diseases, it may be appropriate simply for the adjudication officer to aggregate the resulting disablements under s.103(2) of the Social Security Contributions and Benefits Act 1992 (if all the causes were accidents) or reg. 15A of the Social Security (Industrial Injuries) (Prescribed Diseases) Regulations 1985. However, the total disablement resulting from the two accidents may be greater than the aggregate of the individual disablements; the loss of two eyes is more than twice as disabling as the loss of one eye. Effect must be given to that "connection factor" in assessing the extent of disablement resulting from the latest accident or disease for which it is relevant (*R(I) 3/91*).

Para. (6). This introduces Sched. 2 which sets out the prescribed degrees of disablement. The degree of disablement may be increased or reduced "as may be reasonable in the circumstances of the case" if the prescribed degree of disablement "does not provide a reasonable assessment of the extent of disablement". Thus a right-handed person who loses his or her right hand might be assessed as more disabled than a left-handed person would be, at least at the beginning of the period of assessment. It would also seem appropriate to make a higher assessment in a case where a person has had a limb amputated and has not yet been fitted with an artificial limb. The disabling effect of any unusual amount of pain must also be taken into account.

Para. (7). In a case where the assessment of total disablement is 100 per cent, "not because that in fact is the proper figure, but because the law permits no greater figure" a smaller offset or even no offset at all in respect of a pre-existing injury might be reasonable (*R(I) 34/61*). That reflects the fact that an assessment of 100 per cent does not imply total disability.

Para. (8). In a case where there is no prescribed degree of disablement, the adjudicating medical authority "may have such regard as may be appropriate" to the Schedule. This is necessary in the interests of consistency and fairness as between claimants. In particular, adjudicating medical authorities must bear in mind that 100 per cent disablement under the Schedule does not amount to total disablement and other assessments should take account of that fact (*R(I) 30/61*). In *R(I) 30/61*, the claimant had been assessed as 30 per cent disabled during a period when he had been confined to bed. It was argued on his behalf that that was far too low and that the appropriate disablement would have been 100 per cent because the claimant should be compared with a person who had lost both legs or one leg and a foot. The decision of the medical appeal tribunal was held to be erroneous in point of law because their findings of fact in respect of the relevant period were not adequately recorded so that it was impossible to know on what basis the tribunal had arrived at the figure of 30 per cent. However, the Commissioner went on to consider the broader issue:

> "I do not think that the words 'and other disabilities shall be assessed accordingly' [Social Security Contributions and Benefits Act 1992, Sched. 6, para. 1(d)] are to be read as tying a non-Schedule assessment to a Schedule assessment as closely as is suggested. Regulation [11(8)] indicates the nature of the connection, and I think that where a medical appeal tribunal, whose members are entitled to use their own expertise, or a medical board 'may' have such regards to a Schedule as may be 'appropriate,' the use of these words strongly suggests that the question may be one of fact. I think that the effect of [paragraph 1(d) of Schedule 6] is that such other disabilities are to be assessed in the form of a percentage varying between 1 per cent [. . .] and 100 per cent but that no such disability is tied to 100 per cent or any other percentage as a matter of law. I am therefore not prepared to accept the proposition that the question of the amount of the assessment (where not prescribed by the Schedule) is a question of law."

Nevertheless, he went on to accept that, in principle, there was no reason why there should not be a high assessment for a short period. He also left open the question whether, and if so on what principles and in what circumstances the Commissioner is entitled to set aside an assessment, where it is alleged that there was no evidence to support it, or that it was contrary to the undisputed evidence, or that it was based on an erroneous view of the law or that the tribunal had omitted to take some factor into account. The question as to the principles to be applied was answered in *Murrell v. Secretary of State for Social Services* (reported as an appendix to *R(I) 3/84*). In that case the Court of Appeal declined to interfere with an assessment. Lord Donaldson M.R. and Dunn L.J. took the view that only a medical appeal tribunal had the skill to make assessments. However, they both accepted that, in theory at least, there might be a case where a Commissioner or court could interfere on the ground that the award was so low that no reasonable tribunal could have reached it (*Edwards v. Bairstow* [1956] A.C. 14). Browne–Wilkinson L.J. expressed grave doubts about the view of the other members of the Court that the decision of the medical appeal tribunal was not so wrong as to indicate whether they must have made an error of law but did not feel there was any purpose in airing them given the view of the majority. Thus, a Commissioner could, in appropriate cases decide that an assessment was too low or too high and it would doubtless do something to promote consistency in decision making if the Commissioners did give guidance from time to time. However, the practical difficulty facing Commissioners is that the findings of fact of medical appeal tribunals are seldom detailed enough to enable someone else to hold that an assessment is so low (or high) as to be wrong in law and, as in *R(I) 30/61* and *R(I) 1/95*, decisions are more likely to be overturned on the ground that the reasons are inadequate and that specific contentions advanced by the parties as to the assessment have not been dealt with.

Disablement benefit

12. and **13.** *Revoked.*

Amount of disablement gratuities

14.—(1) Where the extent of a claimant's disablement is assessed at any of the degrees of disablement severally specified in column 1 of Schedule 3 to these regulations, the amount of any disablement gratuity payable shall—

(a) if the period taken into account by that assessment is limited by reference to the claimant's life or is not less than 7 years, be the amount calculated as the percentage of the maximum disablement gratuity (specified in paragraph 2 of Part V of Schedule 4 to the Act) which is shown in column 2 of Schedule 3 to these regulations as being appropriate to that degree of disablement;

(b) in any other case, be the amount calculated as such a percentage of the maximum disablement gratuity as bears the same proportion to the percentage shown in column 2 of Schedule 3 to these regulations as being appropriate to that degree of disablement as the period taken into account by the assessment bears to a period of 7 years, a fraction of 5 pence being, for this purpose, treated as 5 pence.

[[1](1A) Paragraph (1) applies in relation to cases where the claim for benefit was made before 1st October 1986.]

(2) For the purposes of this regulation, whenever such maximum disablement gratuity is altered by virtue of the passing of an Act or the making of an uprating order, corresponding variations in the scale of gratuities payable under this regulation shall be payable only where the period taken into account by the assessment of the extent of disablement in respect of which the gratuity is awarded begins on or after the date of coming into operation of the provision altering the amount of the maximum disablement gratuity.

AMENDMENT

1. Social Security (Industrial Injuries and Diseases) Miscellaneous Provisions Regulations 1986 (S.I. 1986 No. 1561), reg. 7(3) (October 1, 1986).

GENERAL NOTE

This provides that the amount of a gratuity should be calculated by reference to the maximum disablement gratuity specified in Sched. 4 to the Social Security Contributions and Benefits Act 1992 as in force at the beginning of the period of assessment. In *R(I) 4/82*, an earlier provision to the same effect was held valid, in a case where the claimant had had good cause for a delayed claim so that the period of assessment commenced some years before the date of claim.

Despite the fact that this provision is only concerned with claims made before October 1, 1986, a new maximum disablement gratuity is still prescribed each year because, where there have been one or more provisional assessments following a claim made before October 1, 1986, a further period of assessment will commence at their end. That each further assessment is made on the same claim at least seems to be the reasoning of the draftsman, although it is not entirely consistent with the approach taken by the Court of Appeal in *Parker v. Secretary of State for Social Security* (reported as an appendix to *R(I) 2/90*) in a rather different context.

15. and **16.** *Omitted.*

Increase of disablement benefit

Circumstances in which, for the purposes of section 60, a beneficiary may be treated as being incapable of following an occupation or employment notwithstanding that he has worked thereat

17.—(1) For the purposes of [[2]section 59A (reduced earnings allowance)], when it is being determined whether a beneficiary has at all times since the end of [[2]the period of 90 days referred to in section 57(4)] been incapable of following his regular occupation or employment of an equivalent standard which is suitable in his case, and in determining that question only, the fact that since the end of [[1]that period of 90 days] such beneficiary had worked at that occupation or any such employment (as the case maybe)—

(a) for the purpose of rehabilitation or training or of ascertaining whether he had recovered from the effects of the relevant injury; or

(b) before obtaining surgical treatment for the effects of the said injury; shall be disregarded in respect of the periods specified in the next following paragraph.

(2) The periods during which the beneficiary worked at his regular occupation or at employment of equivalent standard, which shall be disregarded in accordance with the provision of the preceding paragraph, shall be—

(a) in any case to which sub-paragraph (a) of that paragraph applies)—

(i) any period during which he worked thereat for any of the said purposes with the approval of the Secretary of State or on the advice of a medical practitioner, and

(ii) any other period or periods during which he worked thereat for any of the said purposes and which did not exceed six months in the aggregate and

(b) in any case to which sub-paragraph (b) of that paragraph applies—

(i) any period during which he worked thereat and throughout which it is shown that having obtained the advice of a medical practitioner to submit himself to such surgical treatment he was waiting to undergo the said treatment in accordance therewith, and

(ii) any other period during which he worked thereat and throughout which it is shown that he was in process of obtaining such advice.

AMENDMENTS

1. Social Security (Abolition of Injury Benefit) (Consequential) Regulations 1983 (S.I. 1983 No. 186), reg. 13(5) (April 6, 1983).

2. Social Security (Industrial Injuries and Diseases) Miscellaneous Provisions Regulations 1986 (S.I. 1986 No. 1561), reg. 7(4) (October 1, 1986).

GENERAL NOTE

Ss.57 and 59A of the Social Security Act 1975 have been replaced by s.103 of, and para. 11 of Sched. 7 to, the Social Security Contributions and Benefits Act 1992.

Payments in respect of special hardship where beneficiary is entitled to a gratuity

18.—(1) Where in any case a beneficiary is entitled to or has received disablement gratuity, such beneficiary shall as respects that gratuity have the like rights to payments in respect of special hardship as he would have had by way of increase of disablement pension under section 60 if the disablement gratuity had been a disablement pension payable during the period taken into account by the assessment.

(2) A beneficiary who is entitled as respects a disablement gratuity to payments in respect of special hardship by virtue of the preceding paragraph shall, if he makes an application in that behalf at any time before that gratuity or any part thereof has been paid to him, be entitled, subject to the proviso to section 57(6), to a disablement pension in lieu of such gratuity for any part of the period taken into account by the assessment during which he may be entitled to an increase of such pension in respect of special hardship under section 60, and the weekly rate of such pension shall be determined in accordance with Schedule 4 of these regulations.

(3) For the purposes of paragraph (2) and notwithstanding the provisions of regulation 14(2) whenever the weekly rate of such pension is altered consequent upon the passing of an Act or the making of an uprating order, such variation shall have effect as from the date on which the provision varying the amount of the disablement pension specified in paragraph 3 of Part V of Schedule 4 to the Act comes into force, whether the period taken into account by the assessment began before or after the date.

(4) Where a pension has been payable under paragraph (2) in lieu of a gratuity for any period and the beneficiary ceases to be entitled to an increase of such pension under the provisions of section 60, the amount of that gratuity shall be treated as reduced by the amounts which have been paid to the beneficiary by way of such pension, other than any increase thereof under the said section 60 and, subject to the provisions of these regulations, the balance (if any) shall then be payable accordingly.

General Note

This now applies as if references to special hardship allowance under s.60 were references to reduced earnings allowance under para. 11 of Sched. 7 to the Social Security Contributions and Benefits Act 1992 (Social Security (Industrial Injuries and Diseases) Miscellaneous Provisions Regulations 1986, reg. 7).

Increase of disablement pension for constant attendance

19. The amount by which the weekly rate of disablement pension may be increased under section 61 where constant attendance is required by a beneficiary as a result of the relevant loss of faculty shall—

(a) where the beneficiary (not being a case to which paragraph (b) of this regulation relates) is to a substantial extent dependent on such attendance for the necessities of life and is likely to remain so dependent for a prolonged period, be the amount specified in paragraph 7(a) of Part V of Schedule 4 to the Act (unless the attendance so required is part-time only, in which case the amount shall be such sum as may be reasonable in the circumstances) or, where the extent of such attendance is greater by reason of the beneficiary's exceptionally severe disablement, a sum not exceeding one and a half times the amount specified in paragraph 7(a) of Part V of the said Schedule, a fraction of five pence being for this purpose treated as five pence;

(b) where the beneficiary is so exceptionally severely disabled as to be entirely, or almost entirely, dependent on such attendance for the necessities of life, and is likely to remain so dependent for a prolonged period and the attendance so required is whole-time, be the amount specified in paragraph 7(b) of Part V of Schedule 4 to the Act.

General Note

S.61 of the Social Security Act 1975 has been replaced by s.104 of the Social Security Contributions and Benefits Act 1992. Sched. 4 to the 1975 Act has been replaced by Sched. 4 to the 1992 Act.

Determination of degree of disablement for constant attendance allowance

20.—(1) For the purpose of determining whether a person is entitled to an increase by way of constant attendance allowance under section 61 or to a corresponding increase by virtue of section 159(3)(b) of the Act or section 7(3)(b) of the Industrial Injuries and Diseases (Old Cases) Act 1975 of any other benefit, the Secretary of State shall, in a case where that person is subject to disabilities in respect of which payments of two or more of the descriptions set out in the next following paragraph of this regulation fall to be made, determine the extent of that person's disablement by taking into account all such disabilities to which that person is subject.

(2) The payments which may be taken into account are those of the following descriptions:—

(a) payments by way of disablement pensions under the Act;

(b) weekly payments to which that person is or has been at any time after July 4, 1948 entitled in respect of injury or disease being payments by way of compensation under the Workmen's Compensation Acts or under any contracting-out scheme duly certified thereunder;

(c) payments to which that person is or has been at any time after July 4, 1948 entitled as a former constable or fireman on account of an injury pension under or by virtue of any enactment in respect of an injury received or disease contracted by that person before July 5, 1948 or in respect of his retirement in consequence of such an injury or disease;

(d) payments by way of benefit under the Industrial Injuries and Diseases (Old Cases) Act 1975; and

(e) payments of personal benefit by way of disablement pension or gratuity under any Personal Injuries Scheme or Service Pensions Instrument or 1914–18 War Injuries Scheme.

(3) In sub-paragraph (2)(e) the expressions "personal benefit", "disablement pension", "Personal Injuries Scheme" and "Service Pensions Instrument" have the meanings which are assigned to them by the Social Security (Overlapping Benefits) Regulations 1979 for the purposes of those regulations.

General Note

S.61 of the Social Security Act 1975 has been replaced by s.104 of the Social Security Contributions and Benefits Act 1992.

Condition for receipt of increase of disablement pension for constant attendance under section 61 while receiving medical treatment as an in-patient

21.—(1) For the purposes of section 61 (increase of disablement pension in respect of the need of constant attendance), subject to paragraph (2) it shall be a condition for the receipt of an increase of disablement pension under the said section 61 for any period in respect of any person that during that period he is not receiving, or has not received, free in-patient treatment, and for this purpose a person shall be regarded as receiving or having received free in-patient treatment if he would be so regarded for the purposes of the Social Security (Hospital In-Patients) Regulations 1975.

(2) Where a person was entitled to an increase of disablement pension under the said section 61 in respect of the period immediately before he commenced to undergo any treatment mentioned in paragraph (1), that paragraph shall not apply in respect of the first 4 weeks of any continuous period during which he is undergoing such treatment.

(3) For the purposes of paragraph (2), 2 or more distinct periods separated by an interval not exceeding 28 days, or by 2 or more such intervals, shall be treated as a continuous period equal in duration to the total of such distinct periods and ending on the last day of the later or last such period.

GENERAL NOTE

S.61 of the Social Security Act 1975 has been replaced by s.104 of the Social Security Contributions and Benefits Act 1992.

22.—37. *Omitted.*

Adjustment of benefit for successive accidents

Adjustment of benefit for successive accidents where a disablement gratuity is payable

38.—(1) In a case where—

(a) a person who is entitled, as a result of an accident, to a disablement pension (hereafter in this paragraph referred to as an "existing pension") which is payable in respect of an assessment for a period which is limited by reference to that person's life, becomes as a result of any other accident, entitled to an award as a result of an assessment of disablement in respect of which a disablement gratuity would, but for this regulation, be payable; and

(b) the aggregate amount of the assessment in respect of the existing pension and of the assessment in respect of which such disablement gratuity would be payable would, if it were the amount of the assessment of the extent of the disablement resulting from any one accident suffered by that person, have entitled him to receive a disablement pension at a higher rate than the rate of such existing pension;

then, if at any time before his claim for disablement benefit is determined he so elects, that person shall be entitled to a disablement pension in lieu of the said disablement gratuity at a rate equal to the difference between the said higher rate and the rate of the existing pension.

(2) In a case in which a person who is entitled as a result of any accident to a disablement pension would but for the provisions of this paragraph become entitled in respect of any other accident to a disablement gratuity (not being a case in which he is entitled to a disablement pension in lieu of such gratuity)—

(a) if the assessment in respect of which such pension is payable to him amounts to not less than 100 per cent., such person shall not be entitled to receive any disablement gratuity in respect of such other accident;

(b) in any other case, such person shall not be entitled to receive, by way of disablement gratuity in respect of such other accident, an amount exceeding that which would be payable in respect of an assessment equal to the difference between 100 per cent. and the percentage of the assessment in respect of which such pension is payable to him.

(3) For the respective purposes of the two preceding paragraphs of this regulation—

(a) references to an existing pension within the meaning of paragraph (1) and to any disablement pension in paragraph (2) respectively shall include references to all such pensions which may be payable to the person concerned, and references to the amount of the assessment in respect of which, and the rate at which, any such pension is payable shall include references to the aggregate amount of the assessments in respect of which or the aggregate of the rates at which all such pensions are payable as aforesaid;

(b) the extent by which an assessment is increased by virtue of the provisions of section 62 of the Act (increase of disablement benefit during hospital treatment) shall be disregarded;

(c) for the purposes of paragraph (1)(a) a person shall be deemed to be entitled to a disablement pension and to an award as described in the said sub-paragraph from the respective dates of commencement of the periods taken into account by the assessment relating to such pension and to such award.

General Note

S.62 of the Social Security Act 1975 has been replaced by para. 10 of Sched. 7 to the Social Security Contributions and Benefits Act 1992.

Adjustment of increase of benefit in respect of successive accidents

39.—(1) *Omitted.*

(2) *Omitted.*

(3) At any time at which the sum total of the several assessments in respect of two or more accidents suffered by any person amounts to not less than 100 per cent during the continuance of the periods respectively taken into account thereby, the weekly rate of any disablement pension which is payable to him may be increased in accordance with the provisions of section 61 if he requires constant attendance as a result of the loss of faculty resulting from any one or more of such accidents, whether or not that pension is payable in respect of an assessment of 100 per cent. or in respect of that loss of faculty.

(4) A beneficiary who has suffered two or more accidents shall not be entitled at any time to more than one of each of the following increases of benefit, that is to say—

(a) *Omitted.*

(b) in respect of the need of constant attendance under section 61;

(c) *Omitted.*

(d) *Omitted.*

General Note

The omitted provisions deal with entitlement to unemployability supplement under paras. 1–8 of Sched. 7 to the Social Security Contributions and Benefits Act 1992. S.61 of the Social Security Act 1975 has been replaced by s.104 of the 1992 Act.

Disqualification for receipt of benefit and suspension of benefit pending appeals etc.

Disqualification for receipt of benefit, suspension of proceedings on claims and suspension of payment of benefit

40.—(1) *Revoked.*

(2) If, without good cause—

(a) a claimant fails to furnish to the prescribed person any information required for the determination of the claim or of any question arising in connection therewith; or

(b) a beneficiary fails to give notice to the prescribed person of any change of circumstances affecting the continuance of the right to benefit or to the receipt thereof, or to furnish as aforesaid any information required for the determination of any question arising in connection with the award; or

(c) a claimant for, or a beneficiary in receipt of, [[1]disablement benefit] fails to comply with any requirement of regulation 26 of the Social Security (Claims and Payments) Regulations 1979 (obligations of claimants for, and beneficiaries in receipt of, [[1]. . .] disablement benefit);

he shall, subject to the following provisions of this regulation, if the [[2]adjudication officer], a [[2]social security appeal tribunal] or the Commissioner so decide, be disqualified for receiving any benefit claimed in respect of the period of such failure.

(3) If a claimant or beneficiary wilfully obstructs, or is guilty of other misconduct in connection with any examination or treatment to which he is required under regulation 26 of the Social Security (Claims and Payments) Regulation 1979 to submit himself, or any proceedings under the Act for the determination of his right to benefit or to the receipt thereof, he shall, subject to the provisions of this regulation, be disqualified for receiving any benefit claimed for such period as the [[2]adjudication officer], a [[2]social security appeal tribunal] or the Commissioner may determine.

(4) In any case to which any of the foregoing paragraphs of this regulation relates, proceedings on the claim or payment of benefit, as the case may be, may be suspended for such period as the [adjudication officer] a [social security appeal tribunal] or the Commissioner may determine.

(5) Nothing in this regulation providing for the disqualification for the receipt of benefit for any of the following matters, that is to say:—

(a) [[1]. . .]

(b) for failure to comply with the requirements of regulation 26 of the Social Security (Claims and Payments) Regulations 1979;

(c) for obstruction of, or misconduct in connection with, medical examination or treatment;

shall authorise the disentitlement of a claimant or beneficiary to benefit for a period exceeding six weeks on any disqualification.

(6) No person shall be disqualified for receiving any benefit for refusal to undergo a surgical operation not being one of a minor character.

(7) A person who would be entitled to any benefit but for the operation of any of the foregoing provisions of this regulation shall be treated as if he were entitled thereto for the purpose of any rights or obligations under the Act (whether of himself or any other person) which depends on his being so entitled, other than the right to payment of that benefit.

AMENDMENTS

1. Social Security (Abolition of Injury Benefit) (Consequential) Regulations 1983 (S.I. 1983 No. 186), reg. 13 (April 6, 1983).

2. Health and Social Services and Social Security Adjudications Act 1983, Sched. 8, para. 1(3)(a) (April 23, 1984).

41. *Revoked.*

42.–47. *Omitted.*

SCHEDULES

Schedule 1. *Omitted.*

SCHEDULE 2 **Regulation 11**

PRESCRIBED DEGREES OF DISABLEMENT

Description of injury	*Degree of disablement per cent.*
1. Loss of both hands or amputation at higher sites	100
2. Loss of a hand and a foot	100
3. Double amputation through leg or thigh, or amputation through leg or thigh on one side and loss of other foot	100
4. Loss of sight to such an extent as to render the claimant unable to perform any work for which eyesight is essential	100
5. Very severe facial disfiguration	100
6. Absolute deafness	100
7. Forequarter or hindquarter amputation	100
Amputation cases—upper limbs (either arm)	
8. Amputation through shoulder joint	90
9. Amputation below shoulder with stump less than 20.5 centimetres from tip of acromion	80
10. Amputation from 20.5 centimetres from tip of acromion to less than 11.5 centimetres below tip of olecranon	70
11. Loss of a hand or of the thumb and four fingers of one hand or amputation from 11.5 centimetres below tip of olecranon	60
12. Loss of thumb	30
13. Loss of thumb and its metacarpal bone	40
14. Loss of four fingers of one hand	50
15. Loss of three fingers of one hand	30
16. Loss of two fingers of one hand	20
17. Loss of terminal phalanx of thumb	20
Amputation cases—lower limbs	
18. Amputation of both feet resulting in end-bearing stumps	90
19. Amputation through both feet proximal to the metatarso-phalangeal joint	80
20. Loss of all toes of both feet through the metatarso-phalangeal joint	40
21. Loss of all toes of both feet proximal to the proximal inter-phalangeal joint	30
22. Loss of all toes of both feet distal to the proximal inter-phalangeal joint	20
23. Amputation at hip	90
24. Amputation below hip with stump not exceeding 13 centimetres in length measured from tip of great trochanter	80
25. Amputation below hip and above knee with stump exceeding 13 centimetres in length measured from tip of great trochanter, or at knee not resulting in end-bearing stump	70
26. Amputation at knee resulting in end-bearing stump or below knee with stump not exceeding 9 centimetres	60
27. Amputation below knee with stump exceeding 9 centimetres but not exceeding 13 centimetres	50

Description of injury	*Degree of disablement per cent.*
28. Amputation below knee with stump exceeding 13 centimetres	40
29. Amputation of one foot resulting in end-bearing stump	30
30. Amputation through one foot proximal to the metatarso-phalangeal joint	30
31. Loss of all toes of one foot through the metatarso-phalangeal joint	20
Other injuries	
32. Loss of one eye, without complications, the other being normal	40
33. Loss of vision of one eye, without complications or disfigurement of the eyeball, the other being normal	30
Loss of:	
A Fingers of right or left hand	
Index finger—	
34. Whole	14
35. Two phalanges	11
36. One phalanx	9
37. Guillotine amputation of tip without loss of bone	5
Middle finger—	
38. Whole	12
39. Two phalanges	9
40. One phalanx	7
41. Guillotine amputation of tip without loss of bone.	4
Ring or little finger—	
42. Whole	7
43. Two phalanges	6
44. One phalanx	5
45. Guillotine amputation of tip without loss of bone	2
B Toes of right or left foot	
Great toe—	
46. Through metatarso-phalangeal joint	14
47. Part, with some loss of bone	3
Any other toe—	
48. Through metatarso-phalangeal joint	3
49. Part, with some loss of bone	1
Two toes of one foot, excluding great toe—	
50. Through metatarso-phalangeal joint	5
51. Part, with some loss of bone	2
Three toes of one foot, excluding great toe—	
52. Through metatarso-phalangeal joint	6
53. Part, with some loss of bone	3
Four toes of one foot, excluding great toe—	
54. Through metatarso-phalangeal joint	9
55. Part, with some loss of bone	3

General Note

See the notes to reg. 11

SCHEDULE 3 — **Regulation 14**

SCALE OF DISABLEMENT GRATUITIES

Degree of disablement (1)	*Appropriate proportion of maximum disablement gratuity (as specified in paragraph 2 of Part V of Schedule 4 to the Act)* (2)
	per cent
1 per cent.	10
2 per cent.	15
3 per cent.	20
4 per cent.	25
5 per cent.	30
6 per cent.	35
7 per cent.	40
8 per cent.	45
9 per cent.	50
10 per cent.	55
11 per cent.	60
12 per cent.	65
13 per cent.	70
14 per cent.	75
15 per cent.	80
16 per cent.	85
17 per cent.	90
18 per cent.	95
19 per cent.	100

SCHEDULE 4 — **Regulation 18**

RATE OF DISABLEMENT PAYABLE IN LIEU OF DISABLEMENT GRATUITY IN ACCORDANCE WITH REGULATION 18

Where the degree of disablement is as specified in column (1) of the following table, the weekly rate of the pension shall be determined in accordance with column (2) of that table:

Degree of displacement (1)	*Rate of pension* (2)
less than 20 per cent. but not less than 16 per cent.	the appropriate weekly amount of disablement pension payable in respect of a degree of disablement of 20 per cent. as specified in paragraph 3 of Part V of Schedule 4 to the Act;

Degree of displacement (1)	*Rate of pension* (2)
less than 16 per cent. but not less than 11 per cent.	75 per cent. of the appropriate weekly amount of disablement pension payable in respect of a degree of disablement of 20 per cent. as specified in the said paragraph 3;
less than 11 per cent. but not less than 6 per cent.	50 per cent. of the appropriate weekly amount of disablement pension payable in respect of a degree of disablement of 20 per cent. as specified in the said paragraph 3;
less than 6 per cent.	25 per cent. of the appropriate weekly amount of disablement pension payable in respect of a degree of disablement of 20 per cent. as specified in the said paragraph 3;
	a fraction of a penny, being for this purpose treated as a penny.

General Note

This remains in force by virtue of reg. 7(5) and (6) of the Social Security (Industrial Injuries and Diseases) Miscellaneous Provisions Regulations 1986.

Schedule 5. *Omitted.*

The Social Security (Industrial Injuries and Diseases) Miscellaneous Provisions Regulations 1986

(S.I. 1986 No. 1561)

Arrangement of Regulations

Part I

General

Part II

Transitional Provisions

The Secretary of State for Social Services, in exercise of the powers set out in the Schedule below, and of all other powers enabling him in that behalf, by this instrument, which contains only provisions consequential upon section 39 of the Social Security Act 1986, makes the following regulations:

PART I

GENERAL

Citation, commencement and interpretation

1.—(1) These regulations may be cited as the Social Security (Industrial Injuries and Diseases) Miscellaneous Provisions Regulations 1986 and shall come into operation on 1st October 1986.

(2) In these regulations, "the 1975 Act" means the Social Security Act 1975 and "the 1986 Act" means the Social Security Act 1986.

2.—12. *Omitted.*

13. *Revoked.*

PART II

TRANSITIONAL PROVISIONS

Claims for disablement benefit made before 1st October 1986

14. Where a claim for disablement benefit is made before 1st October 1986, that claim shall be determined as though—

(a) paragraph 3(1) of Schedule 3 to the 1986 Act had not been enacted,

(b) paragraph 3(2) had been enacted to the extent only of inserting subsection (1B) of section 57 of the 1975 Act but omitting the words "Subject to paragraph (1C)" and the words from "and where it is" to the end of the subsection.

GENERAL NOTE

This still has some effect because a claim is not finally determined until there is a final assessment of disablement. Where there has been a series of provisional assessments following a claim made before October 1, 1986, further awards of disablement benefit are made as though s.57 of the 1975 Act (now s.103 of the Social Security Contributions and Benefits Act 1992) had not been significantly amended. This means that a weekly disablement pension is awarded only if disablement is assessed as at least 20 per cent but that a disablement gratuity is payable if disablement is assessed at anything from 1 per cent to 19 per cent (see Social Security Contributions and Benefits Act 1992, Sched. 7, para. 9).

The Social Security (Industrial Injuries) (Prescribed Diseases) Regulations 1985

(S.I. 1985 No. 967)

ARRANGEMENT OF REGULATIONS

PART I

GENERAL

PART II

PRESCRIPTION OF DISEASES AND PRESUMPTION AS TO THEIR ORIGIN

PART III

DATE OF ONSET AND RECRUDESCENCE

PART IV

APPLICATION OF CHAPTERS IV AND VI OF PART II OF THE ACT AND OF REGULATIONS MADE THEREUNDER

PART V

SPECIAL PROVISIONS AS TO PNEUMOCONIOSIS, BYSSINOSIS, OCCUPATIONAL DEAFNESS AND CERTAIN OTHER DISEASES

Section A—Benefit

The Secretary of State for Social Services, in exercise of powers conferred by sections 76, 77, 78, 113 and 155 of and Schedule 20 to the Social Security Act 1975, and of all other powers enabling him in that behalf, and for the purpose only of consolidating regulations hereinafter revoked, after consultation with the Council of Tribunals in so far as is required by section 10 of the Tribunals and Inquiries Act 1971, hereby makes the following regulations:

PART I

GENERAL

Citation, commencement and interpretation

1.—(1) These regulations may be cited as the Social Security (Industrial Injuries) (Prescribed Diseases) Regulations 1985 and shall come into operation on 31st July 1985.

(2) In these regulations, unless the context otherwise requires—

"the Act" means the Social Security Act 1975;

"the Workmen's Compensation Acts" means the Workmen's Compensation Acts 1925 to 1945, or the enactments repealed by the Workmen's Compensation Act 1925, or the enactments repealed by the Workmen's Compensation Act 1906;

"the Adjudication Regulations" means the Social Security (Adjudication) Regulations 1984;

"the Benefit Regulations" means the Social Security (General Benefit) Regulations 1982;

"the Claims and Payments Regulations" means the Social Security (Claims and Payments) Regulations 1979;

[[3]"adjudicating medical authority" means, as the case may be, an adjudicating medical practitioner, a specially qualified adjudicating medical practitioner, a medical board or a special medical board;]

"asbestosis" means fibrosis of the parenchyma of the lungs due to the inhalation of asbestos dust;

"asbestos textiles" means yarn or cloth composed of asbestos or of asbestos mixed with any other material;

"coal mine" means any mine where one of the objects of the mining operations is the getting of coal (including bituminous coal, cannel coal, anthracite, lignite, and brown coal);

"diffuse mesothelioma" means the disease numbered D3 in Part I of Schedule 1 to these regulations;

"employed earner" means employed earner for the purposes of industrial injuries benefit and the term "employed earner's employment" shall be construed accordingly;

"foundry" means those parts of industrial premises where the production of metal articles (other than pig iron or steel ingots) is carried on by casting (not being diecasting or other casting in metal moulds), together with any part of the same premises where any of the following processes are carried on incidentally to such production, namely, the drying and subsequent preparation of sand for moulding (including the reclamation of used moulding sand), the preparation of moulds and cores, knock-out operations and dressing or fettling operations;

"grindstone" means a grindstone composed of natural or manufactured sandstone and includes a metal wheel or cylinder into which blocks of natural or manufactured sandstone are fitted;

[[5]"knock out and shake out grid" means a grid used for mechanically separating moulding sand from mouldings and castings;]

"a local office" means any office appointed by the Secretary of State as a local office for the purposes of the Act or of these regulations;

[[4]. . .]

"medical board" has the same meaning as in regulation 30 of the Adjudication Regulations;

[[2]"metal" for the purposes of the disease number A10 in Part I of Schedule 1 to these Regulations, does not include stone, concrete, aggregate or similar substances for use in road or railway construction;]

"mine" includes every shaft in the course of being sunk, and every level and inclined plane in the course of being driven, and all the shafts, levels, planes, works, tramways and sidings, both below ground and above ground, in and adjacent to and belonging to the mine, but does not include any part of such premises on which any manufacturing process is carried on other than a process ancillary to the getting or dressing of minerals or the preparation of minerals for sale;

"occupational asthma" means the disease numbered D7 in Part I of Schedule 1 to these regulations;

"occupational deafness" means the disease numbered A10 in Part I of Schedule 1 to these regulations;

"the old regulations" means the Social Security (Industrial Injuries) (Prescribed Diseases) Regulations 1980, as amended by the Social Security (Industrial Injuries) (Prescribed Diseases) Amendment Regulations 1980, the Social Security (Industrial Injuries) (Prescribed Diseases) Amendment Regulations 1982 and the Social Security (Industrial Injuries) (Prescribed Diseases) Amendment (No. 2) Regulations 1982;

"prescribed disease" means a disease or injury prescribed under Part II of these regulations, and references to a prescribed disease being contracted shall be deemed to include references to a prescribed injury being received;

[[4]"primary carcinoma of the lung" means the diseases numbered D8, D10 and D11 in Schedule 1 to these Regulations;]

"the Secretary of State" means the Secretary of State for Social Services;

''silica rock'' means quartz, quartzite, ganister, sandstone, gritstone and chert, but not natural sand or rotten rock;

[[5]''skid transfer bank'' means the area of a steel mill where the steel product is moved from the area of its formation to the finishing area;]

''special medical board'' has the same meaning as in regulation 30 of the Adjudication Regulations;

[[3]''specially qualified adjudicating medical practitioner'' means a specially qualified adjudicating medical practitioner appointed by virtue of section 62 of the Social Security Administration Act 1992;]

''tuberculosis'' in the description of the disease numbered B5 in Part I of Schedule 1 to these regulations means disease due to tuberculosis infection, but when used elsewhere in these regulations in connection with pneumoconiosis means tuberculosis of the respiratory system only;

and other expressions have the same meanings as in the Act.

(3) Unless the context otherwise requires, any reference in these regulations—

(a) to a numbered section or Schedule is to the section of or, as the case may be, the Schedule to the Act bearing that number; and

(b) to a numbered regulation is a reference to the regulations bearing that number in these regulations, and any reference in a regulation to a numbered paragraph is a reference to the paragraph of that regulation bearing that number; and

(c) to any provision made by or contained in any enactment or instrument shall be construed as including a reference to any provision which it re-enacts or replaces, with or without modification.

[[1](4) In these Regulations, any reference to death benefit shall be taken as including also a reference to any benefit in respect of which contribution conditions are taken as having been satisfied in accordance with paragraph 10 of Schedule 3 to the Social Security Act 1986.]

AMENDMENTS

1. Social Security (Industrial Injuries) (Miscellaneous Amendment) Regulations 1988 (S.I. 1988 No. 553), reg. 5 (April 11, 1988).

2. Social Security (Industrial Injuries) (Prescribed Diseases) Amendment Regulations 1990 (S.I. 1990 No. 2269), reg. 2 (December 13, 1990).

3. Social Security (Industrial Injuries and Adjudication) Regulations 1993 (S.I. 1993 No. 861), reg. 17 (April 19, 1993).

4. Social Security (Industrial Injuries) (Prescribed Diseases) Amendment Regulations 1993 (S.I. 1993 No. 862), reg. 2 (April 19, 1993).

5. Social Security (Industrial Injuries) (Prescribed Diseases) Amendment Regulations 1994 (S.I. 1994 No. 2343), reg. 2 (October 10, 1994).

PART II

PRESCRIPTION OF DISEASES AND PRESUMPTION AS TO THEIR ORIGIN

Prescription of diseases and injuries and occupations for which they are prescribed

2. For the purposes of Chapter V of Part II of the Act—

(a) subject to paragraphs (b) and (c) of this regulation and to regulation 43(3), (5) and (6), each disease or injury set out in the first column of Part I of Schedule 1 hereto is prescribed in relation to all persons who have been employed on or after 5th July 1948 in employed earner's employment in any occupation set against such disease or injury in the second column of the said Part;

(b) pneumoconiosis is prescribed—
   (i) in relation to all persons who have been employed on or after 5th July 1948 in employed earner's employment in any occupation set out in Part II of the said Schedule; and
   (ii) in relation to all other persons who have been so employed in any occupation involving exposure to dust and who have not worked at any time (whether in employed earner's employment or not) in any occupation in relation to which pneumoconiosis is prescribed by virtue of regulations (apart from this sub-paragraph) in force—
      (a) in the case of any claim for disablement benefit or a claim for death benefit in respect of the death of a person to whom disablement benefit has been awarded in respect of pneumoconiosis, on the date of the claim for disablement benefit;
      (b) in the case of a claim for death benefit in respect of the death of any other person, on the date of the death of that person;

(c) occupational deafness is prescribed in relation to all persons who have been employed in employed earner's employment—
   (i) at any time on or after 5th July 1948; and
   (ii) for a period or periods (whether before or after 5th July 1948) amounting in the aggregate to not less than 10 years

   in one or more of the occupations set out in the second column of paragraph A10 of Part I of Schedule 1 to these regulations and in the case of a person who during such period as is specified above has been concurrently employed in two or more of the occupations described in sub-paragraphs (a), (b), (d), (e), (f), (g) and (h) of the said paragraph A10 those occupations shall be treated as a single occupation for the purposes of determining whether that person has been employed wholly or mainly in work described in those sub-paragraphs

[[1](d) the disease specified in paragraph D12 of Part I of Schedule 1 is not prescribed in relation to persons to whom regulation 22 applies.]

AMENDMENT

1. Social Security (Industrial Injuries) (Prescribed Diseases) Amendment (No. 2) Regulations 1993 (S.I. 1993 No. 1985), reg. 2 (September 13, 1993).

GENERAL NOTE

This regulation introduces Sched. 1 listing the prescribed diseases. Each disease is prescribed only in relation to claimants who have been employed in the occupations described in the Schedule. That is a significant limitation. It is also necessary for the occupation to have caused the disease but that is usually presumed under reg. 4. The question whether a person is suffering from a disease is determined by an adjudication officer or, on an appeal or reference, the adjudicating medical authorities under regs. 43–54 of the Social Security (Adjudication) Regulations 1995. The question whether the disease is prescribed in relation to the particular claimant (*i.e.* whether he or she was employed in the prescribed occupation) is determined by an adjudication officer but any appeal is considered by a social security appeal tribunal. See the notes to this regulation and to Sched. 1 in Bonner *et al., Non-means-tested Benefits: The Legislation.*

Sequelae or resulting conditions

3. Where a person—

(a) is or was in employed earner's employment and a disease is or was prescribed under the Act and these regulations in relation to him in such employment; and

(b) is suffering from a condition which, in his case, has resulted from that disease;

the provisions of Chapter V of Part II of the Act and of these regulations shall apply to him as if he was suffering from that disease, whether or not the condition from which he is suffering is itself a prescribed disease.

General Note

Disablement resulting from a condition which is not prescribed but which has resulted from a prescribed disease is to be included in any assessment.

Presumption that a disease is due to the nature of employment

4.—(1) Where a person has developed a disease which is prescribed in relation to him in Part I of Schedule 1 hereto, other than the diseases numbered A10, [[1]A12,] B5, D1, D2, [[3]. . .] [[2]D5 and D12] in that Schedule, that disease shall, unless the contrary is proved, be presumed to be due to the nature of his employed earner's employment if that employment was in any occupation set against that disease in the second column of the said Part and he was so employed on, or at any time within one month immediately preceding, the date on which, under the subsequent provisions of these regulations, he is treated as having developed the disease.

(2) Where a person in relation to whom tuberculosis is prescribed in paragraph B5 of Part I of Schedule 1 hereto develops that disease, the disease shall, unless the contrary is proved, be presumed to be due to the nature of his employed earner's employment if the date on which, under the subsequent provisions of these regulations, he is treated as having developed the disease is not less than six weeks after the date on which he was first employed in any occupation set against the disease in the second column of the said Part and not more than two years after the date on which he was last so employed in employed earner's employment.

(3) Where a person in relation to whom pneumoconiosis is prescribed in regulation 2(b)(i) develops pneumoconiosis, the disease shall, unless the contrary is proved, be presumed to be due to the nature of his employed earner's employment if he has been employed in one or other of the occupations set out in Part II of the said Schedule 1 for a period or periods amounting in the aggregate to not less than two years in employment which either—

(a) was employed earner's employment; or

(b) would have been employed earner's employment if it has taken place on or after 5th July 1948.

(4) Where a person in relation to whom byssinosis is prescribed in paragraph D2 of Part I of Schedule 1 hereto develops byssinosis, the disease shall, unless the contrary is proved, be presumed to be due to the nature of his employed earner's employment.

(5) Where a person in relation to whom occupational deafness is prescribed in regulation 2(c) develops occupational deafness the disease shall, unless the contrary is proved, be presumed to be due to the nature of his employed earner's employment.

[[2](6) Where a person in relation to whom chronic bronchitis or emphysema is prescribed in paragraph D12 of Schedule 1 develops chronic bronchitis or emphysema, the disease shall, unless the contrary is proved, be presumed to be due to the nature of his employed earner's employment.]

Amendments

1. Social Security (Industrial Injuries) (Prescribed Diseases) Amendment Regulations 1993 (S.I. 1993 No. 862), reg. 3 (April 19, 1993).

2. Social Security (Industrial Injuries) (Prescribed Diseases) Amendment (No. 2) Regulations 1993 (S.I. 1993 No. 1985), reg. 3 (September 13, 1993).

3. Social Security (Industrial Injuries and Diseases) (Miscellaneous Amendments) Regulations 1996 (S.I. 1996 No. 425), reg. 5(2) (March 24, 1996).

General Note

Except in the case of the diseases listed in para. (1), there is a presumption that the prescribed disease was caused by the prescribed occupation if the date of onset of the disease (see regs. 5 and 6) was no more than a month after the claimant last worked in the occupation. In the cases of tuberculosis, pneumoconiosis (in relation to occupations in Pt. 2 of the Schedule), byssinosis and occupational deafness, there are different conditions. There is no presumption in any cases of diseases D5 (non-infective dermatitis of external origin) or in any case of pneumoconiosis arising from general exposure to dust. Where the presumption applies, it is still open to an adjudication officer to show that, on the balance of probabilities, the occupation did not cause the disease in the particular case under consideration.

Until March 24, 1996, there was also no presumption in any case of disease D4, the prescription of which was altered from the same date (it having been known previously as "inflammation or ulceration of the mucous membrane of the upper respiratory passages or mouth produced by dust, liquid or vapour"). There are certain cases which must still be determined under the law as it existed before the amendments to this regulation and to the prescription (see Social Security (Industrial Injuries and Diseases) (Miscellaneous Amendments) Regulations 1996 (S.I. 1996 No. 425), reg. 7).

Part III

Date of Onset and Recrudescence

Development of disease

5. If on a claim for benefit under Chapter V of Part II of the Act in respect of a prescribed disease a person is found to be or to have been suffering from the disease, or to have died as the result thereof, the disease shall, for the purposes of such claim, be treated as having developed on a date (hereafter in these regulations referred to as "the date of onset") determined in accordance with the provisions of the next two following regulations.

Date of onset

6.—(1) For the purposes of the first claim in respect of a prescribed disease suffered by a person, the date of onset shall be determined in accordance with the following provisions of this regulation, and, save as provided in regulation 7, that date shall be treated as the date of onset for the purposes of any subsequent claim in respect of the same disease suffered by the same person, so however that—

(a) subject to the provisions of section 117(4), as modified by paragraph 1 of Schedule 3 to the Adjudication Regulations, any date of onset determined for the purposes of that claim shall not preclude fresh consideration of the question whether the same person is suffering from the same disease on any subsequent claim for or award of benefit; and

(b) if, on the consideration of a claim, [[1]the degree of disablement is assessed at less than one per cent.], any date of onset determined for the purposes of that claim shall be disregarded for the purposes of any subsequent claim.

(2) Where the claim for the purposes of which the date of onset is to be determined is—

(a) a claim for sickness benefit made by virtue of section 50A of the Act by a person to whom regulation 8(1) applies (except in respect of pneumoconiosis, byssinosis, diffuse mesothelioma, occupational deafness, occupational asthma, [[2]primary carcinoma of the lung][[3], bilateral diffuse pleural thickening or chronic bronchitis or emphysema]) the date of onset shall be the first day on which the claimant was incapable of work as the result of the disease on or after 5th July 1948;

(b) a claim for disablement benefit (except in respect of occupational deafness), the date of onset shall be the day on which the claimant first suffered from the relevant loss of faculty on or after 5th July 1948; and the date of onset so determined shall be the date of onset for the purposes of a claim for sickness benefit made by virtue of section 50A of the Act in respect of pneumoconiosis, byssinosis, diffuse mesothelioma, occupational asthma, [[2] primary carcinoma of the lung][[3], bilateral diffuse pleural thickening or chronic bronchitis or emphysema];

(c) a claim for disablement benefit in respect of occupational deafness, the date of onset shall be the day on which the claimant first suffered from the relevant loss of faculty on or after 3rd February 1975; or, if later—

(i) 3rd September 1979 in the case of a claim made before that date which results in the payment of benefit commencing on that date, and

(ii) in any other case, the date on which such claim is made as results in the payment of benefit; or

(d) a claim for death benefit, the date of onset shall be the date of death.

Amendments

1. Social Security (Industrial Injuries) (Prescribed Diseases) Amendment Regulations 1989 (S.I. 1989 No. 1207), reg. 2 (August 9, 1989).

2. Social Security (Industrial Injuries) (Prescribed Diseases) Amendment Regulations 1993 (S.I. 1993 No. 862). reg. 4 (April 19, 1993).

3. Social Security (Industrial Injuries) (Prescribed Diseases) Amendment (No. 2) Regulations 1993 (S.I. 1993 No. 1985), reg. 4 (September 13, 1993).

General Note

This is an important provision because, under Sched. 2, references in the Act to the date of the relevant accident must, in disease cases, be construed as references to the date of onset. It is also important when reduced earnings allowance is being claimed because the claimant's ''regular employment'' is the employment he had at that date (*CI/285/49*). Under para. (1), once there has been a claim for benefit, the date of onset established for the purposes of that claim applies for any future claim in respect of the same disease unless disablement is assessed at less than 1 per cent. Reg. 7 deals with the distinction between fresh attacks of a disease and recrudescence of an earlier attack.

In *CI/189/94*, it was held that the determination of the date of onset involves the determination of a diagnosis question and, on a claim for disablement benefit, a disablement question. It is, accordingly a matter falling within the jurisdiction of a medical appeal tribunal rather than a social security appeal tribunal. The Commissioner criticised the practice of referring cases to adjudicating medical authorities and medical appeal tribunals with a ''provisional date of onset'' inserted on the relevant form by the local office of the Benefits Agency.

It was clear from *McKiernon v. Secretary of State for Social Services* (*The Times*, November 1, 1989), that reg. 6(2)(c) was originally *ultra vires.* As a result, s.77(2) of the Social Security Act 1975 (now s.109 of the Social Security Contributions and Benefits Act 1992) was amended by para. 4(2) of Sched. 6 to the Social Security Act 1990. Para. 4(3) of Sched. 6 to the 1990 Act provided that reg. 6(2)(c) should be taken always to have been validly made. An argument that the 1990 Act failed to have the desired effect was rejected in *Chatterton v. Chief Adjudication Officer* (Court of Appeal, unreported, July 8, 1993).

S.50A of the Social Security Act 1975 has been replaced by s.102 of the Social Security Contributions and Benefits Act 1992. S.107(4) related to death benefit and was repealed (with a saving) in 1988.

Recrudescence

7.—(1) [[1]Where in respect of a prescribed disease other than pneumoconiosis, byssinosis, diffuse mesothelioma, occupational deafness, occupational asthma,

[2primary carcinoma of the lung][3 bilateral diffuse pleural thickening or chronic bronchitis or emphyrema], a person's disablement has been assessed at not less than one per cent. and he] suffers from another attack of the same disease, or dies as a result thereof, then—

(a) if the further attack commences or the death occurs during a period taken into account by [1that assessment] (which period is in this regulation referred to as a "relevant period") the disease shall be treated as a recrudescence of the attack to which the relevant period relates, unless it is otherwise determined in the manner referred to in the following sub-paragraph;

(b) if the further attack commences or the death occurs otherwise than during a relevant period, or if it is determined in the manner provided in Part IX of the Adjudication Regulations that the disease was in fact contracted afresh, it shall be treated as having been so contracted.

(2) For the purposes of paragraph (1), a further attack of a prescribed disease shall be deemed to have commenced on the date on which the person concerned was first incapable of work or first suffered from the relevant loss of faculty, whichever is earlier, as a result of that further attack.

(3) Where, under the foregoing provisions of this regulation, a disease is treated as having been contracted afresh, the date of onset of the disease in relation to the fresh contraction shall be the date on which the person concerned was first incapable of work or first suffered from the relevant loss of faculty, whichever is earlier as a result of the further attack, or in the event of his death, the date of death.

(4) Where, under the provisions aforesaid, a disease is treated as a recrudescence, any assessment of disablement in respect of the recrudescence during a period taken into account by a previous assessment of disablement shall be by way of review of the assessment relating to the relevant period, and the review shall be subject to the provisions of regulation 49 of the Adjudication Regulations.

(5) This regulation shall not apply in relation to a claim for sickness benefit made by virtue of section 50A of the Act except where such a claim is made by a person to whom regulation 8(1) applies.

AMENDMENTS

1. Social Security (Industrial Injuries) (Prescribed Diseases) Amendment Regulations 1989 (S.I. 1989. No. 1207), reg. 3 (August 9, 1989).

2. Social Security (Industrial Injuries) (Prescribed Diseases) Amendment Regulations 1993 (S.I. 1993 No. 862), reg. 5 (April 19, 1993).

3. Social Security (Industrial Injuries) (Prescribed Diseases) Amendment (No. 2) Regulations 1993 (S.I. 1993 No. 1985), reg. 4 (September 13, 1993).

GENERAL NOTE

Under regs. 43 to 54 of the Social Security (Adjudication) Regulations 1995, any question whether there has been a fresh attack or a recrudescence of an earlier attack arising under this regulation or reg. 8 falls to be decided by an adjudication officer or by adjudicating medical authorities in the same way as a diagnosis question.

Workmen's compensation cases

8.—(1) If under the foregoing provisions of this Part of these regulations a date of onset has to be determined for the purposes of a claim for benefit in respect of a prescribed disease, other than pneumoconiosis or byssinosis, suffered by a person to whom compensation under the Workmen's Compensation Acts has been awarded or paid in respect of the same disease and, at the date of such claim for benefit, or, if it is a claim for death benefit, at the date of death—

(a) that person was in receipt of weekly payments in respect of such compensation; or

(b) any liability or alleged liability for such compensation had been redeemed by the payment of a lump sum, or had been the subject of a composition agreement under the provisions of the said Acts;

the disease in respect of which the claim is made shall be treated for the purposes of these regulations as a recrudescence of the disease in respect of which such compensation was awarded or paid and not as having developed on or after 5th July 1948 unless it is determined in the manner provided in Part IX of the Adjudication Regulations that the disease was in fact contracted afresh.

(2) If it is determined as provided in the foregoing paragraph that the disease was contracted afresh, or if compensation is not being or has not been paid as provided in sub-paragraph (a) or (b) thereof, the date of onset shall be determined in accordance with regulations 5 to 7 as if no compensation under the Workmen's Compensation Acts has been paid in respect of that disease.

(3) If the date of onset has to be determined as aforesaid in respect of pneumoconiosis or byssinosis suffered by a person to whom compensation has been awarded or paid in respect of the same disease or in respect of whose death compensation has been awarded or paid under the provisions of any scheme made under the provisions of the Workmen's Compensation Acts relating to compensation for silicosis, asbestosis, pneumoconiosis or byssinosis, the disease in respect of which the claim is made shall (subject to the provisions of regulation 9(2)(b)) be treated for the purposes of these regulations as not having developed on or after 5th July 1948.

(4) If, after the date of a claim for benefit in respect of a prescribed disease, the claimant receives a weekly payment of compensation in respect of that disease under the Workmen's Compensation Acts which he was not receiving at the date of such claim, or if the amount of any such weekly payment which he was receiving at that date is increased, then any decision on any question arising in connection with that claim, if given before the date of, or in ignorance of the fact of, the receipt of such weekly payment or increased weekly payment, may be reviewed as if it had been given in ignorance of a material fact, and on such review the question may be decided as if the claimant had been in receipt of such weekly payment or increased weekly payment at the date of the claim, and the foregoing provisions of this regulation shall apply accordingly.

(5) For the purposes of this regulation, a person shall be deemed to be, or to have been, in receipt of a weekly payment of compensation if—

(a) he is or was in fact receiving such payment; or

(b) he is or was entitled thereto under an award or agreement made under the Workmen's Compensation Acts.

(6) This regulation shall apply to compensation under any contracting out scheme duly certified under the Workmen's Compensation Acts as it applies to compensation under those Acts.

Re-employment of pneumoconiotics and special provisions for benefit (workmen's compensation cases)

9.—(1) Where a person—

(a) has been certified by a medical board under the provisions of any scheme made under the provisions of the Workmen's Compensation Acts to be suffering from silicosis or pneumoconiosis not accompanied in either case by tuberculosis and has been awarded or paid compensation under the provisions of any such scheme, and by reason of such certification has been suspended from employment in any industry or process or in any particular operation or work in any industry, and

(b) wishes to start work in employed earner's employment in any occupation involving work underground in any coal mine, or the working or handling above ground at any coal mine of any minerals extracted therefrom, or any operation incidental thereto, being an occupation in which he is allowed by certificate of the medical board under the provisions of the scheme to engage,

he shall, before starting any such work, submit himself under arrangements made or approved by the Secretary of State for medical examination by a special medical board.

(2) Where a person submits himself for medical examination in accordance with the provisions of the foregoing paragraph, the provisions of the Act and the regulations made thereunder shall apply to him subject to the following modifications:—

(a) The special medical board shall determine at what degree the extent of disablement resulting from pneumoconiosis at the time of their examination would be assessed in his case, if that question had been referred to them for determination by an adjudication officer on consideration of a claim for disablement benefit, and the provisions of the Act and of the Adjudication Regulations which relate to the determination of disablement questions (other than the provisions relating to the review of assessments on the ground of unforeseen aggravation) shall apply as if the decision of the special medical board were a final assessment of the extent of disablement.

(b) Where the extent of disablement has been determined in his case in accordance with the provisions of the foregoing sub-paragraph by a special medical board or a medical appeal tribunal, and he starts any such work as is mentioned in the foregoing paragraph, the provisions of regulation 38(a) (periodical examinations) shall apply to him as if he were making a claim for benefit in respect of pneumoconiosis, and the provisions of regulation 8(3) (pneumoconiosis shall in certain cases be treated as not having developed on or after 5th July 1948) shall cease to apply to him as from the date of starting such work.

(c) If, after having started work as aforesaid, he makes a claim at any time for disablement benefit in respect of pneumoconiosis, the extent of disablement in his case shall be assessed as if, to the extent certified in the decision of the special medical board or medical appeal tribunal given under sub-paragraph (a) of this paragraph, his disabilities resulting from pneumoconiosis were contracted before the date of onset and were not incurred as the result of the relevant loss of faculty.

(d) A person to whom a disablement pension is payable in respect of an assessment made in accordance with the provisions of the last foregoing sub-paragraph and who requires constant attendance shall, if the sum of that assessment and the assessment made in his case in accordance with the provisions of sub-paragraph (a) of this paragraph is not less than 100 per cent., have the like right to payments in respect of the need of such constant attendance as if the disablement pension were payable in respect of an assessment of 100 per cent.

(3) Where a person to whom sub-paragraph (a) of paragraph (1) applies has started any such work as is mentioned in sub-paragraph (b) thereof without having submitted himself for medical examination in accordance with the provisions of that paragraph, he may nevertheless, at any time whilst he is engaged in any such work, so submit himself for medical examination, and the provisions

of the foregoing paragraph shall, if he continues thereafter to be engaged in any such work, apply to him as if he had started that work immediately after the medical examination.

(4) The Secretary of State, in making or approving any such arrangements for medical examination of any person as are mentioned in paragraph (1) shall, as far as possible, co-ordinate those arrangements with any arrangements for medical examination of that person made or approved under Part V of these regulations or under the Workmen's Compensation Acts.

PART IV

APPLICATION OF CHAPTERS IV AND VI OF PART II OF THE ACT AND OF REGULATIONS MADE THEREUNDER

Definition of "relevant disease"

10. In this Part of these regulations, unless the context otherwise requires, the expression "relevant disease" means, in relation to any claim for benefit in respect of a prescribed disease, the prescribed disease in respect of which benefit is claimed, but does not include any previous or subsequent attack of that disease, suffered by the same person, which, under the provisions of Part III of these regulations, is or has been treated—

(a) as having developed on a date other than the date which, under the said provisions, is treated as the date of onset for the purposes of the claim under consideration;

(b) as a recrudescence of a disease for which compensation has been paid or awarded under the Workmen's Compensation Acts.

Application of Chapters IV and VI of Part II of the Act

11. The provisions of Chapters IV and VI of Part II of the Act which relates to industrial injuries benefit and sickness benefit made by virtue of section 50A of the Act shall, in relation to prescribed diseases, be subject to the following provisions of this Part of these regulations, and, subject as aforesaid, to the additions and modifications set out in Schedule 2 hereto.

GENERAL NOTE

S.50A of the Social Security Act 1975 has been replaced by s.102 of the Social Security Contributions and Benefits Act 1992.

Application of Claims and Payments Regulations and Benefit Regulations

12.—(1) Save in so far as they are expressly varied or excluded by, or are inconsistent with, the provisions of this Part of these regulations or of regulation 25 or 36, the Claims and Payments Regulations and the Benefit Regulations shall apply in relation to prescribed diseases as they apply in relation to accidents.

(2) Save as provided in this Part of these regulations or where the context otherwise requires, references in the aforesaid regulations to accidents shall be construed as references to prescribed diseases, references to the relevant accident shall be construed as references to the relevant disease, references to the date of the relevant accident shall be construed as references to the date of onset of the relevant disease, and in regulation 17 of the Benefit Regulations (increase of disablement pension in cases of special hardship), the reference to the effects of the relevant injury shall be construed as a reference to the effects of the relevant disease.

Benefit not payable in cases covered by the Industrial Injuries and Diseases (Old Cases) Act 1975

13. Benefit shall not be payable by virtue of the provisions of these regulations in respect of the incapacity, disablement or death of any person as a result of any disease, if an award of benefit under the provisions of any Scheme made under the Industrial Injuries and Diseases (Old Cases) Act 1975 (not being an award which is subsequently reversed on review) has at any time been made in respect of any attack of the disease suffered by him, or in respect of his death.

Diseases contracted outside Great Britain

14. For section 50(5) (accidents happening outside Great Britain) there shall be substituted the provision that, subject to the provisions of sections 129, 131 and 132, for the purpose of determining whether a prescribed disease is, or, under the provisions of Part II of these regulations is to be presumed to be, due to the nature of the person's employed earner's employment, that person shall be regarded as not being or as not having been in employed earner's employment during any period for which he is or was outside Great Britain, and accordingly benefit shall not be payable in respect of a prescribed disease which is due to the nature of employment in an occupation in which the person has only been engaged outside Great Britain.

General Note

Ss. 50(5), 129, 131 and 132 of the Social Security Act 1975 have been replaced by ss.94(5), 117, 119 and 120 of the Social Security Contributions Act 1992.

[1Modification of paragraph 11(1) of Schedule 7 to the Social Security Contributions and Benefits Act 1992

14A. The provisions of paragraph 11(1) of Schedule 7 to the Social Security Contributions and Benefits Act 1992 shall be modified by adding after the words "(the day on which section 3 of the Social Security Act 1990 came into force)" the words "and a person shall not be entitled to reduced earnings allowance—

(i) in relation to a disease prescribed on or after 10th October 1994 under section 108(2) above; or

(ii) in relation to a disease prescribed before 10th October 1994 whose prescription is extended on or after that date under section 108(2) above but only in so far as the prescription has been so extended"]

Amendment

1. Social Security (Industrial Injuries) (Prescribed Diseases) Amendment Regulations 1994 (S.I. 1994 No. 2343), reg. 3 (October 10, 1994).

Assessment of extent of disablement

15. For the purposes of paragraph 1(b) of Schedule 8 (disabilities to be taken into account in assessing the extent of the claimant's disablement) and of regulation 11 of the Benefit Regulations (which further defines the principles of assessment of disablement), an injury or disease other than the relevant disease shall be treated as having been received or contracted before the relevant disease if it was received or contracted on or before the date of onset, and as having been received or contracted after the relevant disease if it was received or contracted after that date.

General Note

Sched. 8 to the Social Security Act 1975 has been replaced by Sched. 6 to the Social Security Contributions and Benefits Act 1992.

Aggregation of percentages of disablement

[[1]**15A.**—(1) After the extent of an employed earner's disablement resulting from the relevant disease has been determined, the Adjudication Officer shall add to the percentage of that disablement the assessed percentage of any present disablement of his resulting from—

(a) any accident after 4th July 1948 arising out of and in the course of his employment, being employed earner's employment, or

(b) any other relevant disease due to the nature of that employment and developed after 4th July 1948,

and in respect of which a disablement gratuity was not paid to him under the Act after a final assessment of disablement.

(2) In determining the extent of an employed earner's disablement for the purposes of section 57 of the Act there shall be added to the percentage of disablement resulting from any relevant accident the assessed percentage of any present disablement of his resulting from any disease or injury prescribed for the purposes of Chapter V of Part II of the Act, which was both due to the nature of the employment and developed after 4th July 1948, and in respect of which a disablement gratuity was not paid to him under the Act after a final assessment of his disablement.

(3) This regulation is subject to the provisions of regulation 15B(3).]

Amendment

1. This whole regulation was inserted by the Social Security (Industrial Injuries and Diseases) Miscellaneous Provisions Regulations 1986 (S.I. 1986 No. 1561), reg. 3(2) (October 1, 1986).

General Note

S.57 of the Social Security Act 1975 has been replaced by s.103 of the Social Security Contributions and Benefits Act 1992.

Rounding

[[1]**15B.**—(1) Subject to the provisions of this regulation, where the assessment of disablement is a percentage between 20 and 100 which is not a multiple of 10, it shall be treated—

(a) if it is a multiple of 5, as being the next higher percentage which is a multiple of 10; and

(b) if it is not a multiple of 5 as being the nearest percentage which is a multiple of 10,

and where it is 14 per cent. or more but less than 20 per cent. it shall be treated as 20 per cent.

(2) In a case to which regulation 15A (aggregation of percentages of disablement) applies, paragraph (1) shall have effect in relation to the aggregate percentage and not in relation to any percentage forming part of the aggregate.

(3) [[2]Where an assessment or a reassessment] states the degree of disablement due to occupational deafness as less than 20 per cent. that percentage shall be disregarded for the purposes of regulation 15A and this regulation.]

AMENDMENTS

1. This whole regulation was inserted by the Social Security (Industrial Injuries and Diseases) Miscellaneous Provisions Regulations 1986 (S.I. 1986 No. 1561), reg. 3(2) (October 1, 1986).
2. Social Security (Industrial Injuries) (Prescribed Diseases) Amendment Regulations 1990 (S.I. 1990 No. 2269), reg. 2 (December 13, 1990).

16. and **17.** *Omitted.*

Exception from requirements as to notice

18. Regulation 24 of the Claims and Payments Regulations (giving of notice of accidents in respect of which benefit may be payable) shall not apply in relation to prescribed diseases.

Provisions as to medical examination

19. Those provisions of section 89(1) and (2) which relate to the obligation of claimants to submit themselves to medical examination for the purpose of determining the effect of the relevant accident shall apply also to medical examinations for the purpose of determining whether a claimant or beneficiary is suffering or has suffered from a prescribed disease, and regulation 26 of the Claims and Payments Regulations shall be construed accordingly.

GENERAL NOTE

S.89 of the Social Security Act 1975 has been replaced by s.9 of the Social Security Administration Act 1992.

PART V

SPECIAL PROVISIONS AS TO PNEUMOCONIOSIS, BYSSINOSIS, OCCUPATIONAL DEAFNESS AND CERTAIN OTHER DISEASES

Section A—Benefit

Special conditions for disablement benefit for pneumoconiosis, byssinosis and diffuse mesothelioma

20.—[[1](1) On a claim for disablement pension in respect of pneumoconiosis, byssinosis or diffuse mesothelioma, section 57(1) shall apply as if for "14 per cent." there was substituted "1 per cent.".

(1A) Where on a claim for disablement pension in respect of pneumoconiosis, byssinosis or diffuse mesothelioma the extent of the disablement is assessed at one per cent. or more, but less than 20 per cent., disablement pension shall be payable at the 20 per cent. rate if the resulting degree of disablement is greater than 10 per cent. and if it is not at one-tenth of the 100 per cent. rate, with any fraction of a penny being for this purpose treated as a penny.

(1B) Where immediately before 1st October 1986 a person is entitled to a disablement pension on account of pneumoconiosis, byssinosis or diffuse mesothelioma and in determining the extent of his disablement other disabilities were taken into account in accordance with regulation 11 of the Social Security (General Benefit) Regulations 1982, disablement pension shall continue to be payable on or after 1st October 1986 at the weekly rate applicable to the degree of disablement determined on the last assessment made before 14th October 1986 until—

(a) on a reassessment or review of the extent of disablement the degree of disablement is assessed either as less than 1 per cent. or as equal to or more than that determined on that last assessment, or

(b) the other disability ceases to exist.]

(2) Section 78(4)(b), in so far as it provides that disablement benefit shall not be payable in respect of byssinosis unless the claimant is found to be suffering from loss of faculty which is likely to be permanent, shall not apply.

(3) Notwithstanding paragraph 4(a) of Schedule 8 (period to be taken into account by an assessment of the extent of the claimant's disablement), the period to be taken into account by an assessment of the extent of the claimant's disablement in respect of byssinosis, if not limited by reference to the claimant's life, shall not be less than one year.

[[2](4) On a claim for disablement pension in respect of diffuse mesothelioma—

(a) section 103(6) of the Social Security Contributions and Benefits Act 1992 shall apply as if for the words "after the expiry of the period of 90 days (disregarding Sundays) beginning with the day of the relevant accident" there were substituted the words, "the day on which he first suffers from a loss of faculty due to diffuse mesothelioma";

(b) paragraph 6(1) of Schedule 6 to the Social Security Contributions and Benefits Act 1992 shall apply as if the words "beginning not earlier than the end of the period of 90 days referred to in section 103(6) above and in paragraph 9(3) of that Schedule and" were omitted.]

AMENDMENT

1. Social Security (Industrial Injuries and Diseases) Miscellaneous Provisions Regulations 1986 (S.I. 1986 No. 1561), reg. 3(3) (October 1, 1986).

2. Social Security (Industrial Injuries) (Miscellaneous Amendments) Regulations 1997 (S.I. 1997 No. 810, reg. 5 (April 9, 1997).

GENERAL NOTE

Ss.57(1) and 78(4)(b) of the Social Security Act 1975 have been replaced by ss.103(1) and 110(4) of the Social Security Contributions and Benefits Act 1992. Sched. 8, para. 4(a) has been replaced by Sched. 6, para. 6(2)(a).

Disablement benefit is still payable in respect of pneumoconiosis, byssinosis or diffuse mesothelioma even if the extent of disablement is less than 1 per cent. The amount of disablement benefit payable is calculated under para. (1A) or (1B). An assessment of disablement in respect of byssinosis must be for at least one year. Para. (4) removes the usual 90 day waiting period for disablement benefit in cases where the claim is in respect of diffuse mesothelioma but makes it clear that there can be no entitlement until the disease results in a loss of faculty. Repeated assessments are seldom to be expected once the condition produces symptoms and so assessments should take into account anticipated deterioration in the claimant's condition. Thirty per cent of sufferers die within six months of the onset of symptoms.

Pneumoconiosis—effects of tuberculosis

21. Where any person is found to be suffering from pneumoconiosis accompanied by tuberculosis, the effects of the tuberculosis shall be treated for the purposes of Chapter V of Part II of the Act and of these regulations as if they were effects of the pneumoconiosis.

GENERAL NOTE

Chapter V of Part II of the Social Security Act 1975 has been replaced by ss.108–110 of the Social Security Contributions and Benefits Act 1992.

Pneumoconiosis—effects of emphysema and chronic bronchitis

22.—(1) [[1]Except] in the circumstances specified in paragraph (1A),] where any person is disabled by pneumoconiosis or pneumoconiosis accompanied by tuberculosis to an extent which would, if his physical condition were otherwise normal, be assessed at not less than 50 per cent., the effects of any emphysema and of any chronic bronchitis from which that person is found to be suffering shall be treated for the purposes of Chapter V of Part II of the Act and of these regulations as if they were effects of the pneumoconiosis.

[[1](1A) The circumstances referred to in paragraph (1) are that the person is entitled to industrial injuries disablement benefit on account of the disease set out in paragraph D12 of Part I of Schedule 1.]

(2) Where, on a claim for death benefit, the question arises whether the extent of a person's disablement resulting from pneumoconiosis or from pneumoconiosis accompanied by tuberculosis would, if his physical condition were otherwise normal, have been assessed at not less than 50 per cent.—

(a) if there has been no assessment of disablement resulting from pneumoconiosis or from pneumoconiosis accompanied by tuberculosis made during the person's life, or if there is no such assessment current at the time of death, that question shall be determined by a medical board and the provisions of the Act shall apply as if such question were a disablement question;

(b) if there is an assessment of disablement resulting from pneumoconiosis or from pneumoconiosis accompanied by tuberculosis current at the time of the person's death, that question shall be treated as having been determined by the decision of the medical board or medical appeal tribunal, as the case may be, which made such assessment.

AMENDMENT

1. Social Security (Industrial Injuries) (Prescribed Diseases) Amendment (No. 2) Regulations 1993 (S.I. 1993 No. 1985), reg. 5 (September 13, 1993).

GENERAL NOTE

Chapter V of Part II of the Social Security Act 1975 has been replaced by ss.108–110 of the Social Security Contributions and Benefits Act 1992.

Reduced earnings allowance—special provision for pneumoconiosis cases

[[1]**23.** Where a beneficiary in receipt of a disablement pension in respect of pneumoconiosis receives advice from a special medical board that in consequence of the disease he should not follow his regular occupation unless he complies with certain special restrictions as to the place, duration or circumstances of his work, or otherwise, then for the purpose of determining whether he fulfils the conditions laid down in section 59A (reduced earnings allowance)] and for that purpose only—

(a) the beneficiary shall be deemed, unless the contrary is proved by evidence other than the aforesaid advice—

  (i) to be incapable of following his regular occupation and likely to remain permanently so incapable, and

  (ii) to be incapable of following employment of an equivalent standard which is suitable in his case;

(b) where the beneficiary has ceased to follow any occupation to which the aforesaid special restrictions were applicable, the fact that he had followed such an occupation in the period between the date of onset of the disease and the date of the current assessment of his disablement, or for a reasonable period of trial thereafter, shall be disregarded.

AMENDMENT

1. Social Security (Industrial Injuries and Diseases) Miscellaneous Provisions Regulations 1986 (S.I. 1986 No. 1561), reg. 6 (October 1, 1986).

GENERAL NOTE

S.59A of the Social Security Act 1975 has been replaced by the Social Security Contributions and Benefits Act 1992, Sched. 7, para. 11.

Special requirement for pneumoconiosis claimants in unscheduled occupation cases

24.—(1) Part IX of the Adjudication Regulations shall apply to any claim for disablement benefit in respect of pneumoconiosis by a person in relation to whom the disease is prescribed by virtue of regulation 2(b)(ii) subject to the modification that if the claimant fails to show to the satisfaction of the adjudication officer that there is reasonable cause for suspecting that the claimant is suffering or has suffered from the disease the adjudication officer shall on that ground, and without referring the diagnosis question as provided in regulation 43(2) of the Adjudication Regulations, determine that an award cannot be made.

(2) The provisions of the last foregoing paragraph shall apply to a social security appeal tribunal and a Commissioner as they apply to the adjudication officer.

GENERAL NOTE

Part IX and reg. 43(2) of the Social Security (Adjudication) Regulations 1984 have been replaced by Part IV, Section A and reg. 45(1) of the Social Security (Adjudication) Regulations 1995.

Time for claiming benefit in respect of occupational deafness

25.—(1) Regulation 14 of the Claims and Payments Regulations (time for claiming benefit) shall not apply in relation to occupational deafness except in relation to a claim for sickness benefit payable by virtue of section 50A.

(2) Subject to regulation 27(1)(c), disablement benefit, or sickness benefit payable by virtue of section 50A of the Act, shall not be paid in pursuance of a claim in respect of occupational deafness which is made later than five years after the latest date, before the date of the claim, on which the claimant worked in an occupation prescribed in relation to occupational deafness unless—

- (a) the claimant has been employed in one or more of the occupations so prescribed for a period or periods amounting in aggregate to not less than 10 years, and
- (b) that period or the last of those periods ended on or after 8th October 1977, and
- (c) the claim is made within the period of one year beginning on 3rd October 1983, and
- (d) either—
  - (i) the claimant, not being a person to whom regulation 27(1)(c) applies, has not within the period of three years before the claim was made previously made a claim which was disallowed because he was not suffering from occupational deafness, or
  - (ii) where a previous claim was made by him, a medical board or a medical appeal tribunal have not within the period of three years before the claim was made reassessed the extent of his disablement at less than 20 per cent.

General Note

In *McKiernon v. Secretary of State for Social Services* (*The Times*, November 1, 1989), the Court of Appeal held reg. 25 to be *ultra vires* because it did not allow the time for claiming to be extended if there was good cause for the delay (see s.165A of the Social Security Act 1975, now s.1 of the Social Security Administration Act 1992). As a result, s.77(2) of the Social Security Act 1975 (now s.109 of the Social Security Contributions and Benefits Act 1992) was amended by para. 4(2) of Sched. 6 to the Social Security Act 1990. Para. 4(3) of Sched. 6 to the 1990 Act provided that reg. 25 should be taken always to have been validly made. In *Chatterton v. Chief Adjudication Officer* (unreported, July 8, 1993), the Court of Appeal rejected an argument that para. 4(3) merely had the effect that reg. 25 was validly made but was still subject to s.165A of the 1975 Act so that the time for claiming could be extended. On the same day, in *McKiernon v. Chief Adjudication Officer*, the Court of Appeal held that Mr McKiernon lost his entitlement to disablement benefit upon the 1990 Act coming into force.

Reg. 14 of the Social Security (Claims and Payments) Regulations 1979 has been replaced by reg. 19 of the Social Security (Claims and Payments) Regulations 1987. S.50A of the Social Security Act 1975 has been replaced by s.102 of the Social Security Contributions and Benefits Act 1992.

Claims in respect of occupational deafness

26. Where it appears that a person who has made a claim for sickness benefit by virtue of section 50A of the Act in respect of occupational deafness—

(a) may be entitled to disablement benefit, and

(b) has not previously made a claim for disablement benefit in respect of occupational deafness or such a previous claim has been disallowed,

such a claim for sickness benefit may also be treated as a claim for disablement benefit.

General Note

A claim for sickness benefit on the ground of occupational deafness may be treated as a claim for disablement benefit if the claimant has not already made an unsuccessful claim. This paragraph would seem to apply even if the claimant would have satisfied the contribution conditions under s.14 without the assistance of s.50A.

Further claims in respect of occupational deafness

27.—(1) In the event of disallowance of a claim for disablement benefit or sickness benefit made by virtue of section 50A of the Act in respect of occupational deafness because the claimant has failed to satisfy the minimum hearing loss requirement prescribed in column 1 of paragraph A10 of Part I of Schedule 1 hereto, disablement benefit or sickness benefit made by virtue of section 50A of the Act shall not be paid in pursuance of a further claim in respect of occupational deafness made by or on behalf of that claimant unless—

(a) it is a claim made after the expiration of three years from the date of a claim which was disallowed because the claimant was not suffering from occupational deafness; or

(b) it is a claim made after the expiration of three years from the date of a reassessment by a medical board or medical appeal tribunal of the extent of the claimant's disablement at less than 20 per cent; or

(c) if the claimant would otherwise be precluded by regulation 25(2) from making a further claim after the expiration of three years from the date of the disallowed claim or from the date of a reassessment by a medical board or a medical appeal tribunal of the extent of his disablement at less than 20 per cent. as the case may be, it is the first claim made since that date and within five years from the latest date, before the date of the claim, on which he worked in any occupation specified in column 2 of paragraph A10 of Part 1 of Schedule 1 hereto.

(2) A claim to be paid benefit by virtue of paragraph (1)(c) may be disallowed by the adjudication officer, social security appeal tribunal or Commissioner, as the case may be (hereinafter called "the determining authority"), without referring the disablement question to a medical board or medical appeal tribunal where the determining authority is satisfied from the medical evidence given on the disallowed claim that the claimant is not suffering from occupational deafness.

GENERAL NOTE

S.50A of the Social Security Act 1975 has been replaced by s.102 of the Social Security Contributions and Benefits Act 1992.

Availability of disablement benefit in respect of occupational deafness

28. Where a person is awarded disablement benefit in respect of occupational deafness, section 57(4) (period for which disablement benefit is not available) shall not apply.

GENERAL NOTE

In occupational deafness cases, the date of onset of the disease is deemed to be no earlier than the date of claim (see reg. 6(2)(c)) and so the usual 90-day qualifying period does not apply. S.57(4) of the Social Security Act 1975 has been replaced by s.103(6) of the Social Security Contributions and Benefits Act 1992.

Period to be covered by assessment of disablement in respect of occupational deafness

29. Subject to the proviso to section 57(6) (cessation of pension on death of beneficiary)—

(a) every initial assessment of the extent of a claimant's disablement in respect of occupational deafness shall be a provisional assessment and the period to be taken into account by such an assessment shall be a period of five years;

(b) the period to be taken into account by any subsequent reassessment of the extent of the claimant's disablement in respect of occupational deafness, if not limited by reference to the claimant's life, shall not be less than five years.

GENERAL NOTE

S.57(6) of the Social Security Act 1975 has been replaced by s.103(8) of the Social Security Contributions and Benefits Act 1992.

Review of assessment for unforeseen aggravation in respect of occupational deafness

30.—(1) The provisions of section 110(2) (review of assessment in case of unforeseen aggravation) shall not apply to an assessment of the extent of disablement in respect of occupational deafness until after the expiration of five years from the date of commencement of the period taken into account by that assessment.

(2) The provisions of section 110(2) shall not apply to an assessment of the extent of disablement in respect of occupational deafness which is less than 20 per cent.

31. Subject to the provisions of regulation 30 and notwithstanding the provisions of section 110(5) (leave of medical appeal tribunal required to review assessment in certain cases), a life assessment in respect of occupational deafness made by a medical board or a medical appeal tribunal shall not be reviewed in accordance with section 110(2) (review of assessment in case of unforeseen aggravation) without leave of a medical appeal tribunal, and in the case of a provisional assessment in respect of occupational deafness no such leave shall be required.

General Note

S.110(2) and (5) of the Social Security Act 1975 has been replaced by s.47(4) and (7) of the Social Security Administration Act 1992.

No appeal against initial provisional assessment of disablement in respect of occupational deafness

32. Notwithstanding section 109(2), but subject to the provisions of section 109(3), no appeal shall lie against an initial provisional assessment of the extent of disablement in respect of occupational deafness.

General Note

This provision appears to allow a provisional assessment of disablement in respect of occupational deafness to be referred to a medical appeal tribunal by an adjudication officer but not on appeal by a claimant. It remains open to a claimant to persuade the Secretary of State or an adjudication officer that there should be a reference. S. 109 of the Social Security Act 1975 has been replaced by s. 46 of the Social Security Administration Act 1992.

Cases in which reassessment of disablement in respect of occupational deafness is final

33. Where in any case the extent of disablement in respect of occupational deafness has been provisionally assessed at 20 per cent. or more and on any reassessment the extent of disablement in respect of occupational deafness is assessed at less than 20 per cent. that assessment shall be final.

Assessment of extent of disablement and rate of disablement benefit payable in respect of occupational deafness

34.—(1) Subject to the provisions of Schedule 8 and regulations made thereunder and the following provisions of this regulation, the first assessment of the extent of disablement in respect of occupational deafness made in pursuance of a claim made before 3rd September 1979 by a person to whom disablement benefit in respect of occupational deafness is payable for a period before 3rd September 1979 [[3]shall be the percentage calculated by—

(a) determining the average total hearing loss due to all causes for each ear at 1, 2 and 3 kHz frequencies; and then by

(b) determining the percentage degree of disablement for each ear in accordance with Part I of Schedule 3; and then by

(c) determining the average percentage degree of binaural disablement in accordance with the formula set out in Part III of Schedule 3.]

(2) Except in any case to which paragraph (1) applies and subject to the provisions of Schedule 8 and regulations made thereunder and the following provisions of this regulation, the extent of disablement in respect of occupational deafness [[3]shall be the percentage calculated by—

(a) determining the average total hearing loss due to all causes for each ear at 1, 2 and 3 kHz frequencies; and then by

(b) determining the percentage degree of disablement for each ear in accordance with Part II of Schedule 3; and then by

(c) determining the average percentage degree of binaural disablement in accordance with the formula set out in Part III of Schedule 3.]

(3) In [[3]. . .] Schedule 3 hereto "better ear" means that ear in which the claimant's hearing loss due to all causes is the less and "worse ear" means that ear in which the claimant's hearing loss due to all causes is the more.

[[3](3A) For the purposes of determining the percentage degree of disablement in Parts I and II of Schedule 3 to these Regulations, any fraction of an average hearing loss shall, where the average hearing loss is over 50 dB, be rounded down to the next whole figure.]

(4) The extent of disablement in respect of occupational deafness may be subject to such increase or reduction of the degree of disablement as may be reasonable in the circumstances of the case where, having regard to the provisions of Schedule 8 and to regulations made thereunder, that degree of disablement does not provide a reasonable assessment of the extent of disability resulting from the relevant loss of faculty.

[[1](5) Where on re-assessment of the extent of disability in respect of occupational deafness the average sensorineural hearing loss over 1, 2 and 3 kHz frequencies is not 50 dB or more in each ear, or where there is such a loss but the loss in one or each ear is not 50 dB or more due to occupational noise, the extent of disablement shall be assessed at less than 20 per cent.]

(6) Where the extent of disablement is reassessed at less than 20 per cent. disablement benefit [[2]or reduced earnings allowance] shall not be payable.

(7) In the case of a person to whom disablement benefit by reason of occupational deafness was payable in respect of a period before 3rd September 1979—

(a) if no assessment of the extent of his disability has been made, reviewed or varied on or after that date, the rate of any disablement benefit payable to him shall be the rate payable for the degree of disablement assessed in accordance with paragraph (1), but

(b) if such an assessment has been made, reviewed or varied in respect of a period commencing on or after that date and before 3rd October 1983, the rate of any disablement benefit payable to him shall be either—

(i) the rate which would be payable if an assessment were made in accordance with paragraph (2), or

(ii) the rate which was payable immediately before the first occasion on which such review or variation took place,

whichever is the more favourable to him.

(8) Where in the case of a person to whom disablement benefit by reason of occupational deafness was payable in respect of a period before 3rd September 1979 the extent of his disability is reassessed and the period taken into account on reassessment begins on or after 3rd October 1983 and—

(a) immediately before that date, by virtue of paragraph (7) the rate at which disablement benefit was payable to him was higher than the rate which would otherwise have been payable, or,

(b) the reassessment is the first reassessment for a period commencing after 3rd September 1979,

the rate of disablement benefit payable to him shall be whichever of the rates specified in paragraph (9) is applicable.

(9) The rate of disablement benefit payable in the case of a person to whom paragraph (8) applies shall be—

(a) if the current rate appropriate to the extent of his disability as reassessed is the same as or more than the rate at which disablement benefit was payable immediately before the beginning of the period taken into account on reassessment, the current rate, or

(b) if the current rate is less than the rate at which disablement benefit was payable immediately before the beginning of the period taken into account on reassessment, the lower of the following rates—

(i) the rate at which benefit would have been payable if the reassessment of the extent of his disability had been made in accordance with paragraph (1), or

(ii) the rate at which benefit was payable immediately before the beginning of the period taken into account on reassessment.

AMENDMENTS

1. Social Security (Industrial Injuries and Adjudication) Miscellaneous Amendment Regulations 1986 (S.I. 1986 No. 1374), reg. 3 (September 1, 1986).

2. Social Security (Industrial Injuries and Diseases) Miscellaneous Provisions 1986 (S.I. 1986 No. 1561), reg. 6 (October 1, 1986).

3. Social Security (Industrial Injuries) (Prescribed Diseases) Amendment Regulation 1989 (S.I. 1989 No. 1207), reg. 4 (October 16, 1989).

GENERAL NOTE

This regulation and Sched. 3 govern the assessment of disablement in occupational deafness cases. Note, however, that paras. (1) and (2) are expressed to be subject to Sched. 8 to the Social Security Act 1975 (now Sched. 6 to the Social Security Contributions and Benefits Act 1992) and regulations made thereunder, including reg. 11 of the Social Security (General Benefit) Regulations 1982.

Para. (1) of this regulation and Pt. 1 of Sched. 3 only apply to the first assessment of disablement in respect of claims made before September 3, 1979. Therefore, virtually all assessments are now made under para. (2) of this regulation and Pt. 2 of Sched. 3 which is less generous. The percentage degree of disablement for each ear is calculated separately and the formula in Pt. 3 of Sched. 3 is then applied to give an overall percentage of disablement. However, note that para. (4) of this regulation enables an adjudicating medical authority to depart from the Schedule if the result of applying the Schedule is to give an unreasonable assessment. A tribunal should first assess according to the Schedule and then give a reason for departing from that assessment (*R(I) 1/89*). Para. (5) applies only on a reassessment.

Paras. (7)–(9) are transitional and apply to a person who was in receipt of disablement benefit before September 3, 1979. If there has been no assessment since that date, entitlement to disablement benefit is calculated under the more favourable provisions of para. (1). If there was an assessment between that date and October 3, 1983, disablement benefit is payable either at the rate which would be payable on an assessment calculated under para. (2) or at the rate payable immediately before the review or variation took place, whichever is the more favourable. In view of inflation, the latter option is unlikely to be more favourable. If there has been an assessment on or after October 3, 1983, it will be usual for the claimant to receive the rate appropriate to an assessment under para. (2). However, if that rate is lower than the rate payable immediately before the beginning of the period taken into account on the reassessment, the lower of the two rates mentioned in para. (9)(b) is payable instead. The greater the lapse of time since the review or variation, the less favourable will be the latter option.

The 1989 amendments removed the requirement that hearing loss should be measured by pure tone audiometry as opposed to evoked response audiometry or any other test. In *CI/410/91*, it was held that those amendments (in particular, the introduction of para. (3A)) are procedural and so operate retrospectively in respect of periods before October 16, 1989.

Commencement date of period of assessment in respect of occupational deafness

35. Notwithstanding the provisions of section 108 and Schedule 8, the period to be taken into account by an assessment of the extent of disablement in respect of occupational deafness shall not commence before 3rd February 1975.

GENERAL NOTE

S.108 of the Social Security Act 1975 has been replaced by s.45 of the Social Security Administration Act 1992. Sched. 8 to the 1975 Act has been replaced by Sched. 6 to the Social Security Contributions and Benefits Act 1992.

Time for claiming benefit in respect of occupational asthma

36.—(1) Subject to paragraphs (2) and (3), disablement benefit and sickness benefit payable by virtue of section 50A shall not be paid in pursuance of a claim in respect of occupational asthma which is made later than 10 years after the latest date, before the date of the claim, on which the claimant or, as the case may be, the person in respect of whom the claim is made worked in an occupation prescribed in relation to occupational asthma.

(2) Paragraph (1) shall not apply to any claim made before 29th March 1983 by or in respect of a person who ceased on or after 29th March 1972 to be employed in an occupation prescribed in relation to occupational asthma.

(3) Paragraph (1) shall not apply to any claim made by or in respect of a person who has at any time been found to be suffering from asthma as a result of an industrial accident and by virtue of that finding has been awarded disablement benefit either for life or for a period which includes the date on which the aforesaid claim is made.

(4) Subject to paragraphs (5) and (6), industrial death benefit shall not be paid in pursuance of a claim in respect of occupational asthma where the person in respect of whose death the benefit is being claimed died more than 10 years after the latest day on which he worked in an occupation prescribed in relation to occupational asthma.

(5) Paragraph (4) shall not apply to any claim made in respect of the death of a person who died before 29th March 1983 and who on or after 29th March 1972 had not worked in an occupation prescribed in relation to occupational asthma.

(6) Paragraph (4) shall not apply to any claim made in respect of the death of a person who had at any time been found to be suffering either from asthma as a result of an industrial accident or from occupational asthma and by virtue of that finding had been awarded disablement benefit either for life or for a period which included the date of his death.

(7) Regulation 14 of the Claims and Payments Regulations (time for claiming benefit) shall not apply to a claim in respect of occupational asthma made before 29th March 1983.

General Note

It was clear from *McKiernon v. Secretary of State for Social Services* (*The Times*, November 1, 1989), that reg. 36 was originally *ultra vires*. As a result, s.77(2) of the Social Security Act 1975 (now s.109(2) of the Social Security Contributions and Benefits Act 1992) was amended by para. 4(2) of Sched. 6 to the Social Security Act 1990. Para. 4(3) of Sched. 6 to the 1990 Act provided that reg. 36 should be taken always to have been validly made. See the note to reg. 25.

Section B—Medical examinations and suspension

37. and **38.** *Revoked by Social Security (Industrial Injuries) (Prescribed Diseases) Amendment Regulations 1994 (S.I. 1994 No. 2343), reg. 5 (October 10, 1994).*

Suspension from employment

39. A certificate of suspension issued under the provisions of either regulation 43 or regulation 44 of the National Insurance (Industrial Injuries) (Prescribed Diseases) Regulations 1959 (regulations revoked with effect from 27th November 1974 by regulation 7(1) of the National Insurance (Industrial Injuries) (Prescribed Diseases) Amendment (No. 2) Regulations 1974) and in force immediately before 27th November 1974 shall continue in force subject to and in accordance with the provisions of regulation 40 of these regulations.

Conditions of suspension

40.—(1) A certificate of suspension issued under the provisions of either regulation 43 or regulation 44 of the National Insurance (Industrial Injuries) (Prescribed Diseases) Regulations 1959, and remaining in force by virtue of the last preceding regulation, shall suspend the person to whom it relates from further employment in any occupation in relation to which pneumoconiosis is prescribed, with such exceptions and subject to such conditions (if any) as may be specified in the certificate.

(2) A special medical board may at any time revoke or vary a certificate of suspension on the application of the person to whom it relates, but unless so revoked or varied such certificate shall remain in force throughout the life of such person.

(3) No person who has been suspended from employment may engage or continue in employment, and no employer may employ or continue to employ any such person, in any occupation in relation to which pneumoconiosis is prescribed, except in accordance with the terms of the certificate of suspension in his case.

41. and **42.** *Revoked by Social Security (Industrial Injuries) (Prescribed Diseases) Amendment Regulations 1994 (S.I. 1994 No. 2343), reg. 5 (October 10, 1994).*

PART VI

TRANSITIONAL PROVISIONS AND REVOCATION

Transitional provisions regarding relevant dates

43.—(1) Subject to paragraph (2) the "relevant date", in relation to each disease set out in the first column of Schedule 4 hereto, is the date set against the disease in the second column of that Schedule.

(2) Where a disease set out in the first column of Schedule 4 hereto was prescribed in relation to any person by regulations which came into operation on a date earlier than the date set against that disease in the second column of that Schedule, the "relevant date" in relation to such disease is such earlier date on which the disease was prescribed in relation to the person in question.

(3) It shall be a condition of a person's right to benefit in respect of any disease set out in Schedule 4 that he was—

(a) incapable of work, or

(b) suffering from a loss of faculty,

as a result of that disease on or after the relevant date.

(4) The "relevant date" in relation to byssinosis—

(a) in the case of a person employed in an occupation involving work in any room in which the weaving of cotton or flax or any other process which takes place between, or at the same time as, the winding or beaming and weaving of cotton or flax is carried on in a factory in which any or all of those processes are carried on is 3rd October 1983;

(b) in any other case, is 6th April 1979 except that where the disease was prescribed in relation to any person by regulations which came into operation on a date earlier that 6th April 1979 the relevant date is that earlier date.

(5) Byssinosis is not prescribed in relation to any person if neither of the following conditions is satisfied, namely:—

(a) that he was suffering from a loss of faculty as a result of bysinnosis on or after the relevant date;

(b) that he has been employed in employed earner's employment in any occupation mentioned in regulation 2(c) of the old regulation for a period or periods (whether before or after 5th July 1948) amounting in the aggregate to five years.

(6) Notwithstanding that a person does not satisfy paragraph (3) infection by leptospira is prescribed in relation to any person if he is or has been either incapable of work or suffering from a loss of faculty as a result of infection by—

(a) leptospira icterohaemorrhagiae in the case of a person employed in employed earner's employment before 7th January 1980 in any occupation involving work in places which are or are liable to be, infested by rats, or

(b) leptospira canicola in the case of a person so employed in any occupation involving work at dog kennels or the care or handling of dogs.

(7) A person who, immediately before 3rd October 1983, was in receipt of benefit in respect of a disease or injury which was prescribed by virtue of the old regulations, or who makes a claim for benefit in respect of a prescribed disease after 2nd October 1983 where the date of onset of the disease or injury was before 3rd October 1983, shall be treated for the purpose only of determining whether the disease or injury is in relation to him a prescribed disease by virtue of the occupation in which he is or was engaged as if the old regulations were still in force and these regulations had not come into operation, if that would be more favourable to him.

Transitional provisions regarding dates of development and dates of onset

44. Where a claim for benefit has been made before 6th April 1983 or a date of onset is determined which is before 6th April 1983 or a claim for injury benefit is made after 5th April 1983 for a day falling or a period beginning before 6th April 1983, these regulations shall take effect subject to the provisions of Schedule 5.

45. *Omitted.*

SCHEDULES

SCHEDULE 1 **Regulations 2 and 4**

PART I

LIST OF PRESCRIBED DISEASES AND THE OCCUPATIONS FOR WHICH THEY ARE PRESCRIBED

Prescribed disease or injury	*Occupation*
A. **Conditions due to physical agents**	*Any occupation involving:*
A1. Inflammation, ulceration or malignant disease of the skin or subcutaneous tissues or of the bones, or blood dyscrasia, or cataract, due to electro-magnetic radiations (other than radiant heat), or to ionising particles.	Exposure to electro-magnetic radiations (other than radiant heat) or to ionising particles.
A2. Heat cataract.	Frequent or prolonged exposure to rays from molten or red-hot material.
A3. Dysbarism, including decompression sickness, barotrauma and osteonecrosis.	Subjection to compressed or rarefied air or other respirable gases or gaseous mixtures.
A4. Cramp of the hand or forearm due to repetitive movements.	Prolonged periods of handwriting, typing or other repetitive movements of the fingers, hand or arm.
A5. Subcutaneous cellulitis of the hand (beat hand).	Manual labour causing severe or prolonged friction or pressure on the hand.
A6. Bursitis or subcutaneous cellulitis arising at or about the knee due to severe or prolonged external friction or pressure at or about the knee (beat knee).	Manual labour causing severe or prolonged external friction or pressure at or about the knee.
A7. Bursitis or subcutaneous cellulitis arising at or about the elbow due to severe or prolonged external friction or pressure at or about the elbow (beat albow).	Manual labour causing severe or prolonged external friction or pressure at or about the elbow.
A8. Traumatic inflammation of the tendons of the hand or forearm, or of the associated tendon sheaths.	Manual labour, or frequent or repeated movements of the hand or wrist.
A9. Miner's nystagmus.	Work in or about a mine.
[[6]A10. Sensorineural hearing loss amounting to at least 50 dB in each ear, being the average of hearing losses at 1, 2 and 3 kHz frequencies, and being due in the case of at least one ear to occupational noise (occupational deafness).]	[[3](a) The use of powered (but not hand powered) grinding tools on [[10]metal (other than sheet metal or plate metal)] in the metal producing industry, or work wholly or mainly in the immediate vicinity of those tools whilst they are being so used; or

Prescribed disease or injury	*Occupation*
	Any occupation involving: (b) the use of pneumatic percussive tools on metal, or work wholly or mainly in the immediate vicinity of those tools whilst they are being so used; or (c) the use of pneumatic percussive tools for drilling rock in quarries or underground or in mining coal [[10] or in sinking shafts or for tunnelling in civil engineering works], or work wholly or mainly in the immediate vicinity of those tools whilst they are being so used; or [[10](ca) the use of pneumatic percussive tools on stone in quarry works, or work wholly or mainly in the immediate vicinity of those tools whilst they are being so used; or] (d) work wholly or mainly in the immediate vicinity of plant (excluding power press plant) engaged in the forging (including drop stamping) of metal by means of closed or open dies or drop hammers; or (e) work in textile manufacturing where the work is undertaken wholly or mainly in rooms or sheds in which there are machines engaged in weaving man-made or natural (including mineral) fibres or in the high speed false twisting of fibres; or] (f) the use of, or work wholly or mainly in the immediate vicinity of, machines engaged in cutting, shaping or cleaning metal nails; or (g) the use of, or work wholly or mainly in the immediate vicinity of, plasma spray guns engaged in the deposition of metal; or (h) the use of, or work wholly or mainly in the immediate vicinity of, any of the following machines engaged in the working of wood or material composed partly of wood, that is to say: multi-cutter

Prescribed disease or injury	*Occupation*
	Any occupation involving: moulding machines, planing machines, automatic or semi-automatic lathes, multiple cross-cut machines, automatic shaping machines, double-end tenoning machines, vertical spindle moulding machines (including high speed routing machines), edge banding machines, bandsawing machines with a blade width of not less than 75 millimetres and circular sawing machines in the operation of which the blade is moved towards the material being cut; or
	(i) the use of chain saws in forestry [;[10] or
	(j) air arc gouging or work wholly or mainly in the immediate vicinity of air arc gouging; or
	(k) the use of band saws, circular saws or cutting discs for cutting metal in the metal founding or forging industries, or work wholly or mainly in the immediate vicinity of those tools whilst they are being so used; or
	(l) the use of circular saws for cutting products in the manufacture of steel, or work wholly or mainly in the immediate vicinity of those tools whilst they are being so used; or
	(m) the use of burners or torches for cutting or dressing steel based products, or work wholly or mainly in the immediate vicinity of those tools whilst they are being so used; or
	(n) work wholly or mainly in the immediate vicinity of skid transfer banks; or
	(o) work wholly or mainly in the immediate vicinity of knock out and shake out grids in foundries; or
	(p) mechanical bobbin cleaning or work wholly or mainly in the immediate vicinity of mechanical bobbin cleaning; or

Prescribed disease or injury	*Occupation*
	Any occupation involving: (q) the use of, or work wholly or mainly in the immediate vicinity of, vibrating metal moulding boxes in the concrete products industry; or (r) the use of, or work wholly or mainly in the immediate vicinity of, high pressure jets of water or a mixture of water and abrasive material in the water jetting industry (including work under water); or (s) work in ships' engine rooms; or (t) the use of circular saws for cutting concrete masonry blocks during manufacture, or work wholly or mainly in the immediate vicinity of those tools whilst they are being so used; or (u) burning stone in quarries by jet channelling processes, or work wholly or mainly in the immediate vicinity of such processes; or (v) work on gas turbines in connection with— (i) performance testing on test bed; (ii) installation testing of replacement engines in aircraft; (iii) acceptance testing of Armed Service fixed wing combat planes; or (w) the use of, or work wholly or mainly in the immediate vicinity of— (i) machines for automatic moulding, automatic blow moulding or automatic glass pressing and forming machines used in the manufacutre of glass containers or hollow ware; (ii) spining machines using compressed air to produce glass wool or mineral wool; (iii) continuous glass toughening furnaces.]

REPORT NO. RDA61321
RUN DATE : 04/11/2004

DISABILITY LIVING ALLOWANCE

HIGH PRIORITY WORK AVAILABLE - NEW CLAIM EVENTS : 04/11/2

MANAGEMENT UNIT NO : 09946 SECTION NO : 002

SECTION NAME : EO (2) DAW - GZ

NINO	SURNAME	FORENAME	CASE NO.	CONTROL U/S	U/D	ACTIVITY
PA706566C	DOWNING	SARAH L	0322	N	Y	MANUAL NOTIFICATION REQUIRED
PB672750C	GOLDIE	JACK	0322	N	Y	MANUAL NOTIFICATION REQUIRED

*** END OF REPORT ***

Prescribed disease or injury	*Occupation*
A. 11 Episodic blanching, occurring throughout the year, affecting the middle or proximal phalanges or in the case of a thumb the proximal phalanx, of— (a) in the case of a person with 5 fingers (including thumbs) on one hand, any 3 of those fingers, or (b) in the case of a person with only 4 such fingers, any 2 of those fingers, or (c) in the case of a person with less than 4 such fingers, any one of those fingers or, as the case may be, the one remaining finger (vibration white finger).	*Any occupation involving:* (a) The use of hand-held chain saws in forestry; or (b) the use of hand-held rotary tools in grinding or in the sanding or polishing of metal, or the holding of material being ground, or metal being sanded or polished, by rotary tools; or (c) the use of hand-held percussive metal-working tools, or the holding of metal being worked upon by percussive tools, in riveting, caulking, chipping, hammering, fettling or swaging; or (d) the use of hand-held powered percussive drills or hand-held powered percussive hammers in mining, quarrying, demolition, or on roads or footpaths, including road construction; or (e) the holding of material being worked upon by pounding machines in shoe manufacture.
[[11]A12. Carpal tunnel syndrome.	The use of hand-held powered tools whose internal parts vibrate so as to transmit that vibration to the hand, but excluding those which are solely powered by hand.]
B. **Conditions due to biological agents**	
B1. Anthrax.	Contact with animals infected with anthrax or the handling (including the loading or unloading or transport) of animal products or residues.
B2. Glanders	Contact with equine animals or their carcases.
B3. Infection by leptospira.	(a) Work in places which are, or are liable to be, infested by rats, field mice or voles, or other small mammals; or (b) work at dog kennels or the care or handling of dogs; or (c) contact with bovine animals or their meat products or pigs or their meat products.
B4. Ankylostomiasis.	Work in or about a mine.
B5. Tuberculosis.	Contact with a source of tuberculous infection.

Prescribed disease or injury	*Occupation*
B6. Extrinsic allergic alveolitis (including farmer's lung).	*Any occupation involving:* Exposure to moulds or fungal spores or heterologous proteins by reason of employment in; (a) agriculture, horticulture, forestry, cultivation of edible fungi or malt-working; or (b) loading or unloading or handling in storage mouldy vegetable matter or edible fungi; or (c) caring for or handling birds; or (d) handling bagasse.
B7. Infection by organisms of the genus brucella.	Contact with— (a) animals infected by brucella, or their carcases or parts thereof, or their untreated products; or (b) laboratory specimens or vaccines of, or containing brucella.
B8. Viral hepatitis.	Contact with— (a) human blood or human blood products; or (b) a source of viral hepatitis.
B9. Infection by Streptococcus suis.	Contact with pigs infected by Streptococcus suis, or with the carcases, products or residues of pigs so infected.
[[5]B10. (a) Avian chlamydiosis.	Contact with birds infected with chlamydia psittaci, or with the remains or untreated products of such birds.
B10. (b) Ovine chlamydiosis.	Contact with sheep infected with chlamydia psittaci, or with the remains or untreated products of such sheep.
B11. Q fever.	Contact with animals, their remains or their untreated products.]
[[7]B12. Orf.	Contact with sheep, goats or with the carcasses of sheep or goats.
B13. Hydatidosis.	Contact with dogs.]
C. **Conditions due to chemical agents**	
C1. Poisoning by lead or a compound of lead.	The use or handling of, and exposure to the fumes, dust or vapour of, lead or a compound of lead, or a substance containing lead.

Prescribed disease or injury	*Occupation*
	Any occupation involving:
C2. Poisoning by manganese or a compound of manganese.	The use or handling of, or exposure to the fumes, dust or vapour of, manganese or a compound of manganese, or a substance containing manganese.
C3. Poisoning by phosphorus or an inorganic compound of phosphorus or poisoning due to the anti-cholinesterase or pseudo anti-cholinesterase action of organic phosphorus compounds.	The use or handling of, or exposure to the fumes, dust or vapour of, phosphorus or a compound of phosphorus, or a substance containing phosphorus.
C4. Poisoning by arsenic or a compound of arsenic.	The use or handling of, or exposure to the fumes, dust or vapour of, arsenic or a compound of arsenic, or a substance containing arsenic.
C5. Poisoning by mercury or a compound of mercury.	The use or handling of, or exposure to the fumes, dust or vapour of, mercury or a compound of mercury, or a substance containing mercury.
C6. Poisoning by carbon bisulphide.	The use or handling of, or exposure to the fumes or vapour of, carbon bisulphide or a compound of carbon bisulphide, or a substance containing carbon bisulphide.
C7. Poisoning by benzene or a homologue of benzene.	The use or handling of, or exposure to the fumes of, or vapour containing benzene or any of its homologues.
C8. Poisoning by a nitro- or amino- or chloro- derivative of benzene or of a homologue of benzene, or poisoning by nitrochlorbenzene.	The use or handling of, or exposure to the fumes of, or vapour containing a nitro- or amino- or chloro- derivative of benzene, or of a homologue of benzene, or nitrochlorbenzene.
C9. Poisoning by dinitrophenol or a homologue of dinitrophenol or by substituted dinitrophenols or by the salts of such substances.	The use or handling of, or exposure to the fumes of, or vapour containing, dinitrophenol or a homologue or substituted dinitrophenols or the salts of such substances.
C10. Poisoning by tetrachloroethane.	The use or handling of, or exposure to the fumes of, or vapour containing, tetrachloroethane.
C11. Poisoning by diethylene dioxide (dioxan).	The use or handling of, or exposure to the fumes of, or vapour containing, diethylene dioxide (dioxan).
C12. Poisoning by methyl bromide.	The use or handling of, or exposure to the fumes of, or vapour containing, methyl bromide.
C13. Poisoning by chlorinated naphthalene.	The use or handling of, or exposure to the fumes of, or dust or vapour containing, chlorinated naphthalene.

Prescribed disease or injury	*Occupation*
	Any occupation involving:
C14. Poisoning by nickel carbonyl.	Exposure to nickel carbonyl gas.
C15. Poisoning by oxides of nitrogen.	Exposure to oxides of nitrogen.
C16. Poisoning by gonioma kamassi (African boxwood).	The manipulation of gonioma kamassi or any process in or incidental to the manufacture of articles therefrom.
C17. Poisoning by beryllium or a compound of beryllium.	The use or handling of, or exposure to the fumes, dust or vapour of, beryllium or a compound of beryllium, or a substance containing beryllium.
C18. Poisoning by cadmium.	Exposure to cadmium dust or fumes.
C19. Poisoning by acrylamide monomer.	The use or handling of, or exposure to, acrylamide monomer.
C20. Dystrophy of the cornea (including ulceration of the corneal surface) of the eye.	(a) The use or handling of, or exposure to arsenic, tar, pitch, bitumen, mineral oil (including paraffin), soot or any compound, product or residue of any of these substances, except quinone or hydroquinone; or (b) exposure to quinone or hydroquinone during their manufacture.
C21. (a) Localised new growth of the skin, papillomatous or keratotic; (b) squamous-celled carcinoma of the skin.	The use or handling of, or exposure to, arsenic, tar, pitch, bitumen, mineral oil (including paraffin) soot or any compound, product or residue of any of these substances, except quinone or hydroquinone.
C22. (a) Carcinoma of the mucous membrane of the nose or associated air sinuses; (b) primary carcinoma of a bronchus or of a lung.	Work in a factory where nickel is produced by decomposition of a gaseous nickel compound which necessitates working in or about a building or buildings where that process or any other industrial process ancillary or incidental thereto is carried on.
C23. Primary neoplasm (including papilloma, carcinoma-in-situ and invasive carcinoma) of the epithelial lining of the urinary tract (renal pelvis, ureter, bladder and urethra).	(a) Work in a building in which any of the following substances is produced for commercial purposes: (i) alpha-naphthylamine, beta-naphthylamine or methylene-bis-orthochloroaniline; (ii) diphenyl substituted by at least one nitro or primary amino group or by at least one nitro and primary amino group (including benzidine);

Prescribed disease or injury	*Occupation*
	Any occupation involving: (iii) any of the substances mentioned in sub-paragraph (ii) above if further ring substituted by halogeno, methyl or methoxy groups, but not by other groups; (iv) the salts of any of the substances mentioned in the sub-paragraphs (i) to (iii) above; (v) auramine or magenta; or (b) the use or handling of any of the substances mentioned in sub-paragraph (a)(i) to (iv), or work in a process in which any such substance is used, handled or liberated; or (c) the maintenance or cleaning of any plant or machinery used in any such process as is mentioned in sub-paragraph (b), or the cleaning of clothing used in any such building as is mentioned in sub-paragraph (a) if such clothing is cleaned within the works of which the building forms a part or in a laundry maintained and used solely in connection with such works [[8]; or (d) exposure to coal tar pitch volatiles produced in aluminium smelting involving the Soderberg process (that is to say the method of producing aluminium by electrolysis in which the anode consists of a paste of petroleum coke and mineral oil which is baked *in situ*).]
C24. (a) Angiosarcoma of the liver; (b) osteolysis of the terminal phalanges of the fingers; (c) non-cirrhotic portal fibrosis.	(a) Work in or about machinery or apparatus used for the polymerisation of vinyl chloride monomer, a process which, for the purposes of this provision, comprises all operations up to and including the drying of the slurry produced by the polymerisation and the packaging of the dried product; or (b) work in a building or structure in which any part of that process takes place.

Prescribed disease or injury	*Occupation*
	Any occupation involving:
C25. Occupational vitiligo.	The use or handling of, or exposure to, para–tertiary–butylphenol, para–tertiary–butylcatechol, para–amyl–phenol, hydroquinone or the monobenzyl or monobutyl ether of hydroquinone.
[[4]C26. Damage to the liver or kidneys due to exposure to Carbon Tetrachloride.	The use of or handling of, or exposure to the fumes of, or vapour containing, carbon Tetrachloride.
C27. Damage to the liver or kidneys due to exposure to Trichloromethane (Chloroform).	The use of or handling of, or exposure to the fumes of, or vapour containing, Trichloromethane (Chloroform).
C28. Central nervous system dysfunction and associated gastro-intestinal disorders due to exposure to Chloromethane (Methyl Chloride).	The use of or handling of, or exposure to the fumes of, or vapour containing, chloromethane (Methyl Chloride).
C29. Peripheral neuropathy due to exposure to n-hexane or methyl n-butyl ketone.	The use of or handling of, or exposure to the fumes of, or vapour containing, n-hexane or methyl n-butyl ketone.]
[[11]C30. Chrome dermatitis, or ulceration of the mucous membranes or the epidermis, resulting from exposure to chromic acid, chromates or bi-chromates.	The use or handling of, or exposure to, chromic acid, chromates or bi-chromates.]
D. **Miscellanous Conditions**	
D1. Pneumoconiosis.	*Any occupation—* (a) set out in Part II of this Schedule; (b) specified in regulation 2(b)(ii).
	Any occupation involving:
D2. Byssinosis.	Work in any room where any process up to and including the weaving process is performed in a factory in which the spinning or manipulation of raw or waste cotton or of flax, or the weaving of cotton or flax, is carried on.
D3. Diffuse mesothelioma (primary neoplasm of the mesothelium of the pleura or of the pericardium or of the peritoneum).	[[12]Exposure to asbestos, asbestos dust or any admixture of asbestos at a level above that commonly found in the environment at large.]

Prescribed disease or injury	Occupation
	Any occupation involving:
[11D4. Allergic rhinitis which is due to exposure to any of the following agents— (a) isocyanates; (b) platinum salts; (c) fumes or dusts arising from the manufacture, transport or use of hardening agents (including epoxy resin curing agents) based on phthalic anhydride, tetrachlorophthalic anhydride, trimellitic anhydride or triethylene-tetramine; (d) fumes arising from the use of resin as a soldering flux; (e) proteolytic enzymes; (f) animals including insects and other arthropods used for the purposes of research or education or in laboratories]; (g) dusts arising from the sowing, cultivation, harvesting, drying, handling, milling, transport or storage of barley, oats, rye, wheat or maize, or the handling, milling, transport or storage of meal or flour made therefrom; (h) antibiotics; (i) cimetidine; (j) wood dust; (k) ispaghula; (l) castor bean dust; (m) ipecacuanha; (n) azodicarbonamide]; (o) animals including insects and other arthropods or their larval forms, used for the purposes of pest control or fruit cultivation, or the larval forms of animals used for the purposes of research, education or in laboratories; (p) glutaraldehyde; (q) persulphate slats or henna;	Exposure to any of the agents set out in column 1 of this paragraph.]

Prescribed disease or injury	*Occupation*
	Any occupation involving:
(r) crustaceans or fish or products arising from these in the food processing industry;	
(s) reactive dyes;	
(t) soya bean;	
(u) tea dust;	
(v) green coffee bean dust;	
(w) fumes from stainless steel welding.	
D5. Non-infective dermatitis of external origin [11. . .] but excluding dermatitis due to ionising particles or electro-magnetic radiations other than radiant heat).	Exposure to dust, liquid or vapour or any other external agent capable of irritating the skin (including friction or heat but excluding ionising particles or electro-magnetic radiations other than radiant heat).
D6. Carcinoma of the nasal cavity or associated air sinuses (nasal carcinoma).	(a) Attendance for work in or about a building where wooden goods are manufactured or repaired; or (b) attendance for work in a building used for the manufacture of footwear or components of footwear made wholly or partly of leather or fibre board; or (c) attendance for work at a place used wholly or mainly for the repair of footwear made wholly or partly of leather or fibre board.
D7. Asthma which is due to exposure to any of the following agents:	Exposure to any of the agents set out in column 1 of this paragraph.
(a) isocyanates;	
(b) platinum salts;	
(c) fumes or dusts arising from the manufacture, transport or use of hardening agents (including epoxy resin curing agents) based on phthalic anhydride, tetrachlorophthalic anhydride, trimellitic anhydride or triethylenetetramine;	
(d) fumes arising from the use of resin as a soldering flux;	
(e) proteolytic enzymes;	
[1(f) animals including insects and other arthropods used for the purposes of research or education or in laboratories];	

Prescribed disease or injury	Occupation
	Any occupation involving:
(g) dusts arising from the sowing, cultivation, harvesting, drying, handling, milling, transport or storage or barley, oats, rye, wheat or maize, or the handling, milling, transport or storage of meal or flour made therefrom;	
[[1](h) antibiotics;	
(i) cimetidine;	
(j) wood dust;	
(k) isphaghula;	
(l) castor bean dust;	
(m) ipecacuanha;	
(n) azodicarbonamide];	
[[7](o) animals including insects and other arthropods or their larval forms, used for the purposes of pest control or fruit cultivation, or the larval forms of animals used for the purposes of research, education or in laboratories;	
(p) glutaraldehyde;	
(q) persulphate slats or henna;	
(r) crustaceans or fish or products arising from these in the food processing industry;	
(s) reactive dyes;	
(t) soya bean;	
(u) tea dust;	
(v) green coffee bean dust;	
(w) fumes from stainless steel welding;	
(x) any other sensitising agent]	
(occupational asthma).	
D8. Primary carcinoma of the lung where there is accompanying evidence of one or both of the following:	

Prescribed disease or injury	*Occupation*
(a) asbestosis; [[12]](b) unilateral or bilateral diffuse pleural thickening extending to a thickness of 5mm or more at any point with the area affected as measured by a plain chest radiograph (not being a computerised tomography scan or other form of imaging) which— (i) in the case of unilateral diffuse pleural thickening, covers 50 per cent or more of the area of the chest wall of the lung affected; or (ii) in the case of bilateral diffuse pleural thickening, covers 25 per cent or more of the combined area of the chest wall of both lungs.]	*Any occupation involving:* (a) The working or handling of asbestos or any admixture of asbestos; or (b) the manufacture or repair of asbestos textiles or other articles containing or composed of asbestos; or (c) the cleaning of any machinery or plant used in any of the foregoing operations and of any chambers, fixtures and appliances for the collection of asbestos dust; or (d) substantial exposure to the dust arising from any of the foregoing operations.
[[12]D9. Unilateral and bilateral diffuse pleural thickening extending to a thickness of 5mm or more at any point within the area affected as measured by a plain chest radiograph (not being a computerised tomography scan or other form of imaging) which— (i) in the case of unilateral diffuse pleural thickening, covers 50 per cent or more of the area of the chest wall of the lung affected; or (ii) in the case of bilateral diffuse pleural thickening, covers 25 per cent or more of the combined area of the chest wall of both lungs.]	(a) The working or handling of asbestos or any admixture of asbestors; or (b) the manufacture or repair of asbestos textiles or other articles containing or composed of asbestos; or (c) the cleaning of any machinery or plant used in any of the foregoing operations and of any chambers, fixtures and appliances for the collection of asbestos dust; or (d) substantial exposure to the dust arising from any of the foregoing operations.
D10. [[8]Primary carcinoma of the lung.]	(a) Work underground in a tin mine; or (b) exposure to bis (chloromethyl) ether produced during the manufacture of chloromethyl methyl ether; or (c) exposure to zinc chromate, calcium chromate or stronium chromate in their pure forms.

Prescribed disease or injury	*Occupation*
	Any occupation involving:
[8D11. Primary carcinoma of the lung where there is accompanying evidence of silicosis.	Exposure to silica dust in the course of— (a) the manufacture of glass or pottery; (b) tunnelling in or quarrying sandstone or granite; (c) mining metal ores; (d) slate quarrying or the manufacture of artefacts from slate; (e) mining clay; (f) using siliceous materials as abrasives; (g) cutting stone; (h) stonemasonry; or (i) work in a foundry.]
[12D12. Except in the circumstances specified in regulation 2(d)— (a) chronic bronchitis; or (b) emphysema; or (c) both where there is accompanying evidence of a forced expiratory volume in one second (measured from the position of maximum inspiration with the claimant making maximum effort) which is— (i) at least one litre below the mean value predicted in accordance with "Lung Function: Assessment and Application in Medicine: by J. E. Cotes. (5th ed. 1994) published at Oxford by Blackwell Scientific Publications Limited (ISBN 0-632-03926-9) for a person of the claimant's age, height and sex; or (ii) less than one litre.	Exposure to coal dust by reason of working underground in a coal mine for a period or periods amounting in aggregate to at least 20 years (whether before or after 5th July 1948) and any such period or periods shall include a period or periods of incapacity while engaged in such an occupation.]

PART II

Regulations 2, 4, 38 and 40

OCCUPATIONS FOR WHICH PNEUMOCONIOSIS IS PRESCRIBED

1. Any occupation involving—

(a) the mining, quarrying or working of silica rock or the working of dried quartzose sand or any dry deposit or dry residue of silica or any dry admixture containing such materials (including any occupation in which any of the aforesaid operations are carried out incidentally to the mining or quarrying of other minerals or to the manufacture of articles containing crushed or ground silica rock);

(b) the handling of any of the materials specified in the foregoing sub-paragraph in or incidental to any of the operations mentioned therein, or substantial exposure to the dust arising from such operations.

2. Any occupation involving the breaking, crushing or grinding of flint or the working or handling of broken, crushed or ground flint or materials containing such flint, or substantial exposure to the dust arising from any such operations.

3. Any occupation involving sand blasting by means of compressed air with the use of quartzose sand or crushed silica rock or flint, or substantial exposure to the dust arising from sand and blasting.

4. Any occupation involving work in a foundry or the performance of, or substantial exposure to the dust arising from, any of the following operations:—

(a) the freeing of steel castings from adherent siliceous substance;

(b) the freeing of metal castings from adherent siliceous substance—

(i) by blasting with an abrasive propelled by compressed air, by steam or by a wheel; or

(ii) by the use of power-driven tools.

5. Any occupation in or incidental to the manufacture of china or earthenware (including sanitary earthenware, electrical earthenware and earthenware tiles), and any occupation involving substantial exposure to the dust arising therefrom.

6. Any occupation involving the grinding of mineral graphite, or substantial exposure to the dust arising from such grinding.

7. Any occupation involving the dressing of granite or any igneous rock by masons or the crushing of such materials, or substantial exposure to the dust arising from such operations.

8. Any occupation involving the use, or preparation for use, of a grindstone, or substantial exposure to the dust arising therefrom.

9. Any occupation involving—

(a) the working or handling of asbestos or any admixture of asbestos;

(b) the manufacture or repair of asbestos textiles or other articles containing or composed of asbestos;

(c) the cleaning of any machinery or plant used in any foregoing operations and of any chambers, fixtures and appliances for the collection of asbestos dust;

(d) substantial exposure to the dust arising from any of the foregoing operations.

10. Any occupation involving—

(a) work underground in any mine in which one of the objects of the mining operations is the getting of any mineral;

(b) the working or handling above ground at any coal or tin mine of any minerals extracted therefrom, or any operation incidental thereto;

(c) the trimming of coal in any ship, barge, or lighter, or in any dock or harbour or at any wharf or quay;

(d) the sawing, splitting or dressing of slate, or any operation incidental thereto.

11. Any occupation in or incidental to the manufacture of carbon electrodes by an industrial undertaking for use in the electrolytic extraction of aluminium from aluminium oxide, and any occupation involving substantial exposure to the dust arising therefrom.

12. Any occupation involving boiler scaling or substantial exposure to the dust arising therefrom.

AMENDMENTS

1. Social Security (Industrial Injuries and Adjudication) Miscellaneous Amendment Regulations 1986 (S.I. 1986 No. 1374), reg. 3 (September 1, 1986).

2. Social Security (Industrial Injuries) (Prescribed Diseases) Amendment Regulations 1987 (S.I. 1987 No. 335), reg. 2 (April 1, 1987).

3. Social Security (Industrial Injuries) (Prescribed Diseases) Amendment (No. 2) Regulations 1987 (S.I. 1987 No. 2112), reg. 2 (January 4, 1988).

4. Social Security (Industrial Injuries) (Prescribed Diseases) Amendment (No. 2) Regulations 1987 (S.I. 1987 No. 2112), reg. 3 (January 4, 1988).

5. Social Security (Industrial Injuries) (Prescribed Diseases) Amendment Regulations 1989 (S.I. 1989 No. 1207), reg. 6 (August 9, 1989).

6. Social Security (Industrial Injuries) (Prescribed Diseases) Amendment Regulations 1989 (S.I. 1989 No. 1207), reg. 4 (October 16, 1989).

7. Social Security (Industrial Injuries) (Prescribed Diseases) Amendment Regulations 1991 (S.I. 1991 No. 1938), reg. 2 (September 26, 1991).

8. Social Security (Industrial Injuries) (Prescribed Diseases) Amendment Regulations 1993 (S.I. 1993 No. 862), reg. 6 (April 19, 1993).

9. Social Security (Industrial Injuries) (Prescribed Diseases) Amendment (No. 2) Regulations 1993 (S.I. 1993 No. 1985), reg. 6 (September 13, 1993).

10. Social Security (Industrial Injuries) (Prescribed Diseases) Amendment Regulations 1994 (S.I. 1994 No. 2343), reg. 4 (October 10, 1994).

11. Social Security (Industrial Injuries and Diseases) (Miscellaneous Amendments) Regulations 1996 (S.I. 1996 No. 425), reg. 5 (March 24, 1996 with savings, see reg. 7 below).

12. Social Security (Industrial Injuries) (Miscellaneous Amendments) Regulations 1997 (S.I. 1997 No. 810), reg. 5 (April, 1997).

General Note

The question whether a claimant has been employed in a prescribed occupation falls to be decided by an adjudication officer or a social security appeal tribunal rather than by an adjudicating medical authority or medical appeal tribunal. The prescribed occupations have been the subject of countless Commissioners' decisions and reference should be made to the note to this Schedule in Bonner *et al., Non-means-tested benefits: The Legislation.*

The question whether a claimant is suffering from a prescribed disease (the "diagnosis question") is determined under regs. 43 to 54 of the Social Security (Adjudication) Regulations 1995 and so falls within the jurisdiction of a medical appeal tribunal. Oddly, the question whether the disease is due to the nature of the claimant's employment falls to be decided by an adjudication officer or social security appeal tribunal (*R(I) 4/91*). As is pointed out in *CI/701/93*, a medical appeal tribunal that allows a claimant's appeal on a diagnosis question may be asked to determine the disablement questions (including the assessment of the disablement resulting from the prescribed disease) before the adjudication officer has determined that the disease is prescribed in relation to the particular claimant. However, the cause of the disease is not always irrelevant to the medical appeal tribunal's determination of the diagnosis question because some diseases are prescribed only where the disease is attributable to a particular cause. Thus, on a claim in respect of prescribed disease D4, it is for the medical authorities to consider whether any inflammation or ulceration of the mucous membrane of the upper respiratory passages or mouth was produced by dust, liquid or vapour, but it is for the adjudication officer or social security appeal tribunal to determine whether the claimant's employment involved exposure to dust, liquid or vapour and whether the claimant's condition was due to that employment rather than to contact with dust, liquid or vapour elsewhere (*CI/738/93*). Where a disease is prescribed only when attributable to a particular cause, there is a substantial risk of inconsistency between the medical authorities and the adjudication officer or social security appeal tribunal. S.60(2) of the Social Security Administration Act 1992 has the effect that any finding of fact embodied in, or necessary to, the decision of the adjudication officer or social security appeal tribunal is not conclusive for the purpose of any decision of the medical authorities. In *CI/73/94*, an adjudication officer was satisfied that the claimant making a claim in respect of occupational asthma (prescribed disease D7) had been employed in an occupation involving exposure to a sensitising agent because she had been exposed to tobacco smoke. The Commissioner held that the medical appeal tribunal were entitled to find that the claimant was suffering from asthma but not from the prescribed disease if, in their view, the tobacco smoke was not a sensitising agent. The decision contains an interesting discussion of the meaning of "any other sensitising agent". The diagnosis of pneumoconiosis (prescribed disease D1) was considered in *CSI/78/93* where the Commissioner held that to say that minimal coalworker's pneumoconiosis "is insufficient radiologically for him to be eligible for industrial injuries benefit" is wrong in law. Pneumoconiosis is defined in s.122(1) of the Social Security Contributions and Benefits Act 1992 as "fibrosis of the lungs due to silica dust, asbestos dust or other dust, and includes the condition of the lungs known as dust-reticulation". Either the claimant has fibrosis due to dust or he does not. The International Labour Organisation's "International Classification of Radiographs of Pneumoconiosis" is a diagnostic aid but the radiological category does not determine the diagnosis.

In *CI/414/94*, the Commissioner rejected an argument to the effect that, when a new disease is added to this Schedule, disablement benefit may be payable in respect of a period before the date on which the addition was made.

SCHEDULE 2 — Regulation 11

MODIFICATIONS OF CHAPTERS IV AND VI OF PART II OF THE ACT IN THEIR APPLICATION TO BENEFIT AND CLAIMS TO WHICH THESE REGULATIONS APPLY

In Chapters IV and VI of Part II of the Act references to accidents shall be construed as references to prescribed diseases and references to the relevant accident shall be construed as references to the relevant disease and references to the date of the relevant accident shall be construed as references to the date of onset of the relevant disease.

SCHEDULE 3 — Regulation 34

ASSESSMENT OF THE EXTENT OF OCCUPATIONAL DEAFNESS

PART I

CLAIMS TO WHICH REGULATION 34(1) APPLIES

[[1]*Average of hearing losses (dB) due to all causes at 1, 2 and 3 kHz frequencies*]	*Degree of disablement per cent.*
50–52 dB	20
53–57 dB	30
58–62 dB	40
63–67 dB	50
68–72 dB	60
73–77 dB	70
78–82 dB	80
83–87 dB	90
88 dB or more	100

PART II

CLAIMS TO WHICH REGULATION 34(2) APPLIES

[[1]*Average of hearing losses (dB) due to all causes at 1, 2 and 3 kHz frequencies*]	*Degree of disablement per cent.*
50–53 dB	20
54–60 dB	30
61–66 dB	40
67–72 dB	50
73–79 dB	60
80–86 dB	70
87–95 dB	80
96–105 dB	90
106 dB or more	100

Part III

Formula for Calculating Binaural Disablement

$$\frac{(\text{Degree of disablement of better ear} \times 4) + \text{degree of disablement of worse ear}}{5}$$

Amendment

1. Social Security (Industrial Injuries) (Prescribed Diseases) Amendment Regulations 1989 (S.I. 1989 No. 1207), reg. 4 (October 16, 1989).

Schedule 4 **Regulation 43**

Prescribed Diseases and Relevant Dates of the Purposes of Regulation 43

Description of disease or injury	*Relevant date*
A3. Dysbarism, including decompression sickness, barotrauma and osteonecrosis.	Except in the case of a person suffering from decompression sickness employed in any occupation involving subjection to compressed or rarefied air, 3rd October 1983.
A11. Episodic blanching, occurring throughout the year, affecting the middle or proximal phalanges or in the case of a thumb the proximal phalanx, of— (a) in the case of a person with 5 fingers (including thumb) one hand, any 3 of those fingers, or (b) in the case of person with only 4 such fingers, any 2 of those fingers, or (c) in the case of a person with less than 4 such fingers, any one of those fingers or, as the case may be, the one remaining finger (vibration white finger).	1st April 1985.
B1. Anthrax.	In the case of a person employed in an occupation involving the loading and unloading or transport of animal products or residues, 3rd October 1983.
B3. Infection by leptospira.	(a) In the case of a person employed in an occupation in places which are or are liable to be infested by small mammals other than rats, field mice or voles, 3rd October 1983;

Description of disease or injury	*Relevant date*
	(b) in the case of a person employed in an occupation in any other place mentioned in the second column of paragraph B3 of Part I of Schedule 1 above, 7th January 1980.
B5. Tuberculosis.	In the case of a person employed in an occupation involving contact with a source of tuberculosis infection, not being an employment set out in the second column of paragraph 38 of Part I of Schedule 1 to the old regulations, 3rd October 1983.
B6. Extrinsic allergic alveolitis (including farmer's lung)	In the case of a person suffering from extrinsic allergic alveolitis, not being farmer's lung, employed in any occupation set out in the second column of paragraph B6 of Part I of Schedule 1 above, or in the case of a person suffering from farmer's lung, employed in any occupation involving exposure to moulds or fungal spores or heterologous proteins by reason of employment in cultivation of edible fungi or maltworking, or loading or unloading or handling in storage edible fungi or caring for or handling birds, 3rd October 1983.
B7. Infection by organisms of the genus brucella.	In the case of a person suffering from infection by organisms of the genus brucella, not being infection by Brucella abortus, or employed in an occupation set out in the second column of paragraph B7 of Part I of Schedule 1 above, not being an occupation set out in the second column of paragraph 46 of Part I of Schedule 1 to the old regulations, 3rd October 1983.
B8. Viral hepatitis.	In the case of a person employed in any occupation involving contact with human blood or human blood products, or contact with a source of viral hepatitis, 3rd December 1984.
B9. Infection by Streptococcus suis.	3rd October 1983.
[[4]B10. (a) Avian chlamydiosis.	9th August 1989.
B10. (b) Ovine chlamydiosis.	9th August 1989.
B11. Q fever.	9th August 1989.]

Description of disease or injury	*Relevant date*
C3. Poisoning by phosphorus or an inorganic compound of phosphorus or poisoning due to the anti-cholinesterase or pseudo anti-cholinesterase action of organic phosphorus compounds.	In the case of a person suffering from poisoning by an inorganic compound of phosphorus or poisoning due to the pseudo anti-cholinesterase action or organic phosphorus compounds, 3rd October 1983.
C18. Poisoning by cadmium.	In the case of a person employed in an occupation involving exposure to cadmium dust, 3rd October 1983.
C23. Primary neoplasm (including papilloma, carcinoma-in-situ and invasive carcinoma) of the epithelial lining of the urinary tract (renal pelvis, ureter, bladder and urethra).	In the case of a person employed in an occupation involving work in a building in which methylene-bis-orthochloroaniline is produced for commercial purposes, 3rd October 1983.
C24. (a) Angiosarcoma of the liver; (b) osteolysis of the terminal phalanges of the finger; (c) non-cirrhotic portal fibrosis.	(a) In the case of a person suffering from angiosarcoma of the liver or osteolysis of the terminal phalanges of the fingers, 21st March 1977; (b) in the case of a person suffering from non-cirrhotic portal fibrosis, 3rd October 1983.
C25. Occupational vitiligo.	15th December 1980.
[3C26. Damage to the liver or kidneys due to exposure to Carbon Tetrachloride.	4th January 1988.
C27. Damage to the liver or kidneys due to exposure to Trichloromethane (Chloroform).	4th January 1988.
C28. Central nervous system dysfunction and associated gastro-intestinal disorders due to exposure to chloromethane (Methyl Chloride).	4th January 1988.
C29. Peripheral neuropathy due to exposure to n-hexane or methyl-n-butyl ketone.	4th January 1988.]
D3. Diffuse mesothelioma.	In the case of a person suffering from primary neoplasm of the pericardium, 3rd October 1983.
D6. carcinoma of the nasal cavity or associated air sinuses (nasal carcinoma).	In the case of a person employed in an occupation involving attendance for work in or about a building where wooden goods (other than wooden furniture) are manufactured or where wooden goods are repaired, 3rd October 1983.
D7. Occupational asthma.	[1(a) In the case of a person suffering from asthma due to exposure to any of the following agents:

Description of disease or injury	*Relevant date*
	(i) isocyanates; (ii) platinum salts; (iii) fumes or dusts arising from the manufacture, transport or use of hardening agents (including epoxy resin curing agents) based on phthalic anhydride, tetrachlorophthalic anhydride, trimellitic anhydride or triethylenetetramine; (iv) fumes arising from the use of rosin as a soldering flux; (v) proteolytic enzymes; (vi) animals or insects used for the purposes of research or education or in laboratories; (vii) dusts arising from the sowing, cultivation, harvesting, drying, handling, milling, transport or storage of barley, oats, rye, wheat or maize, or the handling, milling, transport or storage of meal or flour made therefrom, 29th March 1982; (b) In the case of a person suffering from asthma due to exposure to any of the following agents: (i) animals including insects and other anthropods used for the purposes of research or education or in laboratories; (ii) antibiotics; (iii) cimetidine; (iv) wood dust; (v) ispagahula; (vi) castor bean dust;

	(vii) ipecacuanha;
	(viii) azodicarbonamide,
	1st September 1986.]
D8. Primary carcinoma of the lung where there is accompanying evidence of one or both of the following—	1st April 1985.
(a) asbestosis;	
(b) bilateral diffuse pleural thickening.	
D9. Bilateral diffuse pleural thickening.	1st April 1985.
[[2]D10. Lung cancer.	1st April 1987.]

AMENDMENTS

1. Social Security (Industrial Injuries and Adjudication) Miscellaneous Amendment Regulations 1986 (S.I. 1986 No. 1374), reg. 3 (September 1, 1986).
2. Social Security (Industrial Injuries) (Prescribed Diseases) Amendment Regulations 1987 (S.I. 1987 No. 335), reg. 2 (April 1, 1987).
3. Social Security (Industrial Injuries) (Prescribed Diseases) Amendment (No. 2) Regulations 1987 (S.I. 1987 No. 2112), reg. 3 (January 4, 1988).
4. Social Security (Industrial Injuries) (Prescribed Diseases) Amendment Regulations 1989 (S.I. 1989 No. 1207), reg. 6 (August 9, 1989).

SCHEDULE 5 — Regulation 44

TRANSITIONAL PROVISIONS REGARDING DATES OF DEVELOPMENT AND DATES OF ONSET

1. In this Schedule the "date of development" has the meaning attributed to it by regulations 5, 6, 7 and 56 of the old regulations.

2. Where a claim for benefit has been made before 6th April 1983, a date of development shall be determined and regulation 16 of the old regulations shall apply as if the old regulations were still in force.

3. Where a claim for benefit is made after 5th April 1983 and a date of onset is determined which is before 6th April 1983, regulation 16 of the old regulations shall apply as if the old regulations were still in force.

4. Where in pursuance of a claim made before 6th April 1983 a date of development has been determined and an award of benefit has been made these regulations shall have effect in relation to that claim and any subsequent claim made by or on behalf of the same person in respect of the same disease (except where under regulation 7 the disease is treated as having been contracted afresh) as if references to the date of onset were references to that date of development.

5. Subject to paragraph 6, where a claim for injury benefit for a day falling or a period beginning before 5th April 1983 is made after 6th April 1983 and no date of development or date of onset which can be treated as such for the purposes of that claim has already been determined, for the purposes only of determining the date on which the injury benefit period (if any) is to begin, a date of development shall be determined, so however that if it is later than 5th April 1983 no injury benefit period shall begin and injury benefit shall not be payable.

6. There shall be no entitlement, in the following cases, to benefit for any day which is earlier than the date specified:—

(a) in the case of a person who is or has been suffering from

(i) viral hepatitis : 2nd February 1976

(ii) angiosarcoma of the liver : 21st March 1977

(iii) osteolysis of the terminal phalanges of the fingers : 21st March 1977

(iv) carcinoma of the nasal cavity or associated air sinuses (nasal carcinoma) : 8th August 1979

(v) occupational vitiligo : 15th December 1980

[[1](vi) occupational asthma arising otherwise than as described at (vii) below : 29th March 1982;

(vii) occupational asthma which is due to exposure to antibiotics, cimetidine, wood dust, ispaghula, castor bean dust, ipecacuanha or azodicarbonamide : 1st September 1986;]

(b) in the case of a person who is or has been suffering from byssinosis but who has not been employed in employed earner's employment in any occupation mentioned in regulation 2(c) of the old regulations for a period or periods (whether before or after 5th July 1948) amounting in the aggregate to 5 years : 6th April 1979;

(c) in the case of a person who is or has been suffering from infection by leptospira but neither is nor has been either incapable of work or suffering from a loss of faculty as a result of infection by—

(i) leptospira icterohaemorrhagiae in the case of a person employed in employed earner's employment in any occupation involving work in places which are, or are liable to be, infested by rats, or

(ii) leptospira canicola in the case of a person employed in employed earner's employment in any occupation involving work at dog kennels or the care or handling of dogs : 7th January 1980.

AMENDMENT

1. Social Security (Industrial Injuries and Adjudication) Miscellaneous Amendment Regulations 1986 (S.I. 1986 No. 1374), reg. 2 (September 1, 1986).

Schedule 6. *Omitted.*

The Social Security (Industrial Injuries) (Prescribed Diseases) Amendment (No. 2) Regulations 1993

(S.I. 1993 No. 1985, reg. 1)

ARRANGEMENT OF REGULATIONS

The Secretary of State for Social Security, in exercise of the powers conferred by sections 108(2) and (4), 109(2) and (3), 110(1) and (2), 122(1) and 175(1) and (3) of and paragraph 2 of Schedule 6 to the Social Security Contributions and Benefits Act 1992 and sections 5(1)(a) and (b), 58(1)(b) and 189(1) and (4) of the Social Security Administration Act 1992, and of all other powers enabling him in that behalf, after reference to the Industrial Injuries Advisory Council hereby makes the following Regulations:

Citation, commencement and interpretation

1.—(1) These Regulations may be cited as the Social Security (Industrial Injuries) (Prescribed Diseases) Amendment (No. 2) Regulations 1993 and shall come into force on 13th September 1993.

(2) In these Regulations "the principal Regulations" means the Social Security (Industrial Injuries) (Prescribed Diseases) Regulations 1985.

2.–8. *Omitted.*

Transitional provision with respect to claims for prescribed disease D12

9.—(1) In this regulation—

"prescribed disease D12" means the disease bearing that number and listed in Part I of Schedule 1 to the principal Regulations (chronic bronchitis and emphysema);

"relevant claim" means a claim for benefit in respect of prescribed disease D12; and

"relevant date" means 13th September 1993 or the date upon which the claimant in question first satisfies the conditions specified in Schedule 1 to the principal Regulations in respect of prescribed disease D12, whichever is the later.

(2) The provisions of the Social Security (Claims and Payments) Regulations 1987 shall apply in relation to a relevant claim subject to the following provisions of this regulation.

(3) A person who is aged not less than 70 on 13th September 1993 may make a relevant claim at any time in the period beginning with 13th September 1993 and ending with 28th February 1994, and if so made the claim shall be treated as having been made on the relevant date.

(4) A person who is aged less than 70 on 13th September 1993 and who, on the date the claim is made, has an award of attendance allowance at the higher rate under section 65(3) of the Social Security Contributions and Benefits Act 1992 or of the care component of disability living allowance at the highest rate under section 72(4) of that Act, may make a relevant claim at any time in the period beginning with 13th September 1993 and ending with 28th February 1994, and if so made the claim shall be treated as having been made on the relevant date.

(5) A person who does not fall within either of paragraphs (3) and (4) above may not make a relevant claim before 1st March 1994, but if such a person, or a person falling within paragraph (4) above who has not previously made a relevant claim, makes a relevant claim in the period beginning with that day and ending with 31st August 1994 that claim shall be treated as having been made on the relevant date.

The Social Security (Industrial Injuries and Diseases) (Miscellaneous Amendments) Regulations 1996

(S.I. 1996 No. 425)

ARRANGEMENT OF REGULATIONS

The Secretary of State for Social Security, in exercise of the powers conferred by sections 108(2), 109(2) and (3), 113(1)(b), 122(1) and 175(1), (3) and (4) of, and sub-paragraphs (8) and (9) of paragraph 13 of Schedule 7 to, the Social Security Contributions and Benefits Act 1992(**a**) and sections 5(1)(k), 27(1)(b) and 189(1) and (4)(b) of the Social Security Administration Act 1992(**b**), and of all other powers enabling him in that behalf, after reference to the Industrial Injuries Advisory Council(**c**), hereby makes the following Regulations:

Citation and commencement

1. These Regulations may be cited as the Social Security (Industrial Injuries and Diseases) (Miscellaneous Amendments) Regulations 1996 and shall come into force on 24th March 1996.

2.–6. *Omitted.*

Transitional provisions

7.—(1) The amendments made by regulation 5 of these Regulations ("the relevant amendments") to the terms in which each of the prescribed diseases A12, D4 and D5 ("the relevant disease") is prescribed shall not apply in the cases specified in the following provisions of this regulation, and in this regulation "commencement date" means the date on which these Regulations come into force.

(2) The relevant amendments shall not apply in the case of a person—

(a) who had an assessment of disablement in respect of the relevant disease for period which includes commencement date; or

(b) in respect of whom a decision in relation to a relevant disease on a claim for disablement benefit made before commencement date is reviewed on or after that date under section 47 of the Social Security Administration Act 1992 (reviews of medical decisions) which results in an assessment for a period which includes commencement date;

during any period where there is in respect of him a continuous assessment of disablement in respect of that disease which began before commencement date, and for this purpose two or more assessments one of which begins on the day following the end of a preceding assessment shall be treated as continuous.

(3) The relevant amendments shall not apply in the case of a person who makes a claim for disablement benefit in respect of the relevant disease before commencement date which results in an assessment of disablement, where the date of onset of that disease is earlier than commencment date, during any period when there is in respect of him a continuous assessment of disablement in respect of that disease which began not later than 91 days (excluding Sundays) after commencement date, and for this purpose two or more assessments one of which begins on the day following the end of a preceding assessment shall be treated as continuous.

(4) The relevant amendments shall not apply in the case of a person—

(a) who had an assessment of disablement in respect of the relevant disease for a period which ended before commencement date;

(b) who suffers a further attack of that relevant disease before commencement date;

(c) who makes a claim for disablement benefit in respect of that disease after commencement date; and

(d) in respect of whom it is decided, under regulation 7 of the Social Security (Industrial Injuries) (Prescribed Diseases) Regulations 1985 (recrudescence) that the further attack is a recrudescence of that disease.

The Social Security (Invalid Care Allowance) Regulations 1976

(S.I. 1976 No. 409)

ARRANGEMENT OF REGULATIONS

PART I

GENERAL

PART II

MISCELLANEOUS PROVISIONS RELATING TO INVALID CARE ALLOWANCE

The Secretary of State for Social Services, in exercise of the powers conferred upon her by sections 13(4), 37, 40(2), 49, 79(1), 80, 81(1), (2) and (6), 82(1), (5) and (6), 84(1) and (2), 85(1), 86(5) and 119(3) of the Social Security Act 1975, section 36(7) of the National Insurance Act 1965 as continued in force by regulation 2(2) of the Social Security (Graduated Retirement Benefit) Regulations 1975, and of all other powers enabling her in that behalf, and after reference to the National Insurance Advisory Committee, hereby makes the following regulations:

PART I

GENERAL

Citation and commencement

1. These regulations may be cited as the Social Security (Invalid Care Allowance) Regulations 1976 and shall come into operation on 12th April 1976.

Interpretation

2.—[[1](1) In these Regulations, "the Contributions and Benefits Act" means the Social Security Contributions and Benefits Act 1992.].

(2) Any reference in these regulations to any provision made by or contained in any enactment or instrument shall, except in so far as the context otherwise requires, be construed as a reference to that provision as amended or extended by any enactment or instrument and as including a reference to any provision which may re-enact or replace it, with or without modification.

(3) The rules for the construction of Acts of Parliament contained in the Interpretation Act 1889 shall apply for the purposes of the interpretation of these regulations as they apply for the purposes of the interpretation of an Act of Parliament.

AMENDMENT

1. Social Security (Invalid Care Allowance) Amendment Regulations 1996 (S.I. 1996 No. 2744), reg. 2 (November 25, 1996).

PART II

MISCELLANEOUS PROVISIONS RELATING TO INVALID CARE ALLOWANCE

Prescribed payments out of public funds which constitute the persons in respect of whom they are payable as severely disabled persons

3.—(1) For the purposes of [[1]section 70 of the Contributions and Benefits Act] (invalid care allowance) the prescribed payments out of public funds which constitute the persons in respect of whom they are payable as severely disabled persons are—

(a) a payment under [[1]section 104 of the Contributions and Benefits Act] (increase of disablement pension where constant attendance needed);

(b) a payment such as is referred to in section 7(3)(b) of the Industrial Injuries and Diseases (Old Cases) Act 1975 (increase of an allowance under that Act where the person in respect of whom that allowance is payable requires constant attendance as a result of his disablement);

(c) a payment under regulation 44 of the Social Security (Industrial Injuries) (Benefit) Regulations 1975 in respect of the need of constant attendance;

(d) a payment by way of an allowance in respect of constant attendance on account of disablement for which a person is in receipt of a war disablement pension,

being a payment the weekly rate of which is not less than the amount specified in [[1]paragraph 7(a) of Part V of Schedule 4 to the Contributions and Benefits Act].

(2) For the purposes of paragraph (1)(d) of this regulation "war disablement pension" means—

(a) retired pay, pension or allowance granted in respect of disablement under powers conferred by or under the Ministry of Pensions Act 1916, the Air Force (Constitution) Act 1917, the Personal Injuries (Emergency Provisions) Act 1939, the Pensions (Navy, Army, Air Force and Mercantile Marine) Act 1939, the Polish Resettlement Act 1947, the Home Guard Act 1951 or the Ulster Defence Regiment Act 1969,

(b) any retired pay or pension to which section 365(1) of the Income and Corporation Taxes Act 1970 applies, not being retired pay, pension or allowance to which sub-paragraph (a) of this paragraph applies; or

(c) any payment which the Secretary of State has certified can be accepted as being analogous to any such retired pay, pension or allowance as is referred to in sub-paragraph (a) or (b) of this paragraph.

AMENDMENT

1. Social Security (Invalid Care Allowance) Amendment Regulations 1996 (S.I. 1996 No. 2744), reg. (November 25, 1996).

Circumstances in which persons are or are not to be treated as engaged or regularly and substantially engaged in caring for severely disabled persons

4.—(1) [[1] Subject to paragraph (1A) of this regulation,] a person shall be treated as engaged and as regularly and substantially engaged in caring for a severely disabled person on every day in a week if, and shall not be treated as engaged or regularly and substantially engaged in caring for a severely disabled person on any day in a week unless, as at that week he is, or is likely to be, engaged and regularly engaged for at least 35 hours a week in caring for that severely disabled person.

[[1](1A) A person who is caring for two or more severely disabled persons in a week shall be treated as engaged and regularly and substantially engaged in caring for a severely disabled person only where he is engaged and regularly engaged for at least 35 hours in that week in caring for any one severely disabled person, considered without reference to any other severely disabled person for whom he is caring.]

(2) A week in respect of which a person fails to satisfy the requirements of paragraph (1) of this regulation shall be treated as a week in respect of which that person satisfies those requirements if he establishes—

(a) that he has only temporarily ceased to satisfy them; and
(b) that (disregarding the provisions of this sub-paragraph) he has satisfied them for at least 14 weeks in the period of 26 weeks ending with that week and would have satisfied them for at least 22 weeks in that period but for the fact that either he or the severely disabled person for whom he has been caring was undergoing medical or other treatment as an inpatient in a hospital or similar institution.

Amendment

1. Social Security (Invalid Care Allowance) Amendment (No. 2) Regulations 1993 (S.I. 1993 No. 1851), reg. 2 (August 17, 1993).

Circumstances in which persons are to be regarded as receiving full-time education

[[1]**5.**—(1) For the purposes of [[2]section 70(3) of the Contributions and Benefits Act] a person shall be treated as receiving full-time education for any period during which he attends a course of education at a university, college, school or other educational establishment for twenty-one hours or more a week.

(2) In calculating the hours of attendance under paragraph (1) of this regulation—

(a) there shall be included the time spent receiving instruction or tuition, undertaking supervised study, examination or practical work or taking part in any exercise, experiment or project for which provision is made in the curriculum of the course; and
(b) there shall be excluded any time occupied by meal breaks or spent on unsupervised study, whether undertaken on or off the premises of the educational establishment.

(3) In determining the duration of a period of full-time education under paragraph (1) of this regulation, a person who has started on a course of education shall be treated as attending it for the usual number of hours per week throughout any vacation or any temporary interruption of his attendance until the end of the course or such earlier date as he abandons it or is dismissed from it.]

Amendments

1. Social Security (Invalid Care Allowance) Amendment Regulations 1992 (S.I. 1992 No. 470).
2. Social Security (Invalid Care Allowance) Amendment Regulations 1996 (S.I. 1996 No. 2744), reg. 2 (November 25, 1996).

Severely disabled persons prescribed for the purposes of [2section 70(1)(c) of the Contributions and Benefits Act]

[1**6.** For the purposes of [2section 70(1)(c) of the Contributions and Benefits Act] (condition of entitlement to an invalid care allowance that the severely disabled person is either such relative of the person caring for him as may be prescribed or a person of any such other description as may be prescribed) where a severely disabled person is being cared for by another person, that disabled person shall be a prescribed person for the purposes of that section, whether he is related to the person caring for him or not.]

Amendments

1. Social Security (Invalid Care Allowance) Amendment Regulations 1981 (S.I. 1981 No. 655).
2. Social Security (Invalid Care Allowance) Amendment Regulations 1996 (S.I. 1996 No. 2744), reg. 2 (November 25, 1996).

Manner of electing the person entitled to an invalid care allowance in respect of a severely disabled person where, but for [1section 70(7) of the Contributions and Benefits Act], more than one person would be entitled to an invalid care allowance in respect of that severely disabled person

7.—(1) For the purposes of the provision in [1section 70(7) of the Contributions and Benefits Act] which provides that where, apart from that section, two or more persons would be entitled for the same day to an invalid care allowance in respect of the same severely disabled person one of them only shall be entitled, being such one of them as they may jointly elect in the prescribed manner, an election shall be made by giving the Secretary of State a notice in writing signed by the persons who but for the said provision would be entitled to an invalid care allowance in respect of the same severely disabled person specifying one of them as the person to be entitled.

(2) An election under paragraph (1) of this regulation shall not be effective to confer entitlement to invalid care allowance either for the day on which the election is made or for any earlier day if such day is one for which an invalid care allowance has been paid in respect of the severely disabled person in question and has not been repaid or recovered.

Amendment

1. Social Security (Invalid Care Allowance) Amendment Regulations 1996 (S.I. 1996 No. 2744), reg. 2 (November 25, 1996).

Circumstances in which a person is or is not to be treated as gainfully employed

8.—(1) For the purposes of [3section 70(1)(b) of the Contributions and Benefits Act] (condition of a person being entitled to an invalid care allowance for any day that he is not gainfully employed) a person shall not be treated as gainfully employed on any day in a week unless his earnings in the immediately preceding week have exceeded [1£50] and, subject to paragraph (2) of this regulation, shall be treated as gainfully employed on every day in a week if his earnings in the immediately preceding week have exceeded [1£50].

(2) There shall be disregarded for the purposes of paragraph (1) above a person's earnings—

(a) for any week which under paragraph (2) of regulation 4 of these regulations is treated as a week in which that person satisfies the requirements of paragraph (1) of that regulation;

(b) [2. . .]
(c) [3. . .]
(3) *Revoked.*

AMENDMENTS

1. Social Security (Invalid Care Allowance) Amendment Regulations 1993 (S.I. 1993 No. 316), reg. 2 (April 12, 1993).
2. Social Security (Invalid Care Allowance) Amendment Regulations 1995 (S.I. 1995 No. 2935), reg. 2 (December 12, 1995 with saving under reg. 3).
3. Social Security (Invalid Care Allowance) Amendment Regulations 1996 (S.I. 1996 No. 2744), reg. 2 (November 25, 1995 with saving under reg. 3).

GENERAL NOTE

Earnings are calculated under the Social Security Benefit (Computation of Earnings) Regulations 1996 which are not included in this book. See Bonner *et al., Non-means-tested Benefits: The Legislation.*

Conditions relating to residence and presence in Great Britain

9.—(1) Subject to the following provisions of this regulation, the prescribed conditions for the purposes of [4section 70(4) of the Contributions and Benefits Act] (person not to be entitled to an invalid care allowance unless he satisfies prescribed conditions as to residence or presence in Great Britain) in relation to any person in respect of any day shall be—

(a) that he is ordinarily resident in Great Britain; and
[3(aa) subject to paragraph (1A), his right to reside or remain in Gret Britain is not subject to any limitation or condition, and]
(b) that he is present in Great Britain; and
(c) that he has been present in Great Britain for a period of, or periods amounting in the aggregate to, not less than 26 weeks in the 12 months immediately preceding that day.

[3(1A) For the purposes of paragraph (1)(aa), a person's right to reside or remain in Great Britain is not to be treated as if it were subject to a limitation or condition if—

(a) he is a person recorded by the Secretary of State as a refugee within the defintion in Article 1 of the Convention relating to the Status of Refugees done at Geneva on 28th July 1951, as extended by Article 1(2) of the Protocol relating to the Status of Refugees done at New York on 31st January 1967;
(b) he is a person who has been granted exceptional leave outside the provisions of the immigration rules within the meaning of the Immigration Act 1971 to remain in the United Kingdom by the Secretary of State;
(c) he is a national, or a member of the family of a national, of a State contracting party to the Agreement on the European Economic Area signed at Oporto on 2nd May 1992 as adjusted by the Protocol signed at Brussels on 17th March 1993; or
(d) he is a person who is—
   (i) lawfully working in Great Britain and is a national of a State with which the Community has concluded an Agreement under article 238 of the Treaty establishing the European Community providing, in the field of social security, for the equal treatment of workers who are nationals of the signatory State and their families, or
   (ii) a member of the family of, and living with, such a person.]

(2) For the purposes of paragraph (1)(b) and (c) of this regulation, a person who is absent from Great Britain on any day shall be treated as being present in Great Britain—

(a) if his absence is, and when it began was, for a temporary purpose and has not lasted for a continuous period exceeding 4 weeks; or
(b) if his absence is temporary and for the specific purpose of caring for the severely disabled person who is also absent from Great Britain and where attendance allowance [2, or the care component of disability living allowance at the highest or middle rate prescribed in accordance with [4section 72(3) of the Contributions and Benefits Act]] or a payment specified in regulation 3(1) of these regulations is payable in respect of that disabled person for that day.

[1(3) For the purposes of paragraph (1)(b) and (c) notwithstanding that on any day a person is absent from Great Britain he shall be treated as though he were present in Great Britain if his absence is by reason only of the fact that on that day—
(a) he is abroad in his capacity as—
(i) a serving member of the forces within the meaning of the definition of "serving member of the forces" in regulation 1(2) of the Social Security (Contributions) Regulations 1975, as amended, or
(ii) an airman or mariner within the meaning of regulation 72 and regulation 77 respectively of those Regulations; or
(b) he is in prescribed employment in connection with continental shelf operations within the meaning of regulation 76 of those Regulations; or
(c) he is living with a person mentioned in sub-paragraph (a)(i) and is the spouse, son, daughter, father, father-in-law, mother or mother-in-law of that person.]

AMENDMENTS

1. Social Security (Child Benefit Consequential) Regulations 1977 (S.I. 1977 No. 342), reg. 18 (April 4, 1977).
2. Disability Living Allowance and Disability Working Allowance Regulations 1991 (S.I. 1991 No. 2742), reg. 3 (April 6, 1992).
3. Social Security (Persons From Abroad) Miscellaneous Amendments Regulations 1996 (S.I. 1996 No. 30), reg. 9 (February 5, 1996, subject to a saving under reg. 12(3)).
4. Social Security (Invalid Care Allowance) Amendment Regulations 1996 (S.I. 1996 No. 2744), reg. 2 (November 25, 1996).

Circumstances in which a person over [1the age of 65] is to be treated as having been entitled to invalid care allowance immediately before attaining that age

10. A person who has attained [1the age of 65] shall for the purposes of [2section 70(5) of the Contributions and Benefits Act] be treated as having been entitled to an invalid care allowance immediately before attaining that age if immediately before attaining it he would have satisfied the conditions for entitlement to that allowance but for the provisions of the Social Security (Overlapping Benefits) Regulations 1975, as amended.

AMENDMENTS

1. Social Security (Severe Disablement Allowance and Invalid Care Allowance) Amendment Regulations 1994 (S.I. 1994 No. 2556), reg. 5 (October 28, 1994).
2. Social Security (Invalid Care Allowance) Amendment Regulations 1996 (S.I. 1996 No. 2744), reg. 2 (November 25, 1996).

[1Women aged 65 before 28th October 1994

10A. A woman shall be entitled to an invalid care allowance if—
(a) she attained the age of 65 before 28th October 1994;

(b) immediately before attaining the age of 65 she would have satisfied the requirements for entitlement to an invalid care allowance, whether or not she made a claim, but for the condition, which applied prior to 28th October 1994, in section 70(5) of the Contributions and Benefits Act (exclusion of persons who had attained pensionable age and had not been entitled to that allowance immediately before attaining that age); and

(c) she satisfies the requirements for entitlement to an invalid care allowance apart from the conditions in section 70(1)(a) and (b) and (5) of the Contributions and Benefits Act.]

Amendment

1. Social Security (Severe Disablement Allowance and Invalid Care Allowance) Amendment Regulations 1994 (S.I. 1994 No. 2556), reg. 5 (October 28, 1994).

Invalid care allowance for persons over [1the age of 65]

11. Where a person is entitled to an invalid care allowance immediately before he attains [1 the age of 65] he shall not be disentitled to that allowance after he attains that age by reason only of the fact that he is not caring for a severely disabled person or no longer satisfies the requirements of [2section 70(1)(a) or (b) of the Contributions and Benefits Act].

Amendments

1. Social Security (Severe Disablement Allowance and Invalid Care Allowance) Amendment Regulations 1994 (S.I. 1994 No. 2556), reg. 5 (October 28, 1994).
2. Social Security (Invalid Care Allowance) Amendment Regulations 1996 (S.I. 1996 No. 2744), reg. 2 (November 25, 1996).

[1Men aged 65 before 28th October 1994

11A. A man who—

(a) attained the age of 65 before 28th October 1994; and

(b) was entitled to an invalid care allowance immediately before he attained that age,

shall be entitled to that allowance notwithstanding that, after he attained that age, he was not caring for a severely disabled person or no longer satisfied the requirements of section 70(1)(a) or (b) of the Contributions and Benefits Act, if he satisfies the other requirements for entitlement to that allowance.]

Amendment

1. Social Security (Severe Disablement Allowance and Invalid Care Allowance) Amendment Regulations 1994 (S.I. 1994 No. 2556), reg. 5 (October 28, 1994).

12.—21. *Omitted.*

The Social Security (Overlapping Benefits) Regulations 1979

(S.I. 1979 No. 597)

Arrangement of Regulations

The Secretary of State for Social Services, in exercise of powers conferred by sections 83(1) and 85 of the Social Security Act 1975 and of all other powers enabling him in that behalf hereby makes the following regulations which only consolidate the regulations herein revoked and which accordingly by virtue of paragraph 20 of Schedule 15 to the Social Security Act 1975, are not subject to the requirement of section 139(1) of that Act for prior reference to the National Insurance Advisory Committee:

Citation and commencement

1. These regulations may be cited as the Social Security (Overlapping Benefits) Regulations 1979 and shall come into operation on 29th June 1979.

Interpretation

2.—(1) In these regulations, unless the context otherwise requires—
"the Act" means the Social Security Act 1975;
[[2]"the Contributions and Benefits Act" means the Social Security Contributions and Benefits Act 1992;]
"the Pensions Act" means the Social Security Pensions Act 1975;
"benefit under Chapters I and II of Part II of the Act" includes benefit treated as included in Chapter I of Part II of the Act by virtue of section 66(2)(b) of the Pensions Act;
"the Child Benefit Act" means the Child Benefit Act 1975;
"child benefit" means benefit under Part I of the Child Benefit Act;
[[3]"contributory benefit" means any benefit payable under Part II of the Contributions and Benefits Act, and a contribution-based jobseeker's allowance;]
"death benefit" means any benefit, pension or allowance which, apart from these regulations, is payable (whether under the Act or otherwise) in respect of the death of any person;
"the deceased" means, in relation to any death benefit, the person in respect of whose death that benefit, apart from these regulations, is payable;
"dependency benefit" means that benefit, pension or allowance which, apart from these regulations, is payable (whether under the Act or otherwise) to a person in respect of another person who is a child or an adult dependant; it includes child's special allowance and any personal benefit by way of pension payable to a child under any Personal Injuries Scheme, Service Pensions Instrument or 1914–1918 War Injuries Scheme but does not include benefit under section 73 of the Act (allowances to a woman who has care of children of a person who died as a result of an industrial accident);

"disablement pension" includes a disablement payment on a pension basis and retired pay or pension in respect of any disablement, wound, injury or disease;

[3"the Jobseekers Act" means the Jobseekers Act 1995]

"personal benefit" means any benefit, pension or allowance [1(whether under the Act or otherwise)] which is not a dependency benefit [3, and includes a contribution-based jobseeker's allowance but not an income-based jobseeker's allowance.] and which [1, apart from these regulations,] is payable to any person;

"Personal Injuries Scheme" means any scheme made under the Personal Injuries (Emergency Provisions) Act 1939 or under the Pensions (Navy, Army, Air Force and Mercantile Marine) Act 1939;

"Pneumoconiosis and Byssinosis Benefit Scheme" means any scheme made under section 5 of the Industrial Injuries and Diseases (Old Cases) Act 1975;

[1"Service Pensions Instrument" means any instrument described in subparagraphs (a) or (b) below in so far, but only in so far, as the pensions or other benefit provided by that instrument are not calculated or determined by reference to length of service, namely:—

(a) any instrument made in exercise of powers—

(i) referred to in section 12(1) of the Social Security (Miscellaneous Provisions) Act 1977 (pensions or other benefits for disablement or death due to service in the armed forces of the Crown); or

(ii) under section 1 of the Polish Resettlement Act 1947 (pensions and other benefits for disablement or death due to service in certain Polish forces); or

(b) any instrument under which a pension or other benefit may be paid to a person (not being a member of the armed forces of the Crown) out of public funds in respect of death or disablement, wound, injury or disease due to service in any nursing service or other auxiliary service of any of the armed forces of the Crown, or in any other organisation established under the control of the Defence Council or formerly established under the Control of the Admiralty, the Army Council or the Air Council.]

"training allowance" means [*Omitted.*];

"treatment allowance" means [*Omitted.*];

"unemployability supplement" means [*Omitted.*];

"war pension death benefit" means [*Omitted.*];

"1914–1918 War Injuries Scheme" means any scheme made under the Injuries in War (Compensation) Act 1914 or under the Injuries in War Compensation Act 1914 (Session 2) or any Government scheme for compensation in respect of persons injured in any merchant ship or fishing vessel as the result of hostilities during the 1914–1918 War.

(2) *Omitted.*

Amendments

1. Social Security (Overlapping Benefits) Amendment Regulations 1980 (S.I. 1980 No. 1927), reg. 2 (January 5, 1981).

2. Social Security (Overlapping Benefits) Amendments (No. 2) Regulations 1992 (S.I. 1992 No. 3194), reg. 2 (January 13, 1993).

3. Social Security and Child Support (Jobseeker's Allowance) (Consequential Amendments) Regulations 1996 (S.I. 1996 No. 1345), reg. 22(2) (October 7, 1996).

Adjustments of personal benefit under Chapters I and II of Part II of the Act by reference to industrial injuries benefits and benefits not under the Act, and adjustments of industrial injuries benefits

6.—(1)Subject to paragraph (5) and regulation 12, where a personal benefit which is specified in column (1) of Schedule 1 to these regulations ("the column (1) benefit") is, or but for this regulation would be payable to a person for the same period as a personal benefit which is specified in the corresponding paragraph of column (2) of that Schedule ("the column (2) benefit") the column (1) benefit shall be adjusted by deducting from it the amount of the column (2) benefit and, subject to any further adjustment under regulation 4, only the balance, if any, shall be payable.

(2) *Omitted.*

(3) Paragraph (1) and Schedule 1 to these regulations shall have effect in relation to an attendance allowance [[1] or the care component of disability living allowance], and to any benefit by reference to which [[1]that allowance (as the case may be)] is to be adjusted, as requiring adjustment where both that allowance and the benefit are payable in respect of the same person (whether or not one or both of them are payable to him).

(4) and (5) *Omitted.*

AMENDMENT

1. Disability Living Allowance and Disability Working Allowance (Consequential Provisions) Regulations 1991 (S.I. 1991 No. 2742), reg. 5 (April 6, 1992).

7.—13. *Omitted.*

Provisions for adjusting benefit for part of a week

14.—[[1](1) Where an adjustment falls to be made under these regulations for a part of a week, benefit shall be deemed to be payable—

(a) at a daily rate equal to one-seventh of the appropriate weekly rate for each day of the week in respect of any benefit (whether under the Contributions and Benefits Act or otherwise) except when maternity benefit [[2]. . .] falls to be adjusted; or

(b) at a daily rate equal to one-sixth of the appropriate weekly rate for each day of the week except Sunday [[2]where maternity benefits] falls to be adjusted.]

(2) [[2]. . .].

(3) In paragraph (1) "appropriate weekly rate" means the weekly rate at which the benefit in question would be payable but for these regulations.

AMENDMENTS

1. Social Security (Incapacity Benefit) (Consequential and Transitional Amendments and Savings) Regulations 1995 (S.I. 1995 No. 829), reg. 14 (April 13, 1995).

2. Social Security and Child Support (Jobseeker's Allowance) (Consequential Amendments) Regulations 1996 (S.I. 1996 No. 1345), reg. 22(5) (October 7, 1996).

15. *Omitted.*

Persons to be treated as entitled to benefit for certain purposes

16. Any person who would be entitled to any benefit under the Act [[1]or under the Jobseekers Act] but for these regulations shall be treated as if he were entitled thereto for the purpose of any rights or obligations under the Act and the regulations made under it [1, or under the Jobseekers Act and regulations made under it] (whether of himself or some other person) which depend on his being so entitled, other than for the purposes of the right to payment of that benefit.

AMENDMENT

1. Social Security and Child Support (Jobseeker's Allowance) (Consequential Amendments) Regulations 1996 (S.I. 1996 No. 1345), reg. 22(6) (October 7, 1996).

Prevention of double adjustments

17. No adjustment shall be made under regulations 6 to 10 to any benefit under the Act [1or under the Jobseekers Act] by reference to any other benefit, whether under the Act [1or under the Jobseekers Act] or otherwise, where the latter benefit has itself been adjusted by reference to the former benefit.

AMENDMENT

1. Social Security and Child Support (Jobseeker's Allowance) (Consequrntial Amendments) Regulations 1996 (S.I. 1996 No. 1345), reg. 22(7) (October 7, 1996).

18. *Omitted.*

SCHEDULES

SCHEDULE 1 **Regulation 6**

PERSONAL BENEFITS WHICH ARE REQUIRED TO BE ADJUSTED BY REFERENCE TO BENEFITS NOT UNDER CHAPTERS I AND II OF PART II OF THE ACT

Column (1) *Personal benefit under the Act*	Column (2) *Other personal benefit by reference to which the benefit in column (1) is to be adjusted*
[. . .]	[. . .]
5. Attendance allowance [1or the care component of disability living allowance]	5. Any benefit based on need for attendance under section 61 or under any Pneumoconiosis and Byssinosis Benefit Scheme, Personal Injuries Scheme, Service Pensions Instrument or 1914–1918 War Injuries Scheme.
[. . .]	[. . .]

AMENDMENT

1. Disability Living Allowance and Disability Working Allowance (Consequential Provisions) Regulations 1991 (S.I. 1991 No. 2742), reg. 5 (April 6, 1992).

GENERAL NOTE

S.61 of the Social Security Act 1975 has been replaced by s.104 of the Social Security Contributions and Benefits Act 1992.

Schedule 2. *Omitted.*

The Social Security Benefit (Persons Abroad) Regulations 1975

(S.I. 1975 No. 563)

Arrangement of Regulations

The Secretary of State for Social Services, in exercise of powers conferred upon her by sections 21(3), 30(3), 32(5), 82(5), 114(1), 131 and 132 of the Social Security Act 1975 and of all other powers enabling her in that behalf, without having referred any proposals on the matter to the National Insurance Advisory Committee or the Industrial Injuries Advisory Council since it appears to her that by reason of urgency it is inexpedient to do so, hereby makes the following regulations:

Citation, commencement and interpretation

1.(1) These regulations may be cited as the Social Security Benefit (Persons Abroad) Regulations 1975 and shall come into operation on 6th April 1975.

(2) In these regulations, unless the context otherwise requires—

"the Act" means the Social Security Act 1975;

[. . .]

[[3], "the Contributions and Benefits Act" means the Social Security Contributions and Benefits Act 1992;]

"the Contributions Regulations" means the Social Security (Contributions) Regulations [[1]1979];

[. . .]

"the former Principal Act" means the National Insurance Act 1965;

[. . .]

"the Industrial Injuries Employment Regulations" means the Social Security (Employed Earners' Employments for Industrial Injuries Purposes) Regulations 1975;

[. . .]

[[2]"serving member of the forces" has the meaning given to it in regulation 1(2) of the Contributions Regulations;]

[. . .]

and other expressions have the same meanings as in the Act.

(3) Any reference in these regulations to any provision made by or contained in any enactment or instrument shall, except, in so far as the context otherwise requires, be construed as a reference to that provision as amended or extended by any enactment or instrument, and as including a reference to any provision which it re-enacts or replaces, or which may re-enact or replace it, with or without modification.

(4) The rules for the construction of Acts of Parliament contained in the Interpretation Act 1889 shall apply for the purposes of the interpretation of an Act of Parliament.

AMENDMENTS

1. Social Security (Maternity Grant) Regulations 1981 (S.I. 1981 No. 1157), reg. 3(2) (April 1, 1982).
2. Social Security Benefit (Persons Abroad) Amendment Regulations 1990 (S.I. 1990 No. 40), reg. 2(2) (February 8, 1990).
3. Social Security (Miscellaneous Provisions) Amendment (No. 2) Regulations 1992 (S.I. 1992 No. 2595), reg. 9 (November 16, 1992).

Modification of the Act in relation to [6incapacity benefit], unemployability supplement and maternity allowance

2.—(1) [6Except as provided by paragraph (1A) or (1B) below,] [3a person shall not be disqualified for receiving [6any benefit in respect of incapacity]] an unemployability supplement or a maternity allowance by reason of being temporarily absent from Great Britain for any day if—

[1(a) the Secretary of State has certified that it is consistent with the proper administration of the Act that, subject to the satisfaction of one of the conditions in sub-paragraph (b), [2bb][6 and (c)] below, the disqualification under section 82(5)(a) of the Act should not apply, and [5. . .]]

(b) the absence is for the specific purpose of being treated for incapacity which commenced before he left Great Britain, or

[2(bb) in the case [4of [7incapacity benefit]], the incapacity for work is the result of a personal injury of a kind mentioned in section 50(1) of the Act, and the absence is for the specific purpose of receiving treatment which is appropriate to that injury, or]

(c) on the day on which the absence began he was, and had for the past 6 months continuously been, incapable of work and on the day for which benefit is claimed he has remained continuously so incapable [5since the absence began][6. . .]

[6. . .]

[6(1A) Subject to paragraph (1B), a person who is in receipt of attendance allowance or disability living allowance shall not by reason of being temporarily absent from Great Britain be disqualified for receiving any benefit in respect of incapacity if—

(a) the absence is for the specific purpose of being treated for incapacity which commenced before he left Great Britain; or

(b) in the case of [7incapacity benefit] the incapacity for work is the result of a personal injury of a kind mentioned in section 94(1) of the Social Security Contributions and Benefits Act 1992 and the absence is for the specific purpose of receiving treatment which is appropriate to that injury; or

(c) on the day on which the absence began he was, and had for the past 6 months continuously been, incapable of work and on the day for which benefit is claimed he has remained continuously so incapable since the absence began.

(1B) A person who is a member of the family of a serving member of the forces and temporarily absent from Great Britain by reason only of the fact that he is living with that member shall not by reason of being temporarily absent be disqualified—

(a) for receiving any benefit in respect of incapacity except severe disablement allowance if—

(i) the absence is for the specific purpose of being treated for incapacity which commenced before he left Great Britain; or

(ii) in the case of [7incapacity benefit] the incapacity for work is the result of a personal injury of a kind mentioned in section 94(1) of the Social Security Contributions and Benefits Act 1992 and the absence is for the specific purpose of receiving treatment which is appropriate to that injury; or

(iii) on the day on which the absence began he was, and had for the past 6 months continuously been, incapable of work and on the day for which benefit is claimed he has remained continuously so incapable since the absence began; or

(b) for the receipt of severe disablement allowance.]

(2) to (4) *Revoked.*

[1(5) In this regulation—

(a) "benefit in respect of incapacity" means [7incapacity benefit], severe disablement allowance, an unemployability supplement or a maternity allowance;

(b) "member of the family of a serving member of the forces" means the spouse, son, daughter, step-son, step-daughter, father, father-in-law, step-father, mother, mother-in-law or step-mother of such a member; and

(c) "week" means any period of seven days.]

Amendments

1. Social Security Benefit (Persons Abroad) Amendment Regulations 1977 (S.I. 1977 No. 1679), reg. 2(2) (November 14, 1977).

2. Social Security (Abolition of Injury Benefit) (Consequential) Regulations 1983 (S.I. 1983 No. 186), reg. 5(2) (April 6, 1983).

3. Social Security (Severe Disablement Allowance) Regulations 1984 (S.I. 1984 No. 1303), reg. 16 (November 29, 1984).

4. Social Security Benefit (Persons Abroad) Amendment (No. 2) Regulations 1986 (S.I. 1986 No. 1545) (October 1, 1986).

5. Social Security Benefit (Persons Abroad) Amendment Regulations 1990 (S.I. 1990 No. 40), reg. 2(3) (February 8, 1990).

6. Social Security Benefit (Persons Abroad) Amendment Regulations 1994 (S.I. 1994 No. 268), reg. 2 (March 8, 1994 with a saving).

7. Social Security (Incapacity Benefit) (Consequential and Transitional Amendments and Savings) Regulations 1995 (S.I. 1995 No. 829), reg. 16 (April 13, 1995).

General Note

S.82(5) of the Social Security Act 1975 has been replaced by s.113(1) of the Social Security Contributions and Benefits Act 1992.

3.—8. *Omitted.*

Modification of the Act in relation to title to disablement benefit and industrial death benefit

9.—(1) [2. . .]

(2) [1. . .]

(3) A person shall not be disqualified for receiving [3disablement benefit (other than any increase thereof under sections 58, 59, 61, 62, 63 or 66 of the Act)] by reason of being absent from Great Britain.

(4) A person shall not be disqualified for receiving an increase of disablement pension in respect of the need for constant attendance under section 61, or under regulations made under section 159(3), or in respect of exceptionally severe disablement under section 63, of the Act, by reason of being temporarily absent

from Great Britain during the period of six months from the date on which such absence from Great Britain during the period of six months from the date on which such absence commences or during such longer period as the Secretary of State may, having regard to the purpose of the absence and any other factors which appear to him to be relevant, allow.

(5) A person shall not be disqualified for receiving [[1]reduced earnings allowance under section 59A of the Act,] by reason of being temporarily absent from Great Britain during the period of three months from the date on which such absence commences or during such longer period as the Secretary of State may, having regard to the purpose of the absence and any other factors which appear to him to be relevant, allow, so however that—

(a) such absence or any part thereof is not for the purpose of or in connection with any employment, trade or business;

(b) a claim as a result of which a decision is given awarding [[3]such allowance] in respect of such period of absence or part thereof was made before the commencement of such absence; and

(c) the period taken into account by the award of [[3]such allowance] to that person either includes the day of commencement of such absence or follows a period so taken into account which includes that day without there being a break in entitlement by that person to such increase from that day.

(6) *Omitted.*

[[4](7) A person shall not be disqualified for receiving retirement allowance under paragraph 13 of Schedule 7 to the Contributions and Benefits Act by reason of being absent from Great Britain.]

AMENDMENTS

1. Social Security Benefit (Persons Abroad) Amendment Regulations 1977 (S.I. 1977 No. 1679 reg. 2(4) (November 14, 1977).

2. Social Security (Abolition of Injury Benefit) (Consequential) Regulations 1983 (S.I. 1983 No. 186), reg. 5(4) (April 6, 1983).

3. Social Security (Industrial Injuries and Diseases) Miscellaneous Provisions Regulations 1986 (S.I. 1986 No. 1561), reg. 4 (October 1, 1986).

4. Social Security (Miscellaneous Provisions) Amendment (No. 2) Regulations 1992 (S.I. 1992 No. 2595), reg. 9 (November 16, 1992).

GENERAL NOTE

Ss.61 and 63 of the Social Security Act 1975 have been replaced by ss.103 and 104 of the Social Security Contributions and Benefits Act 1992. Ss.58, 59, 62 and 66 of the 1975 Act have replaced by paras. 2, 3, 10 and 6 respectively of Sched. 7 to the 1992 Act.

Modification of the Act in relation to attendance allowance

10. A person shall not be disqualified for receiving attendance allowance [[1]or disability living allowance] by reason of being absent from Great Britain.

AMENDMENT

1. Disability Living Allowance and Disability Working Allowance (Consequential Provisions) Regulations 1991 (S.I. 1991 No. 2742), reg. 2(2) (April 6, 1992).

10A. *Revoked.*

[[1]Modification of the Act in relation to invalid care allowance

10B. A person shall not be disqualified for receiving an invalid care allowance by reason of being absent from Great Britain.]

AMENDMENT

1. This whole regulation was inserted by the Social Security (Invalid Care Allowance) Regulations 1976 (S.I. 1976 No. 409), reg. 20 (April 12, 1976).

[1Modification of Parts II and III of the Act in relation to accidents happening or prescribed diseases contracted outside Great Britain

10C.—(1) In this regulation—

"prescribed area" means an area over which Norway or any member State (other than the United Kingdom) exercises sovereign rights for the purpose of exploring the seabed and subsoil and exploiting their natural resources, being an area outside the territorial seas of Norway or such member State;

"prescribed disease" means a disease or injury prescribed for the purposes of Chapter V of Part II of the Act; and

"prescribed employment" means employment in a prescribed area in connection with the exploration of the seabed and subsoil and the exploitation of the natural resources of that area, or prescribed employment as defined in regulation 11 of these regulations (modification of the Act in relation to the United Kingdom continental shelf).

(2) Where on or after 30th November 1964 a person sustains or has sustained an accident or contracts or has contracted a prescribed disease while outside Great Britain, for the purposes of Chapter IV or V of Part II of the Act (benefit for industrial injuries and diseases) section 50(5) of the Act or regulation 14 of the Social Security (Industrial Injuries) (Prescribed Diseases) Regulations 1975 shall not operate to make benefit not payable in respect of that accident or prescribed disease if that person—

(a) in connection with prescribed employment has sustained the accident or contracted the prescribed disease in a prescribed area, or while travelling between one prescribed area and another, or while travelling between a designated area (as defined in regulation 11 of these regulations) and a prescribed area, or while travelling between Norway or a member State (including the United Kingdom) and a prescribed area; or

(b) has sustained the accident or contracted the prescribed disease while in the territory of a member State (other than the United Kingdom).

[2(2A) Where a person sustains an accident or contracts a prescribed disease while outside Great Britain in circumstances to which paragraph (2)(a) applies and the employment of that person would, but for the employment being outside Great Britain, have been employed earner's employment, that employment shall for the purposes of Chapter IV or V of Part II of the Act (benefit for industrial injuries and diseases) be treated as employed earner's employment if:—

(a) that person is ordinarily resident in Great Britain and immediately before the commencement of the employment was resident therein, and

(b) the employer of that person has a place of business in Great Britain.]

(3) Where, before the date on which this regulation comes into operation, a decision has been given disallowing a claim for industrial injuries benefit in respect of an accident sustained or a prescribed disease contracted on or after 30th November 1964, then notwithstanding the provisions of section 107(6)(b) of the Act (decision that an accident not an industrial accident not reviewable) that decision may be reviewed by an insurance officer under section 104(1)(b) of the Act (review on ground of relevant change of circumstances) if he is satisfied that had paragraphs (1) and (2) of this regulation been in force when that decision was given those paragraphs would have applied, but a decision on review under this paragraph shall not make industrial injuries benefit payable for any period before the date on which this regulation comes into operation.

(4) Paragraph (3) of this regulation shall apply to a decision refusing a declaration that an accident was an industrial accident as it applies to a decision disallowing a claim for industrial injuries benefit.]

[3(5) Where on or after 1st October 1986 a person to whom this paragraph applies sustains an accident arising out of, and in the course of, his employment, or contracts a prescribed disease due to the nature of his employment, such employment shall for the purposes of Chapters IV and V of Part II of the Act (benefit for industrial injuries and diseases) be treated as employed earner's employment notwithstanding that he is employed outside Great Britain, and any benefit which would be payable under those chapters but for the provisions of section 50(5) of the Act and regulation 14 of the Social Security (Industrial Injuries) (Prescribed Diseases) Regulations 1985 shall be payable from the date of his return to Great Britain notwithstanding that the accident happened or the disease was contracted while he was outside it.

(6) Paragraph (5) applies to any person in respect of whom Class 1 contributions are payable by virtue of regulation 120 of the Social Security (Contributions) Regulations 1979 or who is paying Class 2 (volunteer development workers) contributions under Case G of those regulations.]]

AMENDMENTS

1. This whole regulation was inserted by the Social Security Benefit (Persons Abroad) Amendment Regulations 1979 (S.I. 1979 No. 463), reg. 2 (April 17, 1979).

2. Social Security Benefit (Persons Abroad) Amendment Regulations 1982 (S.I. 1982 No. 388), reg. 2 (April 14, 1982).

3. Social Security Benefit (Persons Abroad) Amendment (No. 2) Regulations 1986 (S.I. 1986 No. 1545), reg. 3 (October 1, 1986).

GENERAL NOTE

S.50(5) of the Social Security Act 1975 has been replaced by s.94(5) of the Social Security Contributions and Benefits Act 1992. Ss.104 and 107 of the Social Security Act 1975 have been replaced by ss.25 and 44 of the Social Security Administration Act 1992.

Modification of the Act in relation to employment on the Continental Shelf

11.—(1) In this regulation—

"the Continental Shelf Act" means the Continental Shelf Act 1964;

"designated area" means any area which may from time to time be designated by Order in Council under the Continental Shelf Act as an area within which the rights of the United Kingdom with respect to the seabed and subsoil and their natural resources may be exercised;

"prescribed disease" means a disease or injury prescribed for the purposes of Chapter V of Part II of the Act;

[1"prescribed employment" means any employment (whether under a contract of service or not) in any designated area or prescribed area, being employment in connection with any activity mentioned in section 23(2) of the Oil and Gas (Enterprise) Act 1982 in any designated area or in any prescribed area]; and

[1"prescribed area" means any area over which Norway or any member State (other than the United Kingdom) exercises sovereign rights for the purpose of exploring the seabed and subsoil and exploiting their natural resources, being an area outside the territorial seas of Norway or such member State, or any other area which is from time to time specified under section 22(5) of the Oil and Gas (Enterprise) Act 1982.]

(2) Where benefit under Part II of the Act would, but for the provisions of section 82(5)(a) of the Act (absence from Great Britain), be payable to a person

in a designated area, that benefit shall be payable notwithstanding the absence of that person from Great Britain, if the absence is due to his being or having been in prescribed employment [1 in a designated area].

[1(2A) Subject to paragraph (2B) where benefit under Part II of the Act would be payable to a person were that person in Great Britain, that person shall not be disqualified for receiving such benefit by reason only of the fact that he is, in connection with prescribed employment:—

(a) in a prescribed area; or
(b) travelling between one prescribed area and another; or
(c) travelling between a designated area and a prescribed area; or
(d) travelling between Norway or a member State (including the United Kingdom) and a prescribed area.

(2B) Paragraph (2A) shall not apply where, under the legislation administered by Norway or any member State (other than the United Kingdom) benefit is payable in respect of a person for the same contingency and for the same period for which benefit is claimed under the Act.]

(3) Where benefit under Chapter IV or V of Part II of the Act would, but for the provisions of section 50(5) of the Act, be payable to a person in respect of an accident arising out of and in the course of, or a prescribed disease due to the nature of, any employment by virtue of which any person is treated as an employed earner under paragraph 7 of Part I of Schedule 1 to the Industrial Injuries Employments Regulations, that benefit shall be payable notwithstanding that the accident happens or the disease is contracted while such person is outside Great Britain, if at the time that the accident happens or the disease is contracted the person is either in a designated area or travelling from one designated area to another or from or to Great Britain to or from a designated area.

(4) The provision of the Act of the regulations and orders made thereunder shall, so far as they are not inconsistent with the provisions of this regulation, apply in relation to persons in prescribed employment with this modification, that where such a person is, on account of his being outside Great Britain by reason of his employment, being prescribed employment, unable to perform any act required to be done either forthwith or on the happening of a certain event or within a specified time, he shall be deemed to have complied with that requirement if he performs the act as soon as is reasonably practicable, although after the happening of the event or the expiration of the specified time.

AMENDMENT

1. Social Security and Statutory Sick Pay (Oil and Gas (Enterprise) Act 1982) (Consequential) Regulations 1982 (S.I. 1982 No. 1738), reg. 2 (December 31, 1982).

GENERAL NOTE

S.50 of the Social Security Act 1975 has been replaced by s.94 of the Social Security Contributions and Benefits Act 1992.

Modification of the Act in relation to the Channel Islands

12.—(1) Notwithstanding any provision of the Act or of these regulations a person shall not—

(a) be disqualified for receiving any benefit under the Act by reason of absence from Great Britain [1. . .];
(b) *Omitted.*
(c) *Omitted.*

if that person is, or, as the case may be, that confinement or that death occurred, in any part of the Channel Islands which is not subject to an order made under section 143 of the Act or section 105 of the former Principal Act.

(2) A person who—

(a) (i) is in any part of the Channel Islands which is not the subject of an order made under section 143 of the Act or section 84 of the National Insurance (Industrial Injuries) Act 1965, or

(ii) is going from (or to) Great Britain to (or from) such a part of the Channel Islands; and who

(b) suffers an industrial accident in the course of his employment (being employed earner's employment by virtue of regulation 94 of the Contributions Regulations),

shall, subject to the provisions of section 51 of the Act, be treated as if the employment were employed earner's employment for the purposes of industrial injuries and as if the accident occurred in Great Britain.

Amendment

1. Social Security and Child Support (Jobseeker's Allowance) (Consequential Amendments) Regulations 1996 (S.I. 1996 No. 1345), reg. 15(2) (October 7, 1996).

General Note

S.51 of the Social Security Act 1975 has been replaced by s.95 of the Social Security Contributions and Benefits Act 1992.

13.—15. *Omitted.*

The Social Security (Severe Disablement Allowance) Regulations 1984

(S.I. 1984 No. 1303)

Arrangement of Regulations

Part I

General

Part II

Miscellaneous Provisions Relating to Severe Disablement Allowance

The Secretary of State for Social Services, in exercise of the powers set out in Schedule 1 below, and for all other powers enabling him in that behalf, by this instrument, which contains only provisions consequential on section 11 of the Health and Social Security Act 1984 and regulations made under section 36 of the Social Security Act 1975, makes the following regulations:

PART I

GENERAL

Citation and commencement

1. These regulations may be cited as the Social Security (Severe Disablement Allowance) Regulations 1984 and shall come into operation in the case of regulations 1, 2, 10, 17, 18 and 19 on 10th September 1984, and in the case of the remainder of the regulations on 29th November 1984.

Interpretation

2.(1) In these regulations "the Act" means the Social Security Act 1975, "the 1984 Act" means the Health and Social Security Act 1984 [[3]and "the Contributions and Benefits Act" means the Social Security Contributions and Benefits Act 1992].

[[4](1A) In these Regulations—

"councillor" has the same meaning as in section 171F(2) of the Contributions and Benefits Act; and

"councillor's allowance" has the same meaning as in section 30E(2) of the Contributions and Benefits Act.]

[[1](1B) In these Regulations "disability appeal tribunal" means a tribunal constituted in accordance with Schedule 10A to the Act.]

[[2](1C) In these Regulations—

"voluntary body" means a body the activities of which are carried out otherwise than for the purpose of profit; and "volunteer" means a person who is engaged in voluntary work with a charity or voluntary body, or who is engaged in voluntary work otherwise than for a member of his family, where the only payment received by him or due to be paid to him by virtue of being so engaged, is a payment in respect of any expenses reasonably incurred by him in the course of being so engaged.]

(2) Any reference in these regulations to a person's father, mother, son, or daughter includes a reference to his step-father, step-mother, step-son or step-daughter, as the case may be, and a person shall be treated as such a relative if he would be such a relative if some person born illegitimate had been born legitimate.

[[4](3) In determining whether a day falls within a period of incapacity for work, the provisions of section 30C of the Contributions and Benefits Act (incapacity benefit: days and periods of incapacity for work) and of any regulations made under section 30C(3) and (4) shall have effect for the purposes of severe disablement allowance as they have effect for the purposes of incapacity benefit.]

(4) References in regulations 5(b) and 6 to a person being entitled to a severe disablement allowance and in regulation 20 to a person being entitled to a non-contributory invalidity pension include a reference to a person who would be entitled to a payment of such an allowance or, as the case may be, such a person but for any provision of the Social Security (Overlapping Benefits) Regulations 1979.

(5) Unless the context otherwise required, any reference in these regulations to a numbered regulation is a reference to the regulation bearing that number in these regulations and any reference in a regulation to a numbered paragraph is a reference to the paragraph of that regulation bearing that number.

AMENDMENTS

1. Social Security (Invalidity Benefit and Severe Disablement Allowance) Miscellaneous Amendment Regulations 1992 (S.I. 1992 No. 585), reg. 3 (April 6, 1992).

2. Social Security (Sickness and Invalidity Benefit and Severe Disablement Allowance) Miscellaneous Amendments Regulations 1994 (S.I. 1994 No. 1101), reg. 3 (May 16, 1994).

3. Social Security (Severe Disablement Allowance and Invalid Care Allowance) Amendment Regulations 1994 (S.I. 1994 No. 2556), reg. 4 (October 28, 1994).

4. Social Security (Severe Disablement Allowance) Amendment Regulations 1994 (S.I. 1994 No. 2947), reg. 2(2) (April 13, 1995).

PART II

MISCELLANEOUS PROVISIONS RELATING TO SEVERE DISABLEMENT ALLOWANCE

Conditions relating to residence and presence

3.—

[[1](1) Subject to the following provisions of this regulation, the prescribed conditions for the purposes of section 36(4)(c) of the Act as to residence and presence in Great Britain in relation to any person on any day shall be that—

(a) on that day—

(i) he is ordinarily resident in Great Britain, and

[[3](ia) subject to paragraph (1B), his right to reside or remain in Great Britain is not subject to any limitation or condition, and]

(ii) he is present in Great Britain, and

(iii) he has been present in Great Britain for a period of, or for periods amounting in the aggregate to, not less than 26 weeks in the 52 weeks immediately preceding that day; and

(b) where that day falls within a period in which that person—
(i) receives tax free emoluments, or
(ii) is the spouse of a person who receives tax free emoluments, that period is immediately preceded by a period of 4 years during which the person first mentioned in this sub-paragraph was present in Great Britain for not less than 156 weeks in aggregate.

(1A) In paragraph (1)(b), the expression "tax free emoluments" means emoluments which are exempt from tax under any of the provisions listed in paragraph (1) of regulation 9 of the Child Benefit (General) Regulations 1976.]

[[3](1B) For the purposes of paragraph (1)(a)(ia), a person's right to reside or remain in Great Britain is not to be treated as if it were subject to a limitation or condition if—

(a) he is a person recorded by the Secretary of State as a refugee within the defintion in Article 1 of the Convention relating to the Status of Refugees done at Geneva on 28th July 1951, as extended by Article 1(2) of the Protocol relating to the Status of Refugees done at New York on 31st January 1967;

(b) he is a person who has been granted exceptional leave outside the provisions of the immigration rules within the meaning of the Immigration Act 1971 to remain in the United Kingdom by the Secretary of State.

(c) he is a national, or a member of the family of a national, of a State contracting party to the Agreement on the European Economic Area signed at Oporto on 2nd May 1992 as adjusted by the Protocol signed at Brussles on 17th March 1993; or

(d) he is a person who is—
(i) lawfully working in Great Britain and is a national of a State with which the Community has concluded an Agreement under article 238 of the Treaty establishing the European Community providing, in the field of social security, for the equal treatment of workers who are nationals of the signatory State and their families, or
(ii) a member of the family of, and living with, such a person.]

(2) *Omitted.*

(3) Where a person has been entitled to a severe disablement allowance or a non-contributory invalidity pension for any day, the conditions set out in paragraph (1) of this regulation shall not apply to that person in respect of any subsequent day of incapacity for work falling within the same [[2]period of incapacity for work].

AMENDMENTS

1. Social Security (Severe Disablement Allowance) Amendment Regulations 1992 (S.I. 1992 No. 704), reg. 2 (April 6, 1992 subject to a saving under reg. 3).

2. Social Security (Severe Disablement Allowance) Amendment Regulations 1994 (S.I. 1994 No. 2947), reg. 2(3) (April 13, 1995).

3. Social Security (Persons From Abroad) Miscellaneous Amendments Regulations 1996 (S.I. 1996 No. 30), reg. 11 (February 5, 1996, subject to a saving under reg. 12(3)).

Circumstances in which a person over [[1] the age of 65] is to be treated as having been entitled to a severe disablement allowance immediately before attaining that age

4. A person who has attained [[1] the age of 65] shall for the purposes of section 36(4)(d) of the Act be treated as having been entitled to a severe disablement allowance immediately before attaining that age if immediately before attaining it—

(a) he would have satisfied the conditions for entitlement to that allowance or to a non-contributory invalidity pension but for the provisions of the Social Security (Overlapping Benefits) Regulations 1979, or
(b) he was entitled to a non-contributory invalidity pension.

AMENDMENT

1. Social Security (Severe Disablement Allowance and Invalid Care Allowance) Amendment Regulations 1994 (S.I. 1994 No. 2556), reg. 4 (October 28, 1994).

GENERAL NOTE

S.36 of the Social Security Act 1975 has been replaced by s.68 of the Social Security Contributions and Benefits Act 1992.

[[1]Women aged 65 before 28th October 1994

4A.—(1) A woman shall be entitled to a severe disablement allowance if—
(a) she attained the age of 65 before 28th October 1994;
(b) immediately before attaining the age of 65 she would have satisfied the requirements for entitlement to a severe disablement allowance or, if she attained that age before 29th November 1984, to a non-contributory invalidity pension (whether or not she made a claim) but for—
(i) the condition, which applied prior to 28th October 1994, in section 68(4)(d) of the Contributions and Benefits Act (exclusion of persons who had attained pensionable age and had not been entitled to a severe disablement allowance immediately before attaining that age); or
(ii) the corresponding condition in respect of non-contributory invalidity pension; and
(c) she satisfies the requirements for entitlement to a severe disablement allowance apart from the conditions in section 68(2), (3) and (4)(d) of the Contributions and Benefits Act.

(2) For the purposes of paragraph (1)(b) there shall be excluded from the requirements for entitlement to a non-contributory invalidity pension the condition that the claimant, if she were married or cohabiting with a man, be incapable of performing normal household duties.]

AMENDMENT

1. Social Security (Severe Disablement Allowance and Invalid Care Allowance) Amendment Regulations 1994 (S.I. 1994 No. 2556), reg. 4 (October 28, 1994).

Severe disablement allowance for persons over [[1]the age of 65]

5. A person who—
(a) has attained [[1] the age of 65]; and
(b) was entitled to a severe disablement allowance immediately before he attained that age,

shall continue to be so entitled notwithstanding that he does not satisfy the conditions specified in subsection (2) or (3) of section 36 of the Act if he satisfies the other requirements for entitlement to such an allowance.

AMENDMENT

1. Social Security (Severe Disablement Allowance and Invalid Care Allowance) Amendment Regulations 1994 (S.I. 1994 No. 2556), reg. 4 (October 28, 1994).

General Note

S.36 of the Social Security Act 1975 has been replaced by s.68 of the Social Security Contributions and Benefits Act 1992.

[[1]Men aged 65 before 28th October 1994

5A. A man who—

(a) attained the age of 65 before 28th October 1994; and

(b) was entitled to a severe disablement allowance or a non-contributory invalidity pension immediately before he attained that age,

shall be entitled to a severe disablement allowance notwithstanding that he ceased to satisfy the conditions specified in section 68(2) or (3) of the Contributions and Benefits Act after he attained that age, if he satisfies the other requirements for entitlement to that allowance.]

Amendment

1. Social Security (Severe Disablement Allowance and Invalid Care Allowance) Amendment Regulations 1994 (S.I. 1994 No. 2556), reg. 4 (October 28, 1994).

Modification of section 36(2) and (3) of the Act in relation to persons who have previously been entitled to a severe disablement allowance

6. A person who has previously been entitled to a severe disablement allowance for any day shall be entitled to such an allowance on the relevant day notwithstanding that he does not satisfy—

(a) in the case of a person who on the earlier day satisfied the conditions specified in section 36(2) of the Act, the conditions specified in subsection (2)(b) of that section; or

(b) in the case of a person who on the earlier day satisfied the conditions specified in section 36(3) of the Act, the conditions specified in subsection (3)(b) of that section,

if the relevant day and the earlier day fall within the same [[1]period of incapacity for work] and if he satisfies the other requirements for entitlement to such an allowance.

Amendment

1. Social Security (Severe Disablement Allowance) Amendment Regulations 1994 (S.I. 1994 No. 2947), reg. 2(4) (April 13, 1995).

General Note

S.36 of the Social Security Act 1975 has been replaced by s.68 of the Social Security Contributions and Benefits Act 1992.

Days for which persons are to be regarded as incapable of work for the purposes of severe disablement allowance

7.—[[1](1) Subject to paragraph (3), for the purposes of severe disablement allowance a person shall not be treated as incapable of work for any day which is not to be treated as a day of incapacity for work under regulation 4(1)(c) (Persons attending training courses) of the Social Security (Incapacity Benefit) Regulations 1994.

(1A) Regulation 5 (night workers) of the Social Security (Incapacity Benefit) Regulations 1994 shall apply for the purposes of severe disablement allowance as it applies for the purposes of incapacity benefit.

(2) In determining for the purposes of section 68(2) or (3) of the Contributions and Benefits Act whether a person has been incapable of work for a period of not less than 196 consecutive days, a day shall not be treated as a day on which that person was incapable of work if that day was a day on which he was undergoing imprisonment or detention in legal custody and which was part of a period of imprisonment or detention of more than 6 weeks.]

(3) A person who was incapable of work—

(a) for not less than 196 consecutive days commencing on or before he attained the age of 20, and

(b) for not less than 196 consecutive days immediately preceding the relevant day,

but who was capable of work for a period which does not, or for periods which in the aggregate do not, exceed 182 days where that period or those periods occurred—

(i) after the 196 days mentioned in sub-paragraph (a) but before the 196 days mentioned in sub-paragraph (b), and

(ii) after he attained the age of 15 years 24 weeks,

shall be treated for the purposes of section 36(2)(b) of the Act, and for that purpose only, as incapable of work on each day within that period or those periods.

AMENDMENT

1. Social Security (Severe Disablement Allowance) Amendment Regulations 1994 (S.I. 1994 No. 2947), reg. 2(5) (April 13, 1995).

GENERAL NOTE

S.36 of the Social Security Act 1975 has been replaced by s.68 of the Social Security Contributions and Benefits Act 1992.

7A. *Revoked by Social Security (Severe Disablement Allowance) Amendment Regulations 1994 (S.I. 1994 No. 2947), reg. 3 (April 13, 1995).*

Circumstances in which a person is to be treated as receiving full-time education

8.—(1) A person shall be treated as receiving full-time education for the purposes of severe disablement allowance for any period during which—

(a) he is not less than 16 or more than 19 years of age; and

(b) he attends for not less than 21 hours a week a course of education; so, however, that in calculating the number of hours a week during which he attends that course no account shall be taken of any instruction or tuition which is not suitable for persons of the same age and sex who do not suffer from a physical or mental disability.

(2) In determining the duration of a period of full-time education under paragraph (1), any temporary interruption of that education may be disregarded.

(3) A person over the age of 19 shall be treated as not receiving full-time education.

Severe disablement allowance for persons who are councillors

[[1]**8A.** Where the amount of a councillor's allowance to which a person is entitled in respect of any week exceeds the sum for the time being specified in [2]regulation 8 of the Social Security (Incapacity Benefit) Regulations 1994], then an amount equal to the excess shall be deducted from the amount of any severe disablement allowance to which he is entitled in respect of that week, and only the balance remaining (if any) shall be payable.]

AMENDMENTS

1. Social Security (Severe Disablement Allowance (Amendment) and Local Councillors Consequential) Regulations 1989 (S.I. 1989 No. 1687), reg. 2 (October 9, 1989).
2. Social Security (Severe Disablement Allowance) Amendment Regulations 1994 (S.I. 1994 No. 2947), reg.2(6) (April 13, 1995).

9. *Revoked by Social Security (Severe Disablement Allowance) Amendment Regulations 1994 (S.I. 1994 No. 2947), reg. 3 (April 13, 1995).*

Adjudication

10.—(1) For the purposes of section 36(5) (extent of disablement) of the Act, the evidence required that on any day a person suffers or suffered from loss of physical or mental faculty such that the assessed extent of the resulting disablement amounts or amounted to not less than 80 per cent, shall consist of—

(a) [3. .];

[3(b) evidence that on that day he is or was entitled to the care component of disability living allowance at the highest rate prescribed in accordance with section 72(3) and (4)(a) of the Contributions and Benefits Act;]

(c) evidence that the extent of his disablement on that day has been assessed for the purposes of section 57 of the Act as not less than 80 per cent.;

(d) evidence that that day is or was or is or was later than one in respect of which it has been determined under the Vaccine Damage Payments Act 1979 that he is or was severely disabled as a result of a vaccination against any of the diseases to which that Act applies;

(e) evidence that the degree of his disablement on that day has been assessed for the purposes of Part III of the Naval, Military and Air Forces etc. (Disablement and Death) Service Pensions Order 1983 or of Part III of the Personal Injuries (Civilians) Scheme 1983 as not less than 80 per cent.;

(f) evidence that on that day he is or was registered as a blind [3. . .] person in a register complied under section 29 of the National Assistance Act 1948;

[1(ff) evidence that he has been certified as blind [3. . .] and that in consequence he is or was registered on that day as blind or partially sighted in a register maintained by or on behalf of a regional or islands council;]

(g) evidence that on that day the Secretary of State provides or provided him with an invalid carriage or other vehicle under section 5(2) of the National Health Service Act 1977 or makes or made payments by way of grant to him under paragraph 2 of Schedule 2 to that Act;

[1(gg) evidence that on that day the Secretary of State provides or provided him with an invalid carriage or other vehicle under section 46 of the National Health Service (Scotland) Act 1978 or makes or made payments by way of grant to him under that section;]

(h) evidence that the extent of his disablement on that day has been assessed for the purposes of section 36 of the Act as not less than 80 per cent; or

(i) such other evidence as satisfies an adjudicating medical authority that he so suffers or suffered.

(2) For the purposes of sub-paragraphs (a) to (h) of paragraph (1) an official record of the [2Department of Social Security] of any fact specified in those sub-paragraphs shall be sufficient evidence of that fact.

[1(2A) For the purposes of paragraphs (1)(g) and (1)(gg) "invalid carriage or other vehicle" means a vehicle propelled by petrol engine or by electric power supplied for use on the road and to be controlled by the occupant.]

(3) The disablement questions in relation to severe disablement allowance shall be referred to and determined by an adjudication officer in any case where the Department of Health and Social Security has an official record as specified in paragraph (2).

(4) For the purposes of paragraph (1)(i) "adjudicating medical authority" means an adjudicating medical practitioner, or two or more adjudicating medical practitioners acting as a medical board, or a medical appeal tribunal.

Amendments

1. Social Security (Severe Disablement Allowance) Amendment Regulations 1986 (S.I. 1986 No. 1933), reg. 2 (December 8, 1986).

2. Transfer of Functions (Health and Social Security) Order 1988 (S.I. 1988 No. 1843), art. 3 (November 28, 1988).

3. Social Security (Incapacity for Work and Severe Disablement Allowance) Amendment Regulations 1997 (S.I. 1997 No. 1009), reg. 3 (April 1, 1997, subject to a saving under reg. 4).

General Note

Ss.36 and 57 of the Social Security Act 1975 have been replaced by ss.68 and 103 of the Social Security Contributions and Benefits Act 1992.

Effectively, a person is deemed to be disabled to the extent of 80 per cent if any of sub-paras. (1)(a)–(h) is satisfied in his or her case. Where there is an official record of the Department of Social Security of the relevant fact, an adjudication officer or social security appeal tribunal can be satisfied that the claimant is disabled to the required extent and, by virtue of para. (3), an adjudicating medical authority has no jurisdiction. Otherwise, the disablement questions must be referred, under s.45(2) of the Social Security Administration Act 1992 to an adjudicating medical authority to assess the extent of disablement. By virtue of s.68(6) of the Social Security Contributions and Benefits Act 1992 "assessed" means assessed in accordance with Sched. 6 to that Act. If, perhaps because no official record is available, an adjudicating medical authority is provided with adequate evidence, other than an official record of the Department of Social Security, of any of matters described in sub-paras. (1)(a)–(gg) that authority should assess the extent of disablement as being not less than 80 per cent during the period to which that evidence relates.

Part IIA

Severe Disablement Allowance: Age Related Addition

Circumstances in which a person is to be treated as having qualified for severe disablement allowance

[1**10A.**—(1) A person shall be treated for the purposes of section 36A of the Act (which applies an age related addition to a severe disablement allowance) as having qualified for severe disablement allowance—

(a) where he is a person to whom regulation 20 (persons formerly entitled to non-contributory invalidity pension) applies, on the first day of incapacity for work in a period of not less than 196 consecutive days of incapacity for work which immediately preceded the day he was first entitled to a non-contributory invalidity pension;

(b) where he is a person who qualified for severe disablement allowance by virtue of subsection (3)(b) of section 36 of the Act and was incapable of work on each day in a period which immediately preceded the period of not less than 196 consecutive days mentioned in that subsection, on the first day of incapacity for work in the period first mentioned;

(c) where he is a person to whom regulation 6 (modification of section 36(2) and (3) of the Act etc.) applies, on the first day of incapacity for work in a period of not less than 196 consecutive days of incapacity which immediately preceded the first day on which he was previously entitled to a severe disablement allowance.

(2) Where in any particular case a person satisfies the requirements of two or more sub-paragraphs in paragraph (1), then he shall be treated as having qualified for severe disablement allowance in accordance with that sub-paragraph which produces the earlier or earliest day in his case.]

AMENDMENT

1. Social Security (Severe Disablement Allowance) Amendment Regulations 1991 (S.I. 1991 No. 1747), reg. 3 (October 14, 1991).

GENERAL NOTE

Ss.36 and 36A of the Social Security Act 1975 have been replaced by ss.68 and 69 of the Social Security Contributions and Benefits Act 1992.

Circumstances in which days are to be treated as days of incapacity for work

[[1]**10B.** Where a person is treated as incapable of work for the purposes of section 36(2)(b) of the Act because regulation 7(3) (days for which persons are to be regarded as incapable of work etc.) applies to him, the days on which he was treated as incapable of work under regulation 7(3), shall be treated as days of incapacity for work for the purpose of determining the day on which he qualified for severe disablement allowance under section 36A of the Act.]

AMENDMENT

1. Social Security (Severe Disablement Allowance) Amendment Regulations 1990 (S.I. 1990 No. 2209), reg. 2 (December 3, 1990).

GENERAL NOTE

Ss.36 and 36A of the Social Security Act 1975 have been replaced by ss.68 and 69 of the Social Security Contributions and Benefits Act 1992.

11.—17. *Omitted.*

PART IV

TRANSITIONAL PROVISIONS AND REVOCATIONS

Claims made before 29th November 1984

18.—(1) A claim for a severe disablement allowance may be made in writing before 29th November 1984 on a form approved for the purpose by the Secretary of State by any person in relation to whom the appointed day for the coming into force generally of section 11 of and Schedule 4 to the 1984 Act is 29th November 1984.

(2) Any claim made in accordance with paragraph (1) may be treated as made for a period commencing on or after 29th November 1984.

(3) A decision which is given before 29th November 1984 awarding a severe disablement allowance on such a claim as is referred to in paragraph (1) of this regulation—

(a) may award the allowance from a date not before 29th November 1984 on which it appears probable that the requirements for entitlement will be satisfied;
(b) shall be subject to the condition that those requirements are satisfied on the date from which it is so awarded;
(c) may be reviewed if any question arises as to the satisfaction of those requirements.

Claims made before 28th November 1985

19. In relation to any person other than one to whom paragraph (1) of regulation 18 refers that regulation shall have effect, from a day three months before the day appointed for the coming into force generally in relation to him of the provisions referred to in that paragraph, as if for each reference to 29th November 1984 there were substituted a reference to the day so appointed.

Persons formerly entitled to non-contributory invalidity pension

20.—(1) Any person who, immediately before both 10th September 1984 and 29th November 1984 was entitled to a non-contributory invalidity pension shall be entitled for 29th November 1984, and for any subsequent days which together with 29th November 1984 fall within a single [3 period of incapacity for work, to a severe disablement allowance whether or not—
(a) he is disabled for the purposes of section 36 of the Act, or
(b) 29th November 1984 is appointed for the purposes of section 11 of the 1984 Act in relation to persons of his age,
if he satisfies the other requirements for entitlement to such an allowance.

[1(1A) A woman who—
(a) would have been entitled to a non-contributory invalidity pension immediately before 29th November 1984, but for the requirement that she be incapable of performing normal household duties (whether or not she made a claim for that pension), and
(b) has been continuously incapable of work since that date,
shall be entitled to a severe disablement allowance, whether or not she is disabled for the purposes of section 68 of the Social Security Contributions and Benefits Act 1992 and whether or not she has attained the age referred to in subsection (4)(d) of that section, if she satisfies the other requirements for entitlement to that allowance.]

(2) If in the case of any person a day and an earlier day for which he was entitled to a non-contributory invalidity pension fall within a single [3 period of incapacity for work]—
(a) for the purposes of section 36 of the Act he shall be deemed to be disabled on the day first mentioned whether or not he is suffering from such loss of faculty as is specified in subsection (5) of that section; and
(b) the condition in section 79(1) of the Act (benefit must be duly claimed) shall be deemed to be satisfied for the purposes of his right to a severe disablement allowance for the day first-mentioned if, but for the passing of the 1984 Act, that condition would have been satisfied for the purposes of his right to a non-contributory invalidity pension for that day.

(3) A person who was entitled to a non-contributory invalidity pension immediately before attaining [2 the age of 65] shall be treated for the purposes of regulation 5 as having been entitled to a severe disablement allowance immediately before attaining that age.

(4) A person who was entitled to a non-contributory invalidity pension for any day before 29th November 1984 shall be treated for the purposes of regulation 6 as having been entitled to a severe disablement allowance for that day.

Amendments

1. Social Security (Severe Disablement Allowance) Amendment Regulations 1993 (S.I. 1993 No. 3194), reg. 2 (January 13, 1994).
2. Social Security (Severe Disablement Allowance and Invalid Care Allowance) Amendment Regulations 1994 (S.I. 1994 No. 2556), reg. 4(8) (October 28, 1994).
3. Social Security (Severe Disablement Allowance) Amendment Regulations 1994 (S.I. 1994 No. 2947), reg. 2(7) (April 13, 1995).

General Note

Non-contributory invalidity pension was replaced by severe disablement allowance in 1984 because the old benefit was clearly discriminatory and would have been incompatible with Council Directive 79/7/EEC *on the progressive implementation of the principle of equal treatment for men and women in matters of social security* which came into force on December 22, 1984. S.36 of the Social Security Act 1975 has been replaced by s.68 of the Social Security Contributions and Benefits Act 1992. S.79 of the 1975 Act was repealed in 1985.

21. *Omitted.*

SCHEDULES

Schedule 1

Provisions Covering Powers Exercised in Making These Regulations

Column (1) *Provision*		Column (2) *Relevant Amendment*
The Social Security Act 1975	3(2)	None
	36(4) and (7)	The Health and Social Security Act 1984, section 11.
	40(a)	None.
	79(3)	The Social Security and Housing Benefits Act 1982, section 48(5); Schedule 4, paragraph 14(3). The Health and Social Security Act 1984, section 11(2); Schedule 4, paragraph 3.
	80(1)	The Social Security (Miscellaneous Provisions) Act 1977, section 17(2). The Child Benefit Act 1975, section 21(2); Schedule 5, Part I.
	81	None.
	82	None.
	83(1)	None.
	85	The Child Benefit Act 1975, section 21(1); Schedule 4, paragraph 28.
	108(2)	The Health and Social Services and Social Security Adjudications Act 1983, section 25; Schedule 8, paragraph 21(1). The Health and Social Security Act 1984, section 11(2); Schedule 4, paragraph 6.
	115(1)	None.
	119(3)	The Social Security Act 1979, section 21(4); Schedule 3, paragraph 9(a).
	128(2)	None.
	129(1)	None.

Column (1) *Provision*		Column (2) *Relevant Amendment*
	131	None.
	Schedule 13, paragraph 2	None.
	schedule 20 (definition of ''prescribe'' and ''regulations'')	None.
The Child Benefit Act 1975	17(5)	The Health and Social Security Act 1984, section 11(2); Schedule 4, paragraph 12.
The Social Security (Miscellaneous Provisions) Act 1977	22(1)	None.

SCHEDULES 2. AND **3.** *Omitted.*

PART III

Administration Regulations

The Disability Living Allowance Advisory Board Regulations 1991

(S.I. 1991 No. 1746)

ARRANGEMENT OF REGULATIONS

Whereas a draft of this instrument was laid before Parliament in accordance with section 12(1) of the Disability Living Allowance and Disability Working Allowance Act 1991 and approved by resolution of each House of Parliament;

Now, therefore, the Secretary of State for Social Security in exercise of powers conferred by sections 3(2), (3), (5), (7) and (8) of the Disability Living Allowance and Disability Working Allowance Act 1991 and of all other powers enabling him in that behalf, by this instrument, which is made before the end of a period of six months beginning with the coming into force of those provisions, hereby makes the following Regulations:

Citation and commencement

1. These Regulations may be cited as the Disability Living Allowance Advisory Board Regulations 1991 and shall come into force on 12th August 1991.

Functions and powers

2.—(1) The Board shall have the following functions in relation to disability living allowance and attendance allowance, namely—

(a) to give advice to the Secretary of State on such matters as he may refer to them for consideration;

(b) to give advice to a medical practitioner who is an officer of the Secretary of State on any case or question which he refers to the Board in accordance with section 115C(4) of the Social Security Act 1975; and

(c) to present an annual report on its activities over the year to the Secretary of State.

(2) In carrying out any of its functions under paragraph (1) above the Board may consult persons or bodies on matters as respects which in the Board's opinion, those persons or bodies are especially qualified.

GENERAL NOTE

S.115C(4) of the 1975 Act has been replaced by s.54(4) of the Social Security Administration Act 1992.

Members

3.—(1) The Board shall consist of a chairman appointed by the Secretary of State and not less than 11 and not more than 20 other members so appointed.

(2) The members appointed by the Secretary of State shall include—

(a) members with professional knowledge or experience of—

(i) physiotherapy,

(ii) occupational therapy,
(iii) social work,
(iv) nursing disabled persons,
(v) medical practice;

(b) at least one member with personal experience of caring for a disabled person; and

(c) six or more members who are disabled persons.

(3) All appointments made by the Secretary of State shall be made—

(a) after consultation with such organisations as he thinks fit, and

(b) in writing.

Term of office

4. The chairman and other members of the Board shall hold office for such period of not more than five years as the Secretary of State may determine; but any member—

(a) shall be eligible for re-appointment from time to time on or after the expiration of his term of office; and

(b) may by notice in writing to the Secretary of State resign office at any time, while remaining eligible for re-appointment.

Removal

5. The Secretary of State may remove the chairman or other member of the Board on the grounds of his inability to discharge his functions or of misbehaviour.

Procedure

6.—(1) The Board may make rules for regulating its procedure, including its quorum.

(2) The Board may act notwithstanding any vacancy among its members.

Expenses

7. Persons attending its meetings at the request of the Board may be paid such travelling and other allowances, including compensation for loss of remunerative time, as the Secretary of State may with the consent of the Treasury determine.

Officers and servants

8. The Secretary of State may appoint such officers and servants of the Board as he thinks appropriate.

The Social Security (Adjudication) Regulations 1995

(S.I. 1995 No. 1801)

ARRANGEMENT OF REGULATIONS

PART I

GENERAL

Part II

Common Provisions

2. Procedure in connection with determinations; and right to representation.
3. Manner of making applications, appeals or references; and time limits.
4. Oral hearings and inquiries.
5. Postponement and adjournment.
6. Withdrawal of applications, appeals and references.
7. Striking-out of proceedings for want of prosecution.
8. Non-disclosure of medical evidence.
9. Correction of accidental errors in decisions.
10. Setting aside of decisions on certain grounds.
11. Provisions common to regulations 10 and 11.

12.–17. *Omitted.*

Section B—Adjudication Officers

18. Notification of decisions.
19. Procedure on claim or question involving questions for determination by the Secretary of State.

20.–24 *Omitted.*

Section D—Disability Adjudication

25. Prescribed period.
26. Manner of making applications for review under section 30(1) of the Administration Act.
27. Appeal to a disability appeal tribunal.
28. Persons who may appeal to disability appeal tribunals and appeal tribunals.
29. Procedure for disability appeal tribunals.
30. Examination and report by a medical practitioner.
31. Persons who may not act as members of disability appeal tribunals.
32. Application for leave to appeal from a disability appeal tribunal to a Commissioner.
33. Procedure of a disability appeal tribunal on receipt of a Commissioner's decision.

Section E—Medical Adjudication

34. Construction of Section E.
35. Appointment of adjudicating medical practitioners and specially qualified adjudicating medical practitioners.
36. Determination of medical questions.
37. Decisions of adjudicating medical authorities.
38. Medical appeal tribunals.
39. Application for leave to appeal from a medical appeal tribunal to a Commissioner.
40. Disqualification from acting as an adjudicating medical authority or as a member thereof or as a member of a medical appeal tribunal.
41. Application for review involving review of decision of a medical appeal tribunal.
42. Procedure of a medical appeal tribunal on receipt of a Commissioner's decision.

Part IV

Provisions relating to particular benefits or procedures

Section A—Prescribed Diseases

43. Construction of Section A.
44. Application of Part II of the Administration Act and of these Regulations.
45. Reference of diagnosis and recrudescence questions for medical report.
46. Procedure on receipt of medical report.
47. Restriction of adjudication officer's power to determine diagnosis and recrudescence questions.
48. Appeal against decision of adjudication officer.
49. Appeal or reference to a medical appeal tribunal.
50. Powers of medical appeal tribunal upon determining the question referred.

The Secretary of State for Social Security in exercise of the powers set out in Schedule 1, and of all other powers enabling him in that behalf, after consultation with the Council on Tribunals in accordance with section 8 of the Tribunals and Inquiries Act 1992, hereby makes the following Regulations:

PART I

GENERAL

Citation, commencement and interpretation

1.—(1) These Regulations may be cited as the Social Security (Adjudication) Regulations 1995 and shall come into force on 10th August 1995.

(2) In these Regulations, unless the context otherwise requires–

[[1]"the Acts" means the Social Security Contributions and Benefits Act 1992, the Social Security Administration Act 1992 and the Jobseekers Act 1995;

"the Administration Act" means the Social Security Administration Act 1992;

"adjudicating authority" means, as the case may be, an adjudicating medical practitioner, the Chief or any other adjudication officer, an appeal tribunal, a medical appeal tribunal, a disability appeal tribunal, a medical board or a special medical board;

"adjudicating medical authority" has the meaning assigned to it by regulation 34;

"adjudicating medical practitioner" means a medical practitioner appointed in accordance with section 49(1) of the Administration Act;

"adjudication officer" means an officer appointed in accordance with section 38(1) of the Administration Act;

"appeal tribunal" means a social security appeal tribunal constituted in accordance with section 41(1) to (5) of the Administration Act;

"Chief Adjudication Officer" means the Chief Adjudication Officer appointed under section 39(1) of the Administration Act;

"claimant" means a person who has claimed benefit under the Acts (including, in relation to an award or decision, a beneficiary under the award or a person affected by the decision) or from whom benefit is alleged to be recoverable, and in relation to statutory sick pay and statutory maternity pay includes both the employee alleged to be entitled to and the employer alleged to be liable to pay such pay;

[[2]"clerk to the tribunal" means, as the case may be, a clerk to a social security appeal tribunal, a clerk to a disability appeal tribunal or a clerk to a medical appeal tribunal appointed in accordance with section 41, 43, or 50 of and paragraph 3 of Schedule 2 to, the Administration Act, or a person acting as the clerk to a medical board or special medical board constituted in accordance with these Regulations;]

"Commissioner" means the Chief or any other Social Security Commissioner appointed in accordance with section 52(1) of the Administration Act and includes a Tribunal of 3 such Commissioners constituted in accordance with section 57 of that Act;

"the Contributions and Benefits Act" means the Social Security Contributions and Benefits Act 1992;

"disability appeal tribunal" means a tribunal constituted in accordance with section 43 of the Administration Act;

"disability question" has the meaning assigned by regulation 27(2);

[[3]"full statement of the tribunal's decision" means the statement referred to in regulations 23(3A), 29(6A) and 38(5A)']

"full-time chairman" means a regional or other full-time chairman of appeal tribunals, medical appeal tribunals and disability appeal tribunals appointed under section 51 of the Administration Act;

"income support" means income support under Part VII of the Contributions and Benefits Act and includes personal expenses addition, special transitional addition and transitional addition as defined in the Income Support (Transitional) Regulations 1987;

"Income Support Regulations" means the Income Support (General) Regulations 1987;

"inquiry" means an inquiry held pursuant to section 17(4) of the Administration Act;

[[1]"the Jobseekers Act" means the Jobseekers Act 1995;

"the Jobseeker's Allowance Regulations" means the jobseeker's Allowance Regulations 1996;]

"local office" means an office of the Department of Social Security, an office of the Department for Education and Employment or the office of the Chief Adjudication Officer;

"medical appeal tribunal" means a tribunal constituted in accordance with section 50 of the Administration Act;

"medical board" and "special medical board" have the meanings assigned to them by regulation 34;

"party to the proceedings" means–

(a) the claimant;

(b) in proceedings before an appeal tribunal or a disability appeal tribunal, the adjudication officer;

(c) in proceedings relating to the determination of a question included in section 17(1) of the Administration Act, any person interested within the meaning of regulation 12;

(d) in any other proceedings, the adjudication officer and the Secretary of State except in proceedings in which the adjudication officer or the Secretary of State is the adjudicating authority;

(e) any other person appearing to the Secretary of State, the adjudicating authority or, in the case of a tribunal or board, its chairman or in relation to an inquiry, the person appointed to hold the inquiry, to be interested in the proceedings;

"the Prescribed Diseases Regulations" means the Social Security (Industrial Injuries) (Prescribed Diseases) Regulations 1985;

"President" means the President of social security appeal tribunals, medical appeal tribunals and disability appeal tribunals appointed under section 51(1) of the Administration Act;

"proceedings" means proceedings on a claim, application, appeal or reference to which these Regulations apply;

"specially qualified adjudicating medical practitioner" means a specially qualified adjudicating medical practitioner appointed by virtue of section 62 of the Administration Act; and

"the Supplementary Benefits Act" means the Supplementary Benefits Act 1976.

(3) Where, by any provision of the Acts or of these Regulations–

(a) any notice or other document is required to be given or sent to any office, that notice or document shall be treated as having been so given or sent on the day that it is received in that office; and

(b) any notice or other document is required to be given or sent to any person, that notice or document shall, if sent by post to that person's last known or notified address, be treated as having been given or sent on the day that it was posted.

(4) Unless the context otherwise requires, any reference in these Regulations to a numbered or lettered Part, section, regulation or Schedule is a reference to the Part, Section, regulation or Schedule bearing that number or letter in these Regulations and any reference in a regulation to a numbered paragraph is a reference to the paragraph of that regulation bearing that number.

(5) Unless otherwise provided, where by these Regulations any power is conferred on a chairman of an appeal tribunal, a medical tribunal or a disability appeal tribunal then–

(a) if the power is to be exercised at the hearing of an appeal or application, it shall be exercised by the chairman of the tribunal hearing the appeal or application; and

(b) otherwise, it shall be exercised by a person who is eligible to be nominated to act as a chairman of an appeal tribunal under section 41 of the Administration Act.

AMENDMENTS

1. Social Security (Adjudication) Amendment Regulations 1996 (S.I. 1996 No. 1518), reg. 2(2) (October 7, 1996).

2. Social Security (Adjudication) and Child Support Amendment (No. 2) Regulations 1996 (S.I. 1996 No. 2450), reg. 2 (October 21, 1996).
3. Social Security (Adjudication) and Commissioners Procedure and Child Support Commissioners (Procedure) Amendment Regulations 1996 (S.I. 1997 No. 955), reg. 2 (April 28, 1997).

Part II

Common Provisions

Procedure in connection with determinations; and right to representation

2.—(1) Subject to the provisions of the Administration Act and of these Regulations—

(a) the procedure in connection with the consideration and determination of any claim or question to which these Regulations relate shall be such as the Secretary of State, the adjudicating authority or the person holding the inquiry, as the case may be, shall determine; so however that in the case of a tribunal or board, the procedure shall be such as the chairman shall determine;

[[1](aa) the chairman of a tribunal or board may give directions requiring any party to the proceedings to comply with any provision of these Regulations and may further at any stage of the proceedings either of his own motion or on a written application made to the clerk to the tribunal by any party to the proceedings give such directions as he may consider necessary or desirable for the just, effective and efficient conduct of the proceedings and may direct any party to provide such further particular or to produce such documents as may reasonably be required;

(ab) where under these Regulations the clerk to the tribunal is authorised to take steps in relation to the procedure of the tribunal or board, he may directions requiring any party to the proceedings to comply with any provision of these Regulations.]

(b) any person who by virtue of the provisions of these Regulations has the right to be heard at a hearing or an inquiry may be accompanied and may be represented by another person whether having professional qualifications or not and, for the purposes of the proceedings at any such hearing or inquiry, any such representative shall have all the rights and powers to which the person whom he represents is entitled under the Administration Act and these Regulations.

(2) For the purpose of arriving at their decision an appeal tribunal, a medical board, a special medical board, a medical appeal tribunal or a disability appeal tribunal, as the case may be, shall, and for the purpose of discussing any question of procedure may, notwithstanding anything contained in these Regulations, order all persons not being members of the tribunal or board, other than the person acting as clerk to the tribunal or board, to withdraw from the sitting of the tribunal or board, except that,

(a) a member of the Council on Tribunals or of the Scottish Committee of the Council and the President and any full-time chairman; and

(b) with the leave of the chairman of the tribunal or board, and if no person having the right to be heard objects, any person mentioned in regulation 4(6)(b) and (d) (except a person undergoing training as an adjudication officer or as an adjudicating medical practitioner),

may remain present at any such sitting.

(3) Nothing in these regulations shall prevent a member of the Council on Tribunals or of the Scottish Committee of the Council from being present at a hearing before an appeal tribunal a medical appeal tribunal or a disability appeal

tribunal or at any inquiry, in his capacity as such, notwithstanding that the hearing or inquiry is not in public.

AMENDMENT

1. Social Security (Adjudication) and Child Support Amendment (No. 2) Regulations 1996 (S.I. 1996 No. 2450), reg. 3 (October 21, 1996).

GENERAL NOTE

Para. (1)(a). Matters of procedure are to be decided by the chairman alone, unless the Regulations otherwise provide. However, matters of substance are to be determined by the tribunal as a whole.

Tribunals exercise an inquisitorial jurisdiction rather than an adverserial one, so they must not simply leave it to the parties to present their respective cases. They must investigate cases more deeply, seeking to ascertain the facts and determine the truth (*R(S) 1/87*). They must also pick up points that might not have occurred to the parties. That does not mean that they are expected to question undisputed facts presented to them in case after further investigation they might prove to be materially different, unless the point is obvious or self-evident (*R(SB) 2/83*).

There is a general no smoking policy in tribunal hearing rooms (see *President's Circular No. 3*)

Para. (1)(aa) and (ab). A failure to comply with a direction may lead to a case being struck out under reg. 7.

Para. (2). Note that anyone may, with the permission of all parties present, remain with the tribunal while they confer for the purposes of reaching a decision, except the parties to the case themselves, anyone being trained as an adjudication officer or adjudicating medical practitioner or any of the people identified in reg. 4(6)(c). The people identified in para. (2)(a) have a right to remain irrespective of the views of the parties, and of the chairman, while the clerk has a right to remain subject to the chairman's right to decide matters of procedure. If a matter of procedure is being discussed, no-one need be required to withdraw.

Manner of making applications, appeals or references; and time limits

3.—(1) Any application, appeal or reference mentioned in column (1) of Schedule 2 shall be in writing [[2]and, in the case of appeal, shall be on a form approved by the Secretary of State] and shall be made or given by sending or delivering it to the appropriate office within the specified time.

(2) In this regulation—

(a) "the appropriate office" means the office specified in column (2) of Schedule 2 opposite the description of the relevant application, appeal or reference listed in column (1); and

(b) "the specified time" means the time specified in column (3) of that Schedule opposite the description of the relevant application, appeal or reference so listed.

[[2](3) The time specified by this regulation and Schedule 2 for the making of any application, appeal or reference (except an application to the chairman of an appeal tribunal, a medical appeal tribunal or a disability appeal tribunal for leave to appeal to a Commissioner) may be extended, even though the time so specified may already have expired—

(a) in the case of an application or reference, for special reasons;

(b) in the case of an appeal, provided the conditions set out in paragraphs (3A) to (3E) are satisfied;

and any application for an extension of time under this paragraph shall be made to and determined by the person or body to whom the application, appeal or reference is sought to be made or, in the case of tribunal or board, its chairman.]

[[1](3A) Where the time specified for the making of an appeal has already expired, an application for an extension of time for making an appeal shall not be granted unless the applicant has satisfied the person considering the application that—

(a) if the application is granted there are reasonable prospects that such an appeal will be successful; and

(b) it is in the interests of justice that the application be granted.

(3B) For the purposes of paragraph (3A) it shall not be considered to be in the interests of justice to grant an application unless the person considering the application is satisfied that—

(a) special reasons exist, which are wholly exceptional and which relate to the history or facts of the case; and
(b) such special reasons have existed throughout the period beginning with the day following the expiration of the time specified by Schedule 2 for the making of an appeal and ending with the day on which the application for an extension of time is made; and
(c) such special reasons manifestly constitute a reasonable excuse of compelling weight for the applicant's failure to make an appeal within the time specified.

(3C) In determining whether there are special reasons for granting an applicatin for an extension of time for making an appeal under paragraph (3) the person considering the application shall have regard to the principle that the greater the amount of time that has elapsed between the expiration of the time specified for the making of the appeal and the making of the application for an extension of time, the more cogent should be the special reasons on which the application is based.

(3D) In determining whether facts constitute special reasons for granting an application for an extension of time for making an appeal under paragraph (3) no account shall be taken of the following—

(a) that the applicant or anyone acting for him or advising him was aware of or misunderstood the law applicable to his case (including ignorance or misunderstanding of any time limits imposed by Schedule 2);
(b) that a Commissioner or a court has taken a different view of the law from that prevously understood and applied.

(3E) Notwithstanding paragraph (3), no appeal may in any event be brought later than 6 years after the beginning of the period specified in column (3) of Schedule 2.]

(4) An application under paragraph (3) for an extension of time which has been refused may not be renewed.

[[2](5) Any application, appeal or reference under these Regulations shall contain the following particulars—

(a) in the case of an appeal, the date of the notification of the decision against which the appeal is made, the claim or question under the Acts to which the decision relates, and a summary of the arguments relied on by the person making the appeal to support his contention that the decision was wrong:
(b) in the case of an application under paragraph (3) for an extension of time in which to appeal, in relation to the appeal which it is proposed to bring, the particulars required under sub-paragraph (a) together with particulars of the special reasons on which the application is based;
(c) in the case of any other application or any reference, the grounds on which it is made or given.

(5A) Where an appeal is not made on the form approved for the time being, but is made in writing and contains all the particulars required under paragraph (5), the chairman of the tribunal may treat that appeal as duly made.

(6) Where it appears—

(a) to the chairman of a tribunal or board or the clerk to the tribunal that an application, appeal or reference which is made to him or to the tribunal or board; or
(b) to the Secretary of State or an adjudication officer that an application or reference which is made to him,

does not contain the particulars required under paragraph (5), he may direct the person making the application, appeal to provide such particulars.

(6A) Where further particulars are required under paragraph (6), the chairman of the tribunal or board, the clerk to the tribunal, the Secretary of State or the adjudication officer, as the case may be, may extend the time specified by this regulation and Schedule 2 for making the application, appeal or reference by a period of not more than 14 days.

(6B) Where further particulars are required under paragraph (6), in the case of an appeal they shall be sent or delivered to the clerk to the tribunal within such period as the chairman or the clerk to the tribunal may direct.

(6C) The date of an appeal shall be the date on which all the particulars required under paragraph (5) are recieved by the clerk to the tribunal.]

(7) A chairman of an appeal tribunal, a medical appeal tribunal or a disability appeal tribunal] may give directions for the disposal of any purported appeal where he is satisfied that the tribunal does not have jurisdiction to entertain the appeal.

[[1](8) In the case of an application under paragraph (3) for an extension of time for making an appeal, the person who determines that application shall record his decision in writing together with a statement of the reasons for the decison.

(9) As soon as practicable after the decision has been made it shall be communicated to the applicant and to every other party to the proceedings and if within 3 months of such communication being sent the applicant or any other party to the proceedings so requests in writing, a copy of the record referred to in paragraph (8) shall be supplied to him.]

Amendments

1. Social Security (Adjudication) and Child Support Amendment Regulations 1996 (S.I. 1996 No. 182), reg. 2(2) (February 28, 1996).

2. Social Security (Adjudication) and Child Support Amendment (No. 2) Regulations 1996 (S.I. 1996 No. 2450), reg. 4 (appeals, applications or references made on or after October 21, 1996).

General Note

Paras. (1) and (2). Note reg. 1(3) which has the effect that a notice of application or appeal is deemed to be given on the date it is received. The provision requiring an appeal to be on a proper form is probably merely directory as it seems unlikely that a notice of appeal will be held to be invalid merely because it is not on an official form, provided it contains the particulars required by para. (5), particularly as para. (6) even permits some of the particulars to be provided later.

Paras. (3) to (3E). Unitl 1996 there was a broad discretion to admit late appeals which was probably exercised more liberally than was wise. The consequence has been a massive tightening up of the legislation and a substantial restriction on the power of a chairman to admit a late appeal. Para. (3D)(a) and (b) both seem particularly unfair, although each may be subject to more than one interpretation. If sub-para. (a) is interpreted broadly, there would hardly be any scope for admitting late appeals, for there are few cases where a claimant's ignorance of his or her rights is not a factor in delay. However, it is arguable that it is to be construed more narrowly and applies only where a claimant or advisor had a particular statutory provision or authority in mind and either misunderstood it or was unaware of some other relevant provision or authority which would have had some bearing on its relevance. The narrow construction might be said to be supported by the existence of sub-para. (b). Either construction might be thought to be unfair because some statutory provisions relating to social security are so obscure it is more surprising when people are aware of them than when they are not. Sub-para. (b) immediately raises the question of whose understanding it is that is relevant. It is extremely rare for a Commissioner or court to make a decision which is contrary to the understanding of virtually everybody. It is rather naïve to think that there is ever a completely unanimous view as to what the law is. If the understanding is that of persons who has previously applied the law, then it must be the understanding of adjudication officers, tribunals and Commissioners. How is that to be proved? What if Commissioners have reached different conclusions in the past? It seems unlikely that such a contentious matter can be considered properly without an oral hearing of the application for leave to appeal. On the other hand, it is arguable that what is relevant is how the individual chairman considering the application had previously understood and applied the law. That might produce some arbitrary results but whether they would be any more arbitrary than those produced by any other approach is doubtful.

Para. (4). An application for an extension of time may not be renewed. Nor is possible to apply for a refusual (or grant) of an extension of time to be set aside under reg. 10, because a chairman is not an "adjudicating authority" (see reg. 1(2)). Nor is it possible to appeal to a Commisioner against a refusal (or grant) of such an application, because an appeal does not lie from a decision of a chairman and, in any event, a refusal of an extension of time is probably not a "decision" at all (*Bland v. Chief Supplementary Benefit Officer* [1983] 1 W.L.R. 262, also reported as *R(SB) 12/83*. The only remedy is judicial review. Note that para. (9) requires the chairman to give reasons upon which an application for judicial review might be based.

Paras. (5) and *(6).* It is now possible for a party to be required to give reasons for an application, appeal or reference. It is usually pretty obvious from the surrounding circumstances what the case is about but the power to require particulars may be helpful in a few cases. If a party fails to give particulars, the application, appeal or reference may be struck out under reg. 7 for want of prosecution.

Para. (7). This is a power to be used sparingly. It is not intended to be used merely because an appeal seems hopeless. It should be used only when the tribunal has no jurisdiction to consider the case because some other body, such as the Secretary of State, is required to deal with it. Unless the position is absolutely clear, which it seldom is, it will usually be better to list the case and for the whole tribunal to deal with the issue of jurisdiction at the hearing. This provision applies only to appeals and not also to references to medical appeal tribunals made at the instance of the Secretary of State (*R(I) 3/92*).

Paras. (8) and (9). A chairman must record reasons for refusing or granting an extension of time. This is to enable a party to know whether or not the chairman made an error of law that might give grounds for applying for judicial review. Although para. (9) requires that a claimant be sent the record if a request is made within 3 months of the decision being issued, it would be hard to justify a refusal to send a copy of the record after that period had expired unless, of course, the record had been destroyed. An application for leave to apply for judicial review must nearly always be made within 3 months of the relevant decision but a judge does have the power to extend the time for applying.

Oral hearings and inquiries

4.—(1) This regulation applies to any oral hearing of an application, appeal or reference and to any inquiry.

(2) [[1]Except where paragraph 2C applies, not less than 7 notice notice] (beginning with the day on which the notice is given and ending on the day before the hearing of the case or, as the case may be, the inquiry is to take place) of the time and place of any oral hearing before an adjudicating authority or of an inquiry shall be given to every party to the proceedings, and if such notice has not been given to a person to whom it should have been given under the provisions of this paragraph the hearing or inquiry may proceed only with the consent of that person.

[[1](2A) The chairman of an appeal tribunal, a medical appeal tribunal or a disability appeal tribunal may give notice for the determination forthwith, in accordance with the provisions of these Regulations, of an appeal notwithstanding that a party to the proceedings has failed to indicate his availability for a hearing or to provide all the information which may have been requested, if the chairman is satisifed that such party—

(a) has failed to comply with a direction regrading his availability or requiring information under regulation 2(1)(aa) or (ab); and

(b) has not given any explanation for his failure to comply with such a direction;

provided that the chairman is satisfied that the tribunal has sufficient particulars in order for the appeal to be determined.

(2B) the chairman of an appeal tribunal, a medical appeal tribunal or a disability appeal tribunal may give notice for the determination forthwith, in accordance with the provisions of these Regulations, of an appeal which he believes has no reasonable prospect of success.

(2C) Any party to the proceedings may waive his right to receive not less than 7 days notice of the time and place of any oral hearing as specified in paragraph (2).]

(3) If a party to the proceedings to whom notice has been given under paragraph (2) [[1]fails to appear] at the hearing or inquiry the adjudicating authority or the person holding the inquiry may, having regard to all the circumstances including any explanation offered for the absence, [[1]and where applicable the circumstances set out in sub-paragraphs (a) and (b) of paragraph (2A) proceed with the hearing or inquiry] notwithstanding his absence, or give such directions with a view to the determination of the case or conduct of the inquiry as it or he may think proper.

[[1](3A) If a party to the proceedings has waived his right to be given notice under paragraph (2C) the adjudicating authority or the person holding the inquiry or hearing may proceed with the hearing or inquiry notwithstanding his absence.]

(4) Any oral hearing before an adjudicating authority and any inquiry shall be in public except where (in the case of an oral hearing) the claimant requests a private hearing or (in any case) the chairman or the person holding the inquiry is satisfied that intimate personal or financial circumstances may have to be disclosed or that considerations of public security are involved, in which case the hearing or inquiry shall be in private.

(5) At any oral hearing or inquiry any party to the proceedings shall be entitled to be present and be heard.

(6) The following persons shall also be entitled to be present at an oral hearing (whether or not it is otherwise in private) but shall take no part in the proceedings:—

(a) the President and any full-time chairman;

(b) any person undergoing training as a chairman or other member of an appeal tribunal, a medical appeal tribunal or a disability appeal tribunal, or as a clerk to any such tribunal, or as an adjudication officer or an adjudicating medical practitioner;

(c) any person acting on behalf of the President, the Chief Adjudication Officer or the Secretary of State in the training or supervision of clerks to appeal tribunals medical appeal tribunals or disability appeal tribunals or of adjudication officers or officers of the Secretary of State or in the monitoring of standards of adjudication by adjudication officers; and

(d) with the leave of the chairman of the tribunal or board, as the case may be, and the consent of every party to the proceedings actually present, any other person.

(7) At any inquiry (whether or not it is otherwise in private) the following persons shall be entitled to be present but shall take no part in the proceedings—

(a) any person undergoing training as an officer of the Secretary of State; and

(b) any person acting on behalf of the Secretary of State in the training or supervision of officers of the Secretary of State; and

(c) with the leave of the person holding the inquiry and the consent of all parties to the proceedings actually present, any other person.

(8) Nothing in paragraph (6) affects the rights of any person mentioned in sub-paragraphs (a) and (b) at any oral hearing where he is sitting as a member of the tribunal or acting as its clerk, and nothing in this regulation prevents the presence at an oral hearing or an inquiry of any witness.

(9) Any person entitled to be heard at an oral hearing or inquiry may address the adjudicating authority or person holding the inquiry, may give evidence,

may call witnesses and may put questions directly to any other person called as a witness.

Amendment

1. Social Security (Adjudication) and Child Support Amendment (No. 2) Regulations 1996 (S.I. 1996 No. 2450), reg. 5 (October 21, 1996).

General Note

Para. (2). Note the provision of reg. 1(3) deeming notice of a hearing to be given when it is sent. That applies even if it is never received. In such a case a claimant should apply for the decision to be set aside under reg. 10(1)(a) or (b) rather than appealing (*R(SB) 55/83*). If a party does not attend, a tribunal should always ask the clerk whether notification was properly sent (*R(SB) 19/83*). For the practice where a domiciliary hearing is requested, see *President's Circular No. 4*.

Para. (2A). Claimants are asked whether they wish to attend an oral hearing and, if they do, when they will be available. Para (2A) makes express (but possibly unnecessary) provision for a case to be listed if no reply is received but it is to be noted that notice under para. (2) must still be given. If the claimant then fails to appear, the case may be considered in his or her absence (see para. (3)).

Para. (2B). It is unclear quite what the purpose of this paragraph is. Notice of a hearing must be given under para. (2) and, if a claimant fails to appear, the lack of apparent prospects of success is doubtless a matter that can be considered when considering how to proceed under para. (3). If para. (2B) is intended to allow a case to be listed without the claimant being given the usual opportunity to say when he or she will be available to attend a hearing, it is suggested that it should be used sparingly.

Para. (2C). The parties may waive their right to notice of a hearing, in which case the "oral" hearing will effectively be a hearing on the papers in the absence of the parties unless the tribunal considering the case directs otherwise (see para. 3A). This provision has been criticised because the fact that a claimant is offered the opportunity of having a case heard in his or her absence may suggest that his or her attendance at the hearing is not only unnecessary but would not increase his or her chances of success. There are few cases (other than those that have no prospect of success whatsoever) in which the claimant's chances of success are not increased if he or she attends and there are many cases where a failure to attend utterly destroys any such chances.

Para. (3). If a claimant has been given the opportunity of saying when he or she will be available for a hearing and either failed to reply at the proper time or else has indicated availability on the date the case is listed, there is no reason in the vast majority of cases why the tribunal should not proceed in the unexplained absence of the claimant. However, if a new point emerges that has not previously been put to the claimant, it may, depending on the circumstances, be necessary for compliance with the rules of natural justice to adjourn the hearing.

In considering whether or not to adjourn a case because of a gap in the evidence which could have been filled had a party attended the hearing, a tribunal may wish to consider making a finding on the relevant issue on such evidence as there is, but drawing the party's attention to the right to apply for a review of the tribunal's decision on the ground of ignorance or mistake of the fact (ss.35(1)(a) or 47(1) of the Social Security Administration Act 1992 for disability appeal tribunals and medical appeal tribunals respectively).

Commissioners have frequently deplored the failure of the Benefits Agency to ensure that adjudication officers are represented before tribunals (*e.g. CI/11449/95*). Not only does the lack of a presenting officer mean that important matters may not be drawn to the attention of a tribunal but also there may be an injustice to a claimant because presenting officiers often know more about a claim than appears in the papers.

Para. (3A). Note that a tribunal considering a case on the papers is entitled to decide that is is inappropriate to do so and to adjourn so that the parties may be given notice of an oral hearing. If they do so, it will be helpful if they give reasons so that the paries may understand the importance of their attending the next hearing.

Paras. (4), (5) and *(6).* See reg. 2(2) for the power to require people to withdraw during deliberations.

Para. (9). A claimant's own verbal account of events or circumstances is evidence and need not be corroborated (*R(I) 2/51*) although a tribunal is not bound to accept it if it is inherently improbable or is challenged. A chairman's note of evidence taken at one hearing is also evidence which may be considered at a later hearing (*R(S) 1/87*).

Postponement and adjournment

5.—[[1](1) Where a person to whom notice of an oral hearing or inquiry has been given wishes to request a postponement of that hearing or inquiry—

(a) in the case of an oral hearing be an adjudicating authority, he shall do so in writing to the clerk to the tribunal stating his reasons for the request, and the clerk to the tribunal may grant or refuse the request as he thinks fit or may pass the request to the chairman, who may grant or refuse the request as he thinks fit;

(b) in the case of an inquiry, he shall do so in writing to the person appointed to hold the inquiry stating his reasons for the request, and the person appointed may grant or refuse the request as he thinks fit.]

(2) A chairman [[1]or the clerk to the tribunal] may of his own motion at any time before the beginning of the hearing postpone the hearing.

(3) An oral hearing or an inquiry may be adjourned by the adjudicating authority or, as the case may be, the person appointed to hold the inquiry at any time on the application of any party to the proceedings or of its or his own motion.

Amendment

1. Social Security (Adjudication) and Child Support Amendment (No. 2) Regulations 1996 (S.I. 1996 No. 2450), reg. (October 21, 1996).

General Note

Paras. (1) and (2). The amendments allow a clerk to postpone, or refuse to postpone, a hearing. It is suggested that a clerk should not usually *refuse* to postpone a hearing without referring the matter to a chairman, unless there is not time to do so. If either a clerk or chairman refuses to postpone a hearing, it is suggested that the tribunal should be informed so that they may consider whether to adjourn the hearing.

Para. (3). The distinction between a postponement (paras. (1) and (2)) and an adjournment (para. (3)). is that the former is considered by a clerk or chairman *before* the commencement of the hearing and the latter is considered by the whole tribunal *after* the commencement of the hearing. Whether an application made at the beginning of a hearing is to be considered by the chairman under para. (1) or by the whole tribunal under para. (3) is a moot point.

A tribunal should not automatically adjourn because a piece of evidence is not available. The need for the evidence should be weighed against the desirability of not delaying the decision, bearing in mind that an error of fact on the part of a tribunal.may be corrected on review (see s. 35(1)(a) of the Social Security Administration Act 1992 in respect of disability appeal tribunals and the more restricted power under s. 47(1) in respect of medical appeal tribunals). The likelihood of the evidence becoming available should be considered as should the question whether a party could reasonably have been expected to bring the evidence to the hearing. Tribunals should also have regard to *President's Circular No. 1* and, where appropriate, *No. 7* and *No. 13.*

Withdrawal of applications, appeals and references

6.—(1) A person who has made an application to the chairman of the tribunal for leave to appeal to a Commissioner against a decision of an appeal tribunal, a medical appeal tribunal or a disability appeal tribunal may withdraw his application at any time before it is determined by giving written notice of intention to withdraw to the chairman.

(2) Any appeal to an adjudicating authority made under the Administration Act [[1]or section 11(3) of the Jobseekers Act 1995] or these Regulations may be withdrawn by the person who made the appeal—

[[2](a) before the hearing begins, provided that, in the case of a tribunal or board, the clerk to the tribunal has not received any notice under paragraph (2A), by giving written notice of intention to withdraw to the adjudicating authority to whom the appeal was made and with the consent in writing of any other party to the proceedings other than—

(i) in a case which originated in a decision of an adjudication officer, an adjudication officer;

(ii) in any other case; the Secretary of State; or]

(b) after the hearing has begun, with the leave of the adjudicating authority or, in the case of a tribunal or board, its chairman, at any time before the determination is made.

[[2](2A) An appeal to a tribunal or board shall not be withdrawn under sub-paragraph (a) of paragraph (2) if the clerk to the tribunal has previously received notice opposing a withdrawal of such appeal from—

(a) in a case which originated in a decision of an adjudication officer, an adjudication officer; or

(b) in any other case, the Secretary of State.]

(3) A reference by an adjudication officer to an appeal tribunal under section 21(2) of the Administration Act or to a medical board under regulation 45(3) or to a medical appeal tribunal under section 46(3) of the Administration Act may be withdrawn by him at any time before the reference is determined by giving written notice of intention to withdraw to the adjudicating authority to whom the reference was made, but in the case of a reference under section 46(3) of the Administration Act made at the instance of the Secretary of State only with his consent.

(4) An application under regulation 13 for a decision of the Secretary of State on any question may, with his leave, be withdrawn at any time before the decision is given.

AMENDMENTS

1. Jobseeker's Allowance Regulations 1996 (S.I. 1996 No. 207), reg. 42(a) (October 7, 1996).

2. Social Security (Adjudication) and Child Support Amendment (No. 2) Regulations 1996 (S.I. 1996 No. 2450), reg. 7 (October 21, 1996).

GENERAL NOTE

Para. (1). An application for leave to appeal to a Commissioner can be withdrawn at any time before a decision is given. The consent of other parties is not required.

Para. (2). Before amendment, an appeal could be withdrawn under para. (2)(a) before a hearing only with the consent of the adjudication officer or, as the case might have been, the Secretary of State. Now the appeal may be withdrawn unless there is positive opposition. This does not make a great deal of difference because silence cannot be construed as a lack of opposition, until the last minute. However, it does make it unnecessary to begin a hearing if there has been no opposition up to that point. After a hearing has begun, the appeal may be withdrawn only with the leave of the chairman, who will doubtless consider the views of the other paries. There is no automatic right to withdraw an appeal because other parties may have an interest in an appeal continuing.

Striking-out of proceedings for want of prosecution

7.—(1) The chairman of an appeal tribunal, a medical appeal tribunal or a disability appeal tribunal may, subject to paragraph (2), on the application of any party to the proceedings or of his own motion, strike out any application, appeal or reference for want of prosecution including the failure of a claimant to comply with a direction given by the chairman [[1]or the clerk to the tribunal] under regulation 2(1)[[1](aa) or (bb)].

[[1](1A) Where the chairman decides not to strike out an appeal under paragraph (1) he shall consider whether the appeal should be determined forthwith in accordance with these Regulations.

(1B) Where the chairman decides that an appeal should not be detemined forthwith under paragraph (1A) he shall consider whether he should make further directions with a view to expediting the hearing of the appeal.]

(2) The chairman shall not make an order under paragraph (1) before a notice has been sent to the person against whom it is proposed that any such order should be made giving him a reasonable opportunity to show cause why such an order should not be made.

[[1](2A) Paragraph (2) shall not apply where the address of the person against whom it is proposed that an order under paragraph (1) should be made is unknown to the chairman or to the clerk to the tribunal and cannot be ascertained by reasonable enquiry.]

(3) The chairman of an appeal tribunal, a medical appeal tribunal or a disability appeal tribunal may, on application by the party concerned, made not later than [[1]3 months] beginning with the date of the order made under paragraph (1), give leave to reinstate any application, appeal or reference which has been struck out in accordance with paragraph (1) [[1]if he is satisfied that the party concerned did not receive a notice under paragraph (2) and that the conditions in paragraph (2A) were not met].

AMENDMENT

1. Social Security (Adjudication) and Child Support Amendment (No. 2) Regulations 1996 (S.I. 1996 No. 2450), reg. 8 (October 21, 1996).

GENERAL NOTE

Para. (1). Want of prosecution implies a failure to take some necessary preliminary step in an application, appeal or reference, so it will be rare for it to be appropriate to strike out a case rather than simply have it listed for hearing and deciding it on the material available (see paras. (1A) and (1B)). Use of this power is most appropriate where a person has failed to give particulars required under reg. 3(6). Although there is no specific requirement to obtain the views of the adjudication officer or Secretary of State, as there is in reg. 6(2)(a), it is suggested that it cannot be right to strike out an appeal for any reason other than a failure to comply with a direction under reg. 3(6), unless the adjudication officer or Secretary of State is at least given the opportunity to comment. It may be simpler just to list the case for hearing.

Para. (1A). Presumably, determining an appeal "forthwith" means listing it with 7 days notice under reg. 4(2A) or (2B).

Para. (3). An application that has been struck out may be reinstated only on the ground that the claimant did not receive the requisite notice. In an important case, a chairman may wish to hold an oral hearing before finding that a person did not receive such a notice, if the point is disputed. If the claimant replied to a notice but the reply was lost, there is no remedy under the Regulations, although it is arguable that a power to set aside the striking out in such circumstances could be implied. On the other hand, it might be more appropriate simply to admit a fresh appeal, which does not appear to be prohibited if the stringent conditions in reg. 3 are met.

Non-disclosure of medical evidence

8.—(1) Where, in connection with the consideration and determination of any claim or question there is before an adjudicating authority medical advice or medical evidence relating to a person which has not been disclosed to him and in the opinion of the adjudicating authority or, in the case of a tribunal or board, its chairman, the disclosure to that person of that advice or evidence would be harmful to his health, such advice or evidence shall not be required to be disclosed to that person.

(2) Evidence such as is mentioned in paragraph (1) shall not be disclosed to any person acting for or representing the person to whom it relates or, in a case where a claim for benefit is made by reference to the disability of a person

other than the claimant and the evidence relates to that other person, shall not be disclosed to the claimant or any person acting for or representing him, unless the adjudicating authority, or in the case of a tribunal or board its chairman, is satisfied that it is in the interests of the person to whom the evidence relates to do so.

(3) An adjudicating authority shall not be precluded from taking into account for the purposes of the determination evidence which has not been disclosed to a person under the provisions of paragraphs (1) or (2).

(4) In this regulation "adjudicating authority" includes the Secretary of State in a case involving a question which is for determination by him.

General Note

In *R(A) 4/89*, the Attendance Allowance Board withheld from a claimant "additional information" supplied by a doctor who in effect said that when he arrived outside the claimant's house the claimant was sitting with his back to a window but when he went in the claimant was lying on a couch claiming to be unable to respond to the doctor's questions. The doctor was therefore implying that the claimant was a fraud. The Commissioner held that this was not "medical evidence", but was factual evidence and that, in any event, the power to withhold evidence that was prejudicial, rather than helpful, to a claimant should be exercised with caution. He held the Board to have erred in law because it was common fairness to let the claimant be aware of the allegation that he was a fraud. It is difficult to see how evidence of the sort considered in that case could possibly be harmful to the claimant's health. A doctor's wish to avoid embarrassment is not a ground for withholding evidence.

In most cases concerning disability living allowance, this regulation will not give rise to great problems because evidence that a claimant is seriously ill, which is the sort of evidence that would normally be withheld, is evidence that is likely to assist the claimant rather than the reverse. It is in cases before medical appeal tribunals, where causation is often in issue, that the problem arises most acutely.

However, it was in the context of a disability living allowance case, *CSDLA/5/95*, that the scope of reg. 8 was most recently considered. In that case, there was withheld evidence that the child claimant was not seriously ill but that her mother, who was acting on her behalf, was suffering from Munchausen By Proxy Syndrome. The Deputy Commissioner pointed out that the fact a senior medical officer was of the view that disclosure would cause "considerably difficulty and distress" did not mean that it would be harmful to the health of any person. However, more fundamently, he held that, while a claimant was not necessarily entitled to see the whole evidence in the case:—

> ". . . . no adversarial dispute should be decided against a party on the basis of evidence not disclosed to them unless that party has been given sufficient indication of the gist of that evidence to give them a proper opportunity to put forward their case."

He added that non-disclosure to a representative must be considered "quite separately to, and perhaps even more cautiously than, non-disclosure to a claimant" and that the regulation should be operated "in a manner consistent with the principles of natural justice". Further, he held that a claimant to whom material is not being disclosed should be told that fact, and the tribunal's record of reasons should refer to it and no part of that reasoning should not be disclosed to the claimant. It is arguable that that is going too far. The very existence of reg. 8 suggests that a breach of the rules of natural justice may be considered the lesser of two evils in some cases. To tell a claimant that evidence is being withheld will often be tantamount to telling him or her what the evidence is. It is suggested that the regulation anticipates that a tribunal will approach the case inquisitorially, bearing in mind the best interests of the claimant. As the Deputy Commissioner also said, expected harm must be "substantial" before reg. 8 is applied and it is arguable that the real problem in *CSDLA/5/95* was that there was no clear explanation before the Deputy Commissioner as to why it was considered that substantial harm would be caused if there were disclosure and there were reasons to doubt that there would be such harm. If a tribunal are satisifed that evidence should be withheld but would be likely to be contested by a claimant if he or she knew of it, it is suggested that they should take care to ensure that it is properly tested by, for example, obtaining a second opinion. If proceedings cannot properly be adversarial, they must be truly inquisitorial. Indeed, if there were contradictory evidence and the claimant would be likely to contest the withheld evidence, a tribunal might well be particularly slow to conclude that reg. 8 should be applied and might choose either to disclose the evidence or else to disregard it.

Correction of accidental errors in decisions

9.—(1) Subject to regulation 11 (provisions common to regulations 9 and 10), accidental errors in any decision or record of a decision may at any time be corrected by the adjudicating authority who gave the decision or by an authority of like status.

(2) A correction made to, or to the record of, a decision shall be deemed to be part of the decision or of that record and written notice of it shall be given as soon as practicable to every party to the proceedings.

General Note

Only slips of the pen, arithmetical errors or a genuine failure to record something that was actually decided may be corrected under this provision (*CM/209/1987*).

Any correction must be agreed to by the whole tribunal, not just the chairman, and the tribunal must be sitting together and cannot agree a correction by post (*CSSB/76/93*). The normal practice is for the application for a correction to be considered by a tribunal with the same chairman as the original tribunal, but the other members may well be different (see *President's Circular No. 4*).

A decision is only effective when it is sent out (*R(I) 14/74*). Until then, it may be altered informally. Even if an oral "decision" has been given, the case may be recalled by the tribunal before it is sent out, if it appears to them that they have made a serious mistake (*CI/141/87*, applying *Re Harrison's Share* [1955] Ch. 260). Generally it would then be necessary to have a rehearing.

The time for appealing against a decision of a tribunal is extended if it is corrected (reg. 11(2)). There is no right of appeal against a refusal to correct a decision (reg. 11(3)); a dissatisfied party must either appeal against the original decision or seek judicial review of the refusal to make the correction.

Setting aside of decisions on certain grounds

10.—(1) Subject to regulation 11 (provisions common to regulations 9 and 10), on an application made by a party to the proceedings, a decision may be set aside by the adjudicating authority who gave the decision or by an authority of like status in a case where it appears just to set the decision aside on the ground that—

(a) a document relating to the proceedings in which the decision was given was not sent to, or was not received at an appropriate time by, a party to the proceedings or to the party's representative or was not received at an appropriate time by the adjudicating authority who gave the decision; or

(b) a party to the proceedings in which the decision was given or the party's representative was not present at a hearing or inquiry relating to the proceedings; or

(c) the interests of justice so require.

[[1](1A) In determining whether it is just to set aside a decision on the ground set out in paragraph (1)(b), the adjudicating authority shall determine whether the party making the application gave notice that he wished an oral hearing to be held, and if that party did not give such notice the adjudicating authority shall not set the decision aside unless it is satisfied that the interests of justice manifestly so require.]

(2) An application under this regulation shall be made in accordance with regulation 3 and Schedule 2.

(3) Where an application to set aside a decision is entertained under paragraph (1), every party to the proceedings shall be sent a copy of the application and shall be afforded a reasonable opportunity of making representations on it before the application is determined.

(4) Notice in writing of a determination on an application to set aside a decision shall be given to every party to the proceedings as soon as may be practicable and the notice shall contain a statement giving the reasons for the determination.

(5) For the purposes of determining under these regulations an application to set aside a decision there shall be disregarded regulation 1(3)(b) and any provision in any enactment or instrument to the effect that any notice or other document required or authorised to be given or sent to any person shall be deemed to have been given or sent if it was sent by post to that person's last known or notified address.

AMENDMENT

1. The Social Security (Adjudication) and Child Supoort Amendment (No. 2) Regulations 1996 (S.I. 1996 No. 2450), reg. 9 (October 21, 1996).

GENERAL NOTE

Para. (1)(a). Note that para. (5) excludes the effect of any provision deeming a document to have been given or sent.

Para. (1)(b). The fact that a party could well have attended the hearing does not necessarily mean that a decision cannot be set aside but it may be difficult for a claimant who has deliberately not attended to persuade a tribunal that "it appears just to set the decision aside" and this will particularly be the case where para. (1A) applies. However, if a tribunal is satisfied that it is just to set a decision aside because a claimant was not present, the tribunal cannot then refuse to do so on the ground that his or her evidence would have made no difference to the outcome (*R(S) 12/81*). In *CIS/14192/96*, a claimant did not appear at a hearing but he had asked for a postponement and the tribunal were unaware of the request. His appeal was decided in his absence. The Commissioner suggested that the tribunal considering his application to have the decision set aside should have considered para. (1)(a) as well as para. (1)(b).

Para. (1)(c). It is now quite clear that "the interests of justice so require" refers only to matters of procedural justice and that a decision may be set aside on this ground only where there has been some procedural irregularity (*R(SB) 4/90*). Nevertheless, a decision to set aside an earlier decision on this ground which is made in appropriate circumstances cannot be ignored and remains effective. Therefore, if one tribunal allows an appeal, a second tribunal sets aside the decision of the first tribunal and a third tribunal then sits to hear the appeal afresh, the third tribunal is not entitled to inquire whether the second tribunal ought to have set aside the decision of the first tribunal, except to inquire whether the second tribunal acted altogether outside its jurisdiction. A tribunal acts outside its jurisdiction if (a) there is no valid application, (b) the application has already been determined, (c) the tribunal is not properly constituted or (d) the tribunal fails to make a determination on the application (*CI/79/90*). For the procedure where an application is made on the ground of misconduct by a member of a tribunal or a clerk, see *President's Circular No. 6*.

Para. (1A). As para. (1)(b) requires a decision to be set aside on the ground of the absence of a party or representative only where it "appears just" to do so, it may be thought that para. (1A) does not add a great deal. However, it is clearly intended that there should be a greater degree of certainty on the part of the tribunal that justice requires the setting aside of an earlier decision. This may, in some cases, make it particularly necessary for a tribunal to ensure that an applicant has a proper opportunity of satisfying them of the merits of his or her case, which an entirely written procedure may not do.

Para. (3). There is no general right to an oral hearing of an application set aside (since regs. 22(1), 29(1) and 38(1) do not apply to applications as opposed to appeals) but a tribunal may decide that one is necessary. For instance, if, on an application under para. (1)(b), a claimant asserts that he or she did not attend a hearing through illness, it is suggested that a tribunal should not usually dismiss the application on the ground that they do not believe the claimant was ill unless the claimant has been offered an oral hearing of the application. Adjudication officers have been encouraged to make representations when offered the opportunity to do so (*R(S) 12/81*).

Para. (4). There is no appeal against a determination under this regulation (reg. 11(3)). Such a determination could be challenged by way of judicial review. If a tribunal wrongly refuses to set aside a decision, it will often be possible to appeal against the original decision on the ground that there has been a breach of the rules of natural justice. The three month time limit for seeking leave to appeal runs from the date of the determination not to set the decision aside (reg. 11(2)).

Provisions common to regulations 9 and 10

11.—(1) In regulations 9 and 10 "adjudicating authority" includes the Secretary of State.

(2) In calculating any time specified in Schedule 2 there shall be disregarded any day falling before the day on which notice was given of a correction of a decision or the record thereof pursuant to regulation 9 or on which notice is given of a determination that a decision shall not be set aside following an application made under regulation 10, as the case may be.

(3) There shall be no appeal against a correction made under regulation 9 or a refusal to make such a correction or against a determination given under regulation 11.

(4) Nothing in this Part shall be construed as derogating from any power to correct errors or set aside decisions which is exercisable apart from these Regulations.

12.—17. *Omitted.*

Section B—Adjudication Officers

Notification of decisions

18.—(1) Subject to paragraph (2) and regulation 55 the decision of an adjudication officer on any claim or question and the reasons for it shall be notified in writing to the claimant who shall at the same time be informed.

(a) in the case of a decision of an adjudication officer—
   (i) under section 21 of the Administration Act relating to attendance allowance, disability living allowance or disability working allowance, or
   (ii) on a review under section 30(2) or (4) or section 35 of the Administration Act,

of his right to a review under section 30(1) of that Act;

(b) in the case of a decision of an adjudication officer under section 30(1) of that Act, of his right of appeal—
   (i) to a disability appeal tribunal where the appeal relates to the determination of a disability question, and
   (ii) to an appeal tribunal in any other case;

(c) in all other cases, of his right of appeal to an appeal tribunal under section 22 of that Act.

(2) Paragraph (1) does not apply in relation to a decision (other than a decision given on review) awarding benefit for a period which begins immediately after a period in respect of which the claimant had been awarded benefit of the same kind and at the same rate as that awarded by the first-mentioned decision.

Procedure on claim or question involving questions for determination by the Secretary of State

19.—(1) Where an adjudication officer has decided any claim or question on an assumption of facts as to which there appeared to him to be no dispute, but concerning which, had a question arisen, that question would have fallen for determination by the Secretary of State, it shall be deemed to be a sufficient compliance with the requirements of regulation 18 as to notification to the claimant, to give him notice in writing informing him of the decision and of the reasons for it and that, if he is dissatisfied with the decision, he should reply to that effect, giving the reasons for his dissatisfaction.

(2) Where—

(a) the claimant replies to the notice referred to in paragraph (1) expressing his dissatisfaction with the decision, and

(b) after any appropriate investigations and explanations have been made, the claimant nonetheless remains dissatisfied with the decision, and

(c) an adjudication officer certifies that the sole ground for dissatisfaction appears to be the assumption referred to in paragraph (1),

the claimant shall be notified in writing of his right to apply for the determination by the Secretary of State of the question arising on the assumption.

(3) Where the Secretary of State's decision—

(a) upholds the assumption, section 22(3) of the Administration Act shall apply as if the adjudication officer had given the certificate therein referred to;

(b) does not uphold the assumption, the Secretary of State's decision may be treated by the adjudication officer as an application for the review of the adjudication officer's decision, and for the purposes of regulation 59, the date of the claimant's application for the Secretary of State's decision shall be treated as the date of the application for review.

20.—24. *Omitted.*

Section D—Disability Adjudication

Prescribed period

25.—(1) Subject to paragraph (2), the prescribed period for the purposes of section 30(1), (2) and (4) of the Administration Act shall be three months beginning with the date on which notice in writing of the decision of an adjudication officer under section 21 of that Act was given to the claimant.

(2) Where a claimant submits an application for review under section 30(1) of the Administration Act by post which would have arrived in a local office in the ordinary course of the post within the period prescribed by paragraph (1) but is delayed by postal disruption caused by industrial action whether within the postal service or elsewhere, that period shall expire on the day the application is received in the local office if that day does not fall within the period prescribed by paragraph (1).

Manner of making applications for review under section 30(1) of the Administration Act

26. An application for a review of a decision of an adjudication officer under section 30(1), (2) and (4) of the Administration Act shall be made to a local office.

Appeal to a disability appeal tribunal

27.—(1) The claimant may appeal to a disability appeal tribunal from a decision of an adjudication officer under section 30(1) of the Administration Act in any case in which there arises—

(a) a disability question; or

(b) both a disability question and any other question relating to attendance allowance, disability living allowance or disability working allowance.

(2) In this regulation "disability question" means a question as to—

(a) whether the claimant satisfies the conditions for entitlement to—

(i) the care component of a disability living allowance specified in section 72(1) and (2) of the Contributions and Benefits Act, or

(ii) the mobility component of a disability living allowance specified in section 73(1), (8) and (9) of the Contributions and Benefits Act, or

(iii) an attendance allowance specified in sections 64 and 65(1) of the Contributions and Benefits Act; or

(iv) a disability working allowance specified in sections 129(1)(b) of the Contributions and Benefits Act;

(b) the period throughout which the claimant is likely to satisfy the conditions for entitlement to an attendance allowance or a disability living allowance;

(c) the rate at which an attendance allowance is payable; and

(d) the rate at which the care component or the mobility component of a disability living allowance is payable.

General Note

Para. (1). In any case concerning attendance allowance, disability living allowance or disability working allowance, an appeal may be brought against a decision of an adjudication officer under s.33(1) of the Social Security Administration Act 1992 only if there has first been an application for a review under s.30(1) of the 1992 Act within the period prescribed by reg. 25.

Under s.33(1), an appeal lies to a disability appeal tribunal if a disability question arises whether with, or without, any other question. If no disability question arises, the appeal lies to a social security appeal tribunal.

Para. (2). The principal disability questions are broadly whether, and for what period, the claimant satisfies:

(i) for the care component of disability living allowance, the attendance conditions;

(ii) for the mobility condition of disability living allowance, the basic mobility conditions and the condition that his or her condition should be such as permits the claimant from time to time to benefit from enhanced facilities for locomotion;

(iii) for attendance allowance, the attendance conditions;

(iv) for disability working allowance, the condition that he or she should have a physical or mental disability which puts him or her at a disadvantage in getting a job.

It is not entirely clear why specific provision is made to include questions as to the rate of attendance allowance or disability living allowance, but it may have been simply for certainty.

Persons who may appeal to disability appeal tribunals and appeal tribunals

28. A person purporting to act on behalf of a person who is terminally ill as defined in section 66(2) of the Administration Act, whether or not that other person is acting with his knowledge or authority, may appeal to a disability appeal tribunal or an appeal tribunal, as appropriate, in accordance with section 33(1) of that Act in any case where the ground of appeal is that that person is or was at any time terminally ill.

General Note

Usually a claim or appeal must be made by the claimant in person but ss.66(2)(b) and 76(3) of the Social Security Contributions and Benefits Act 1992 permit claims to be made on behalf of terminally ill people with or without their knowledge. This regulation enables an appeal in such a case to be brought on behalf of the claimant with or without the claimant's knowledge. There does not appear to be any similar provision in respect of appeals to a Commissioner.

Procedure for disability appeal tribunals

29.—[[2](1) Where an appeal is made to a disability appeal tribunal, the clerk to the tribunal shall direct every party to the proceedings to notify him if that party wishes an oral hearing of that appeal to be held.

(1A) A notification under paragraph (1) shall be made within 10 days of receipt of the direction from the clerk to the tribunal or within such other period as the clerk to the tribunal or the chairman of the tribunal may direct.

(1B) Where the clerk to the tribunal receives notification in accordance with paragraph (1A) the disability appeal tribunal shall hold an oral hearing.

(1C) The chairman of a disability appeal tribunal may of his own motion require an oral hearing to be held if he is satisfied that such a hearing is necessary to enable the tribunal to reach a decision.]

(2) Where any member of a disability appeal tribunal is not present at the consideration of a case the tribunal shall not proceed to determine that case but shall instead adjourn it for consideration by another tribunal.

(3) Where an oral hearing is adjourned and at the hearing after the adjournment the tribunal is differently constituted, otherwise than through the operation on that occasion of paragraph (2), the proceedings at that hearing shall be by way of a complete rehearing of the case.

(4) Where a disability appeal tribunal is unable to reach a unanimous decision on any case the decision of the majority of its members shall be the decision of the tribunal.

[2(5) Every decision of a disability appeal tribunal shall be recorded in summary by the chairman in such written form of decision notice as shall have been approved by the President, and such decision notice shall be signed by the chairman.

(6) As soon as may be practicable after a case has been decided by a disability appeal tribunal, a copy of the decision notice made in accordance with paragraph (5) shall be sent or given to every party to the proceedings who shall also be informed of—

(a) his right under paragraph (6C); and

(b) the conditions governing appeals to a Commissioner.

(6A) A statement of the reasons for the tribunal's decision and of its findings on questions of fact material thereto may be given—

(a) orally at the hearing; or

(b) in writing at such later date as the chairman may determine.

(6B) Where the statement referred to in paragraph (6A) is given orally, it shall be recorded in such medium as the chairman may determine.

(6C) A copy of the statement referred to in paragraph (6A) shall be supplied to the parties to the proceedings if requested by any of them within 21 days after the decision notice has been sent or given, and if the statement is one to which sub-paragraph (a) of that paragraph applies, that copy shall be supplied in such medium as the chairman may direct.

(6D) If a decision is not unanimous, the statement referred to in paragraph (6A) shall record that one of the members dissented and the reasons given by him for dissenting.]

[1(7) A record of the proceedings at the hearing shall be made by the chairman in such medium as he may direct and preserved by the clerk to the tribunal for 18 months, and a copy of such record [2. . .] shall be supplied to the parties if requested by any of them them within that period.]

AMENDMENTS

1. The Social Security (Adjudication) and Child Support Amendment Regulations 1996 (S.I. 1996 No. 182), reg. 2(4) (February 28, 1996).

2. The Social Security (Adjudication) and Child Support Amendment (No. 2) Regulations 1996 (S.I. 1996 No. 2450), reg. 12 (October 21, 1996).

GENERAL NOTE

Paras. (1) to (1C). For the procedure on oral hearings, see reg. 4. Note that no oral hearing is required on an application (*e.g.* to set aside an earlier decision) as opposed to an appeal. Note also *President's Circular No. 4* in respect of domiciliary hearings.

S.32(7)(a) of the Social Security Administration Act 1992 provides that an appeal shall lapse if an adjudication officer reviews the decision under appeal and considers that the decision made on the review gives the claimant everything he or she seeks on the appeal.

Para. (2). Unlike a social security appeal tribunal, a disability appeal tribunal cannot function with one member missing.

Para. (3). If a tribunal is differently constituted after an adjournment, the new tribunal must start from scratch, even if one or two of the members of the new tribunal were also members of the earlier one. In *R(U) 3/88*, it was suggested that, if it was not possible to have the same tribunal as before, an effort should be made to have a completely different one so that all members of the tribunal have then heard exactly the same evidence. The chairman's note of evidence from the earlier hearing is itself evidence for the new tribunal (*R(S) 1/89*), but the parties at the new hearing should be given a proper opportunity to comment upon it. They may agree that it should be accepted as an agreed statement of facts and it may, therefore, not be necessary to go through all the evidence orally again. However, a tribunal should make it plain that all issues are at large again and that the new tribunal is not fettered by anything said by the earlier tribunal during the course of discussion (*R(U) 3/88*). Generally, a tribunal adjourning a case should not make findings of fact, but there is no reason in principle why, if a number of issues are before the tribunal, they should not make decisions on some questions and adjourn consideration of others (compare an adjudication officer's position under s.20 of the Social Security Administration Act 1992). The wisdom of doing that may depend on the extent to which the issues are really separate from each other, as any risk of inconsistent decisions should be avoided. If a disability appeal tribunal is able to determine any disability question as defined in reg. 27(2) but is unable to determine some other question without adjourning, it would appear that that other question must still be determined by a disability appeal tribunal rather than a social security appeal tribunal because the claimant will have appealed "to a disability appeal tribunal". A power to transfer appeals might occasionally be useful.

The reference to para. (2) is a little strange as an incomplete tribunal can never have considered the merits of a case.

Para. (5). The fact that a decision must be recorded in writing does not mean that it cannot also be given orally. Indeed, it is the policy of the Independent Tribunal Service that decisions should usually be given orally at the end of the hearing (see *President's Circular No. 2*). However, the decision is not effective until it is recorded in writing and it may be recalled at any time until the chairman signs the record if the tribunal realises that it has made an error (*CI/141/87*).

It is the responsibility of the chairman to record the decision of the tribunal, and not the responsibility of the whole tribunal. If an appeal is dismissed, it may be necessary to say no more than "appeal dismissed" because the adjudication officer's decision stands. However, if the appeal is allowed, a decision should be recorded in clear terms making it quite clear what has been decided. The terms may need to be quite technical and should include any relevant dates. A defective decision may be corrected under reg. 9.

Paras. (6A) and (6B). Note that reasons given orally under para. (6A)(a) must be recorded under para. (6B). In the light of the right to request reasons under para. (6C), the word "may" in para. (6A) makes it a matter of discretion whether the reasons be given orally or in writing but does not permit no reasons at all to be given, at least if a request is made within the permitted time. *President's Circular No. 2* envisages short reasons being given on the notice of decision issued under paras. (5) and (6) if the chairman does not propose to issue a full statement under para. (6A) unless requested to do so.

If a full statement of reasons is inadequate, the tribunal's decision is rendered erroneous in point of law and will be liable to be set aside on appeal to a Commissioner (*R(A) 1/72, R(SB) 26/83*. The extent to which reasons need be provided varies immensely depending on the nature of the evidence and the case (*R(SB) 5/81*). In some cases, it may be sufficient simply to adopt the reasoning set out in a written submission of the successful party. In other cases, more detailed reasons may be required. In *R(A) 1/72*, the Commissioner said that the "obligation to give reasons for the decision . . . imports a requirement to do more than only to state the conclusion . . . the minimum requirement must at least be that the claimant looking at the decision should be able to discern on the face of it the reasons why . . . evidence has failed to satisfy the authority". In *Baron v. Secretary of State for Social Services* (reported as an appendix to *R(M) 6/86*), the Court of Appeal referred to an approach previously adopted in the context of both industrial tribunals and immigration appeal tribunals. "The overriding test must always be: is the tribunal providing both parties with the materials which will enable them to know that the tribunal has made no error of law in reaching its findings of fact?". That test is most likely to be satisfied if the reasons deal with specific contentions advanced by the parties and make clear findings on those points most obviously in issue. Attempts to fudge findings to avoid embarrassing the parties are likely to lead to errors of law. A tribunal should state what evidence was accepted and what was rejected (*R(SB) 8/84*). There is now a statutory duty to make a record of the proceedings (see para. (7)) and, if reference is made to that note, the reasoning required under para. (6A) can often be quite brief. That being so, it will often be much easier for a chairman to give a full statement of reasons without waiting for a request, rather than giving only partial reasons in the notice of decision with the risk of having to give fuller reasons much later. The guidance given to medical appeal tribunals in *Kitchen and Others v. Secretary of State for Social Services* (*The Times*, September 14, 1993) (see the note to reg. 38(4)) is equally applicable to disability appeal tribunals and, indeed, it was suggested in *R(M) 1/93* (decided before *Kitchen*) that disability appeal tribunals have a greater obligation to give reasons for rejecting other medical opinions than medical appeal tribunals have. The medical member of a disability appeal tribunal was said to be ''an expert juryman rather than an expert witness'', there being no medical examination. Claims for disability living allowance also throw up special problems. There are two components and, even though a claimant may specifically claim entitlement only to one, if the evidence raises the serious possibility of entitlement to the other, the tribunal must deal with it in their decision (*R(DLA)*1/95). Similarly, they must deal with all possibly relevant grounds upon which the claimant might be entitled to either component. However, a tribunal does not err in law if the reasons do not deal with an issue that did not fairly arise on the evidence. In *CDLA/899/94*, a tribunal did not consider whether there was a need for supervision arising from a tendency on the part of the claimant to fall but the Commissioner dismissed the claimant's appeal because, on the undisputed evidence, it was not arguable that the claimant reasonably reqired supervision throughout the day to avoid substantial danger to himself or others. Continuation claims also give rise to difficulties if a tribunal decide that no, or a lower, award should be made on the new claim. The claimant is entitled to an explanation for the decision not to continue the earlier award (*CM/20/94*).

Para. (6C). This is a highly contentious provision. At first sight, it implies that no statement need be issued after 21 days. However, it does not say that no statement may be issued after that date and *President's Circular No. 2* suggests that ''a chairman may, at his/her discretion, agree to issue decision even though the request is made outside the 21 day period''. Until these amendments were made, claimants always received a full statement of reasons with the notice of decision and the time for appealing was three months from the date the notice was sent. Now a statement of reasons need not be issued unless it is requested and the request is expected to be made within three weeks of the notice being sent. The time for appealing may have been extended to three months from the date the *statement of reasons* is sent, but the right of appeal is conditional on a statement being obtained. The three week time-limit is, therefore, as important as the formal three month time-limit for lodging an appeal. It is arguable that, unless there is a particular reason why a chairman is unable to provide a statement of reasons after the 21 day period has elapsed (in which case he or she could make the reason known), he or she should provide a statement if asked to do so within three months or so of the hearing, so as not unreasonably to deprive the applicant of the right to make an appeal. See further the note to reg. 32.

Para. (7). Until this paragraph was inserted, it was not an express statutory requirement that a record of proceedings had to be kept, although it had been held that a failure to do so could, where there was a dispute as to had happened at the hearing, lead to a decision being held to be erroneous in point of law (*CSSB/212/87*). The record should include a note of evidence, a note of the submissions of each party and a note of any procedural matter that arose and was resolved during the hearing. The notes need not be verbatim. The record of proceedings is likely to be particularly important if an appeal is brought without a full statement of reasons having been provided by the chairman. Even where there is a full statement of reasons, a proper record of proceedings is required where the question on the appeal is whether the reasons are adequate for compliance with the duty to provide reasons under either para. (6A) or para. (6C) (*CDLA/16902/96*). It is suggested that the record of proceedings should always be provided with any written statement of reasons.

Examination and report by a medical practitioner

30. The condition which must be satisfied if a person who may be nominated as chairman of a disability appeal tribunal is to refer a claimant to a medical practitioner for examination and report is that the person who may be so nominated is satisfied that an appeal by the claimant cannot be properly determined unless the claimant is examined by a medical practitioner and the medical practitioner has provided the disability appeal tribunal with information for use in determining the appeal.

General Note

This regulation establishes the condition which must be satisfied before a chairman may refer a claimant for a medical report under s.55(1) of the Social Security Administration Act 1992. S.55(1) is concerned with references made before a hearing takes place, as s.53 of the Social Security Administration Act 1992 permits a tribunal (not just the chairman) to refer a claimant for examination and report, whether or not the condition set out in this regulation is satisfied.

Persons who may not act as members of disability appeal tribunals

31.—(1) A person shall not act as a member of a disability appeal tribunal in any case if he—

(a) is or may be directly affected by that case; or

(b) has taken any part in such case as an assessor, a medical practitioner who has regularly attended the claimant or to whom any question has been referred for report or advice, or as a witness.

(2) If a disability appeal tribunal is unable to determine a question by reason of the provisions of paragraph (1) the case shall be referred to another such tribunal.

General Note

This regulation is not exhaustive but makes it clear that certain people may not act as members of tribunals in particular cases. The rules of natural justice may prevent other people from sitting because they know one of the parties personally or professionally. A doctor who has attended a claimant once or twice but not "regularly", and not as a consultant asked to report or advise, is not excluded by the regulation but should declare his or her knowledge of the claimant. The tribunal would then have to consider whether he or she should sit to hear that particular appeal, bearing in mind that the rules of natural justice prohibit the appearance of bias as well as actual bias and considering the date and extent of the attendance and its connection with the issues before the tribunal. In *CDLA/224/94*, it was held that being an adjudicating medical practitioner appointed under s. 49 of the Social Security Administration Act 1992 was not a bar *per se* to being a member of a disability appeal tribunal.

Application for leave to appeal from a disability appeal tribunal to a Commissioner

32. [[1](1) Subject to the following provisions of the regulation, and application to the chairman of a disability appeal tribunal for leave to appeal to a Commissioner from a decision of a disability appeal tribunal shall—

(a) be made in accordance with regulations 3 and Schedule 2; and

(b) have annexed to it a copy of the full statement of the tribunal's decision.]

(2) Where an application in writing for leave to appeal is made by an adjudication officer, the clerk to the tribunal shall, as soon as may be practicable, send a copy of the application to every other party to the proceedings.

(3) The decision of the chairman on an application for leave to appeal shall be recorded in writing and notice of it shall be given to every party to the proceedings.

(4) Where in any case it is impracticable, or it would be likely to cause undue delay, for an application for leave to appeal against a decision of a disability appeal tribunal to be determined by the person who was the chairman of that tribunal, that application shall be determined by any other person qualified under section 43(5) of the Administration Act to act as a chairman of disability appeal tribunals.

Amendment

1. The Social Security (Adjudication) and Commissioners Procedure and Child Support Commissioners (Procedure) Amendment Regulations 1997 (S.I. 1997 No. 955), reg. 4 (April 28, 1997).

GENERAL NOTE

Para. (1). Under the new para. (1), an application may no longer be made orally. It must be made in writing and be sent to the clerk to the tribunal, within three months of the full statement of reasons being issued under reg. 29(6A) (see reg. 3 and Para. 9 of Sched. 2). The requirement that the application have annexed to it a full statement of reasons (which, by reg. 1(2), means a statement issued under reg. 29(6A)) has effectively reduced the time for considering whether or not to appeal because reg. 29(6A) requires a statement to be issued only if it is requested within 21 days of the issue of the tribunal's decision. Formally, the time for appealing has been enlarged because the three months now runs from the date the full statement of reasons under reg. 29(6A) was issued. This is all very well if the claimant is represented or immediately appreciates that he or she might have grounds for appealing, but it may take an unrepresented claimant longer than 21 days to obtain advice and it will then be too late to *require* the chairman to issue a statement, However, it is open to a chairman to issue a full statement of reasons if it is requested after 21 days has expired and it is suggested that he or she should consider doing so whenever an application for leave to appeal is received in a case where full reasons have not been given. It is arguable that, if a chairman considers it appropriate to reject an application because there is no statement of reasons, he or she should not refuse to admit the application at all but should admit it and then refuse leave so that the applicant can renew the application to a Commissioner who may consider whether to waive the irregularity. It would be open to the chairman to make it plain that he or she had decided not to provide a full statement of reasons and that the lack of the full statement of reasons was the reason why leave was being refused. In many cases, it will be possible to deal with an appeal without a full statement of reasons and so the lack of such a statement need not be fatal. There seems no reason why a chairman should not grant leave to appeal in such a case on the ground that nothing is required beyond the brief reasons provided in the decision notice.

There is no right of appeal against a refusal of leave by a chairman. Instead, an unsuccessful applicant should make a fresh application for leave direct to a Commssioner, in writing within 42 days of notification of the chairman's refusal (reg. 3 of the Social Security Commissioners Procedure Regulations 1987).

A party may appeal to a Commissioner only on the ground that the tribunal's decision was erroneous in point of law (s.34 of the Social Security Administration Act 1992), so leave to appeal should not be given unless the applicant has an arguable point of law.

Para. (2). This simply warns other parties of the application. See reg. 37 of the Social Security (Claims and Payments) Regulations 1987 for circumstances in which payment may be suspended pending the determination of an application for leave to appeal and any subsequent appeal. A failure to comply with this paragraph does not render invalid a chairman's grant of leave to appeal (*CDLA/1215/96*).

Para. (3). There is no requirement to give reasons for a grant or refusal of leave to appeal. It may occasionally be helpful for a chairman to explain briefly why leave has been given if a claimant has an arguable point of law which is not well expressed in his or her grounds for applying for leave.

Para. (4). Generally, an application for leave to appeal is considered by the chairman who actually sat on the tribunal whose decision is being challenged. However, if that is not practical, or would cause undue delay, the application will be determined by another chairman, usually by a full-time chairman.

Procedure of a disability appeal tribunal on receipt of a Commissioner's decision

33.—(1) Subject to the following provisions of this regulation, the provisions of these Regulations apply for the disposal by a disability appeal tribunal of a case remitted to it following an appeal to a Commissioner as if it were an original hearing of an appeal to the disability appeal tribunal.

(2) If the case is remitted to the disability appeal tribunal following an appeal to the Commissioner in which it was decided that the decision of the disability appeal tribunal was erroneous in point of law the proceedings shall, subject to any direction of the Commissioner, be by way of a complete rehearing of the appeal by persons who were not members of the tribunal which gave the erroneous decision.

General Note

Unless the Commissioner directs otherwise, any case remitted for rehearing should be completely reheard from the beginning by a tribunal consisting of people who were not members of the tribunal whose decision has been set aside by the Commissioner. Ideally, they should also not have been members of any other tribunal that has ever considered the appeal (*R(U) 3/88*).

Section E—Medical Adjudication

Construction of Section E

34. In this Section—

''adjudicating medical authority'' means, as the case may be, an adjudicating medical practitioner, a specially qualified adjudicating medical practitioner, a medical board or a special medical board;

''medical board'' means 2 or more adjudicating medical practitioners nominated by the Secretary of State to act jointly in the consideration of a case; and

''special medical board'' means a medical board of which at least 2 of the members are specially qualified adjudicating medical practitioners.

Appointment of adjudicating medical practitioners and specially qualified adjudicating medical practitioners

35.—(1) Adjudicating medical practitioners shall be appointed by the Secretary of State to act for such area or areas as may be specified in the instrument of appointment.

(2) Specially qualified adjudicating medical practitioners shall be appointed by the Secretary of State to act for such area or areas as may be specified in the instrument of appointment.

Determination of medical questions

36.—(1)(a) (i) Section 47(1) of the Administration Act shall have effect as if for the words ''an adjudicating medical practitioner'' in the second place where they occur there are substituted the words ''a medical board'';

(ii) section 47(2) of the Administration Act shall have effect as if for the words ''such a practitioner if he'' there are substituted the words ''a medical board if it'';

(b) any case which in the opinion of the Secretary of State, should be determined by more than one adjudicating medical practitioner, shall be referred to and determined by a medical board.

(2) Subject to the provisions of Section A of Part IV any question arising in connection with a claim made in respect of any of the diseases numbered B6, C15, C17, C18, C22, D1, D2, D3, D7, D8, D9, D10, D11 or D12 in Part I of Schedule 1 to the Prescribed Diseases Regulations shall be referred to an determined by a specially qualified adjudicating medical practitioner except where a question mentioned in paragraph (1) arises, in which case it shall be referred to and determined by a special medical board.

(3) Any question which falls to be determined by an adjudicating medical authority other than those within paragraphs (1) and (2) shall be referred to and determined by an adjudicating medical practitioner.

(4) Where a case has been referred to an adjudicating medical practitioner for determination the Secretary of State may, at any time before the determination is made, revoke that reference and refer the case instead to a medical board.

(5) Where a case has been referred to a medical board or a special medical board consisting of 2 members and they are unable to agree, the reference to that board shall be revoked and the case shall be referred to a board consisting of 3 members and if they are not unanimous the decision of the majority shall be the decision of the board.

(6) The Secretary of State shall appoint one of the members of any medical board or special medical board to act as chairman.

(7) A medical board or special medical board shall not determine any question unless all the members thereof are present at the consideration of that question, and if any member of the board is absent the reference to that board shall be revoked and the case shall be referred to another such board.

(8) Reasonable notice (being not less than 10 days beginning with the day on which the notice is given and ending on the day before the sitting is to take place) of the time and place at which an adjudicating medical authority will sit for the consideration of any case shall be given to the claimant and if such notice is not given or if, after such notice has been given, the claimant should fail to appear at the sitting of the authority, the authority may proceed to determine the questions referred to him or them only with the claimant's consent.

(9) For the purposes of these regulations a sitting of an adjudicating medical authority is not an oral hearing, and the only persons entitled to be present and be heard during the consideration of any question by such an authority are the claimant and any other person whom the authority may, with the consent of the claimant, allow to be present as being a person who, in his or their opinion, is likely to assist him or them in the determination of that question.

General Note

Paras. (1)–(4). These paragraphs deal with the distribution of cases between single adjudicating medical practitioners, medical boards, specially qualified adjudicating medical practitioners and special medical boards, any of which is known as an ''adjudicating medical authority'' (reg. 27). The general rule is that cases should be considered by a single adjudicating medical practitioner or specially qualified adjudicating medical practitioner unless the case concerns a review on the ground of error of fact or law, although under paras. (1)(b) and (4), the Secretary of State may decide that any other case should be determined by a medical board. Cases concerned with any of the prescribed diseases mentioned in para. (2) (all respiratory or other lung conditions) are considered by a specially qualified adjudicating medical practitioner or, in the case of a review, by a special medical board.

For the procedure to be followed in industrial disease cases, see regs. 40–51.

Paras. (5)-(7). A medical board or special medical board consists simply of two or more adjudicating medical practitioners, or as the case may be specially qualified adjudicating medical practitioners, considering a case together (regs. 34 and 35).

Para (8). A case cannot be considered in the claimant's absence without the claimant's consent. An adjudicating medical authority does *not* have the power to strike out proceedings for want of prosecution as reg. 7 applies only to tribunals.

Para. (9). Consideration of a case by an adjudicating medical authority consists primarily of a medical examination rather than a judicial hearing. Parties wishing to address arguments to an adjusting medical authority may be best advised to do so in writing.

Decisions of adjudicating medical authorities

37.—(1) An adjudicating medical authority shall in each case record his or their decision in writing in such form as may from time to time be approved by the Secretary of State and shall include in such record (which shall be signed by all members of the authority)—

(a) a statement of his or their findings on all questions of fact material to such decision; and

(b) in a case in which the decision of a medical board or special medical board consisting of three members was not unanimous, a statement that one of the members dissented and of the reasons given by him for dissenting.

(2) As soon as may be practicable, the claimant shall be sent written notice of the decision of the adjudicating medical authority, and such notice shall be in such form as may from time to time be approved by the Secretary of State and shall contain a summary of the findings of the authority, including, where the decision was not unanimous, a statement that one of the members dissented and of the reasons given by him for dissenting.

(3) A person to whom written notice of the decision of an adjudicating medical authority is sent in accordance with paragraph (2) shall be informed in writing of the conditions governing an appeal to a medical appeal tribunal.

Medical appeal tribunals

38. [[2](1) Where an appeal or reference is made to a medical appeal tribunal, the clerk to the tribunal shall direct every party to the proceedings to notify him if that party wishes an oral hearing of that appeal or reference to be held.

(1A) A notification under paragraph (1) shall be in writing and shall be made within 10 days of receipt of the direction from the clerk to the tribunal or within such other period as the clerk to the tribunal or the chairman of the tribunal may direct.

(1B) Where the clerk to the tribunal receives notification in accordance with paragraph (1A) the medical appeal tribunal shall hold an oral hearing.

(1C) The chairman of a medical appeal tribunal may of his own motion require an oral hearing to be held if he is satisfied that such a hearing is necessasry to enable the tribunal to reach a decision.]

(2) Where any member of a medical appeal tribunal is not present at the consideration of a case the tribunal shall not proceed to determine that case but shall instead adjourn it for consideration by another tribunal.

(3) Where a medical appeal tribunal are unable to reach a unanimous decision on any case the decision of the majority of its members shall be the decision of the tribunal.

[[2](4) Every decision of a medical appeal tribunal shall be recorded in summary by the chairman in such written form of decision notice as shall have been approved by the President, and such decision notice shall be signed by the chairman.

(5) As soon as may be practicable after a case has been decided by a medical appeal tribunal, a copy of the decision notice made in accordance with paragraph (4) shall be sent or given to every party to the proceedings who shall also be informed of—

(a) his right under paragraph (5C); and

(b) the conditions governing appeals to a Commissioner.

(5A) A statement of the reasons for the tribunal's decision and of its findings on questions of fact material thereto may be given—

(a) orally at the hearing; or

(b) in writing at such later date as the chairman may determine.

(5B) Where the statement referred to in paragraph (5A) is given orally, it shall be recorded in such medium as the chairman may determine.

(5C) A copy of the statement referred to in paragraph (5A) shall be supplied to the parties to the proceedings if requested by any of them within 21 days after the decison notice has been sent or given, and if the statement is one to which sub-paragraph (a) of that paragraph applies, that copy shall be supplied in such medium as the chairman may direct.

(5D) If a decision is not unanimous, the statement referred to in paragraph (5A) shall record that one of the members dissented and the reasons given by him for dissenting.]

[1(6) A record of the proceedings at the hearing shall be made by the chairman in such medium as he may direct and preserved by the clerk to the tribunal for 18 months, and a copy of such record [2. . .] shall be supplied to the parties if requested by any of them within that period.]

AMENDMENTS

1. Social Security (Adjudication) and Child Support Amendment Regulations 1996 (S.I. 1996 No. 182, reg. 2(5) (February 28, 1996).

2. Social Security (Adjudication) and Child Support Amendment (No. 2) Regulations 1996 (S.I. 1996 No. 2450, reg. 13 (October 21, 1996).

GENERAL NOTE

For the right to appeal to a medical appeal tribunal, see s.46 of the Social Security Administration Act 1992 (which is applied by reg. 44(2) to cases concerning prescribed diseases) in respect of the disablement questions and reg. 49 in respect of the diagnosis and recrudescence questions.

Paras. (1) to (1C). For the procedure on an oral hearing, see reg. 4. In addition, the medical members usually carry out a medical examination of the claimant.

Paras. (2) and (3). A medical appeal tribunal cannot proceed in the absence of a member, but its decision need not be unanimous.

Para. (4). Decisions should also be given orally unless there are good reasons for not doing so (see *President's Circular No. 2*). A decision is not invalid merely because the chairman's name is typed and his signature is not on the document (*CDLA/6166/95*).

Paras. (5A) to (5C). See the notes to the similar provisions relating to disability appeal tribunals in reg. 29(6A) to (6C). The standard of reasoning required from medical appeal tribunals was considered by the Court of Appeal in *Kitchen and Others v. Secretary of State for Social Services* (*The Times*, September 14, 1993). Neill L.J. gave the following guidance:

> "(1) The decision should record the medical question or questions which the tribunal is required to answer. Provided the questions are set out and the answers are directed to the questions it should then be possible for the parties to know the issues to which the tribunal have addressed themselves.
>
> (2) In cases where the tribunal have medically examined a claimant they should record their findings. These findings by themselves may be sufficient to demonstrate the reason why they have reached a particular conclusion.
>
> (3) Where, however, the clinical findings do not point to some obvious diagnosis it may well be necessary for the tribunal to give a short explanation as to why they have made one diagnosis rather than another. Such an explanation will be important in cases where the tribunal's diagnosis differs from a reasoned diagnosis reached by another qualified practitioner who has examined the claimant on an earlier occasion.
>
> (4) A decision on a question of causation may pose particular difficulties when one is examining the adequacy of the reasons for the decision. In some cases it may be sufficient for the tribunal to record that it is not satisfied that the present condition was caused by the relevant trauma. Where, however, a claimant has previously been in receipt of some benefit or allowance (particularly if the benefit or allowance has been paid over a long period) and there is no question of malingering or bad faith it seems to me that the tribunal should go further than merely to state a conclusion. If one accepts that the underlying principle is fairness the claimant should be given some explanation, which may be very short, to enable him or his advisers to know where the break in the chain of causation has been found. Thus it may well be that the claimant will wish to reapply and for this purpose fairness requires that, if possible, he should be told why his claim has failed."

In *CSI/36/94*, it was held that the obligation to record the tribunal's findings on examination did not preclude them from simply adopting the findings of the adjudicating medical authority if they agreed with them and they were sufficiently full. Equally, the duty to explain why the tribunal's diagnosis differs from a reasoned diagnosis given by another medical practitioner does not require a tribunal to explain why they have differed from a diagnosis given by an adjudicating medical authority without any explanation beyond bare clinical findings (*CI/422/94*). A medical appeal tribunal are regarded as an expert body (*per* Diplock J. in *R. v. Medical Appeal Tribunal, ex p. Hubble* [1958] 2 Q.B. 1) and, provided their findings of fact are clear, they are not expected to give detailed reasons for their medical judgments. The assessment of disablement is not entirely a matter of medical expertise but there is a limit to the extent to which reasons can be given for the sort of value judgments involved in such assessments. What is important is that the factual basis of the assessment should be clear and that it should also be clear that the tribunal have not erred in law in their approach to the case (see *Baron v. Secretary of State for Social Services*, reported as an appendix to *R(M) 6/86)*. It is more likely to be accepted that the tribunal considered the legislation properly if some reference is made to it.

In *CI/636/93*, a Commissioner has reiterated that the assessment of disablement is a matter of medical judgment. At para. 10, he siad:

> "Whether or how far the duty in law to give reasons for their decision extends beyond saying that the particular percentage arrived at is in the medical judgment of the tribunal a fair one on these particular facts must depend on the nature of the individual case and the issues that have been raised in it. It seems to me that the position is correctly summarised by the Commissioner in *R(I) 30/61* at paragraph 8: there may well be cases where a mere statement that the tribunal makes an assessment of a particular percentage is in itself a sufficeint record, since it implies that they think that is a fair assessment; but in other cases findings of fact and an explanation of reasons will be needed to show what evidence the tribunal have accepted or rejected as justifying the making of a smaller or larger assessment, since otherwise the claimant will be left guessing as to the basis on which the decision has been arrived at. And in a case where specific submissions backed with expert medical evidence have been addressed to them on the basis of assessment to be used, it will normally be an error of law for the tribunal simply to state their conclusion in the form of a percentage without making it clear to what extent and for what reasons they are accepting or rejecting the suggested basis, since they will not have carried out the general duty to give reasons on a material issue raised before them: see *R(I) 18/61* para. 13."

Application for leave to appeal from a medical appeal tribunal to a Commissioner

39.—[[1](1) Subject to the following provisions of this regulation, an application to the chairman of a medical appeal tribunal for leave to appeal to a Commissioner from a decision of a medical appeal tribunal shall—

(a) be made in accordance with regulation 3 and Schedule 2; and

(b) have annexed to it a copy of the full statement of the tribunal's decision.]

(2) Where an application in writing for leave to appeal is made by the Secretary of State or an adjudicating officer the clerk to the tribunal shall, as soon as may be practicable, send a copy of the application to every other party to the proceedings.

(3) The decision of the chairman on an application for leave to appeal shall be recorded in writing and notice of it shall be given to every party to the proceedings.

(4) Where in any case it is impracticable, or it would be likely to cause undue delay, for an application for leave to appeal against decision of a medical appeal tribunal to be determined by the person who was the chairman of that tribunal, that application shall be determined by any other person qualified under section 50(4) of the Administration Act to act as a chairman of medical appeal tribunals.

AMENDMENT

1. Social Security (Adjudication) and Commissioners Procedure and Child Support Commissioners (Procedure) Amendment Regulations 1997 (S.I. 1997 No. 955, reg. 5 (April 28, 1997).

GENERAL NOTE

Para. (1). See the note to reg. 32(1) which is an identical provision relating to disability appeal tribunals. There is no right of appeal against a refusal of leave by a chairman. Instead, an unsuccessful applicant should make a fresh application direct to a Commissioner, in writing within 42 days of notification of the chairman's refusal (reg. 3 of the Social Security Commissioners Procedure Regulations 1987).

A party may appeal to a Commissioner only on the ground that the tribunal's decision was erroneous in point of law (s.49 of the Social Security Administration Act 1992), so leave to appeal should not be granted unless the applicant has an arguable point of law.

Para. (2). This warns the other parties about the application. See reg. 37 of the Social Security (Claims and Payments) Regulations 1987 for the power to suspend payment pending the determination of an application for leave and any subsequent appeal. A failure to comply with this paragraph does not render invalid a chairman's grant of leave to appeal (*CDLA/1212/96*).

Para. (3). There is no requirement to give reasons for a grant or refusal to leave. It may occasionally be helpful to do so, particularly to explain why leave has been given if the point of law has not been well expressed by the applicant.

Para. (4). Generally, an application for leave to appeal is considered by the chairman who actually sat on the tribunal whose decision is being challenged. However, if that is not practical, or would cause undue delay, the application will be determined by another chairman, usually a full-time chairman.

Disqualification from acting as an adjudicating medical authority or as a member thereof or as a member of a medical appeal tribunal

40.—(1) Subject to paragraphs (2) and (3), a person shall not act as an adjudicating medical authority or as a member thereof or as a member of a medical appeal tribunal in any case if he—

(a) is or may be directly affected by that case;
(b) has taken any part in such case as a medical assessor or as a medical practitioner who has regularly attended the claimant or to whom any question has been referred for report or as an employer or as a witness; or
(c) in the case only of a medical appeal tribunal, has acted as an adjudicating medical authority, or a member thereof, to whom the case was referred.

(2) A medical practitioner to whom a question has been referred under regulation 45(1) (reference of diagnosis and recrudescence questions for medical report) shall not be precluded from acting as an adjudicating medical practitioner or a specially qualified adjudicating medical practitioner solely by reason of his having prepared, under that regulation, a report on the case of the claimant (whether in relation to the question for determination or otherwise) if he proposes to determine the question in favour of the claimant.

(3) A medical practitioner shall not be precluded from acting as a member of a special medical board for the purpose of the consideration of a case solely because he has taken part in that case as a medical practitioner to whom a question relating to any of the diseases numbered B6, C15, C17, C18, C22(b), D1, D2, D3, D7, D8, D9, D10, D11 or D12 in Part I of Schedule 1 to the Prescribed Diseases Regulations has been referred for report.

(4) If an adjudicating medical authority or a medical appeal tribunal is unable to determine a question by reason of the provisions of paragraph (1) the reference to that authority or tribunal shall be revoked and the case shall be referred to another such authority or tribunal.

General Note

This regulation is not exhaustive but it makes it clear that certain people may not act as adjudicating medical authorities or members of medical appeal tribunals in particular cases. Para. (3) is necessary because of the relatively few medical practitioners who are qualified to sit on special medical boards. A doctor who has attended the claimant once or twice but not "regularly", and not as a consultant asked to prepare a report, is not excluded from being a member of the tribunal by the regulation. Nevertheless, the rules of natural justice may still mean that it is unwise for him or her to sit as they prohibit the appearance of bias as well as actual bias. A doctor in such a situation should declare his or her position. The tribunal will then have to consider the position, taking into account the views of the parties, the date and extent of the medical attention given, its relevance to the issues before the tribunal and the likelihood of there being a suitable person on the panel of tribunal members who has not considered the claimant's case before.

Application for review involving review of decision of a medical appeal tribunal

41. Where, in the opinion of the adjudication officer, an application made under the provisions of section 47(4) of the Administration Act raises a question as to the review of a decision of a medical appeal tribunal and, by virtue of section 47(7) of that Act, such a decision may not be reviewed without the leave of a medical appeal tribunal, the adjudication officer shall submit the application to a medical appeal tribunal so that such tribunal may consider whether such leave shall be granted and shall not refer the question to an adjudicating medical authority with a view to review of that decision unless the medical appeal tribunal grant such leave.

General Note

An application for review on the ground of "unforeseen aggravation" of a medical appeal tribunal's decision on the disablement questions cannot be considered by a medical board unless a medical appeal tribunal has given leave. It is not necessary for the tribunal to hold an oral hearing for the purpose of considering the application. An unsuccessful applicant has no right of appeal but he or she could apply for judicial review of the tribunal's refusal of leave (*Bland v. Chief Supplementary Benefit Officer* [1983] 1 W.L.R. 262, also reported as *R(SB) 12/83*). As long as the claimant has an arguable case, even if it appears weak, leave to apply for the review should be given because it is not the function of the tribunal at that stage to determine the application for review itself. There may be cases where a tribunal considers it right to give reasons for a refusal so that a claimant understands the decision. Nothing in these Regulations requires a tribunal to give reasons for refusing leave to apply for a review but it is suggested that there is an obligation to give brief reasons by virtue of the Tribunals and Inquiries Act 1992, s.10, applied in *CCR/5336/95*.

Procedure of a medical appeal tribunal on receipt of a Commissioner's decision

42.—(1) Subject to the following provisions of this regulation the provisions of these regulations apply for the disposal by a medical appeal tribunal of a case remitted to it following an appeal to a Commissioner as if it were an original hearing of an appeal to the medical appeal tribunal.

(2) If, on appeal from the medical appeal tribunal to him, the Commissioner has decided that the decision of the medical appeal tribunal is not erroneous in point of law, the medical appeal tribunal need not hold a hearing for the purpose of confirming its decision.

(3) If the case is remitted to the medical appeal tribunal following an appeal to the Commissioner in which it was decided that the decision of the medical appeal tribunal was erroneous in point of law the proceedings shall, subject to any direction of the Commissioner, be by way of a complete rehearing of the appeal by persons who were not members of the tribunal which gave the erroneous decision.

General Note

Para. (1). Under s.48(6) of the Social Security Administration Act 1992, any medical appeal tribunal to whom a case is remitted must consist of persons who were not members of the tribunal which gave the erroneous decisions unless the Commissioner otherwise directs.

Para. (2). Until April 6, 1990, a Commissioner was obliged to remit a case to a tribunal even if he or she had held there to be no error of law. Since the amendment of s.112(4) of the Social Security Act 1975, this paragraph has lost its purpose. At least, it is to be hoped that there is not still a case where a decision needs to be confirmed following a Commissioner's decision that it was not erroneous in point of law.

Para. (3). A Commissioner usually directs a rehearing but may occasionally not do so where the facts found by the previous tribunal are clear. Because a Commissioner cannot give the decision which the medical appeal tribunal could have given, as is possible in the case of an appeal from a decision of a disability appeal tribunal, he or she has to remit the case to the tribunal but may direct it to proceed without a rehearing.

Part IV

Provisions Relating to Particular Benefits or Procedures

Section A—Prescribed Diseases

Construction of Section A

43.—(1) Regulation 34 applies for the construction of this Section as it applies for the construction of Section E of Part III.

(2) Except as provided in this Section any reference in Part II of the Administration Act or in these Regulations to the relevant accident shall be construed as a reference to the relevant disease and any reference to the date of the relevant accident shall be construed as a reference to the date of onset of the relevant disease.

(3) In the following provisions of this Section any question arising in connection with a claim for or award of disablement benefit—

(a) whether any person is suffering or has suffered from a prescribed disease, is referred to as a diagnosis question;

(b) whether a prescribed disease has, in fact, been contracted afresh in a case where the question arises under the provisions of regulation 7 or 8 of the Prescribed Diseases Regulations is referred to as a recrudescence question.

General Note

When considering the diagnosis question, an adjudicating medical authority or medical appeal tribunal are concerned only with the narrow question whether the claimant is suffering or has suffered from the prescribed disease. They are not concerned with the cause of the disease which is a matter for a social security appeal tribunal save to the extent that the disease is defined in Schedule 1 to the Social Security (Industrial Injuries) (Prescribed Diseases) Regulations 1985 by reference to its cause (*R(I) 4/91*). Determining the "date of onset" of a prescribed disease (see reg. 6 of the 1985 Regulations) for the purpose of a claim for disablement benefit involves the determination of a diagnosis question (*CI/189/94*).

Application of Part II of the Administration Act and of these Regulations

44.—(1) Subject to regulation 52 (review on ground of unforeseen aggravation) the provisions of section 47(5) of the Administration Act (effect of decisions as to a loss of faculty) and of section 44 of that Act (declaration that an accident is an industrial accident) shall not apply in relation to prescribed diseases.

(2) The provisions of—

(a) Part II of the Administration Act, subject to the provisions of this Section and of Schedule 3; and

(b) these regulations, subject, in the case of the diseases numbered B6, C15, C17, C18, C22(b), D1, D2, D7, D8, D9, D10, D11 and D12 in Part I of Schedule 1 to the Prescribed Diseases Regulations, to the provisions of Part V of those Regulations,

shall apply for the determination of any question arising in connection with a claim for benefit under sections 108, 109, and 110 of the Contributions and Benefits Act in respect of a prescribed disease.

General Note

Para. (1). This has the effect that the provisions for determining whether there has been an industrial accident do not apply to cases concerning prescribed diseases. Instead, the "diagnosis" and "recrudescence" questions (defined in reg. 43(3)) are determined in accordance with regs. 45–51 and 53.

Para. (2). Taken with reg. 43(1) and (2), this has the effect that the provisions for determining the disablement questions in respect of industrial accidents apply equally to cases arising out of prescribed industrial diseases.

Reference of diagnosis and recrudescence questions for medical report

45.—(1) Subject to paragraph (2), if a diagnosis or recrudescence question arises in any case, the adjudication officer shall forthwith refer that question for report to one or more medical practitioners who, in the case of each of the diseases numbered B6, C15, C17, C18, C22(b), D1, D2, D3, D7, D8, D9, D10, D11 and D12 in Part I of Schedule 1 to the Prescribed Diseases Regulations shall be a specially qualified adjudicating medical practitioner or practitioners and shall have power, if he or they consider it to be necessary to do any or all of the following, namely—

(a) to make or cause to be made a radiological examination of the person's lungs;

(b) to obtain the report of a radiologist or other physician on the case;

(c) to make or cause to be made serological or lung function tests or such other tests as he or they consider necessary;

(d) to obtain reports upon the results of such tests.

(2) The adjudication officer may determine a diagnosis or recrudescence question without referring it as provided by paragraph (1) if he is satisfied that such reference can be dispensed with having regard to—

(a) a medical report signed by a medical practitioner on the staff of a hospital at which the claimant is receiving or has received treatment for a condition due to a prescribed disease, or by a medical officer engaged at the place of work where the claimant is or was employed; or

(b) the decision on any similar diagnosis or recrudescence question which has been determined on the consideration of any previous claim or question arising in respect of the same disease suffered by the same person (including the date and terms of any medical reports on which such previous decision was based and of any medical certificates submitted by the claimant),

so however that a reference for report shall not be dispensed with on the grounds specified in sub-paragraph (a) of this paragraph except where a diagnosis question is determined in favour of the claimant or where a recrudescence question arises in connection with a diagnosis question which has been so determined under this regulation.

(3) The adjudication officer may, if he is satisfied that a reference for report as provided in paragraph (1) may be dispensed with on any of the grounds specified in paragraph (2), refer for the decision of a special medical board any diagnosis or recrudescence question in connection with a claim in respect of each of the diseases numbered B6, C15, C17, C18 and C22(b), without having referred such a question for report.

(4) If the adjudication officer is of the opinion that the claim or question submitted to him or any part thereof can be disposed of without determining any diagnosis or recrudescence question, he may make an award or determine that an award cannot be made or may determine the question submitted to him accordingly without referring such diagnosis or recrudescence question for report as aforesaid or before so referring it.

(5) Where the assessed extent of a person's disablement in respect of a prescribed disease amounts to one per cent. or more and during the period taken into account by that assessment, the beneficiary either—

(a) applies for a review of such assessment; or

(b) makes a further claim for disablement benefit in respect of a fresh attack of the disease;

any recrudescence question arising on such application or further claim instead of being referred for report as aforesaid shall be referred for decision to a medical board together with any disablement question which arises.

(6) The provisions of this regulation apply to an appeal tribunal as they apply to an adjudication officer with the modification that an appeal tribunal, instead of themselves referring a diagnosis or recrudescence question to a medical practitioner in accordance with paragraph (1), shall direct the adjudication officer to refer it to an adjudicating medical authority in accordance with regulation 46.

General Note

Paras. (1)–(3). The first step in determining these questions is taken by the adjudication officer obtaining a medical report. However, such a report need not be obtained if there is other medical evidence as specified in para. (2) *and* it is proposed either to determine the question in the claimant's favour or to refer it to a special medical board under para. (3).

Para. (4). No report need be obtained if it is not necessary to determine the diagnosis or recrudescence question.

Para. (5). If a recrudescence question arises on an application for a review of an assessment of disablement, or a fresh claim during the period of an existing assessment, the recrudescence question may be referred to the medical board dealing with the disablement questions instead of being referred separately to a medical practitioner for a report.

Para. (6). "Appeal tribunal" means a social security appeal tribunal (reg. 1(2)), so this refers only to a case where the diagnosis or recrudescence question first arises in the course of an appeal to such a tribunal.

Procedure on receipt of medical report

46.—(1) If a diagnosis or recrudescence question has been referred as provided by regulation 45(1), the adjudication officer shall, subject to the provisions of paragraph (4) [[1]and of regulation 47(1)], proceed with the consideration of that question as soon as possible after he has received the report of the medical practitioner or practitioners to whom it was so referred.

(2) If the question so referred was a diagnosis question, then, subject to regulation 47(1), the adjudication officer may himself determine the question or refer it to an adjudicating medical authority for decision.

(3) If the question so referred was a recrudescence question, then, subject to regulation 47, the adjudication officer—

(a) if he is satisfied having regard to the report that the disease ought to be treated as having been, in fact, contracted afresh, shall so treat it and shall determine the question accordingly;

(b) if he is not so satisfied, shall treat the disease as a recrudescence of the previous attack or as not having developed on or after 5th July 1948, as the case may require, and shall determine the question accordingly.

(4) Subject to the provisions of these Regulations, the provisions of sections 22, 25 to 29, 37 and 69 of the Administration Act shall apply as if a diagnosis or recrudescence question were a question such as is referred to in section 37(1) of that Act and as if references in those sections to the determination of, or to the review of the decision of, such a question included references to the determination of, or to the review of the decision of, a diagnosis or recrudescence question under these regulations.

Amendment

1. Social Security (industrial Injuries) (Miscellaneous Amendments) Regulations 1997 (S.I. 1997 No. 810), reg. 2 (April 9, 1997).

General Note

Para. (2). The adjudication officer will usually either determine the question or refer it to a medical board. Reg. 47 provides for circumstances in which the question *must* be referred.

Para. (3). See regs. 5–7 of the Social Security (Industrial Injuries) (Prescribed Diseases) Regulations 1985 for the significance of the recrudescence question.

Para. (4). This provision is necessary because appeals from, or reviews of, diagnosis and recrudescence questions are, by virtue or regs. 48 and 53, considered by medical boards (and not by social security appeal tribunals and adjudication officers as would have been required by the Social Security Administration Act 1992).

Restriction of adjudication officer's power to determine diagnosis and recrudescence questions

47.—[[1](1) Where a diagnosis or recrudescence question is referred to one or more medical practitioners for report under regulation 45(1) and they consider that a disablement question arises they shall refer the diagnosis or recrudescence question and the disablement question to an adjudicating medical authority.]

(2) If a diagnosis question is referred to a medical board under the provisions of regulations 46 or 48, the adjudication officer shall not himself determine any recrudescence question which arises in connection therewith but shall refer it to the medical board together with the diagnosis question.

Amendment

1. Social Security (Industrial Injuries) (Miscellaneous Amendments) Regulations 1997 (S.I. 1997 No. 810), reg. 3 (April 9, 1997).

General Note

Para. (1). A disablement question (see s.45(1) of the Social Security Administration Act 1992) will always arise if a diagnosis question is determined in the claimant's favour on a claim for disablement benefit. It follows that an adjudication officer may determine a diagnosis question on a claim for disablement benefit only if he or she proposes to find that the claimant is not suffering and has not suffered from the prescribed disease. In any other case, the diagnosis question must be referred to the adjudicating medical authority.

Appeal against decision of adjudication officer

48.—(1) Where, under the provisions of regulation 45 or 46, an adjudication officer has decided a diagnosis question or a recrudescence question the claimant shall be notified in writing of the decision, of the reasons for it and of his right of appeal under paragraph (2).

(2) A claimant may appeal any decision mentioned in paragraph (1) to a medical board in accordance with the provisions of regulation 3 and Schedule 2.

(3) If an appeal is made against a decision on a recrudescence question, the adjudication officer shall also refer the diagnosis question, and the adjudicating medical authority may confirm, reverse or vary the decision on that question as on an appeal.

(4) If a diagnosis or recrudescence question is referred to an adjudicating medical authority to which there is also referred a disablement question and the decision of the adjudicating medical authority on the diagnosis or recrudescence question enables the case to be decided adversely to the claimant, the adjudicating medical authority shall not determine the disablement question.

General Note

Para. (4). A medical board is expressly forbidden to determine a disablement question if it is not necessary to do so. There does not appear to be any equivalent provision in respect of medical appeal tribunals, but the same approach would be justified.

[[1]Powers of adjudicating medical authority upon determining the question referred

48A. Where a diagnosis or recrudescence question is referred to an adjudicating medical authority, that authority upon determining the question referred—

(a) may proceed to determine any diagnosis or recrudescence question which arises in connection therewith and any disablement question which arises in consequence thereof; and

(b) if it is determined that the disease is a recrudescence of an attack to which an earlier decision of an adjudicating medical authority or a medical appeal tribunal relates, may proceed to review that earlier decision under the provisions of section 47(4) of the Administration Act.]

AMENDMENT

1. Social Security (Industrial Injuries) (Miscellaneous Amendments) Regulations 1997 (S.I. 1997 No. 810), reg. 4 (April 9, 1997).

GENERAL NOTE

Where there is a decision that there has been a recrudescence, it will often follow that there should be consideration whether an existing assessment of disablement should be reviewed. This new regulation enables that question to be considered at once.

Appeal or reference to a medical appeal tribunal

49.—(1) A claimant may appeal the decision of an adjudicating medical authority on a diagnosis or recrudescence question and in that event the case shall be referred to a medical appeal tribunal.

(2) If the adjudication officer is of the opinion, or if the Secretary of State notifies the adjudication officer that he is of the opinion, that any decision of an adjudicating medical authority on a diagnosis or recrudescence question ought to be considered by a medical appeal tribunal, the adjudication officer shall refer the case to a medical appeal tribunal for their consideration and the tribunal may confirm, reverse or vary the decision as on an appeal.

GENERAL NOTE

This provision is necessary because s.46 of the Social Security Administration Act 1992 is concerned only with appeals on the disablement questions.

An appeal must be brought, or a reference sought, by giving notice in writing to the local office within three months of notification of the medical board's decision being sent to the parties (reg. 3 and Sched. 2, applied by reg. 44(2)(b)).

For the procedure before, and the powers and duties of, medical appeal tribunals, see regs. 4, 38 and 50.

Powers of medical appeal tribunal upon determining the question referred

50. Where a diagnosis or recrudescence question is referred to a medical appeal tribunal that tribunal, upon determining the question referred—

(a) may proceed to determine any diagnosis or recrudescence question which arises in connection therewith and any disablement question which arises in consequence thereof and where a decision on any such question has been given by an adjudicating medical authority, may confirm, reverse or vary that decision; and

(b) if it is determined that the disease is a recrudescence of an attack to which an earlier decision of a medical board or a medical appeal tribunal relates, may proceed to review that earlier decision under the provisions of section 47(4) of the Administration Act.

General Note

A medical appeal tribunal allowing a claimant's appeal on a diagnosis question may go on to determine the disablement questions notwithstanding that the adjudicating medical practitioner has not made any decision on those questions due to reg. 48(4). Logically, there falls to be determined between the diagnosis and disablement questions the question whether the prescribed disease has been caused by the relevant occupation. That question does not fall within the jurisdiction of a medical appeal tribunal (*R(I) 4/91*). If a tribunal determine the diagnosis question in favour of the claimant, they may nevertheless go on to determine the disablement questions without waiting for the question of causation to be determined, particularly if they are of the opinion that the causation question is likely to be resolved in the claimant's favour. However, they may adjourn consideration of the disablement questions until the issue of causation has been determined if they consider it impractical to make a proper assessment before the causation question has been determined (*CI/701/93, CI/738/93*).

If an attack of an industrial disease is not a recrudescence of an earlier one, entitlement to disablement benefit is determined on the basis of a new claim. However, if it is a recrudescence of an old attack, any assessment of disablement in respect of the earlier attack may fall to be reviewed on the ground that there has been unforeseen aggravation of the effects of the old attack. A medical appeal tribunal finding that there has been recrudescence may proceed to carry out the necessary review, notwithstanding that question has not been determined by a medical board. For the period to be covered by the review, see reg. 62(b).

Review of previous assessment following recrudescence decision

51. Where, by reason of the provisions of regulation 7(4) of the Prescribed Diseases Regulations, the decision on a recrudescence question necessitates the review of a previous assessment of disablement, the adjudicating medical authority may review such previous assessment, as provided by section 47 of the Administration Act, so however that, in any such case, notwithstanding the provisions of subsection (7) of that section, a previous assessment may be reviewed as provided by this regulation at any time without the leave of a medical appeal tribunal.

General Note

If there is a finding that an attack of an industrial disease is a recrudescence of an earlier attack, it is likely to be necessary to review any assessment of disablement made in respect of the old attack. This regulation permits a medical board to do so, notwithstanding the absence of an application for a review and, in a case where it would otherwise be necessary, the consent of a medical appeal tribunal. Note that the reference in reg. 7(4) of the Prescribed Diseases Regulations to "regulation 49 of the Adjudication Regulations" referred to the 1984 Adjudication Regulations and should now be construed as a reference to this regulation.

Review on ground of unforeseen aggravation

52. Section 47(8) of the Administration Act shall have effect as if–

(a) after the words "this section" there are inserted the words "and of subsection 8A"; and

(b) the following subsection is inserted after subsection (8)–

"(8A) Where–

(a) a final assessment of the extent of disablement resulting from a loss of faculty has been made for a period limited by reference to a definite date, and

(b) an application for review on the ground that there has been unforeseen aggravation of the results of the relevant disease is made within a period of 3 months immediately following that date, the adjudicating medical authority shall determine the extent of disablement resulting from the relevant loss of faculty [[1]for the period of one month before the date of the application for review, and for any time after that date.]"

AMENDMENT

1. Social Security (Miscellaneous Amendments) (No. 2) Regulations 1997 (S.I. 1997 No. 793), reg. 8 (April 7, 1997).

GENERAL NOTE

This provision is necessary because s.47(5) and (6) does not apply to cases involving prescribed diseases. However, it only applies if the application for review is made within three months of the end of the previous period of assessment. Otherwise, a recrudescence question must be determined. The amendment brings the provision into line with reg. 62.

Review of decision on diagnosis or recrudescence question

53.—(1) Any decision on a diagnosis or recrudescence question of an adjudication officer, adjudicating medical authority or medical appeal tribunal may be reviewed at any time by a medical board if they are satisfied by fresh evidence that the decision was given in ignorance of, or was based on mistake as to, some material fact, so however that a decision of a medical appeal tribunal on a diagnosis or recrudescence question shall not be reviewed by a medical board without the leave of a medical appeal tribunal.

(2) A question may be raised with a view to the review of any decision on a diagnosis or recrudescence question by means of an application in writing to an adjudication officer, and on receipt of such application the adjudication officer shall proceed to refer such question to a medical board, so however that where in the opinion of the adjudication officer such application raises a question as to the review of a decision of a medical appeal tribunal on a diagnosis or recrudescence question, the adjudication officer shall submit the application to a medical appeal tribunal so that such tribunal may consider whether leave shall be granted and shall not refer the question to a medical board unless the medical appeal tribunal grant leave.

(3) Subject to the foregoing provisions of this regulation, a medical board may deal with a case on review in any manner in which they could deal with it on an original reference to them, and regulation 49 shall apply to a decision of a medical board in connection with an application for review as it applies to a decision on an original reference to them.

GENERAL NOTE

Para. (1). A decision on a diagnosis or recrudescence question may be reviewed only if there is "fresh evidence" which "means some evidence which the claimant was unable to produce before the decision was given, or which he could not reasonably be expected to have produced in the circumstances of the case" (*R. v. Medical Appeal Tribunal (North Midland Region), ex p. Hubble* [1959] 2 Q.B. 408, applied in *Saker v. Secretary of State for Social Services* (reported as an appendix to *R(I) 2/88*)). Whether evidence is "fresh" is a question of fact (*R(I) 27/61*).

Para. (2). A decision of a medical appeal tribunal on a diagnosis or recrudescence question may be reviewed only with the leave of such a tribunal. It is not necessary for the tribunal to hold an oral hearing or to give reasons for their decision. There is no appeal against a refusal of leave but such a refusal may be subject to judicial review (*Bland v. Chief Supplementary Benefit Officer* [1983] 1 W.L.R. 262, also reported as an appendix to *R(SB) 12/83*). If a party has an arguable case, even if it appears weak, leave should be granted as it is the function of the review medical board to decide whether the application for review should ultimately succeed. A tribunal may wish to give reasons for a refusal of leave and is arguably obliged to do so by s.10 of the Tribunals and Inquiries Act 1992.

Additional provisions relating to the powers and decisions of specially qualified adjudicating medical practitioners and special medical boards

54.—(1) Specially qualified adjudicating medical practitioners and special medical boards shall have power to make or cause to be made a radiological examination of the lungs of the claimant, and to obtain the report of a radiologist on the case, and to make or cause to be made serological, lung function and such other tests as they consider necessary and to obtain reports upon the results of such tests.

(2) Where in respect of a claim for disablement benefit by reason of prescribed disease D1 (pneumoconiosis) or D2 (byssinosis) a specially qualified adjudicating medical practitioner, special medical board or a medical appeal tribunal gives a decision under the foregoing provisions of these regulations that the claimant is or, as the case may be, was suffering from one or other of those diseases—

(a) that practitioner board or medical appeal tribunal may, on the evidence before it at the time of its decision, determine also the date from which the claimant has or, as the case may be, had suffered from that disease; and

(b) notwithstanding the provisions of section 60(1) of the Administration Act (finality of decisions), in making that determination, the practitioner board or the medical appeal tribunal shall not be bound by any previous decision of an adjudication officer, specially qualified adjudicating medical practitioner or special medical board that the claimant was not suffering from that disease; and

(c) any such previous decision, in so far as inconsistent with the said determination, shall cease to have effect.

General Note

Para. (1). Medical appeal tribunals have the power to refer claimants for examination and report under s.53 of the Social Security Administration Act 1992. So do special medical boards and it is difficult to see that reg. 54(1) adds anything.

Para. (2). This applies to medical appeal tribunals as well as special medical boards. It gives tribunals considering pneumoconiosis and byssinosis cases the power to override previous decisions to the effect that the claimant was not suffering from those diseases.

55. and **56.** *Omitted.*

Section C—Review of Decisions

Date from which revised decision has effect on a review

57.—(1) In the case of review to which either paragraph (2) or paragraph (3) applies, the decision given shall have effect from the date from which the decision being reviewed had effect or from such earlier date as the authority giving the decision being reviewed could have awarded benefit had that authority taken account of the evidence mentioned in paragraph (2) or not overlooked or misconstrued some provision or determination as mentioned in paragraph (3).

(2) This paragraph applies to a review under sections 25(1)(a), [1 30(2)(a), (4) and (5)(a), and 35(1)(a) and (3)(a)] of the Administration Act (review for error of fact) of any decision, whether that decision was made before or after the coming into force of this regulation, where the reviewing authority, that is to say the adjudication officer or, as the case may be, the appeal tribunal, is satisfied that—

(a) the evidence upon which it is relying to revise the decision under review is specific evidence which the authority which was then determining the claim or question had before it at the time of making the decision under review and which was directly relevant to the determination of that claim or question but which that authority failed to take into account; or

(b) the evidence upon which it is relying to revise the decision under review is a document or other record containing such evidence which at the time of making the submission to the authority which was then to determine the claim or question, the officer of the Department of Social Security, the Department of Employment or the former Department of Health and Social Security who made the submission had in his possession but failed to submit; or

(c) the evidence upon which it is relying to revise the decision under review did not exist and could not have been obtained at that time, but was produced to an officer of one of those Departments or to the authority which made that decision as soon as reasonably practicable after it became available to the claimant.

(3) This paragraph applies to a review under sections 25(2) and 30(2)(d) [[1]and (5)(c)] of the Administration Act (review for error of law) of any decision, whether that decision was made before or after the coming into force of this regulation, where the adjudication officer or, as the case may be, the appeal tribunal, is satisfied that the adjudication officer, in giving the decision under review, overlooked or misconstrued either—

(a) some provision in an Act of Parliament or in any Order or Regulations; or

(b) a determination of the Commissioner or the court,

which, had he taken it properly into account, would have resulted in a higher award or benefit or, where no award was made, an award of benefit.

(4) The following provisions of this section, including regulation 63, are subject to the provisions of this regulation.

(5) In this regulation "court" has the same meaning as it has in section 68 of the Administration Act.

Amendment

1. Social Security (Miscellaneous Amendments) (No. 2) Regulations 1997 (S.I. 1997 No. 793), reg. 9 (April 7, 1997).

General Note

Para. (1). The normal restrictions on the payment of arrears of benefit where a decision is revised on review (regs. 59 and 60) do not apply where paras. (2) or (3) are satisfied.

Para. (2). This is concerned with reviews on the ground of error of fact. Sub-para. (a) looks clear enough at first sight, but it is possible to foresee difficulties in deciding what is "directly relevant" and also determining whether an authority failed to take the evidence into account at all or merely gave it insufficient weight. Sub-para. (b) is clearer although the words "containing such evidence" would have been better omitted. Sub-para. (c) seems particularly tough, because it does not allow for the possibility of evidence existing which the claimant could not reasonably have obtained. The words "could not have obtained" appear, in this context, to mean "could not have been brought into existence".

Para. (3). This is concerned with reviews on the ground of error of law. Generally, this will have the effect that a claimant should not be penalised because the adjudication officer made an error of law. However, this is subject to reg. 58.

Review of decisions in cases to which section 69(1) of the Administration Act applies

58. In any case to which section 69(1) of the Administration Act applies, the decision given on review shall have effect from the date of the relevant determination within the meaning of that subsection whether the decision which is being reviewed was made before, on or after 9th March 1992.

Review of decisions involving payment or increase of benefit other than industrial injuries benefit [[1]except reduced earnings allowance], disability working allowance, income support [[2], jobseeker's allowance] or family credit

59.—(1) Where on a review a decision relating to benefit other than industrial injuries benefit [[1]except reduced earnings allowance], disability working allowance, income support [[2], jobseeker's allowance] or family credit is revised so as to make benefit payable, or to increase the rate of benefit, then subject to the following provisions of this regulation, the decision given on the review shall have effect from such date as may be specified in the decision, being [[3]one month before the date of the application for the review.]

[[3](1A) A determination on a claim or question relating to incapacity benefit may be revised on a review so as to increase the amount of incapacity benefit payable in respect of a period which falls more than one month before the date of the application for the review where the reason for the revised determination is that section 30B(4) of the Contributions and Benefits Act(**d**) applies to the claimant because he has become entitled to the highest rate of the care component of disability living allowance.

(1B) A determination on a claim or question relating to incapacity benefit or severe disablement allowance may be revised on a review so as to make incapacity benefit or severe disablement allowance payable in respect of a period which falls more than one month before the date of the application for the review where on a review under section 25(1)(a) of the Administration Act (review for error of fact), it is determined that the claimant is to be treated as incapable of work under regulation 10 of the Social Security (Incapacity for Work) (General) Regulations 1995(**e**) (certain persons with a severe condition to be treated as incapable of work).]

[[4](1C) Subject to regulation 58, where, in the case of attendance allowance or disability living allowance, the decision is reviewed under section 30(1) of the Administration Act (application within the prescribed period), or under that subsection as applied by section 31(2) or 35(8) of that Act, the decision given on review shall have effect from such date as may be specified in the decision, being a date not earlier than—

(a) where the decision being reviewed is also a review decision or a refusal to review ("the first review"), one month before the date of application for the first review;

(b) in any other case, the date of claim.]

(2) [[3]. . .]

[[3](3) A review may have effect from a date earlier than one month before the date of the application where—

(a) regulation 57 or 58 applies; or

(b) it is certified in the decision on review that the original decision was revised by reason only of—

(i) a matter specified in section 17(1)(b) of the Administration Act (contributions and earnings factors); or

(ii) a matter relating to the number of days in respect of which the claimant has been entitled or deemed to be entitled to short-term incapacity benefit.]

(4) In any case other than a case to which paragraph (5) applies in which the review to which the foregoing provisions of this regulation relate was based on a material change of circumstances subsequent to the date from which the original decision took effect, it shall not have effect for any period before the date

declared by the adjudicating authority making the review to be the date on which that change took place.

(5) In any case relating to attendance allowance or disability living allowance in which the review to which the foregoing provisions of this regulation relate was based on a relevant change of circumstances to which this paragraph applies subsequent to the date from which the original decision took effect, the decision on review shall not have effect for any period before—

(a) the date declared by the adjudicating authority making the review to be the date on which that change took place, or

(b) if more than one change has taken place between the date from which the original decision took effect and the date of the application for review, the date declared by the adjudicating authority making the review to be the date on which the most recent change took place, or

(c) the date [3one month] before the date of the application for review, whichever is the later.

(6) Paragraph (5) applies only to a relevant change of circumstances which relates to a deterioration in a person's physical or mental condition.

(7) Where a claim for an attendance allowance or a disability living allowance has been refused and either—

(a) an application for review of the decision is made under section 30(1) of the Administration Act; or

(b) a further claim for an attendance allowance or a disability living allowance is made within the period prescribed under section 30(1) of the Administration Act and is accordingly treated as an application for review in accordance with section 30(13) of that Act

then, if that review results in an award of an attendance allowance or a disability living allowance, the decision on review shall have effect from the date specified in paragraph (8).

(8) The date referred to in paragraph (7) is such date as may be specified in the decision on review being a date not later than—

(a) in the case of an attendance allowance, 6 months; and

(b) in the case of a disability living allowance, 3 months

after the date on which the application for review is made or the further claim is made which ever is appropriate.

(9) For the purposes of this regulation, where a decision is reviewed at the instance of an adjudication officer under section 25(1) or (2) of the Administration Act, the date on which the adjudication officer decided to make that review shall be deemed to be the date of the application for the review.

(10) In any case to which paragraph (1) applies, the decision on review shall not in any event have effect for any period before the date on which the original decision took effect or would have taken effect if any award had been made.

AMENDMENTS

1. Social Security (Industrial Injuries and Diseases) (Miscellaneous Amendments) Regulations 1996 (S.I. 1996 No. 425), reg. 2 (March 24, 1996).

2. Social Security (Adjudication) Amendment Regulations 1996 (S.I. 1996 No. 1518), reg. 2(4) (October 7, 1996).

3. Social Security (Miscelleaneous Amendments) (No. 2) Regulations 1997 (S.I. 1992 No. 793), reg. 10 (April 7, 1997).

4. Social Security (Claims and Payments and Adjudication) Amendment No. 2 Regulations 1997 (S.I. 1997 No. 2290), reg. 2 (October 13, 1997).

GENERAL NOTE

Para. (1). This has the effect that most reviews in favour of claimants can be effective in respect of a period no more than one month before the date of the application. Where the review is carried out by an adjudication officer of his or her own motion under s.25 of the Social Security Administration Act 1992, the date he or she decided to carry out the review is treated as the date of the application. An application for review is not required to be in any particular form and the provision of relevant information to the Benefits Agency is often treated as an application for review. A tribunal is entitled to decided what does, or does not, amount to an application for review because that question is not reserved to the Secretary of State. Para. (2), which provided for the period in respect of which arrears might be paid to be extended if there was good cause for the delay in applying for the review, has been revoked. This makes it particularly important to establish the true date of application for review. The only circumstances in which arrears may be paid in respect of a period more than than one month before the date of application for review are those set out in paras. (1A), (1B), (IC) (3)(b) and, most importantly, regs. 57 and 58.

Para (1C). This enables second tier reviews to be effective from the same date as the decision under review could have been. Reg. 7 of the Social Security (Claims and Payments and Adjudication) Amendment No. 2 Regulations 1997 makes transitional provision where the application for the first review was made on or before April 6, 1997.

Paras. (4) to (8). These have the general effect of ensuring that, where a review is based on a change of circumstances, no effect is given to that change for any period before it occurred.

Para. (9). This is limited to reviews under s.25 because reviews under ss.30 and 35 may be made only on an application.

Review of decisions involving payment or increase of industrial injuries benefit [[1]except reduced earnings allowance]

60.—(1) Except in a case to which regulation 57(2) or (3) or regulation 58 applies where on a review a decision of an adjudication officer, an appeal tribunal or a Commissioner is revised so as to make industrial injuries benefit [[1]except reduced earnings allowance] payable or to increase the rate of such benefit, the decision on review shall, subject to paragraph (2), have effect [[2]from such date as may be specified in that decision, being a date not earlier than one month before the date of the application for the review.]

(2) Paragraph (1)—

(a) shall not permit benefit to become payable from a date earlier than the earliest date from which it could have been payable had it been awarded in the decision being reviewed;

(b) in the case of a review made by virtue of section 60(5)(a) of the Administration Act (which permits the review of a decision given before the passing of the National Insurance Act 1972 that a claimant was not entitled to industrial death benefit) shall not permit benefit to become payable for any period earlier than 9th August 1972.

(3) Where a decision is reviewed at the instance of an adjudication officer under section 25(1) of the Administration Act, the date on which it was first decided by the adjudication officer that the decision should be reviewed shall be treated for the purposes of this regulation as the date of application for review.

AMENDMENTS

1. Social Security (Industrial Injuries and Diseases) (Miscellaneous Amendments) Regulations 1996 (S.I. 1996 No. 425), reg. 2 (March 24, 1996).

2. Social Security (Miscellaneous Amendments) (No. 2) Regulations 1997 (S.I. 1997 No. 793), reg. 11 (April 7, 1997).

GENERAL NOTE

This applies only to reviews of decisions of adjudication officers, social security appeal tribunals and Commissioners. Reviews of decisions of adjudicating medical authorities or medical appeal tribunals on the ground of unforeseen aggravation are also limited in their effect (see reg. 62). Reviews of decisions of adjudicating medical authorities or medical appeal tribunals on other grounds are not limited as to the period that may be considered. However, the amount of additional benefit that may be paid in consequence of such reviews will be limited because either there will be an existing award which falls to be reviewed under s.25 so that reg. 60 applies or else there will be a new claim so that reg. 19 of the Social Security (Claims and Payments) Regulations 1987 applies.

Review of medical decisions on grounds of ignorance of or mistake as to a material fact

61. A decision of an adjudicating medical authority or a medical appeal tribunal may not be reviewed under section 47(1) of the Administration Act unless the adjudicating medical authority is satisfied as mentioned in that subsection by fresh evidence.

General Note

For the meaning of "fresh evidence", see the annotation to s.47 of the Social Security Administration Act 1992. There is no provision restricting the period that may be considered by a review medical board under s.47(1) of the Social Security Administration Act 1992 but see the note to reg. 60.

Period to be taken into account by assessments revised on ground of unforeseen aggravation

62. On review of any assessment under section 47(4) of the Administration Act (review on ground of unforeseen aggravation) the period to be taken into account by any revised assessment may include any period not exceeding [1one month] before—

(a) if the review was in consequence of an application by a claimant, or a person acting on his behalf, the date of that application; or

(b) if the review was in consequence of a decision on a recrudescence question, within the meaning of regulation 43(3)(b) given under regulation 7(4) of the Prescribed Diseases Regulations (recrudescence of a prescribed disease), the date of the claim on which that decision was given,

if the medical board are satisfied that throughout that period there has been unforeseen aggravation of the results of the relevant injury since the making of the assessment under review.

Amendment

1. Social Security (Miscellaneous Amendments) (No. 2) Regulations 1997 (S.I. 1992 No. 793), reg. 12 (April 7, 1997).

General Note

A review medical board cannot consider any period more than one month before the date of the application for review, if the review is based on the ground of "unforeseen aggravation", except in those industrial disease cases where para. (b) may apply. In an industrial disease case, where the application is made within three months after the end of a period of assessment, see reg. 52.

63.—65. *Omitted.*

Review in disability working allowance cases

66.—[2(1) Where a claim for disability working allowance has been refused and a further claim for disability working allowance is made within the period prescribed under section 30(1) of the Administration Act and is accordingly treated as an application for review in accordance with section 30(13) of that Act, then if that further claim results in an award of disability working allowance, the decision on review shall have effect from the date on which the further claim is made.]

(2) Where a review under section 30(1) or (5)(a) or section 35(3)(a) of the Administration Act of a decision relating to disability working allowance arises from a disclosure of a material fact of which the person who claimed disability working allowance was, or could reasonably have been expected to be, aware but of which he previously failed to furnish information to the Secretary of State, then if that review would result in either a new award of disability working allowance or an increase in the amount of disability working allowance payable, the decision on review shall not have effect in respect of any period earlier than [[1]one month] before the date on which that person first furnished that information.

AMENDMENTS

1. Social Security (Miscellaneous Amendments) (No. 2) Regulations 1997 (S.I. 1992 No. 793), reg. 10 (April 7, 1997).
2. Income-related Benefits and Jobseeker's Allowance (Miscellaneous Amendments) Regulations 1997 (S.I. 1996 No. 65), reg. 16 (April 8, 1997).

GENERAL NOTE

Para. (1). The object of the paragraph is to enable a claimant to make a new claim within the three-month prescribed period if an initial claim was rightly rejected. It is necessary because entitlement to disability working depends very much on the claimant's circumstances at the date of claim and s.30(13) of the Social Security Administration Act 1992 would otherwise prevent the claimant from having a new date of claim. If the initial claim was *wrongly* rejected, see the note to reg. 6(11) of the Social Security (Claims and Payments) Regulations 1987.

Para. (2). This limits the effect of a review applied for within the three-month prescribed period if the review "arises from" a material fact about which the claimant could have provided information earlier. The words "arises from" are a little vague.

67. *Omitted.*

[[1]Review in attendance allowance and disability living allowance cases

67A.—(1) Failure by a person to attend for, or submit to, a medical examination under the provisions made under section 57A of the Administration Act(**a**) (medical examinations) is prescribed as a relevant change of circumstances for the purposes of section 30(2)(b) or 35(1)(b) of the Administration Act (review on the grounds of relevant change of circumstances).

(2) In the case where an award of attendance allowance or disability living allowance falls to be reviewed under section 30(2)(b) or 35(1)(b) of the Administration Act (review on the grounds of relevant change of circumstances) in the circumstances prescribed under paragraph (1), the decision given on review shall have effect from the date determined by the Secretary of State under regulation 8D(1) of the Social Security (Attendance Allowance) Regulations 1991 or regulation 5B(1) of the Social Security (Disability Living Allowance) Regulations 1991, as the case may be.]

AMENDMENT

1. Social Security (Attendance Allowance and Disability Living Allowance) (Miscellaneous Amendments) Regulations 1997 (S.I. 1997 No. 1839), reg. 4 (August 25, 1997).

GENERAL NOTE

See regs. 8C to 8D of the Social Security (Attendance Allowance) Regulations 1991 and regs. 5A to 5C of the Social Security (Disability Living Allowance) Regulations 1991.

PART V

TRANSITIONAL PROVISIONS, SAVINGS AND REVOCATIONS

Transitional provisions

68.—(1) The Social Security (Adjudication) Regulations 1986 as originally made, shall continue to apply to the adjudication of any claim or question under the National Assistance Act 1948 or the Supplementary Benefit Act 1966 as they apply to a corresponding claim or question under the Supplementary Benefits Act 1976 and to the adjudication of any claim or question under the Supplementary Benefits Act 1976 as if the present Regulations had not been made.

(2) Anything done, begun or deemed to be done or begun under the Social Security (Adjudication) Regulations 1986 shall be deemed to have been done or continued under the corresponding provisions of these Regulations.

(3) So much of any document as refers expressly or by implication to any regulation revoked by these Regulations shall, if and so far as the context permits, for the purposes of these Regulations be treated as referring to the corresponding provision of these Regulations.

(4) Nothing in paragraphs (2) and (3) shall be taken as affecting the general application of the rules for the construction of Acts of Parliament contained in sections 15 to 17 of the Interpretation Act 1978 (repealing enactments) with regard to the effect of revocations.

(5) Without prejudice to the powers conferred on the Lord Chancellor or the Lord President of the Court of Session by section 6 of the Tribunals and Inquiries Act 1992 or on the Secretary of State or the President by Part II of and Schedule 2 to the Administration Act, any person who, immediately before the coming into force of section 25 of and Schedule 8 to the 1983 Act, held a subsisting appointment as—

(a) a member of any of the panels of persons constituted under the said section 7 from which were selected chairmen of National Insurance Local Tribunals (constituted under section 97(2) of the Social Security Act 1975) or, as the case may be, of Supplementary Benefit Appeal Tribunals (constituted under Schedule 4 to the Supplementary Benefits Act) shall be deemed to have been appointed to the panel from which chairmen of appeal tribunals are selected for a period corresponding to that of his subsisting appointment;

(b) a member of either of the tribunal membership panels mentioned in section 97(2)(a) of the Social Security Act 1975 and paragraph 1(a) of Schedule 4 to the Supplementary Benefits Act (representing employers and earners other than employed earners) shall be deemed to have been appointed to the panel constituted by the President under paragraph 1(4) of Schedule 10 to the 1975 Act for a period corresponding to that of his subsisting appointment;

(c) a member of either of the tribunal membership panels mentioned in section 97(2)(b) of the Social Security Act 1975 and paragraph 1(b) of Schedule 4 to the Supplementary Benefits Act (representing employed earners) shall be deemed to have been appointed to the panel constituted by the President under paragraph 1(3) of Schedule 10 to the 1975 Act for a period corresponding to that of his subsisting appointment;

(d) a clerk to any National Insurance Local Tribunal or Supplementary Benefit Appeal Tribunal shall be deemed to have been assigned by the President as a clerk to the appeal tribunal for the area in question;

(e) a member of a pneumoconiosis medical panel (under regulation 49 of the Prescribed Diseases Regulations) shall be deemed to have been appointed as a specially qualified adjudicating medical practitioner.

69. *Omitted.*

SCHEDULES

Schedule 1

Provisions Conferring Powers Exercised in making these Regulations

Column (1)	*Column (2)*
Social Security Administration Act 1992	section 17(3) section 20(3)(b) section 22(2) and (4) section 23(9) and (10) section 26(3) section 27(1) section 30 section 31 section 32(8) section 33 section 34(4) section 35(10) section 45 section 46(2) and (3) section 47(3), (7) and (9) section 48(3) and (4) section 49 section 50(6) section 55(1) section 58 section 59 section 61(1), (2) and (3) section 62(1) and (2) section 70(1) section 159 section 189 section 190(3) section 191 Schedule 3 Schedule 10, Paragraph 3

SCHEDULE 2 **Regulation 3**

TIME LIMITS FOR MAKING APPLICATIONS, APPEALS OR REFERENCES

Column (1) *Application, appeal or reference*	Column (2) *Appropriate Office*	Column (3) *Specified time*
1. Appeal to a medical board from an adjudication officer's determination of a diagnosis or recrudescence question (regulation 48).	A local office.	3 months beginning with the date when notice in writing of the decision was given to the appellant.
2. Appeal to a medical appeal tribunal from a decision of an adjudicating medical authority, as defined in regulation 34 (section 46(2) of the Administration Act).	A local office.	3 months beginning with the date when notice in writing of the decision was given to the appellant.
3. Reference by the Secretary of State notifying the adjudication officer that a decision of an adjudicating medical practitioner ought to be considered by a medical appeal tribunal (section 46(3) of the Administration Act).	A local office.	3 months beginning with the date of the decision of the adjudicating medical practitioner.
4. Appeal to an appeal tribunal from a decision of an adjudicating officer (section 22(1) of the Administration Act).	A local office.	3 months beginning with the date when notice of the decision was given to the appellant.
5. Appeal to a disability appeal tribunal from a decision on review of an adjudication officer under section 30(1) of the Administration Act.	A local office.	3 months beginning with the date when notice in writing of the decision was given to the appellant.
6. Appeal to an appeal tribunal from a decision on a review of an adjudication officer under section 30(1) of the Administration Act.	A local office.	3 months beginning with the date when notice in writing of the decision was given to the appellant.
7. Application to the chairman for leave to appeal to a Commissioner from the decision of an appeal tribunal (regulation 24(1)).	The office of the clerk to the appeal tribunal.	3 months beginnning with the date when [[3]a copy of the full statement of the tribunal's decision was given or sent to the applicant]

Column (1) *Application, appeal or reference*	Column (2) *Appropriate Office*	Column (3) *Specified time*
8. Application to the chairman for leave to appeal to a Commissioner from the decision of a medical appeal tribunal (regulation 39(1)).	The office of the clerk to the medical appeal tribunal.	3 months beginning with the date when [[3]a copy of the full statement of the tribunal's decision was given or sent to the applicant].
9. Application to the chairman for leave to appeal to a Commissioner from the decision of a disability appeal tribunal (regulation 32(1)).	The office of the clerk to the disability appeal tribunal.	3 months beginning with the date when [[3]a copy of the full statement of the tribunal's decision was given or sent to the applicant].
10. Application to the Secretary of State with a view to a review under section 19(1) of the Administration Act of a decision under section 17(1) of that Act (regulation 16(1)).	The office of the Department of Social Security or the Department for Education and Employment from which notice of the decision was issued.	3 months beginning with the date when the Secretary of State gave the applicant notice in writing of the decision.
11. Application to an adjudicating authority to set aside decision (regulation 10(2)).	A local office of the Department of Social Security or, in the case of unemployment benefit [[2]or jobseeker's allowance], either at such an office or at a local office of the Department for Education and Employment or, in any case, at the office of the authority who gave the decision.	3 months beginning with the date when notice in writing of the decision was given to the applicant.
[[1]Appeal to an appeal tribunal against any determination of, or direction given by, and adjudication officer on a review under section 11 of the Jobseekers Act 1995	The office of the Department for Education and Employment which the claimant is required to attend in accordance with a notice under regulation 23 of the Jobseeker's Allowance Regulations 1996 (S.I. 1996/207), or any other place which he is so required to attend.	3 months beginning with the date when notice in writing of the determination or direction was given to the claimant].

AMENDMENTS

1. Jobseeker's Allowance Regulations 1996 (S.I. 1996 No. 207), reg. 42(b) (October 7, 1996).

2. Social Security (Adjudication) Amendment Regulations 1996 (S.I. 1996 No. 1518), reg. 2(8) (October 7, 1996).
3. Social Security (Adjudication) and Commissioners Procedure and Child Support Commissioners (Procedure) Amendment Regulations 1997 (S.I. 1997 No. 955), reg. 6 (April 28, 1997).

General Note

It is arguable that the requirement that a would-be appellant obtain a full statement of the tribunal's reasons is directory rather than mandatory and that, if a would-be appellant fails to do so the irregularity can be wavied. The time for appealing would then not have started to run but that is not necessarily fatal (see *CI/337/92*). Presumably the length of time that had elapsed since the decision was given and the obviousness of an error by the tribunal would be among the matters to be taken into account when considering whether to waive the irregularity.

Schedule 3 **Regulation 44(2)**

Modification of Part II of the Administration Act in its Application to Benefit and Claims and Questions to which Part IV of these Regulations Apply

1. Section 60(4) of the Administration Act shall have effect as if for the words "an accident" there were substituted the words "a prescribed disease"; as if for the words "an injury resulted in whole or in part from the accident" there were substituted the words "a person suffered from a prescribed disease"; as if for the words "that accident" there were substituted the words "that disease"; and as if for the words "the injury did so result" there were substituted the words "the person did so suffer".

2. There shall be included in the questions to be determined under the Administration Act any question—

(a) whether a person is suffering or has suffered from a prescribed disease or injury;
(b) whether a prescribed disease or injury, suffered by a person who has previously been awarded benefit under the National Insurance (Industrial Injuries) Act 1946, under the National Insurance (Industrial Injuries) Act 1965, under the Social Security Act 1975 or who is or has been in receipt of compensation under the Workmen's Compensation Acts 1925 to 1945 or under any contracting out scheme duly certified thereunder in respect of the same disease or injury, has been contracted or received afresh if and in so far as regulations made under sections 108, 109, or 110 of the Contributions and Benefits Act or section 62(1) of the Administration Act necessitate the determination of that question);

which shall, where the question arises in connection with claim for or award of sickness benefit made by virtue of section 102 of the Contributions and Benefits Act or disablement benefit, be determined as provided by regulations, by an adjudication officer in the light of medical advice or by a medical board or a medical appeal tribunal, so however that no appeal shall lie under the provisions of section 22 or 23 of the Administration Act from a decision of an adjudication officer on any such question.

Schedule 4. *Omitted.*

The Social Security (Claims and Payments and Adjudication) Amendment No. 2 Regulations 1997

(S.I. 1997 No. 2290)

The Secretary of State for Social Security, in exercise of the powers conferred by sections 5(1)(a) and (b), 27(1), 61(1), 189(1) and (3) to (5) and 191 of the Social Security Administration Act 1992, and of all other powers enabling her in that behalf, after agreement by the Social Security Advisory Committee that proposals to make these Regulations should not be referred to it, hereby makes the following Regulations:

Citation, commencement and interpretation

1.—(1) These Regulations may be cited as the Social Security (Claims and Payments and Adjudication) Amendment No. 2 Regulations 1997 and shall come into force—

(a) for the purposes of this regulation and regulation 8, on 24th September 1997.

(b) for the purposes of regulations 2 to 7, on 13th October 1997.

(2) In these Regulations—

"the Adjudication Regulations" means the Social Security (Adjudication) Regulations 1995;

"the Claims and Payments Regulations" means the Social Security (Claims and Payments) Regulations 1987.

2.—6. *Omitted.*

Transitional provision

7. In a case to which regulation 59(1)(a) of the Adjudication Regulations applies, where the application for the first review referred to in that provision was made on or before 6th April 1997, regulation 59 of the Adjudication Regulations shall apply with the following modifications—

(a) as if in paragraph (1C)(a), for the words "one month" there were substituted the words "subject to paragraph (1D), three months";

(b) as if after paragraph (1C) there were inserted the following paragraph—

"(1D) Subject to the following provisions of this regulation, in a case to which paragraph (1C)(a) applies where the claimant proves that—

(a) on a date earlier than three months before the date of the application for the first review, he was (apart from the condition of making a claim) entitled to benefit or to a higher rate of benefit; and

(b) throughout the period between that earlier date and the date on which the applications for the first review was made, there was good cause for delay in making the application,

the decision given on review shall have effect either on that earlier date or twelve months before the date on which the application for the first review was made, whichever is the later."; and

(c) as if in paragraph (5)(c) for the words "one month" there were substituted the words "three months".

8. *Omitted.*

The Social Security (Claims and Payments) Regulations 1979

(S.I. 1979 No. 628)

ARRANGEMENT OF REGULATIONS

PART I

GENERAL

PART IV

SPECIAL PROVISIONS RELATING TO INDUSTRIAL INJURIES BENEFIT ONLY

PART V

MISCELLANEOUS PROVISIONS

SCHEDULES

The Secretary of State for Social Services, in exercise of powers conferred upon him by sections 45(3), 79 to 81, 88 to 90, 146(5), and 115(1) of, and Schedule 13 to, the Social Security Act 1975 and paragraphs 9(1)(a) and (c) of Schedule 3 to the Social Security (Consequential Provisions) Act 1975 and of all other powers enabling him in that behalf, hereby makes the following regulations, which consolidate the regulations hereby revoked and which accordingly by virtue of sections 139(2) and 141(2) of the Social Security Act 1975—and paragraphs 20 of Schedule 15 and 12 of Schedule 16—are not subject to the requirements of section 139(1) and 141(2) of that Act for prior reference to the National Insurance Advisory Committee and the Industrial Injuries Advisory Council respectively:

PART I

GENERAL

Citation and commencement

1. These regulations may be cited as the Social Security (Claims and Payments) Regulations 1979 and shall come into operation on 9th July 1979.

Interpretation

2.—(1) In these regulations, unless the context otherwise requires—
"the Act" means the Social Security Act 1975;
[. . . .]
and other expressions have the same meaning as in the Act.

(1A) *Omitted.*

(2) Unless the context otherwise requires, any reference in these regulations to—

(a) a numbered section is a reference to the section of the Social Security Act 1975 bearing that number;
(b) a numbered regulation is a reference to the regulation bearing that number in these regulations and any reference in a regulation to a numbered paragraph is a reference to the paragraph of that regulation bearing that number;

(c) any provision made by or contained in an enactment or instrument shall be construed as a reference to that provision as amended or extended by any enactment or instrument and as including a reference to any provision which it re-enacts or replaces, or which may re-enact or replace it, with or without modification.

(3) and (4) *Omitted.*

3.—23. *Revoked.*

PART IV

SPECIAL PROVISIONS RELATING TO INDUSTRIAL INJURIES BENEFIT ONLY

Notice of accidents

24.—(1) Every employed earner who suffers personal injury by accident in respect of which benefit may be payable shall give notice of such accident either in writing or orally as soon as is practicable after the happening thereof:

Provided that any such notice required to be given by an employed earner may be given by some other person acting on his behalf.

(2) Every such notice shall be given to the employer, or (if there is more than one employer) to one of such employers, or to any foreman or other official under whose supervision the employed earner is employed at the time of the accident, or to any person designated for the purpose by the employer, and shall give the appropriate particulars.

(3) Any entry of the appropriate particulars of an accident made in a book kept for that purpose in accordance with the provisions of regulation 25 shall, if made as soon as practicable after the happening of an accident by the employed earner or by some other person acting on his behalf, be sufficient notice of the accident for the purposes of this regulation.

(4) In this regulation—

''employer'' means, in relation to any person, the employer of that person at the time of the accident and ''employers'' shall be construed accordingly; and

''employed earner'' means a person who is or is treated as an employed earner for the purposes of industrial injuries benefit.

(5) In this regulation and regulation 25, ''appropriate particulars'' mean the particulars indicated in Schedule 4 to these regulations.

GENERAL NOTE

This regulation does not apply in respect of industrial diseases not caused by accident (see reg. 18) of the Social Security (Industrial Injuries) (Prescribed Diseases) Regulations 1985).

Obligations of employers

25.—(1) Every employer shall take reasonable steps to investigate the circumstances of every accident of which notice is given to him or to his servant or agent in accordance with the provisions of regulation 24 and, if there appear to him to be any discrepancies between the circumstances found by him as a result of his investigation and the circumstances appearing from the notice so given, he shall record the circumstances so found.

(2) Every employer who is required to do so by the Secretary of State shall furnish to an officer of the Department within such reasonable period as may be required, such information and particulars as shall be required—

(a) of any accident or alleged accident in respect of which benefit may be payable to, or in respect of the death of, a person employed by him at the time of the accident or alleged accident; or

(b) of the nature of and other relevant circumstances relating to any occupation prescribed for the purposes of Chapter V of Part II of the Act in which any person to whom or in respect of whose death benefit may be payable under that Chapter was or is alleged to have been employed by him.

(3) Every owner or occupier (being an employer) of any mine or quarry or of any premises to which any of the provisions of the Factories Act 1961 applies and every employer by whom 10 or more persons are normally employed at the same time on or about the same premises in connection with a trade or business carried on by the employer shall, subject to the following provisions of this paragraph—

[[1]](a) keep readily accessible a means (whether in a book or books or by electronic means), in a form approved by the Secretary of State, by which a person employed by the employer or some other person acting on his behalf may record the appropriate particulars (as defined in regulation 24) of any accident causing personal injury to that person; and

(b) preserve every such record for the period of at least 3 years from the date of its entry.]

Amendment

1. Social Security (Claims and Payments) Amendment (No. 3) Regulations 1993 (S.I. 1993 No. 2113), reg. 2 (September 27, 1993).

General Note

Chapter V of Part II of the Social Security Act 1975 has been replaced by ss.108–110 of the Social Security Contributions and Benefits Act 1992.

Obligations of claimants for, and beneficiaries in receipt of [[1]. . .] disablement benefit

26.—(1) Subject to the following provisions of this regulation, every claimant for, and every beneficiary in receipt of [[1]. . .] disablement benefit shall comply with every notice given to him by the Secretary of State which requires him either—

(a) to submit himself to a medical examination by a medical authority for the purpose of determining the effects of the relevant accident or the treatment appropriate to the relevant injury or loss of faculty; or

(b) to submit himself to such medical treatment for the said injury or loss of faculty as is considered appropriate in his case by the medical practitioner in charge of the case or by any medical authority to whose examination he has submitted himself in accordance with the foregoing provisions of this regulation.

(2) Every notice given to a claimant or beneficiary requiring him to submit himself to medical examination shall be given in writing and shall specify the time and place for examination and shall not require the claimant or beneficiary to submit himself to examination—

(a) by a Medical Board, before the expiration of the period of six days beginning with the date of the notice or such shorter period as may be reasonable in the circumstances;

(b) in any other case, on a date earlier than the third day after the day on which the notice was sent.

(3) Every claimant and every beneficiary who, in accordance with the foregoing provisions of this regulation, is required to submit himself to a medical examination or to medical treatment—

(a) shall attend at every such place and at every such time as may be required; and

(b) may, in the discretion of the Secretary of State, be paid such travelling and other allowances (including compensation for loss of remunerative time) as the Secretary of State may with the consent of the Minister for the Civil Service determine.

[[2](4) In this regulation—

"medical authority" means a medical appeal tribunal, an adjudicating medical authority or any medical practitioner appointed or nominated by the Secretary of State; and

"adjudicating medical authority" has the meaning assigned to it by regulation 30 of the Social Security (Adjudication) Regulations 1984.]

AMENDMENTS

1. Social Security (Abolition of Injury Benefit) (Consequential) Regulations 1983 (S.I. 1983 No. 186), reg. 11 (April 6, 1983).

2. Social Security Adjudication (Consequential Amendments) Regulations 1984 (S.I. 1984 No. 458), reg. 5 (April 23, 1984).

GENERAL NOTE

This regulation applies also to examination in respect of prescribed diseases (see reg. 19 of the Social Security (Industrial Injuries) (Prescribed Diseases) Regulations 1985).

27. *Revoked.*

PART V

MISCELLANEOUS PROVISIONS

28.—30. *Revoked.*

Breach of regulations

31. If any person contravenes or fails to comply with any requirement of these regulations (not being a requirement to give notice of an accident or a requirement to submit himself to medical treatment or examination) in respect of which no special penalty is provided, he shall for such offence be liable on summary conviction to a penalty not exceeding [[1]£200] or, where the offence consists of continuing any such contravention or failure after conviction thereof, [[1]£20] for each day on which it is so continued.

AMENDMENT

1. Social Security (Claims and Payments) Amendment Regulations 1982 (S.I. 1982 No. 1241), reg. 7 (October 4, 1982).

32. *Revoked*

SCHEDULES

Schedules 1.—3. *Revoked.*

SCHEDULE 4 **Regulations 24 and 25**

PARTICULARS TO BE GIVEN OF ACCIDENTS

(1) Full name, address and occupation of injured person;
(2) Date and time of accident;
(3) Place where accident happened;
(4) Cause and nature of injury;
(5) Name, address and occupation of person giving the notice, if other than the injured person.

Schedule 5. *Revoked.*

The Social Security (Claims and Payments) Regulations 1987

(S.I. 1987 No. 1968, reg. 2)

ARRANGEMENT OF REGULATIONS

PART 1

GENERAL

PART II

CLAIMS

Whereas a draft of this instrument was laid before Parliament and approved by resolution of each House of Parliament:

Now therefore, the Secretary of State for Social Services, in exercise of the powers conferred by sections 165A and 166(2) of the Social Security Act 1975, section 6(1) of the Child Benefit Act 1975, sections 21(7), 51(1)(a) to (s), 54(1) and 84(1) of the Social Security Act 1986 and, as regards the revocations set out in Schedule 10 to this instrument, the powers specified in that Schedule, and all other powers enabling him in that behalf, by this instrument which contains only regulations made under the sections of the Social Security Act 1986 specified above and provisions consequential on those sections and which is made before the end of a period of 12 months from the commencement of those sections, makes the following Regulations:

PART I

GENERAL

Citation and commencement

1. These Regulations may be cited as the Social Security (Claims and Payments) Regulations 1987 and shall come into operation on 11th April 1988.

Interpretation

2.–(1) In these Regulations unless the context otherwise requires—

''adjudicating authority'' means any person or body with responsibility under the Social Security Acts 1975 to 1986, and regulations made thereunder, for the determination of claims for benefit and questions arising in connection with a claim for, or award of, or disqualification for receiving benefits;

''appropriate office'' means an office of the [[2]Department of Social Security] or [[10]the Department for Education and Employment]

[[11]''claim for asylum'' has the same meaning as in the Asylum and Immigration Appeals Act 1993];

''claim for benefit'' includes—

(a) an application for a declaration that an accident was an industrial accident;

(b) [[3]. . .]

(c) an application for the review of an award or a decision for the purpose of obtaining any increase of benefit [[6]in respect of a child or adult dependant under the Social Security Act 1975 or an increase in disablement benefit under section 60 (special hardship), 61 (constant attendance), 62 (hospital treatment allowance) or 63 (exceptionally severe disablement) of the Social Security Act 1975], but does not include any other application for the review of an award or a decision;

[[8]''instrument for benefit payment'' means an instrument issued by the Secretary of State under regulation 20A on the presentation of which benefit due to a beneficiary shall be paid in accordance with the arrangements set out in that regulation.]

[10"the Jobseekers Act" means the Jobseekers Act 1995;
"Jobseeker's Allowance" means an allowance payable under Part I of the Jobseekers Act'
"the Jobseeker's Allowance Regulations" means the Jobseeker's Allowance Regulations 1996;]
"long-term benefits" means any retirement pension, a widowed mother's allowance, a widow's pension, attendance allowance, [5 disability living allowance], invalid care allowance, guardian's allowance, any pension or allowance for industrial injury or disease and any increase in any such benefit;
"married couple" means a man and a woman who are married to each other and are members of the same household;
"partner" means one of a married or unmarried couple;
[9 "pension fund holder" means with respect to a personal pension scheme or retirement annuity contract, the trustees, managers or scheme administrators, as the case may be, of the scheme or contract concerned;
"personal pension scheme" has the same meaning as in section 1 of the Pension Schemes Act 1993 in respect of employed earners and in the case of self-employed earners, includes a scheme approved by the Board of Inland Revenue under Chapter IV of Part XIV of the Income and Corporation Taxes Act 1988;]
[11"refugee" means a person recorded by the Secretary of State as a refugee within the definition of Article 1 of the Convention relating to the Status of Refugees done at Geneva on July 28 1951 as extended by Article 1(2) of the Protocol relating to the Status of Refugees done at New York on January 31, 1967;]
"retirement annuity contract" means a contract or trust scheme approved under Chapter III of Part XIV of the Income and Corporation Taxes Act 1988;]
[4...]
"unmarried couple" means a man and a woman who are not married to each other but are living together as husband and wife otherwise than in prescribed circumstances; and
"week" means a period of seven days beginning with midnight between Saturday and Sunday.

(2) Unless the context otherwise requires, any reference in these Regulations to—

(a) a numbered regulation, Part or Schedule is a reference to the regulation, Part or Schedule bearing that number in these Regulations and any reference in a regulation to a numbered paragraph is a reference to the paragraph of that regulation having that number;

(b) a benefit includes any benefit under the Social Security Act 1975, child benefit under Part I of the Child Benefit Act 1975, income support [5, family credit and disability working allowance under the Social Security Act 1986 and any social fund payments such as are mentioned in section 32(2)(a) [1and section 32(2A)] of that Act [10and a jobseeker's allowance under Part I of the Jobseekers Act]

[10(2A) References in regulations 20, 21 (except paragraphs (3) and (3A)), 29, 30, 32 to 34, 37 (except paragraph (1A)), 37A, 37AA (except paragraph (3)), 37AB, 37B, 38 and 47 to "benefit", "income support" or "a jobseeker's allowance", include a reference to a back to work bonus which, by virtue of regulation 25 of the Social Security (Back to Work Bonus) Regulations 1996(**b**), is to be treated as payable as income support or, as the case may be, as a jobseeker's allowance.]

(3) For the purposes of the provisions of these Regulations relating to the making of claims [6every increase of benefit in respect of a child or adult

dependant under the Social Security Act 1975 or an increase of disablement benefit under sections 60 (special hardship), 61 (constant attendance), 62 (hospital treatment allowance) or 63 (exceptionally severe disablement) of the Social Security Act 1975] shall be treated as a separate benefit [12. . .]

Amendments

1. Social Security (Common Provisions) Miscellaneous Amendment Regulations 1988 (S.I. 1988 No. 1725), reg. 3 (November 7, 1988).

2. Transfer of Functions (Health and Social Security) Order 1988 (S.I. 1988 No. 1843), art. 3(4) (November 28,1988).

3. Social Security (Medical Evidence, Claims and Payments) Amendment Regulations 1989 (S.I. 1989 No. 1686), reg. 3 (October 9, 1989).

4. Social Security (Miscellaneous Provisions) Amendment Regulations 1991 (S.I. 1991 No. 2284, reg. 5 (November 1, 1991).

5. Social Security (Claims and Payments) Amendment Regulations 1991 (S.I. 1991 No. 2741), reg. 2 (February 3, 1992, with a saving under reg. 29 until April 6, 1992).

6. Social Security (Claims and Payments) Amendment Regulations 1991 (S.I. 1991 No. 2741), reg. 2 (March 10, 1992).

7. Social Security (Miscellaneous Provisions) Amendment Regulations 1992 (S.I. 1992 No. 247), reg. 9 (March 9, 1992).

8. Social Security (Claims and Payments) Amendment (No. 4) Regulations 1994 (S.I. 1994 No. 3196), reg. 2 (January 10, 1995).

9. Income-related Benefits Schemes and Social Security (Claims and Payments) (Miscellaneous Amendments) Regulations 1995 (S.I. 1995 No. 2303), reg. 10(2) (October 2, 1995).

10. Social Security (Claims and Payments) (Jobseeker's Allowance Consequential Amendments) Regulations 1996 (S.I. 1996 No. 1460), reg. 2(2) (October 7, 1996).

11. Income Support and Social Security (Claims and Payments) (Miscellaneous Amendments) Regulations 1996 (S.I. 1996 No. 2431), reg. 7(a) (October 15, 1996).

12. Child Benefit, Child Support and Social Security (Miscellaneous Amendments) Regulations 1996 (S.I. 1996 No. 1803), reg. 18 (April 7, 1997).

General Note

The Social Security Acts 1975 to 1986 have been replaced by the Social Security Contributions and Benefits Act 1992 and the Social Security Administration Act 1992. S.60 of the 1975 Act was repealed before the 1992 consolidation. Ss.61 and 63 of the 1975 Act have been replaced by ss.104 and 105 of the 1992 Contributions and Benefits Act and s.62 has been replaced by Sched. 7, para. 10.

Part II

Claims

3. *Omitted.*

Making a claim for benefit

4.—(1) Every claim for benefit [5other than a claim for income support or jobseeker's allowance] shall be made in writing on a form approved by the Secretary of State [3 for the purpose of the benefit for which the claim is made], or in such other manner, being in writing, as the Secretary of State may accept as sufficient in the circumstances of any particular case.

(1A) to (3) *Omitted.*

[2 (3A) In the case of a married or unmarried couple where both partners satisfy the conditions set out in Section 20(6A) of the Social Security Act 1986, a claim for disability working allowance shall be made by whichever partner they agree should so claim, or in default of agreement, by such one of them as the Secretary of State shall determine.]

(3B) to (4) *Omitted.*

[5(5) Where a person who wishes to make a claim for benefit and who has not been supplied with an approved form of claim notifies an appropriate office (by whatever means) of his intention to make a claim, he shall be supplied, without charge, with such form of claim by such person as the Secretary of State may appoint or authorise for that purpose.]

[4(6) A person wishing to make a claim shall—

(a) if it is a claim for a jobseeker's allowance, unless the Secretary of State otherwise directs, attend in person at an appropriate office or such other place, and at such time, as the Secretary of State may specify in his case in a notice under regulation 23 of the Jobseeker's Allowance Regulations:

(b) if it is a claim for any other benefit, deliver or send the claim to an appropriate office.]

(7) If a claim [5other than a claim for income support or jobseeker's allowance] is defective at the date when it is received or has been made in writing but not on the form approved for the time being, the Secretary of State may refer the claim to the person making it or, as the case may be, supply him with the approved form, and if the form is received properly completed within one month, or such longer period as the Secretary of State may consider reasonable, from the date on which it is so referred or supplied, the Secretary of State shall treat the claim as if it has been duly made in the first instance.

(7A) *Omitted.*

[5(8) A claim, other than a claim for income support or jobseeker's allowance, which is made on the form approved for the time being is, for the purposes of these Regulations, properly completed if completed in accordance with the instructions on the form and defective if not so completed.]

(9) *Omitted.*

Amendments

1. Social Security (Miscellaneous Provisions) Amendment Regulations 1990 (S.I. 1990 No. 2208), reg. 8 (December 5, 1990).

2. Social Security (Claims and Payments) Amendment Regulations 1991 (S.I. 1991 No. 2741), reg. 3 (March 10, 1992).

3. Social Security (Miscellaneous Provisions) Amendment Regulations 1992 (S.I. 1992 No. 247), reg. 10 (March 9, 1992).

4. Social Security (Claims and Payments) (Jobseeker's Allowance Consequential Amendments) Regulations 1996 (S.I. 1996 No. 1460), reg. 2(4) (October 7, 1996).

5. Social Security (Miscellaneous Amendments) (No. 2) Regulations 1997 (S.I. 1997 No. 793, reg. 2 (April 7, 1997).

General Note

Para. (1). A claim must be in writing but it need not necessarily be on the proper form. However, if it is not on the proper form, it is for the Secretary of State to decide whether the document is acceptable to him as a claim. If the Secretary of State has not considered that question, it is necessary for the tribunal to adjourn to allow him to do so. Even if the Secretary of State does accept the document as sufficient, it is still a matter for an adjudication officer or tribunal to decide whether the document *does* constitute a claim (*R(U) 9/60*). Other questions as to whether a claim has been made and, if so, when it was received are also to be determined by an adjudication officer and a tribunal, rather than by the Secretary of State (*R(SB) 5/89*). See also para. (7).

Para. (3A). Only one member of a couple can claim disability working allowance. In a case where only one member of the couple is both disabled and in work, that person will make the claim. If both members could qualify, they must either decide between themselves who is to claim or else the Secretary of State will decide for them. S.20(6A) of the Social Security Act 1986 has been replaced by s.129(1) of the Social Security Contributions and Benefits Act 1992.

Para. (6). In *CS/175/88*, it was held that a claim was not delivered when a claim form was merely shown to a clerk and then taken away for amendment. It may be necessary for an adjudication officer or tribunal to decide exactly what has been done in a similar situation because there seems no reason in principle why a claim should not be regarded as having been delivered merely because it has been given back to the claimant, particularly having regard to para. (7).

Para. (7). If a claim is defective (see para. 8), it may simply be treated as not being a claim at all. However, the Secretary of State can refer the claim back to the claimant so that it can be made properly. If the claim is then made properly within a month (or longer if the Secretary of State considers it reasonable), it is treated as having been properly made at the date when the defective claim was received (reg. 6(1)(b)).

Amendment and withdrawal of claim

5.—(1) A person who has made a claim may amend it at any time by notice in writing received in an appropriate office before a determination has been made on the claim, and any claim so amended may be treated as if it had been so amended in the first instance.

(2) A person who has made a claim may withdraw it at any time before a determination has been made on it, by notice to an appropriate office, and any such notice of withdrawal shall have effect when it is received.

Date of claim

6.—(1) [[3]Subject to the following provisions of this regulation,] the date on which a claim is made shall be—

(a) in the case of a claim which meets the requirements of regulation 4(1), the date on which it is received in a appropriate office;

[[10](aa) in the case of a claim for—

family credit;

disability working allowance;

jobseeker's allowance if first notification is received before 6th October 1997; or

income support if first notification is received before 6th October 1997;

which meets the requirements of regulation 4(1) and which is received in an appropriate office within one month of first notification in accordance with regulation 4(5), whichever is the later of—

(i) the date on which that notification is received; and

(ii) the first date on which that claim could have been made in accordance with these Regulations;]

(b) in the case of a claim which does not meet the requirements of regulation 4(1) but which is treated, under regulation 4(7) as having been duly made, the date on which the claim was received in an appropriate office in the first instance.

(1A) *Omitted.*

(2) [[1]. . .]

[[1](3) In the case of a claim for income support, family credit [[5]disability working allowance] [[10]or jobseeker's allowance] [[4]. . .], where the time for claiming is extended under regulation 19 the claim shall be treated as made on the first day of the period in respect of which the claim is, by reason of the operation of that regulation, timeously made.

(4) Paragraph (3) shall not apply when the time for claiming income support, [[5]family credit] [[9]disability working allowance or jobseeker's allowance] has been extended under regulation 19 and the failure to claim within the prescribed time for the purposes of that regulation is for the reason only that the claim has been sent by post.]

(4A) to (4D) *Omitted.*

[[3](5) Where a person submits a claim for attendance allowance [[5]or disability living allowance or a request under paragraph (8)] by post and the arrival of that [[5]claim or request] at an appropriate office is delayed by postal disruption caused by industrial action, whether within the postal service or elsewhere, the

[5claim or request] shall be treated as received on the day on which it would have been received if it had been delivered in the ordinary course of post.]

(6) and (7) *Omitted.*

[5(8) [7Subject to paragraph (8A)] where—

(a) a request is received in an appropriate office for a claim form for disability living allowance or attendance allowance; and

(b) in response to the request a claim form for disability living allowance or attendance allowance is issued from an appropriate office; and

(c) within the time specified the claim form properly completed is received in an appropriate office,

the date on which the claim is made shall be the date on which the request was received in the appropriate office.

[7(8A) Where, in a case which would otherwise fall within paragraph (8), it is not possible to determine the date when the request for a claim form was received in an appropriate office because of a failure to record that date, the claim shall be treated as having been made on the date 6 weeks before the date on which the properly completed claim form is received in an appropriate office.]

(9) [8In paragraphs (8) and (8A)]—

"a claim form" means a form approved by the Secretary of State under regulation 4(1);

"properly completed" has the meaning assigned by regulation 4(8);

"the time specified" means six weeks from the date on which the request was received or such longer period as the Secretary of State may consider reasonable.]

[6(10) Where a person starts a job on a Monday or Tuesday in any week and he makes a claim for disability working allowance in that week the claim shall be treated as made on the Tuesday of that week.

(11) Where a claim for disability working allowance in respect of a person has been refused and a further claim for the same allowance is made in respect of him within the period prescribed under section 100A(1) of the Social Security Act 1975 and that further claim has been treated as an application for review in accordance with section 100A(12) of that Act then the original claim shall be treated as made on the date on which the further claim is made or treated as made.]

[10(12) Subject to paragraph (14), where a person has claimed disability working allowance and that claim ("the original claim") has been refused, and a further claim is made in the circumstances speccified in paragraph (13), that further claim shall be treated as made—

(a) on the date of the original claim; or

(b) on the first date in respect of which the qualifying benefit was payable, whichever is the later.

(13) The circumstances referred to in paragraph (12) are that—

(a) the original claim was refused on the ground that the claimant did not qualify under section 129(2) of the Contributions and Benefits Act;

(b) at the date of the original claim the claimant had made a claim for a qualifying benefit and that claim had not been determined;

(c) after the original claim had been determined, the claim for the qualifying benefit was determined in the claimant's favour; and

(d) the further claim for disability working allowance was made within three months of the date that the claim for qualifying benefit was determined.

(14) Paragraph (12) shall not apply in a case where the further claim for disability working allowance is made within the period prescribed under section 30(1) of the Social Security Administration Act 1992, and is accordingly treated as an application for a review under section 30(13) of that Act.

(15) In paragraphs (12) and (13) ''qualifying benefit'' means any of the benefits referred to in section 129(2) of the Contributions and Benefits Act.

(16) Where a person has claimed severe disablement allowance and that claim (''the original claim'') has been refused, and a further claim is made in the circumstances specified in paragraph (17), that further claim shall be treated as made—

(a) on the date of the original claim; or

(b) on the first date in respect of which the highest rate of the care component of disability living allowance was payable,

whichever is the later.

(17) The circumstances referred to in paragraph (16) are that—

(a) the original claim was refused on the ground that the claimant's disablement was less than 80 per cent.;

(b) at the date of the original claim the claimant had made a claim for disabilty living allowance, and that claim had not been determined;

(c) after the original claim had been determined, the claimant was awarded the highest rate of the care component of disability living allowance; and

(d) the further claim for severe disablement allowance was made within three months of the date that the claim for disability living allowance was determined.]

(18) to (20) *Omitted.*

[[10](21) Where a person has claimed invalid care allowance and that claim (''the original claim'') has been refused, and a further claim is made in the circumstances specified in paragraph (22), that further claim shall be treated as made—

(a) on the date of the original claim; or

(b) on the first date in respect of which the qualifiy benefit was payable in respect of the disabled person,

whichever is the later.

(22) The circumstances referred to in paragraph (21) are that—

(a) the original claim was refused on the ground that the disabled person was not a severely disabled person within the meaning of section 70(2) of the Contributions and Benefits Act;

(b) at the date of the orginal claim the disabled person had made a claim for a qualifying benefit, and that claim had not been determined;

(c) after the original claim had been determined, the claim for the qualifying benefit was determined in the diabled person's favour; and

(d) the further claim for invalid care allowance was made within three months of the date that the claim for the qualifying benefit was determined.

(23) In paragraphs (21) and (22)—

(a) ''the disabled person'' means the person for whom the invalid care allowance claimant is caring in accordance with section 70(1)(a) of the Contributions and Benefits Act; and

(b) ''qualifying benefit'' means any benefit or payment referred to in section 70(2) of the Contributions and Benefits Act.]

(24) to (26) *Omitted.*

[[10](27) Where a claim is made for family credit or disability working allowance, and—

(a) the claimant had previously made a claim for income support or jobseeker's allowance (''the original claim'');

(b) the original claim was refused on the ground that the claimant or his partner was in remunerative work; and

(c) the claim for family credit or disability working allowance was made within 14 days of the date that the original claim was determined, that claim shall be treated as made on the date of the original claim, or, if the claimant so requests, on a later specified by the claimant.

(28) Where a claim is made for income support or jobseeker's allowance, and—

(a) the claimant had previously made a claim for family credit or disability working allowance ("the original claim");

(b) the original claim was refused on the ground that the claimant or his partner was not in remunerative work; and

(c) the claim for income support or jobseeker's allowance was made within 14 days of the date that the original claim was determined,

that claim shall be treated as made on the date of the original claim, or, if the claimant so requests, on a later date specified by the claimant.]

[[11](29) In the case of a claim for an increase of severe disablement allowance or of invalid care allowance in respect of a child or adult dependant, paragraphs (16) and (21) shall apply to the claim as if it were a claim for severe disablement allowance or, as the case may be, invalid care allowance.]

AMENDMENTS

1. Social Security (Claims and Payments) Amendment Regulations 1988 (S.I. 1988 No. 522), reg. 2 (April 11, 1988).
2. Social Security (Medical Evidence, Claims and Payments) Amendment Regulations 1989 (S.I. 1989 No. 1686), (October 9, 1989).
3. Social Security (Claims and Payments) Amendment Regulations 1990 (S.I. 1990 No. 725), reg. 2 (April 9, 1990).
4. Social Security (Miscellaneous Provisions) Amendment Regulations 1991 (S.I. 1991 No. 2284), reg. 6 (November 1, 1991).
5. Social Security (Claims and Payments) Amendment Regulations 1991 (S.I. 1991 No. 2741), reg. 4 (February 3, 1992).
6. Social Security (Claims and Payments) Amendment Regulations 1991 (S.I. 1991 No. 2741), reg. 4 (March 10, 1992).
7. Social Security (Claims and Payments) Amendment (No. 3) Regulations 1993 (S.I. 1993 No. 2113), reg. 3(2) (September 27, 1993).
8. Social Security (Claims and Payments) Amendment Regulations 1994 (S.I. 1994 No. 2319), reg. 2 (October 3, 1994).
9. Social Security (Claims and Payments) (Jobseeker's Allowance Consequential Amendments) Regulatins 1996 (S.I. 1996 No. 1460), reg. 2(5) (October 7, 1996).
10. Social Security (Miscellaneous Amendments) (No. 2) Regulations 1997 (S.I. 1997 No. 793, reg. 3 (April 7, 1997).
11. Social Security (Claims and Payments and Adjudication) Amendment No. 2 Regulations 1997 (S.I. 1997 No. 2290), reg. 6 (October 13, 1997).

GENERAL NOTE

Even by the standards of social security legislation, this is a long regulation.

Para. (1). Generally a claim is made when it is received. In the circumstances specified, a claim is treated as received when the claimant first asks for a claim form.

Para. (3). If the time for claiming is extended, the claim is treated as having been made at the beginning of the usual period for claiming. This enables the claim to backdated, but it does not apply where a claim for an income-related benefit is delayed in the post (see para. (4)).

Paras. (8) and *(9).* There is a large claim pack for disability living allowance and attendance allowance. A claimant who requests one from any office of the Department of Social Security (see the definition of "appropriate office" in reg. 2(1)), then has six weeks from the date of the request (*not* the date on which the pack was sent out) in which to fill in the claim form and return it to the Department. The six-week period may be extended by the Secretary of State. Provided the claim form is returned within the correct period, the claim is treated as having been made on the date the original request was received by the Department. There is no reason why the request should be in writing; an oral one will do.

Para. (10). In reg. 2(1), a "week" is defined so as to run from Sunday to Saturday. If a claimant starts a job on the Monday or Tuesday, any claim for disability working allowance received during that week is treated as having been made on the Tuesday (the pay-day for disability working allowance under reg. 27). It is not clear why this does not apply to a person who starts work on a Sunday.

Para. (11). This appears to be a strange provision. If a person has been refused disability working allowance and, instead of applying for a review, makes a new claim within three months of the refusal, the second claim is treated as an application for a review (Social Security Administration Act 1992, s.30(13), formerly Social Security Act 1975, s.100A(12)). One would therefore expect that, if the application was successful, benefit would be paid from the date of the original claim. However, this provision requires the original claim to be treated as having been made on the date the second claim was made or treated as made. If the claimant is relying on having been entitled to, say, invalidity benefit within the eight weeks before the date of claim, he or she may be unfairly prejudiced and, or course, there is always the question of payment in respect of the period between the two claims. The way out of this dilemma is to consider whether reg. 19(5)(d) might apply. If so, the second claim may be treated as having been made on the date of the first claim (reg. 6(3)). This paragraph seems to be based on an assumption that the first claim was rightly refused (see the note to reg. 66(1) of the Social Security (Adjudication) Regulations 1995).

Paras. (12) to (29). These paragraphs have been introduced to counteract the effect of the tightening up of the circumstances in which arrears may be paid following a review and, indeed, they solve some problems that existed even before that tightening up. They are concerned with situations where entitlement to one benefit depends on the entitlement of the claimant or some other person to another benefit. Broadly, if a claim is rejected because there was at the time no award of the other benefit and the other benefit is subsequently awarded, the first benefit may be awarded on the basis of the original claim. It should be noted that a claimant must make a claim for the first benefit as soon as possible; benefit will be lost if the claimant awaits the determination of the claim to the second benefit.

Evidence and information

7.—(1) [3Subject to paragraph (7),] every person who makes a claim for benefit shall furnish such certificates, documents, information and evidence in connection with the claim, or any question arising out of it, as may be required by the Secretary of State and shall do so within one month of being required to do so or such longer period as the Secretary of State may consider reasonable.

(2) [3Subject to paragraph (7),] where a benefit may be claimed by either of two partners or where entitlement to or the amount of any benefit is or may be affected by the circumstances of a partner, the Secretary of State may require the partner other than the claimant to certify in writing whether he agrees to the claimant making the claim or, as the case may be, that he confirms the information given about his circumstances.

(3) In the case of a claim for family credit [1or disability working allowance], the employer of the claimant or, as the case may be, of the partner shall furnish such certificates, documents, information and evidence in connection with the claim or any question arising out of it as may be required by the Secretary of State.

[2(4) In the case of a person who is claiming disability working allowance, family credit [3income support or jobseeker's allowance], where that person or any partner is aged not less than 60 and is a member of, or a person deriving entitlement to a pension under, a personal pension scheme, or is a party to, or a person deriving entitlement to a pension under, a retirement annuity contract, he shall where the Secretary of State so requires furnish the following information—

(a) the name and address of the pension fund holder;

(b) such other information including any reference or policy number as is needed to enable the personal pension scheme or retirement annuity contract to be identified.

(5) Where the pension fund holder receives from the Secretary of State a request for details concerning the personal pension scheme or retirement annuity contract relating to a person or any partner to whom paragraph (4) refers, the

pension fund holder shall provide the Secretary of State with any information to which paragraph (6) refers.

(6) The information to which this paragraph refers is—

(a) where the purchase of an annuity under a personal pension scheme has been deferred, the amount of any income which is being withdrawn from the personal pension scheme;

(b) in the case of—

(i) a personal pension scheme where income withdrawal is available, the maximum amount of income which may be withdrawn from the scheme; or

(ii) a personal pension scheme where income withdrawal is not available, or a retirement annuity contract, the maximum amount of income which might be withdrawn from the fund if the fund were held under a personal pension scheme where income withdrawal was available.

calculated by or on behalf of the pension fund holder by means of tables prepared from time to time by the Government Actuary which are appropriate for this purpose.]

{[3](7) Paragraphs (1) and (2) do not apply in the case of jobseeker's allowance.]

Amendments

1. Social Security (Claim and Payments) Amendment Regulations 1991 (S.I. 1991 No. 2741) reg. 5 (March 10, 1992).

2. Income-related Benefits Schemes and Social Security (Claims and Payments) (Miscellaneous Amendments) Regulations 1995 (S.I. 1995 No. 2303), reg. 10(3) (October 2, 1995).

3. Social Security (Claims and Payments) (Jobseeker's Allowance Consequential Amendmants) Regulations 1996 (S.I. 1996 No. 1460), reg. 2(6) (October 7, 1996).

General Note

A failure to provide proper information does not disentitle a claimant from benefit. An adjudication officer or tribunal simply has to make a decision on such information as is available (*R(SB) 29/83*). A failure to provide information which would, if the claim were well founded, be readily available to the claimant is likely to lead to an inference that the evidence does not exist. However, an adjudication officer or tribunal must consider all the surrounding circumstances and also consider whether the requests for information were in sufficiently specific terms to justify the inference.

Attendance in person

8.—(1) [[1]. . .]

(2) Every person who makes a claim for benefit [[1](other than a jobseeker's allowance)] shall attend at such office or place and on such days and at such times as the Secretary of State may direct, for the purpose of furnishing certificates, documents, information and evidence under regulation 7, if reasonably so required by the Secretary of State.

Amendment

1. Social Security (Claims and Payments) (Jobseeker's Allowance Consequential Amendments) Regulations 1996 (S.I. 1996 No. 1460), reg. 2(7) (October 7, 1996).

Interchange with claims for other benefits

9.—(1) Where it appears that a person who has made a claim for benefit specified in column (1) of Part I of Schedule 1 may be entitled to the benefit specified opposite to it in column (2) of that Part, any such claim may be treated by the Secretary of State as a claim alternatively, or in addition, to the benefit specified opposite to it in that column.

(2) to (6) *Omitted.*

[[1](7) In determining whether he should treat a claim alternatively or in addition to another claim (the original claim) under this regulation the Secretary of State shall treat the alternative or additional claim, whenever made, as having been made at the same time as the original claim.]

AMENDMENT

1. Social Security (Miscellaneous Provisions) Amendment Regulations 1992 (S.I. 1992 No. 247), reg. 12 (March 9, 1992).

10. and **11.** *Omitted.*

12. *Revoked.*

13. *Omitted.*

[[1]Advance award of disability living allowance

13A.—(1) Where, although a person does not satisfy the requirements for entitlement to disability living allowance on the date on which the claim is made, the adjudicating authority is of the opinion that unless there is a change of circumstances he will satisfy those requirements for a period beginning on a day (''the relevant day'') not more than three months after the date on which the claim is made, then that authority may award disability living allowance from the relevant day subject to the condition that the person satisfies the requirements for entitlement on the relevant day.

(2) Where a person makes a claim for disability living allowance on or after 3rd February 1992 and before 6th April 1992 the adjudicating authority may award benefit for a period beginning on any day after 5th April 1992 being a day not more than three months after the date on which the claim was made, subject to the condition that the person satisfies the requirements for entitlement when disability living allowance becomes payable under the award.

(3) An award under paragraph (1) or (2) shall be reviewed by the adjudicating authority if the requirements for entitlement are found not to have been satisfied when disability living allowance becomes payable under the award.]

AMENDMENT

1. This whole regulation was inserted by the Social Security (Claims and Payments) Amendment Regulations 1991 (S.I. 1991 No. 2741), reg. 7(1) (February 3, 1991).

GENERAL NOTE

Para. (1) permits an advance award of disability living allowance to be made if a claim is made during the three-month qualifying period.

[[1]Advance claim for and award of disability working allowance

13B.—(1) Where a person makes a claim for disability working allowance on or after 10th March 1992 and before 7th April 1992 the adjudicating authority may—

(a) treat the claim as if it were made for a period beginning on 7th April 1992; and

(b) award benefit accordingly, subject to the condition that the person satisfies the requirements for entitlement on 7th April 1992.

(2) An award under the paragraph (1)(b) shall be reviewed by the adjudicating authority if the requirements for entitlement are found not to have been satisfied on 7th April 1992.]

AMENDMENT

1. This whole regulation was inserted by the Social Security (Claims and Payments) Admendment Regulations 1991 (S.I. 1991 No. 2742), reg. 7(2) (March 10, 1992).

[[1]Further claim for and award of disability living allowance

13C.—(1) A person entitled to an award of disability living allowance may make a further claim for disability living allowance during the period of six months immediately before the existing award expires.

(2) Where a person makes a claim in accordance with paragraph (1) the adjudicating authority may—

(a) treat the claim as if made on the first day after the expiry of the existing award (''the renewal date''); and

(b) award benefit accordingly, subject to the condition that the person satisfies the requirements for entitlement on the renewal date.

(3) An award under paragraph (2)(b) shall be reviewed by the adjudicating authority if the requirements for entitlement are found not to have been satisfied on the renewal date.]

AMENDMENT

1. This whole regulation was inserted by the Social Security (Claims and Payments) Amendment Regulations 1991 (S.I. 1991 No 2741), reg. 8 (March 10, 1992).

GENERAL NOTE

This permits a continuation claim for disability living allowance to be made during the last six months of an existing award.

In *CDLA/14895/96*, it was held that reg. 13C(2) should not be applied until it has been considered whether, if the claim were treated as an application for review under s.30(13) of the Social Security Administration Act 1992, there would be grounds for review. If there are grounds for review, the existing award should be reviewed. Otherwise, the claim should be treated as a renewal claim, effective only from the end of the existing award.

14. and **15.** *Omitted.*
15A. *Revoked.*

Date of entitlement under an award for the purpose of payability of benefit and effective date of change of rate

16.—(1) For the purpose only of determining the day from which benefit is to become payable, where a benefit other than one of those specified in paragraph (4) is awarded for a period of a week, or weeks, and the earliest date on which entitlement would otherwise commence is not the first day of a benefit week, entitlement shall begin on the first day of the benefit week next following.

[[1](1A) Where a claim for family credit is made in accordance with paragraph 7(a) [[2]or (aa)] of Schedule 4 for a period following the expiration of an existing award of family credit [[2]or disability working allowance], entitlement shall begin on the day after the expiration of that award.

(1B) Where a claim for family credit [[2]or disability working allowance] is made on or after the date when an uprating order is made under section 63(2) of the Social Security Act 1986, but before the date when that order comes into force, and—

(a) an award cannot be made on that claim as at the date it is made but could have been made if that order were then in force, and
(b) the period beginning with the date of claim and ending immediately before the date when the order came into force does not exceed 28 days,

entitlement shall begin from the date the up-rating order comes into force.]

[2(1C) Where a claim for disability working allowance is made in accordance with paragraph 11(a) or (b) of Schedule 4 for a period following the expiration of an existing award of disability working allowance or family credit, entitlement shall begin on the day after the expiration of that award.]

(2) Where there is a change in the rate of any benefit to which paragraph (1) applies the change, if it would otherwise take effect on a day which is not the appropriate pay day for that benefit, shall take effect from the appropriate pay day next following.

[1(3) For the purposes of this regulation the first day of the benefit week—
(a) in the case of child benefit is Monday,
(b) in the case of family credit [2or disability working allowance] is Tuesday, and
(c) in any other case is the day of the week on which the benefit is payable in accordance with regulation 22 (long-term benefits).]

(4) The benefits specified for exclusion from the scope of paragraph (1) are [4jobseeker's allowance], [3incapacity benefit], maternity allowance, [1. . .] severe disablement allowance, income support [1. . .] and any increase of those benefits.

AMENDMENTS

1. Social Security (Claims and Payments) Amendment Regulations 1988 (S.I. 1988 No. 522), reg. 3 (April 11, 1988).
2. Social Security (Claims and Payments) Amendment Regulations 1991 (S.I. 1991 No. 2741), reg. 9 (March 10, 1992).
3. Social Security (Claims and Payments) Amendment (No. 2) Regulations 1994 (S.I. 1994 No. 2943), reg. 6 (April 13, 1995).
4. Social Security (Claims and Payments) (Jobseeker's Allowance Consequential Amendments) Regulations 1996 (S.I. 1996 No. 1460), reg. 2(9) (October 7, 1996).

GENERAL NOTE

This regulation has the effect that entitlement to disability working allowance always begins on a Tuesday (which is the pay-day under reg. 27, although payment is always in arrears). Under para. (1), if a claim is made on a Tuesday, that day is the first day of entitlement. Otherwise entitlement commences on the next Tuesday. Para. (1C) deals with continuation claims.

Duration of awards

17.—(1) Subject to the provisions of this regulation and of section [137ZA(3) of the Social Security Act 1975 (disability living allowance) and section] 20(6) [2 and (6F)] of the Social Security Act 1986 (family credit [2 and disability working allowance]) a claim for benefit shall be treated as made for an indefinite period and any award of benefit on that claim shall be made for an indefinite period.

(1A) *Omitted.*

(2) [3. . .]

(3) If [3. . .] it would be inappropriate to treat a claim as made and to make an award for an indefinite period (for example where a relevant change of circumstances is reasonably to be expected in the near future) the claim shall be treated as made and the award shall be for a definite period which is appropriate in the circumstances.

(4) In any case where benefit is awarded in respect of days subsequent to the date of claim the award shall be subject to the condition that the claimant satisfies the requirements for entitlement; and where those requirements are not satisfied the award shall be reviewed.

(5) *Omitted.*

Amendments

1. Social Security (Claims and Payments) Amendment Regulations 1991 (S.I. 1991 No. 2741), reg. 10 (February 3, 1992).

2. Social Security (Claims and Payments) Amendment Regulations 1991 (S.I. 1991 No. 2741), reg. 10 (March 10, 1992).

3. Social Security (Claims and Payments) (Jobseeker's Allowance Consequential Amendments) Regulations 1996 (S.I. 1996 No. 1460), reg. 2(10) (October 7, 1996).

General Note

*Para. (1).*The general rule is that awards are made for an indefinite period. However, that does not apply to awards of disability living allowance (s.71(3) of the Social Security Contributions and Benefits Act 1992, formerly s.37ZA(3) of the Social Security Act 1975 provides that awards shall either be for a fixed period or for life), or family credit or disability working allowance (ss.128(3) and 129(6) of the Social Security Contributions and Benefits Act 1992, formerly s.20(6) and (6F) of the Social Security Act 1986 provides that awards shall be for 26 weeks).

Para. (4). In *R(S) 5/89*, a Tribunal of Commissioners held that this power of review was wholly independent of the power to review under the predecesser of s. 25 of the Social Security Administration Act 1992. However, is *CSIS/137/94*, another Tribunal of Commissioners have held *R(S) 5/89* to have been wrongly decided. They have held that reg. 17(4) merely acts as a trigger for the operation of s.25 or s.30 of the 1992 Act.

18. *Revoked.*

[1Time for claiming benefit

19.—(1) Subject to the following provisions of this regulation, the prescribed time for claiming any benefit specified in column (1) of Schedule 4 is the appropriate time specified opposite that benefit in column (2) of that Schedule.

(2) The prescribed time for claiming the benefits specified in paragraph (3) is three months beginning with any day on which, apart from satisfying the condition of making a claim, the claimant is entitled to the benefit concerned.

(3) The benefits to which paragraph (2) applies are—

(a) child benefit;

(b) guardian's allowance;

(c) graduated retirement benefit(**d**);

(d) invalid care allowance;

(e) maternity allowance;

(f) retirement pension of any category;

(g) widow's benefit;

(h) except in a case to which section 3(3) of the Social Security Administration Act 1992 applies (late claims for widowhood benefits where death is difficult to establish), any increase in any benefit (other than support or jobseeker's allowance) in respect of a child or adult dependant.

(4) Subject to paragraph (8), in the case of a claim for income support, jobseeker's allowance, family credit or disability working allowance, where the claim is not made within the time specified for that benefit in Schedule 4, the prescribed time for claiming the benefit shall be extended, subject to a maximum extension of three months, to the date on which the claim is made, where—

(a) any of the circumstances specified in paragraph (5) applies or has applied to the claimant; and

(b) as a result of that circumstances or those circumstances the clamant could not reasonably have been expected to make the claim earlier.

(5) The circumstances referred to in paragraph (4) are—

(a) the claimant has difficulty communicating because—

(i) he has learning, language or literacy difficulties; or

(ii) he is deaf or blind,

and it was not reasonably practicable for the claimant to obtain assistance from another person to make his claim;

(b) except in the case of a cliam for jobseeker's allowance, the claimant was ill or disabled, and it was not reasonably practicable for the claimant to obtain assistance from another person to make his claim;

(c) the claimant was caring for a person who is ill or disabled, and it was not reasonably practicable for the claimant to obtain assistance from another person to make his claim;

(d) the claimant was given information by an officer of the Department of Social Security or of the Department for Educaiton and Employment which led the claimant to believe that a claim for benefit would not succeed;

(e) the claimant was given written advice by a solicitor or other professional adviser, a medical practitioner, a local authority, or a person working in a Citizens Advice Bureau or a similar advice agency, which led the claimant to believe that claim for benefit would not succeed;

(f) the claimant or his partner was given written information about his income or capital by his employer or former employer, or by a bank or building society, which led the claimant to believe that a claim for benefit would not succeed;

(g) the claimant was required to deal with a domestic emergency affecting him and it was not reasonably practicable for him to obtain assistance from another person to make his claim; or

(h) the claimant was prevented by adverse weather conditions from attending the appropriate office.

(6) In the case of a claim for income support, jobseeker's allowance, family credit or disability working allowance, where—

(a) the claim is not made within the time specified for that benefit in Schedule 4, but is made within one month of the expiry of that time; and

(b) the Secretary of State considers that to do so would be consistent with the proper administration of benefit,

the Secretary of State may direct that the prescribed time for claiming shall be extended by such period as he considers appropriate, subject to a maximum of one month, where any of the circumstances specified in paragraph (7) applies.

(7) The circumstances referred to in praragraph (6) are—

(a) the appropriate office where the claimant would be expected to make a claim was closed and alternative arrangements were not available;

(b) the claimant was unable to attend the appropriate office due to difficulties with his normal mode of transport and there was no reasonable alternative available;

(c) there were adverse postal conditions;

(d) the claimant was previously in receipt of another benefit, and notification of expiry of entitlement to that benefit was not sent to the claimant before the date that his entitlement expired;

(e) in the case of a claim for family credit, the claimant had previously been entitled to income support or jobseeker's allowance (''the previous benefit''), and the claim for family credit was made within one month of expiry of entitlemt to the previous benefit;

(f) except in the case of a claim for family credit or disability working allowance, the claimant had ceased to be a member of a married or unmarried couple within the period of one month before the claim was made; [2. . .]

(g) during the period of one month before the claim was made a close relative of the claimant had died, and for this purpose "close relative" means partner, parent, son, daughter, brother or [2sister; or]

[2(h) in the case of a claim for disability working allowance, the claimant had previously been entitled to income support, jobseeker's allowance, incapacity benefit or severe disablement allowance ("the previous benefit"), and the claim for disability working allowance was made within one month of expiry of entitlement to the previous benefit.]

(8) This regulation shall not effect with respect to a claim to which regulation 21ZA(2) of the Income Support (General) Regulations 1987 (treatment of refugees) applies.]

AMENDMENT

1. This regulation was substituted by Social Security (Miscellaneous Amendments) (No. 2) Regulations 1997 (S.I. 1997 No. 793, reg. 6 (April 7, 1997).

2. Social Security (Claims and Payments and Adjudication) Amendment No. 2 Regulations 1997 (S.I. 1997 No. 2290), reg. 2 (October 13, 1997).

GENERAL NOTE

This new provision represents a radical change in the approach to late claims. Gone is the concept of "good cause" on which there had been been countless Commissioners' decisions since 1948. Now the time for claiming most benefits is three months and cannot be extended (save where section 3 of the Social Security Administration Act 1992 applies in respect of widow's benefit). For incapacity benefit or severe disablement allowance, it is one month and cannot be extended (Sched. 4, para. 2). For income support, jobseeker's allowance, family credit or disability allowance, it is the first day in respect of which benefit is claimed, although there is an extra 14 days' grace in the case of repeat claims for disability working allowance and family credit (Sched. 4). The time for claiming any of those four benefits may be extended to one month under para. (6), in the circumstances mentioned in para. (7), or to three months under para. (4) in the circumstances mentioned in para. (5). If a claim is late, para. (6) should be considered by the Secretary of State, before the case is referred to an adjudication officer (*CSIS/61/92*). The circumstances set out in para. (5) are analogous to some of those in which it had been held that there was "good cause" for delay under the old regime. However, the list of circumstances is restricted and is exhaustive. Some of the sub-paragraphs require a judgement as to whether it was reasonably practicable for the claimant to obtain assistance. It has been held that it is not reasonably practicable for a person to make enquiries or make a claim if he or she reasonably believes that there is nothing about which to enquire or that might be claimed (*R(P) 1/79, R(I) 1/90*). It is arguable that the same approach might be appropriate under the new legislation.

It must be emphasised that the backdating possible under reg. 19 is from the date of claim and, under reg. 6, the date on which a claim may be treated as made is often very much earlier than the actual date of claim. In practical terms, reg. 6 may be far more important than reg. 19 if a claimant is seeking benefit in respect of a period before the date of claim. This is particularly so where entitlement to one benefit depends on entitlement to another (see reg. 6(12) to (29)), but it is still vital to claim both benefits at the earliest possible opportunity.

Reg. 19 has no application to attendance allowance or disability living allowance which cannot usually be paid in respect of any period before the date of claim (see ss. 65(4) and 76 of the Social Security Contributions and Benefits Act 1992 although, again, the claim may be treated under reg. 6 as having been made before the actual date of claim).

PART III

PAYMENTS

Time and manner of payment: general provision

20. Subject to the provisions of [1regulations 20A to 27], benefit shall be paid in accordance with an award as soon as is reasonably practicable after the award has been made, by means of an instrument of payment or by such other means as appears to the Secretary of State to be appropriate in the circumstances of any particular case.

Amendment

1. Social Security (Claims and Payments) Amendment (No. 4) Regulations 1994 (S.I. 1994 No. 3196), reg. 3 (January 10, 1995).

[1Payment on presentation of an instrument for benefit payment

20A.—(1) Where it appears to the Secretary of State to be appropriate in any class of case, benefit due to a beneficiary falling within such a class shall be paid on presentation of an instrument for benefit payment in accordance with the arrangements set out in this regulation.

[2(2) When a beneficiary falls within a class mentioned in paragraph (1) the Secretary of State shall issue an instrument for benefit payment to whichever one or more of the following persons seems to him to be approrpaite in the circumstances of the case—

(a) that beneficiary;
(b) in England and Wales, the receiver appointed by the Court of Protection with power to receive benefit on behalf of that claimant;
(c) in Scotland, the tutor, curator or other guardian acting or appointed in terms of law to administer the estate of that beneficiary;
(d) the person appointed by the Secretary of State under regulation 33 to act on behalf of that beneficiary;
(e) subject to paragraph (4A), the person authorised by that beneficiary to act on his behalf;
(f) the person to whom benefit is to be paid on that beneficiary's behalf further to a direction by the Secretary of State under regulation 34; and
(g) the alternative payee under regulation 36.]

(3) Instruments for benefit payment shall be in such form as the Secretary of State may from time to time approve.

(4) Benefits shall not be paid under this regulation other than to—

(a) a person to whom an instrument for benefit payment has been issued in accordance with paragraph (2); or
(b) subject to paragraph (4A), a person not falling within sub-paragraph (a) who has been authorised by a beneficiary to whom an instrument for benefit payment has been issued to act on his behalf.

[2(4A) A person authorised by the beneficiary to act on his behalf under paragraph (2)(e) must be so authorised in respect of all benefits, payment of which may be obtained by means of that instrument for benefit payment.]

(5) The Secretary of State shall provide the paying agent with information as to the amount of benefit, if any, due to the beneficiary where the paying agent uses the instrument for benefit payment to request that information.

[2(5A) When an instrument for benefit payment is presented for payment the Secretary of State may require the person presenting that instrument to accept payment—

(i) for the purpose of obtaining payment of any benefit to which the person presenting it is entitled in his own right; or
(ii) by a person such as is mentioned in paragraph (2)(b), (c), (d), (e) or (f) for the purpose of obtaining payment of any benefit to which the person in respect of whom the appointment, authorisation or, as the case may be, direction mentioned in those provisions relate is so entitled.

of all monies then due in respect of such benefits; or

(b) if the instrument is presented for the purpose of obtaining payment of any benefit which that person is entitled to receive by virtue of regulation 36 (payment to a partner as alternative payee), of all monies then due in respect of such benefits,

payments of which may be obtained by means of that instrument.]

(6) Where a paying agent pays benefit in accordance with this regulation, the person receiving it shall sign a receipt in a form approved by the Secretary of State and such signature shall be sufficient discharge to the Secretary of State for any sum so paid.

(7) In this regulation, "paying agent" means a person authorised by the Secretary of State to make payments of benefit in accordance with the arrangements for payment set out in this regulation.]

AMENDMENT

1. Social Security (Claims and Payments) Amendment (No. 4) Regulations 1994 (S.I. 1994 No. 3196), reg. 4 (January 10, 1995).

2. Social Security (Claims and Payments, etc.) Amendment Regulations 1996 (S.I. 1996 No. 672), reg. 2(2) (April 4, 1996).

Direct credit transfer

21.—(1) Subject to the provisions of this regulation, [1benefit [4to which this regulation applies]] may, on the application of the person claiming, or entitled to it, and with the consent of the Secretary of State, be paid by way of automated [1. . .] credit transfer into a bank or other account—

- (a) in the name of the person entitled to benefit, or his spouse [3or partner], or a person acting on his behalf, or
- (b) in the joint names of the persons entitled to benefit and his spouse [3or partner], or the person entitled to benefit and a person acting on his behalf.

(2) An application for the benefit to be paid in accordance with paragraph (1)—

- (a) shall be in writing on a form approved for the purpose by the Secretary of State or in such other manner, being in writing, as he may accept as sufficient in the circumstances, and
- (b) shall contain a statement or be accompanied by a written statement made by the applicant declaring that he has read and understood the conditions applicable to payment of benefit in accordance with this regulation.

(3) [2Subject to paragraph (3A)] benefit shall be paid in accordance with paragraph (1) within seven days of the last day of each successive period of entitlement as may be provided in the application.

[2(3A) Income Support shall be paid in accordance with paragraph (1) within 7 days of the time determined for the payment of income support in accordance with Schedule 7.]

(4) In respect of benefit which is the subject of an arrangement for payment under this regulation, the Secretary of State may make a particular payment by credit transfer otherwise than is provided by paragraph (3) if it appears to him appropriate to do so for the purpose of—

- (a) paying any arrears of benefit, or
- (b) making a payment in respect of a terminal period of an award or for any similar purpose.

(5) The arrangement for benefit to be payable in accordance with this regulation may be terminated—

- (a) by the person entitled to benefit or a person acting on his behalf by notice in writing delivered or sent to an appropriate office or
- (b) by the Secretary of State if the arrangement seems to him to be no longer appropriate to the circumstances of the particular case.

[1(6) [4. . .]]

AMENDMENTS

1. Social Security (Miscellaneous Provisions) Amendment Regulations 1992 (S.I. 1992 No. 247), reg. 15 (March 9, 1992).
2. Social Security (Claims and Payments) Amendment (No. 2) Regulations 1993 (S.I. 1993 No. 1113), reg. 2 (May 12, 1993).
3. Social Security (Claims and Payments) Amendment Regulations 1994 (S.I. 1994 No. 2319), reg. 4 (October 3, 1994).
4. Social Security (Claims and Payments, etc.) Amendment Regulations 1996 (S.I. 1996 No. 672), reg. 2(3) (April 4, 1996).

Long-term benefits

22.—(1) Subject to the provisions of [1regulations 21 and 25(1)] long-term benefits shall be paid at intervals of four weeks in the case of [1disability living allowance] but otherwise weekly in advance, by means of benefit orders [2or on presentation of an instrument for benefit payment] at such place as the Secretary of State, after enquiry of the beneficiary, may from time to time specify, unless in any particular case the Secretary of State arranges otherwise.
(2) Where the amount of long-term benefit payable is less than [3£5.00] a week the Secretary of State may direct that it shall be paid (whether in advance or in arrears) at such intervals as may be specified not exceeding 12 months.
(3) Schedule 6 specifies the days of the week on which the various long-term benefits are payable.

AMENDMENTS

1. Social Security (Claims and Payments) Amendment Regulations 1991 (S.I. 1991 2741), reg. 12 (February 3, 1992 with a saving under reg. 29 until April 16, 1992).
2. Social Security (Claims and Payments) Amendment (No. 4) Regulations 1994 (S.I. 1994 No. 3196), reg. 4 (January 10, 1995).
3. Social Security (Claims and Payments and Adjudication) Amendment Regulations 1996 (S.I. 1996 No. 2306), reg. 3 (October 7, 1996).

23. and **24.** *Omitted.*

Payment of attendance allowance and constant attendance allowance at a daily rate

25.—(1) Attendance allowance [1or disability living allowance [2. . .] shall be paid in respect of any person, for any day falling within a period to which paragraph (2) applies, at the daily rate (which shall be equal to 1/7th of the weekly rate) and attendance allowance [1or disability living allowance [2. . .] payable in pursuance of this regulation shall be paid weekly or as the Secretary of State may direct in any case.
(2) This paragraph applies to any period which—
(a) begins on the day immediately following the last day of a period during which a person was living in [1a hospital specified in or other accommodation provided as specified in regulations made under section 37ZB(8) of the Social Security Act 1975 (''specified hospital or other accommodation'')]; and
(b) ends—
(i) if the first day of the period was a day of payment, at midnight on the day preceding the [14th] following day of payment, or
(ii) if that day was not a day of payment, at midnight on the day preceding the [15th] following day of payment, or

(iii) if earlier, on the day immediately preceding the day on which [[1]he next lives in specified hospital or other accommodation];

if on the first day of the period it is expected that, before the expiry of the period of [[1]28 days] beginning with that day, he will return to [[1]specified hospital or other accommodation].

(3) An increase of disablement pension under section 61 of the Social Security Act 1975 where constant attendance is needed (''constant attendance allowance'') shall be paid at a daily rate of 1/7th of the weekly rate in any case where it becomes payable for a period of less than a week which is immediately preceded and immediately succeeded by periods during which the constant attendance allowance was not payable because regulation 21(1) of the Social Security (General Benefit) Regulations 1982 applied.

AMENDMENT

1. Social Security (Claims and Payments) Amendment Regulations 1991 (S.I. 1991 No. 2741), reg. 13 (April 6, 1992).
2. Social Security (Disability Living Allowance and Claims and Payments) Amendment Regulations 1996 (S.I. 1996 No. 1436), reg. (July 31, 1996).

GENERAL NOTE

Ss.37ZB(8) and 61 of the Social Security Act 1975 have been replaced by ss.72(8) and 104 of the Social Security Contributions and Benefits Act 1992.

26. and **26A.** *Omitted.*

[[1]Family credit and disability working allowance

27.—(1) Subject to regulation 21 [[3]and paragraph (1A)], family credit and disability working allowance shall be payable in respect of any benefit week on the Tuesday next following the end of that week by means of a book of serial orders [[2]or on presentation of an instrument for benefit payment] unless in any case the Secretary of State arranges otherwise.

[[3](1A) Subject to paragraph (2), where an amount of family credit or disability working allowances becomes payable which is at a weekly rate of not more than £4.00, that amount shall, if the Secretary of State so directs, be payable as soon as practicable by means of a single payment; except that if that amount represents an increase in the amount of either of those benefits which has previously been paid in respect of the same period, this paragraph shall apply only if that previous payment was made by means of a single payment.]

(2) Where the entitlement to family credit or disability working allowance is less than 50 pence a week that amount shall not be payable.]

AMENDMENTS

1. Social Security (Claims and Payments) Amendment Regulations 1991 (S.I. 1991 No. 2741), reg. 14 (April 6, 1992).
2. Social Security (Claims and Payments) Amendment (No. 3) Regulations 1993 (S.I. 1993 No. 2113), reg. 3(4) (October 25, 1993).
3. Social Security (Claims and Payments) Amendment (No. 4) Regulations 1994 (S.I. 1994 No. 3196), reg. 7 (January 10, 1995).

Fractional amounts of benefit

28. Where the amount of any benefit payable would, but for this regulation, include a fraction of a penny, that fraction shall be disregarded if it is less than a half penny and shall otherwise be treated as a penny.

[1Payment to a person under age 18

29. Where benefit is paid to a person under the age of 18 (whether on his own behalf or on behalf of another) the receipt of that person shall be sufficient discharge to the Secretary of State.]

AMENDMENT

1. Social Security (Claims and Payments, etc.) Amendment Regulations 1996 (S.I. 1996 No. 672), reg. 2(4) (April 4, 1996).

Payments on death

30.—(1) On the death of a person who has made a claim for benefit, the Secretary of State may appoint such person as he may think fit to proceed with the claim.

(2) Subject to paragraph (4), any sum payable by way of benefit which is payable under an award on a claim proceeded with under paragraph (1) may be paid or distributed by the Secretary of State to or amongst persons over the age of 16 claiming as personal representatives, legatees, next of kin, or creditors of the deceased (or, where the deceased was illegitimate, to or amongst other persons over the age of 16), and the provisions of regulation 38 (extinguishment of right) shall apply to any such payment or distribution; and

(a) the receipt of any such person shall be a good discharge to the Secretary of State for any sum so paid; and

(b) where the Secretary of State is satisfied that any such sum or part thereof is needed for the benefit of any person under the age of 16, he may obtain a good discharge therefor by paying the sum or part thereof to a person over that age who satisfies the Secretary of State that he will apply the sum so paid for the benefit of the person under the age of 16.

(3) Subject to paragraph (2), any sum payable by way of benefit to the deceased, payment of which he had not obtained at the date of his death may, unless the right thereto was already extinguished at that date, be paid or distributed to or amongst such persons as are mentioned in paragraph (2), and regulation 38 shall apply to any such payment or distribution, except that, for the purpose of that regulation, the period of 12 months shall be calculated from the date on which the right to payment of any sum is treated as having arisen in relation to any such person and not from the date on which that right is treated as having arisen in relation to the deceased.

(4) Paragraphs (2) and (3) shall not apply in any case unless written application for the payment of any such sum is made to the Secretary of State within 12 months from the date of the deceased's death or within such longer period as the Secretary of State may allow in any particular case.

(5) Where the conditions specified in paragraph (6) are satisfied, a claim may be made on behalf of the deceased to any benefit other than [6jobseeker's allowance,] income support [3, family credit or disability working allowance] or a social fund payment such as is mentioned in section 32(2)(a) [1and section 32(2A)] of the Social Security Act 1986 [2, or reduced earnings allowance or disablement benefit], to which he would have been entitled if he had claimed it in the prescribed manner and within the prescribed time.

(6) [4Subject to the following provisions of this regulation,] the following conditions are specified for the purposes of paragraph (5)—

(a) within 6 months of the death an application must have been made in writing to the Secretary of State for a person, whom the Secretary of State thinks fit to be appointed to make the claim, to be so appointed;

(b) a person must have been appointed by the Secretary of State to make the claim;

(c) there must have been no longer period than six months between the appointment and the making of the claim.

[[2](6A) Where the conditions specified in paragraph (6B) are satisfied, a person may make a claim for reduced earnings allowance or disablement benefit, including any increase under section 61 or 63 of the Social Security Act 1975, in the name of a person who has died.

(6B) [[4]Subject to the following provisions of this regulation] the conditions specified for the purposes of paragraph (6A) are—

(a) that the person who has died would have been entitled to the benefit claimed if he had made a claim for it in the prescribed manner and within the prescribed time;

(b) that within 6 months of a death certificate being issued in respect of the person who has died, the person making the claim has applied to the Secretary of State to be made an appointee of the person who has died [[5]. . .];

[[5](ba) that that person has been appointed by the Secretary of State to make the claim;]

(c) the claim is made within 6 months of the appointment.

(6C) Subject to paragraph (6D), where the Secretary of State certifies that to do so would be consistent with the proper administration of the Social Security Contributions and Benefits Act 1992 the period specified in paragraphs (6)(a) and (c) and (6B)(b) and (c) shall be extended by such period, not exceeding 6 months, as may be specified in the certificate.

(6D) (a) Where a certificate is given under paragraph (6C) extending the period specified in paragraph (6)(a) or (6B)(b), the period specified in paragraph (6)(c) or (6B)(c) shall be shortened by a period corresponding to the period specified in the certificate;

(b) no certificate shall be given under paragraph (6C) which would enable a claim to be made more than 12 months after the date of death (in a case falling within paragraph (6)) or the date of a death certificate being issued in respect of the person who has died (in a case falling within paragraph (6B)); and

(c) in the application of sub-paragraph (b) any period between the date when an application for a person to be appointed to make a claim is made and the date when that appointment is made shall be disregarded.]

(7) A claim made in accordance with paragraph (5) [[2]or paragraph (6A)] shall be treated, for the purposes of these regulations, as if made by the deceased on the date of his death.

(8) The Secretary of State may dispense with strict proof of the title of any person claiming in accordance with the provisions of this regulation.

(9) In paragraph (2) "next of kin" means—

(a) in England and Wales, the persons who would take beneficially on an intestacy; and

(b) in Scotland, the persons entitled to the moveable estate of the deceased on intestacy.

AMENDMENTS

1. Social Security (Common Provisions) Miscellaneous Amendment Regulations 1988 (S.I. 1988 No. 1725), reg. 3 (April 11, 1988).

2. Social Security (Miscellaneous Provisions) Amendment Regulations 1990 (S.I. 1990 No. 2208), reg. 11 (December 5, 1990).

3. Social Security (Claims and Payments) Amendment Regulations 1991 (S.I. 1991 No. 2741), reg. 15 (March 10, 1992).

4. Social Security (Claims and Payments) Amendments (No. 3) Regulations 1993 (S.I. 1993 No. 2113), reg. 3(5) (September 27, 1993).

5. Social Security (Claims and Payments) Amendment Regulations 1994 (S.I. 1994 No. 2319), reg. 5 (October 3, 1994).

6. Social Security (Claims and Payments) (Jobseeker's Allowance Consequential Amendments) Regulations 1996 (S.I. 1996 No. 1460), reg. 2(15) (October 7, 1996).

Time and manner of payments of industrial injuries gratuities

31.—(1) This regulation applies to any gratuity payable under Chapter IV or V of Part II of the Social Security Act 1975.

(2) Subject to the following provisions of this regulation, every gratuity shall be payable in one sum.

(3) A gratuity may be payable by instalments of such amounts and at such times as appear reasonable in the circumstances of the case to the adjudicating authority awarding the gratuity if—

- (a) the beneficiary to whom the gratuity has been awarded is, at the date of the award, under the age of 18 years, or
- (b) in any other case, the amount of the gratuity so awarded (not being a gratuity payable to the widow of a deceased person or her remarriage) exceeds £52 and the beneficiary requests that payments should be made by instalments.

(4) An appeal shall not be brought against any decision that a gratuity should be payable by instalments or as to the amounts of any such instalments or the time of payment but any such decision may be varied by the adjudicating authority by whom the award of that gratuity is varied.

(5) Subject to the provisions of regulation 37 (suspension), a gratuity shall—

- (a) if it is payable by equal weekly instalments, be paid in accordance with the provisions of regulation 22 insofar as they are applicable; or
- (b) in any case, be paid by such means as may appear to the Secretary of State to be appropriate in the circumstances.

Information to be given when obtaining payment of benefit

32.—(1) [[2]Except in the case of a jobseeker's allowance,] every beneficiary and every person by whom or on whose behalf sums payable by way of benefit are receivable shall furnish in such manner and at such times as the Secretary of State may determine such certificates and other documents and such information or facts affecting the right to benefit or to its receipt as the Secretary of State may require (either as a condition on which any sum or sums shall be receivable or otherwise), and in particular shall notify the Secretary of State of any change of circumstances which he might reasonably be expected to know might affect the right to benefit, or to its receipt, as soon as reasonably practicable after its occurrence, by giving notice in writing of any such change to the appropriate office.

(2) Where any sum is receivable on account of an increase of benefit in respect of an adult dependant, the Secretary of State may require the beneficiary to furnish a declaration signed by such dependant confirming the particulars respecting him, which have been given by the claimant.

[[1](3) In the case of a person who is claiming income support [[2]on a jobseeker's allowance], where that person or any partner is aged not less than 60 and is a member of, or a person deriving entitlement to a pension under, a personal pension scheme, or is a party to, or a person deriving entitlement to a pension under, a retirement annuity contract, he shall where the Secretary of State so requires furnish the following information—

- (a) the name and address of the pension fund holder;
- (b) such other information including any reference or policy number as is

needed to enable the personal pension scheme or retirement annuity contract to be identified.

(4) Where the pension fund holder receives from the Secretary of State a request for details concerning a personal pension scheme or retirement annuity contract relating to a person or any partner to whom paragraph (3) refers, the pension fund holder shall provide the Secretary of State with any information to which paragraph (5) refers.

(5) The information to which this paragraph refers is—

(a) where the purchase of an annuity under a personal pension scheme has been deferred, the amount of any income which is being withdrawn from the personal pension scheme;

(b) in the case of—

(i) a personal pension scheme where income withdrawal is available, the maximum amount of income which may be withdrawn from the scheme; or

(ii) a personal pension scheme where income withdrawal is not available, or a retirement annuity contract, the maximum amount of income which might be withdrawn from the fund if the fund were held under a personal pension scheme where income withdrawal was available,

calculated by or on behalf of the pension fund holder by means of tables prepared from time to time by the Government Actuary which are appropriate for this purpose.]

AMENDMENT

1. Income-related Benefits Schemes and Social Security (Claims and Payments) (Miscellaneous Amendments) Regulations 1995 (S.I. 1995 No. 2303), reg. 10(4) (October 2, 1995).

2. Social Security (Claims and Payments) (Jobseeker's Allowance Consequential Amendments) Regulations 1996 (S.I. 1996 No. 1460), reg. 2(16) (October 7, 1996).

PART IV

THIRD PARTIES

Persons unable to act

33.—(1) Where—

(a) a person is, or is alleged to be, entitled to benefit, whether or not a claim for benefit has been made by him or on his behalf; and

(b) that person is unable for the time being to act; and either

(c) no receiver has been appointed by the Court of Protection with power to claim, or as the case may be, receive benefit on his behalf; or

(d) in Scotland, his estate is not being administered by any tutor, curator or other guardian acting or appointed in terms of law,

the Secretary of State may, upon written application made to him by a person who, if a natural person, is over the age of 18, appoint that person to exercise, on behalf of the person who is unable to act, any right to which that person may be entitled and to receive and deal on his behalf with any sums payable to him.

(2) Where the Secretary of State has made an appointment under paragraph (1)—

(a) he may at any time revoke it;

(b) the person appointed may resign his office after having given one month's notice in writing to the Secretary of State of his intention to do so;

(c) any such appointment shall terminate when the Secretary of State is notified that a receiver or other person to whom paragraph (1)(c) or (d) applies has been appointed.

(3) Anything required by these regulations to be done by or to any person who is for the time being unable to act may be done by or to the receiver, tutor, curator or other guardian, if any, or by or to the person appointed under this regulation or regulation 43 [[1]{disability living allowance for a child)] and the receipt of any person so appointed shall be a good discharge to the Secretary of State for any sum paid.

Amendment

1. Social Security (Claims and Payments) Amendment Regulations 1991 (S.I. 1991 No. 2741), reg. 16 (February 3, 1992, with a saving under reg. 29 until April 6, 1992).

Payment to another person on the beneficiary's behalf

34. The Secretary of State may direct that benefit shall be paid, wholly or in part, to [[1]another natural person] on the beneficiary's behalf if such a direction as to payment appears to the Secretary of State to be necessary for protecting the interests of the beneficiary, or any child or dependant in respect of whom benefit is payable.

Amendment

1. Social Security (Miscellaneous Provisions) Amendment (No.2) Regulations 1992 (S.I. 1992 No. 2595), reg. 5 (January 4, 1993).

35. and **35A.** *Omitted.*

Payment to a partner as alternative payee

36. Where one of a married or unmarried couple residing together is entitled to child benefit [[1], family credit or disability working allowance] the Secretary of State may make arrangements whereby that benefit, as well as being payable to the person entitled to it, may, in the alternative, be paid to that person's partner on behalf of the person entitled.

Amendment

1. Social Security (Claims and Payments) Amendment Regulations 1991 (S.I. 1991 No. 2741), reg. 17 (March 10, 1992).

36A. *Revoked by Social Security (Claims and Payments) Amendment Regulation 1991 (S.I. 1991 No. 2741), reg. 18 (April 6, 1992).*

Part V

Suspension and Extinguishment

[[1]Suspension in individual cases

37.—(1) [[3]Subject to paragraph (1A),] where—
it appears to the Secretary of State that a question arises whether—

(a) the conditions for entitlement are or were fulfilled

(b) an award ought to be revised; or

(c) subject to paragraph (2), an appeal ought to be brought against an award the Secretary of State may direct that payment of benefit under an award be suspended, in whole or in part, pending the determination of that question on review, appeal or reference.

[[3](1A) Where, in the case of a person who is in receipt of a jobseeker's allowance, it appears to the Secretary of State that a question arises whether that person is or was available for employment or whether he is or was actively seeking employment, payment of benefit shall be suspected until such time as that question has been determined.]

(2) Where it appears to the Secretary of State that a question arises under paragraph (1)(c), he may only give directions that payment of benefit under the award be suspended [[2]within the relevant period].

(3) A suspension under paragraph (1)(c) shall cease unless, [[2]within the relevant period], the claimant is given notice in writing that either an appeal or an application or petition for leave to appeal, whichever is appropriate, has been made against that decision.

(4) Where the claimant has been given notice [[2]within the relevant period] that either an appeal or an application or petition for leave to appeal has been made, the suspension may continue until the appeal or the application or the petition and any subsequent appeal have been determined.

[[2](5) For the purposes of this regulation—

[[4](a) "relevant period" means the period of 3 months beginning with the date on which notice in writing of the decision in question and of the reasons for it is received by the adjudication officer; and]

(b) a claimant is to be treated as having been given the notice required by paragraph (3) on the date that it is posted to him at his last known address.]]

AMENDMENTS

1. Social Security (Miscellaneous Provisions) Amendment Regulations (S.I. 1992 No. 247), reg. 16 (March 9, 1992).

2. Social Security (Claims and Payments) Amendment (No. 3) Regulations 1993 (S.I. 1993 No. 2113), reg. 3(6) (September 27, 1993).

3. Social Security (Claims and Payments) (Jobseeker's Allowance Consequential Amendments) Regulatins 1996 (S.I. 1996 No. 1460), reg. 2(17) (October 7, 1996).

4. Social Security (Claims and Payments and Adjudication) Amendment Regulations 1996 (S.I. 1996 No. 2306), reg. 4 (October 7, 1996).

Suspension in identical cases

[[1]**37A.**—(1) Where it appears to the Secretary of State that—

(a) an appeal has been brought or a question arises whether an appeal ought to be brought against a decision of a Social Security Commissioner or of the appropriate court in relation to a case ("the primary case"); and

(b) if such an appeal were to be allowed a question would arise in relation to another case ("the secondary case") whether the award of benefit (whether the same benefit as in the primary case or not) in that case ought to be revised,

he may direct that payment of benefit under the award in the secondary case be suspended, in whole or in part—

(i) until the time limit for making an application or lodging a petition for leave to appeal in the primary case has expired; or

(ii) if such an application is made or petition lodged, until that application or petition and any consequent appeal has been determined,

whichever is the later.

(2) In this regulation "appeal" includes an appeal in relation to an application for judicial review made in accordance with Order 53 of the Rules of the Supreme Court 1965 or, in Scotland, an appeal in relation to such an application under the supervisory jurisdiction of the Court of Session, and, in relation to such an application "the appropriate court" includes the High Court or, as the case may be, the Court of Session.]

AMENDMENT

1. Social Security (Claims and Payments) Amendment (No. 3) Regulations 1993 (S.I. 1993 No. 2113), reg. 3(7) (September 27, 1993).

[[1]Withholding of benefit in prescribed circumstances

37AA.—(1) Where a person who is in receipt of benefit fails to comply with the provisions of regulation 32(1), in so far as they relate to documents, information or facts required by the Secretary of State, that benefit may be withheld, in whole or in part, from a date not earlier than 28 days after the date on which the requirement is imposed.

(2) Where the Secretary of State is satisfied that the last known address of a person who is in receipt of benefit is not the address at which that person is residing or that a serious doubt exists as to whether that person is residing at that address, that benefit may be withheld from the date on which the Secretary of State is so satisfied or such later date as he may determine.

(3) and (3A) *Omitted.*

(4) Where a person—

(a) claims any benefit, and entitlement to that benefit depends on his being incapable of work during the period to which his claim relates; or

[[2](b) claims income support, and qualifies for income support by virtue of paragraph 7 of Schedule 1B to the Income Support (General) Reglations 1987]

and that person fails to provide evidence of incapacity in accordance with regulation 2 of the Social Security (Medical Evidence) Regulations 1976 (evidence of incapacity for work), that benefit may be withheld from the date from which he has ceased to comply with the requirements of that regulation, or as soon as practicable thereafter.]

AMENDMENTS

1. Social Security (Claims and Payments) Amendment Regulations 1994 (S.I. 1994 No. 2319), reg. 6 (October 3, 1994).

2. Social Security (Clainms and Payments and Adjudication) Amendment Regulations 1996 (S.I. 1996 No. 2306), reg. 5 (October 7, 1996).

[[1]Payment of withheld benefit

37AB.—(1) Subject to paragraph (2), where the circumstances in which any benefit that has been withheld under the provisions of regulation 37AA no longer exist, and—

(a) the Secretary of State is satisfied that no question arises in connection with the award of that benefit, payments of that benefit shall be made;

(b) a question arises in connection with the award of that benefit and that question has been determined, payments of benefit that the beneficiary is entitled to in accordance with that determination shall be made.

(2) Subject to paragraph (3)—

(a) a payment of any sum by way of benefit shall not be made under paragraph (1) after the expiration of a period of 12 months from the date the right to that payment arose;

(b) where a person from whom benefit has been withheld satisfies the adjudicating authority that there was good cause for his failure to act from a day within the period specified in sub-paragraph (a) and continuing after the expiration of that period, the period specified in that sub-paragraph shall be extended to the date on which the adjudicating authority is so satisfied, or the date on which good cause ceases, whichever is the earlier.

(3) For the purposes of paragraph (2), the following periods shall be disregarded—

(a) any period during which the Secretary of State possesses information which is sufficient—

(i) to enable him to be satisfied that no question arises in connection with the award of that benefit, or

(ii) to enable him to decide that a question does arise in connection with the award of that benefit;

(b) in a case where a question in connection with the award of the benefit arises, the period commencing on the date the question is submitted to an adjudication officer and ending on the date that question is finally determined.]

AMENDMENT

1. Social Security (Claims and Payments) Amendment Regulations 1994 (S.I. 1994 No. 2319), reg. 6 (October 3, 1994).

[[1]Withholding payment of arrears of benefit

37B. Where it appears to the Secretary of State that a question arises whether any amount paid or payable to a person by way of, or in connection with, a claim for benefit is recoverable under section 27 or section 53 of the Social Security Act 1986, or regulations made under either section, he may direct that any payment of arrears of benefit to that person shall be withheld in whole or in part, pending determination of that question.]

AMENDMENT

1. This whole regulation was inserted by the Social Security (Miscellaneous Provisions) Amendment Regulations 1992 (S.I. 1992 No. 247), reg. 16 (March 9, 1992).

GENERAL NOTE

Ss.27 and 53 of the Social Security Act 1986 have been replaced by ss.74 and 71 respectively of the Social Security Administration Act 1992.

Extinguishment of right to payment of sums by way of benefit where payment is not obtained within the prescribed period

38.—(1) [[1]Subject to paragraph (2A), the right to payment of any sum by way of benefit shall be extinguished] where payment of that sum is not obtained within the period of 12 months from the date on which the right is to be treated as having arisen; and for the puposes of this regulation the right shall be treated as having arisen—

(a) in relation to any such sum contained in an instrument of payment which has been given or sent to the person to whom it is payable, or to a place approved by the Secretary of State for collection by him (whether or not received or collected as the case may be)—

(i) in the date of the said instrument of payment, or

(ii) if a further instrument of payment has been so given or sent as a replacement, on the date of the last such instrument of payment;

(b) in relation to any such sum to which sub-paragraph (a) does not apply, where notice is given (whether orally or in writing) or is sent that the sum contained in the notice is available for collection on the date of the notice or, if more than one such notice is given or sent, the date of the first such notice;

(c) in relation to any such sum to which neither (a) nor (b) applies, on such date as the Secretary of State determines.

(2) The giving or sending of an instrument of payment under paragraph 1(a), or of a notice under paragraph (1)(b), shall be effective for the purposes of that paragraph, even where the sum contained in that instrument, or notice, is more or less than the sum which the person concerned has the right to receive.

[[1](2A) Where a question arises whether the right to payment of any sum by way of benefit has been extinguished by the operation of this regulation and the adjudicating authority is satisfied that—

(a) the Secretary of State has first received written notice requesting payment of that sum after the expiration of 12 months; and

(b) from a day within that period of 12 months and continuing until the day the written notice was given, there was good cause for not giving the notice; and

[[2](c) the Secretary of State has certified either—

(i) that no instrument of payment has been given or sent to the person to whom it is payable and that no payment has been made under the provisions of regulation 21 (automated credit transfer); or

(ii) that such instrument has been produced to him and that no further instrument has been issued as a replacement,]

the period of 12 months shall be extended to the date on which the adjudicating authority decides that question, and this regulation shall accordingly apply as though the right to payment had arisen on that date.]

(3) For the purposes of paragraph (1) the date of an instrument of payment is the date of issue of that instrument or, if the instrument specifies a date which is the earliest date on which payment can be obtained on the instrument and which is later than the date of issue, that date.

(4) This regulation shall apply to a person authorised or appointed to act on behalf of a beneficiary as it applies to a beneficiary.

(5) This regulation shall not apply to the right to a single payment of any industrial injuries gratuity or in satisfaction of a person's right to graduated retirement benefit.

AMENDMENTS

1. Social Security (Medical Evidence, Claims and Payments) Amendment Regulations 1989 (S.I. 1989 No. 1686), reg. 7 (October 9, 1989).

2. Social Security (Claims and Payments) Amendment (No. 3) Regulations 1993 (S.I. 1993 No. 2113), reg. 3(8) (September 27, 1993).

3. Social Security (Claims and Payments, etc) Amendment Regulations 1996 (S.I. 1996 No. 672), reg. 2(5) (April 4, 1996).

PART VI

MOBILITY COMPONENT OF DISABILITY LIVING ALLOWANCE

AND

DISABILITY LIVING ALLOWANCE FOR CHILDREN

39.–41. *Revoked by the Social Security (Claims and Payments) Amendment Regulations 1991 (S.I. 1991 No. 2741), reg. 19 (February 3, 1992, with a saving under reg. 29 until April 6, 1992).*

Cases where allowance not to be payable

42.—(1) Subject to the provisions of this regulation, [[1]disability living allowance by virtue of entitlement to the mobility component] shall not be payable to any person who would otherwise be entitled to it in respect of any period—

(a) during which that person has the use of an invalid carriage or other vehicle provided by the Secretary of State under section 5(2) of and Schedule 2 to the National Health Service Act 1977 or section 46 of the National Health Service (Scotland) Act 1978 which is a vehicle propelled by petrol engine or by electric power supplied for use on the road and to be controlled by the occupant; or

(b) in respect of which that person has received, or is receiving, any payment—

  (i) by way of grant under the said section 5(2) and Schedule 2 or section 46 towards the costs of running a private car, or

  (ii) of mobility supplement under the Naval, Military and Air Forces etc., (Disablement and Death) Service Pensions Order 1983 or the Personal Injuries (Civilians) Scheme 1983, or under the said Order by virtue of the War Pensions (Naval Auxiliary Personnel) Scheme 1964, the Pensions (Polish Forces) Scheme 1964, the War Pensions (Mercantile Marine) Scheme 1964 or an Order of Her Majesty in relation to the Home Guard dated 21st December 1964 or 22nd December 1964, or in relation to the Ulster Defence Regiment dated 4th January 1971,

or any payment out of public funds which the Secretary of State is satisfied is analogous thereto.

(2) A person who has notified the Secretary of State that he no longer wishes to use such an invalid carriage or other vehicle as is referred to in paragraph (1)(a) and has signed an undertaking that he will not use it while it remains in his possession awaiting collection, shall be treated, for the purposes of this regulation, as not having the use of that invalid carriage or other vehicle.

(3) Where a person in respect of whom [[1]disability living allowance] is claimed for any period has received any such payment as referred to in paragraph (1)(b) for a period which, in whole or in part, covers the period for which the allowance is claimed, such payment shall be treated as an aggregate of equal weekly amounts in respect of each week in the period for which it is made and, where in respect of any such week a person is treated as having a weekly amount so calculated which is less than the weekly rate of [[1]mobility component of disability living allowance to which, apart from paragraph (1), he would be entitled], any allowance to which that person may be entitled for that week shall be payable at a weekly rate reduced by the weekly amount so calculated.

(4) In a case where the Secretary of State has issued a certificate to the effect that he is satisfied—

(a) that the person in question either—
   (i) has purchased or taken on hire or hire-purchase or
   (ii) intends to purchase or take on hire or hire-purchase a private car or similar vehicle ("the car") for a consideration which is more than nominal, on or about a date (not being earlier than 13th January 1982) specified in the certificate ("the said date");

(b) that that person intends to retain possession of the car at least during, and to learn to drive it within, the period of six months or greater or lesser length of time as may be specified in the certificate ("the said period") beginning on the said date; and

(c) that that person will use [[1]disability living allowance by virtue of entitlement to the mobility component] in whole or in part during the said period towards meeting the expense of acquiring the car,

paragraph (1)(a) shall not apply, and shall be treated as having never applied, during a period beginning on the said date and ending at the end of the said period or (if earlier) the date on which the Secretary of State cancels the certificate because that person has parted with possession of the car or for any other reason.

AMENDMENT

1. Social Security (Claims and Payments) Amendment Regulations 1991 (S.I. 1991 No. 2741), reg. 20 (February 3, 1992).

Children

43.—(1) In any case where a claim for [[1]disability living allowance] for a child is received by the Secretary of State, he shall, in accordance with the following provisions of this regulation, appoint a person to exercise, on behalf of that child, any right to which he may be entitled under the Social Security Act 1975 in connection with [[1]disability living allowance] and to receive and deal on his behalf with any sums payable by way of [[1]that allowance].

(2) Subject to the following provisions of this regulation, a person appointed by the Secretary of State under this regulation to act on behalf of the child shall—

(a) be a person with whom the child is living; and

(b) be over the age of 18; and

(c) be either the father or mother of the child, or, if the child is not living with either parent, be such other person as the Secretary of State may determine; and

(d) have given such undertaking as may be required by the Secretary of State as to the use, for the child's benefit, of any allowance paid.

(3) For the purpose of paragraph (2)(a), a person with whom a child has been living shall, subject to paragraph (4) and to the power of the Secretary of State to determine in any case that the provisions of this paragraph should not apply, be treated as continuing to live with that child during any period—

(a) during which that person and the child are separated but such separation has not lasted for a continuous period exceeded [[1]12 weeks], or

(b) during which the child is absent by reason only of the fact that he is receiving full-time education at a school; or

(c) during which the child is absent and undergoing medical or other treatment as an in-patient in a hospital or similar institution; or

(d) during such other period as the Secretary of State may in any particular case determine:

Provided that where the absence of the child under (b) has lasted for a continuous period of 26 weeks or the child is absent under (c), that person shall only be treated as continuing to live with that child if he satisfies the Secretary of State that he has incurred, or has undertaken to incur, expenditure for the benefit of the child of an amount not less than the allowance payable in respect of such period of absence.

(4) Where a child, in respect of whom an allowance is payable, is, by virtue of any provision of an Act of Parliament—

(a) committed to, or received into the care of, a local authority; or

(b) subject to a supervision requirement and residing in a residential establishment under arrangements made by a local authority in Scotland;

any appointment made under the foregoing provisions of this regulation shall terminate forthwith:

Provided that, when a child is committed to, or received into, care or is made subject to a supervision requirement for a period which is, and when it began was, not intended to last for more than [[1]12 weeks] the appointment shall not terminate by virtue of this paragraph until such period has lasted for [[1]12 weeks].

(5) In any case where an appointment on behalf of any child in the care of, or subject to a supervision requirement under arrangements made by, a local authority is terminated in accordance with paragraph (4), the Secretary of State may, upon application made to him by that local authority or by an officer of such authority nominated for the purpose by that authority, appoint the local authority or nominated officer thereof or appoint such other person as he may, after consultation with the local authority, determine, to exercise on behalf of the child any right to which that child may be entitled under the Act in connection with the allowance and to receive and deal on his behalf with any sums payable to him by way of [[1]disability living allowance] for any period during which he is in the care of, or, as the case may be, subject to a supervision requirement under arrangements made by, that authority.

(6) Where a child is undergoing medical or other treatment as an in-patient in a hospital or similar institution and there is no other person to whom [[1]disability living allowance] may be payable by virtue of an appointment under this regulation, the Secretary of State may, upon application made to him by the district health authority [[1], National Health Service Trust] or, as the case may be, social services authority, controlling the hospital or similar institution in which the child is an in-patient, or by an officer of that authority [[1]or Trust] nominated for the purpose by the authority [[1]or Trust], appoint that authority [[1]or Trust] or the nominated officer thereof or such other person as the Secretary of State may, after consultation with that authority [[1]or Trust], determine, to exercise on behalf of the child any right to which that child may be entitled in connection with the allowance and to receive and deal on his behalf with any sums payable to him by way of [[1]disability living allowance] for any period during which he is an in-patient in a hospital or similar institution under the control of that authority [[1]or Trust].

(7) For the purposes of this regulation—

"district health authority" means, in relation to England and Wales a District Health Authority within the meaning of the National Health Service Act 1977 and, in relation to Scotland, a Health Board within the meaning of the National Health Services (Scotland) Act 1978;

"child's father" and "child's mother" include a person who is a child's father or mother by adoption or would be such a relative if an illegitimate child had been born legitimate;

"hospital or similar institution" means any premises for the reception of and treatment of persons suffering from any illness, including any mental disorder, or of persons suffering from physical disability, and any premises used for providing treatment during convalescence or for medical rehabilitation;

"local authority' means, in relation to England and Wales, a local authority as defined in the Local Government Act 1972 and, in relation to Scotland, a local authority as defined in the Local Government (Scotland) Act 1973;

"social services authority" means—

(a) in relation to England and Wales, the social services committee established by a local authority under section 2 of the Local Authority Social Services Act 1970; and

(b) in relation to Scotland, the social work committee established by a local authority under section 2 of the Social Work (Scotland) Act 1968.

AMENDMENT

1. Social Security (Claims and Payments) Amendment Regulations 1991 (S.I. 1991 No. 2741), reg. 21 (February 3, 1992).

Payment of [2disability living allowance] on behalf of a beneficiary

44.—(1) Where, under arrangements made or negotiated by Motability, an agreement has been entered into by or on behalf of a beneficiary in respect of whom [2disability living allowance is payable by virtue of entitlement to the mobility component at the higher rate] for the hire or hire-purchase of a vehicle, the Secretary of State may arrange that any [1disability living allowance by virtue of entitlement to the mobility component at the higher rate payable] to the beneficiary shall be paid in whole or in part on behalf of the beneficiary in settlement of liability for payments due under that agreement.

(2) Subject to regulations 45 and 46 an arrangement made by the Secretary of State under paragraph (1) shall terminate at the end of whichever is the relevant period specified in paragraph (3), in the case of hire, or paragraph (4), in the case of a hire-purchase agreement.

(3) In the case of hire the relevant period shall be:—

(a) where the vehicle is returned to the owner at or before the expiration of the original term of hire, the period of the original term; or

(b) where the vehicle is retained by or on behalf of the beneficiary with the owner's consent after the expiration of the original term of hire, the period of the original term; or

(c) where the vehicle is retained by or on behalf of the beneficiary otherwise than with the owner's consent after the expiration of the original term of hire or its earlier termination, whichever is the longer of the following periods

(i) the period ending with the return of the vehicle to the owner; or

(ii) the period of the original term of hire.

(4) In the case of a hire-purchase agreement, the relevant period shall be:—

(a) the period ending with the purchase of the vehicle; or

(b) where the vehicle is returned to the owner or is repossessed by the owner under the terms of the agreement before the completion of the purchase, the original period of the agreement.

[1(5) In this regulation "Motability" means the company, set up under that name as a charity and originally incorporated under the Companies Act 1985 and subsequently incorporated by Royal Charter.]

AMENDMENTS

1. Social Security (Miscellaneous Provisions) Amendment Regulations 1990 (S.I. 1990 No. 2208), reg. 13 (December 5, 1990).

2. Social Security (Claims and Payments) Amendment Regulations 1991 (S.I. 1991 No. 2741), reg. 22 (February 3, 1992).

Power for the Secretary of State to terminate an arrangement

45. The Secretary of State may terminate an arrangement for the payment of [[1]disability living allowance by virtue of entitlement to the mobility component at the higher rate] on behalf of a beneficiary under regulation 44 on such date as he shall decide—

(a) if requested to do so by the owner of the vehicle to which the arrangement relates, or

(b) where it appears to him that the arrangement is causing undue hardship to the beneficiary and that it should be terminated before the end of any of the periods specified in regulation 44(3) or 44(4).

AMENDMENT

1. Social Security (Claims and Payments) Amendment Regulations 1991 (S.I. 1991 No. 2741), reg. 23 (February 3, 1992).

Restriction on duration of arrangements by the Secretary of State

46. The Secretary of State shall end an arrangement for the payment of [[1]disability living allowance by virtue of entitlement to mobility component at the higher rate] on behalf of a beneficiary made under regulation 44, where he is satisfied that the vehicle to which the arrangement relates has been returned to the owner, and that the expenses of the owner arising out of the hire or hire-purchase agreement have been recovered following the return of the vehicle.

AMENDMENT

1. Social Security (Claims and Payments) Amendment Regulations 1991 (S.I. 1991 No. 2741), reg. 24 (February 3, 1992).

PART VII

MISCELLANEOUS

[[1]Instruments of payment, etc. and instruments for benefit payment

47.—(1) Instruments of payment, books of serial orders and instruments for benefit payment issued by the Secretary of State shall remain his property.

(2) Any person having an instrument of payment or book of serial orders shall, on ceasing to be entitled to the benefit to which such instrument or book relates, or when so required by the Secretary of State, deliver it to the Secretary of State or such other person as he may direct.

(3) Any person having an instrument for benefit payment shall, when so required by the Secretary of State, deliver it to the Secretary of State or such other person as he may direct.]

AMENDMENT

1. Social Security (Claims and Payments) Amendment (No. 4) Regulations 1994 (S.I. 1994 No. 3196), reg. 8 (January 10, 1995).

48. and **49.** *Omitted.*

SCHEDULES

SCHEDULE 1 — Regulation 9(1)

PART I

BENEFIT CLAIMED AND OTHER BENEFIT WHICH MAY BE TREATED AS IF CLAIMED IN ADDITION OR IN THE ALTERNATIVE

Benefit Claimed (1)	*Alternative benefit* (2)
[*entries omitted*]	
Attendance allowance.	An increase of disablement pension where constant attendance is needed.
An increase of disablement pension where constant attendance is needed.	Attendance allowance [[2]or disability living allowance].
[*entries omitted*]	
[[1]Disability living allowance.	Attendance allowance or an increase of disablement pension where constant attendance is needed.
Attendance allowance or an increase of disablement pension where constant attendance is needed.	Disability living allowance.]
[[2]Disability working allowance.	Family credit.
Family credit.	Disability working allowance.]

AMENDMENTS

1. Social Security (Claims and Payments) Amendment Regulations 1991 (S.I. 1991 No. 2741), reg. 25(a)(i) and (b) (February 3, 1992).
2. Social Security (Claims and Payments) Amendment Regulations 1991 (S.I. 1991 No. 2741), reg. 25(c) (March 10, 1992).

SCHEDULES 2. AND **3.** *Omitted.*

SCHEDULE 4 **Regulation 19(1)**

PRESCRIBED TIMES FOR CLAIMING BENEFIT

Description of benefit (1)	*Prescribed time for claiming benefit* (2)
3. Disablement benefit (not being an increase of benefit).	As regards any day on which, apart from satisfying the condition of making a claim, the claimant is entitled to benefit, that day and the period of 3 months immediately following it.
4. Increase of disablement benefit under section 61 (constant attendance), or 63 (exceptionally severe disablement) of the Social Security Act 1975.	As regards any day on which apart from satisfying the conditions that there is a current award of disablement benefit and making of a claim, the claimant is entitled to benefit, that day and the period of 3 months immediately following it.
5. Reduced earnings allowance.	As regards any day on which apart from satisfying the conditions that there is an assessment of disablement of not less than one per cent. and the making of a claim, the claimant is entitled to the allowance, that day and the period of 3 months immediately following it.
[[1]**11.** Disability working allowance.	(a) Where disability working allowance has previously been claimed and awarded the period beginning 42 days before and ending 14 days after the last day of that award; (b) where family credit has previously been claimed and awarded the period beginning 28 days before and ending 14 days after the last day of that award of family credit; (c) subject to (a) and (b), the first day of the period in respect of which the claim is made; (d) where a claim for disability working allowance is made by virtue of regulation 13B(1), the period beginning on 10th March 1992 and ending on 6th April 1992.]

AMENDMENT

1. Social Security (Claims and Payments) Amendment Regulations 1991 (S.I. 1991 No. 2741), reg. 26 (March 10, 1992).

Schedule 5. *Omitted.*

SCHEDULE 6 **Regulation 22(3)**

DAYS FOR PAYMENT OF LONG-TERM BENEFITS

[[1]Attendance allowance and disability living allowance

1. Subject to the provisions of regulation 25 (payment of attendance allowance, constant attendance allowance and the care component of a disability living allowance at a daily rate) attendance allowance shall be payable on Mondays and disability living allowance shall be payable on Wednesdays, except that the Secretary of State may in any particular case arrange for either allowance to be payable on any other day of the week and where it is in payment to any person and the day on which it is payable is changed, it shall be paid at a daily rate of 1/7th of the weekly rate in respect of any of the days for which payment would have been made but for that change.]

2.—6. *Omitted.*
7. [[1]. . .]

AMENDMENT

1. Social Security (Claims and Payments) Amendment Regulations 1991 (S.I. 1991 No. 2741), reg. 27 (April 6, 1992).

Schedules 7.—10. *Omitted.*

The Social Security Commissioners Procedure Regulations 1987

(S.I. 1987 No. 214)

ARRANGEMENT OF REGULATIONS

PART I

INTRODUCTION

PART II

MAKING APPLICATIONS, APPEALS AND REFERENCES

PART III

GENERAL PROCEDURE

The Lord Chancellor, in exercise of the powers conferred by the provisions set out in the Schedule to these Regulations and now vested in him and of all other powers enabling him in that behalf, after consultation with the Lord Advocate and, in accordance with section 10 of the Tribunals and Inquiries Act 1971, with the Council on Tribunals, hereby makes the following Regulations.

PART I

INTRODUCTION

Citation and commencement

1. These Regulations may be cited as the Social Security Commissioners Procedure Regulations 1987 and shall come into force on 6th April 1987.

Interpretation

2. In these Regulations, unless the context otherwise requires:—
"the Act" means the Social Security Act 1975;
"adjudicating authority" means, as the case may be, the Chief or any other adjudication officer, an appeal tribunal, the Attendance Allowance Board, or a medical tribunal and, in cases where a forfeiture rule question arises, includes the Secretary of State;

"adjudication officer" means an officer appointed in accordance with section 97(1) of the Act;

[1"appeal tribunal" means a social security appeal tribunal constituted in accordance with section 97(2) to (2E) of the Act or a disability appeal tribunal constituted in accordance with Schedule 10A to the Act];

"the Attendance Allowance Board" means the Board constituted in accordance with section 105 of the Act and for the purpose of section 106(2) of the Act, unless the context otherwise requires, includes a delegate appointed in pursuance of paragraph 5 of Schedule 11 to the Act;

"the chairman" for the purposes of Regulations 3 and 4 means:

(i) the person who was the chairman of the appeal tribunal or medical appeal tribunal, as the case may be, when the decision was given against which leave to appeal is being sought; or

(ii) any other chairman of an appeal tribunal or medical appeal tribunal, as the case may be, duly authorised for the purposes of applications for leave to appeal to a Commissioner under the Social Security (Adjudication) Regulations 1986;

"Chief Adjudication Officer" means the Chief Adjudication Officer appointed under section 97(1B) of the Act;

"Chief Commissioner" means the Chief Social Security Commissioner appointed under section 97(3) of the Act;

"Commissioner" means the Chief or any other Social Security Commissioner appointed in accordance with section 97(3) of the Act or section 13(5) of the Social Security Act 1980 and includes a Tribunal of three such Commissioners constituted in accordance with section 116 of the Act;

"forfeiture rule question" means any question referred to in section 4(1) or 4(1A) to 4(1H) of the Forfeiture Act 1982;

[2"full statement of the tribunal's decison" has the same meaning as in the Social Security (Adjudication) Regulations 1995;]

"medical appeal tribunal" means a medical appeal tribunal constituted in accordance with Schedule 12 to the Act;

"nominated officer" means an officer authorised by the Lord Chancellor (or in Scotland, by the Secretary of State) in accordance with section 114(2C) of the Act;

"proceedings" means any proceedings before a Commissioner, whether by way of an application for leave to appeal to, or from, a Commissioner, by way of an appeal or reference, or otherwise;

"respondent" means any person or organisation other than the applicant, appellant or person making the reference who would be entitled under Regulation 17(5) to be present and to be heard at any oral hearing;

"the specified time" for the purposes of Regulations 3(2) and 4(3) means the time specified under the Social Security (Adjudication) Regulations 1986 for applying to a chairman of an appeal tribunal or, as the case may be, a medical appeal tribunal for leave to appeal to a Commissioner;

"summons", in relation to Scotland, means "citation" and Regulation 18 shall be construed accordingly.

AMENDMENTS

1. Social Security Commissioners Procedure (Amendment) Regulations 1992 (S.I. 1992 No. 1121), reg. 2 (June 1, 1992).

2. Social Security (Adjudication) and Commissioners Procedure and Child Support Commissioners (Procedure) Amendment Regulations 1997 (S.I. 1997 No. 955), reg. 7 (April 28, 1997).

Part II

Making Applications, Appeals and References

Application to a Commissioner for leave to appeal

3.—(1) Subject to paragraph (2) of this Regulation, an application may be made to a Commissioner for leave to appeal against a decision of an appeal tribunal or a medical appeal tribunal only where the applicant has been refused leave to appeal by the chairman of an appeal tribunal or, as the case may be, of a medical appeal tribunal.

(2) Where there has been a failure to apply to the chairman for such leave within the specified time, an application for leave to appeal may be made to a Commissioner who may, if for special reasons he thinks fit, accept and proceed to consider and determine the application.

(3) An application for leave to appeal under paragraph (1) above must be made within 42 days from the date on which notice in writing of the refusal of leave to appeal was given to the applicant.

(4) An application to a Commissioner for leave to appeal against a determination by the Attendance Allowance Board of any question of law arising:

(i) on a review by the Board in pursuance of section 106(1) of the Act; or

(ii) in connection with a refusal by the Board to review a determination made in pursuance of section 105(3) of the Act,

must be made within three months from the date on which notice in writing of the determination was given to the applicant.

(5) A Commissioner may accept and proceed to consider and determine an application for leave to appeal under paragraphs (1) and (4) above notwithstanding that the period specified for making the application has expired, if for special reasons he thinks fit.

Notice of application to a Commissioner for leave to appeal

4.—(1) Subject to the following provisions of this Regulation, an application to a Commissioner for leave to appeal shall be brought by a notice to a Commissioner containing:

(a) the name and address of the applicant;

(b) the grounds on which the applicant intends to rely;

(c) an address for service of notices and other documents on the applicant;

and the notice shall have annexed to it [[1]a copy of the full statement of the tribunal's decision against which leave to appeal is being sought].

(2) Where the applicant has been refused leave to appeal by the chairman of an appeal tribunal or of a medical appeal tribunal [[1]. . .] the notice shall also have annexed to it a copy of the decision refusing leave and shall state the date on which the applicant was given notice in writing of the refusal of leave.

(3) Where the applicant has failed:

(i) to apply within the specified time to the chairman of an appeal tribunal or of a medical appeal tribunal for leave to appeal; or

(ii) to comply with Regulation 3(3) above; or

(iii) to apply within the period specified in Regulation 3(4) to a Commissioner for leave to appeal against a determination by the Attendance Allowance Board,

the notice of application for leave to appeal shall, in addition to complying with paragraphs (1) and (2) above, state the grounds relied upon for seeking acceptance of the application notwithstanding that the relevant period has expired.

(4) Where an application for leave to appeal is made by an adjudication officer or by the Secretary of State the applicant shall, as soon as may be practicable, send each respondent a copy of the notice of application for leave to appeal.

AMENDMENT

1. Social Security (Adjudication) and Commissioners Procedure and Child Support Commissioners (Procedure) Amendment Regulations 1997 (S.I. 1997 No. 955), reg. 8 (April 28, 1997).

Determination of application

5.—(1) The office of the Social Security Commissioners shall notify the applicant and each respondent in writing of the determination by a Commissioner of the application.

(2) Subject to a direction by a Commissioner to the contrary, where a Commissioner grants leave to appeal on an application made in accordance with Regulation 4 above, notice of appeal shall be deemed to have been duly given on the date when notice of the determination is given to the applicant and the notice of application shall be deemed to be a notice of appeal duly served under Regulation 7 below.

(3) If on consideration of an application for leave to appeal to him from the decision of an adjudicating authority the Commissioner grants leave he may, with the consent of the applicant and each respondent, treat the application as an appeal and determine any question arising on the application as though it were a question arising on an appeal.

Notice of appeal

6. Subject to Regulation 5(2) above, an appeal shall be brought by a notice to a Commissioner containing:

(a) the name and address of the appellant;

(b) the date on which leave to appeal was granted;

(c) the grounds on which the appellant intends to rely;

(d) an address for service of notices and other documents on the appellant;

and the notice shall have annexed to it a copy of the determination granting leave to appeal and a copy of the [1full statement of the tribunal's decision] against which leave to appeal has been granted.

AMENDMENT

1. Social Security (Adjudication) and Commissioners Procedure and Child Support Commissioners (Procedure) Amendment Regulations 1997 (S.I. 1997 No. 955), reg. 9 (April 28, 1997).

Time limit for appealing

7.—(1) Subject to paragraph (2) below a notice of appeal shall not be valid unless it is served on a Commissioner within 42 days of the date on which the applicant was given notice in writing that leave to appeal had been granted.

(2) A Commissioner may accept a notice of appeal served after the expiry of the period prescribed by paragraph (1) above if for special reasons he thinks fit.

References

8.—(1) Where a forfeiture rule question arises in a case before an adjudicating authority and that authority is not satisfied that the case can be disposed of without that question being determined, the adjudicating authority shall—

(a) if not the Secretary of State, require the Secretary of State to arrange for the case to be referred to a Commissioner to determine the forfeiture rule question; and

(b) if the Secretary of State, refer the case to a Commissioner to determine that question,

and shall inform the person in relation to whom the forfeiture rule question arises that his case is being referred to a Commissioner to determine that question.

(2) Any reference to a Commissioner under the Forfeiture Act 1982 or from a medical appeal tribunal shall be made in writing and shall include:

(a) a statement of the question for determination by the Commissioner and the facts upon which it arises;
(b) the grounds upon which the reference is made;
(c) the address for service of notices and other documents on the person making the reference and on any respondent.

Acknowledgement of a notice of appeal or a reference and notification to each respondent

9. There shall be sent by the office of the Social Security Commissioners:

(a) to the appellant or person making the reference an acknowledgement of the receipt of the notice of appeal or the reference; and
(b) to each respondent a copy of the notice of appeal or of the reference.

PART III

GENERAL PROCEDURE

Respondent's written observations

10.—(1) A respondent who wishes to submit to a Commissioner written observations on the appeal or on the reference shall do so within 30 days of being given notice in writing of it.

(2) Any such written observations shall include:

(a) the respondent's name and address and address for service; and
(b) in the case of observations on an appeal, a statement as to whether or not he opposes the appeal, and
(c) in any case, the grounds upon which the respondent proposes to rely.

(3) A copy of any written observations from a respondent shall be sent by the office of the Social Security Commissioners to the other parties.

Written observations in reply

11.—(1) Any party may, within 30 days of being sent written observations submitted in accordance with Regulation 10 above, submit to a Commissioner written observations in reply.

(2) Regulation 10(3) above shall apply in relation to written observations in reply as it does in relation to written observations under Regulation 10 above.

Directions

12.—(1) Where it appears to a Commissioner that an application, appeal or reference which is made to him gives insufficient particulars to enable the question at issue to be determined, he may direct the party making the application, appeal or reference, or any respondent, to furnish such further particulars as may reasonably be required.

(2) In the case of an application for leave to appeal, or an appeal, from the Attendance Allowance Board, or of an application for leave to appeal or an appeal from, or of a reference by, a medical appeal tribunal, a Commissioner may, before determining the application, appeal or reference, direct the Board or tribunal, as the case may be, to submit a statement of such facts as he considers necessary for the proper determination of that application, appeal or reference.

(3) At any stage of the proceedings, a Commissioner may, either of his own motion or on application, give such directions as he may consider necessary or desirable for the efficient and effective despatch of the proceedings.

(4) Without prejudice to the provisions of Regulations 10 and 11, or to paragraph (3) above, a Commissioner may direct any party to any proceedings before him to make such written observations as may seem to him necessary to enable the question at issue to be determined.

(5) An application under paragraph (3) above shall be made in writing to a Commissioner and shall set out the direction which the applicant is seeking to have made and the grounds for the application.

(6) Unless a Commissioner shall otherwise determine, an application made pursuant to paragraph (3) above shall be copied by the office of the Social Security Commissioners to the other parties.

Medical references

13. A Commissioner may refer to a medical practitioner for examination and report any question arising in proceedings before him except in proceedings on an application for leave to appeal, or an appeal, from a medical appeal tribunal or the Attendance Allowance Board or on a reference by a medical appeal tribunal.

Non-disclosure of medical evidence

14.—(1) Where, in connection with any application, appeal or reference there is before a Commissioner medical advice or medical evidence relating to a person which has not been disclosed to that person and in the opinion of the Commissioner the disclosure to that person of that advice or evidence would be harmful to his health, such advice or evidence shall not be required to be disclosed to that person.

(2) Advice or evidence such as is mentioned in paragraph (1) above:

(a) shall not be disclosed to any person acting for or representing the person to whom it relates

(b) in a case where a claim for benefit is made by reference to the disability of a person other than the claimant and the advice or evidence relates to that other person, shall not be disclosed to the claimant or any person acting for or representing the claimant

unless the Commissioner is satisfied that it is in the interests of the person to whom the advice or evidence relates to do so.

(3) The Commissioner shall not by reason of non-disclosure under paragraphs (1) or (2) above be precluded from taking the advice or evidence concerned into account for the purpose of the proceedings.

Requests for oral hearings

15.—(1) Subject to paragraphs (2) and (3) below, a Commissioner may determine an application for leave to appeal or an appeal or a reference without an oral hearing.

(2) Where, in any proceedings before a Commissioner, a request is made by any party thereto for an oral hearing the Commissioner shall grant the request unless, after considering all the circumstances of the case and the reasons put forward in the request for the hearing, he is satisfied that the application or appeal or reference can properly be determined without a hearing, in which event he may proceed to determine the case without a hearing and he shall in writing either before giving his determination or decision, or in it, inform the person making the request that it has been refused.

(3) A Commissioner may of his own motion at any stage, if he is satisfied that an oral hearing is desirable, direct such a hearing.

Representation at an oral hearing

16. At any oral hearing a party may conduct his case himself (with assistance from any person if he wishes) or be represented by any person whom he may appoint for the purpose.

Oral hearings

17.—(1) This Regulation applies to any oral hearing of an application, appeal or reference to which these Regulations apply.

(2) Reasonable notice (being not less than 10 days beginning with the day on which notice is given and ending on the day before the hearing of the case is to take place) of the time and place of any oral hearing before a Commissioner shall be given to the parties by the office of the Social Security Commissioners.

(3) If any party to whom notice of an oral hearing has been given in accordance with these Regulations should fail to appear at the hearing, the Commissioner may, having regard to all the circumstances including any explanation offered for the absence, proceed with the case notwithstanding that party's absence, or may give such directions with a view to the determination of the case as he thinks fit.

(4) Any oral hearing before a Commissioner shall be in public except where the Commissioner is satisfied that intimate personal or financial circumstances may have to be disclosed or that considerations of public security are involved, in which case the hearing or any part thereof shall be in private.

(5) Where a Commissioner holds an oral hearing the following persons or organisations shall be entitled to be present and be heard;—

(a) the person or organisation making the application, appeal or reference;
(b) the claimant;
(c) the Secretary of State;
(d) an adjudication officer;
(e) a trade union, employers association or other association which would have had a right of appeal under sections 101(2) and 101(4) of the Act (including those sections as substituted by section 52(7)(d) of the Social Security Act 1986);
(f) in cases concerning statutory sick pay and statutory maternity pay, the alleged employer and the alleged employee concerned;
(g) a person from whom it is determined that any amount is recoverable under or by virtue of section 27 or 53 of the Social Security Act 1986;
(h) any other person with the leave of a Commissioner.

(6) Any person entitled to be heard at an oral hearing may:

(i) address the Commissioner;
(ii) with the leave of the Commissioner but not otherwise, give evidence, call witnesses and put questions directly to any other person called as a witness.

(7) Nothing in these Regulations shall prevent a member of the Council on Tribunals or of the Scottish Committee of the Council in his capacity as such from being present at an oral hearing before a Commissioner, notwithstanding that the hearing is not in public.

General Note

S.101 of the Social Security Act 1975 has been replaced by s.23 of the Social Security Administration Act 1992. Ss.27 and 53 of the Social Security Act 1986 have been replaced by ss.74 and 71 respectively of the Social Security Administration Act 1992.

Summoning of witnesses

18.—(1) A Commissioner may summon any person to attend as a witness, at such time and place as may be specified in the summons, at an oral hearing of an application to a Commissioner for leave to appeal, or of an appeal or of a reference, to answer any questions or produce any documents in his custody or under his control which relate to any matter in question in the proceedings.

Provided that no person shall be required to attend in obedience to such a summons unless he has been given at least seven days' notice of the hearing or, if less than seven days, has informed the Commissioner that he accepts such notice as he has been given.

(2) A Commissioner may upon the application of a person summoned under this Regulation set the summons aside.

Postponement and adjournment

19.—(1) A Commissioner may, either of his own motion or on an application by any party to the proceedings, postpone an oral hearing.

(2) An oral hearing, once commenced, may be adjourned by the Commissioner at any time either on the application of any party to the proceedings or of his own motion.

Withdrawal of applications for leave to appeal, appeals and references

20.—(1) At any time before it is determined, an application to a Commissioner for leave to appeal against a decision of an appeal tribunal, a medical appeal tribunal or the Attendance Allowance Board may be withdrawn by the applicant by giving written notice to a Commissioner of his intention to do so.

(2) At any time before the decision is made, an appeal or reference made to a Commissioner under these Regulations may be withdrawn by the appellant or person making the reference, with the leave of a Commissioner.

(3) A Commissioner may, on application by the party concerned, give leave to reinstate any application, appeal or reference which has been withdrawn in accordance with paragraphs (1) and (2) above and, on giving leave, he may make such directions as to the future conduct of the proceedings as he thinks fit.

Irregularities

21. Any irregularity resulting from failure to comply with the requirements of these Regulations before a Commissioner has determined the application, appeal or reference shall not by itself invalidate any proceedings, and the Commissioner, before reaching his decision, may waive the irregularity or take such steps as he thinks fit to remedy the irregularity whether by amendment of any document, or the giving of any notice or directions or otherwise.

PART IV

DECISIONS

Determinations and decisions of a Commissioner

22.—(1) The determination of a Commissioner on an application for leave to appeal shall be in writing and signed by him.

(2) The decision of a Commissioner on an appeal or on a reference shall be in writing and signed by him and, except in respect of a decision made with the consent of the parties, he shall record the reasons.

(3) A copy of the determination or decision and any reasons shall be sent to the parties by the office of the Social Security Commissioners.

(4) Without prejudice to paragraphs (2) and (3) above, a Commissioner may announce his determination or decision at the conclusion of an oral hearing.

Procedure after determination of a forfeiture rule question

23.—(1) Subject to paragraph (2) below, the Commissioner who has determined a forfeiture rule question shall remit the case to the adjudicating authority which caused it to be referred to him together with a copy of his decision on that question and that authority shall then dispose of the case in the light of the Commissioner's decision on the forfeiture rule question.

(2) Where, disregarding the forfeiture rule question, the case referred to a Commissioner is one where an appeal tribunal has, or in the event of an appeal from a decision of an adjudication officer would have, jurisdiction to dispose of the case, the Commissioner may, with the consent of the parties, dispose of the case.

Correction of accidental errors in decisions

24.—(1) Subject to Regulation 26, accidental errors in any decision or record of a decision may at any time be corrected by the Commissioner who gave the decision.

(2) A correction made to, or to the record of, a decision shall become part of the decision or record thereof and written notice thereof shall be given by the office of the Social Security Commissioners to any party to whom notice of the decision had previously been given.

Setting aside of decisions on certain grounds

25.—(1) Subject to this Regulation and Regulation 26, on an application made by any party a decision may be set aside by the Commissioner who gave the decision in a case where it appears just to do so on the ground that—

(a) a document relating to the proceedings was not sent to, or was not received at an appropriate time by, a party or his representative or was not received at an appropriate time by the Commissioner; or

(b) a party or his representative had not been present at an oral hearing which had been held in the course of the proceedings; or

(c) the interests of justice so require.

(2) An application under this Regulation shall be made in writing to a Commissioner, within 30 days from the date on which notice in writing of the

decision was given by the office of the Social Security Commissioners to the party making the application.

(3) Where an application to set aside a decision is made under paragraph (1), each party shall be sent by the office of the Social Security Commissioners a copy of the application and shall be afforded a reasonable opportunity of making representations on it before the application is determined.

(4) Notice in writing of a determination of an application to set aside a decision shall be given by the office of the Social Security Commissioners to each party and shall contain a statement giving the reasons for the determination.

Provisions common to Regulations 24 and 25

26.—(1) In Regulations 24 and 25 the word "decision" shall include determinations of applications for leave to appeal as well as decisions on appeals and on references.

(2) Subject to a direction by a Commissioner to the contrary, in calculating any time for applying for leave to appeal against a Commissioner's decision there shall be disregarded any day falling before the day on which notice was given of a correction of a decision or the record thereof pursuant to Regulation 24 or on which notice was given of a determination that a decision shall not be set aside under Regulation 25, as the case may be.

(3) There shall be no appeal against a correction or a refusal to correct under Regulation 24 or a determination given under Regulation 25.

(4) If it is impracticable or likely to cause undue delay for a decision or record of a decision to be dealt with pursuant to Regulation 24 or 25 by the Commissioner who gave the decision, the Chief Commissioner or another Commissioner may deal with the matter.

Part V

Miscellaneous and Supplementary

General powers of a Commissioner

27.—(1) Subject to the provisions of these Regulations, and without prejudice to Regulation 12, a Commissioner may adopt such procedure in relation to any proceedings before him as he sees fit.

(2) A Commissioner may, if he thinks fit:

(a) subject to Regulations 3(5) and 7(2) above, extend the time specified by or under these Regulations for doing any act, notwithstanding that the time specified may have expired;

(b) abridge the time so specified;

(c) expedite the proceedings in such manner as he thinks fit.

(3) A Commissioner may, if he thinks fit, either on the application of a party or of his own motion, strike out for want of prosecution any application for leave to appeal, appeal or reference.

Provided that before making any such order, the Commissioner shall send notice to the party against whom it is proposed that it shall be made giving him an opportunity to show cause why it should not be made.

(4) A commissioner may, on application by the party concerned, give leave to reinstate any application, appeal or reference which has been struck out in accordance with paragraph (3) above and, on giving leave, he may make such directions as to the future conduct of the proceedings as he thinks fit.

(5) Nothing in these Regulations shall be construed as derogating from any inherent or other power which is exercisable apart from these Regulations.

28.—*Omitted.*

Delegation of functions to nominated officers

29.—(1) All or any of the following functions of a Commissioner may be exercised by a nominated officer, that is to say:

(a) making any direction under Regulations 12(1), (3) and (4);
(b) making orders for oral hearings under Regulations 15(2) and (3);
(c) summoning witnesses under Regulation 18(1) and setting aside a summons made by a nominated officer under Regulation 18(2);
(d) ordering the postponement of oral hearings under Regulation 19(1);
(e) giving leave for the withdrawal of any appeal or reference under Regulation 20(2);
(f) making any order for the extension or abridgement of time, or for expediting the proceedings, under Regulations 27(2)(a), (b) and (c);
(g) making an order under paragraph (2) of this Regulation.

(2) Any party may, within 10 days of being given the decision of a nominated officer, in writing request a Commissioner to consider, and confirm or replace with his own, that decision, but such a request shall not stop the proceedings unless so ordered by the Commissioner.

Manner of and time for service of notices, etc.

30.—(1) Any notice or other document required or authorised to be given or sent to any party under the provisions of these Regulations shall be deemed to have been given or sent if it was sent by post properly addressed and pre-paid to that party at his ordinary or last notified address.

(2) Any notice or other document given, sent or served by post shall be deemed to have been given on the day on which it was posted.

(3) Any notice or document required to be given, sent or submitted to or served on a Commissioner:—

(a) shall be given, sent or submitted to an office of the Social Security Commissioners;
(b) shall be deemed to have been given, sent or submitted if it was sent by post properly addressed and pre-paid to an office of the Social Security Commissioners.

Application to a Commissioner for leave to appeal to the Courts

31.—(1) An application to a Commissioner under section 14(3) of the Social Security Act 1980 for leave to appeal against a decision of a Commissioner shall be made in writing and shall be made within three months from the date on which the applicant was given written notice of the decision.

(2) In a case where the Chief Commissioner considers that it is impracticable, or would be likely to cause undue delay, for such an application to be determined by the Commissioner who decided the case, that application shall be determined—

(a) where the decision was a decision of an individual Commissioner, by the Chief Commissioner or a Commissioner selected by the Chief Commissioner, and
(b) where the decision was a decision of a Tribunal of Commissioners, by a differently constituted Tribunal of Commissioners selected by the Chief Commissioner.

(3) If the office of Chief Commissioner is vacant, or if the Chief Commissioner is unable to act, paragraph (2) above shall have effect as if the expression "the Chief Commissioner" referred to such other of the Commissioners as may

have been nominated to act for the purpose either by the Chief Commissioner or, if he has not made such a nomination, by the Lord Chancellor.

(4) Regulation 28 of the Social Security (Claims and Payments) Regulations 1979 (persons unable to act) shall apply to the right of appeal conferred by section 14 of the Social Security Act 1980 (appeal from Commissioners etc. on point of law) as it applies to rights arising under the Act.

(5) In relation to a decision of a Commissioner which was given in consequence of a reference under section 112(4) of the Act (references of questions of law by medical appeal tribunals), section 14(3) of the Social Security Act 1980 shall have effect with the modification that an application for leave to appeal against the Commissioner's decision may be made only by—

(a) the claimant in relation to whose claim the question of law arose before the medical appeal tribunal; or
(b) a person appointed to apply on behalf of the claimant under paragraph (4) above; or
(c) a trade union of which the claimant is a member at the material time; or
(d) any other association which exists to promote the interests and welfare of its members and of which the claimant is a member at the material time; or
(e) an adjudication officer; or
(f) the Secretary of State.

(6) In paragraph (5)(c) and (d), "the material time" means, where the question of law arose in relation to—

(a) an accident, the time of that accident; or
(b) a prescribed disease, the date of onset (within the meaning of the Social Security (Industrial Injuries) (Prescribed Diseases) Regulations 1985) of that disease; or
(c) a claim for mobility allowance, the date on which the reference was made.

(7) In relation to such a decision of a Commissioner as is referred to in paragraph (5), section 14(5) of the Social Security Act 1980 shall have effect with the modification that "the relevant place" means the premises where the medical appeal tribunal which has referred the question of law to the Commissioner usually exercises its functions.

(8) A person in respect of whom a forfeiture rule question arises and, as appropriate, an adjudication officer or the Secretary of State shall be authorised to apply for leave to appeal from a Commissioner's decision of a forfeiture rule question.

(9) Regulations 20(1) and 20(3) shall apply to applications to a Commissioner for leave to appeal from a Commissioner as they do to the proceedings therein set out.

General Note

S.112(4) of the Social Security Act 1975 was repealed with effect from April 6, 1990 by the Social Security Act 1989. S.14 of the Social Security Act 1980 has been replaced by ss.23 and 34(5) of the Social Security Administration Act 1992.

Revocation

32. The following Regulations are hereby revoked to the extent that they relate to proceedings before the Commissioners:

(i) the Statutory Sick Pay (Adjudication) Regulations 1982;
(ii) the Social Security (Adjudication) Regulations 1984;
(iii) the Social Security (Adjudication) Amendment Regulations 1984;

(iv) the Social Security (Adjudication) Amendment (No. 2) Regulations 1984.

Transitional provisions

33.—(1) Subject to paragraphs (2) and (3) below, these Regulations shall apply to proceedings before the Commissioners commenced before the date on which they come into operation as well as to proceedings commenced on or after that date.

(2) Where he considers that the application of these Regulations to proceedings before a Commissioner would be inappropriate, a Commissioner may give such directions for the future conduct of the proceedings as he thinks fit and, in particular, he may order the proceedings to continue as if the Social Security (Adjudication) Regulations 1984 were still applicable to the proceedings to such extent as he may specify.

(3) Notwithstanding paragraphs (1) and (2) above, where before these Regulations came into operation the time limit for making an application, appeal or reference to a Commissioner had begun to run, then nothing in these Regulations shall operate so as to reduce that time limit.

Schedule

Provisions Conferring Powers Exercised in Making These Regulations

Section 6 of the National Insurance Act 1974.

Sections 101(5A), 101(5B), 106(2), 112(3), 114(2C) and (5) and 115(1), (5) and (6) of, and the definitions of "prescribed" and "regulations" in Schedule 20 to, the Social Security Act 1975.

Sections 14 and 15 of the Social Security Act 1980.

Section 4 of the Forfeiture Act 1982.

The Social Security (Introduction of Disability Living Allowance) Regulations 1991

(S.I. 1991 No. 2891)

Arrangement of Regulations

Part I

Introduction

Part II

Attendance Allowance

PART III

MOBILITY ALLOWANCE

PART IV

PROVISIONS COMMON TO PARTS II AND III

PART V

CLAIMS, PAYMENTS AND ADJUDICATION

Whereas a draft of the following Regulations was laid before Parliament in accordance with the provisions of section 12(1) of the Disability Living Allowance and Disability Working Allowance Act 1991 and approved by resolution of each House of Parliament:

Now, therefore, the Secretary of State for Social Security, in exercise of the powers conferred by sections 37ZD and 166(1), (2) and (3A) of the Social Security Act 1975, section 51(1)(g) and (k) of the Social Security Act 1986 and sections 5 and 11 of the Disability Living Allowance and Disability Working Allowance Act 1991, and of all other powers enabling him in that behalf, by this instrument, which contains only regulations made by virtue of, or consequential upon, section 5 of the Act of 1991, hereby makes the following Regulations:

PART I

INTRODUCTION

Citation, commencement and interpretation

1.—(1) These Regulations may be cited as the Social Security (Introduction of Disability Living Allowance) Regulations 1991 and shall come into force on 3rd February 1992.

(2) In these Regulations—
"the Act" means the Disability Living Allowance and Disability Working Allowance Act 1991;
"the 1975 Act" means the Social Security Act 1975;
"the 1986 Act" means the Social Security Act 1986;
"care component" means the care component of a disability living allowance;
"mobility component" means the mobility component of a disability living allowance;
"adjudicating authority" means, as the case may require, an adjudication officer, a social security appeal tribunal, a disability appeal tribunal or the chief or any other Social Security Commissioner appointed in accordance with section 97(3) of the 1975 Act, including a Tribunal of three such Commissioners constituted in accordance with section 116 of that Act;
"second tier adjudication" has the meaning given to it in regulation 15.

(3) In these Regulations, unless the context otherwise requires, a reference—
(a) to a numbered regulation is to the regulation bearing that number in these Regulations;
(b) in a regulation to a numbered paragraph is to the paragraph bearing that number in that regulation.

(4) Any sum payable in accordance with these Regulations is payable subject to the provisions of chapters II and VI of Part II of the 1975 Act, and of any regulations made thereunder.

General Note

Chapters II and VI of Part II of the Social Security Act 1975 have been replaced by Parts III and VI of the Social Security Contributions and Benefits Act 1992. Ss.97(3) and 116 of the Social Security Act 1975 have been replaced by ss.52(1) and 57 of the Social Security Administration Act 1992.

Part II

Attendance Allowance

Termination or cancellation of awards of attendance allowance

2.—(1) Any award of attendance allowance to a person to whom paragraph (2) applies for a period—
(a) part of which falls after 5th April 1992, shall terminate immediately before 6th April 1992; or
(b) the whole of which falls after 5th April 1992, shall be cancelled.

(2) This paragraph applies to a person who has not attained the age of 65 on 6th April 1992.

General Note

No-one under 65 is entitled to attendance allowance after April 6, 1992. Existing awards beyond that date are treated as awards of the care component of disability living allowance under reg. 3.

Award of disability living allowance

3.—(1) Subject to the following provisions of this regulation, a person whose award of attendance allowance is terminated under regulation 2 shall be treated as having been awarded the care component for the period commencing on 6th April 1992 and ending on the day the period of the award of attendance allowance would have been ended but for regulation 2.

(2) Subject to the following provisions of this regulation and regulation 4 (claims for, and applications for reviews of decisions relating to, attendance allowance), a person whose award of attendance allowance is cancelled under regulation 2 shall be treated as having been awarded the care component for a period commencing on whichever of the following dates is the latest, namely—

(a) 6th April 1992, or

(b) the date which precedes by three months the date the award of attendance allowance would have commenced but for regulation 2, or

(c) where on 6th April 1992 the person has an award of the care component under paragraph (1), the day following the day that award ends,

and ending on the date the award of attendance allowance would have ended but for regulation 2.

(3) Where the award of attendance allowance which has been terminated or cancelled under regulation 2 was made to the person in respect of a child who, on the date the award is terminated or cancelled, has not attained the age of 16 years, then that child, and not the person to whom the award was made, shall be treated for the purposes of paragraph (1) or (2) as having been awarded the care component.

(4) The weekly rate of disability living allowance payable by virtue of this regulation shall be—

(a) in the case of a person to whom attendance allowance was payable, immediately before the award was terminated in accordance with regulation 2, at the higher rate specified in paragraph 1 of Part III of Schedule 4 to the 1975 Act, the highest of the three weekly rates of care component prescribed in accordance with section 37ZB(3) of the 1975 Act;

(b) in the case of a person to whom attendance allowance was payable, immediately before the award of attendance allowance was terminated in accordance with regulation 2, at the lower rate specified in paragraph 1 of Part III of Schedule 4 to the 1975 Act, the middle of the three weekly rates of care component prescribed in accordance with section 37ZB(3) of the 1975 Act;

(c) at the highest of the three weekly rates of care component where the award which was cancelled in accordance with regulation 2 was to be payable at the higher rate of attendance allowance and at the middle of those rates where the award which was cancelled was to be payable at the lower rate.

(5) Where immediately before 6th April 1992 a person had an award of attendance allowance but no benefit was payable under the award by virtue of regulations made under any provision mentioned in paragraph (6), benefit under the award of disability living allowance treated as made under this regulation shall likewise not be payable; but, subject to the following provisions of this regulation, for any parts of the period during which those regulations do not apply in his case, disability living allowance shall be payable—

(a) at the highest of the three weekly rates of the care component prescribed in accordance with section 37ZB(3) of the 1975 Act if attendance allowance would, immediately before 6th April 1992 have been payable at the higher rate but for those regulations, or

(b) at the middle of those rates if attendance allowance would immediately before 6th April 1992 have been payable at the lower rate but for those regulations.

(6) The provisions are—

(a) section 35(6) of the 1975 Act (persons for whom accommodation is provided under certain enactments):

(b) section 82(5) of the 1975 Act (persons undergoing detention in legal custody);

(c) section 85(1) of the 1975 Act (overlapping benefits).

(7) For the purposes of determining the weekly rate of disability living allowance payable to a person under the age of 16 such as is mentioned in paragraph (3), paragraphs (4) and (5) shall apply as if he was the person to whom the attendance allowance was payable immediately before the award was terminated or would have been payable if the award had not been cancelled in accordance with regulation 2.

(8) Disability living allowance awarded in accordance with this regulation shall continue for the period of the award only so long as the person to whom the award is treated as made continues to satisfy conditions as to residence and presence prescribed under section 37ZA(6) of the 1975 Act and—

(a) in the case of a person to whom the care component is payable at the highest rate, also continues to satisfy the conditions mentioned in section 37ZB(1)(b) and (c) of that Act, or

(b) in the case of a person to whom the care component is payable at the middle of the three rates, also continues to satisfy one or other of the conditions mentioned in section 37ZB(1)(b) or (c) of that Act.

(9) Subject to paragraph (10), paragraph (8) shall apply to a person who—

(a) before 6th April 1992 was entitled to an attendance allowance by virtue of section 35(1)(b) of the 1975 Act as enacted, and

(b) is awarded disability living allowance in accordance with this regulation,

as if section 37ZB(1)(c)(ii) was modified to read—

"(a) he requires continual supervision in order to avoid substantial danger to himself or others."

(10) Paragraph (9) shall not apply where the award of disability living allowance is reviewed in accordance with provisions in Part III of the 1975 Act.

GENERAL NOTE

Ss.35(1)(b), 35(6), 37ZA, 37ZB, 82(5) and 85(1) of the Social Security Act 1975 have been replaced by ss.64(3), 67(2), 71, 72, 113(1) of the Social Security Contributions and Benefits Act 1992 and s.73(1) of the Social Security Administration Act 1992 respectively.

Paras. (1) and *(4)*. The general rule is that an existing award of attendance allowance becomes an award of the care component of disability living allowance at the equivalent rate as from April 6, 1992. Para. (4)(c) is concerned with advance awards.

Para. (2). This makes technical provision for different starting dates for awards of the care component of disability living allowance. Sub-paras. (b) and (c) are concerned with awards made in advance.

Paras. (3) and *(7)*. Awards of attendance allowance for children were made to adults; awards of disability living allowance are made to children.

Paras. (5) and *(6)*. These make provisions for people entitled to an allowance but in respect of whom it is not payable because they are in hospital or other relevant accommodation or prison or are affected by the Social Security (Overlapping Benefits) Regulations 1979.

Para. (8). The award of disability living allowance is conditional on the claimant continuing to satisfy the usual residence and presence conditions and the appropriate attendance conditions.

Paras. (9) and *(10)*. Para. (9) preserves the position of claimants awarded attendance allowance before s.35(1)(b) of the Social Security Act 1975 was amended by s.1 of the Social Security Act 1988 so as to replace the night "supervision" condition with a "watching over" condition. However, the protection is lost if the award is reviewed.

Claims for, and applications for reviews of decisions relating to, attendance allowance

4.—(1) Subject to paragraph (4), the replacement of attendance allowance by disability living allowance shall be disregarded in a case to which paragraph (2) or paragraph (3) applies.

(2) This paragraph applies in a case where a person—

(a) is under the age of 65 on 6th April 1992;

(b) has an award of attendance allowance which expires after 5th April 1992; and

(c) makes a claim for attendance allowance for a period commencing immediately after that award expires.

(3) This paragraph applies in a case where—

(a) a person is under the age of 65 on 6th April 1992;

(b) that person has an award of attendance allowance or is the subject of a decision given on a claim or application either not to award benefit or that conditions of entitlement to attendance allowance were not satisfied;

(c) an application is made either—

(i) to the adjudication officer in accordance with section 104(2) of the 1975 Act for the decision to award, or as the case may be, not to award benefit to be reviewed, or

(ii) to the Attendance Allowance Board in accordance with regulation 38(2) of the Social Security (Adjudication) Regulations 1986 for a decision of theirs given in accordance with section 105(3) or section 106(1) of the 1975 Act (matters for determination by the Attendance Allowance Board), to be reviewed.

(4) Any award of attendance allowance made pursuant to this regulation shall be subject to the provisions of regulations 2 and 3 (termination or cancellation of awards of attendance allowance and award of disability living allowance as from 6th April 1992).

General Note

This regulation is concerned only with people under the age of 65 on April 6, 1992. Although it does not say so clearly, it follows that it is also concerned only with continuation claims and applications made for review made *before* that date. That inference is to be drawn primarily because paras. (2)(b) and (3)(b) both refer to a claimant who "has an award of attendance allowance" and a person under the age of 65 cannot have had such an award after April 5, due to the effect of reg. 2. The reference to the Attendance Allowance Board in para. (3)(c)(ii) is a further indication.

Para. (2). A continuation claim made in advance before April 6, 1992, in respect of a period beginning on or after that date is treated as a claim for attendance allowance and is then converted under regs. 2 and 3. Reg. 22 makes provision for adjudication.

Para. (3). Similar provision is made in respect of applications for review made before April 6.

Claim for care component treated as having been made

5.—(1) Paragraph (2) applies where—

(a) a person who—

(i) does not have an award of attendance allowance, or

(ii) does have an award of attendance allowance, but that award is due to expire before 6th April 1992,

makes a claim for attendance allowance, or an application in writing is made in accordance with section 104(2) of the 1975 Act for the decision to award or, as the case may be, not to award attendance allowance to him to be reviewed;

(b) the claim or application is made after 2nd February 1992 or is made before 3rd February 1992 but has not been determined by that date; and

(c) at the time the claim, or as the case may be, the application is determined the person to whom the claim or application relates has not made a claim for disability living allowance.

(2) Where the adjudication officer who is determining the claim or application such as is mentioned in paragraph (1) is satisfied that—

(a) the person does not satisfy the conditions of entitlement to attendance allowance, but

(b) solely on the evidence before him and apart from the requirement that he makes a claim for disability living allowance in the manner and within the time prescribed, the person would as from 6th April 1992 or from such later date as the adjudication officer may in any particular case determine, satisfy the conditions of entitlement to the care component which qualify him for the lowest, but not the middle or higher, rate of that component,

a claim for the care component only shall be treated as having been made on 3rd February 1992, and an adjudication officer shall determine it.

(3) Where a person has before 3rd February 1992 applied to the Attendance Allowance Board for a decision given pursuant to section 105(3) or 106(1) of the 1975 Act to be reviewed, and the question arising thereon has not been determined by 3rd February 1992, then—

(a) if the Secretary of State is notified that the question is determined against that person, and

(b) at the time he is notified, the person has not made a claim for disability living allowance, but

(c) the Secretary of State is satisfied solely on the evidence before him and apart from any requirement that he makes a claim for disability living allowance in the manner and within the time prescribed, that the person may nonetheless satisfy the conditions of entitlement to the care component which qualify him for the lowest, but not the middle or higher rate, of that component,

a claim for care component only shall be treated as having been made on 3rd February 1992 and the Secretary of State shall refer that claim to an adjudication officer for his determination.

General Note

If a claimant with no existing award of attendance allowance effective from April 6, 1992, makes an unsuccessful claim or application for review in respect of attendance allowance which falls to be determined after February 2, 1992, the adjudication officer or, as the case might be, the Secretary of State, is obliged to consider, "solely on the evidence before him", whether the claimant might qualify for the lowest rate of the care component of disability living allowance. If so, the claim for attendance allowance is treated as a claim for disability living allowance made on February 3, 1992, and an adjudication officer must determine that claim.

Termination of awards of attendance allowance when beneficiary aged 65 or over

6.—(1) This regulation applies where a person—

(a) has attained the age of 65 but not the age of 66, on 6th April 1992;

(b) makes a claim for the mobility component by virtue of Parts IV or V of these Regulations or of any regulation made under section 37ZD of the 1975 Act (persons aged 65 or over); and

(c) is entitled to attendance allowance on the day the claim is made.

(2) Where in connection with a claim such as is mentioned in paragraph (1)(b) an adjudicating authority makes an award of the mobility component, the person's award of attendance allowance shall, if it has not already been terminated, terminate as from the day which immediately precedes the day the period of the award of the mobility component commences.

(3) Where a person whose award of attendance allowance has been terminated in accordance with paragraph (2) also has a further award of attendance allowance due to commence on the day following the day the first award would have ended but for paragraph (2), the further award shall be cancelled.

(4) A person whose award of attendance allowance has been terminated in accordance with paragraph (2) or cancelled in accordance with paragraph (3)

shall be treated as having been awarded the care component for the period specified in paragraph (5).

(5) The period the award commences is the day immediately following the day the award of attendance allowance is terminated in accordance with paragraph (2) and the award ends—

(a) except in a case to which sub-paragraph (b) applies, on the day the award of attendance allowance mentioned in paragraph (1)(c) would have ended but for paragraph (2), or

(b) where the person also had an award of attendance allowance to which paragraph (3) applies, on the day that award of attendance allowance would have ended but for paragraph (3).

(6) Paragraphs (4), (5), (6), (8), (9) and (10) of regulation 3 shall apply to awards of the care component having effect under this regulation as they apply to awards having effect under that regulation but as if references to 6th April 1992 were references to the date the period of the award of the care component commenced.

GENERAL NOTE

This ensures that a claimant over 65 cannot simultaneously be entitled to attendance allowance and the mobility component of disability living allowance. The award of attendance allowance is converted to an award of the care component of disability living allowance.

S.37ZD of the Social Security Act 1975 has been replaced by s.75 of the Social Security Contributions and Benefits Act 1992.

PART III

MOBILITY ALLOWANCE

Termination or cancellation of awards of mobility allowance

7.—(1) Any award of mobility allowance to a person for a period part of which falls after 5th April 1992, shall terminate immediately before 6th April 1992.

(2) Any award of mobility allowance to a person for a period the whole of which falls after 5th April 1992 shall be cancelled.

GENERAL NOTE

Mobility allowance was abolished from April 6, 1992. Under reg. 8, existing awards were converted to awards of the mobility component of disability living allowance.

Disability living allowance to replace mobility allowance

8.—(1) Subject to paragraph (4), a person whose award of mobility allowance is terminated in accordance with regulation 7(1) shall be treated as having been awarded the mobility component—

(a) for a period commencing on 6th April 1992 and ending on the day the period of the award of mobility allowance would have ended but for regulation 7(1), or

(b) for life, where the award of mobility allowance was for, or had effect as if for, a period ending on the day before the day on which the person would have attained the age of 80.

(2) Subject to paragraph (4) a person whose award of mobility allowance is cancelled in accordance with regulation 7(2) shall be treated as having been awarded the mobility component—

(a) except where sub-paragraph (b) applies, for a period commencing on the date the award of mobility allowance would have commenced, and ending on the date that award would have ended, but for regulation 7(2);

(b) where the award of mobility allowance was for a period ending with the day before the day the person would have attained the age of 80, for life, commencing on the date the award of mobility allowance would have commenced but for regulation 7(2).

(3) The weekly rate of disability living allowance payable by virtue of this regulation shall be the higher of the two weekly rates of mobility component prescribed in accordance with section 37ZC(10) of the 1975 Act.

(4) Disability living allowance awarded in accordance with this regulation shall continue for the period of the award only so long as the person to whom the award is treated as made continues—

(a) to satisfy conditions as to residence and presence prescribed under section 37ZA(6) of the 1975 Act, and

(b) to satisfy or be deemed in accordance with section 13(1) of the Social Security (Miscellaneous Provisions) Act 1977 (mobility component for certain persons eligible for invalid carriages) to satisfy one of the conditions mentioned in paragraphs (a) to (c) of subsection (1) of section 37ZC of the 1975 Act.

General Note

Awards of mobility allowance terminated under reg. 7 are converted into awards of the mobility component of disability living allowance, at the higher rate. An award of mobility allowance to the age of 80 (the maximum age for entitlement to mobility allowance) is converted to a life award of the mobility component. The award of the mobility component depends on the continued satisfaction of the usual residence and presence conditions for disability living allowance, and the appropriate mobility conditions (*i.e.* those which are the same both for mobility allowance and for disability living allowance).

A disability appeal tribunal considering a claim for mobility allowance may award mobility allowance in respect of the period beginning after April 5, 1992, if not satisfied that the conditions of entitlement were met from an earlier date. The award is then converted to an award of disability living allowance under this regulation. Technically the tribunal does not award disability living allowance but they may explain the effect of this regulation on their award of mobility allowance (*CM/95/94*).

Claims for, and applications for reviews of decisions relating to, mobility allowance

9.—(1) The replacement of mobility allowance by disability living allowance shall except to the extent specified in paragraphs (4) and (5) be disregarded in a case to which paragraph (2) or paragraph (3) applies.

(2) This paragraph applies in a case where a person—

(a) is under the age of 65 on 6th April 1992;

(b) has an award of mobility allowance which expires after 5th April 1992; and

(c) makes a claim for mobility allowance for a period commencing immediately after that award expires.

(3) This paragraph applies in a case where—

(a) a person is under the age of 65 on 6th April 1992;

(b) that person has an award of mobility allowance or is the subject of a decision given on a claim or application not to award benefit; and

(c) an application is made to an adjudication officer in accordance with section 104(2) of the 1975 Act for the decision to award, or as the case may be, not to award benefit to be reviewed.

(4) Any award of mobility allowance made pursuant to this regulation shall be subject to the provisions of regulations 7 and 8 (termination or cancellation of awards of mobility allowance and disability living allowance to replace mobility allowance as from 6th April 1992).

(5) In determining under this regulation a person's entitlement to mobility allowance for any period after 5th April 1992—

(a) the conditions as to residence and presence prescribed under section 37ZA(6) of the 1975 Act (which relates to residence and presence conditions for disability living allowance) and not those prescribed under section 37A(1) of that Act (mobility allowance) shall apply; and

(b) for the reference to 12 months in section 37A(2)(a) of the 1975 Act there shall be substituted a reference to nine months.

GENERAL NOTE

Like reg. 4, this is concerned with claims or applications for review made *before* April 6, 1992. No person "has an award of mobility allowance" after that date due to the operation of reg. 7.

Para. (2). A continuation claim, made in advance in respect of a period commencing after April 6, is treated as a claim for mobility allowance, any award being converted to an award of the mobility component of disability living allowance, under regs. 7 and 8. See reg. 24 for provisions concerning adjudication.

Para. (3). Similar provision is made in respect of applications for review. In *CM/95/94* the Commissioner held that an appeal brought before April 6, 1992 in respect of the medical questions for mobility allowance should also be treated as an application under s.104 of the 1975 Act for a review of the adjudication officer's decision on the claim.

Para. (5). Entitlement to an award under this regulation in respect of any period after April 5, 1992 requires satisfaction of the residence and presence conditions for disability living allowance rather than mobility allowance. Inability or virtual inability to walk must be expected to last for at least nine months, which is a compromise between the 12 months for mobility allowance and the six months for disability living allowance.

Claim for mobility component treated as having been made

10.—(1) Paragraph (2) applies where—

(a) a person who—

(i) does not have an award of mobility allowance, or

(ii) does have an award of mobility allowance, but that award is due to expire before 6th April 1992,

makes a claim for mobility allowance or an application in writing is made in accordance with section 104(2) of the 1975 Act for a decision on a claim for mobility allowance relating to him to be reviewed or a question has been referred to a medical board or a case to a medical appeal tribunal in accordance with section B of Part IV of the Social Security (Adjudication) Regulations 1986;

(b) the claim, application or reference is made after 2nd February 1992, or is made before 3rd February 1992 but has not been determined by that date; and

(c) at the time the claim, application or reference is determined, the person to whom it relates has not made a claim for disability living allowance.

(2) Where an adjudication officer is determining a claim or application such as is mentioned in paragraph (1) and he is satisfied that—

(a) the person does not satisfy conditions for entitlement to mobility allowance, but

(b) solely on the evidence before him, and apart from the requirement that the person makes a claim for disability living allowance in the manner and within the time prescribed, the person would as from 6th April 1992 or from such later date as the adjudication officer may in any particular case determine, satisfy those conditions of entitlement to the mobility component which qualify him for—

(i) the lower, but not the higher rate of mobility component, or

(ii) the higher rate of mobility component but only by virtue of being a person who falls within section 37ZC(3) of the 1975 Act (which relates to persons severely mentally impaired),

a claim for the mobility component only shall be treated as having been made on 3rd February 1992, and an adjudication officer shall determine it.

(3) Where a claim, application or reference is being determined by a Board or Tribunal, and they are satisfied that—

(a) the question before them be determined against the person claiming mobility allowance, but

(b) solely on the evidence before them, the person may, as from April 6, 1992, or from such later date as they may in any particular case determine, satisfy the conditions of entitlement to mobility component specified in section 37ZC(1)(c) or (d),

they shall refer the case to an adjudication officer.

(4) Where a case is referred to an adjudication officer in accordance with paragraph (3), a claim for mobility component shall be treated as having been made on 3rd February 1992, and the adjudication officer shall determine that claim.

General Note

This regulation is concerned with a claimant who had no existing award of mobility allowance effective from April 6, 1992, and has made a claim, or application for review, in respect of mobility allowance which has resulted in an unfavourable determination after February 2,1992. The adjudicating authority making that determination is obliged to consider, "solely on the evidence before [the authority]", whether the claimant might qualify for the mobility component of disability living allowance (*i.e.* on one of the grounds that had no equivalent in the mobility allowance scheme). If so, the adjudication officer must determine that issue. Note that, under para. (3), a medical appeal tribunal considering this question is bound to refer the claimant's case to an adjudication officer and cannot determine entitlement to the mobility component itself.

There appears to be some overlap between this regulation and reg. 25, but, if so, it is academic because, despite the use of the word "may" in reg. 25(2), a medical appeal tribunal, unlike a disability appeal tribunal, can never have jurisdiction to consider entitlement to the mobility component.

S.37ZC of the Social Security Act 1975 has been replaced by s.73 of the Social Security Contributions and Benefits Act 1992.

Part IV

Provisions Common to Parts II and III

Separate awards of attendance allowance and mobility allowance

11.—(1) Where—

(a) a person has an award of attendance allowance terminated or cancelled under Part II of these Regulations and an award of mobility allowance terminated or cancelled under regulation 7, and

(b) awards of disability living allowance are treated as made in accordance with Parts II and III of these Regulations,

those awards shall be separate awards.

(2) Where a person—

(a) has an award of attendance allowance or mobility allowance, but not both for a period commencing before 6th April 1992;

(b) in accordance with Parts II and III of these Regulations is treated as from 6th April 1992 as having one award of disability living allowance consisting of either the care component or the mobility component;

(c) claims, or is treated as claiming, disability living allowance but only in respect of the component which is not the subject of the award mentioned in sub-paragraph (b) above; and

(d) is awarded disability living allowance for that component on that claim for a period beginning on or after 6th April 1992, but before 5th April 1993,

the award so made shall be in addition to the award of disability living allowance treated as arising under Parts II and III of these Regulations.

General Note

Under s.71 of the Social Security Contributions and Benefits Act 1992 (formerly s.37ZA of the Social Security Act 1975), on a claim for disability living allowance, there cannot be awarded the care component and the mobility component for different fixed periods and there is only one overall award of the allowance. Mobility allowance and attendance allowance had no connection with each other and were always liable to be awarded for different periods. Where awards of attendance allowance and mobility allowance are converted to disability living allowance, this regulation permits the awards to co-exist as separate awards for different periods.

Under reg. 13, the two awards are converted to one single award from April 5, 1993.

Backdating of awards of disability living allowance

12.—(1) This regulation applies where—

(a) a person claims or is treated as claiming attendance allowance or mobility allowance before 6th April 1992;

(b the decision on the claim is given after 2nd February 1992; and

(c) the decision on the claim was that the person was not entitled to either of those benefits.

(2) Where such a person submits a claim for disability living allowance within three months of the date the decision on the claim was notified to him, any award of disability living allowance arising from the later claim may, notwithstanding section 37ZE(1) of the 1975 Act, be for a period commencing on such earlier date (but not before 6th April 1992) as the authority determining the claim decide the person satisfied the appropriate conditions of entitlement thereto.

(3) Notwithstanding section 37ZD(1) of the 1975 Act, a person who has attained the age of 65, but not the age of 66, on 6th April 1992, shall be entitled to disability living allowance where, in addition to satisfying the appropriate conditions of entitlement to that allowance, he made a claim for it within three months of the date on which he was so notified of the decision on the claim for attendance allowance or mobility allowance.

(4) Any award made by virtue of paragraph (3) shall, notwithstanding section 37ZE(1) of the 1975 Act be for a period commencing on—

(a) 6th April 1992, or, if later,

(b) the date he first satisfies the appropriate conditions of entitlement to disability living allowance (other than the need to make a claim for it).

(5) In this regulation, the "claim" in the expression "decision on the claim" is the claim referred to in sub-paragraph (a) of paragraph (1) and the "decision" is the first decision given on that claim by an adjudicating authority after 2nd February 1992.

(6) This regulation applies to an application made under section 104(2) or 106(1) of the 1975 Act for a review of a determination as it applies to a claim for benefit but as if the application was the claim and the decision was the decision given on that application.

General Note

This regulation is concerned with a claimant who has delayed a claim for disability living allowance until a pending claim or application for review (made before April 6, 1992, and concerning attendance allowance or mobility allowance) has been determined, and that determination is unfavourable. Provided a claim for disability living allowance is made within three months of the unfavourable determination, the claim may be backdated as far as April 6, 1992.

Note that, under para. (5), "decision" is not the final decision on the claim or application, but the first decision after February 2, 1992. It would appear that a claimant who has pending claims for both attendance allowance and mobility allowance, can obtain the benefit of this regulation by submitting the claim for disability living allowance within three months of the later of the two first decisions, provided, of course, that it was unfavourable. Nothing in the regulation prevents the claim for disability living allowance from being in respect of both components.

If the claimant is successful on a claim for either attendance allowance or mobility allowance so that the award is converted into an award of either the care component or the mobility component of disability living allowance, a claim may be made for the other component under reg. 16 and be backdated under reg. 16(5).

Regs. 5, 10 and 25 deem claims to have been made in limited circumstances and in respect of one component only. This regulation assists those to whom regs. 5, 10 and 25 do not apply.

Ss.37ZD and 37ZE of the Social Security Act 1975 have been replaced by ss.75 and 76 of the Social Security Contributions and Benefits Act 1992.

Treatment of two awards of disability living allowance

13.—(1) Where a person has two awards of disability living allowance both of which are for periods which commence before [[1]27th December 1993] and expire after [[1]26th December 1993], then [[2]subject to paragraph (1A)] those awards shall both terminate immediately before [[1]27th December 1993].

[[2](1A) Paragraph (1) shall not apply where the two awards referred to in paragraph (1) are for fixed periods ending on different days.]

(2) A person whose awards of disability living allowance have been terminated by virtue of paragraph (1) shall be treated, as from [[1]27th December 1993], as having been granted one award of disability living allowance—

(a) where both the awards terminated by virtue of paragraph (1) were for life, consisting of both components for life, payable at a weekly rate which is the aggregate of the appropriate weekly rate for each of those components;

(b) where one of the awards terminated by virtue of paragraph (1) was for life and the other was for a fixed period, consisting of one component for life, corresponding to the component which was for life under the terminated award, and the other component for a fixed period ending on the day the award for the fixed period would have ended but for the termination of the award under paragraph (1), and payable at the weekly rate which is the aggregate of the appropriate weekly rate for each of the components from [[1]27th December 1993] until the day the period of the fixed award ends, and thereafter at the weekly rate which is the appropriate weekly rate for the component awarded for life;

(c) [[2]. . .];

(d) where both awards terminated by virtue of paragraph (1) were for fixed periods ending on the same day, consisting of both components for a period ending on that day, payable at the weekly rate which is the aggregate of the appropriate weekly rate for each of those components.

[[2](2A) Where, after 26th December 1993, a person has two awards of disability living allowance for fixed periods ending on different days those awards shall terminate on the day the shorter period ends if the adjudication officer has determined that an award for the component corresponding to the award which was for the shorter period should be made—

(a) for life, or

(b) for a period ending on the day the award for the longer fixed period ends.

(2B) A person whose awards of disability living allowance have been terminated by virtue of paragraph (2A) shall be treated, as from the day referred to in paragraph (2A), as having one award of disability living allowance—

(a) where sub-paragraph (2A)(a) applies, consisting of one component for life corresponding to the component which was for the shorter period under the terminated award and the other component for a fixed period ending on the day the award for that component would have ended but for the termination of the award under sub-paragraph (2A)(a) payable at the weekly rate which is the aggregate of the appropriate weekly rate for each of the components until the day on which the award for the fixed period ends and thereafter at the weekly rate which is the appropriate weekly rate for the component awarded for life;

(b) where sub-paragraph (2A)(b) applies, consisting of two components both of which are for fixed periods ending on the day the period the award for the component corresponding to the component which was for the longer period under the terminated award ends payable at the weekly rate which is the aggregate of the appropriate weekly rate for each of the components.

(2C) Where, after 26th December 1993, a person has two awards of disability living allowance for fixed periods ending on different days the adjudication officer shall not make an award following review or make a new award for a period ending on a date after the date on which the award for the longer period ends unless either—

(a) both awards are reviewed or made as the case may be for a period ending on the same date; or

(b) one award is for life.

(2D) Where, after 26th December 1993, a person who had two awards of disability living allowance for fixed periods ending on different days is awarded two awards of disability living allowance where either—

(a) both awards are for fixed periods ending on the same day; or

(b) one award is for life and one award is for a fixed period,

those awards shall terminate immediately after they are made and the person shall be treated, as from that date, as having one award of disability living allowance consisting of either both components for a fixed period ending on the day the two awards of disability living allowance would have ended but for the termination of the awards under this paragraph or one component for life and one component for a fixed period ending on the day the two awards of disability living allowance would have ended but for the termination of the awards under this paragraph whichever is appropriate.

(2E) Where a person is treated as having one award of disability living allowance under paragraph (2D) the award shall be payable at the weekly rate which is the aggregate of the appropriate weekly rate for each of those components until the award for the fixed period ends and, if one component has been awarded for life, thereafter at the appropriate weekly rate for the component awarded for life.]

(3) In this regulation, the "appropriate weekly rate" in relation to either component of disability living allowance is the rate which corresponds to the rate payable for that component under any award terminated in accordance with [[3]paragraph (1), (2A) or (2D)].

[[2](3A) In this regulation, in relation to references to two awards for fixed periods ending on different days, a reference to the shorter period is a reference to the award which ends first and a reference to the longer period is a reference to the award that ends second notwithstanding that the shorter period may be of longer duration.]

(4) An award of disability living allowance granted in accordance with this regulation shall continue for the period of the award only so long as the person to whom the award is treated as having been granted continues to satisfy—

(a) conditions as to residence and presence prescribed under section 37ZA(6) of the 1975 Act, and

(b) any other conditions of entitlement appropriate to that award specified in sections 37ZA to 37ZE of the 1975 Act.

AMENDMENTS

1. Social Security (Introduction of Disability Living Allowance) (Amendment) Regulations 1993 (S.I. 1993 No. 408), reg. 2(2) (April 1, 1993).

2. Social Security (Introduction of Disability Living Allowance) (Amendment) (No. 2) Regulations 1993 (S.I. 1993 No. 1739), reg. 2(3) (August 6, 1993).

3. Social Security (Introduction of Disability Living Allowance) (Amendment) (No. 3) Regulations 1993 (S.I. 1993 No. 2704), reg. 2(3) (November 25, 1993).

GENERAL NOTE

By virtue of s.71(3) of the Social Security Contributions and Benefits Act 1992, a person may not be awarded the two components of disability living allowance for different periods. However, Parts II and III of these Regulations operate so that former beneficiaries of attendance allowance or mobility allowance may have been treated as having two awards of disability living allowance ending on different dates. This regulation is intended to convert the two awards to a single one.

Ss.37ZA to 37ZE of the Social Security Act 1975 have been replaced by ss.71, 72, 73, 75 and 76 of the Social Security Contributions and Benefits Act 1992.

Reviews

14.—(1) Where a person is treated as having been awarded disability living allowance under any of the preceding provisions of these Regulations, sections 100A(1), (2) and (4) and 104A(1) of the 1975 Act (reviews of decision given by the adjudication officer and the appellate authorities) shall have effect in his case as if the decision there mentioned was the decision which was referable to the award of disability living allowance.

(2) For the purposes of this regulation, a decision is referable to an award of disability living allowance if—

(a) it was a decision awarding attendance allowance or mobility allowance to such a person and the decision was terminated or cancelled in accordance with Part II or Part III of these Regulations and replaced by the person's current award of disability living allowance, or was so terminated or cancelled and replaced by an award of disability living allowance which was itself terminated under regulation 13 and replaced by the person's current award of disability living allowance; or

(b) it was a decision awarding disability living allowance to such a person which was terminated in accordance with regulation 13 and replaced by the person's current award of disability living allowance.

(3) A decision is also referable to an award of disability living allowance where it was—

(a) a decision of the Attendance Allowance Board on a matter reserved for the Board's determination under section 105(3) of the 1975 Act and the decision to award attendance allowance mentioned in paragraph (2)(a) was dependent upon the Board's decision; or

(b) a decision of a medical board or a medical appeal tribunal on a medical question and the decision awarding mobility allowance mentioned in paragraph (2)(a) was dependent upon the board's or, as the case may be, the tribunal's decision.

(4) In paragraph (3) ''medical board'' means two or more adjudicating medical practitioners appointed by the Secretary of State to act jointly in consideration of the medical question, and ''medical question'' has the meaning it bore in regulation 53 of the Social Security (Adjudication) Regulations 1986 on 3rd February 1992.

General Note

This regulation is concerned with decisions awarding benefit, decisions of the Attendance Allowance Board and decisions on the medical questions for mobility allowance, where the award flowing from the decision has been converted under regs. 3, 8 or 13 into a different award. The provisions of ss.100A and 104A (now ss.30 and 35 of the Social Security Administration Act 1992) are applied to the original decision, notwithstanding the conversion.

Part V

Claims, Payments and Adjudication

Second tier adjudication

15. For the purposes of this Part of these Regulations, the expression ''second tier adjudication'' means adjudication by an adjudication officer; and for those purposes section 100D(1) of the 1975 Act (appeals following reviews) shall apply to any decision given by the adjudication officer as if it was a decision given by him on a review under section 100A(1) of that Act (review of a decision on any ground).

General Note

''Second tier adjudication'' is useful shorthand for adjudication equivalent to that type of determination on review against which an appeal may be brought to a social security appeal tribunal or disability appeal tribunal under s.33 of the Social Security Administration Act 1992. Ss.100A and 100D of the Social Security Act 1975 have been replaced by ss.30 and 33 of the Social Security Administration Act 1992.

Claims for a single component of disability living allowance

16.—(1) Where a person—

(a) had an award of attendance allowance or mobility allowance, but not both for a period commencing before 6th April 1992; and

(b) in accordance with the above regulations is treated as from 6th April 1992 as having one award of disability living allowance at the weekly rate applicable in his case to either the care component or the mobility component,

he may submit a claim for a disability living allowance relating solely to that component to which he has no entitlement.

(2) Any such claim made after 4th April 1993 shall be treated as an application for a review under section 100A(1) of the 1975 Act, if made within the period prescribed under that provision, or if not, under section 100A(2) of that Act, of an award of disability living allowance in force at the time the claim is made.

(3) Subject to paragraph (4), an award of disability living allowance consisting of one component may be made by virtue of this regulation in addition to any award of disability living allowance consisting only of the other component which is treated as having been made to the claimant in accordance with the preceding provisions of these Regulations.

(4) An award shall not be made in accordance with paragraph (3) where the period of the award would commence after 4th April 1993.

(5) Where a claim submitted in accordance with paragraph (1) is received in an office of the Department of Social Security or the Department of Employment before 5th April 1993, any award on that claim may, notwithstanding anything in section 37ZE(1) of the 1975 Act, commence on a date not earlier than 6th April 1992.

General Note

Para. (1). Normally a claim cannot be made in respect of one component only. This paragraph permits such a claim to be made where the claimant has an award of the other component following the conversion of an award of attendance allowance or mobility allowance under reg. 3 or 8.

Para. (2). If made after April 4, the claim is treated as an application for a review (which is the way a person originally awarded one component would usually apply for the other). S.100A of the Social Security Act 1975 has been replaced by s.30 of the Social Security Administration Act 1992.

Paras. (3) and *(4).* An award on a claim under para. (1) may be made separately from the existing award if it begins before April 5, 1993. Under reg. 13, the two awards will then be converted to one from that date.

Para. (5). This permits a claim under para. (1) to be backdated as far as April 6, 1992, if it is received by the Department before April 5, 1993. S.37ZE of the Social Security Act 1975 has been replaced by s.76 of the Social Security Contributions and Benefits Act 1992.

Claims in addition

17.—(1) This regulation applies in a case where an adjudicating authority in determining a person's claim for, or application for a review of a decision relating to, disability living allowance is satisfied that the person satisfies the conditions of entitlement to the care component which qualify him for the highest or the middle of the three rates prescribed under section 37ZB(3) of the 1975 Act or to the mobility component which qualify him for the higher of the two rates prescribed under section 37ZC(10) of that Act or to both, and that the person is neither—

(a) entitled to attendance allowance or mobility allowance or both, nor

(b) awaiting a determination by an adjudicating authority on—

(i) a claim made by him or on his behalf for one or both of those benefits, or

(ii an application for review, made in accordance with section 104(2) of the 1975 Act, of a decision relating to one or both of those benefits, or

(iii) an appeal from a decision given on a claim or application for review of a decision relating to one or both of those benefits.

(2) Subject to paragraphs (3) and (4), where in determining a person's claim for, or application for a review of a decision relating to, disability living allowance in a case to which this regulation applies, an adjudicating authority is satisfied that the person—

(a) in addition to satisfying the conditions of entitlement to the care component, also satisfied the conditions of entitlement to attendance allowance for a period before 6th April 1992; or

(b) in addition to satisfying the conditions of entitlement to the mobility component, also satisfied conditions of entitlement to mobility allowance, for a period before 6th April 1992,

other than the condition that he makes a claim for the benefit in question in the manner and within the time prescribed in relation thereto, the authority shall treat the claim for disability living allowance, or in the case of an application for review of the decision relating to disability living allowance, the claim on which that decision was made, as a claim also for—

(i) attendance allowance, where sub-paragraph (a) above is satisfied,

(ii) mobility allowance, where sub-paragraph (b) above is satisfied,
(iii) attendance allowance and mobility allowance, where sub-paragraph (a) and sub-paragraph (b) are satisfied,

and determine that claim accordingly.

(3) Where a claim for disability living allowance is a claim for a single component in accordance with regulation 16 then paragraph (2) shall apply only where the adjudicating authority is satisfied the person fulfils or fulfilled the conditions of entitlement to—

(a) attendance allowance, where the claim is for the care component, or
(b) mobility allowance where the claim is for the mobility component.

(4) Any award of mobility allowance or attendance allowance arising on a claim treated as made in accordance with paragraph (2) shall be for a period ending not later than 5th April 1992.

(5) Where an adjudicating authority is satisfied that the person whose claim or application he is determining satisfies the conditions of entitlement to mobility allowance for a period before 6th April 1992, then he shall determine that claim or application as if in section 37ZC of the 1975 Act, paragraph (a) of subsection (9) was omitted.

General Note

Ss.37ZB and 37ZC of the Social Security Act 1975 have been replaced by ss.72 and 73 of the Social Security Contributions and Benefits Act 1992.

This regulation enables a claim for disability living allowance also to be treated as a claim for attendance allowance of mobility allowance. The need to do this will arise if the claim for disability living allowance was made before April 6, 1992, or if it was delayed in the post or was made within six months of a previous period of entitlement to either attendance allowance or mobility allowance (which were the grounds of which claims for attendance allowance or mobility allowance could be backdated).

An adjudicating authority awarding the care component of disability living allowance at the highest or middle rates must also consider entitlement to attendance allowance. An adjudicating authority awarding the mobility component of disability living allowance at the higher rate must also consider entitlement to mobility allowance.

Para. (5). If the claimant satisfies the conditions for mobility allowance, the usual three months qualifying period for the mobility component of disability living allowance (which had no equivalent for mobility allowance) is ignored.

Claim for disability living allowance treated as not having been made

18.—(1) Subject to the following provisions of this regulation, a claim for a disability living allowance shall be treated as not having been made where the person who made the claim, or on whose behalf the claim was made—

(a) has an award of both attendance allowance and mobility allowance and each award is for a period due to expire after 5th April 1992, or
(b) has an existing award of disability living allowance, consisting of both components, or
(c) has two existing awards of disability living allowance, where one award consists of the care component and the other award consists of the mobility component, or
(d) has an award of disability living allowance consisting of one component and has in addition submitted another claim for a single component of that benefit in accordance with regulation 16.

(2) Paragraph (1) shall not apply where the claim for a disability living allowance is made in anticipation of the expiration of the award of attendance allowance or of mobility allowance or of disability living allowance.

General Note

A claim for disability living allowance is treated as not having been made where it is unnecessary due to the effect of these Regulations.

Claims for attendance allowance or mobility allowance treated as not having been made

19. Where after 2nd February 1992 a person has made a claim for disability living allowance, then any claim [[1]for attendance allowance or mobility allowance made on or after the day on which the claim for disability living allowance was made shall be treated as not having been made].

Amendment

1. Social Security (Introduction of Disability Living Allowance) Miscellaneous Amendment Regulations 1992 (S.I. 1992 No. 728), reg. 2 (March 16, 1992).

General Note

In view of reg. 17, claims for attendance allowance and mobility allowance are unnecessary if a claim for disability living allowance has been made.

Claims for disability living allowance where person has an award of attendance allowance or mobility allowance

20.—(1) Subject to paragraph (3) where a person—

(a) has an award of attendance allowance, and

(b) makes a claim for disability living allowance,

the claim for the care component shall be treated as not having been made.

(2) Subject to paragraph (3) where a person—

(a) has an award of mobility allowance, and

(b) makes a claim for disability living allowance,

the claim for the mobility component shall be treated as not having been made.

(3) Where the claim for disability living allowance is made in anticipation of the expiry of an award of attendance allowance or of mobility allowance, then paragraph (1) or, as the case may be, paragraph (2) shall not apply.

General Note

This refers to claims for disability living allowance made before April 6, 1992 (which is the only period for which it can be said that a claimant ''has'' an award of attendance allowance or mobility allowance as such awards were converted from that date by regs. 3 and 8). Effectively, awards of attendance allowance and mobility allowance are treated as existing awards of the appropriate component of disability living allowance so that the adjudication officer is required only to consider entitlement to the other component. A claimant seeking an increased rate of attendance allowance could apply for a review.

Claims for both old and new benefits outstanding

21.—(1) This regulation applies where—

(a) a claim to either mobility allowance or attendance allowance, or both has been made by or on behalf of a person;

(b) the claim or claims have not been determined by 3rd February 1992, or if it or they have been determined the decision given was that no award be made and an application for review of that decision or an appeal to an appeal tribunal from that decision awaits determination on or after 3rd February 1992; and

(c) a claim for disability living allowance is made by the person mentioned in sub-paragraph (a) before the determination on the claim or, as the case may be, the application or appeal, is made.

(2) Where the person mentioned in paragraph (1)(a) has claimed—

(a) attendance allowance, but not mobility allowance, the claim for disability living allowance shall be treated, until the claim, application or appeal is determined, as a claim for mobility component only;

(b) mobility allowance, but not attendance allowance, the claim for disability living allowance shall be treated, until the claim, application or appeal is determined, as a claim for care component only;

(c) attendance allowance and mobility allowance, the claim for disability living allowance shall be treated, until the claims, applications or appeals in respect of both those benefits are determined, as not having been made.

(3) When the claim, application or appeal is or both are determined and—

(a) the person is awarded attendance allowance, then the claim for care component shall be treated as not having been made;

(b) the person is awarded mobility allowance, then the claim for mobility component shall be treated as not having been made;

(c) the person is awarded both attendance allowance and mobility allowance, then the claim for disability living allowance shall continue to be treated as not having been made;

(d) no award is made, the claim for disability living allowance in so far as it has not been determined, shall then be referred to the adjudication officer for his determination.

General Note

If a person claims disability living allowance at a date when he or she still has an outstanding claim for attendance allowance or mobility allowance which has not been determined, consideration of the claim for the appropriate component of the disability living allowance is deferred until the outstanding claim is determined. If an award is made on the outstanding claim, the claim for the appropriate component of disability living allowance is then treated as not having been made (because it is unnecessary).

Determination of claims for, or of applications for review of decisions relating to, attendance allowance

22.—(1) The Attendance Allowance Board shall not consider any question reserved for their determination under section 105(3) of the 1975 Act where the claim for, or application for a review of a decision relating to, attendance allowance was made after 15th March 1992, whether or not the person to whom the question refers has attained the age of 65.

(2) In a case to which paragraph (1) applies, the adjudication officer shall determine the claim or application in accordance with the system of adjudication for attendance allowance introduced by the Act.

(3) Any question referred for determination by the Attendance Allowance Board in accordance with section 105(3) or 106(1) of the 1975 Act which has not been determined by 5th April 1992, shall be determined as soon as reasonably practicable thereafter in accordance with paragraph (4).

(4) For the purposes of paragraph (3), the question shall be determined—

(a) except in a case to which sub-paragraph (b) applies, by the adjudication officer, or

(b) where the application for review of a decision of the Attendance Allowance Board is made within three months of that decision being given, as a second tier adjudication.

(5) For the purposes of this regulation, any application for a review of a decision which required the leave of the Attendance Allowance Board shall itself be treated as an application for review.

(6) In determining any question in accordance with paragraph (4) any correspondence issuing from the Attendance Allowance Board indicating the matters which, in the Board's opinion arise on a question before it, together with the submissions (if any) made by or on behalf of the claimant in response to that correspondence, may be taken into account by the adjudication officer as evidence relating to the question to be determined.

(7) Where before 6th April 1992, the Board has issued a certificate in accordance with section 35(2) of the 1975 Act, but the adjudication officer has not determined the claim or as the case may be the application for review to which the certificate relates, then in determining that claim or application the adjudication officer shall treat the certificate—

(a) if it specifies both the conditions mentioned in section 35(1)(a) and (b) of the 1975 Act, as evidence that the person satisfies or is likely to satisfy both the conditions mentioned in subsections (1)(a) and (1)(b) of section 35 throughout the period mentioned in the certificate; and

(b) if it specifies one or other of them, but not both, as evidence of his falling within that subsection by virtue of having satisfied or being likely to satisfy one or other of those conditions throughout the period mentioned in the certificate.

(8) Where the Board has before 6th April 1992 determined a question referred to them in accordance with section 105(3) of the 1975 Act and the decision is such that no award of attendance allowance could have been made on the basis of it, then in determining on or after April 6th 1992 any claim for, or application for review of a decision relating to attendance allowance to which the Board's decision relates, the adjudication officer shall treat the decision of the Board, and any reasons given by the Board in support of their decision, as evidence that the person does not satisfy those requirements to which the decision relates.

[[1](9) For the purposes of the provisions of Part III of the 1975 Act in so far as they relate to the review of decisions of adjudication officers, any decision made by the former Attendance Allowance Board under section 105(3) or 106(1) of the 1975 Act together (if applicable) with any certificate issued or altered in consequence of that decision shall, after 5th April 1992, be treated as a decision of an adjudication officer and as such shall be subject to review on the same grounds and in the same circumstances as decisions of an adjudication officer.]

Amendment

1. Social Security (Introduction of Disability Living Allowance) Miscellaneous Amendments Regulations 1992 (S.I. 1992 No. 728), reg. 3 (March 16, 1992).

General Note

Paras. (1) and *(2)*. Any new claim or application for review in relation to attendance allowance made *after* March 15, 1992, is determined under the new procedure introduced by the Disability Living Allowance and Disabililty Working Allowance Act 1991 (now to be found in ss.30 to 35 of the Social Security Administration Act 1992). Para. (5) means that it does not matter that, under the old régime, leave would have been required for the application for review.

Paras. (3) and *(4)*. Any claim or application for review made *before* March 16, 1992, could still be determined under the old procedure until April 5, 1992. If the decision had not been made at that date, it was transferred to the new system of adjudication. An application for review made within three months of a decision of the Attendance Allowance Board was treated as an application for the equivalent type of review under the new regime (see the definition of "second tier adjudication" in reg. 15). Again, para. (5) provides for cases where leave would have been required for an application for review.

Para. (5). Leave was required under reg. 38(4) of the Social Security (Adjudication) Regulations 1986 if more than one application for review was made within a year.

Para. (6). An adjudication officer considering a case transferred under para. (4) must have regard to any draft decision and other correspondence which came from the Board and also to the claimant's submissions. Such documents should be included in the papers for a disability appeal tribunal and should be considered by the tribunal in the event of an appeal.

Paras. (7) and *(8).* Under the old régime, although questions relating to satisfaction of the attendance conditions fell to be decided by the Board, the final decision on any claim was a matter for the adjudication officer. Awards of benefit following reviews were also matters for adjudication officers rather than the Board. This paragraph is concerned with cases where the Board issued, or refused, a certificate before April 6, 1992, but the consequential decision had not been made by the adjudication officer before that date. Under these paragraphs, the certificate issued by the Board or the refusal to issue a certificate is evidence which the adjudication officer is still bound to take into account. However, these paragraphs do not say that that evidence is to be regarded as conclusive (which it would have been under the old régime).

Para. (9). A certificate issued by the Board is treated as a decision of an adjudication officer for the purpose of permitting it to be reviewed.

Appeals to Commissioners from decisions of the Attendance Allowance Board

23.—[[1](1) Subject to paragraph (1A), after the 5th April 1992 an appeal lies to a Commissioner, with his leave or that of another Commissioner, against a determination by the Attendance Allowance Board of any question of law arising from either—

(a) a review made by the Attendance Allowance Board under section 106(1) of the 1975 Act, or

(b) a refusal by the Attendance Allowance Board to review a determination made by them under section 105(3) or 106(1) of the 1975 Act,

at the instance of the claimant in question or the Secretary of State.

(1A) Those provisions of the Social Security Commissioners Procedure Regulations 1987 which on 5th April 1992 applied to applications of appeals made under section 106(2) of the 1975 Act shall apply in like manner to applications and appeals made under paragraph (1).]

(2) [[1]On or after 16th March 1992], where the Commissioner holds that the Board's decision was erroneous in point of law, he shall set it aside and—

(a) he shall have the power—

(i) to give the decision which he considers the Board should have given, if he can do so without making fresh or further findings of fact; or

(ii) if he considers it expedient, to make such findings and to give such decision as he considers appropriate in the light of them; or

(b) in any other case he shall refer the case for second tier adjudication with directions for its determination.

(3) Where in accordance with paragraph (2)(a) the Commissioner gives the decision himself, he shall refer that decision to the adjudication officer with directions to determine the claim or application for review from which the appeal to the Commissioner arose.

AMENDMENT

1. Social Security (Introduction of Disability Living Allowance) Miscellaneous Amendments Regulations 1992 (S.I. 1992 No. 728), reg. 4 (March 16, 1992).

GENERAL NOTE

For the meaning of "second tier adjudication", see reg. 15. The case is remitted to an adjudication officer rather than to a disability appeal tribunal so that the whole claim or application for review (and not just the questions formerly within the jurisdication of the Attendance Allowance Board) can be considered at the same time.

Persons claiming mobility allowance

24.—(1) In this regulation, the expression "medical question" has the meaning it bore in regulation 53 of the Social Security (Adjudication) Regulations 1986 on 3rd February 1992.

(2) Any claim for mobility allowance made after 15th March 1992, or any application made after 9th February 1992 for a review of a decision relating to the medical question or otherwise to mobility allowance, shall be subject to adjudication in accordance with the provisions of the 1975 Act relating to disability living allowance, and the modification, additions and exclusions set out in Section B of Part IV of the Social Security (Adjudication) Regulations 1986 shall be disregarded.

(3) Subject to the following provisions of this regulation, where a claim for, or an application for a review of a decision relating to, mobility allowance, other than a claim or application mentioned in paragraph (2), has not been determined as at 6th April 1992, then that claim or application shall as from that date be subject to adjudication in accordance with provisions in the 1975 Act relating to disability living allowance.

(4) Where a medical question arose on a claim or question to which paragraph (3) refers, then, in determining that claim or question the adjudication officer—

(a) shall have regard to any report received from the medical practitioner to whom the medical question has been referred;

(b) if a report of a medical practitioner to whom the medical question has been referred has not been received by the adjudication officer may—

(i) subject to sub-paragraph (ii) below, await the report and have regard to it before determining the claim or application, or

(ii) where the report has not been received by the adjudication officer within six weeks of the question being referred to the medical practitioner, determine the claim without waiting for the report;

(c) where the medical question has been determined by the medical board before 6th April 1992, shall have regard to any report made by the board on that question;

(d) where the medical question has been referred to a medical board otherwise than on an appeal by the person claiming the allowance, but the board has not determined that question by 6th April 1992, shall consider the question as though—

(i) the reference had not been made, and

(ii) the provisions in section 115C of the 1975 Act (references of claims to medical practitioners and the Disability Living Allowance Advisory Board) relating to disability living allowance applied also to the medical question;

(e) where the medical question was referred to the medical board following an appeal by the person claiming the allowance but the board has not determined that question by 6th April 1992, shall consider the question as though—

(i) it was an application for a review under section 100A(1) of the 1975 Act (reviews of decisions by adjudication officers) of the decision appealed against, and

(ii) the provisions in section 115C of the 1975 Act relating to disability living allowance applied also to the medical question;

(f) where the medical question has been referred to a medical appeal tribunal, shall be bound by any decision given by the Tribunal on the matters to which it relates.

(5) No reference on a medical question to a medical board shall be made by an adjudication officer after 9th February 1992.

(6) Any medical question which would but for paragraph (5) have been referred to a medical board shall be subject to adjudication in accordance with the provisions of the 1975 Act relating to disability living allowance, and for this purpose the medical question shall be determined as though it was a second tier adjudication.

(7) Any appeal on a medical question from a decision of a medical board which is made on or after 10th February 1992 shall be subject to adjudication in accordance with the provisions of the 1975 Act relating to disability living allowance and the provisions of Section B of Part IV of the Social Security (Adjudication) Regulations 1986 shall be disregarded.

(8) Section 100D(1) of the 1975 Act shall apply to the appeal mentioned in paragraph (7) as if the decision appealed against was the decision of an adjudication officer given on review under section 100A(1) of the 1975 Act and the appeal shall be to a disability appeal tribunal.

(9) Any medical question referred to a medical appeal tribunal which has not been determined by 6th April 1992 shall—

(a) where the person to whom the question relates to consents, continue to be heard by the medical appeal tribunal, or

(b) where he does not consent, be subject to adjudication in accordance with the provisions of the 1975 Act relating to disability living allowance, and for this purpose, the medical question shall be determined by a disability appeal tribunal and not by a medical appeal tribunal.

(10) Where a disability appeal tribunal is determining, pursuant to paragraph (9), a medical question which was considered by a medical appeal tribunal but adjourned with a request for further information or a report, then the disability appeal tribunal shall await the submission of that information or report but not for more than three months from the date the information or report was requested, and shall if it is available take it into account in determining the question before them.

(11) Any decision of an adjudication officer, a medical board or a medical appeal tribunal on a medical question may be reviewed at any time by an adjudication officer if—

(a) he is satisfied, in the case of a decision of a medical appeal tribunal by fresh evidence, that the decision was given in ignorance of, or was based upon a mistake as to, a material fact; or

(b) there has been a relevant change of circumstances since the decision was given.

(12) Subsections (3), (4) and (6) to (9) of section 104A of the 1975 Act shall apply to reviews under paragraph (11) as they apply to reviews under that section.

(13) Section 112 of the 1975 Act (appeal on a question of law to the Commissioner) shall have effect in relation to a decision of a medical appeal tribunal on a medical question subject to the modifications that in subsection (6) for the words "a medical appeal tribunal" there were substituted the words "an adjudication officer" and as though subsection (7) were omitted.

(14) Where the Commissioner returns a question to an adjudication officer pursuant to paragraph (11), section 100D(1) of the 1975 Act (appeals following reviews) shall apply to the decision of the adjudication officer on that question as if it were a decision given by him on a review under section 100A(1) of that Act (review of a decision on any ground).

General Note

Para. (2). A *claim* for mobility allowance made after March 15, 1992, or an *application for review* relating to mobility allowance made after February 9, 1992, is determined under the new régime applicable to disability living allowance.

Paras. (3) and *(4)*. A claim or application made earlier than the above dates could still be determined under the old procedure until April 5, 1992. If it has not been finally determined by then, it was transferred to the new régime. For the old procedure requiring the report referred to in para. (4)(a) and (b), see regs. 56 and 57 of the Social Security (Adjudication) Regulation 1986 in the 1993 edition of this book. If the medical question had been determined by a medical board before April 6, an adjudication officer making the final determination on the claim or application for review was bound to have regard to the medical board's decision but the decision was not conclusive (para. (4)(c)). However, a decision of a medical appeal tribunal (or a disability appeal tribunal considering the medical questions under para. (9)(b)) is conclusive (para. (4)(f)). A reference to a medical board as a result of an appeal which has not been heard before April 6, was determined by an adjudication officer as though it was an application for a review under s.100A(1) of the Social Security Act 1975 (which means that an appeal against an adverse decision may be brought to a disability appeal tribunal—see now s.30(1) of the Social Security Administration Act 1992) (para. (4)(e)). On the other hand, a reference which was made by an adjudication officer without an initial determination ever having been made was simply withdrawn (para. (4)(d)). For appeals and references to medical boards, see reg. 59 of the 1986 Regulations. S.115C of the 1975 Act has now been replaced by s.54 of the Social Security Administration Act 1992.

Paras. (5) and *(6)*. No reference to a medical board could be made after February 9, 1992, and so any appeal from a decision of an adjudication officer on a medical question (which would have resulted in such a reference under the old régime) is treated as an application for a review (see the definition of "second tier adjudication" in reg. 15).

Paras. (7) and *(8)*. Any appeal from a decision of a medical board made *on or after* February 10, 1992, is heard by a disability appeal tribunal and not by a medical appeal tribunal. The relevant date is the date the appeal is lodged—not the date of the decision (*CM/091A/93*). Nevertheless, the disability appeal tribunal is concerned only with the medical questions and has no power to award benefit on the claim or application for review. Ss.100A(1) and 100D(1) of the 1975 Act have been replaced by ss.30(1) and 33(1) of the Social Security Administration Act 1992.

Para. (9). Any appeal from a decision of a medical board made *before* February 10, 1992, could be determined only by a medical appeal tribunal until April 6, 1992. Since then, claimants have had a choice. If they consent, their appeals are still heard by medical appeal tribunals. Otherwise, they are heard by disability appeal tribunals. A disability appeal tribunal has no jurisdiction unless the claimant has been given the opportunity of having the appeal heard by a medical appeal tribunal (*CM/409/92*). When a disability appeal tribunal is considering an appeal under this paragraph, it does not have power to make an award of either mobility allowance or disability living allowance, because it has before it only the medical questions and not the whole claim. For the right of appeal to a medical appeal tribunal under the old régime see reg. 60 of the Social Security (Adjudication) Regulations 1986 but note that that regulation has been revoked without any saving in respect of reg. 60(3).

Para. 11. For the meaning of "fresh evidence", see the annotation to s.47 of the Social Security Administration Act 1992.

Para. 12. S.104A of the 1975 Act has been replaced by s.35 of the Social Security Administration Act 1992.

Paras. (13) and *(14)*. A Commissioner who on appeal under reg. 61 of the 1986 Regulations (which applied s.112 of the 1975 Act to mobility allowance cases), finds a decision of a medical appeal decision to be erroneous in point of law must remit the case to an adjudication officer who can then both determine the medical questions and make the final decision on the claim or application for review. However, the right of appeal to a disability appeal tribunal conferred by para. (14) applies only to the medical questions which were previously before the medical appeal tribunal. Any other question or a refusal to award benefit on the claim or application for review must first be challenged by way of an application for review under s.30(1) of the Social Security Administration Act 1992. Ss.100A(1), 100d(1), 112(B) and 112(7) of the 1975 Act have been replaced by ss.30(1), 33(1), 48(5) and 48(6) of the 1992 Act.

Reference to an adjudication officer

25.—(1) This regulation applies where, on or after 3rd February 1992 a disability appeal tribunal are determining an appeal which relates to a claim for attendance allowance or a disability appeal tribunal or a medical appeal tribunal are determining an appeal which relates to a claim for mobility allowance.

(2) Where an appeal tribunal are unable to make an award of the benefit claimed, but, solely on the evidence before them they are satisfied that the claimant may qualify for—

(a) where the claim relates to attendance allowance, the lowest of the three rates of care component prescribed under section 37ZB(3) of the 1975 Act; or

(b) where the claim relates to mobility allowance—

(i) the lower of the two rates of mobility component prescribed under section 37ZC(6) of the 1975 Act, or

(ii) the higher rate of the two rates of mobility component because he may fall within section 37ZC(1)(c) of the 1975 Act (entitlement to mobility component for the severely mentally impaired).

the appeal tribunal may refer to an adjudication officer the question of his entitlement to disability living allowance.

(3) Where an adjudication officer has a question referred to him in accordance with paragraph (2), he shall treat—

(a) the claim for attendance allowance as being also a claim for disability living allowance relating solely to the care component, or

(b) the claim for mobility allowance as being also a claim for disability living allowance relating solely to the mobility component,

made on 3rd February 1992 and proceed to determine that claim in accordance with section 99 of the 1975 Act.

(4) An award made in accordance with paragraph (3) may be for a period commencing on 6th April 1992 or on such later date as the adjudication officer may, in the circumstances of the particular case, determine.

GENERAL NOTE

If a tribunal decides that a person does not satisfy the relevant conditions for attendance allowance or mobility allowance but might qualify for disability living allowance (on one of the grounds that had no equivalent in respect of the old benefits), the tribunal may refer the case to an adjudication officer who should then treat the claim for the old benefit as a claim for the appropriate component of disability living allowance. There appears to be some overlap with reg. 10(3). It should be noted that the tribunal *may* refer the case. The use of the word "may" can be contrasted with the use of the word "shall" in reg. 10(3) and is clearly intended to confer a discretionary power rather than a duty to refer. However, it will always be right for the tribunal to refer the case unless both parties have had the opportunity of dealing with the new point, at least at the hearing. Furthermore, any medical appeal tribunal, or a disability appeal tribunal hearing a case under reg. 24(9) or in any other circumstances where it is considering only certain questions (and not the whole claim or application for review), *must* refer the case to an adjudication officer, because it has no power to make an award of any benefit.

A reference need be made only where there is a serious possibility that the claimant may qualify for disability living allowance on one of the new grounds. A tribunal whose chairman has failed to record that they have considered whether to make a reference under this regulation, where the issue arose on the evidence, are liable to have their decision set aside for want of compliance with the duty imposed by reg. 29(5)(b) of the Social Security (Adjudication) Regulations 1995 to record reasons for the decision (*CSM/14/93, CM/43/93*).

Ss.37ZB, 37ZC and 99 of the Social Security Act 1975 have been replaced by ss.72 and 73 of the Social Security Contributions and Benefits Act 1992 and s.21 of the Social Security Administration Act 1992. Presumably the reference in para. (2)(b)(i) to s.37ZC(6) is a misprint in the statutory instrument. The reference should be to s.37ZC(10) (now s.73(10) of the 1992 Act).

Payments of disability living allowance

26.—(1) This regulation applies to the payment of awards of disability living allowance where the award arises in accordance with Parts II or III of these Regulations.

(2) Subject to paragraphs (3), (4) and (5), where a person has an award of attendance allowance, mobility allowance or disability living allowance which—

(a) is payable by direct credit transfer in accordance with regulation 21 of the Social Security (Claims and Payments) Regulations 1987, and

(b) is superseded by an award treated as made under Parts II or III of these Regulations,

the award mentioned in sub-paragraph (b) above shall continue to be paid by direct credit transfer into the same bank or other account as the award it superseded; and for this purpose, any application made or treated as made and any consent given or treated as given in relation to the terminated award shall be treated as made or given in relation to the award mentioned in sub-paragraph (b) above.

(3) Where a person—

(a) has two awards of disability living allowance, and

(b) those awards are paid separately but into the same account by direct credit transfer in accordance with regulation 21 of the Social Security (Claims and Payments) Regulations 1987,

then those payments may at any time before [[1] 28th December 1993] be combined into one payment, equal to the aggregate of the two payments, payable by direct credit transfer into that account.

(4) Where a person has two awards of disability living allowance paid by direct credit transfer in accordance with regulation 21 of the Social Security (Claims and Payments) Regulations 1987 into different accounts, those payments may, with the consent of the Secretary of State, be made into such one account as the person to whom the payments are made may specify in a notice in writing to the Secretary of State.

(5) For the purposes of paragraph (3) any application made or treated as made and any consent given or treated as given in relation to a terminated or cancelled award shall be treated as made or given in relation to the award treated as having been made by virtue of these Regulations.

(6) Where a person has an award of disability living allowance which is payable by direct credit transfer in accordance with regulation 21 of the Social Security (Claims and Payments) Regulations 1987, any further award of disability living allowance made to that person shall be paid by direct credit transfer into the same bank or other account as the award first mentioned; and any application made or treated as made and any consent given or treated as given in relation to the first mentioned award shall be treated as made or given also in relation to the further award.

(7) Subject to the following provisions of this regulation, where attendance allowance was payable to a person otherwise than by direct credit transfer, any disability living allowance arising in accordance with Part II of these Regulations shall be payable on the day of the week the attendance allowance was or would have been payable.

(8) Subject to paragraph (9), where mobility allowance was payable to a person otherwise than by direct credit transfer, any disability living allowance arising in accordance with regulation 8 shall be payable on a Wednesday.

(9) Where both attendance allowance and mobility allowance were payable to a person otherwise than by direct credit transfer, any disability living allowance payable in accordance with an award treated as made by virtue of these Regulations shall be payable—

(a) from such date before [[1]28th December 1993] as the Secretary of State may in any particular case determine—

(i) except in a case to which head (ii) below applies, on a Wednesday; or

(ii) where in any particular case payment of attendance allowance was combined with the payment of another benefit and that benefit was payable on a day of the week other than Wednesday, the care component shall be payable on that day and the mobility component shall be payable on a Wednesday;

(b) until that day, care component shall be payable in the manner and at the time when attendance allowance was payable and mobility component shall likewise be payable in the manner and at the time when mobility allowance was payable.

(10) Where attendance allowance was payable to a person otherwise than by direct credit transfer and an award of mobility component is made to that person, any award of disability living allowance treated as having been made by virtue of these Regulations shall be payable, from such date before [[1]28th December 1993] as the Secretary of State may in any particular case determine—

(a) except in a case to which sub-paragraph (b) applies, on a Wednesday; or

(b) where in any particular case the payment of attendance allowance was combined with the payment of another benefit and that benefit was payable on a day of the week other than Wednesday, the care component shall be payable on that day and the mobility component shall be payable on a Wednesday.

(11) Where in accordance with this regulation payment of a person's award of disability living allowance is changed to a Wednesday, and because of this change in pay day the interval between the first Wednesday pay day and the last previous pay day (referred to in this paragraph as "the relevant period") is greater than it would have been but for that change, then the first Wednesday payment of disability living allowance shall include by way of adjustment an additonal payment which is equal to the daily rate for the benefit or part of a benefit which is subject to that change, multiplied by a number determined by deducting from the number of days in the relevant period, the number of days which would have been in that period but for the change in pay days.

[[2](12) Where a person—

(a) before 6th April 1992 has an award of attendance allowance and of mobility allowance and—

(i) those awards are paid in a different manner, and

(ii) both awards are terminated [[3]or cancelled] in accordance with Parts II and III of these Regulations; or

(b) has been awarded disability living allowance under regulation 11,

then the awards of disability living allowance shall be paid in accordance with paragraph (13).]

(13) In cases to which this paragraph refers, disability living allowance shall be paid—

[[2](a) from such date before 27th December 1993 as the Secretary of State may in any particular case determine, on the day, for the period and, subject to paragraph (13A), in the manner determined by the Secretary of State;]

(b) until that date, on such days, at such intervals and in such manner as the former awards of attendance allowance and mobility allowance were paid.

[[2](13A) Where [[3]the person to whom the allowance is payable (whether for himself or another)] has within 4 weeks of receiving notice of the Secretary of State's determination under paragraph (13)(a) made an election which has been approved by the Secretary of State that he wishes the allowance to be paid in a manner other than that determined under paragraph (13)(a), the allowance shall be paid in the manner specified in the election from a date determined by the Secretary of State.]

(14) Where a person who has not attained the age of 65 on 6th April 1992—

(a) has claimed attendance allowance or disability living allowance and pursuant to that claim an award of attendance allowance was made after 2nd February 1992, or

(b) has applied for a review of a decision of the Attendance Allowance Board or the adjudication officer not to award attendance allowance and pursuant to that application an award of attendance allowance is made after 2nd February 1992, and that award is for a period commencing before 6th April 1992, both the attendance allowance and any disability living allowance granted in place of the award of attendance allowance shall be payable at four weekly intervals on a Wednesday, unless in any particular case the Secretary of State arranges otherwise.

(15) For the purpose of paragraph (11), the "daily rate" is an amount equal to one-seventh of the weekly rate, rounded up to the next 1p.

AMENDMENTS

1. Social Security (Introduction of Disability Living Allowance) (Amendment) Regulations 1993 (S.I. 1993 No. 408), reg. 2(3) (April 1, 1993).

2. Social Security (Introduction of Disability Living Allowance) (Amendment) (No. 2) Regulations 1993 (S.I. 1993 No. 1739), reg. 2(4) (August 6, 1993).

3. Social Security (Introduction of Disability Living Allowance) (Amendment) (No. 3) Regulations 1993 (S.I. 1993 No. 2704), reg. 2(4) (November 25, 1993).

Persons unable to act

27.—(1) [[1]Except as provided in paragraph (3)] a person who before regulation 3(2) came into force was entitled to attendance allowance in respect of a child shall, after 5th April 1992 be regarded for the purposes of regulation 43 of the Claims and Payments Regulations as the person appointed on behalf of that child.

(2) An appointment having effect in accordance with paragraph (1) may be terminated when the child attains the age of 16 or ceases to be entitled to disability living allowance, or in accordance with regulation 43 of the Claims and Payments Regulations.

(3) Where on 5th April 1992 a person holds an appointment in respect of a child under regulation 43 of the Claims and Payments Regulations (mobility allowance) and that person is different from the person mentioned in paragraph (1) as being entitled to an attendance allowance in respect of that same child, then that appointment shall terminate on 6th April 1992 and the Secretary of State shall make a new appointment under regulation 43 of the Claims and Payments Regulations to take effect on that day.

(4) [[1]. . .]

(5) In this regulation, the "Claims and Payments Regulations" means the Social Security (Claims and Payments) Regulations 1987.

AMENDMENT

1. Social Security (Introduction of Disability Living Allowance) Miscellaneous Amendment Regulations 1992 (S.I. 1992 No. 728), reg. 5 (March 16, 1992).

The Social Security (Payments on account, Overpayments and Recovery) Regulations 1988

(S.I. 1988 No. 664)

ARRANGEMENT OF REGULATIONS

PART I

GENERAL

Whereas a draft of the following Regulations was laid before Parliament in accordance with the provisions of section 83(3)(b) of the Social Security Act 1986 and approved by resolution of each House of Parliament.

Now, therefore, the Secretary of State for Social Services, in exercise of the powers conferred on him by sections 23(8), 27, 51(1)(t) and (u), 53, 83(1), 84(1) and 89 of that Act and all other powers enabling him in that behalf, by this instrument, which contains only regulations made under the sections of the Social Security Act 1986 specified above and provisions consequential on those sections and which is made before the end of a period of 12 months from the commencement of those sections, makes the following Regulations:

PART I

GENERAL

Citation, commencement and interpretation

1.—(1) These Regulations may be cited as the Social Security (Payments on account, Overpayments and Recovery) Regulations 1988 and shall come into force on 11th April 1988.

(2) In these Regulations, unless the context otherwise requires—

"the Act" means the Social Security Act 1986;

"adjudicating authority" means, as the case may be, the Chief or any other adjudication officer, a social security appeal tribunal, [[2]a disability appeal tribunal,] the Chief or any other Social Security Commissioner or a Tribunal of Commissioners;

"benefit" means [[4]a jobseeker's allowance and] any benefit under the Social Security Act 1975, child benefit, family credit, income support and [[1]any social fund payment under sections 32(2)(a) and 32(2A) of the Act [[3] and any incapacity benefit under sections 30A(1) and (5) of the Contributions and Benefits Act];

"child benefit" means benefit under Part I of the Child Benefit Act 1975;

"the Claims and Payments Regulations" means the Social Security (Claims and Payments) Regulations 1987;

[[3]"the Contributions and Benefits Act" means the Social Security Contributions and Benefits Act 1992;]

[[2]"disability living allowance" means a disability living allowance under section 37ZA of the Social Security Act 1975;

"disability working allowance" means a disability working allowance under section 20 of the Act;]

"family credit" means family credit under Part II of the Act;

"guardian's allowance" means an allowance under section 38 of the Social Security Act 1975;

"income support" means income support under Part II of the Act and includes personal expenses addition, special transitional addition and transitional addition as defined in the Income Support (Transitional) Regulations 1987;

"Income Support Regulations" means the Income Support (General) Regulations 1987;

[[4]"Jobseeker's Allowance" Regulations means the Jobseeker's Allowance Regulations 1996]

"severe disablement allowance" means an allowance under section 36 of the Social Security Act 1975.

(3) Unless the context otherwise requires, any reference in these Regulations to a numbered Part or regulation is a reference to the Part or regulation bearing that number in these Regulations and any reference in a regulation to a numbered paragraph is a reference to the paragraph of that regulation bearing that number.

Amendments

1. Social Security (Claims and Payments and Payments on Account, Overpayments and Recovery) Amendment Regulations 1989 (S.I. 1989 No. 136), reg. 3 (February 27, 1989).

2. Disability Living Allowance and Disability Working Allowance (Consequential Provisions) Regulation 1991 (S.I. 1991 No. 2742), reg. 15 (April 6, 1992).

3. Social Security (Incapacity Benefit) (Consequential and Transitional Amendments and Savings) Regulations 1995 (S.I. 1995 No. 829), reg. 21 (April 13, 1995).

4. Social Security and Child Support (Jobseeker's Allowance) (Consequential Amendments) Regulations 1996 (S.I. 1996 No. 1345), reg. 23(2) (October 7, 1996).

Part II

Interim Payments

Making of interim payments

2.—(1) [[2]Subject to paragraph (1A),] the Secretary of State may, in his discretion, make an interim payment, that is to say a payment on account of any benefit to which it appears to him that a person is or may be entitled, in the following circumstances—

(a) a claim for that benefit has not been made in accordance with the Claims and Payments Regulations and it is impracticable for such a claim to be made immediately; or

(b) a claim for that benefit has been so made, but it is impracticable for it or a reference, review, application or appeal which relates to it to be determined immediately; or

(c) an award of that benefit has been made but it is impracticable for the beneficiary to be paid immediately, except by means of an interim payment.

[[2](1A) Paragraph (1) shall not apply pending the determination of an appeal unless the Secretary of State is of the opinion that there is entitlement to benefit.]

(2) [[1]Subject to paragraph (3),] on or before the making of an interim payment the recipient shall be given notice in writing of his liability under this Part to have it brought into account and to repay any overpayment.

(3) Where the recipient of an interim payment of disability living allowance—

(a) is terminally ill within the meaning of section 35(2C) of the Social Security Act 1975; or

(b) had an invalid carriage or other vehicle provided by the Secretary of State under section 5(2)(a) of the National Health Service Act 1977 and Schedule 2 to that Act or under section 46 of the National Health Service (Scotland) Act 1978,

the requirement to give notice in paragraph (2) of this regulation shall be omitted.

AMENDMENTS

1. Disability Living Allowance and Disability Working Allowance (Consequential Provisions) Regulations 1991 (S.I. 1991 No. 2742), reg. 15 (April 6, 1992).

2. Social Security (Persons From Abroad) Miscellaneous Amendment Regulation 1996 (S.I. 1996 No. 30), reg. 10 (February 5, 1996).

Bringing interim payments into account

3. Where it is practicable to do so and notice has been given as required by regulation 2(2), the interim payment shall be brought into account as follows—

(a) any interim payment made in anticipation of an award of benefit shall be offset by the adjudicating authority in reduction of the benefit to be awarded; and

(b) any interim payment (whether or not made in anticipation of an award) which is not offset under paragraph (a) shall be deducted by the Secretary of State from—

  (i) the sum payable under the award of benefit on account of which the interim payment was made; or

  (ii) any sum payable under any subsequent award of the same benefit to the same person.

Recovery of overpaid interim payments

4.—(1) Where the adjudicating authority has determined that an interim payment has been overpaid in circumstances which fall within paragraph (3) and that notice has been given as required by regulation 2(2), that authority shall determine the amount of the overpayment.

(2) The amount of the overpayment shall be recoverable by the Secretary of State by the same procedures and subject to the same conditions as if it were recoverable under section 53(1) of the Act.

(3) The circumstances in which an interim payment may be determined to have been overpaid are as follows—

(a) an interim payment has been made under regulation 2(1)(a) or (b) but—

(i) the recipient has failed to make a claim in accordance with the Claims and Payments Regulations as soon as practicable or has made a claim which is either defective or is not made on the form approved for the time being by the Secretary of State and the Secretary of State has not treated the claim as duly made under regulation 4(7) of the Claims and Payments Regulations, or

(ii) it has been determined that there is no entitlement on the claim, or that the entitlement is less than the amount of the interim payment, or that benefit on the claim is not payable, or

(iii) the claim has been withdrawn under regulation 5(2) of the Claims and Payments Regulations; or

(b) an interim payment has been made under regulation 2(1)(c) which exceeds the entitlement under the award of benefit on account of which the interim payment was made.

(4) For the purposes of this regulation a claim is defective if it is made on the form approved for the time being by the Secretary of State but is not completed in accordance with the instructions on the form.

General Note

S.53 of the Social Security Act 1986 has been replaced by s. 71 of the Social Security Administration Act 1992.

Part III

Offsetting

Offsetting prior payment against subsequent award

5.—(1) Subject to regulation 6 (exception from offset of recoverable overpayment, any sum paid in respect of a period covered by a subsequent determination in any of the cases set out in paragraph (2) shall be offset against arrears of entitlement under the subsequent determination and, except to the extent that the sum exceeds the arrears, shall be treated as properly paid on account of them.

(2) Paragraph (1) applies in the following cases—

Case 1: Payment under an award which is revised, reversed or varied

Where a person has been paid a sum by way of benefit under an award which is subsequently varied on appeal or revised on a review.

Case 2: Award or payment of benefit in lieu

Where a person has been paid a sum by way of benefit under the original award and it is subsequently determined, on review or appeal, that another benefit should be awarded or is payable in lieu of the first.

Case 3: Child benefit and severe disablement allowance

Where either—

(a) a person has been awarded and paid child benefit for a period in respect of which severe disablement allowance is subsequently determined to be payable to the child concerned; or

(b) severe disablement allowance is awarded and paid for a period in respect of which child benefit is subsequently awarded to someone else, the child concerned in the subsequent determination being the beneficiary of the original award.

Case 4: Increase of benefit for dependant

Where a person has been paid a sum by way of an increase in respect of a dependent person under the original award and it is subsequently determined that that other person is entitled to benefit for that period, or that a third person is entitled to the increase for that period in priority to the beneficiary of the original award.

Case 5: Increase of benefit for partner

Where a person has been paid a sum by way of an increase in respect of a partner (as defined in regulation 2 of the Income Support Regulations) and it is subsequently determined that that other person is entitled to benefit for that period.

(3) Where an amount has been deducted under regulation 13(b) (sums to be deducted in calculating recoverable amounts) an equivalent sum shall be offset against any arrears of entitlement of that person under a subsequent award of income support [[1]or income-based jobseeker's allowance] for the period to which the deducted amount relates.

(4) Where child benefit which has been paid under an award in favour of a person (the original beneficiary) is subsequently awarded to someone else for any week, the benefit shall nevertheless be treated as properly paid if it was received by someone other than the original beneficiary, who—

(a) either had the child living with him or was contributing towards the cost of providing for the child at a weekly rate which was not less than the weekly rate under the original award, and

(b) could have been entitled to child benefit in respect of that child for that week had a claim been made in time.

(5) Any amount which is treated under paragraph (4) as properly paid shall be deducted from the amount payable to the beneficiary under the subsequent award.

Amendment

1. Social Security and Child Support (Jobseeker's Allowance) (Consequential Amendments) Regulations 1996 (S.I. 1996 No. 1345), reg. 23(5) and (6) (October 7, 1996).

Exception from offset of recoverable overpayment

6. No amount may be offset under regulation 5(1) which has been determined to be a recoverable overpayment for the purposes of section 53(1) of the Act.

General Note

S. 53 of the Social Security Act 1986 has been replaced by s. 71 of the Social Security Administration Act 1992.

7.—10. *Omitted.*

Part V

Direct Credit Transfer Overpayments

Recovery of overpayments by automated or other direct credit transfer

11.—(1) Where it is determined by the adjudicating authority that a payment in excess of entitlement has been credited to a bank or other account under an arrangement for automated or other direct credit transfer made in accordance with regulation 21 of the Claims and Payments Regulations and that the conditions prescribed by paragraph (2) are satisfied, the excess, or the specified part of it to which the Secretary of State's certificate relates, shall be recoverable under this regulation.

(2) The prescribed conditions for recoverability under paragraph (1) are as follows—

(a) the Secretary of State has certified that the payment in excess of entitlement, or a specified part of it, is materially due to the arrangement for payments to be made by automated or other direct transfer; and

(b) notice of the effect which this regulation would have in the event of an overpayment, was given in writing to the beneficiary, or to a person acting for him, before he agreed to the arrangement.

(3) Where the arrangement was agreed to before 6th April 1987 the condition prescribed by paragraph 2(b) need not be satisfied in any case where the application for benefit to be paid by automated or other direct credit transfer contained a statement, or was accompanied by a written statement made by the applicant, which complied with the provisions of regulation 16A(3)(b) and (8) of the Social Security (Claims and Payments) Regulations 1979 or, as the case may be, regulation 7(2)(b) and (6) of the Child Benefit (Claims and Payments) Regulations 1984.

Part VI

Revision of Determination and Calculation of Amount Recoverable

Circumstances in which determination need not be revised

12. Section 53(4) of the Act (recoverability dependent on reversal, variation or revision of determination) shall not apply where the fact and circumstances of the misrepresentation or non-disclosure do not provide a basis for reviewing and revising the determination under which payment was made.

General Note

S. 53 of the Social Security Act 1986 has been replaced by s. 71 of the Social Security Administration Act 1992.

Sums to be deducted in calculating recoverable amounts

13. In calculating the amounts recoverable under section 53(1) of the Act or regulation 11, where there has been an overpayment of benefit, the adjudicating authority shall deduct—

(a) any amount which has been offset under Part III;

(b) any additional amount of income support [[1]or income-based jobseeker's allowance] which was not payable under the original, or any other, determination, but which should have been determined to be payable—

(i) on the basis of the claim as presented to the adjudicating authority, or

(ii) on the basis of the claim as it would have appeared had the misrepresentation or non-disclosure been remedied before the determination;

but no other deduction shall be made in respect of any other entitlement to benefit which may be, or might have been, determined to exist.

Amendment

1. Social Security and Child Support (Jobseeker's Allowance) (Consequential Amendments) Regulations 1996 (S.I. 1996 No. 1345), reg. 23(5) and (6) (October 7, 1996).

GENERAL NOTE

S. 53 of the Social Security Act 1986 has been replaced by s. 71 of the Social Security Administration Act 1992.

Quarterly diminution of capital

14.—(1) For the purposes of section 53(1) of the Act, where income support, [1family credit or disability working allowance] has been overpaid in consequence of a misrepresentation as to the capital a claimant possesses or a failure to disclose its existence, the adjudicating authority shall treat that capital as having been reduced at the end of each quarter from the start of the overpayment period by the amount overpaid by way of income support, [1family credit or disability working allowance] within that quarter.

(2) Capital shall not be treated as reduced over any period other than a quarter or in any circumstances other than those for which paragraph (1) provides.

(3) In this regulation—

''a quarter'' means a period of 13 weeks starting with the first day on which the overpayment period began and ending on the 90th consecutive day thereafter;

'overpayment period'' is a period during which income support [2or an income-based jobseeker's allowance], [1family credit or disability working allowance] is overpaid in consequence of a misrepresentation as to capital or a failure to disclose its existence.

AMENDMENTS

1. Disability Living Allowance and Disability Working Allowance (Consequential Provisions) Regulations 1991 (S.I. 1991 No. 2742), reg. 15 (April 6, 1992).

2. Social Security (Jobseeker's Allowance and Payments on Account) (Miscellaneous Amendments) Regulations 1996 (S.I. 1996 No. 2519), reg. 3(2) (October 7, 1996).

GENERAL NOTE

S. 53 of the Social Security Act 1986 has been replaced by s. 71 of the Social Security Administration Act 1992.

PART VII

THE PROCESS OF RECOVERY

Recovery by deduction from prescribed benefits

15.—(1) Subject to regulation 16, where any amount is recoverable under sections 27 or 53(1) of the Act, or under these Regulations, that amount shall be recoverable by the Secretary of State from any of the benefits prescribed by the next paragraph to which the person to whom [1the amount is determined] to be recoverable is entitled.

(2) The following benefits are prescribed for the purposes of this regulation—

(a) subject to paragraphs (1) and (2) of regulation 16, any benefit under the Social Security Act 1975;

(b) subject to paragraphs (1) and (2) of regulation 16, any child benefit;

(c) any family credit;

(d) subject to regulation 16, any income support [4or a jobseeker's allowance];

[2(e) any disability working allowance];

[3(f) any incapacity benefit].

AMENDMENTS

1. Social Security (Payments on Account, Overpayments and Recovery) Amendment Regulations 1988 (S.I. 1988 No. 688), reg. 2 (April 11, 1988).
2. Disability Living Allowance and Disability Working Allowance (Consequential Provisions) Regulations 1991 (S.I. 1991 No. 2742), reg. 15 (April 6, 1992).
3. Social Security (Incapacity Benefit) (Consequential and Transitional Amendments and Savings) Regulations 1995 (S.I. 1995 No. 829), reg. 21 (April 13, 1995).
4. Social Security (Jobseeker's Allowance and Payments on Account) (Miscellaneous Amendments) Regulations 1996 (S.I. 1996 No. 2519), reg. 3(3) (October 7, 1996).

GENERAL NOTE

Ss. 27 and 53 of the Social Security Act 1986 have been replaced by ss. 74 and 71 of the Social Security Administration Act 1992.

Limitations on deductions from prescribed benefits

16.—(1) Deductions may not be made from entitlement to the benefits prescribed by paragraph (2) except as a means of recovering an overpayment of the benefit from which the deduction is to be made.

(2) The benefits [[1]prescribed] for the purposes of paragraph (1) are guardian's allowance [[2]. . .] and child benefit.

(3) Regulation 15 shall apply without limitation to any payment of arrears of benefit other than any arrears caused by the operation of regulation 37(1) of the Claims and Payments Regulations (suspension of payments).

(4) Regulation 15 shall apply to the amount of [[5]benefit] to which a person is presently entitled only to the extent that there may, subject to paragraphs 8 and 9 of Schedule 9 to the Claims and Payments Regulations, be recovered in respect of any one benefit week—

(a) in a case to which paragraph (5) applies, not more than the amount there specified; and

(b) in any other case, three times five per cent. of the personal allowance for a single claimant aged not less than 25, that five per cent. being, where it is not a multiple of five pence, rounded to the next higher such multiple.

[[5](4A) Paragraph (4) shall apply to the following benefits—

(a) income support;

(b) an income-based jobseeker's allowance;

(c) where, if there was no entitlement to a contribution-based jobseeker's allowance at the same rate, a contribution-based jobseeker's allowance.]

(5) Where a person responsible for the misrepresentation of or failure to disclose a material fact has, by reason thereof, been found guilty of an offence under section 55 of the Act or under any other enactment, or has made a written statement after caution in admission of deception or fraud for the purpose of obtaining benefit, the amount mentioned in paragraph (4)(a) shall be four times five per cent. of the personal allowance for a single claimant aged not less than 25, that five per cent. being, where it is not a multiple of 10 pence, rounded to the nearest such multiple or, if it is a multiple of five pence but not of 10 pence, the next higher multiple of 10 pence.

[[5](5A) Regulation 15 shall apply to an amount of a contribution-based jobseeker's allowance, other than a contribution-based jobseeker's allowance to which paragraph (4) applies in accordance with paragraph (4A)(c), to which a person is presently entitled only to the extent that there may, subject to paragraphs 8 and 9 of Schedule 9 to the Claims and Payments Regulations be recovered in respect of any one benefit week a sum equal to one third of the age-related amount applicable to the claimant under section 4(1)(a) of the Jobseekers Act 1995(a).

(5B) For the purposes of paragraph (5A) where the sum that would otherwise fall to be deducted includes a fraction of a penny, the sum to be deducated shall be rounded down to the nearest whole penny.]

(6) [[4]Where—

(a) in the calculation of the income of a person to whom the income support is payable, the amount of earnings or other income falling to be taken into account is reduced by paragraphs 4 to 9 of Schedule 8 to the Income Support Regulations (sums to be disregarded in the calculation of earnings) or paragraphs 15 and 16 of Schedule 9 to those Regulations (sums to be disregarded in the calculation of income other than earnings); or

(b) in the calculation of the income of a person to whom income-based jobseeker's allowance is payable, the amount of earnings or other income falling to be taken into account is reduced by paragraphs 5 to 12 of Schedule 6 to the Jobseeker's Allowance Regulations (sums to be disregarded in the calculation of earnings) or paragraphs 15 and 17 of Schedule 7 to those Regulations (sums to be disregarded in the calculation of income other than earnings),

the weekly amount] applicable under paragraph (4) may be increasded by not more than half the amount of the reduction, and any increase under this paragraph has priority over any increase which would, but for this paragraph, be made under paragraph 6(5) of Schedule 9 to the Claims and Payments Regulations.

(7) Regulation 15 shall not be applied to a specified benefit so as to reduce the benefit in any one benefit week to less than 10 pence.

(8) In this regulation—

"benefit week" means the week corresponding to the week in respect of which the benefit is paid;

'personal allowance for a single claimant aged not less than 25" means the amount specified in paragraph 1(1)(c) of column 2 of Schedule 2 to the Income Support Regulations [[4]or, in the case of a person who is entitled to income-based jobseeker's allowance, the amount for the time being specified in paragraph 1(1)(e) of column (2) of Schedule 1 to the Jobseeker's Allowance Regulations;]

[[3]"specified benefit" means—

(a) in respect of any period during which benefit is paid by means of an instrument of payment, [[5]a jobseeker's allownace, or] income support either alone or together with any [[5]. . .], incapacity benefit, retirement pension or severe disablement allowance which is paid by means of the same instrument of payment; and

(b) in respect of any period during which benefit is paid by means of an instrument for benefit payment, [[5]a jobseeker's allowance,] income support and, where paid concurrently with income support, [[5]. . .], incapacity benefit, retirement pension or severe disablement allowance;]

'written statement after caution" means—

(i) in England and Wales, a written statement made in accordance with the Police and Criminal Evidence Act 1984 (Codes of Practice) (No. 1) Order 1985, or, before that Order came into operation, the Judges Rules;

(ii) in Scotland, a written statement duly witnessed by two persons.

AMENDMENTS

1. Social Security (Payments on Account, Overpayments and Recovery) Amendment Regulations 1988 (S.I. 1988 No. 688), reg. 2 (April 11, 1988).

2. Disability Living Allowance and Disability Working Allowance (Consequential Provisions) Regulations 1991 (S.I. 1991 No. 2742), reg. 15 (April 6, 1992).
3. Social Security (Incapacity Benefit) (Consequential and Transitional Amendments and Savings) Regulations 1995 (S.I. 1995 No. 829), reg. 21 (April 13, 1995).
4. Social Security (Claims and Payments, etc.) Amendment Regulations 1996)S.I. 1996 No. 672), reg. 4 (April 4, 1996).
5. Social Security abd Child Support (Jobseeker's Allowance) (Consequential Amendments) Regulations 1996 (S.I. 1996 No. 1345), reg. 23(4) (October 7, 1996).
6. Social Security (Jobseeker's Allowance and Payments on Account) (Miscellaneous Amendments) Regulations 1996 (S.I. 1996 No. 2519), reg. 3(4) (October 7, 1996).

General Note

S. 55 of the Social Security Act 1986 has been replaced by s.112 of the Social Security Administration Act 1992.

Recovery from couples

17. In the case of an overpayment of income support, [1family credit or disability working allowance] to one of a married or unmarried couple, the amount recoverable by deduction, in accordance with regulation 15, may be recovered by deduction from income support [2or income-based jobseeker's allowance], [1family credit or disability working allowance] payable to either of them, provided that the two of them are a married or unmarried couple at the date of the deduction.

Amendments

1. Disability Living Allowance and Disability Working Allowance (Consequential Provisions) Regulations 1991 (S.I. 1991 No. 2742), reg. 15 (April 6, 1992).
2. Social Security and Child Support (Jobseeker's Allowance) (Consequential Amendments) Regulations 1996 (S.I. 1996 No. 1345), reg. 23(5) and (6) (October 7, 1996).

18.—31. *Omitted.*

The Social Security (Recovery of Benefits) Regulations 1997

(S.I. 1997 No. 2205)

Arrangement of Regulations

The Secretary of State for Social Security, in exercise of the powers conferred by section 189(4), (5) and (6) of the Social Security Administration Act 1992(**a**) and sections 4(9), 14(2), (3) and (4), 16(1) and (2), 18, 19, 21(3), 23(1), (2), (5) and (7), 29 and 32 of, and paragraphs 4 and 8 of Schedule 1 to, the Social

Security (Recovery of Benefits) Act 1997**(b)**, and of all other powers enabling her in that behalf, hereby makes the following Regulations:

Citation, commencement and interpretation

1.—(1) These Regulations may be cited as the Social Security (Recovery of Benefits) Regulations 1997 and shall come into force on 6th October 1997.

(2) In these Regulations—

"the 1992 Act" means the Social Security Administration Act 1992;

"the 1997 Act" means the Social Security (Recovery of Benefits) Act 1997;

"commencement day" means the day these Regulations come into force;

"compensator" means a person making a compensation payment;

"Compensation Recovery Unit" means the Compensation Recovery Unit of the Department of Social Security at Reyrolle Building, Hebburn, Tyne and Wear NE31 1XP.

(3) A reference in these Regulations to a numbered section or Schedule is a reference, unless the context otherwise requires, to that section of or Schedule to the 1997 Act.

Exempted trusts and payments

2.—(1) The following trusts are prescribed for the purposes of paragraph 4 of Schedule 1:

(a) the Macfarlane Trust established on 10th March 1988 partly out of funds provided by the Secretary of State to the Haemophilia Society for the relief of poverty or distress among those suffering from haemophilia;

(b) the Macfarlane (Special Payments) Trust established on 29th January 1990 partly out of funds provided by the Secretary of State, for the benefit of certain persons suffering from haemophilia;

(c) the Macfarlane (Special Payments) (No. 2) Trust established on 3rd May 1991 partly out of funds provided by the Secretary of State for the benefit of certain persons suffering from haemophilia and other beneficiaries;

(d) the Eileen Trust established on 29th March 1993 out of funds provided by the Secretary of State for the benefit of persons eligible for payment in accordance with its provisions.

(2) The following payments are prescribed for the purposes of paragraph 8 of Schedule 1:

(a) any payment to the extent that it is made—

(i) in consequence of an action under the Fatal Accidents Act 1976; or

(ii) in circumstances where, had an action been brought, it would have been brought under that Act;

(b) any payment to the extent that it is made in respect of a liability arising by virtue of section 1 of the Damages (Scotland) Act 1976;

(c) any payment made under the Vaccine Damage Payments Act 1979 to or in respect of the injured person;

(d) any award of compensation made to or in respect of the injured person under the Criminal Injuries Compensation Act 1995 or by the Criminal Injuries Compensation Board under the Criminal Injuries Compensation Scheme 1990 or any earlier scheme;

(e) any compensation payment made by British Coal in accordance with the NCB Pneumoconiosis Compensation Scheme set out in the Schedule to an agreement made on the 13th September 1974 between the National Coal Board, the National Union of Mine Workers, the National Association of Colliery Overmen Deputies and Shot-firers and the British Association of Colliery Management;

(f) any payment made to the injured person in respect of sensorineural hearing loss where the loss is less than than 50 dB in one or both ears;
(g) any contractual amount paid to an employee by an employer of his in respect of a period of incapacity for work;
(h) any payment made under the National Health Service (Injury Benefits) Regulations 1995 or the National Health Service (Scotland) (Injury Benefits) Regulations 1974;
(i) any payment made by or on behalf of the Secretary of State for the benefit of persons eligible for payment in accordance with the provisions of a scheme established by him on 24th April 1992 or, in Scotland, on 10th April 1992.

Information to be provided by the compensator

3. The following information is prescribed for the purposes of section 23(1):
(a) the full name and address of the injured person;
(b) where known, the date of birth or national insurance number of that person, or both if both are known;
(c) where the liability arises, or is alleged to arise, in respect of an accident or injury, the date of the accident or injury;
(d) the nature of the accident, injury or disease; and
(e) where known, and where the relevant period may include a period prior to 6th April 1994, whether, at the time of the accident or injury or diagnosis of the disease, the person was employed under a contract of service, and, if he was, the name and address of his employer at that time and the person's payroll number.

Information to be provided by the injured person

4. The following information is prescribed for the purposes of section 23(2):
(a) whether the accident, injury or disease resulted from any action taken by another person, or from any failure of another person to act, and, if so, the full name and address of that other person;
(b) whether the injured person has claimed or may claim a compensation payment, and, if so, the full name and address of the person against whom the claim was or may be made;
(c) the amount of any compensation payment and the date on which it was made;
(d) the listed benefits claimed, and for each benefit the date from which it was first claimed and the amount received in the period beginning with that date and ending with the date the information is sent;
(e) in the case of a person who has received statutory sick pay during the relevant period and prior to 6th April 1994, the name and address of any employer who made those payments to him during the relevant period and the dates the employment with that employer began and ended; and
(f) any changes in the medical diagnosis relating to the condition arising from the accident, injury or disease.

Information to be provided by the employer

5. The following information is prescribed for the purposes of section 23(5):
(a) the amount of any statutory sick pay the employer has paid to the injured person since the first day of the relevant period and before 6th April 1994;
(b) the date the liability to pay such statutory sick pay first arose and the rate at which it was payable;

(c) the date on which such liability terminated; and
(d) the causes of incapacity for work during any period of entitlement to statutory sick pay during the relevant period and prior to 6th April 1994.

Provision of information

6. A person required to give information to the Secretary of State under regulations 3 to 5 shall do so by sending it to the Compensation Recovery Unit not later than 14 days after—
(a) where he is a person to whom regulation 3 applies, the date on which he receives a claim for compensation from the injured person in respect of the accident, injury or disease;
(b) where he is a person to whom regulation 4 or 5 applies, the date on which the Secretary of State requests the information from him.

Application for a certificate of recoverable benefits

7.—(1) The following particulars are prescribed for the purposes of section 21(3)(a) (particulars to be included in an application for a certificate of recoverable benefits):
(a) the full name and address of the injured person;
(b) the date of birth and, where known, the national insurance number of that person;
(c) where the liability arises or is alleged to arise in respect of an accident or injury, the date of the accident or injury;
(d) the nature of the accident, injury or disease;
(e) where the person liable, or alleged to be liable, in respect of the accident, injury or disease, is the employer of the injured person, or has been such an employer, the information prescribed by regulation 5.

(2) An application for a certificate of recoverable benefits is to be treated for the purposes of the 1997 Act as received by the Secretary of State on the day on which it is received by the Compensation Recovery Unit, or if the application is received after normal business hours, or on a day which is not a normal business day at that office, on the next such day.

Payments into court

8.—(1) Subject to the provisions of this regulation, where a party to an action makes a payment into court which, had it been paid directly to another party to the action ("the relevant party"), would have constituted a compensation payment—
(a) the making of that payment shall be treated for the purposes of the 1997 Act as the making of a compensation payment;
(b) a current certificate of recoverable benefits shall be lodged with the payment; and
(c) where the payment is calculated under section 8, the compensator must give the relevant party the information specified in section 9(1), instead of the person to whom the payment is made.

(2) The liability under section 6(1) to pay an amount equal to the total amount of the recoverable benefits shall not arise until the person making the payment into court has been notified that the whole or any part of the payment into court has been paid out of court to or for the relevant party.

(3) Where a payment into court in satisfaction of his claim is accepted by the relevant party in the initial period, then as respects the compensator in question, the relevant period shall be taken to have ended, if it has not done so already, on the day on which the payment into court (or if there were two or more such payments, the last of them) was made.

(4) Where, after the expiry of the initial period, the payment into court is accepted in satisfaction of the relevant party's claim by consent between the parties, the relevant period shall end, if it has not done so already, on the date on which application to the court for the payment is made.

(5) Where, after the expiry of the initial period, payment out of court is made wholly or partly to or for the relevant party in accordance with an order of the court and in satisfaction of his claim, the relevant period shall end, if it has not done so already, on the date of that order.

(6) In paragraphs (3), (4) and (5), "the initial period" means the period of 21 days after the receipt by the relevant party to the action of notice of the payment into court having been made.

(7) Where a payment into court is paid out wholly to or for the party who made the payment (otherwise than to or for the relevant party to the action) the making of the payment into court shall cease to be regarded as the making of a compensation payment.

(8) A current certificate of recoverable benefits in paragraph (1) means one that is in force as described in section 4(4).

Reduction of compensation: complex cases

9.—(1) This regulation applies where—

(a) a compensation payment in the form of a lump sum (an "earlier payment") has been made to or in respect of the injured person; and

(b) subsequently another such payment (a "later payment") is made to or in respect of the same injured person in consequence of the same accident, injury or disease.

(2) In determining the liability under section 6(1) arising in connection with the making of the later payment, the amount referred to in that subsection shall be reduced by any amount paid in satisifaction of that liability as it arose in connection with the earlier payment.

(3) Where—

(a) a payment made in satisfaction of the liability under section 6(1) arising in connection with an earlier payment is not reflected in the certificate of recoverable benefits in force at the time of a later payment, and

(b) in consequence, the aggregate of payments made in satisifaction of the liability exceeds what it would have been had that payment been so reflected,

the Secretary of State shall pay the compensator who made the later payment an amount equal to the excess.

(4) Where—

(a) a compensator receives a payment under paragraph (3), and

(b) the amount of the compensation payment made by him was calculated under section 8,

then the compensation payment shall be recalculated under section 8, and the compensator shall pay the amount of the increase (if any) to the person to whom the compensation payment was made.

(5) Where both the earlier payment and the later payment are made by the same compensator, he may—

(a) aggregate the gross amounts of the payments made by him;

(b) calculate what would have been the reduction made under section 8(3) if that aggregate amount had been paid at the date of the last payment on the basis that—

(i) so much of the aggregate amount as is attributable to a head of compensation listed in column (1) of Schedule 2 shall be taken to be the part of the gross amount which attributable to that head, and

(ii) the amount of any recoverable benefits shown against any head in column (2) of that Schedule shall be taken to be the amount determined in accordance with the most recent certificate of recoverable benefits;

(c) deduct from that reduction calculated under sub-paragraph (b) the amount of the reduction under section 8(3) from any earlier payment; and

(d) deduct from the latest gross payment the net reduction calculated under sub-paragraph (c) (and accordingly the latest payment may be nil).

(6) Where the Secretary of State is making a refund under paragraph (3), he shall send to the compensator (with the refund) and to the person to whom the compensation payment was made a statement showing—

(a) the total amount that has already been paid by that compensator to the Secretary of State;

(b) the amount that ought to have been paid by that compensator; and

(c) the amount to be repaid to that compensator by the Secretary of State.

(7) Where the reduction of a compensation payment is recalculated by virtue of paragraph (4) or (5) the compensator shall give notice of the calculation to the injured person.

Structured settlements

10.—(1) This regulation applies where—

(a) in final settlement of an injured person's claim, an agreement is entered into—

(i) for the making of periodical payments (whether of an income or capital nature); or

(ii) for the making of such payments and lump sum payments; and

(b) apart from the provisions of this regulation, those payments would fall to be treated for the purposes of the 1997 Act as compensation payments.

(2) Where this regulation applies, the provisions of the 1997 Act and these Regulations shall be modified in the following way—

(a) the compensator in question shall be taken to have made on that day a single compensation payment;

(b) the relevant period in the case of the compensator in question shall be taken to end (if it has not done so already) on the day of settlement;

(c) payments under the agreement referred to in paragraph (1)(a) shall be taken not to be compensation payments;

(d) paragraphs (5) and (7) of regulation 11 shall not apply.

(3) Where any further payment falls to be made to or in respect of the injured person otherwise than under the agreement in question, paragraph (2) shall be disregarded for the purpose of determining the end of the relevant period in relation to that further payment.

(4) In any case where—

(a) the person making the periodical payments ("the secondary party") does so in pursuance of arrangements entered into with another ("primary party") (as in a case where the primary party purchases an annuity for the injured person from the secondary party), and

(b) apart from those arrangements, the primary party would have been regarded as the compensator,

then for the purposes of the 1997 Act, the primary party shall be regarded as the compensator and the secondary party shall not be so regarded.

(5) In this regulation "the day of settlement" means—

(a) if the agreement referred to in paragraph (1)(a) is approved by a court, the day on which that approval is given; and

(b) in any other case, the day on which the agreement is entered into.

Adjustments

11.—(1) Where the conditions specified in subsection (1) and paragraphs (a) and (b) of subsection (2) of section 14 are satisfied, the Secretary of State shall pay the difference between the amount that has been paid and the amount that ought to have been paid to the compensator.

(2) Where the conditions specified in subsection (1) and paragraphs (a) and (b) of subsection (3) of section 14 are satisfied, the compensator shall pay the difference between the total amounts paid and the amount that ought to have been paid to the Secretary of State.

(3) Where the Secretary of State is making a refund under paragraph (1), or demanding payment of a further amount under paragraph (2), he shall send to the compensator (with the refund or demand) and to the person to whom the compensation payment was made a statement showing—

(a) the total amount that has already been paid to the Secretary of State;

(b) the amount that ought to have been paid; and

(c) the difference, and whether a repayment by the Secretary of State or a further payment to him is required.

(4) This paragraph applies where—

(a) the amount of the compensation payment made by the compensator was calculated under section 8; and

(b) the Secretary of State has made a payment under paragraph (1).

(5) Where paragraph (4) applies, the amount of the compensation payment shall be recalculated under section 8 to take account of the fresh certificate of recoverable benefits and the compensator shall pay the amount of the increase (if any) to the person to whom the compensation payment was made.

(6) This paragraph applies where—

(a) the amount of the compensation payment made by the compensator was calculated under section 8;

(b) the compensator has made a payment under paragraph (2); and

(c) the fresh certificate of recoverable benefits issued after the review or appeal was required as a result of the injured person or other person to whom the compensation payment was made supplying to the compensator information knowing it to be incorrect or insufficient with the intent of enhancing the compensation payment calculated under section 8, and the compensator supplying that information to the Secretary of State without knowing it to be incorrect or insufficient.

(7) Where paragraph (6) applies, the compensator may recalculate the compensation payment under section 8 to take account of the fresh certificate of recoverable benefits and may require the repayment to him by the person to whom he made the compensation payment of the difference (if any) between the payment made and the payment as so recalculated.

Transitional provisions

12.—(1) In relation to a compensation payment to which by virtue of section 2 the 1997 Act applies and subject to paragraph (2), a certificate of total benefit issued under Part IV of the 1992 Act shall be treated on or after the commencement date as a certificate of recoverable benefits issued under the 1997 Act and the amount of total benefit treated as that of recoverable benefits.

(2) Paragraph (1) shall not apply to a certificate of total benefit which specifies an amount in respect of disability living allowance without specifying whether that amount was, or is likely to be, paid wholly by way of the care component or the mobility component or (if not wholly one of them) specifying the relevant amount for each component.

(3) Any appeal under section 98 of the 1992 Act made on or after the commencement date shall be referred to and determined by a medical appeal tribunal notwithstanding that it would otherwise have been referred by the Secretary of State to a social security appeal tribunal.

(4) Paragraph (5) applies where—

(a) an amount has been paid to the Secretary of State under section 82(1)(b) of the 1992 Act,

(b) liability arises on or after the commencement day to make a payment under section 6(1), and

(c) the compensation payments which give rise to the liability to make both payments are to or in respect of the same injured person in consequence of the same accident, injury or disease.

(5) Where this paragraph applies, the liability under section 6 shall be reduced by the payment (or aggregate of the payments, if more than one) described in paragraph (4)(a).

(6) Where—

(a) a payment into court has been made on a date prior to the commencement day but the initial period, as defined in section 93(6) of the 1992 Act, in relation to that payment, expires on or after the commencement day; and

(b) the payment into court is accepted by the other party to the action in the initial period,

that payment into court shall be treated as a compensation payment to which the 1992 Act, and not the 1997 Act, applies.

(7) Where a payment into court has been made prior to the commencement day, remains in court on that day and paragraph (6) does not apply, that payment into court shall be treated as a payment to which the 1997 Act applies, but paragraph (1) (b) and (c) of regulation 8 shall not apply.

The Social Security (Recovery of Benefit) (Appeals) Regulations 1997

(S.I. 1997 No. 2237)

Arrangement of Regulations

The Secretary of State for Social Security, in exercise of the powers conferred by sections 23(9) and (10) and 189(4), (5) and (6) of the Social Security Administration Act 1992 and by sections 11(5), 12(6) and 29 of the Social Security (Recovery of Benefits) Act 1997, and of all other powers enabling her in that behalf, after consultation with the Council on Tribunals in accordance with section 8 of the Tribunals and Inquiries Act 1992, hereby makes the following Regulations:

Citation, commencement and interpretation

1.—(1) These Regulations may be cited as the Social Security (Recovery of Benefits) (Appeals) Regulations 1997 and shall come into force on 6th October 1997.

(2) In these Regulations—

"the 1997 Act" means the Social Security (Recovery of Benefits) Act 1997;

"clerk to the tribunal" means a clerk to a medical appeal tribunal appointed in accordance with section 50 of, and paragraph 3 of Schedule 2 to, the Social Security Administration Act 1992;

"Commissioner" has the meaning given in section 191 of the Social Security Administration Act 1992;

"Compensation Recovery Unit" means the Compensation Recovery Unit of the Department of Social Security at Reyrolle Building, Hebburn, Tyne and Wear NE31 1XB;

"compensator" means a person making a compensation payment;

"full-time chairman" means a regional or other full-time chairman of medical appeal tribunals appointed under section 51(1) of the Social Security Administration Act 1992;

"President" means the President of social security appeal tribunals, medical appeal tribunals and disability appeal tribunals appointed under section 51(1) of the Social Security Administration Act 1992.

(3) A reference in these Regulations to the parties to the proceedings is a reference to the Secretary of State and any person entitled under section 11(2) of the 1997 Act to make an appeal.

(4) Where, by any provision of these Regulations—

(a) any notice or other document is required to be given or sent to the Compensation Recovery Unit, or the clerk to or a chairman of a tribunal, that notice or document shall be treated as having been so given or sent on the day that it is received in the office of the Compensation Recovery Unit or of the clerk to the relevant tribunal, as appropriate; and

(b) any notice or other document is required to be given or sent to any other person, that notice or document shall, if sent by post to that person's last known or notified address, be treated as having been given or sent on the day that it was posted.

(5) Subject to regulation 13(3), where by these Regulations any power is conferred on a chairman of a tribunal then—

(a) if the power is to be exercised at the hearing of an appeal or application, it shall be exercised by the chairman of the tribunal hearing the appeal or application; and

(b) otherwise, it shall be exercised by a person who is eligible to be nominated to act as a chairman of a medical appeal tribunal under section 50(4) of the Social Security Administration Act 1992.

Manner of making appeals and time limits

2.—(1) Any appeal against a certificate of recoverable benefits shall, subject to paragraph (11), be in writing on a form approved by the Secretary of State and shall be given or sent to the Compensation Recovery Unit—

(a) not later than 3 months after the date the compensator discharged the liability under section 6 of the 1997 Act;

(b) where the certificate is reviewed by the Secretary of State in accordance with regulations made under section 11(5)(c) of the 1997 Act, not later than 3 months after the date the certificate is confirmed, or, as the case may be, a fresh certificate is issued; or

(c) where an agreement is made under which an earlier compensation payment is treated as having been made in final discharge of a claim made by or in respect of an injured person and arising out of the accident, injury or disease, not later than 3 months after the date of that agreement.

(2) The time specified by this regulation for the making of any appeal may be extended, even though the time so specified may already have expired, provided the conditions set out in paragraphs (3) to (7) are satisfied; and any application for an extension of time under this paragraph shall be made to the Compensation Recovery Unit and shall be determined by a chairman of a medical appeal tribunal.

(3) Where the time specified for the making of an appeal has already expired, an application for an extension of time for making an appeal shall not be granted unless the applicant has satisfied the chairman considering the application that—

(a) if the application is granted there are reasonable prospects that such an appeal will be successful; and

(b) it is in the interests of justice that the application be granted.

(4) For the purposes of pargraph (3) it shall not be considered to be in the interests of justice to grant an application unless the chairman considering the application is satisfied that—

(a) special reasons exist, which are wholly exceptional and which relate to the history or facts of the case; and

(b) such special reasons have existed throughout the period beginning with the day following the expiry of the time specified by paragraph (1) for the making of an appeal and ending with the day on which the application for an extension of time is made; and

(c) such special reasons manifestly constitute a reasonable excuse of compelling weight for the applicant's failure to make an appeal within the time specified.

(5) In determining whether there are special reasons for granting an application for an extension of time for making an appeal under paragraph (2) the chairman considering the application shall have regard to the principle that the greater the amount of time that has elapsed between the expiry of the time specified for the making of the appeal and the making of the application for an extension of time, the more cogent should be the special reasons on which the application is based.

(6) In determining whether facts constitute special reasons for granting an application for an extension of time for making an appeal under paragraph (2) no account shall be taken of the following—

(a) that the applicant or anyone acting for him or advising him was unaware of or misunderstood the law applicable to his case (including ignorance or misunderstanding of any time limits imposed by paragraph (1));

(b) that a Commissioner or a court has taken a different view of the law from that previously understood and applied.

(7) Notwithstanding paragraph (2), no appeal may in any event be brought later than 6 years after the beginning of the period specified in paragraph (1) or if more than one such period is relevant, the one beginning later or latest.

(8) An application under paragraph (2) for an extension of time which has been refused may not be renewed.

(9) Any appeal or application under these Regulations shall contain the following particulars—

(a) in the case of an appeal, the date of the certificate of recoverable benefits or review decision of the Secretary of State against which the appeal is made, the question under section 11 of the 1997 Act to which the appeal relates, and a summary of the arguments relied on by the person making the appeal to support his contention that the certificate is wrong;

(b) in the case of an application under paragraph (2) for an extension of time in which to appeal, in relation to the appeal which it is proposed to bring, the particulars required under sub-paragraph (a) together with particulars of the special reasons on which the application is based.

(10) Where the appeal or application under paragraph (2) for an extension of time is made by the injured person or other person to whom a compensation payment has been made, there shall be sent with that appeal or application a copy of the statement given to that person under section 9 of the 1997 Act or if that statement was not in writing, a written summary of it.

(11) Where an appeal is not made on the form approved for the time being, but is made in writing, contains all the particulars required under paragraph (9) and, where applicable, is accompanied by the document required under paragraph (10), the Secretary of State may treat that appeal as duly made.

(12) Where it appears to the Secretary of State that an appeal or application does not contain the particulars required under paragraph (9) or is not accompanied by the document required under paragraph (10) he may direct the person making the appeal or application to provide such particulars or such document.

(13) Where paragraph (12) applies, the Secretary of State may extend the time specified by this regulation for making the appeal or application by a period of not more than 14 days.

(14) Where further particulars or a document are required under paragraph (12) they shall be sent or delivered to the Compensation Recovery Unit within such period as the Secretary of State may direct.

(15) The date of an appeal shall be the date on which all the particulars required under paragraph (9) and, where applicable, the document required under paragraph (10) are received by the Compensation Recovery Unit.

(16) In the case of an application under paragraph (2) for an extension of time for making an appeal, the chairman who determines that application shall record his decision in writing together with a statement of the reasons for the decision.

(17) As soon as practicable after the decision has been made, it shall be communicated to the applicant and to the Secretary of State and if within 3 months of such communication being sent the applicant or the Secretary of State so requests in writing, a copy of the record referred to in paragraph (16) shall be supplied to the person making that request.

(18) The Secretary of State may treat any appeal as an application for review under section 10 of the 1997 Act, notwithstanding that a condition specified in paragraph (a) or (b) of section 10(1) is not satisfied.

GENERAL NOTE

Paras. (1) to (17). These are substantially in the same terms as reg. 3 of the Social Security (Adjudication) Regulations 1995 and reference should be made to the notes to that provision. However, note that paras. (10) and (11) require that an appeal by a person to whom compensation has been paid *must* be accompanied by the compensator's statement given under s. 9 of the Social Security (Recovery of Benefits) Act 1997, unless the statement was not given in writing, in which case a written summary must be provided instead.

Para. (18). This provision, made under s. 11(6) of the 1997 Act, allows the Secretary of State to treat an appeal as an application to review the certificate of recoverable benefits under appeal and to review that certificate on any ground, without regard to the restrictions otherwise imposed by s. 10(1) of the Act.

General provisions relating to the procedure of tribunals

3.—(1) Subject to the provisions of the 1997 Act and of these Regulations—

(a) the procedure in connection with the consideration and determination of any reference to a medical appeal tribunal under section 12 of the 1997 Act shall be such as the chairman of the tribunal shall determine;

(b) the chairman of a tribunal may give directions requiring any party to the proceedings to comply with any provision of these Regulations and may further at any stage of the proceedings either of his own motion or on a written application made to the clerk to the tribunal by any such party give such directions as he may consider necessary or desirable for the just, effective and efficient conduct of the proceedings and may direct any party to provide such further particulars or to produce such documents as may reasonably be required;

(c) where under these Regulations the clerk to the tribunal is authorised to take steps in relation to the procedure of the tribunal, he may give directions requiring any party to the proceedings to comply with any provision of these Regulations;

(d) any person who by virtue of the provisions of these Regulations has the right to be heard at a hearing may be accompanied and may be represented by another person whether having professional qualifications or not and, for the purposes of the proceedings at any such hearing, any such representative shall have all the rights and powers to which the person whom he represents is entitled under the 1997 Act and these Regulations.

(2) For the purpose of arriving at its decision a tribunal shall, and for the purpose of discussing any question of procedure may, notwithstanding anything contained in these Regulations, order all persons not being members of the tribunal, other than the person acting as clerk to the tribunal, to withdraw from the sitting of the tribunal, except that—

(a) a member of the Council on Tribunals or of the Scottish Committee of the Council and the President and any full-time chairman; and

(b) with the leave of the chairman of the tribunal,

(i) any person undergoing training as a chairman or other member of a medical appeal tribunal or as a clerk to such a tribunal, and

(ii) any other person to whose presence every party to the proceedings actually present consents,

may remain present at any such sitting.

(3) Nothing in these Regulations shall prevent a member of the Council on Tribunals or of the Scottish Committee of the Council from being present at a hearing before a tribunal, in his capacity as such, notwithstanding that the hearing is not in public.

(4) Where a reference is made to a tribunal by the Secretary of State, the clerk to the tribunal shall give notice of it to the other parties to the proceedings.

General Note

Paras. (1) to (3). See the notes to reg. 2 of the Social Security (Adjudication) Regulations 1995 which is in similar terms.

Requirement for oral hearings

4.—(1) Where a reference is made to a tribunal, the clerk to the tribunal shall direct every party to the proceedings to notify him if that party wishes an oral hearing of that reference to be held.

(2) A notification under paragraph (1) shall be in writing and shall be made within 10 days of receipt of the direction from the clerk to the tribunal or within such other period as the clerk to the tribunal or the chairman of the tribunal may direct.

(3) Where the clerk to the tribunal receives a notification in accordance with paragraph (2) the tribunal shall hold an oral hearing.

(4) The chairman of a tribunal may of his own motion require an oral hearing to be held if he is satified that such a hearing is necessary to enable the tribunal to reach a decision.

General Note

This regulation is in the same terms as reg. 38(1) to (1C) of the Social Security (Adjudication) Regulations 1995.

Procedure at oral hearings

5.—(1) Except where paragraph (4) applies, not less than 7 days notice, beginning with the day on which the notice is given and ending on the day before the hearing, of the time and place of any oral hearing before a tribunal shall be given to every party to the proceedings, and if such notice has not been given to a person to whom it should have been given under the provisions of this paragraph the hearing may proceed only with the consent of that person.

(2) The chairman of a tribunal may give notice before or during an oral hearing for the determination at that hearing by the tribunal, in accordance with the provisions of these Regulations, of any question referred under section 12 of the 1997 Act notwithstanding that a party to the proceedings has failed to indicate his availability for a hearing or to provide all the information which may have been requested, if the chairman is satisfied that such party—

(a) has failed to comply with a direction regarding his availability or requiring information under regulation 3(1)(b) or (c); and

(b) has not given any explanation for his failure to comply with such a direction;

provided that the chairman is satisfied that the tribunal has sufficient particulars in order for the question to be determined.

(3)The chairman of a tribunal may give notice before or during, an oral hearing for the determination at that hearing by the tribunal, in accordance with the provisions of these Regulations, of any question where he believes the appeal on that ground has no reasonable prospect of success.

(4) Any party to the proceedings may waive his right to receive not less than 7 days notice of the time and place of any oral hearing as specified in paragraph (1).

(5) If a party to the proceedings to whom notice has been given under paragraph (1) fails to appear at the hearing the tribunal may, having regard to all the circumstances including any explanation offered for the absence and, where applicable, the circumstances set out in paragraph (2)(a) and (b), proceed with the hearing notwithstanding his absence, or give such directions with a view to the determination of any question referred to it as it may think proper.

(6) If a party to the proceedings has waived his right to be given notice under paragraph (4), the tribunal may proceed with the hearing notwithstanding his absence.

(7) Any oral hearing before a tribunal shall be in public except where the person making the appeal requests a private hearing or the chairman is satisfied that intimate personal or financial circumstances may have to be disclosed or that considerations of public security are involved, in which case the hearing shall be in private.

(8) At any oral hearing any party to the proceedings shall be entitled to be present and be heard.

(9) The following persons shall also be entitled to be present at an oral hearing (whether or not it is otherwise in private) but shall take no part in the proceedings—

(a) the President and any full-time chairman;
(b) any person undergoing training as a chairman or other member of a medical appeal tribunal or as a clerk to such a tribunal;
(c) any person acting on behalf of the President or the Secretary of State in the training or supervision of clerks to medical appeal tribunals or of officers of the Secretary of State;
(d) any person undergoing training as an officer of the Secretary of State; and
(e) with the leave of the chairman of the tribunal and the consent of every party to the proceedings actually present, any other person.

(10) Nothing in paragraph (9) affects the rights of any person mentioned in sub-paragraph (a) and (b) of that paragraph at any oral hearing where he is sitting as a member of the tribunal or acting as its clerk, and nothing in this regulation prevents the presence at an oral hearing of any witness.

(11) Any person entitled to be heard at an oral hearing may address the tribunal, may give evidence, may call witnessess and may put questions directly to any other person called as a witness.

General Note

See the notes to reg. 4 of the Social Security (Adjudication) Regulations 1995 which is in similar terms.

Postponement and adjournment

6.—(1) Where a person to whom notice of an oral hearing by a tribunal has been given wishes to apply for that hearing to be postponed, he shall do so in writing to the clerk to the tribunal stating his reasons for the application, and the clerk may grant or refuse the request as he thinks fit or may pass the request to the chairman, who may grant or refuse the request as he thinks fit.

(2) The chairman or the clerk to the tribunal may of his own motion at any time before the beginning of an oral hearing postpone that hearing.

(3) An oral hearing may be adjourned by the tribunal at any time on the application of any party to the proceedings or of its own motion.

(4) Where an oral hearing is adjourned and at the hearing after the adjournment the tribunal is differently constituted, the proceedings at that hearing shall be by way of a complete rehearing of the case.

General Note

Paras. (1) to (3). See the notes to reg. 6 of the Social Security (Adjudication) Regulations 1995 which is in similar terms.

Withdrawal of appeals

7. Any appeal may be withdrawn by the person who made the appeal—

(a) before a question has been referred to a tribunal under section 12 of the 1997 Act, by written notice in writing to the Compensation Recovery Unit and with the consent of the Secretary of State;
(b) after the reference has been made and before the hearing begins, by written notice to the chairman of the tribunal to which a question was referred and with the written consent of the Secretary of State;
(c) after the hearing has begun, at any time before the determination is made

with the leave of the chairman of the tribunal and the consent of the Secretary of State.

General Note

An appeal cannot be withdrawn without the consent of the Secretary of State, but withdrawal does not require the consent of any other party. The consent of a tribunal chairman is also required unless the appeal is withdrawn before the case has been referred to a tribunal. For withdrawal of an application for leave to appeal to a Commissioner, see reg. 13(4).

Non-disclosure of medical evidence

8.—(1) Where, in connection with the consideration of any question, there is before a tribunal medical advice or medical evidence relating to a person which has not been disclosed to him, and in the opinion of the chairman of the tribunal the disclosure to that person of that advice or evidence would be harmful to his health, such advice or evidence shall not be required to be disclosed.

(2) Evidence such as is mentioned in paragraph (1) shall not be disclosed to any person acting for or representing the person to whom it relates unless the chairman is satisfied that it is in the interests of the person to whom the evidence relates to do so.

(3) A tribunal shall not be precluded from taking into account for the purposes of the determination evidence which has not been disclosed to a person under the provisions of paragraph (1) or (2).

General Note

See the notes to reg. 8 of the Social Security (Adjudication) Regulations 1995 which is in similar terms.

Decisions of tribunals

9.—(1) The decision of the majority of the tribunal shall be the decision of the tribunal.

(2) Every decision of a tribunal shall be recorded in summary by the chairman in such written form of decision notice as shall have been approved by the President, and such decision notice shall be signed by the chairman.

(3) As soon as may be practicable after a case has been decided by a tribunal, a copy of the decision notice made in accordance with paragraph (2) shall be sent or given to every party to the proceedings who shall also be informed of—

(a) his right under paragraph (6); and

(b) the conditions governing appeals to a Commissioner.

(4) A statement of the reasons for the tribunal's decision and of its findings on questions of fact material thereto may be given—

(a) orally at the hearing; or

(b) in writing at such later date as the chairman may determine.

(5) Where the statement referred to in paragraph (4) is given orally, it shall be recorded in such medium as the chairman may determine.

(6) A copy of the statement referred to in paragraph (4) shall be supplied to the parties to the proceedings if requested by any of them within 21 days after the decision notice has been sent or given, and if the statement was given orally at the hearing, that copy shall be supplied in such medium as the chairman may direct.

(7) If a decision is not unanimous, the statement referred to in paragraph (4) shall record that one of the members dissented and the reasons given by him for dissenting.

(8) A record of the proceedings at the hearing shall be made by the chairman in such medium as he may direct and preserved by the clerk to the tribunal for

18 months, and a copy of such record shall be supplied to the parties if requested by any of them within that period.

General Note

See the notes to reg. 38(3) to (6) of the Social Security (Adjudication) Regulations 1995 which is in similar terms. There is no equivalent to reg. 38(2) of the 1995 Regulations but the latter provision is probably unnecessary anyway as there is no power in the primary legislation for an incomplete medical appeal tribunal to determine an appeal.

Correction of Accidental errors in decisions

10.—(1) Subject to regulation 12 (provisions common to regulations 10 and 11) accidental errors in any decision or record of a decision may at any time be corrected by the tribunal which gave the decision or by another medical appeal tribunal.

(2) A correction made to, or to the record of, a decision shall be deemed to be part of the decision or of that record and written notice of it shall be given as soon as practicable to every party to the proceedings.

General Note

See the notes to reg. 9 of the Social Security (Adjudication) Regulations 1995 which is in similar terms.

Setting aside decisions on certain grounds

11.—(1) Subject to regulation 12 (provisions common to regulations 10 and 11), on an application made by a party to the proceedings, a decision may be set aside by the tribunal which gave the decision or by another medical appeal tribunal in a case where it appears just to set the decision aside on the ground that—

(a) a document relating to the proceedings in which the decision was given was not sent to, or was not received at an appropriate time by, a party to the proceedings or the party's representative or was not received at an appropriate time by the tribunal which gave the decision; or

(b) a party to the proceedings in which the decision was given or the party's representative was not present at a hearing relating to the proceedings; or

(c) the interests of justice so require.

(2) In determining whether it is just to set aside a decision on the ground set out in paragraph (1)(b), the tribunal shall determine whether the party making the application gave a notification to the clerk of the tribunal that he wished an oral hearing to be held, and if that party did not give such a notification the tribunal shall not set the decision aside unless it is satisfied that the interests of justice manifestly so require.

(3) An application under this regulation shall—

(a) be made in writing;

(b) be given or sent to the office of the clerk to the tribunal which made the relevant decision not later than 3 months after the date when notice of the tribunal's decision was sent or given to the applicant;

(c) contain particulars of the grounds on which it is made.

(4) The time specified in paragraph (3) for the making of an application may be extended for special reasons, even though the time so specified may already have expired, by the chairman of the tribunal; and regulation 2(16) and (17) (recording reasons for a decision and providing a copy of the record) shall apply in relation to any determination by a chairman.

(5) Where an application to set aside a decision is entertained under paragraph (1), every party to the proceedings shall be sent a copy of the application and shall be afforded a reasonable opportunity of making representations on it before the application is determined.

(6) Notice in writing of a determination on an application to set aside a decision shall be given to every party to the proceedings as soon as may be practicable and the notice shall contain a statement giving the reasons for the determination.

(7) For the purposes of determining under these Regulations an application to set aside a decision there shall be disregarded regulation 1(4) and any provision in any enactment or instrument to the effect that any notice or other document required or authorised to be given or sent to any person shall be deemed to have been given or sent if it was sent by post to that person's last known or notified address.

General Note

See the notes to reg. 10 of the Social Security (Adjudication) Regulations 1995 which is in similar terms.

Provisions common to regulation 10 and 11

12.—(1) In calculating any time specified in regulation 11 or 13, there shall be disregarded any day falling before the day on which notice was given of a correction of a decision or the record thereof pursuant to regulation 10 or on which notice is given of a determination that a decision shall not be set aside following an application made under regulation 11, as the case may be.

(2) Without prejudice to provisions for appeals to Commissioners, there shall be no other appeal against a correction made under regulation 10 or a refusal to make such a correction or against a determination given under regulation 11.

(3) Nothing in regulation 10 or 11 shall be construed as derogating from any power to correct errors or set aside decisions which is exercisable apart from these Regulations.

General Note

This is in similar terms to reg. 11 of the Social Security (Adjudication) Regulations 1995, save that it is arguable that para. (2) does not exclude the possibility of an appeal under s.12 of the Social Security (Recovery of Benefits) Act 1997 against a decision under regs. 10 and 11 and, particularly, against a refusal to set aside a decision. This will not make much difference in most cases, as an appeal against the original decision is as effective but there are a few cases where there was no breach of natural justice in the original decision but a setting aside would be justified.

Application to a chairman for leave to appeal to a Commissioner

13.—(1) Subject to the following provisions of this regulation, an application to the chairman of a tribunal for leave to appeal to a Commissioner from a decision of a tribunal shall—

(a) be made in writing;

(b) be given or sent to the office of the clerk to the tribunal which made the relevant decision not later than 3 months after the date when a notice of the tribunal's decision was sent or given to the applicant;

(c) contain particulars of the grounds on which it is made;

(d) have annexed thereto a copy of the statement of the reasons for the tribunal's decision referred to in regulation 9(4).

(2) Where an application for leave to appeal is made by the Secretary of State, the clerk to the tribunal shall, as soon as may be practicable, send a copy of the application to every other party to the proceedings.

(3) The decision of the chairman on an application for leave to appeal shall be recorded in writing and copies shall be given or sent to every party to the proceedings.

(4) Where in any case it is impracticable, or it will be likely to cause undue delay, for an application for leave to appeal against the decision of a tribunal to be determined by the person who was the chairman of that tribunal, that application shall be determined by any other person eligible to be nominated to act as a chairman of a medical appeal tribunal under section 50(4) of the Social Security Administration Act 1992.

(5) A person who has made an application to the chairman of the tribunal for leave to appeal to a Commissioner against a decision of a tribunal may withdraw his application at any time before it is determined by giving written notice of intention to withdraw to the chairman.

GENERAL NOTE

Paras. (1) to (4). See the notes to reg. 39 of the Social Security (Adjudication) Regulations 1995 which is in similar terms.

Para. (5). This is in similar terms to reg. 6(1) of the 1995 Regulations.

PART IV

Legislation relating to Vaccine Damage Payments

Vaccine Damage Payments Act 1979

(1979 c. 17)

Arrangement of Sections

An Act to provide for payments to be made out of public funds in cases where severe disablement occurs as a result of vaccination against certain diseases or of contact with a person who has been vaccinated against any of those diseases; to make provision in connection with similar payments made before the passing of this Act; and for purposes connected therewith.

[22nd March 1979]

Payments to persons severely disabled by vaccination

1.—(1) If, on consideration of a claim, the Secretary of State is satisfied—

(a) that a person is, or was immediately before his death, severely disabled as a result of vaccination against any of the diseases to which this Act applies; and

(b) that the conditions of entitlement which are applicable in accordance with section 2 below are fulfilled,

he shall in accordance with this Act make a payment of [the relevant statutory sum] to or for the benefit of that person or to his personal representatives.

[[1](1A) In subsection (1) above "statutory sum" means £10,000 or such other sum as is specified by the Secretary of State for the purposes of this Act by order made by statutory instrument with the consent of the Treasury; and the relevant statutory sum for the purposes of that subsection is the statutory sum at the time when a claim for payment is first made.]

(2) The diseases to which this Act applies are—

(a) diphtheria,
(b) tetanus,
(c) whooping cough,
(d) poliomyelitis,
(e) measles,
(f) rubella,
(g) tuberculosis,
(h) smallpox, and
(i) any other disease which is specified by the Secretary of State for the purposes of this Act by order made by statutory instrument.

(3) Subject to section 2(3) below, this Act has effect with respect to a person who is severely disabled as a result of a vaccination given to his mother before he was born as if the vaccination had been given directly to him and, in such circumstances as may be prescribed by regulations under this Act, this Act has effect with respect to a person who is severely disabled as a result of contracting

a disease through contact with a third person who was vaccinated against it as if the vaccination had been given to him and the disablement resulted from it.

(4) For the purposes of this Act, a person is severely disabled if he suffers disablement to the extent of 80 per cent. or more, assessed as for the purposes of section 57 of the Social Security Act 1975 or the Social Security (Northern Ireland) Act 1975 (disablement gratuity and pension).

[[1](4A) No order shall be made by virtue of subsection (1A) above unless a draft of the order has been laid before Parliament and been approved by a resolution of each House.]

(5) A statutory instrument under subsection (2)(i) above shall be subject to annulment in pursuance of a resolution of either House of Parliament.

AMENDMENT

1. Social Security Act 1985, s.23.

GENERAL NOTE

Subs. (1A). The statutory sum was increased to £30,000 by the Vaccine Damage Payments Act 1979 Statutory Sum Order 1991 (S.I. 1991 No. 939).

Subs. (2). Mumps is added to the lists of diseases by the Vaccine Damage Payments (Specified Disease) Order 1990 (S.I. 1990 No. 623) and haemophilus influenza type b infection is added by the Vaccine Damage Payments (Specified Disease) Order 1995 (S.I. 1995 No. 1164).

Conditions of entitlement

2.—(1) Subject to the provisions of this section, the conditions of entitlement referred to in section 1(1)(b) above are—

(a) that the vaccination in question was carried out—
   (i) in the United Kingdom or the Isle of Man, and
   (ii) on or after 5th July 1948, and
   (iii) in the case of vaccination against smallpox, before 1st August 1971;

(b) except in the case of vaccination against poliomyelitis or rubella, that the vaccination was carried out either at a time when the person to whom it was given was under the age of eighteen or at the time of an outbreak within the United Kingdom or the Isle of Man of the disease against which the vaccination was given; and

(c) that the disabled person was over the age of two on the date when the claim was made or, if he died before that date, that he died after 9th May 1978 and was over the age of two when he died.

(2) An order under section 1(2)(i) above specifying a disease for the purposes of this Act may provide that, in relation to vaccination against that disease, the conditions of entitlement specified in subsection (1) above shall have effect subject to such modifications as may be specified in the order.

(3) In a case where this Act has effect by virtue of section 1(3) above, the reference in subsection (1)(b) above to the person to whom a vaccination was given is a reference to the person to whom it was actually given and not to the disabled person.

(4) With respect to claims made after such date as may be specified in the order and relating to vaccination against such disease as may be so specified, the Secretary of State may by order made by statutory instrument—

(a) provide that, in such circumstances as may be specified in the order, one or more of the conditions of entitlement appropriate to vaccination against that disease need not be fulfilled; or

(b) add to the conditions of entitlement which are appropriate to vaccination against that disease, either generally or in such circumstances as may be specified in the order.

(5) Regulations under this Act shall specify the cases in which vaccinations given outside the United Kingdom and the Isle of Man to persons defined in the regulations as serving members of Her Majesty's forces or members of their families are to be treated for the purposes of this Act as carried out in England.

(6) The Secretary of State shall not make an order containing any provision made by virtue of paragraph (b) of subsection (4) above unless a draft of the order has been laid before Parliament and approved by a resolution of each House; and a statutory instrument by which any other order is made under that subsection shall be subject to annulment in pursuance of a resolution of either House of Parliament.

Determination of claims

3.—(1) Any reference in this Act, other than section 7, to a claim is a reference to a claim for a payment under section 1(1) above which is made—

(a) by or on behalf of the disabled person concerned or, as the case may be, by his personal representatives; and
(b) in the manner prescribed by regulations under this Act; and
(c) within the period of six years beginning on the latest of the following dates, namely, the date of the vaccination to which the claim relates, the date on which the disabled person attained the age of two and 9th May 1978;

and, in relation to a claim, any reference to the claimant is a reference to the person by whom the claim was made and any reference to the disabled person is a reference to the person in respect of whose disablement a payment under subsection (1) above is claimed to be payable.

(2) As soon as practicable after he has received a claim, the Secretary of State shall give notice in writing to the claimant of his determination whether he is satisfied that a payment is due under section 1(1) above to or for the benefit of the disabled person or to his personal representatives.

(3) If the Secretary of State is not satisfied that a payment is due as mentioned in subsection (2) above, the notice in writing under that subsection shall state the grounds on which he is not so satisfied.

(4) If, in the case of any claim, the Secretary of State—

(a) is satisfied that the conditions of entitlement which are applicable in accordance with section 2 above are fulfilled, but
(b) is not satisfied that the disabled person is or, where he has died, was immediately before his death severely disabled as a result of vaccination against any of the diseases to which this Act applies,

the notice in writing under subsection (2) above shall inform the claimant that, if an application for review is made to the Secretary of State, the matters referred to in paragraph (b) above will be reviewed by an independent medical tribunal in accordance with section 4 below.

(5) If in any case a person is severely disabled, the question whether his severe disablement results from vaccination against any of the diseases to which this Act applies shall be determined for the purposes of this Act on the balance of probability.

Review of extent of disablement and causation by independent tribunals

4.—(1) Regulations under this Act shall make provision for independent medical tribunals to determine matters referred to them under this section, and such regulations may make provision with respect to—

(a) the terms of appointment of the persons who are to serve on the tribunals;
(b) the procedure to be followed for the determination of matters referred to the tribunals;

(c) the summoning of persons to attend to give evidence or produce documents before the tribunals and the administration of oaths to such persons.

(2) Where an application for review is made to the Secretary of State as mentioned in section 3(4) above, then, subject to subsection (3) below, the Secretary of State shall refer to a tribunal under this section—

(a) the question of the extent of the disablement suffered by the disabled person;

(b) the question whether he is or, as the case may be, was immediately before his death disabled as a result of the vaccination to which the claim relates; and

(c) the question whether, if he is or was so disabled, the extent of his disability is or was such as to amount to severe disablement.

(3) The Secretary of State may refer to differently constituted tribunals the questions in paragraphs (a) to (c) of subsection (2) above, and the Secretary of State need not refer to a tribunal any of those questions if—

(a) he and the claimant are not in dispute with respect to it; or

(b) the decision of a tribunal on another of those questions is such that the disabled person cannot be or, as the case may be, could not immediately before his death have been severely disabled as a result of the vaccination to which the claim relates.

(4) For the purposes of this Act, the decision of a tribunal on a question referred to them under this section shall be conclusive except in so far as it falls to be reconsidered by virtue of section 5 below.

Reconsideration of determinations and recovery of payments in certain cases

5.—(1) Subject to subsection (2) below, the Secretary of State may reconsider a determination that a payment should not be made under section 1(1) above on the ground—

(a) that there has been a material change of circumstances since the determination was made, or

(b) that the determination was made in ignorance of, or was based on a mistake as to, some material fact,

and the Secretary of State may, on the ground set out in paragraph (b) above, reconsider a determination that such a payment should be made.

(2) Regulations under this Act shall prescribe the manner and the period in which—

(a) an application may be made to the Secretary of State for his reconsideration of a determination; and

(b) the Secretary of State may of his own motion institute such a reconsideration.

(3) The Secretary of State shall give notice in writing of his decision on a reconsideration under this section to the person who was the claimant in relation to the claim which gave rise to the determination which has been reconsidered and also, where the disabled person is alive and was not the claimant, to him; and the provisions of subsections (3) to (5) of section 3 and section 4 above shall apply as if—

(a) the notice under this subsection were a notice under section 3(2) above; and

(b) any reference in those provisions to the claimant were a reference to the person who was the claimant in relation to the claim which gave rise to the determination which has been reconsidered.

(4) If, whether fraudulently or otherwise, any person misrepresents or fails to disclose any material fact and in consequence of the misrepresentation or

failure a payment is made under section 1(1) above, the person to whom the payment was made shall be liable to repay the amount of that payment to the Secretary of State unless he can show that the misrepresentation or failure occurred without his connivance or consent.

(5) Except as provided by subsection (4) above, no payment under section 1(1) above shall be recoverable by virtue of a reconsideration of a determination under this section.

Payments to or for the benefit of disabled persons

6.—(1) Where a payment under section 1(1) above falls to be made in respect of a disabled person who is over eighteen and capable of managing his own affairs, the payment shall be made to him.

(2) Where such a payment falls to be made in respect of a disabled person who has died, the payment shall be made to his personal representatives.

(3) Where such a payment falls to be made in respect of any other disabled person, the payment shall be made for his benefit by paying it to such trustees as the Secretary of State may appoint to be held by them upon such trusts or, in Scotland, for such purposes and upon such conditions as may be declared by the Secretary of State.

(4) The making of a claim for, or the receipt of, a payment under section 1(1) above does not prejudice the right of any person to institute or carry on proceedings in respect of disablement suffered as a result of vaccination against any disease to which this Act applies; but in any civil proceedings brought in respect of disablement resulting from vaccination against such a disease, the court shall treat a payment made to or in respect of the disabled person concerned under section 1(1) above as paid on account of any damages which the court awards in respect of such disablement.

Payments, claims etc. made prior to the Act

7.—(1) Any reference in this section to an extra-statutory payment is a reference to a payment of £10,000 made by the Secretary of State to or in respect of a disabled person after 9th May 1978 and before the passing of this Act pursuant to a non-statutory scheme of payments for severe vaccine damage.

(2) No such claim as is referred to in section 3(1) above shall be entertained if an extra-statutory payment has been made to or for the benefit of the disabled person or his personal representatives.

(3) For the purposes of section 5 above, a determination that an extra-statutory payment should be made shall be treated as a determination that a payment should be made under section 1(1) above; and in relation to the reconsideration of such a determination references in subsection (3) of section 5 above to the person who was the claimant in relation to the determination which has been reconsidered shall be construed as references to the person who made the claim for the extra-statutory payment.

(4) Subsections (4) and (5) of section 5 above and section 6(4) above shall apply in relation to an extra-statutory payment as they apply in relation to a payment made under section 1(1) above.

(5) For the purposes of this Act (other than this section) regulations under this Act may—

(a) treat claims which were made in connection with the scheme referred to in subsection (1) above and which have not been disposed of at the commencement of this Act as claims falling within section 3(1) above; and

(b) treat information and other evidence furnished and other things done before the commencement of this Act in connection with any such claim as is referred to in paragraph (a) above as furnished or done in connection with a claim falling within section 3(1) above.

Regulations

8.—(1) Any reference in the preceding provisions of this Act to regulations under this Act is a reference to regulations made by the Secretary of State.

(2) Any power of the Secretary of State under this Act to make regulations—

(a) shall be exercisable by statutory instrument which shall be subject to annulment in pursuance of a resolution of either House of Parliament; and

(b) includes power to make such incidental or supplementary provision as appears to the Secretary of State to be appropriate.

(3) Regulations made by the Secretary of State may contain provision—

(a) with respect to the information and other evidence to be furnished in connection with a claim;

(b) requiring disabled persons to undergo medical examination before their claims are determined or for the purposes of a reconsideration under section 5 above;

(c) restricting the disclosure of medical evidence and advice tendered in connection with a claim or a reconsideration under section 5 above; and

(d) conferring functions on the tribunals constituted under section 4 above with respect to the matters referred to in paragraphs (a) to (c) above.

Fraudulent statements etc.

9.—(1) Any person who, for the purpose of obtaining any payment under this Act, whether for himself or some other person,—

(a) knowingly makes any false statement or representation, or

(b) produces or furnishes or causes or knowingly allows to be produced or furnished any document or information which he knows to be false in a material particular,

shall be liable on summary conviction to a fine not exceeding £1,000.

(2) In the application of subsection (1) above to the Isle of Man, for the words following "liable" there shall be substituted the words "on summary conviction, within the meaning of the Interpretation Act 1976 (an Act of Tynwald), to a fine of £400 and on conviction on information to a fine".

10. and **11.** *Omitted.*

Financial provisions

12.—(1) The Secretary of State shall pay to persons appointed to serve on tribunals under section 4 of this Act such remuneration and such travelling and other allowances as he may, with the consent of the Minister for the Civil Service, determine.

(2) The Secretary of State shall pay such fees as he considers appropriate to medical practitioners, as defined in [[1]section 191 of the Social Security Administration Act 1992] who provide information or other evidence in connection with claims.

(3) The Secretary of State shall pay such travelling and other allowances as he may determine—

(a) to persons required under this Act to undergo medical examinations;

(b) to persons required to attend before tribunals under section 4 above; and

(c) in circumstances where he considers it appropriate, to any person who accompanies a disabled person to such a medical examination or tribunal.

(4) There shall be paid out of moneys provided by Parliament—
(a) any expenditure incurred by the Secretary of State in making payments under section 1(1) above;
(b) any expenditure incurred by the Secretary of State by virtue of subsections (1) to (3) above; and
(c) any increase in the administrative expenses of the Secretary of State attributable to this Act.

(5) Any sums repaid to the Secretary of State by virtue of section 5(4) above shall be paid into the Consolidated Fund.

AMENDMENT

1. Social Security (Consequential Provisions) Act 1992, Sched. 2, para. 54 (July 1, 1992).

Short title and extent

13.—(1) This Act may be cited as the Vaccine Damage Payments Act 1979.
(2) This Act extends to Northern Ireland and the Isle of Man.

The Vaccine Damage Payments Regulations 1979

(S.I. 1979 No. 432)

ARRANGEMENT OF REGULATIONS

The Secretary of State for Social Services in exercise of powers conferred on him by sections 2(5), 3(1)(b), 4(1), 5(2), 7(5) and 8(3) of the Vaccine Damage

Payments Act 1979 and of all other powers enabling him in that behalf, hereby makes the following regulations:

PART I

GENERAL

Citation, commencement and interpretation

1.—(1) These regulations may be cited as the Vaccine Damage Payments Regulations 1979 and shall come into operation on 6th April 1979.

(2) In these regulations, unless the context otherwise requires—

"the Act" means the Vaccine Damage Payments Act 1979;

"hearing" means oral hearing;

"medical practitioner" means registered medical practitioner;

"payment" means a payment under section 1(1) of the Act;

[[1]"the President" means—

(a) in relation to England, Wales and Scotland, the President of social security appeal tribunals and medical appeal tribunals appointed under paragraph 1A(1)(a) of Schedule 10 to the Social Security Act 1975;

(b) in relation to Northern Ireland, the President of social security appeal tribunals and medical appeal tribunals appointed for Northern Ireland under paragraph 1A(1)(a) of Schedule 10 to the Social Security (Northern Ireland) Act 1975]

"tribunal" means a vaccine damage tribunal constituted under regulation 7 of these regulations.

(3) Any notice required to be given to any person under the provisions of these regulations may be given by being sent by post to that person at his ordinary or last known address.

AMENDMENT

1. Vaccine Damage Payments (Amendment) Regulations 1988 (S.I. 1988 No. 1169), reg. 2(2) (August 1, 1988).

PART II

CLAIMS

Claims to be made to the Secretary of State in writing

2.—(1) Every claim for payment shall be made in writing to the Secretary of State on the form approved by him, or in such other manner, being in writing, as he may accept as sufficient in the circumstances of any particular case or class of cases.

(2) Any person who has made a claim in accordance with the provisions of this regulation may amend his claim, at any time before a decision has been given thereon, by notice in writing delivered or sent to the Secretary of State, and any claim so amended may be treated as if it had been so amended in the first instance.

Information to be given when making a claim

3. Every person who makes a claim shall furnish such certificates, documents, information and evidence for the purpose of determining the claim as may be required by the Secretary of State.

Obligations of disabled person

4.—(1) Subject to the following provisions of this regulation, every disabled person in respect of whom a claim has been made under section 3 of the Act shall comply with every notice given to him or, where he is not the claimant, to the claimant by the Secretary of State which requires such disabled person to submit himself to a medical examination either by a medical practitioner appointed by the Secretary of State or by a tribunal for the purposes of determining whether he is severely disabled as a result of vaccination against any of the diseases to which the Act applies.

(2) Every notice given under the preceding paragraph shall be given in writing and shall specify the time and place of examination and shall not require the disabled person to submit himself to examination before the expiration of the period of fourteen days beginning with the date of the notice or such shorter period as may be reasonable in the circumstances.

Vaccinations to be treated as carried out in England

5.—(1) Vaccinations given outside the United Kingdom and the Isle of Man to serving members of Her Majesty's forces or members of their families shall be treated for the purposes of the Act as carried out in England where the vaccination in question has been given as part of medical facilities provided under arrangements made by or on behalf of the service authorities.

(2) For the purposes of section 2(5) of the Act—

(a) "serving members of Her Majesty's forces" means a member of the naval, military or air forces of the Crown or of any women's service administered by the Defence Council;

(b) the family of a serving member of Her Majesty's forces shall consist of the spouse of such member and the child or children whose requirements are provided by him.

Circumstances prescribed in relation to cases of damage through contact

[[1]**5A.** The circumstances prescribed for the purposes of section 1(3) of the Vaccine Damage Payments Act 1979 (Act to have effect with respect to a person severely disabled as a result of contracting a disease through contact with a third person who was vaccinated against it) are that:—

(1) the disabled person has been in close physical contact with a person who has been vaccinated against poliomyelitis with orally administered vaccine;

(2) that contact occurred within a period of sixty days beginning with the fourth day immediately following such vaccination; and

(3) the disabled person was, within the period referred to in paragraph (2) of this regulation, either—

(a) looking after the person who has been vaccinated, or

(b) himself being looked after together with the person who has been vaccinated.]

Amendment

1. Vaccine Damage Payments (Amendment) Regulations 1979 (S.I. 1979 No. 1441), reg. 2 (December 13, 1979).

Claims made prior to the passing of the Act

6.—(1) A claim made before the passing of the Act in connection with the non-statutory scheme of payments for severe vaccine damage established by the Secretary of State for Social Services in anticipation of the passing of the Act and which has not been disposed of at the commencement of the Act shall be treated as a claim falling within section 3(1) of the Act.

(2) Any information and other evidence furnished and other things done before the commencement of the Act in connection with any such claim made

before the passing of the Act shall be treated as furnished or done in connection with a claim falling within section 3(1) of the Act.

PART III

REVIEW BY TRIBUNALS

Vaccine damage tribunals

7.—[[1](1) Matters arising under section 4 of the Act shall be determined by tribunals to be known as vaccine damage tribunals constituted in accordance with the following provisions of this regulation.

(1A) A vaccine damage tribunal shall consist of a chairman and two other persons.

(1B) The chairman shall—

(a) in Northern Ireland, be appointed by the Secretary of State;

(b) in England, Wales and Scotland, be nominated by the President of social security appeal tribunals and medical appeal tribunals appointed under paragraph 1A(1) of Schedule 10 to the Social Security Act 1975, who may nominate either himself or any person who by virtue of paragraph 2(4)(a) or (b) of Schedule 12 to that Act may be nominated as a chairman of a medical appeal tribunal.]

[[2](1C) The members of the tribunal other than the chairman shall be medical practitioners appointed by the President after consultation with such academic medical bodies as appear to him to be appropriate.

(1D) The President may—

(a) except in Northern Ireland, appoint such officers and staff for vaccine damage tribunals as he thinks fit, subject to the consent of the Secretary of State and the Treasury as to numbers and as to remuneration and other terms and Conditions of Service;

(b) in Northern Ireland, appoint such officers and staff for vaccine damage tribunals as he thinks fit, with the consent of the Department of Health and Social Services for Northern Ireland and the Department of Finance and Personnel as to numbers and as to remuneration and other terms and Conditions of Service;

(c) arrange—

(i) such meetings of chairmen and other members of vaccine damage tribunals, and

(ii) such training for such chairmen and other members,

as he considers appropriate; and

(d) secure that such works of reference as he considers appropriate are available for the use of chairmen and other members of vaccine damage tribunals.]

(2) A person shall not act as a member of a tribunal for the purpose of the consideration of any case referred to them if he—

(a) is or may be directly affected by that case; or

(b) has taken part in such a case as a medical practitioner who has regularly attended the disabled person or whose opinion has been sought on any matter in connection with the said case.

(3) Where any member of a tribunal is not present at the consideration of a case, the reference to that tribunal shall be revoked and the case shall forthwith be referred to another such tribunal.

(4) Where the tribunal are unable to reach a unanimous decision on any case the decision of the majority of its members shall be the decision of the tribunal.

AMENDMENTS

1. Vaccine Damage Payments (Amendment) Regulations 1984 (S.I. 1984 No. 442) (April 23, 1984).
2. Vaccine Damage Payments (Amendment) Regulations 1988 (S.I. 1988 No. 1169), reg. 2(2) (August 1, 1988).

Procedure of vaccine damage tribunals

8.—(1) If the Secretary of State or the claimant, as the case may be, makes a request to a tribunal for a hearing in connection with any question referred to the tribunal under section 4 of the Act such request shall be granted and a tribunal may of its own motion if satisfied that a hearing is desirable, hold a hearing.

(2) Where, in accordance with the provisions of the preceding paragraph, a tribunal holds a hearing, reasonable notice of the time and place of the hearing shall be given to the Secretary of State and the claimant and except with the consent of the claimant, the tribunal shall not proceed with the hearing unless such notice has been given.

(3) Every hearing held by a tribunal shall be in public except in so far as the chairman may for special reasons otherwise direct and, subject to the provisions of this regulation, the procedure shall be such as the tribunal shall determine.

(4) Nothing in the preceding paragraph shall prevent a member of the Council on Tribunals or of the Scottish Committee of the Council from being present at a hearing in his capacity as such notwithstanding that the hearing is not in public.

(5) The Secretary of State and the claimant shall have the right to be heard at a hearing of a tribunal.

(6) If a claimant, to whom notice of hearing has been duly given should fail to appear at the hearing, the tribunal may proceed to determine the case notwithstanding his absence, or may give such directions with a view to the determination of the case as they may think proper having regard to all the circumstances including any explanation offered for the absence.

(7) Any person having the right to be heard who appears at a hearing before a tribunal may call witnesses and shall be given an opportunity of putting questions directly to any witnesses called at the hearing and of addressing the tribunal.

(8) Any person who by virtue of the provisions of these regulations has a right to be heard at a hearing may be represented at a hearing by another person whether having professional qualifications or not and, for the purposes of the proceedings at the hearing, any such representative shall have all the rights and powers to which the person whom he represents is entitled under the Act and these regulations.

(9) Where a tribunal hold a hearing they shall, for the purpose of arriving at their decision or discussing any question of procedure and notwithstanding anything contained in these regulations, order all persons not being members of the tribunal other than the person acting as a clerk of the tribunal to withdraw from the sitting of the tribunal provided that, if all the members of the tribunal agree and if no person having the right to be heard objects, they may permit a member or members of the Council on Tribunals, or of the Scottish Committee of the Council, present only in that capacity, to remain present at any such sitting even though by virtue of this paragraph other persons are ordered to withdraw.

Notice of decision of tribunal

9.—(1) A tribunal shall in each case record their decision in writing in such form as may from time to time be approved by the Secretary of State and shall include in such a record which shall be signed by all the members of the tribunal a statement of the reasons for their decision.

(2) As soon as may be practicable, the claimant shall be sent written notice of the decision of a tribunal and such notice shall be in such form as may from time to time be approved by the Secretary of State and shall contain a summary of the record of that decision made in accordance with this regulation.

Non-disclosure of evidence

10. Where, in connection with the consideration and determination of any matter there is before a tribunal medical advice or medical evidence relating to the claimant or the disabled person which has not been disclosed to the claimant and in the opinion of the chairman of the tribunal it would be undesirable in the interests of the claimant or the disabled person to disclose that advice or evidence to the claimant such advice or evidence shall not be required to be disclosed, but the tribunal shall not by reason of such non-disclosure be precluded from taking it into account for the purpose of the said determination.

Part IV

Reconsideration

Application for reconsideration under section 5 of the Act

11.—(1) An application for reconsideration of a determination may be made to the Secretary of State within 6 years of the date of the notice of that determination and shall be made in writing stating the grounds of the application.

(2) Where the Secretary of State of his own motion institutes a reconsideration of a determination he shall give notice in writing of his intention to the person who was the claimant in relation to the claim which gives rise to the reconsideration and also, where the disabled person is alive and was not the claimant, to him and any such reconsideration shall, subject to paragraph (3) of this regulation, be instituted within 6 years of the date of the notice of that determination.

(3) Notwithstanding paragraph (2) of this regulation, where it appears to the Secretary of State that a payment was made in consequence of a misrepresentation or failure to disclose any material fact he may institute a reconsideration of a determination at any time.

The Vaccine Damage Payments (Specified Disease) Order 1990

(S.I. 1990 No. 623)

Arrangement of Order

The Secretary of State for Social Security, in exercise of the powers conferred by section 1(2)(i) of the Vaccine Damage Payments Act 1979 and of all other powers enabling him in that behalf, hereby makes the following Order:

Citation and commencement

1. This Order may be cited as the Vaccine Damage Payments (Specified Disease) Order 1990 and shall come into force on 9th April 1990.

(S.I. 1990 No. 623, reg. 2)

Addition to the diseases to which the Vaccine Damage Payments Act applies

2. Mumps is specified as a disease to which the Vaccine Damage Payments Act 1979 applies.

The Vaccine Damage Payments (Specified Disease) Order 1995

(S.I. 1995 No. 1164)

The Secretary of State for Social Security, in exercise of powers conferred by section 1(2)(i) of the Vaccine Damage Payments Act 1979(**a**) and of all other powers enabling him in that behalf, hereby makes the following Order:

Citation and commencement

1. This Order may be cited as the Vaccine Damage Payments (Specified Disease) Order 1995 and shall come into force on 31st May 1995.

Addition to the diseases to which the Vaccine Damage Payments Act applies

2. Haemophilus influenza type b infection is specified as a disease to which the Vaccine Damage Payments Act 1979 applies.

The Vaccine Damage Payments Act 1979 Statutory Sum Order 1991

(S.I. 1991 No. 939)

Arrangement of Order

Whereas a draft of the following Order was laid before Parliament in accordance with section 1(4A) of the Vaccine Damage Payments Act 1979 and was approved by resolution of each House of Parliament:

Now, therefore, the Secretary of State for Social Security with the consent of the Treasury, in exercise of the powers conferred by section 1(1A) of the Vaccine Damage Payments Act 1979 and of all other powers enabling him in that behalf, hereby makes the following Order:

Citation and commencement

1. This Order may be cited as the Vaccine Damage Payments Act 1979 Statutory Sum Order 1991 and shall come into force on 15th April 1991.

Statement of the statutory sum for the purposes of the Vaccine Damage Payments Act 1979

2. For the purposes of the Vaccine Damage Payments Act 1979 the statutory sum is £30,000.

3. *Omitted.*

PART V

President's Circulars

President's Circulars

Index

PRESIDENT'S CIRCULAR No. 1

ADJOURNMENTS

Generally

1. Tribunals have the power to adjourn hearings, either of their own motion or upon application of a party and it will often be necessary for the tribunal, in the interests of justice, to exercise that power.

2. Tribunals should, however, remind themselves that the unnecessary adjournment of a hearing should always be avoided; the consequent delay can cause hardship or distress to a party, and can waste valuable public resources which could be more efficiently and properly used.

3. Tribunals will wish, therefore, to articulate very carefully the reason for an adjournment before initiating or agreeing to that action, and to be sure, in those cases where the seeking or obtaining of additional evidence [medical or otherwise] is the reason for the adjournment, that that additional evidence is likely to be available without unreasonable delay, is likely to assist the tribunal in its deliberations and is relevant to the issue to be decided.

4. I regard it as good practice in the fulfilment of the judicial role to articulate the reason for the adjournment in the written decision, and I would hope that tribunal chairmen would follow that practice. An entry reading simply "adjourned for additional evidence", I would not regard as meeting that criterion of good judicial practice. A form now exists [ITS/ADJ] which is to be used on every occasion when a tribunal adjourns a hearing and which is to be

handed to the parties who are present before the tribunal or sent within two days of the hearing to any absent party.

Where the Tribunal Accepts That it Needs Further Evidence

5. The tribunal's judicial task is to determine an appeal before it, on the basis of its assessment of the evidence produced, its findings of fact following such assessment and its application of the relevant law to those findings. Experience shows that in the normal course of events the evidence produced is such as to enable the tribunal properly to complete this task without an adjournment for the purpose of producing further evidence.

6. However, there may be circumstances where the available evidence is insufficient so that it is in the interest of justice for the tribunal to exercise its discretion to adjourn.

7. It is important for the adjournment decision to record who should supply any further evidence i.e. the appellant, his representative or the AO and by when it should be supplied; it is also important to impose a timescale for the case to be relisted. The direction should always make it clear whether the case is to be listed before the same or a differently constituted tribunal. The reservation of cases to the same tribunal should only be done in exceptional circumstances i.e. where substantial oral evidence has been taken or complex legal argument is under consideration.

8. If the tribunal is exercising its power under Section 53 of the Social Security Administration Act 1992 so that the ITS is required to take some action that exercise of power should be expressly indicated on the form ITS [ADJ] and attention should be drawn to the need for the ITS administration to take relevant action and to the form which that action should take.

9. Where the tribunal adjourns for the ITS to obtain a medical report it is important that the report is obtained expeditiously, so that the matter can be relisted without unnecessary delay. There is, therefore, a need to publicise the ways in which the tribunal's decision to adjourn to obtain a medical report may be formulated in such a way as to minimise any such delay.

10. As a first step the form ITS/ADJ on which the chairman records the tribunal's decision to adjourn, should clearly summarise the reasons why the tribunal considered that it should adjourn and why it considered that the ITS should obtain a medical report. Form ITS/FME 1 should be contemporaneously completed in all such cases. The purpose of the form is to specify the kind of report being sought, from whom, whether it requires fresh examination or review of existing medical records, what aspects of the claimed benefit it addresses and to what questions such as diagnosis or treatment, it should be directed. This information is essential to enable the formulation of a proper request for a medical report.

11. It is the chairman's responsibility to complete ITS/FME1, which should be done in the hearing room and in the presence of any party who has attended the hearing so that a medical member of the tribunal or the medical assessor can advise upon its content. The use of form DAT 32 is now discontinued.

Further Considerations

12. Tribunals should always remind themselves that where benefit has been withdrawn upon review, the burden of providing that that action was justified, upon the balance of probabilities, lies upon the AO. Where the tribunal is of the opinion that the AO should have sought medical or other evidence to put before the tribunal in order to discharge that burden, but has failed to do so without good cause, the tribunal will always want to ask itself [albeit recognising that they exercise an inquisitorial jurisdiction] whether the tribunal should

expend resources in and cause further delay by seeking evidence which the AO should have obtained in order to support the review decision. The preferable course may be either to adjourn to enable the AO to seek the necessary evidence within a specified timescale [if a just decision cannot be reached without that evidence and if the PO can offer an acceptable explanation for the failure to produce it] or to decide the case by reference to the facts before the tribunal and the applicable burden of proof.

13. A similar problem may arise where an appellant, on first application for the benefit, appeals against the disallowance, produces no medical evidence yet suggests that it is available and that the tribunal should seek it. It may also occur that, during the course of the hearing, the tribunal identifies a need for additional medical evidence. Tribunals should remind themselves that in these cases the burden of proof lies with the appellant [also on the balance of probabilities] and that they should then consider the extent to which public resources should be expended if what is then proposed is the seeking of evidence which, strictly, the appellant should have sought and produced before the hearing. That consideration may not be appropriate where the tribunal itself identifies the need for further evidence. In deciding whether or not to adjourn and, if so, for what purpose, tribunals should, while reminding themselves that they exercise an inquisitorial jurisdiction, consider the likely availability of the suggested evidence within a reasonable timescale, its relevance to the issues before the tribunal and [where appropriate] the appellant's reasons for not providing that evidence to the tribunal. If the tribunal decides to adjourn for evidence to be obtained, the adjournment decision should make it clear whether the ITS or the appellant is to obtain the evidence and should impose realistic timescales for evidence provision and relisting of the hearing.

14. The practical directions for the obtaining of medical reports and other medical evidence are contained in President's Circular No. 13.

June 1997 **His Honour Judge Keith Bassinghtwaighte**
President

PRESIDENT'S CIRCULAR No. 2

RECORDING AND NOTIFYING TRIBUNAL PROCEEDINGS AND DECISIONS: FORM AND CONTENT

1. Record of Proceedings

In this area amendments occurred by virtue of the Social Security [Adjudication] and Child Support Amendment Regulations 1996 which came into force on 28 February 1996. As a result of those regulations, chairmen should keep a written record of evidence [both oral and written], submissions and the progress of the hearing [a "record of proceedings"] on form ITS[RP]; that record will be kept for 18 months and supplied in its handwritten form to any party to the proceedings who requests them.

2. Chairmen are reminded that the presence of the regulation does not mean that the record of proceedings should never be issued. It is a chairman's decision whether to do so and he/she might consider it prudent [and a saving of administrative resources] to request that a copy of that record be supplied in particularly contentious cases where an appeal—and a request for a copy of the record of proceedings—is likely. If that is done, the full decision [see paragraph 12 below]

should record that a copy of the manuscript note of proceedings on form ITS[RP] is attached.

3. Oral Notification

Whenever an appellant or his/her representative attends a tribunal hearing, I regard it as good judicial practice and in the interests of the appellant for a tribunal chairman orally to announce the result at the conclusion of the hearing, unless there are compelling reasons to the contrary. This applies whatever the nature of the tribunal's decision.

4. The following are examples of "compelling reasons":

(a) An appellant/representative does not or cannot wait to hear the decision.
(b) An appellant/representative cannot hear or understand the decision.
(c) There is reason to believe that, if told the decision, a party will become distressed or distraught.
(d) There is reason to believe that a party will become violent to himself or another, or to property, if told the decision at the conclusion of the hearing.
(e) The decision is too complex to explain to a party without causing undue confusion or anxiety.

5. The chairman should normally use non-technical ordinary language to indicate the decision and its effect, and should explain the procedures for written notification.

6. Written Notification

As a result of further Adjudication Regulation changes following the enactment of Statutory Instrument 1996 No. 2450, new written decision procedures come into effect on and from 21 October 1996. The new procedures apply to SSATs, MATs, DATs and CSATs but not to VDTs. The Adjudication Regulations provided, inter alia, for the introduction of decision notices on the day of the hearing and for statements of the tribunal's findings of fact and reasons for its decision to be provided later, either on request or of a chairman's own motion. In this Circular, the latter document is referred to, for convenience, as a "full decision".

7. **Decision Notices.** A decision notice is a form which the regulation gives me the power to approve. I have approved a form of decision notice for use in each jurisdiction to be known respectively as ITS[DN] [SSAT], [CSAT] etc.; only that form as drafted has my approval under the Adjudication Regulations. That printed form should not be amended nor should anything [other than an AWT schedule] be attached to it. The decision notice is to be legibly handwritten by the chairman; the tribunal clerk will hand a copy of the carbonised decision notice to the parties as they leave the hearing. They will, either at the same time or earlier, have been advised in writing of their right to appeal and to apply for a record of proceedings and a full decision, but tribunal chairmen may want specifically to enquire of the parties whether they want a full decision, since the earlier such a request is notified, the less the effort expended in producing it. The decision notice dispenses with the need for separate forms AT3A or DAT28A [the use of which has been discontinued].

8. **Decision notices must be written and issued in every case** and at the hearing where the decision has been announced. If the decision has not been announced or following determination of a case in the absence of a party or by consideration of the papers alone, the decision notice should be written by the chairman on the day of the hearing and sent by the clerk to any party who was not present at the hearing on the next working day following the hearing. The decision notice will record the decision of the tribunal [in sufficient detail, where an appellant is successful, to enable immediate payment of benefit] and will

provide for inclusion of a summary of the tribunal's reasons for that decision [see paragraph 9. below].

9. Where there has been no request for a full decision at the hearing and the chairman does not intend to issue one, the decision notice will contain a summary of the tribunal's reasons for its decision: that summary is not intended to be an exhaustive recital of the tribunal's process of reasoning but to be a two or three sentence explanation of the reasons for success or failure. For example, in an IB case, the relevant paragraph could read "After examining all the claimed and relevant descriptor areas, we were satisfied that the appellant could not be awarded sufficient points to reach the AWT threshold of 15" or "After examining all the claimed and relevant descriptor areas, the appellant satisfied the AWT as a result of our award of points with reference to the following physical functions i.e. walking [7 points], standing [7 points] and hearing [8 points]." Where a full decision is to be issued or where an extempore decision has been given and taped, the relevant paragraph of the decision notice could read "A written document, which includes the reasons for our decision, will be issued to the parties later" or "The reasons for our decision were explained to the parties at the hearing."

10. There are three decision notices for use in DATs: the ITS/DN/DAT/REF, the ITS/DN/DAT/DLA/AW and the ITS/DN/DAT/AA/AW, the first recording a refusal for both DLA and AA, the second an award of DLA and the third an award of AA. In those cases where the award of both care and mobility components of DLA are in issue, but the tribunal awards one and not the other, chairmen should be aware that **both** DLA decision notices should be issued and that on the award notice the box marked "linked decision" should be ticked.

11. It is always for a chairman to decide whether only a decision notice, or a decision notice and full decision, needs to be issued in any particular case. He/she should always consider very carefully to what extent the decision notice alone is appropriate for the case which the tribunal has just decided, bearing in mind the area and scope of dispute, and the likelihood of appeal.

12. There may be some cases which are so straightforward that, even if requested to provide a full decision, the chairman will not be able to add anything to what is contained in the decision notice. Where that is the case, the decision notice should clearly state on its face that it "includes the full statement of the reasons for the tribunal's decision and of its findings on questions of fact material thereto to which Regulation 23[3A] of the Social Security [Adjudication] Regulations 1995 refers".

13. **Full Decisions.** A chairman will need to prepare a decision which contains "the reasons for the tribunal's decision and its findings on questions of fact material thereto" only if he/she decides to do so or if a party, either at the hearing or within 21 days of issue of a decision notice, so requests. Chairmen will note that the full decision incorporates, by specific reference therein, the terms of the decision notice already issued.

14. If a chairman wishes to give a full decision at the hearing, the regulations provide that he/she may choose to deliver an extempore decision which can be tape-recorded. If a chairman chooses that option and if a request is made for a transcript of that record, it will be typed and sent to the chairman for signature. **It will not be possible for the chairman to correct or alter the typed transcript, except in the case of typing errors.**

15. If a chairman decides upon, or a party requests, preparation of a full decision at the hearing, I would expect it to be ordinarily available within 14 days of the hearing. Chairmen may use any of the currently approved methods for preparation of that decision and should ensure that that decision is provided to the ITS office concerned within 3 working days. The chairman should ensure, whenever a clerk is not present in the tribunal room to appreciate that a full decision will be issued, that the clerk is so advised; the intention to issue a full

decision should also be apparent from the face of the decision notice [see paragraph 9. above].

16. If a party requests preparation of a full decision within 21 days of the issue of the decision notice, the chairman concerned must be notified of that request within 3 days of its receipt in ITS offices and he/she must be sent, within that same timescale, a copy of the tribunal papers [and of any additional written evidence received thereat], of the record of proceedings, of the decision notice and of the written request for the full decision. Chairmen should aim to provide that full decision to the ITS office within 3 working days of receipt of the request. I consider that a chairman may, at his/her discretion, agree to issue a full decision even though the request is made outside the 21 day period. If such a request is made, but refused, I do not, however, consider that a chairman is obliged to give reasons for that decision.

17. Chairmen will no doubt wish to keep some personal record of the identities of those present at the hearing and of the rationale of decisions and closed session discussion against the possibility that a full decision may be later requested. For that reason, judicial notebooks have been acquired and will be available to all chairmen. They are personal records to be kept by chairmen and are *not* to be deposited in ITS offices for safekeeping; it should be noted that it is my opinion that these notebooks will not contain formal records, the production of which I would expect to be compellable either by parties or by the appellate jurisdictions.

18. **I regret that ITS resources cannot be used for the precautionary recording of full decisions simply in case one should later be requested.** Clerks have, therefore, been advised to decline the use of ITS recording equipment unless it is indicated in the decision notice that a full decision will be issued or the chairman, having initially decided not to issue a full decision, changes his/her mind on the day of the hearing and so advises the clerk. If chairmen wish to do so on their own equipment, that is a matter for them but it would obviously assist if it was ensured that that equipment is compatible with that in use in ITS offices.

19. The issue of a decision notice does not affect rights of appeal against the tribunal's decision. Time limits for appeal now run from the date of issue of the full decision.

November 1997 **His Honour Judge Keith Bassingthwaighte**
President

PRESIDENT'S CIRCULAR No. 3

NO SMOKING POLICY

1. For the health and comfort of all who use tribunal hearing rooms, there shall be no smoking in these rooms whether or not a hearing is in progress.

2. Chairmen and members should accept it as their personal responsibility to ensure compliance with the rule. Observance of this rule is a condition of continued appointment to the tribunals operated by the Independent Tribunal Service.

3. Administrative arrangements already ensure that appropriate notices are posted to discourage smoking in all parts of tribunal suites.

October 1995 **His Honour Judge Keith Bassingthwaighte**
President

PRESIDENT'S CIRCULAR No. 4

DOMICILIARY HEARINGS

1. Tribunals have the power to hold a hearing at a claimant's home in appropriate cases: they are known as domiciliary visits [DVs]. A tribunal is never under a legal obligation to hold such a hearing.

2. Administrative staff of the ITS are not to arrange a DV before the tribunal has convened to hear the case, unless the President, a regional or any full-time chairman has so instructed. That instruction will generally not be given unless it is obvious that there are no other reasonable means of ensuring that a just decision is made by the tribunal, taking into account the principles of natural justice.

3. A tribunal or chairman should always give very careful consideration to the facts before directing a DV. In particular, consider whether:

(a) there is already sufficient evidence on which to allow an appeal in full,
(b) sufficient evidence to reach a just decision can reasonably be obtained in some other way, including those indicated in paragraph 4 below, and
(c) there is any other reasonable way to obtain the attendance of the parties, including those indicated in paragraph 5 below.

4. "Other ways of obtaining evidence" include:

(a) requesting the attendance of a family member, a carer or some other witness who could give the evidence that could be given by the parties;
(b) requesting written or recorded evidence from the parties, a carer or some other witness;
(c) referring a question of special difficulty to an expert [including a general practitioner] for report under section 53 of the Social Security Administration Act 1993;
(d) the exercise of the power of the chairman to give such directions as he may consider necessary or desirable for just, effective and efficient conduct of the proceedings under Regulation 2[1][aa] of S.I. 1996 No. 2450.

5. "Other ways of obtaining the attendance of the parties" include:

(a) providing a taxi or a private hire car to bring the parties from home to the tribunal hearing, and
(b) arranging for the parties to be brought from home to the usual venue by St John's Ambulance or similar suitable vehicle.

6. In deciding whether to adjourn and order a DV, a tribunal, in particular, should also take into account:

(a) that members of the tribunal may have disabilities which would cause difficulties in arranging a DV, and
(b) that it may often be preferable to adjourn for another hearing at the usual venue, rather than to arrange an unnecessary DV.

7. There may be occasions when only the obtaining of a General Practitioner's report will enable a tribunal or chairman to make an informed decision. Provided that unacceptable delay will not be occasioned by such a request, such a report may be requested before a tribunal or chairman makes the decision.

June 1997 **His Honour Judge Keith Bassingthwaighte**
President

PRESIDENT'S CIRCULAR No. 6

SETTING-ASIDE APPLICATIONS: CONDUCT OF TRIBUNAL CHAIRMEN/MEMBERS/ASSESSORS/ITS STAFF

1. Regulations provide that a tribunal may set aside the decision of its own or of another tribunal where it is just to do so on the grounds that:

(a) a relevant document was not sent or received at the appropriate time by a party [or a representative] or by the adjudicating authority who gave the decision,
(b) a party [or a representative] was not present, or
(c) the interests of justice so require.

The latter ground has been interpreted to relate only to procedural irregularities, since to do otherwise would undermine the right of appeal to a Commissioner and the finality of tribunal decisions [subject to appeal or review].

2. The tribunal must firstly decide and make appropriate findings of fact, in respect of sub-para a, b or c above. Then, if one [or more] sections is satisfied, the tribunal should consider whether it is *just* to set aside the earlier decision on that ground. The tribunal has discretion; a useful test to be applied in all setting aside decisions is *whether any party had reasonable grounds to believe that there has or may not have been unfair prejudice as a result of what occurred.*

3. Tribunals will be very familiar with the operation of the regulation in routine cases. This circular also draws to your attention the issues which arise where the basis of the setting-aside application is an allegation concerning the conduct of a tribunal chairman/member/assessor or other member of ITS staff on the day of the hearing.

4. A different tribunal should always deal with such a case; it will have no way of knowing whether the complaint is true, misconceived or malicious. Such allegations are easy to make and it would be unfortunate if it ever became the case that, whenever such allegations were made, the application was automatically granted, since it would encourage the making of false allegations where an appellant had lost his/her earlier appeal.

5. Whenever a complaint about the conduct of tribunal personnel or staff on the day of the hearing forms the basis for a setting aside application, the tribunal should first decide, in the event that the complaint should be correct, whether what is complained of amounts to a procedural irregularity, such that it is just to set aside the previous decision.

6. If the tribunal decides that the complaint could properly lead to the decision being set aside, the tribunal should adjourn the application to enable responses to be sought from the appropriate tribunal personnel in accordance with President's Instruction No. 10 and for the application to be heard by a different tribunal.

7. If the tribunal decides that, even if correct, the complaint could not properly lead to the decision being set aside, it should so record in its decision rejecting the application.

October 1995 **His Honour Judge Keith Bassingthwaighte**
President

PRESIDENT'S CIRCULAR No. 7

TRIBUNALS' USE OF "LIBERTY TO RESTORE"

1. The order "Liberty to restore" is a common one in civil jurisdictions: it has not had extensive use in ITS tribunals but it is appropriate to give guidance about its use.

2. There is a proper use of the order where a hearing is adjourned sine die, when no relisting action is anticipated unless a party so requests. Its use in these circumstances will be rare in the ITS jurisdictions.

3. Tribunals should beware of too-ready use of the order in other circumstances. It can be a proper order, but tribunals should be aware:

(a) that it is good judicial practice to specify when making the order for what purpose the hearing may be restored,
(b) that it is good judicial practice to use the order only when, for some specified reason, part of the original hearing remains unsettled, and
(c) that it is never good judicial practice to use the order when the result of it, consciously or otherwise, is the avoidance of otherwise proper review or appeal procedures.

4. Where a tribunal uses the order [other than as envisaged in paragraph 2 above], it will have embarked upon the hearing, yet will have decided that, for some reason, its order is incomplete. It will have decided not to adjourn. In consequence, where a tribunal has given liberty to restore in such circumstances it is appropriate for the *same tribunal* to consider the restored issue[s] in the light of the evidence which it has already heard.

5. A tribunal making such an order should therefore give appropriate instructions to the listing officer, so that the file may be marked accordingly.

October 1995 **His Honour Judge Keith Bassingthwaighte**
President

PRESIDENT'S CIRCULAR No. 9

ACTION IN MULTIPLE CASES WHERE THE DECISION OF A COMMISSIONER OR OF A SUPERIOR COURT IS AWAITED

1. Where these cases are concerned, [which are referred to generically as "appeal dependent cases"] it is always necessary to consider the best way of dealing with them. On many occasions, I will agree that it is desirable that they should not be listed for hearing until the decision in the lead case is known.

2. Where that action has been taken, appellants and their representatives will have been informed of the reason for that action in the terms of the specimen letter attached, and will also have been informed of their right to require a case to be listed despite my direction to the contrary.

3. Such cases may, therefore, come before a tribunal. If that occurs, tribunals will have before them a copy of the ITS letter to the appellant/representative and of any additional information, giving the full context of the case and its likely progress through the appellate levels beyond the ITS. It will then be necessary for the tribunal to decide whether to hear the case or to adjourn it, pending resolution of the relevant issue[s].

4. Tribunals should ensure that they are in possession of all such additional information before making a decision. They must make that decision judicially on the facts before them, having considered the submissions of the presenting officer and/or the appellant and his/her representative.

5. Tribunals should bear in mind that, although delay will occur if there is an adjournment:

(a) a successful appellant [if the case had been heard] is likely to have gained little, since the Secretary of State may well appeal the tribunal's decision, which will permit the suspension of payment of any awarded benefit in such disputed circumstances, and
(b) all benefit routes are not closed to an appellant who alleges that he/she suffers financial hardship as a result of the delay in resolution of the appeal.

6. It sometimes occurs that a party or representative before the tribunal will allege that "there is a lead case pending", although the tribunal has no information before it of the type mentioned in the preceding paragraphs. Tribunals

should be wary of acting upon unsubstantiated suggestion and should, unless compelling detail is provided and if there is sufficient information and evidence before it, decide the case according to the existing law.

June 1997 **His Honour Judge Keith Bassingthwaighte**
President

Specimen Letter

Dear

Important Information about your Appeal

1. I am writing about your appeal against [*here describe the nature of the appeal*].

2. Your appeal, with many others, involves a difficult point of law. [*Here describe the legal issue*]. Consequently, [*here describe who has appealed, to which court and the time frame for appeal*]. Until then, therefore, the law is not clear or settled.

3. If your case was to come before a tribunal and be decided in your favour, I understand that the Adjudication Officer is likely to appeal that decision to the Commissioners. Any advantage you may have gained as a result of the decision could then be lost, since, pending the appeal in your case being decided by the Commissioner, the Secretary of State has, by law, the power to suspend payment of any benefit awarded by the tribunal. In view of that, and of the number of similar cases, a great deal of time and energy could be wasted with little positive outcome for any of the parties. For this reason, we consider that it is in the interests of all concerned not to hear your case—or that of any of the other similar place appellants—until this period of uncertainty is resolved by the decision of the [*here insert identity of appeal court*]. You have my assurance that your appeal will then be dealt with urgently.

4. I appreciate that this letter may come as a disappointment to you. However, I hope that you will accept our concern about delays which arise when difficult questions have to be resolved in the Courts.

5. I will keep you informed from time to time about how the lead appeal is progressing. However, it may be some months before I have any new information to report. You should be aware that if you disagree with the decision not to list your case for hearing for the present, you can request the Independent Tribunal Service [ITS] to list it for hearing. If you do, I am informed that the department's representative is likely to apply for an adjournment; if that is granted by the tribunal, it means that resources have been used which could have been applied to the determination of other cases not affected by pending legislation. I hope, therefore, that you will agree that the decision taken is in the best interests of all concerned.

6. It may also help you to know that not all benefit routes are closed to you while the legal issue is going through the Courts. You should contact your local office of the Benefits Agency for advice or seek that advice from representative sources, such as the Citizens' Advice Bureau or a local welfare rights' organisation. The Secretary of State does also have the discretion to decide not to suspend any benefit which may be awarded by a tribunal if hardship is caused by that suspension. You may, therefore, use that argument if you ask for your case to be listed, despite this letter, and if the Department's representative seeks to persuade the tribunal to adjourn your application. You should realise, how-

ever, that the discretion has only been exercised in severe cases in the recent past.

7. I am sending a copy of this letter to major representatives' organisations, although not necessarily to individual representatives. Any enquiries should be addressed to this office.

Yours sincerely,

PRESIDENT'S CIRCULAR No. 10

CORRECTING ACCIDENTAL ERRORS IN TRIBUNAL DECISIONS

1. Regulation 9 of the Social Security [Adjudication] Regulations 1995 permits the above procedure to be carried out by the original tribunal or by a tribunal of like status.

2. Commissioner's decision *CSSB/76/93* requires that procedure to be effected by a sitting tribunal and indicates that it should not be done by postal confirmation, as previously occurred.

3. Wherever possible, correction of a decision should be put to a tribunal which is chaired by the chairman of the original tribunal, since he/she will have prepared the relevant decision.

4. If, for any reason, unacceptable delay will occur in seeking a correction decision from a tribunal chaired by the original chairman, a differently constituted tribunal of like status may be asked to make that decision after the reaction of the original chairman has been obtained, either in writing or by telephone. His/her comment should be put before the correcting tribunal and it is within the judicial discretion of that tribunal to decide whether it feels competent to make the suggested, or any, correction to the original decision.

5. If, for any reason, the reaction of the original chairman cannot be obtained without unacceptable delay, a correction decision may be sought from any differently constituted tribunal of like status without the original chairman's comment. If that occurs, it is within the judicial discretion of the latter tribunal to decide whether it feels competent to make the suggested, or any, correction to the original decision.

6. A failure accurately and correctly to type a chairman's handwritten decision is not an error in the tribunal's decision requiring correction under regulation 9. In that case a correctly typed copy of the decision can be prepared and made available to the parties without formality.

7. In this Circular "unacceptable delay" means a delay of more than one calendar month.

September 1996 **His Honour Judge Keith Bassingthwaighte**
President

PRESIDENT'S CIRCULAR No. 12

REFERENCES TO THE COURT OF JUSTICE OF THE EUROPEAN COMMUNITIES [ECJ]

1. Chairmen will all be aware that, in cases where appropriate guidance is sought, tribunals are empowered to make a direct reference to the European Court of Justice [ECJ].

2. Guidance in the procedures to be followed and about occasions on which such a reference may be appropriate is contained in the attached note, which has been issued by the ECJ.

3. The decision whether to make a reference to the ECJ must be a matter for an individual tribunal to decide. However, chairmen may consider it advisable to discuss whether a reference would be appropriate with me, or with their regional chairman, before making that decision.

4. The fact that such a reference has been made should always be notified to my office, together with a copy of all supporting and relevant papers.

November 1996 **His Honour Judge Keith Bassingthwaighte President**

Court of Justice of the European Communities

Note for Guidance on References by National Courts for Preliminary Rulings

The development of the Community legal order is largely the result of cooperation between the Court of Justice of the European Communities and national courts and tribunals through the preliminary ruling procedure under Article 177 of the E.C. Treaty and the corresponding provisions of the ECSC and Euratom Treaties.[1]

In order to make this cooperation more effective, and so enable the Court of Justice better to meet the requirements of national courts by providing helpful answers to preliminary questions, this Note for Guidance is addressed to all interested parties, in particular to all national courts and tribunals.

It must be emphasised that the Note is for guidance only and has no binding or interpretative effect in relation to the provisions governing the preliminary ruling procedure. It merely contains practical information which, in the light of experience in applying the preliminary ruling procedure, may help to prevent the kind of difficulties which the Court has sometimes encountered.

1. Any court or tribunal of a Member State may ask the Court of Justice to interpret a rule of Community law, whether contained in the Treaties or in acts of secondary law, if it considers that this is necessary for it to give judgment in a case pending before it.

Courts or tribunals against whose decisions there is no judicial remedy under national law must refer questions of interpretation arising before them to the Court of Justice, unless the Court has already ruled on the point or unless the correct application of the rule of Community law is obvious.[2]

2. The Court of Justice has jurisdiction to rule on the validity of acts of the Community institutions. National courts or tribunals may reject a plea challenging the validity of such an act. But where a national court (even one whose decision is still subject to appeal) intends to question the validity of a Community act, it must refer that question to the Court of Justice.[3]

Where, however, a national court or tribunal has serious doubts about the validity of a Community act on which a national measure is based, it may, in exceptional cases, temporarily suspend application of the latter measure or grant other interim relief with respect to it. It must then refer the question of validity to the Court of Justice, stating the reasons for which it considers that the Community act is not valid.[4]

3. Questions referred for a preliminary ruling must be limited to the interpretation or validity of a provision of Community law, since the Court of Justice does not have jurisdiction to interpret national law or assess its validity. It is

for the referring court or tribunal to apply the relevant rule of Community law in the specific case pending before it.

4. The order of the national court or tribunal referring a question to the Court of Justice for a preliminary ruling may be in any form allowed by national procedural law. Reference of a question or questions to the Court of Justice generally involves stay of the national proceedings until the Court has given its ruling, but the decision to stay proceedings is one which it is for the national court alone to take in accordance with its own national law.

5. The order for reference containing the question or questions referred to the Court will have to be translated by the Court's translators into the other official languages of the Community. Questions concerning the interpretation or validity of Community law are frequently of general interest and the Member State and Community institutions are entitled to submit observations. It is therefore desirable that the reference should be drafted as clearly and precisely as possible.

6. The order for reference should contain a statement of reasons which is succinct but sufficiently complete to give the Court, and those to whom it must be notified (the Member States, the Commission and in certain cases the Council and the European Parliament), a clear understanding of the factual and legal context of the main proceedings.[5]

In particular, it should include:

— a statement of the facts which are essential to a full understanding of the legal significance of the main proceedings;
— an exposition of the national law which may be applicable;
— a statement of the reasons which have prompted the national court to refer the question or questions to the Court of Justice; and
— where appropriate, a summary of the arguments of the parties.

The aim should be to put the Court of Justice in a position to give the national court an answer which will be of assistance to it.

The order for reference should also be accompanied by copies of any documents needed for a proper understanding of the case, especially the text of the applicable national provisions. However, as the case-file or documents annexed to the order for reference are not always translated in full into the other official languages of the Community, the national court should ensure that the order for reference itself includes all the relevant information.

7. A national court or tribunal may refer a question to the Court of Justice as soon as it finds that a ruling on the point or points of interpretation or validity is necessary to enable it to give judgment. It must be stressed, however, that it is not for the Court of Justice to decide issues of fact or to resolve disputes as to the interpretation or application of rules of national law. It is therefore desirable that a decision to refer should not be taken until the national proceedings have reached a stage where the national court is able to define, if only as a working hypothesis, the factual and legal context of the question; on any view, the administration of justice is likely to be best served if the reference is not made until both sides have been heard.[6]

8. The order for reference and the relevant documents should be sent by the national court directly to the Court of Justice, by registered post, addressed to:

The Registry
Court of Justice of the European Communities
L-2925 Luxembourg
Telephone: (352) 43031

The Court Registry will remain in contact with the national court until judgment is given, and will send copies of the various documents (written observations, Report for the Hearing, Opinion of the Advocate General). The Court will also send its judgment to the national court. The Court would appreciate being informed about the application of its judgment in the national proceedings and being sent a copy of the national court's final decision.

9. Proceedings for a preliminary ruling before the Court of Justice are free of charge. The Court does not rule on costs.

[1] A preliminary ruling procedure is also provided for by protocols to several conventions concluded by the Member States, in particular the Brussels Convention on Jurisdiction and the Enforcement of Judgments in Civil and Commercial Mattes.

[2] Judgment in Case 283/81 *CILFIT v. Ministry of Health* [1982] E.C.R. 3415.

[3] Judgment is Case 314/85 *Foto-Frost v. Hauptzollamt Lübeck-ost* [1987] E.C.R. 4199.

[4] Judgments in Joined Cases C-143/88 and C-92/89 *Zuckerfabrik Soest* [1991] E.C.R. I-415 and in Case C-465/93 *Atlanta Fruchthandelsgesellschaft* [1995] E.C.R. I-3761.

[5] Judgment in Joined Cases C-320/90, C-321/90 and C-322/90 *Telemarsicabruzzo* [1993] E.C.R. 1-393.

[6] Judgment in Case 70/77 *Simmenthal v. Amministrazione delle Finanze dello Stato* [1978] E.C.R. 1453.

PRESIDENT'S CIRCULAR No. 13

THE OBTAINING OF FURTHER MEDICAL EVIDENCE [ALL JURISDICTIONS] BY ORDER OF THE TRIBUNAL

1. The ITS has now introduced new procedures where a tribunal decides that the ITS should obtain further medical evidence following an adjournment of an appeal. Requests for medical reports will be actioned by the ITS administrative staff [not BAMS/DBC as was previously the case] and issued direct to the medical profession. Requests for Examining Medical Practitioner [EMP] reports in DATs and Hospital Case Notes' [HCNs] extracts in MATs will, in the future, be processed by the ITS administration via a medical services' contract with the private sector [these requests are still currently being processed via BAMS until the new contract is in place, however administrative staff will prepare the request before issuing to BAMS/DBC].

2. Further changes are as follows:

(a) **Form DAT 32**—this is now obsolete,

(b) **Introduction of form ITS/FME 1**—this form should be used in all jurisdictions when FME is required in the form of:
Examining Medical Practitioner [EMP] reports
GP factual reports
Hospital factual reports
Consultant reports
Any other specialist reports, for example, school reports, and

(c) It is the chairman's responsibility to complete the ITS/FME1, which should be done in the hearing room and in the presence of any party who has attended the hearing so that the medical member/assessor of the tribunal can advise upon the content of the questions to be addressed.

3. Tribunals should remind themselves, in the interests of a prompt resolution of an appeal, that GP factual and EMP reports can usually be received within 4 weeks, whereas other reports can often take several months to obtain.

4. **Referrals back to BAMS for the All Work Test [AWT] [IB cases only].** AWT referrals should continue to be requested in the usual way on the ITS/DN/ADJ. Administrative staff will continue to forward these requests to the originating Benefit Agency [BA] office as is currently the case.

5. **X-rays** [MAT cases only]. Form MAT 5 series should continue to be used and requests issued directly to the owner of the x-rays. Requests for new x-rays will also continue to be processed in the usual way.

6. **Hospital Case Notes** [MAT cases only]. Sight of the original case notes can be requested where needed but tribunals should always consider very carefully whether those notes are needed. It is the case that notes of treatment at

the time of injury will not always be helpful. MATs are often concerned not with the treatment of the injury but with the resultant disablement, which they have to assess. If production of HCNs is considered relevant, wherever possible an extract of HCNs should be requested, as suggested in my memorandum of 1 April 1997 [a copy of which is attached to this Circular]. These requests should be made on the ITS/DN/ADJ. Another alternative to sight of the HCNs is the hospital factual report, see paragraph 2b. above.

June 1997 **His Honour Judge Keith Bassingthwaighte**
President

Memorandum

From: **THE PRESIDENT**

To: **ALL FULL-TIME CHAIRMEN**
MAT AND DAT PART-TIME CHAIRMEN

CC: **REGIONAL CHAIRMEN**
CHIEF EXECUTIVE

References: 25/10/1, 25/24/1

Requests for Hospital Case Notes [HCNs]

1. As you will by now be aware, the ITS is changing the procedures for requesting further medical evidence. Historically, all requests for further medical evidence [FME] have been processed by the Benefits Agency Medical Service [BAMS]. From1 April 1997 the ITS takes responsibility for processing requests for FME with the exception of Examining Medical Practitioner [EMP] reports in DAT cases only and HCNs in MAT cases only. EMPs and HCNs will be processed via a medical services' contract with the private sector.

2. It is on the subject of HCN requests that I write to you now. It is recognised that on some occasions the MAT consider that reference to HCNs is essential in determining an appeal. Unless the tribunal specifically request that the actual HCNs are put before them, BAMS request the HCNs and prepare an extract of the notes which are relevant to the medical issues before the tribunal. Experience within the ITS suggests that the tribunal's needs are normally met by this procedure.

3. Under the terms of the new contract the contractor will only provide the ITS with an extract of the case notes.

4. Where the tribunal request sight of the actual HCNs these will be requested by the ITS direct from the hospital concerned, but this is not without problems for the ITS. The two main problems are:

(a) that the HCNs are provided to the ITS by the hospital under an arrangement which provides for their return to the hospital within 10 days. If this arrangement is not honoured by the ITS, the hospital has the right to withdraw the loan facility from the DSS in general, and

(b) that the ITS would be responsible for the safe custody of HCNs. Should the ITS lose HCNs within its possession, it could find itself involved in significant and costly liability.

5. While, for the reasons mentioned above, I would wish you to consider carefully whether original HCNs are necessary rather than extracts from HCNs,

I would, of course, wish to make it plain that the decision to obtain an extract or production of the original HCN is purely a matter for the tribunal's judicial discretion.

6. These arrangements and the wider topic of medical evidence generally will be confirmed shortly in a President's Instruction.

1 April 1997

INDEX

Page references in **bold type** are references to actual statutory material